PIMLICO

4

THE ENGLISHMAN'S FOOD

Jack Cecil Drummond was born in 1891 and educated at King's College, London, where he studied chemistry. His working life was spent at the leading edge of theoretical nutrition. For twenty years he was Professor of Biochemistry at University College, London, where he met his wife Anne Wilbraham. During the Second World War he worked as scientific adviser to the Ministry of Food. He was knighted in 1944 and in 1945 he embarked on a new post-war career as research director of the Boots Pure Drug Company. An early member of André Simon's Wine and Food Society, he was a man of well-rounded interests with a remarkable gift for communication.

Tom Jaine was brought up in and around The Hole in the Wall, the famous Bath restaurant owned by his stepfather George Perry-Smith. After reading history at Balliol College, Oxford, he worked for six years with the Royal Commission on Historical Documents. In 1973 he became partner in The Carved Angel Restaurant in Dartmouth and in 1984 he started *The Three Course Newsletter*, a bi-monthly publication which carries articles on food and food history.

Tom Jaine is Editor of the *Journal* of the International Wine and Food Society. His publications include *Cooking in the Country* and *Cosmic Cuisine*. Since 1989 he has been Editor of *The Good Food Guide*.

La destinée des nations dépend de la manière dont elles se nourissent.

Brillat-Savarin, *Physiologie du Gôut,* 1825

THE ENGLISHMAN'S FOOD

A History of Five Centuries of English Diet

TOM POCOCK
and
ANNE WILBRAHAM

Revised by Dorothy Hollingsworth
Preface by Norman C. Wright
Introduction by Tom Jaine

PIMLICO

PIMLICO

20 Vauxhall Bridge Road, London SW1V 2SA

London Melbourne Sydney Auckland Johannesburg
and agencies throughout the world

First published by Jonathan Cape Ltd 1939
New and revised edition 1957
Pimlico edition 1991

4

ISBN 978-0-7126-5025-0

Penguin Random House is committed to a sustainable future for
our business, our readers and our planet. This book is made from
Forest Stewardship Council® certified paper.

Printed and bound in Great Britain by Clays Ltd, St Ives plc

CONTENTS

ACKNOWLEDGMENTS

PREFACE

PART ONE

MEDIEVAL AND TUDOR ENGLAND

I	PRODUCTION OF FOOD	17
II	QUALITY OF FOOD	34
III	MEALS OF THE PEOPLE	47
IV	DIET AND HEALTH	65

PART TWO

THE SEVENTEENTH CENTURY

V	FOOD AND MEALS	91
VI	DIET AND HEALTH	121
VII	SCURVY	133
VIII	RICKETS	147

PART THREE

THE EIGHTEENTH CENTURY

IX	RISE OF ENGLISH AGRICULTURE	171
X	EIGHTEENTH-CENTURY FOOD	185
XI	EIGHTEENTH-CENTURY MEALS	206
XII	VIEWS ON DIET	232
XIII	DIET AND HEALTH	250
XIV	SCURVY	259
XV	RICKETS	271

PART FOUR

THE NINETEENTH CENTURY

XVI	INDUSTRY AND AGRICULTURE	279
XVII	QUALITY OF FOOD	288
XVIII	PRESERVATION OF FOOD	313
XIX	FOOD OF THE PEOPLE	327
XX	RISE OF THE SCIENCE OF NUTRITION	343
XXI	DIET IN INSTITUTIONS	363
XXII	DETERIORATION OF PHYSIQUE	373

CONTENTS

PART FIVE

THE TWENTIETH CENTURY

XXIII THE TURN OF THE TIDE   403

XXIV THE APPLICATION OF THE NEWER KNOWLEDGE OF
      NUTRITION   428

APPENDIX A   465

APPENDIX B   468

APPENDIX C   469

INDEX   471

ILLUSTRATIONS

ANDREW BOORDE
> *(By permission of the British Museum)*

A THIRTEENTH-CENTURY MINIATURE SHOWING AN INFANT BEING FED FROM A COW'S HORN
> *(By permission of the Wellcome Historical Medical Museum)*

SANCTORIUS
> He is shown seated in the chair attached to a yard-arm by which he recorded his changes of weight after eating

VIRGIN AND CHILD
> (Hans Bergmaier, Nuremberg, 1500?) This picture shows a typically rachitic infant
> *(By permission of the American Medical Association)*

BROADSHEET SATIRIZING THE INTRODUCTION OF FRENCH COOKING
> *(By permission of the British Museum)*

THE EVOLUTION OF THE FEEDING-BOTTLE
> *(From the collection in the Wellcome Historical Medical Museum)*

ACCUM LECTURING AT THE SURREY INSTITUTION
> *(By permission of Mr R. B. Pilcher, Registrar of the Institute of Chemistry)*

FRONTISPIECE TO 'THE FAMILY ORACLE OF HEALTH'
> Dr Kitchiner is about to be arrested for eating live oysters and thereby contravening Martin's Bill for the Prevention of Cruelty to Animals

ACKNOWLEDGMENTS

In their preface to the first edition of *The Englishman's Food*, Sir Jack and Lady Drummond acknowledged with gratitude the guidance and help they had received from Professor J. E. Neale, M.A., Astor Professor of English History at University College, London, from Mr S. T. Bindoff, M.A., and Dr M. A. Thomson, of the Department of History, University College, and from Dr Rosenstein-Rodan of the Department of Political Economy, University College. They also expressed their thanks to Professor R. H. Tawney, of the London School of Economics, for his advice on certain points, to Dr H. E. Magee, of the Ministry of Health, for information supplied, and to Miss Gladys Scott Thomson and Messrs Jonathan Cape and Mr C. Bruyn Andrews and Messrs Eyre & Spottiswoode, for permission to publish extracts from *Life in a Noble Household, 1641-1700* and *The Torrington Diaries*. They expressed their appreciation of the unfailing courtesy and willing assistance they had received from the Library Staff of the British Museum and of University College.

In preparing the second edition, I have received much help from many friends and colleagues. In particular, I should like to thank Dr H. M. Sinclair, Vice-President of Magdalen College, Oxford, Dr T. Moran, C.B.E., Director of Research at the Cereals Research Station, St Albans, Dr T. Moore of the Dunn Nutritional Laboratory, Cambridge, and Miss Dorothy Hartley for advice on my revisions to certain technical points in the earlier chapters, Dr H. R. Barnell of the Ministry of Agriculture, Fisheries and Food, Mr F. Le Gros Clark, M.A., and Mr E. M. H. Lloyd, C.B., C.M.G., for their advice in the preparation of the new last chapter, and Dr N. C. Wright, C.B., Chief Scientific Adviser (Food) of the Ministry of Agriculture, Fisheries and Food, for his help and encouragement throughout.

I should also like to thank the Library Staff of the Ministry of Agriculture, Fisheries and Food for their constant and willing help, Miss Margaret C. Vaughan for assistance in making nutritional calculations, and Mrs C. M. Back for reading and checking manuscripts and typescripts.

D. H.

PREFACE

THE first edition of *The Englishman's Food* was published in 1939 shortly before the outbreak of war. The unique character of the work created a wide interest which has not died in the intervening years and in response to a widespread demand the publishers decided that it was desirable to issue a second edition.

Sir Jack Drummond had intended to produce such an edition himself, but his tragic death, together with that of his wife and daughter, came before he had found time to make the necessary revisions — or indeed to make any notes for a revision. In the circumstances the publishers have been fortunate in securing the services of Miss Dorothy Hollingsworth to prepare the new edition. Miss Hollingsworth had the opportunity of working in association with Drummond at the Ministry of Food throughout the greater part of the war and was in close touch with him after he left the Ministry and until the time of his death; she therefore not only had the benefit of participating in some of the events which she describes, but was aware of Drummond's own reaction to these events, both during and after the war.

Advances in the science of nutrition and improvements in its application since 1939 have made it necessary for Miss Hollingsworth to modify all the sections on nutrition and to revise all the nutritional calculations given in the first edition. In making these changes she has tried to retain the character of the original volume, though in a few places she felt it right to make alterations in emphasis. The most important changes of this kind are slight toning down of statements about the possible incidence of scurvy in medieval England, made necessary both by present knowledge of the amounts of vitamin C necessary to prevent and to cure scurvy and by uncertainty regarding medieval vegetable consumption; modification of degree, but not of kind, in the nutritional consequences attributed to the alterations in the composition of flour which followed the introduction of the new milling technique in about 1880; and reservation of judgment on the question whether there has been any change in adult stature in England over the centuries.

Owing to the extravagant increases in present printing costs it was necessary to reduce the length of the original work. On the other hand, it was felt that the story would be incomplete without some reference to developments in this country during and after the Second World War, particularly as Drummond himself, as Scientific Adviser at the Ministry of Food from 1940 to 1946, played such a notable part in British achievements in this field. Miss Hollingsworth has tried to meet these conflicting demands by shortening the earlier chapters (chiefly by the omission of some of the quotations), by reducing the length of many of the revised sections, and by incorporating relevant parts of the original last two chapters into a completely new chapter which also includes new material relating to the war and post-war years and, in addition, a discussion on trends in British food consumption during the last seventy-five years.

It is always hard to attempt a revision of the work of others and on this occasion the lack of records relating to the first edition added to the difficulties. I feel sure, however, that the readers of this new edition will be grateful to Miss Hollingsworth for undertaking the task not only with such competence but with such a sensitive appreciation of the character of the original.

NORMAN C. WRIGHT

January 1957

INTRODUCTION

by

Tom Jaine

The Englishman's Food has enjoyed the esteem of readers from the moment of its first publication in 1939. Although re-issued in 1957 (the edition printed here), it has been sensibly hoarded by its owners so that second-hand copies are never easily come by. It is one of those rare books that manages at once to be the first in a particular field and has not been speedily dislodged from its position. Testimonials drop like locusts from footnotes of other writers; quotation is almost supererogatory, but the comments of one, a Frenchman (and how flattering the attention is to an English gastronomic breast), point to its particular merit. In 1970 Louis Stouff wrote a magnificent study of the diet of Provence in the late Middle Ages. 'A new direction is opening up to research: a history of food which, while giving famines and feast-days their due, is preoccupied with day-to-day reality, calculates budgets and dietary regimes, tries to estimate calories, proteins, glucosides and lipids. Conceived thus, the history of diet will move towards the reconstruction of the totality of the past, and not remain an antiquarian exercise preoccupied with the picturesque or the tragic. Until now, there have been few books that have followed this line', one was Maria Dembinska's study of Poland, the other was Drummond.

Jack Cecil Drummond was a scientist, not an historian. He was born in 1891 and died at the hand of a French peasant in the summer of 1952. His career was impressive, its crowning achievement his work as scientific adviser to the Ministry of Food during the Second World War, and spanned twenty years as Professor of Biochemistry at University College, London until 1945 as well as a vigorous post-war career with Boots Pure Drug Company as their research director. The composition of *The Englishman's Food* should be seen in the context of a life at the leading edge of theoretical and practical nutrition. For a research scientist, Drummond was a man of well-rounded interests and a gift for communication. Historical work was but another plank in his ideal springboard towards the better feeding of the whole community.

After gaining a first-class degree in chemistry from King's College, London in 1912, his first job was with the Research Institute of the London Cancer Hospital, becoming a director in 1918 before moving to the academic staff of University College. Promotion was rapid: Reader in 1920, Professor of Biochemistry in 1922. His interests were from the outset nutritional, working for example on butter and margarine substitutes and infant feeding. A humane concern with the wider issues of the history of nutrition, both the development of the science itself and the question of how people actually fared in past centuries, was evident long before 1939. He produced, as an instance, a paper (again with Anne Wilbraham) on the life of the pioneer dietician William Stark who died from the results of experiments upon himself in 1770 and to whose memory Drummond and Wilbraham's own book is dedicated.

This interest in food extended to his own table. Drummond was an early member of the Wine & Food Society, founded in 1933 by the French vintner and gastronome André L. Simon, himself a noted amateur of food and wine history. Drummond contributed a couple of papers to the Society's *Journal*, as well as a posthumous communication recounting the circumstances surrounding the granting of a drinks licence to a restaurant in Nottingham – 'to lovers of good food his place became a welcome oasis in a rather bare gastronomic desert'.

Control of food had been anticipated as an inevitable consequence of war after the experience of the 1914-18 conflict, when muddled measures of across-the-board restriction based on inadequate nutritional understanding and insufficient planning had caused hardship and hunger to much of the population. Britain was not to be caught out again and preparations were well advanced (down to the printing of ration books) by the outbreak of the Second World War in 1939. Jack Drummond's appointment as scientific adviser to successive Ministers of Food, first W.S. Morrison, then Lord Woolton (himself a scientist by training), fits in with his crusading urge to apply scientific knowledge to the rigours of practical circumstance anticipated in the closing chapters of *The Englishman's Food*.

Nutrional studies combine purely scientific investigation – the discovery of vitamins or the analysis of proteins – with a possibility, some would say necessity, of implementing the fruits of research to everyone's benefit. Certainly during the Twenties and Thirties, after half a century of tremendous scientific gain, the tilt of nutritional work was towards discovering the degree of malnourishment in contemporary Britain and persuading the political community that remedies were to hand. Drummond was as much part of this as the more polemical Sir John Orr (later Lord Boyd-Orr), author of *Food, Health and Income* published in 1936. Drummond's first job at the ministry was as chief adviser on food contamination. But his brief was widened when he took the post of scientific adviser and his early memoranda ranged over the whole question of dietary sufficiency – for example, the beneficial consequences of reducing the extraction rate of bread flour. They were in keeping with this desire to intervene in the diet of the nation and they ensured that wartime food control was not merely a system of ensuring equitable distribution of supplies to the shops but underpinned a wholesale experiment in creative nutrition. The political consequences of avoiding hunger were self-evident, as Drummond himself noted, 'if people are properly nourished, cold and unhygienic conditions are much less likely to harm them'.

An advantage of reading the second edition is that it includes the final chapter by Dorothy Hollingsworth with some account of Drummond's work during this period. This lays down a skeleton of fact – more generously clothed in various official histories of food control – but makes small mention of the evidently creative aspect of Drummond's success. As this book so amply demonstrates, he had a gift for clear exposition with a gentle yet pointed humour. Explanation and public relations were essential for his ideas to prosper. He had first to persuade the Minister, who in turn needed to convince the Premier, Sir Winston Churchill; and the ministry depended largely on the goodwill of the food industry and other trade interests as well as the co-operation of the public at large. As one commentator put it, 'He was able to understand and help to solve the problems of housewives with families to feed in wartime, and gradually his name began to creep into the columns of the newspapers through his commonsense pronouncements in his capacity as government expert . . . In the days when most people had to turn to bread and potatoes to take the place of rationed meat, it was Professor Drummond who reassured the public: "Surely foods do not make you fat unless you eat too much. Starch is not more fat-making than butter: it is only over-eating which puts weight on the average person." ' The use by the Ministry of Food of popular entertainers, cartoonists and resourceful writing to put over its message of creative optimism on the kitchen front was as inventive as were its more heavyweight schemes of dietary supplements, national catering through British Restaurants or 'points' control of luxury foodstuffs. Drummond was by no means the chief or only architect of this great achievement, but his role was significant and many-faceted.

Sir Jack Drummond's (he was knighted in 1944) last two years in public service saw greater responsibility when he was appointed adviser on nutrition to SHAEF and to the British Control Commission in defeated Germany. He organised, for instance, special feeding measures for the starving cities of newly liberated Holland and for the surviving victims of Belsen and other concentration camps – just as, before the siege of Malta in 1942, he had counselled the supply of vitaminised chocolate to the island's children – a practical suggestion, among others, that enabled them to endure the months of privation.

When the war was over, Sir Jack did not return to full academic life, nor did he remain with the Ministry. He cast his lot with commerce. This chimes with his appreciation of the potential for good of large-scale commercial enterprise. He sought, throughout the years of war, to involve the food industry at every turn of events. As a card-carrying dietary interventionist, he appreciated that well-organised, powerful and industrialised food production was much more susceptible to control and influence than countless one-man bands working in unregulated workshops. For example, had flour milling not been virtually monopolised, the manipulation of extraction rates and, subsequently, the addition of calcium, vitamins and other nutrients to denatured white flour would have been infinitely more difficult to effect. He wrote in *The Endlishman's Food*, 'It is almost a law of political economy that as the scale of capitalistic enterprise grows the petty dishonesty and fraud which very often characterize its early stages tend to disappear. It is usually the small food manufacturer, or more frequently the proprietor of the little street corner shop in the poor locality, who is responsible for the comparatively rare cases of adulteration found today.' Food and consumerist agitators of the 1990s would not tend to agree with this statement.

By contrast, Drummond valued the principle of enlightened self-interest. Life in commerce also agreed with his practical bent. He had never been a 'conventional scientist of fiction', a colleague remarked, 'he was a great mixer and a shrewd man of affairs . . . who did more than anyone else to introduce science into the food industries.' In the war years this practically took the form of encouragement of research into spray-dried egg and other forms of dehydration and food preservation.

In August 1952 Sir Jack was on a motoring holiday in France. He was in the company of his second wife, the Anne Wilbraham who was joint author of this book, and their ten-year-old daughter Elizabeth. Anne Wilbraham had met Sir Jack at University College, where she was a student of his. Their academic co-operation and subsequent marriage were evidently exceptionally happy. In the winter of 1951-52 Sir Jack had not been well; the holiday was considered as much recuperative as pure pleasure or education. The intention was to drive down to friends with a house at Villefranche on the Côte d'Azur, camping or staying in hotels as the spirit moved them. Exchange control for British travellers was then in force so that camping was a very necessary alternative in order to hoard precious francs. The Drummonds got to Villefranche but wished to return to the mountains to witness the corrida at Digne in Haute Provence. Returning thence by a roundabout but less vertiginous route, they elected to pitch camp in a small field by the road rather than persevere through valley and mountain to the hotels of Manosque or Aix-en-Provence. It was, after all, high summer and holidays. The next morning they were found dead. Sir Jack and Lady Drummond had been shot, Elizabeth was bludgeoned.

The episode lived long in the subconscious of many post-war British tourists.

INTRODUCTION

The family were blameless and middle class; the investigation was horribly botched over several years (the eventual culprit was an old peasant, almost a patriarch, called Gaston Domenici, who lived in the house nearest the campsite); the real circumstances were never properly clarified. It was, and remains, a senseless tragedy and reading about it even today makes one rail at the pointless loss.

Dorothy Hollingsworth was asked by the publishers to prepare a second edition. She is herself a nutritionist, latterly working for the British Nutrition Foundation, though now retired. She had worked with Sir Jack at the Ministry of Food. The preface to this edition explains some of her alterations, the most important of which was the final chapter that sketched in developments through the war and into the Fifties. This meant a substantial change to Drummond's own peroration which was, in its way, the very reason for the book in the first place, but Hollingsworth's work made the book accessible to a new generation of readers.

The Englishman's Food has a subtitle: *A History of Five Centuries of English Diet*. It is not a history of cookery, nor is it an antiquarian mish-mash of anecdote and lore relating to feeding habits. It attempts two things: to relate the new discoveries about dietary requirements to historical fact and to give some account of the development of nutritional science. By the way, because Drummond was a man of broad culture and because the facts would have been mute without it, there is incorporated a vast amount of evidence that touches on the wider questions of cookery and meal habits. It cannot be stressed enough that the book addresses quite different issues than do other pioneering food histories, for instance Florence White's *Good Things in England*, published in 1932, an admirable repository of traditional recipes, or Dorothy Hartley's *Food in England* which came out in 1954 replete with information about domestic economy as well as recipes.

Drummond was working during the heroic period of nutritional science when the constituents of food necessary to maintain, and then to improve, the quality of life were finally defined. Proteins, fats, carbohydrates, water and mineral salts, the five 'proximate principles' essential to any diet, were satisfactorily classified in the closing years of the nineteenth century and nutritionists laboured initially to absorb the meaning of calories and protein to ideas of dietary sufficiency. Experiments showed, however, that subjects fed on materials that had these principles in generous quantity none the less did not flourish. The search for the missing magic ingredient led to the discovery of vitamins – properly defined by the biochemist Sir Frederick Hopkins in 1912. Once dealt a full hand of components, nutritionists got to work to assess how far lack of any one of them would affect the life and health of a population. This, then, was the era when deficiency diseases received their full investigation. For centuries rickets, scurvy, pellagra, beri-beri, night-blindness and hunger-oedema had been the scourge of various societies. Sometimes, remedy had been chanced upon by empirical means – the British navy's eventual adoption of lemon juice as an anti-scorbutic for example – but it needed the new nutrition to fully explain the treatment and to rapidly extend the benefits of cure to as many populations as possible. *The Englishman's Food* attempted to describe how such deficiencies affected the health of earlier centuries, how a proper diet *might* have changed the course of history.

This emphasis on what was missing is different to our own nutritional preoccupations. Today, we are far more interested in the consequences of excess, in how the interaction of various components may itself give rise to illness: cancer, heart and circulatory disease, intestinal troubles, obesity. Whereas Drummond and his colleagues were anxious to supplement diet, for example by extending consumption of green vegetables, fruit, high protein and milk and dairy products, as well as introduce added vitamins to necessary staples such as flour or margarine, we are far more worried by how too much of any of these things may cause us to operate below par. The intellectual transition has been very rapid and is a measure of the success of those first scholars in explaining then eradicating deficiency diseases. *The Englishman's Food* put this process into a proper perspective.

Drummond's work came before there was any substantial body of literature on food history. Even today, it is a discipline imperfectly pursued by British academics, with far greater strides being made in Europe and America. With the help of his colleagues in the history department of University College and excavation of literary sources by other assistants, he constructed a workable account of diet, but not cookery, in earlier periods. Since 1939, a deal of work has been undertaken on early cookery books – see, as high points of this, C. Anne Wilson's *Food and Drink in Britain* (1973), or the sociological perspective of Stephen Mennell in *All Manners of Food* (1985) – and other forms of historical evidence, such as archaeology and the archives of great country houses, have been mobilised to deepen our knowledge or to open up different avenues of approach. History is no longer the blind parroting of dates or the mere detailing of political events; there is a desire for Stouff's 'reconstruction of the totality of the past' and food evidently forms part of this. It may take the form of assessing the role of a particular ingredient (Salaman's work on the potato, Hobhouse's on 'seeds of change', or Forrest's study of tea); the economic development of a specific industry or trade (Perren on the meat trade; Vaisey or Matthias on the brewing industry; Clark on alehouses); the role of food marketing within an economic system (Joan Thirsk on the history of agriculture; Blackman, Minchinton or Fisher's studies of the markets of Sheffield, Bristol and London); or the part of food in social or intellectual change (Lawrence Stone on the English aristocracy; Felicity Heal on hospitality; or Sir Keith Thomas on the interplay between man and his – consumable – environment). All these come after *The Englishman's Food* but they do not weaken its arguments nor destroy the force of its narrative. Had it been written today, it might have ranged more widely than literature for illustration, but could not have expressed more gracefully its underlying message: it may taste nice, but lunch is a bundle of chemicals whose impact we should seek to understand.

Dedicated to

WILLIAM STARK

1740-70

'Wherefore let us neither with the impudent, call diet a frivolous knowledge, or a curious science with the imprudent: but embrace it as the leader to perfit health, (which as the wise man saith) is above gold, and a sound body above all riches.'

THOMAS MUFFETT, 1655

PART ONE

MEDIEVAL AND TUDOR ENGLAND

CHAPTER I

PRODUCTION OF FOOD

§ 1 MEDIEVAL AGRICULTURE

IN medieval times the cultivated lands of England were divided into two categories, those which formed part of the demesne lands of the great manors and those which the common people, still bound by serfdom to the manor, were entitled to work for their own benefit. The former were cultivated by the manor servants assisted by the villagers, who were obliged to provide their lord with a specified number of days' labour or its equivalent in money or kind. The latter, quite considerable in extent as can still be seen from the ribbed markings which survive in so many shires, were farmed by the villagers themselves under a primitive communal system.

The manor farms appear to have consisted in some cases of large fields, many acres in extent and roughly fenced off one from the other, and in others of strips scattered among those of the villagers. The village common fields were divided into long strips, usually of about half an acre each. Each family held a certain number of these strips distributed over the various fields so that none should benefit exclusively from the best sites. The majority of the villagers seem to have held four to six strips but many of them had rights over larger areas and there had grown up an 'aristocracy' of peasants who tilled as much as twenty or thirty acres. The villagers cultivated their common fields according to a conventional plan, regardless of the size of their holdings.

There still remains one survival of this system in England today at Laxton in Nottinghamshire. The strips, which are still of the original dimensions and of which some farmers hold as many as ten, are cultivated according to the plan adopted by the elected village jury. Originally four common fields were cultivated on a simple system of rotation; today one is kept permanently as grazing land and is fenced in, two of the others are under crop and one is lying fallow.[1]

Under the medieval system the villagers were free to till their own land only when they had discharged their duties to the manor estates, which meant that at busy times, such as ploughing and harvesting, the labour was very heavy. Everybody turned to, often lending a neighbour a helping hand.

[1] The system was briefly described in an article in *The Times*, December 2nd, 1937. A complete study of the interesting survivals of the medieval system at Laxton has been published by C. S. and C. S. Orwin, *The Open Fields*, 1938.

Quod Perkyn the Plowman,
'By Seint Peter of Rome!
I have an half acre to erie [plough]
By the heighe waye.'

.   .   .   .   .

Now is Perkyn and hise pilgrimes
To the plow faren; [gone]
To erie his half acre.
Holpen hym manye;
Dikeres and delveres
Digged up the balkes.[1]

But whether it was manor farm or common field, agricultural practice
was the same and little more advanced than it had been in Roman days.
Few crops were grown and only the simplest systems of rotation were
followed. Under the 'two-field' system one half of the plot of land was
cultivated while the other lay fallow; autumn wheat or rye alternated with
spring corn, oats or vetch. The 'three-field' system was based on the division
of the land into areas devoted to spring corn and autumn corn with a third
partition lying fallow. Such primitive rotation of crops survived until well
into Tudor times as can be seen from Thomas Tusser's doggerel verses:

First barlie, then pease,
then wheat, if ye please.

Two crops and alway,
must champion saye.

Where barlie did growe,
laie wheate to sowe.
Yet better I thinke,
some pease, after drinke.
And then, if ye please,
some wheat after pease.

What champion knowes
that custome showes.

First barlie er rie,
then pease by and by.

[1] *The Vision of Piers Plowman*, William Langland, *circa* 1360, edited by T. Wright, 1843.

> Then fallow for wheat,
> is husbandrie great.[1]

For the peasants the usual method of restoring the fertility of their strips was to allow them to lie fallow, although a certain amount of manuring resulted from turning the livestock on to the stubble after harvest. The lord of the manor could if he wished claim any manure that was available and exercise the right (*jus faldae*) of folding the village sheep and cattle on his arable land.[2] The liming of soils and the practice of 'marling', in which heavy sub-soils are dug up and used to give more 'heart' to the surface, seem rarely to have been used to improve the fertility of the land, although early writings on agriculture mention them.

> So that ever the thycker the
> felde is marled the better
> the corn it will bere.[3]

It is possible to get a very clear picture of medieval agricultural practice from contemporary writings, of which the most important are those of Walter of Henley, the *Fleta*, and the *Boke of Husbandry*, attributed to Grosse-teste, Bishop of Lincoln. These are all thirteenth-century works but they seem to have been widely used throughout the two following centuries; Wynkyn de Worde printed the *Boke of Husbandry* in 1510, when it was still regarded as a leading authority on the subject.

The crops grown on the manor lands and by the villagers were wheat, barley, oats, rye, vetches and beans. Wheat and rye were the important crops in the south and seem not infrequently to have been grown from a mixed sowing. The crop was known as *maslin*, a word which is found in many forms but which seems to be derived through the Norman French from the Latin *miscere*, to mix.[4] In the north oats replaced the wheat of the south.

The yields were usually poor, and it seems to have been a good year when a three-fold return, giving about $7\frac{1}{2}$ bushels to the acre, was obtained. The peasant was obliged to take his corn to the manor mill and to pay, sometimes heavily, for the grinding. The chaff was treasured as food for his cattle, for which he also saved the bines of his crop of beans.

---

[1] *Fiue hundred pointes of good Husbandrie, as well for the Champion, or open countrie, as also for the Woodland, or Seuerall*, Thomas Tusser, 1580.

[2] *Life on the English Manor, 1150-1400*, H. S. Bennett, 1937.

[3] *Polycronycon*, Ranulphus Higden, fourteenth century (Wynkyn de Worde's edition of 1495 has been used throughout).

[4] The derivation of this word and its significance is fully discussed by Sir William Ashley in *Bread of Our Forefathers*, 1928.

B

§ 2 MEDIEVAL GARDENS

It is difficult to find clear evidence of what was grown at this period, apart from field crops. The manors and monasteries had herb gardens and orchards and in addition the monasteries often had their own vineyards. Many villagers had an enclosed plot (*curtilage*) adjoining their primitive homes and they doubtless grew there such herbs, fruits and vegetables as they could obtain. But it seems that there was very little to grow. Medieval sources refer to plums, apples and cherries, which seem to have been quite common, but vegetables, with the exception of onions, garlic, leeks and cabbages, are rarely mentioned.[1]

A passage in Harrison's *Description of England* (1577) is often quoted as evidence that vegetables were widely grown and popular in England in the thirteenth and fourteenth centuries and that later they fell into disuse.

> Such herbes, fruits, & roots also, as grow yeerelie out of the ground, of seed, haue been verie plentifull in this land in the time of the first Edward, and after his daies: but in processe of time they grew also to be neglected, so that from Henrie the fourth till the latter end of Henrie the seuenth, & beginning of Henrie the eight, there was little or no vse of them in England, but they remained either vknowne, or supposed as food more meet for hogs & sauage beasts to feed vpon, than mankind.

Johnson held that the decline of gardening came about by 'a still lingering taste for hunting, chivalry and War; by Crusades to the Holy Land, and as wild expeditions to the Continent: and above all by the civil horrors induced by the contest between the houses of York and Lancaster';[2] but we know very little of the details of medieval English gardening. Sir Frank Crisp, in his comprehensive study of the subject,[3] shows that almost all the existing information refers to Continental gardens and practice. The art of gardening at that time was much more advanced in Italy, France and Flanders than it was in England.

The earliest surviving English works on gardening are fifteenth-century MSS, of which one, written about 1440 by 'Mayster Ion Gardener',[4] gives a list of 78 plants suitable for cultivation. Most of them are savoury herbs to be used in the kitchen or for the preparation of simples. Of what might be

---

[1] A twelfth-century recipe which is in keeping with this summary is given by Dorothy Hartley in *Food in England*, 1954. She described how to 'Boyl a Flank with Worts': the flank of mutton was boiled with turnips, parsnips, young onions and herbs and served with shredded cabbage which had been cooked rapidly in milk and butter.

[2] *A History of English Gardening*, G. W. Johnson, 1829.

[3] *Mediaeval Gardens*, Sir Frank Crisp, 1924.

[4] *A History of Gardening in England*, Hon. Mrs Evelyn Cecil, 3rd edition, 1910.

called ordinary garden vegetables the only ones mentioned are radishes, spinach, cabbage and lettuce, besides onions, garlic and leeks, which we know to have been widely grown. Another MS. of about the same date refers to 'rotys [roots] for a gardyne' and names 'parsenepys', 'turnepez', 'karettes' and 'betes'.[1] But so rarely does one find these vegetables mentioned that it is reasonable to suppose that they were only occasionally grown, even in well-stocked gardens such as those of the great monasteries. There are scattered references in fourteenth- and fifteenth-century writings to 'caboches' and 'cabogis', and with these one must associate the more frequent mention of 'wurtys', 'woortes' and 'coleworts'. The name colewort was applied rather indiscriminately both to wild and to cultivated species of the cabbage family (*Brassica*), although when Piers Plowman referred to a few 'cole plants' he probably meant garden cabbages. These seem to have been used mainly for soups, although Miss Dorothy Hartley has stated recently[2] that medieval instructions on cooking shredded 'worts' in butter read like modern directions on conservative vegetable cookery.

The kitchen garden of the fourteenth and fifteenth century supplied chiefly herbs, onions and leeks. The former included not only the ordinary savoury herbs with which we are familiar today, sage, marjoram, rosemary, but also cultivated varieties of many which we know only as common roadside plants, such as bugloss, borage, fennel and even 'chykynweed' and 'rokett'. These were grown partly to provide savoury flavourings for meat, which was not infrequently 'high' in summer and, because most of it had been salted for several months, rather insipid in winter, and partly to provide the materials for home-made remedies and medicaments. Even the gardens of the monasteries, usually the best stocked of all, were sometimes curiously deficient in vegetables. The famous physician, Andrew Boorde, must have known much about kitchen gardens because for a number of years he was a Carthusian and lived on their simple and essentially vegetarian diet. We do not know whether it was this restriction or others that his order imposed — he was an amorous gentleman whose philanderings landed him in a good many awkward situations and finally, ignominiously, in the Fleet prison — which he found intolerable, but we do know that he wrote to the Prior of Hinton Charterhouse in Somerset that 'I am nott able to byd the rugorosite off your relygyon'. He left England and wandered all over the Continent studying at foreign universities. While at Montpelier he wrote his *Compendyous Regyment, or a Dyetary of Helth* (1542), one of the earliest English books on diet. In it he devotes a good deal of attention to herbs but very little to vegetables. One gets the impression that he regarded rape, onions, garlic and leeks as the only ones of importance. Clearly the onion family

[1] Ibid.   [2] *Food in England*, Dorothy Hartley, 1954.

was very popular everywhere. 'Wel loved he garlike, onions, and lekes', wrote Chaucer of his Sompnour. Thorold Rogers in his exhaustive analysis of early manorial and other records found few references to the purchase of seed other than onion.[1]

Fruit, at any rate apples, plums and cherries, seems to have been plentiful in medieval England. The poor people brought Piers Plowman 'baken apples' and 'chiries' when he told them of his hardships. Except in the orchards of the monasteries, where a good deal of skill and knowledge was applied to the care of the trees, its cultivation was probably happy-go-lucky and the quality of most of the produce poor.

There is little information about the supply of fruit and vegetables in English towns during this period. It seems to have been a small trade entirely in the hands of a few countrymen or local gardeners who brought their produce into the towns and sold it for what they could get. Only the wealthy could afford a garden inside the city walls, but there were a number in the 'suburbs' of London which were 'planted with trees, spacious and fair, adjoining one another'.[2] The gardens inside the city walls were probably for the most part purely decorative, but vegetables and fruit must sometimes have been grown, for the gardeners of the 'Earls, Barons, and Bishops, and of the Citizens' of London used to sell their masters' 'pulse, cherries, vegetables and other wares to their trade pertaining' near the gate of St Paul's Churchyard. In 1345 a protest was made on the grounds that their noise disturbed the worshippers and the Mayor and Aldermen ordered them to move to a more open place by the 'garden-wall of the Friars Preachers at Baynard's Castle'.[3]

The famous Gerard for many years supervised the gardens of Lord Burghley's house in the Strand, and Stow refers to the many 'garden plottes'[4] in the newly developing areas to the east of and outside the City of London, notably at Aldgate and Hackney. These were probably market gardens, the produce of which was brought into the City and 'cried' in the streets.

During the sixteenth century it was not uncommon to import fruit, often at considerable expense, from Holland. Catharine Parr used regularly to send messengers to that country when she required a salad.[5] Dried fruits, raisins, prunes, etc., were imported from Portugal and the Levant in considerable amounts as early as the thirteenth century,[6] and by the sixteenth

---

[1] *History of Agriculture and Prices*, J. E. Thorold Rogers, 1866-87.
[2] *A Description of London*, William Fitz Stephen, *circa* 1183, translated by H. E. Butler, Historical Association Leaflet, 1934.
[3] *Memorials of London*, H. T. Riley, 1868.
[4] *A Survay of London*, John Stow, 1598.
[5] *A History of English Gardening*, G. W. Johnson, 1829.
[6] *Of the Commodities of Portugal, The Principall Navigations . . . of the English Nation*, Richard Hakluyt, 1598-1600.

century every large household had stores of 'datys, fieggs, and great ray-syngs'[1] which were used in sweet puddings and as 'Lenten meats'.[2] Lemons were obviously a great luxury, for the Leathersellers' Company gave six silver pennies for one for a civic feast given to Henry VIII and Anne Boleyn in honour of their Coronation.[3]

The penalty for giving short weight of fruit was the pillory.

> The furst day of July [1552] ther was a man and a woman on the pelere in Chepe-syd; the man sold potts of straberries, the whyche the pott was nott alff fulle, but fyllyd with forne [fern].[4]

§ 3 LIVESTOCK

Considerable numbers of livestock were kept by the owners of the manors and in good times many of the villagers were also well off in this respect. The lord of the manor had draught oxen, cows, sheep, pigs and poultry; the villagers seem usually to have kept pigs and poultry, and some-times an ox, a cow and a few sheep. The 'poure widewe ... dwelling in a narwe cotage', whom Chaucer so graphically portrays in the opening lines of the *Nonnes Preestes Tale*, was only a 'maner dey', that is she was a kind of lowly farm servant (Eden says the wages of 'deyes' were generally lower than those of other servants[5]), but she was able to boast of owning 'three large sows ... three kine, and eke a sheep', as well as a 'cok' and 'seven hennes', all of which probably shared her 'souty boure' with her two daughters and herself. The records of the village of Crawley in Hampshire show that it was common for tenants in medieval times to have a cow, a horse, pigs and as many as twenty-five sheep. The lord of the manor could claim payment if a larger number of sheep were kept.[6]

The cattle that were not working grazed during the spring and summer and were turned on to the stubble after the harvest and gleaning. The pigs, long-snouted, razor-backed runts, were seldom specially fed unless they belonged to the manor, where grain, skim milk or brewing residues might be available. Those owned by the villagers scavenged the byways and rooted in the woods in charge of the village swineherd. Enormous numbers of poultry were kept and these too lived to a large extent on what they could

[1] *Regulations and Establishment of the Household of Henry Algernon Percy, 5th Earl of Northumberland, 1512*, edited by T. P. (Thomas Percy, Bishop of Dromore), 1827.
[2] *The Paston Letters*, CCCCIV, CCCCV, 1477-78.
[3] *A History of English Gardening*, G. W. Johnson, 1829.
[4] *Diary of Henry Machin, 1550-1563* (Camden Society Publication, No. 42, 1848).
[5] *The State of the Poor*, Sir Frederic Eden, 1797.
[6] *The Economic and Social History of an English Village*, N. S. B. Gras, 1930.

pick up. The feeding of farm animals was so little understood that the approach of winter was a serious time. The only foodstuffs available for feeding them in stall or in the shelter of the manor yard were beans, dried bines, hay, chaff and straw. Only a strong young animal could survive and this being so it was customary to slaughter all the old or weakly head in the late autumn.

Great distress was caused when epidemics of cattle disease swept the country. Some lasted for years. Stow refers to a 'murrain' which began in 1275 and had not disappeared by 1300. The memory of it seems to have survived for centuries, so terrible were the losses. There is no means of telling what the 'great rot' was, but according to Stow it was attributed to a foreign importation.

> A rich man of France brought into Northumberland a Spanish ewe, as bigge as a calfe of two yeeres, which Ewe being rotten, infected so the country, that it spread ouer all the realme.[1]

The medieval English peasant knew all too often what hard times were. When harvest failed there was nothing to be done but to kill off the livestock and eke out his meals with the animals, herbs and roots of the countryside. Chaucer draws a pathetic picture of the poverty-stricken Grisildis.

> And whan she homward came, she wolde bring
> Wortes and other herbes times oft,
> The which she shred and sethe for hire living.[2]

When his own stocks were short the lord of the manor seldom hesitated to draw upon the poor man's reserve. Usually this amounted to confiscation. Piers Plowman described the plight of one left with nothing but a worthless 'tally' in exchange for the goods removed.

> Bothe my gees and my grys [pigs]
> Hise gadelynges [associates] feccheth.
>
> .   .   .   .   .
>
> And bereth awey my whete
> And taketh me but a taillé
> For ten quarters of otes.

At all times, but particularly when there was a dearth, the poorer people snared and trapped rabbits, birds and game. This must be taken into account when we are discussing diet because although poaching was generally pro-hibited and often punished severely there is no doubt that most of the

[1] *The Annales of England*, John Stow, 1604.   [2] The Clerkes Tale.

villagers added to their slender meals by this means. Thomas Tusser, the poet of Elizabethan agriculture, recorded that 'good peason and leakes' make 'poredge in Lent and pescods in July save fish to be spent'. Miss Dorothy Hartley[1] used this as a text to her statement that pease-pudding and peas and bacon are two of the oldest of English dishes. Baked beans and bacon is a dish which has been made for centuries by country people, for example, as 'Staffordshire blanks and prizes', a mixture of peas and beans and small pieces of fried bacon. These dishes are interesting early examples of ways of eking out scarce or expensive animal protein foods with vegetable protein foods.

The methods of keeping livestock made little progress in Tudor times and it was still difficult to provide adequate winter food for the animals.

> From Christmas to May
> Weak cattle decay.[2]

The weaker ones were therefore slaughtered in the fall and the meat salted or pickled.

> At Hallowmas, slaughter time, sone commeth in:
> and than doth the husbande mans, feasting begin.
> From that time to Candlemas, weekely kill some:
> their offal for household, the better shal come.[3]

The pigeon-loft was still a prominent feature of the farmyard of big estates. It housed hundreds of birds, and provided one source of fresh meat throughout the winter. Another source was the countryside itself. All manner of birds and beasts were hunted, snared and trapped, not only by the farmers but by the villagers as well.

Except for a few cities such as London and York the medieval towns were so small that their food supply could be derived without difficulty from the immediate neighbourhood. This simple economic system became increasingly difficult to maintain as the larger towns grew with the development of trade. Difficulties arose as inevitable consequences of this development and of the growth of urban populations. The fact that no means of preserving perishable food were available other than drying, salting or pickling, did not greatly worry the country dweller, but it was a serious matter in the towns where a carcass or a consignment of fish might be several days old before being disposed of.

[1] *Food in England*, Dorothy Hartley, 1954.
[2] *Fiue hundred pointes of good Husbandrie*, Thomas Tusser, 1580.
[3] *A Hundreth good pointes of husbandrie*, Thomas Tusser, 1557.

§ 4 RISE OF THE TENANT FARMER

From the middle of the fourteenth century we detect a marked change in the structure of English country life which ultimately brought about the disintegration of the manorial system. There was, even in the thirteenth century, a small class of tenant farmers, villagers who had acquired the means to buy their freedom from the obligation to provide so many days' work in the year and to hold land on a rental from their lord. Their numbers increased steadily during the first half of the fourteenth century, most of the landowners looking favourably on a villager who cleared waste land and then held it for his own use on payment of a yearly rent. There is little doubt that the rise of this class of tenant farmers would inevitably have brought about the collapse of the medieval manorial system, but that it did so in so surprisingly short a time can be attributed to two events, the Black Death in 1348-49 and the Wars of the Roses. Of the two, the former was the more important. The devastation was fearful; some authorities think the population of the country was halved in the eighteen months the epidemic raged. There was a serious shortage of labour and widespread discontent and unrest. It is not, therefore, surprising that the landowners were tempted to rent a considerable proportion of their farm land, preferring an assured income in rentals to the worry and expense of managing an estate under exceedingly difficult conditions.

In this manner the numbers of the tenant farmers, or yeomen, grew and the size of their holdings increased as the Middle Ages merged with the Tudor period. By the middle of the fifteenth century so many villeins had purchased their freedom or escaped from bondage, so many landlords had found it more profitable to employ hired rather than forced labour, and so many of the yeomen had gained a position of independence and importance, that little was left of the old feudal or manorial system.

§ 5 TUDOR ENCLOSURES

One of the outstanding developments in the sixteenth century was the increase in trade, particularly in wool. This, more than any other agricultural development, was responsible for farming becoming a national rather than a local concern. People began to think in terms of national markets and international trade. The profits of the wool trade were so tempting that estate owners turned in every direction to find land suitable for grazing. Sometimes they sacrificed arable land, thereby causing not only local shortage of corn but unemployment. More often they cleared and enclosed waste land or forced tenants out by ruthless rent-raising. In some parts of the country, particularly in the south and south-west, covetous eyes were turned on the villagers' common fields and land was forcibly enclosed. Some say that the Tudor enclosures did not adversely affect the countryman. It is true that the amount of land lost by the common people at this date was a drop in the ocean compared with that which was taken from them in the eighteenth and nineteenth centuries, and it is also fair to say that more misery was caused by land being turned over from cultivation to pasture than by the loss of village fields, but directly or indirectly the Tudor enclosures brought much distress to the countryside.

Latimer, who spoke strongly from the pulpit against the enclosures, drew a striking picture of the changed conditions.

> My father was a Yoman, and had no landes of his owne, onlye he had a farme of iii. or iiii. pound by yere at the vttermost, and here vpon he tilled so muche as kepte halfe a dosen men. He had walke for a hundred shepe, and my mother mylked xxx. kyne. He was able and did finde the king a harnesse, wyth hym selfe, and hys horsse, whyle he came to the place that he should receyue the kynges wages . . . He kept me to schole . . . He maryed my systers with v. pounde or xx. nobles a pece . . . He kept hospitalitie for his pore neighbours. And sum almes he gaue to the poore, and all thys did he of the sayd farme. Wher he that now hath it, paieth xvi. pounde by yere and more, and is not able to do any thing for his Prynce, for himselfe, nor for his children, or geue a cup of drincke to the pore.[1]

There was a great public outcry against the enclosures and raising of rents, and serious disturbances occurred in some counties, Oxfordshire and Northamptonshire, for example, where conditions became particularly bad. The landlords were reviled in no uncertain terms.

> Cormerauntes, gredye gulles; yea men that would eate vp menne, women and chyldren, are the cause of Sedition! They take our houses ouer our headdes, they bye our growndes . . . they reyse our rentes . . . they enclose oure commens![2]

Nearly every protest blamed the increase in the flocks of sheep for the depressed state of the countryside. One such document calls attention to 'certayne causes gathered together, wherein is shewed the decaye of England,

[1] *Seven Sermons before Edward VI, 1549* (First Sermon), by Master Hugh Latimer, ex-Bishop of Worcester, edited by Edward Arber, 1869.
[2] *The Way to Health*, Robert Crowley, 1550 (*Tudor Economic Documents*, Vol. III, edited by R. H. Tawney and E. Power, 1924).

only by the great multitude of shepe, to the vtter decay of household keeping, mayntenaunce of men, dearth of corn, and other notable dyscom-
modityes, approued by syxe old Prouerbes'.[1]

> The more shepe, the dearer is the woll.
> The more shepe, the dearer is the mutton.
> The more shepe, the dearer is the beffe.
> The more shepe, the dearer is the corne.
> The more shepe, the skanter is the whit meate.
> The more shepe, the fewer egges for a peny.

More specifically this work goes on to say:

... where as catle was wont to be fede and brede; by reason of kepyng
of catle shulde increase whyt meate; and now there is nothyng kept
there but only shepe ... And furthermore, where householdes be kept,
there is hogges, pygges, and bakon, capons, hennes, duckes, egges,
frute, and many other commodityes, that is necessary and nedeful to
be had for the maintenaunce and lyuinge of the Kynges Maiesties poore
subiectes to lyue by.

Modern authorities do not agree that the development of sheep-rearing
under the Tudors was the chief cause of the depression which hit the villages
so hardly. Though it was a factor, others were even more important, such
as the debasement of the coinage and the financial instability of the Government. One of the few people to appreciate this fact was the author of *A
Discourse of the Common Weal of this Realm of England*, published in 1581.
The pamphlet was signed with the initials W. S., and for this reason it has
been attributed to William Stafford. Historians are, however, inclined to
believe that the author was John Hales (rightly regarded as one of the fathers
of political economy) who was a member of the Commission appointed in
1548 to inquire into the popular outcry against enclosures. Whoever he
was, he saw beyond the superficial view that sheep farming was the primary
cause of the depression.

... the cheife cause of all this dearth of thinges ... is the basinge or
rather corruptynge of our coine and treasure.[2]

This was to a great extent the cause of the sharp rise in the price of food which
hit the poor people so badly in the latter part of the Tudor era, and to which
we shall have occasion to refer later.

[1] *The Decaye of England only by the Great Multitude of Sheep, 1550-1553* (*Tudor Economic
Documents*, Vol. III, edited by R. H. Tawney and E. Power, 1924).
[2] *A Discourse of the Common Weal of this Realm of England*, W. S., 1581, edited by E. Lamond,
1893.

At the same time Hales (or Stafford) realized that the countryside was in a distressed condition as a result of arable land having passed out of cultivation.

> So that I haue knowen of late a docen plowes with in lesse compasse than 6 myles about me laide downe with in theise (vij) yeares; and wheare xl persons had theire lyvinges, nowe one man and his shepard hathe all.[1]

It is not surprising that the poor saw in the enclosures the source of all their troubles, for the land meant everything to them. To lose even their grazing lands meant that a cow could no longer be kept, and a cow provided the 'white meat', as dairy produce was called, for the whole family.

> Why, sir, alasse my Cow is a commonwealth to mee, for first sir, she allowes me, my wife and sonne, for to banket our selues withall, butter, cheese, whay, curds, creame, sod [boiled] milke, raw-milke, sower-milke, sweete-milke, and butter-milke.[2]

The storm of protests, backed by such influential men as Wolsey and Thomas More, at last forced the Government to take some action. A Commission was appointed in 1548 with instructions to examine all enclosures since 1485. Little came of their labours apart from a few rather half-hearted measures aimed at reducing the area of land given over to sheep and the size of flocks. Meanwhile, because the real causes were so much more deep-rooted, depression and unemployment increased, and the price of foodstuffs rose steadily.

§6 DEVELOPMENT OF GARDENS IN THE SIXTEENTH CENTURY

During the Tudor era the methods of growing and harvesting the main crops did not materially change although the more progessive owners were paying greater attention to manuring and marling. The acreage of arable under wheat was tending to increase and better yields were being obtained. The main crops were still wheat (oats in the north), barley, rye, beans and vetches.

It was in garden management that the big changes were taking place. In Flanders gardening had reached a remarkable level of development as early as the fourteenth century. Flemish knowledge and skill was introduced to England partly as a result of Alva's reign of terror from 1568-72, which drove many refugees to our shores, and partly as a direct consequence of

[1] Ibid.
[2] *A Looking Glasse, for London and Englande*, made by Thomas Lodge, Gentleman, and Robert Greene, 1598.

trade contacts with the Continent. Many owners of great estates and large farms began to take an interest in the design and cultivation of their gardens and orchards. The influence of 'certayne Dutch practises' was widespread.[1]

It seems certain that about this time a large number of flowers and vegetables were brought into England and grown there for the first time. How far this also applies to fruit it is difficult to say, but the following quotation suggests that we grew some fruit as yet unknown in France:

> Item, we have almaner of graynes and fruites, and more plenty than you; for, thanked be God! England is a fruitful and plenteous region, so that we have sum fruites whereof you have fewe, as wardeines, quynces, peches, medlers, chestnottes, and other delycious fruytes serving for all seasons of the yere, and so plenty of peres and aples, that in the weste partes of England and Sussex they make pirry and sydre, and in such habundaunce that they convaye parte over the sea, where by the Monseurs of France it is coveted for theyr beverages and drynkes.[2]

The practice of growing vegetables, not only in the gardens of the big houses but in the plots of the cottagers, developed rapidly during the latter part of the sixteenth century.

> Whereas in my time their vse is not onlie resumed among the poore commons, — I meane of melons, pompions, gourds, cucumbers, radishes, skirets, parsneps, carrets, cabbages, naeuewes [rape], turneps, and all kinds of salad herbes, — but also fed vpon as deintie dishes at the tables of delicate merchants, gentlemen, and the nobilitie, who make for their prouision yearelie for new feeds out of strange countries, from whence they haue them aboundantlie.[3]

William Bullein[4] tells much the same story, and although we have to take a great deal that Gerard wrote in his *Herball* with a grain of salt, because of his flagrant plagiarism from Continental authors, we can accept his statement about the cabbage family, 'euery of them grow in our English gardens'.[5] Isaac D'Israeli in his *Curiosities of Literature* mentions 'Sir Anthony Ashley of Wimborne St. Giles, Dorset, d. 1627, [who] first planted cabbages in this country, and a cabbage at his feet appears on his monument'. Mrs Cecil

[1] *A Booke of the Art and Maner howe to plante and grasse all sortes of Trees*, L. Mascall, 1569.
[2] *A Debate between the Heralds of England and France*, John Coke, 1549 (*Tudor Economic Documents*, Vol. III, edited by R. H. Tawney and E. Power, 1924).
[3] *Harrison's Description of England in Shakespeare's Youth*, *1577*, edited by F. J. Furnivall, 1877.
[4] *The Gouernment of Health*, William Bullein, 1595. (This was first published in 1558, but throughout we have used the later edition.)
[5] *The Herball or Generall Historie of Plantes*, John Gerard, 1597.

suggests that D'Israeli is referring to some improved variety of cabbage, for it is certain they were grown in England long before this date.[1]

The potato which 'Mr. John Hawkins Esquire . . . Captaine of the Jesus of Lubek' brought back from his voyage to 'the coast of Guinea, and the Indies of Nova Hispania' in 1564 would seem to have been the sweet potato, *Ipomea batata*.

> These Potatoes be the most delicate rootes that may be eaten, and doe farre exceed our passeneps or carets. Their pines be of the bignes of two fists . . . and the inside eateth like an apple, but it is more delicious then any sweet apple sugred.[2]

It is thought that the potato first reached Spain in about 1580 and that thence it spread to Italy. Carolus Clusius working at the Imperial gardens in Vienna obtained two tubers from Italy early in 1588. There is no clear evidence when or how the common potato, *Solanum tuberosum*, first came to England. It was mentioned by Gerard in the *Catalogue* published in 1596 and in the first edition of his *Herball* of 1597. Redcliffe Salaman[3] has discussed his description of them as 'Potatoes of Virginia' and has suggested that potatoes whose origin is acknowledged to be Peru were by that time growing in Virginia and were thence conveyed to Gerard or that they merely reached him via Virginia. Salaman also suggested that Gerard's tuber might have come from Thomas Harriott, geographer appointed by Sir Walter Raleigh who accompanied Sir Richard Greville on the second expedition to Virginia and who returned to England the following year with Sir Francis Drake. The origin of Gerard's tuber might either have been the cookhouse stores of Drake's ship or Virginia. William Cobbett believed that 'Ireland's lazy root', as he called it, was introduced into England by Sir Walter Raleigh: 'It was one of the greatest villains upon earth (Sir Walter Raleigh), who (they say) first brought this root to England.'[4] Although unable to verify this legend, Salaman has provided weighty evidence that Raleigh personally introduced the potato on to his lands at Youghal in Ireland sometime between 1586 and 1588. He has also made the alternative suggestion that when scattered ships from the Armada foundered on the west coast of Ireland their stores were plundered by peasants who may have found potatoes and planted them along the coast of Kerry and Cork. In spite of many efforts to encourage its cultivation nearly two hundred years passed before the potato became a field crop in England.

---

[1] *A History of Gardening in England*, Hon. Mrs Evelyn Cecil, 3rd Edition, 1910.
[2] *The Principall Navigations . . . of the English Nation*, Richard Hakluyt, 1598-1600.
[3] *The History and Social Influence of the Potato*, Redcliffe N. Salaman, 1949.
[4] *Rural Rides*, William Cobbett, 1830 (1853 Edition).

§ 7 ALE, BEER, WINE

Another change which this period saw was the disappearance of the vineyards. They had been characteristic features of the great religious houses in medieval times and large amounts of wine, mainly white, were made and drunk in England at that time. An account of fifteenth-century practice in vine growing is given in a MS. which was discovered in the library of Colchester Castle.[1] This work is a very full treatise of agriculture, but it is obviously compiled from Mediterranean sources for it deals with the growing of olives, oranges and lemons. It probably represents the type of work that guided the English monks in the care of their vines.

It seems likely that the dissolution of the monasteries dispersed those who had kept alive the art of tending the vines.

> ... manie Monastries in the Kingdome hauing Vineyards, had as much wine made therefrom, as sufficed their couents yeare by yeare: but long since they haue been destroyed, and the knowledge how to order a Vineyard is also vtterly perished with them.[2]

In medieval times the lord of the manor and his guests drank ale, cider, perry, metheglin (a kind of mead), or wine. All except the wine were made on his own estate. Sometimes he made his own wine but more often it was imported, for by the fourteenth century there was already a flourishing trade in wine brought from the Continent, mainly from France and the Rhineland.[3] Sweet wines were also brought from the Levant. Malmsey from Crete became very popular in the fifteenth and sixteenth centuries and a big trade was built up.

The well-to-do villagers brewed a crude ale in their own houses from barley, wheat or oats, but it is doubtful if the poorer ones were often able to spare the necessary grain. The manors brewed prodigious quantities of ale which was often supplied to the village ale-house; less frequently the proprietor was permitted to brew his own. When the tenant farmers and the villagers had become independent ale and later beer was brewed in almost every home and in larger amounts by the owners of the many inns and hostelries. Harrison gives a very detailed account of the domestic brewing of beer in a sixteenth-century household, as 'practised by my wife and hir maid seruantes'. Each brew gave the best part of 200 gallons and if we take

---

[1] *Palladius on Husbondrie*, MS. *circa* 1420, edited by the Rev. Barton Lodge, Early English Text Society, 1873-79.

[2] *Paradisi in Sole, Paradisus Terristris*, John Parkinson, 1629.

[3] A very full account of this trade is given in André Simon's scholarly work, *The History of the Wine Trade in England*, 1906.

literally the statement that it was 'practised once a moneth' the total quantity is a prodigious one for the modest household.[1]

Judging from contemporary writings wine was little drunk by comparison with ale, beer and cider.

Item, for your wyne, we have good-ale, beer, metheghelen, sydre, and pirry, beyng more holsome beverages for us then your wynes, which maketh your people dronken, also prone and apte to all fylthy pleasures and lustes.[2]

[1] *A Description of England*, William Harrison, 1577.
[2] *A Debate between the Heralds of England and France*, John Coke, 1549 (*Tudor Economic Documents*, Vol. III, edited by R. H. Tawney and E. Power, 1924).

CHAPTER II

QUALITY OF FOOD

§ 1 PROTECTION OF THE PURCHASER

EARLY in the history of civic government we find references to measures taken to protect the purchaser against the devices of those dishonest tradesmen who tried to sell him short-weight bread, watered beer, or tainted meat.

> To punysshe on pillories
> And pynynge-stooles, [stools of punishment]
> Brewesters and baksters,
> Bochiers and cokes,
> For thise are men on this molde
> That moost harm wercheth
> To the povere peple.[1]

The markets of the large cities and of some of the country towns were supervised by officials. The records of the activities of the civic authorities of London date back to very early times. As far back as 1319 the sworn wardens of the City appointed for 'overseeing' the flesh markets condemned two carcasses of beef seized from 'William Sperlyng of West Hamme' as being 'putrid and poisonous'. The jury would not accept his plea that they were fit to be eaten and he was duly convicted of attempting to sell 'bodies that have died of disease'.[2] William was put in the pillory and suffered the appropriate punishment of having the offending carcasses burnt beneath him, a popular form of humiliation. This supervision was maintained throughout the period we are considering, and it was the practice of the Mayor and his officers to visit the meat markets to watch for abuses.

> The officers charged with the ouersight of the markets in this Citie, did diuers times take from the markets pigs sterued, or otherwise unwholesome for men's sustenance, these they did slit in the eare.

At one time there was an ordinance in force prohibiting the sale of meat by candlelight. The butchers were suspected, not without reason, of being up to all sorts of tricks.

[1] *Piers Plowman.*
[2] *Memorials of London and London Life in the 13th, 14th and 15th Centuries,* H. T. Riley, 1868.

... to sell a piece of old Cow for a chop of a young Oxe, to wash your olde meate that hath hung weltring in the shop with new bloud, to trusse away an old eaw, [ewe] instead of a young weather.[1]

Sometimes, particularly when there was a shortage and consequently a temptation to profiteer, prices were controlled. In 1549, for example, the Court of Aldermen of the City of London ordained that certain commoners should be appointed to 'peruse the flesshe shambles and fishe market weekly ... that the people may haue reasonable peniworthes for their mony, and not pay above theise prices following, that is to saye:

The best beefe to be sould not above iii. qd. et di. le lb. [3½d. lb.].
The best mutton not above 1d. qd. le lb. [1½d. lb.]
All other mutton not above 1d. di qd. le lb. [1¼d. lb.]
The best veale to be sould not above, the carkasse ready dressed, vis. viiid. [6s. 8d.].[2]

Another regulation was made a few years later.

The v day of September [1552] was a proclamasyon made that the bochers of London shuld selle beyffe and motun and velle, the best for 1[d] fardyng the lb., and nekes and legs at iij fardynges the lb., and the best lam the [quarter] viij[d]. and yff thay wyll nott thay to loysse ther fredom for ever and ever.[3]

§ 2 COOKSHOPS

Partly because of the difficulty of keeping meat fresh, but also because only the larger houses had adequate means for cooking, a considerable amount of food was sent to the cookshops where a wide selection of pies, puddings and baked meats was prepared. A customer could either buy a hot dish ready for eating or he could send his own joint to be cooked. An ordinance of the Cooks and Pastelers, or Piebakers, dated 1378, gives the prices for various dishes.

The best roast pig, for 8d. Three roast thrushes, 2d. Ten eggs, one penny. For the paste, fire and trouble upon a goose, 2d. [In this case the customer provided his own goose.] The best capon baked in a pasty, 8d.[4]

[1] *A Quip for an Upstart Courtier*, Robert Greene, 1592.
[2] *A Chronicle of England, 1485-1559*, Vol. II, Charles Wriothesley (Camden Society Publication, New Series, No. 20, 1877).
[3] *Diary of Henry Machin, 1550-1563* (Camden Society Publication, No. 42, 1848).
[4] *Memorials of London*, H. T. Riley, 1868.

That these cookshops had been known in London since very early times is shown by the following quotation from William Fitz Stephen's *Description of London*, written in the twelfth century.[1]

> Moreover there is in London upon the river's bank, amid the wine that is sold from ships and wine-cellars, a public cook-shop. There daily, according to the season, you may find viands, dishes roast, fried and boiled, fish great and small, the coarser flesh for the poor, the more delicate for the rich, such as venison, and birds both big and little. If friends, weary with travel, should of a sudden come to any of the citizens, and it is not their pleasure to wait fasting till fresh food is bought and cooked and
>
> > 'till servants bring
> > Water for hands and bread'
>
> they hasten to the river bank, and there all things desirable are ready to their hand. However great the infinitude of knights or foreigners that enter the city or are about to leave it, at whatever hour of day or night, that the former may not fast too long nor the latter depart without their dinner, they turn aside thither, if it so please them, and refresh themselves each after his own manner. Those who desire to fare delicately, need not search to find sturgeon or 'Guinea-fowl' or 'Ionian francolin', since all the dainties that are found there are set forth before their eyes. Now this is a public cook-shop, appropriate to a city and pertaining to the art of civic life.

The cheaper cookshops often prepared pies and other dishes from tainted meat; there are fourteenth- and fifteenth-century regulations against such practices and occasionally a prosecution, but detection was difficult and the temptation correspondingly great.

§ 3 USE OF SPICES

It is not surprising to find that the recipe books of these times give numerous suggestions for making tainted meat edible. Washing with vinegar was an obvious, and one of the commonest, procedures. A somewhat startling piece of advice is given in the curious collection of recipes and miscellaneous information published under the title of *The Jewell House of Art and Nature* by 'Hugh Platt, of Lincolnes Inne Gentleman' in 1594. If you had venison that was 'greene' you were recommended to 'cut out all the bones, and bury [it] in a thin olde course cloth a yard deepe in the ground for 12 or 20 houres'. It would then, he asserted, 'bee sweet enough to be eaten'.

---

[1] *A Description of London*, William Fitz Stephen, *circa* 1183, translated by H. E. Butler, Historical Association Leaflet, 1934.

The popularity of strong seasoning for meat was undoubtedly due to the frequency with which it was necessary to mask taint. Onions, garlic and spices not only did this but they added relish to the rather insipid salted and pickled meats of the winter. A large trade in hot spices was carried on with the Mediterranean countries and had been in existence as far back as the eleventh century. Onions were always very popular. In the sixteenth century the demand in London was so great that large quantities were imported from Flanders and landed at Queenhythe for sale in the neighbouring market.

Saffron was grown in considerable quantities in the Eastern Counties. It was used for flavouring and colouring dishes and was very popular in the sixteenth century. It commanded a high price at that time, as much as 20s. a pound being paid for it, and for many years the trade was a flourishing one. The 'briefe Remembrance of things to be indevoured at Constantinople ... drawn by Mr. Richard Hakluyt of the middle Temple, and given to a friend that was sent into Turkie 1582' contains a clause to the effect that he was to 'endevor a vent of our Saffron for the benefit of our poore people: for a large vent found, it setteth many on worke'.[1]

The great importance of the trade in spices is shown by the antiquity of the laws aiming at control of their quality. The Pepperers, already organized in the eleventh century, were early in the fourteenth century given charge of the *peso grosso*, or Great Beam, so named because larger weights were employed and a pound of 15 ounces, which later gave rise to our avoirdupois system. From this they became known as the *Grossarii*, from which our name grocer is thought to be derived. In the twenty-sixth year of Henry VI's reign they were given, as Freemen of the Mistery of Grocers, the exclusive privilege of 'garbelling' the spices and certain drugs which were imported and sold in London. The word is certainly derived initially from the Arabic *gharbala*, possibly through the Italian *garbellare*, both of which mean to sift, but it was used in medieval England in the wider sense of inspecting or testing. The Grocers received approved fees for their duties and were empowered to confiscate on behalf of the City authorities any consignments considered to be of bad quality or adulterated. There is a long record of their activities during the next three hundred years.

Among the 'spices' sold by the Grocers was sugar; this was cane-sugar imported from India or Arabia, which usually passed through 'the Poole at Venys thorowt Almaigne by marte into Flaunders'.[2] It was used principally for making marzipan and other sweetmeats, for spices and sugar were

[1] *The Principall Navigations ... of the English Nation*, Richard Hakluyt, 1598-1600.
[2] *A Treatise concerning the Staple and the Commodities of this Realme*, Clement Armstrong (?), circa 1519-35 (*Tudor Economic Documents*, Vol. III, edited by R. H. Tawney and E. Power, 1924).

luxuries in these early times. Edward I spent the relatively enormous sum of £1600 on spices in one year. Loaf sugar cost from 1s. to 2s. a pound in the thirteenth and fourteenth centuries.[1] With the development of the trade with Madeira and the Canaries by the Portuguese in the fifteenth century the price of sugar fell, and Tudor records show that it could be bought in London for from 4d. to 10d. a pound until the sharp rise in prices in the second half of the sixteenth century.[2]

> The sugar that I have knowne at iiij[d] the li. [lb.] is nowe at xiiij[d].[3]

§4 FISH SOLD IN THE TOWNS

The supply of fresh fish to inland towns was limited to what could be caught in the immediate locality, but it seems always to have been a popular dish. Andrew Boorde speaks of the variety of fish eaten in England.

> Of all nacyons and countres, England is best serued of Fysshe, not onely of al maner of see-fysshe, but also of fresshe-water fysshe, and of all maner of sortes of salte-fysshe.[4]

Transportation of fresh fish over any distance was impracticable. Most of the fish landed at Queenhythe, the chief water gate of the City of London, where the fish market was situated, was salted or pickled unless it came from the fishing grounds off the nearby Essex or Kentish coasts. London's fresh fish came from the rivers, brooks and ponds of the surrounding country — Stow says that in 1549 there was a 'great store of very good fish of diuers sortes' in the 'towne ditch' outside the walls of London[5] — and from the nets which were set in the Thames in the vicinity of London Bridge. The latter were controlled by regulations fixing the size of the mesh in order to prevent depletion of stock. Thus, we learn from an early City record,[6] that 'John de Goldstone of Berkyng, John de Clayhurst of Grenewyche, and Walter Sprot of the same place' were convicted in 1349 of catching 'too small fish' on the east side of London Bridge. The punishment for catching 'too small fish' was sometimes picturesquely appropriate.

[1] *Manners and Household Expenses in the thirteenth to fifteenth Centuries*, Beriah Botfield, 1841, Roxburghe Club Publication.

[2] *English Trade in the Middle Ages*, L. F. Salzmann, 1931.

[3] *The Request and Suite of a True-Hearted Englishman*, William Cholmeley, 1553 (*Camden Miscellany*, Vol. II, Camden Society Publication, No. 55, 1853).

[4] *A Compendyous Regyment, or a Dyetary of Helth*, Andrew Boorde, 1542, edited by F. J. Furnivall, 1870.

[5] *A Survay of London*, John Stow, 1598.

[6] *Memorials of London*, H. T. Riley, 1868.

The xxij day of Marche [1561] dyd a woman ryd a-bowt Chepesyd and Londun for bryngyng yonge frye of dyvers kynd unlafull, with a garland a-pone her hed with strynges of the small fysse.[1]

It is not surprising that the market overseers had frequently to condemn and confiscate fish because it was stinking and unfit for consumption. They were concerned not only with the recognized danger to health of eating decomposed food but perhaps even more with the current belief that a bad smell might give rise to an epidemic. The odour of putrefaction was then regarded as one cause of outbreaks of the plague. Confiscated fish was, therefore, burnt or taken outside the City 'lest the air might become infected through the stench arising therefrom'.[2]

Fresh water fish such as carp, tench and eels were often kept in artificial ponds or 'stews' until required for the table. In the fifteenth century the 'Kings Pike Ponds' at Southwark supplied the royal table.

Oysters and mussels were plentiful, very popular and on the whole inexpensive, at any rate in London; in 1491 the former were sold at 4d. a bushel. Rathgreb, travelling in England in the late sixteenth century, was struck by the fine quality of the oysters 'which are cried in every street'.[3] He thought them larger and better than those he had seen in Italy. Sir Hugh Platt says they were kept 'fresh' for as long as twelve days by immersion in brackish water.[4] An early measure of protection was provided in 1577 by a law prohibiting the dredging of the oyster beds at the mouth of the Medway between Easter and Lammas.[5]

That fresh fish formed relatively a small part of the fishmongers' trade at this date is indicated by the character of the City Companies which then controlled it. For many years two companies existed: the Stockfishmongers, dealing in dried fish (Norwegian: *stokfisk*), mainly cod, haddock, pollack and ling, coming for the most part from Iceland and Norway,[6] and the Saltfishmongers who handled the large quantities of salted and pickled herrings, cod, eels, whiting and mackerel, coming from the East Coast, or Holland and the Baltic. In 1536 the two became united as the Fishmongers' Company. The large trade in salt required for the preservation of meat and fish explains the antiquity of the Salters' Company, incorporated in 1394.

There was a very large trade in herrings, both salted and 'white' (pickled).

[1] *The Diary of Henry Machin, 1550-1563* (Camden Society Publication, No. 42, 1848).
[2] *Memorials of London*, H. T. Riley, 1868.
[3] *A True and Faithful Narrative*, Jacob Rathgreb, 1604, cited in *England as Seen by the Foreigners in the Days of Elizabeth and James I*, W. B. Rye, 1865.
[4] *The Jewell House of Art and Nature*, Sir Hugh Platt, 1594.
[5] *English Industries of the Middle Ages*, L. F. Salzmann, 1923.
[6] *Of the Commodious Stockfish of Island, The Principall Navigations . . . of the English Nation*, Richard Hakluyt, 1598-1600.

The centre of the fishing industry was Yarmouth, where the fishermen held important rights. The price of herrings seems to have varied considerably. At times they were so cheap that forty could be bought for a penny; at other times this sum would only buy two.

It is sometimes stated that salmon was very cheap in London in the fifteenth and sixteenth centuries, and that the apprentices protested on more than one occasion at the frequency with which it appeared in their diet. This seems extremely unlikely in view of the fact that salmon fetched as much as 3s. to 5s. each in the markets.[1] Powdered salmon, that is salmon preserved by powdering with crushed salt, was cheaper, but it was by no means a common food.

The Fishmongers' Company took a prominent part in providing the public with some measure of protection against fraudulence as well as against the sale of bad fish. There are many records in the fourteenth and fifteenth centuries of confiscations of baskets and measures found to hold too small a weight of fish. They examined the quality of imported preserved fish and regulated its sale. A Proclamation of 1382 refers to conditions for the sale of 'Herrings from Scone', 'Jernemouthe' [Yarmouth], 'Holyland' [Heligoland] and 'Sounde' [between Denmark and Sweden].[2] (There was a considerable import of salted or pickled herrings from across the North Sea.) One merchant, Thomas Welford, fell foul of this order, for he was caught selling herrings to 'hukkesteres' at the Wharf of Queenhythe on Saturday, the Eve of St Lawrence, at the rate of five for a penny, so that they could only afford to re-sell them at four a penny. He was fined and ordered to give his customers nine for a penny.[3]

§ 5 MILK AND BUTTER IN THE TOWNS

Milk, unless it was obtained quite fresh from the farms just outside the towns, could not be kept. Although comparatively little seems to have been sold its price in the fifteenth and sixteenth centuries was low. Stow tells how he used to fetch fresh milk from a farm near the Minories.

> ...neare adioyning to this Abbey on the South side thereof, was sometime a Farme belonging to the said Nunrie, at the which Farme I my selfe in my youth haue fetched many a halfe pennie worthe of Milke, and neuer had lesse than three Ale pints for a half pennie in the Sommer, nor lesse than one Ale quart for a halfe pennie in the Winter, always hote from the Kine, as the same was milked and strained.[4]

[1] *English Industries of the Middle Ages*, L. F. Salzmann, 1923.
[2] *Memorials of London*, H. T. Riley, 1868.   [3] Ibid.
[4] *A Survay of London*, John Stow, 1598.

Large quantities of butter were salted in the country, thus enabling the farmers to keep it throughout the winter when none other was available. It seems to have been used chiefly for cooking. Harrison mentions 'pestiferous purueiours' and 'buttermen' who travelled from farm to farm buying up eggs, chickens and butter so that 'our butter [which] was scarcelie woorth eighteene pence the gallon . . . is now worth three shillings foure pence, & perhaps fiue shillings.[1] Salted butter formed the bulk of that sold in the towns and there can be little doubt that much of it was to a greater or lesser degree rancid. It was often sold in a half liquid condition.

§6 THE TOWN BAKERS

Bread, made in the home almost everywhere in the country — in medieval times it was sometimes baked in a manorial or communal village oven — was obtained by townspeople from quite early times, at any rate in the south, from the bakers. The trade was already organized in London in the eleventh century and two Companies, the White Bakers and the Brown Bakers, were incorporated about 1307. They united two hundred years later. Although a good part of London's bread was baked in the City, in bakehouses approved by the Guilds, some of it was baked in the villages east of London, Newington, Hackney and Stratford (the Stratford-atte-Bowe of Chaucer), by 'outside' bakers who sent the loaves in 'diuerse long cartes'[2] to be sold at certain street corners. The City bakers, however, objected to this competition and made several attempts to have it stopped.

Bread was indeed the staff of life in those days and it is understandable that its quality and sale were the concern of the governing authorities. As far back as the reign of King John there are records relating to the price of bread, but the most important date is that of the famous Assize of Bread (51. Hen. II) in 1266. From that date down to as late as 1822, when the first Bread Act replaced the Assize, there is a long list of changes and modifications of the regulations governing the weight and sale of bread. The original Act fixed the weight of various types of loaves and authorized the punishment of the pillory for false weight.

. . . the poore crie out, the rich find fault, and the Lord Maior and the Sherifs like honorable and worshipful Maiestrats, euery day walke abroad and weigh your bread, and yet al will not serue to make you honest men.[3]

[1] *A Description of England*, William Harrison, 1577.
[2] *A Survay of London*, John Stow, 1598.
[3] *A Quip for an Upstart Courtier*, Robert Greene, 1592.

Prosecutions were frequent and not only the pillory but the punishment of being 'drawn upon a hurdle from the Guildhall to his own house, through the great streets, where there may be most people assembled, and through the great streets that are most dirty, with the faulty loaf hanging from his neck'[1] was enforced in the case of a dishonest or careless baker.

There is an amusing account of a 'theevish miller' in the pillory in an incomplete poem by John Lydgate, written about 1450.

> Put out his hed lyst nat for to dare,
>   But lyk a man upon that tour to abyde,
> For cast of eggys wil not oonys spare,
>   Tyl he be quaylled, body, bak and syde;
> His hed endooryd, and of verray pryde,
>   Put out his armys, shewith abroad his face,
> The fenestrallys he made for him so wyde,
> Clemyth to been a capteyn of that place.[2]

The women were usually dealt with more leniently, if we can generalize from two recorded cases. Juliana, la Pestour Neutone, that is, a bakeress of Newington, 'brought a cart laden with six shillings' worth of bread' into the City in 1298. In 'West Chepe' it was examined and the white bread found to be wanting in weight, according to the size of the halfpenny loaf. Her brown bread was passed. The white bread was confiscated and given to the prisoners in Newgate, a practice which seems to have been fairly common. On the Monday before the Feast of St Hilary, 1310, nine bakeresses were taken by Roger de Paunier, Sheriff of London, and their bread seized and weighed before the Mayor and Aldermen. It was found to be of short weight but because it was cold and should not have been weighed in that condition they were let off without a fine on condition that they sold three halfpenny loaves for a penny.[3]

Broadly speaking, the many types of bread sold at this date could be classified as 'white', 'brown' or 'black'. It must not be thought that these names refer to products similar in character to those in use today. Modern white breads are made from wheaten flour from which much of the bran and germ has been removed during milling. The bran and germ contain higher proportions of some mineral salts, vitamins and good quality proteins than the rest of the grain, and if they are removed bread becomes a foodstuff providing relatively more starch and relatively less of other nutrients. For this

---

[1] *Liber Albus*, compiled by John Carpenter and Richard Whittington, 1419, translated by H. T. Riley, 1861.
[2] *The Deserts of Theevish Millers and Bakers, Lydgate's Minor Poems*, edited by J. O. Halliwell, 1840.
[3] *Memorials of London*, H. T. Riley, 1868.

reason white bread on sale in the United Kingdom in 1956 is restored with vitamin B_1, nicotinic acid and iron in specified amounts. The best quality 'white' flour, prior to the middle of the nineteenth century, was a wholemeal flour, produced by stone grinding, from which the coarse particles of the bran were removed by 'bolting' through fine linen or woollen cloths. It contained a good deal of finely ground bran and most of the germ, and was very pale cream in colour owing to the presence of the yellow pigment of the germ. Such 'stone-ground' flour can still be obtained from a few surviving mills in England today. Less fine grades of 'white' flour ranging in colour from 'dirty white' to grey were produced by 'bolting' through coarser cloths, thus allowing more of the bran to pass through. The finest 'white' flour was used in Early English and Tudor times for making the best quality bread, which was called 'paindemaigne' ('painmain', 'pandemayn' and many other spellings are encountered). It was often stamped with a figure of Our Saviour. By the fifteenth century this type of bread was generally known as 'manchet'.

Flours of second or third quality were used to bake the darker breads which went by a variety of names, 'cheat', 'cocket', etc. 'Brown' breads were sometimes wholly wheaten; they contained the whole of the ground grain and were very coarse and rather dark. One early name for such breads was 'tourte', but this name was more generally applied to dark maslin or rye breads which were also referred to as 'brown' or 'black', 'bis' or 'trete'. Oats, in the south, were usually given only to horses; in the north oatmeal was the staple cereal.[1]

§ 7 SOPHISTICATION OF ALE AND BEER

The importance of ale and beer in the everyday life of these times can be judged from the fact that the list of acts, ordinances and regulations aimed at protecting the customer against fraud and bad quality is nearly as extensive as the corresponding list relating to bread. One of the earliest references to a control of the quality of ale is that contained in the *Liber Albus* compiled in 1419 by John Carpenter and Richard Whittington, which mentions the 'Aleconners of the Ward' whose duty it was to taste each brew and report on it to the Mayor. Ale was not supposed to be sold before it had been passed by the 'ale-conner'.

Until the end of the fifteenth century little beer was brewed and the practice of adding bitter herbs, particularly hops, which were introduced

[1] Cf. Samuel Johnson's *Dictionary*, 1st Edition 1755: 'Oats — a grain, which in England is generally given to horses, but in Scotland supports the people.'

from Flanders early in the century,[1] was at first regarded with grave suspicion. Charges of adulteration with hops were made against brewers in 1424 and protests against the introduction of the new drink were made not only by the ale-brewers but by the authorities of the City of London. Henry VI, in a Royal Writ dated 1436, tried to help forward the innovation by commending the new drink 'called biere' as 'notable, healthy and temperate', but it was many years before it became popular. Andrew Boorde praised ale and condemned 'bere' which he described as the 'naturall drynke for a Dutche man. And nowe of late days it is moche vsed in Englande to the detryment of many Englysshe men'.[2] By 1598, however, a foreign visitor was writing that 'The general drink is beer, which is prepared from barley, and is excellently well tasted, but strong and what soon fuddles.'[3]

Henry VIII made an unsuccessful attempt to proscribe the use of hops in beer and his own brewer was forbidden to use either hops or brimstone.[4] A wide variety of bitter substances was employed instead of hops. Sir Hugh Platt advised those who wished to 'brew good and wholsome Beere, without any Hoppes at al' to use an extract of wormwood.[5] Probably the reason why beer steadily replaced ale is that hops contain resinous constituents which exert a marked preservative action on the brew. This was an important discovery in an age when unless ale was brewed strong it would not keep for more than a few days in warm weather.

Judging by the records of charges and convictions much inferior, watered or bad ale and beer was sold. There was, however, some excuse for the brewers. In warm weather a brew would soon 'go off' as a result of bacterial action, the beer turning cloudy, sour, or 'vinegary'. Even in cool weather badly contaminated casks might cause the beer to turn acid in a few days. But we can scarcely blame the Tudor brewers for ignorance of a fact which was not discovered until Pasteur's work three centuries later. On the other hand, there was unquestionably fraudulent practice which not infrequently aroused the wrath of the public. Robert Greene has some amusing remarks to make in the discourse between 'Cloth-breeches' and 'Velvet-breeches' which forms the main part of his *Quip for an Upstart Courtier.* It is a quaint volume in which he professes to expose the fraudulent practices of many trades.

And you, masser Brewer, that growe to be worth forty thousand pounds by your selling of soden water, what subtilty haue you in

[1] Cf. the old rhyme: '*Turkies,* carps, hoppes, picarell and beere, Came into England all in one yeare.'
[2] *A Compendyous Regyment, or a Dyetary of Helth,* Andrew Boorde, 1542.
[3] *A Journey into England, 1598,* Paul Hentzner, translated by Horace Walpole, 1757.
[4] *Manners and Household Expenses in the thirteenth to fifteenth Centuries,* Beriah Botfield, 1841, Roxburghe Club Publication.
[5] *Sundrie new and Artificiall remedies against Famine,* Sir Hugh Platt, 1596.

making your beare, to spare the malt, and put in the more of the hop
to make your drinke, (be barly neuer so cheape) not a whit the stronger,
yet neuer sel a whit the more measure for mony, you can when you haue
taken all the hart of the malt away, then clap on store of water tis
cheape enough, and mash a tunning of small beare, that it scoures a
mans mawe like rennish wine: in your conscience how many barrels
draw you out of a quarter of malt? fie, fie, I conceale your falshood,
least I should bee too broad in setting downe your faults.

The 'ale-conners' or 'ale-tasters' were able to deal with complaints of the
sale of sour or murky beer but the detection of watering and of the use of
prohibited bitter herbs or other brewing materials was more difficult. In
the absence of any tests which could be applied to beer they had to rely on
information and a search of the premises. It is sometimes stated that these
officials made use of a primitive test for the presence of added sugar. Some
of the suspected beer was spilt on a wooden stool and the 'ale-taster' sat
himself down. If after a time, he found the seat of his leather breeches
glued to the stool the brewer was accused of adding sugar. We have been
unable to trace the source from which this amusing but improbable story is
derived.

§ 8 FAKED AND ADULTERATED WINES

There was widespread sophistication of imported wines, particularly
with a view to passing off an inferior product as one of better quality. Sir
Hugh Platt, disgusted with what he had learnt of the methods of the fraudulent vintners, wished he could 'drawe my Countrey men into such a liking
of our Royston Grape, that in the ende they woulde for the most part content themselues with their English and naturall drinke'.[1] There is evidence
of an extensive manufacture and sale of 'concocted' wines. Sometimes these
were cheap, thin French wines to which more 'body' was given by adding
starch, gum, sugar or essences. Other preparations were horrible mixtures
compounded from wine dregs, vinegar or oil of vitriol, and coloured with
sugar, blackberry juice or 'turnsel' (*Tournesole*, a dyestuff obtained from the
Mediterranean plant *Crozophora tinctoria*).

To quote again from *A Quip for an Upstart Courtier*.

Now sir for the Ventner ... I hold him as deceitful as any of the rest,
what, the vintner, why, he is a kind of Negromancer, for at midnight
when al men are in bed, then he forsooth fals to his charmes and spels,

[1] *The Jewell House of Art and Nature*, Sir Hugh Platt, 1594.

so that he tumbles one hogshead into another, and can make a cup of
Claret that hath lost his colour to looke high with a dash of red wine
at his pleasure, if he hath a strong gascoigne wine, for feare it should
make his guests to soone drunke, he can allay it with a small rochel wine
he can cherish up white wine with sack, and perhaps if you bid him wash
the pot cleane when hee goes to drawe you a quart of wine, hee will
leaue a little water in the bottome, and then draw it ful of wine, and
what and if he do? tis no harme, wine and water is good against the heat
of the liuer.

The quality of the wine sold in the towns was to some extent the concern
of the civic officials, but the Vintners Company was the chief body in
authority. Persons convicted of the sale of bad wine or of falsification were
subjected to an appropriate punishment. John Penroe came before the Mayor
and Aldermen of the City of London on November 11th, 1350, charged with
selling unsound wine. He was found guilty and sentenced to drink a copious
draught, to have the rest poured over his head and to 'forswear the calling of
a vintner . . . unless he can obtain the favour of our Lord the King as to the
same'. By what means fair or foul he succeeded we do not know but the
record states that he was readmitted as a vintner on the 24th day of February
five years later.[1]

A charge of compounding artificial 'wine' was brought against William
Horold, who suffered the pillory in 1419 'for that he falsly and deceyuably
gummyd and raysyd two buttes with diuers gummes and unholsome other
thynges for mannys body, and feld hem ful of old and feble Spaynissh wyn,
to have a lykly manere taste and smell to the drynkyng of Romeney'.[2]

[1] *Memorials of London*, H. T. Riley, 1868.   [2] Ibid.

CHAPTER III

MEALS OF THE PEOPLE

§ 1 FOOD OF PEASANTS AND VILLAGERS

In considering the typical meals of the Englishman in these times it is convenient to divide the population into four classes: the village labourer and the lord of the manor in the country, and the artisan and the wealthy merchant or nobleman in the towns. It is, of course, generally recognized that the tables of the rich were lavishly spread, but what emerges rather strikingly from the records and writings of foreign visitors to England is the unanimity of their opinion that the Englishman of every class fed better than his counterpart on the Continent. The only thing that seems to have impressed them as much as the richness of the English diet was the dirt. Of course the peasants suffered badly, as they still do today in primitive agricultural countries, when harvests failed, but in the good years they were well nourished, probably considerably better than the poor country people in the rest of Europe.

A flourishing countryside is described in the fourteenth-century *Polycronycon*.

> Also Englonde is beauteuous of londe/floure of londes all about that londe is full payed with fruyte and good of his owen/that londe releueth strange men that hath nede thereto. And when honger greueth other londes/that londe fedeth them/that londe bereth fruyt and corn good ynoughe/ . . . hony mylke and cheese/this Ilonde thereof shall bere the pryse.
>
> .   .   .   .
>
> For this Ilonde is best to bryng forth trees and fruyte . . . and beestes. And wyn groweth therein in some place. The londe hath plente of fowles and of beestes of dyuerse maner kynde. The londe is plentueous and the see also . . . There is grete plente of small fysshe of samen and of eeles. So that the people in some place fedeth thyr swyne with fysshe.

A dispatch from the Venetian Ambassador at the opening of the sixteenth century contains the following passage:

> The English, being great epicures and very avaricious by nature, indulge in the most delicate fare themselves and give their households

the coarsest bread and beer and cold meat baked on Sunday for the week, which, however, they allow them in great abundance.

Chaucer and the author of *Piers Plowman* give some interesting information about the daily food of the peasant and village labourer. Of the 'poure widewe' in the *Nonnes Preestes Tale* the former says:

> No win ne dranke she, neyther white ne red:
> Hire bord was served most with white and black.
> Milk and broun bread, in which she fond no lack,
> Seinde [singed] bacon, and somtime an ey or twey.

Such were her 'slender meles'. The 'white and black' refers, of course, to milk and coarse brown or 'black' rye or maslin bread. The bacon was from the pig she had salted down the previous autumn. There are so many references to bacon in contemporary writings that there can be no doubt that it was the chief meat on the peasant's table.

Much the same type of staple foods are referred to in the lines in which Piers Plowman deplores his shortage of food until the next harvest comes.

> 'I have no peny', quod Piers,
> 'Pulettes to bugge, [buy]
> Ne neither gees ne grys, [pigs]
> But two grene [fresh] cheses,
> A few cruddes [curds] and creme,
> And an haver cake, [oat-cake]
> And two loves of benes and bran
> Y-bake for my fauntes; [infants]
> And yet I seye, by my soule!
> I have no salt bacon,
> Ne no cokeney [egg] by Crist!
> Coloppes for to maken.
> Ac [but] I have percile [parsley] and porettes, [leeks]
> And manye cole plauntes,
> And ek a cow and a calf.
> And a cart mare
> To drawe a-feld my donge,
> The while the droghte lasteth;
> And by this liflode [state of life] we mote lyve
> Til Lammesse tyme.
> And by that, I hope to have
> Hervest in my crofte.'

These passages, both of which refer to the ordinary country people, justify the view that their general diet was of coarse 'black bread' (maslin, barley, rye or beanflour), milk, cheese, eggs and occasionally bacon or a fowl. Dairy produce was generally known as 'white meat' and the view has been expressed that 'white meats' were extensively consumed by all classes in the country in medieval times but that with the rising prosperity of the early sixteenth century they came to be regarded as inferior food and fit only for the use of the common people. The chief authority for this statement appears to be a passage from Harrison's *Description of England*.

> ... white meats, milke, butter & cheese, which were woont to be accounted of as one of the chief staies throughout the Iland, are now reputed as food appertinent onelie to the inferiour sort, whilest such as are more wealthie, doo feed vpon the flesh of all kindes of cattell accustomed to be eaten, all sorts of fish taken vpon our coasts and in fresh riuers, and such diuersitie of wild and tame foules as are either bred in our Iland, or brought vnto vs from other countries of the maine.

It is doubtful whether we are justified in accepting this view, for all the indications are that the tables of the rich were heavily laden with meat and fish from the earliest times. The quotation is of more value in strengthening our conviction that 'white meats', that is, dairy produce, had formerly been commonly eaten by the poor country people, although at the date that Harrison was writing their consumption by this class was falling. In the middle ages the peasant seldom ate meat except when he did a little successful poaching or when the lord of the manor gave a feast to celebrate the harvest home or some other such occasion. The food given to the tenants at times of 'boon-work' seems to have been barley, oatmeal, wheat, herrings and ale or beer.[1] Prodigious quantities of ale were drunk at these feasts but at other times the peasants rarely drank anything stronger than whey, butter-milk, or simply water.

The general character of the poor countryman's food seems to have changed steadily for the better during the greater part of the fifteenth century. There is little doubt that larger quantities of beef, mutton and veal were being eaten at this time, because the protests in the sixteenth century against enclosures and the consequent dearth and high prices almost invariably declare that the countryman is no longer able to afford these meats. It seems probable, therefore, that the villagers were better fed during the fifteenth and early sixteenth centuries than they had been earlier.

The second half of the sixteenth century saw a sharp turn for the worse. It was a period of depression for which the sheep-farmer was popularly

[1] *The Economic and Social History of an English Village*, N. S. B. Gras, 1930.

blamed but which, in fact, was caused by the financial insecurity of the country. Prices rose alarmingly and there was widespread unemployment. Town and countryside were badly affected by the depression. For the first time in England the numbers of out-of-works roaming the countryside as 'rogues and vagabonds' became so large that a serious national problem was created. These miserable creatures, more often than not driven to crime to keep body and soul together, were the subject of a great deal of primitive poor-law legislation from about 1550.

For the poorer people the most serious matter was the rise in prices, which was alarming, many commodities increasing twofold in less than a decade.

> Remember that within these viij yeares youe could bie the best pigge, or goose, that I could laie my handes one, for iiij^d., which nowe cost me viij^d., and a good Capon for iij or iiij^d., a chicken for a peny, a hen for ij^d., which nowe will cost me double the mony; and yt is likewise of great ware, as of mutton and beife.[1]

Records of the purchases for the kitchen at Woollaton Hall, Nottingham-shire, show chickens at 1d. each in 1515 and 3d. each in 1603. A capon cost 6d. in 1597; by 1603 the price had risen to 1s. 2½d. Geese were 4d. each in 1515 and 1s. 4d. in 1597.[2]

The economist, John Hales, thought the financial insecurity of the country primarily responsible, but he realized that other causes were at work, among them profiteering.

> Ther be thre thynges that be the cause of the Vnyuersall dearthe of vytelles in the Realme. The first is Lack of breadyng and rearyng of catell & pultrie ware . . . The seconde is Regratyng when the most part of vyteyls be gathered into a fewe mens hands who may differ [defer] to sell, but when they see ther most profet. And the third is the kynges prouysions, when vyteyle is taken from the poore people that be the breaders agents ther willes.[3]

Many of the villagers were no longer able to keep a cow to provide them with 'white meats', and meat soon reached a price beyond their slender wages. They had to fall back on the simple diet of earlier times, bread, peas and beans, and what they could gather or trap in wood or field, river or pond.

[1] *Tract on Causes of Dearth*, John Hales, 1548, printed in *A Discourse of the Common Weal of this Realm of England, 1581*, edited by E. Lamond, 1893.
[2] Report on MSS of Lord Middleton, Historical MSS Commission, 1911.
[3] *Tract on Causes of Dearth*, John Hales, 1548, printed in *A Discourse of the Common Weal of this Realm of England, 1581*, edited by E. Lamond, 1893.

Owre Englische nature cannot lyue by Rooats,
by water, herbys or suche beggerye baggage,
that may well serue for vile owtelandische Cooatis;
geeue Englische men meate after their old vsage,
Beiff, Mutton, Veale, to cheare their courage.[1]

It is far from being the 'Merrie England' of popular fancy that is portrayed in Churchyard's poem, written towards the end of Queen Elizabeth's reign.

England was cald, a librall countrey rich,
That tooke great ioy, in spending beefe and bred.
In deede this day, the countrey spendeth mich,
But that expense, stands poore in little sted.
For they finde nought, where hounds and hawks are fed,
But hard colde posts, to leane at in great lacke;
Who wants both foode, and clouts to cloth their backe.[2]

Some rather grim pictures can be drawn from the advice given by H. P. Esq. (Sir Hugh Platt) in his *Sundrie new and Artificiall remedies against Famine, written . . . vppon thoccasion of this present Dearth* in 1596. Those who were short of corn were recommended to 'boile your beanes, pease, beechmast, &c. in faire water . . . and the second or third boyling, you shall finde a strange alteration in taste, for the water hath sucked out & imbibed the greatest part of their ranknesse, then muste you drie them . . . and make bread thereof'. When these substitutes gave out you did not lose heart for you could make 'excellent bread of the rootes of Aaron called Cuckow pit, or starch rootes' (the wild lily of the hedgerows, *arum maculatum*).

Soups seem always to have been very popular and Andrew Boorde says 'Potage is not so moch vsed in al Crystendom as it is vsed in Englande.'[3] He commends heartily 'potages', 'stewpottes', 'grewell', 'fyrmentye', 'pease potage', 'beane potage', 'almon mylke' and 'ryce potage'. Fennel, the 'erbe precyows' as it is called in a fourteenth-century MS. now in the Royal Library at Stockholm, was in great demand for flavouring soups. Since soup was a common dish of the poor it is curious that none has survived as a characteristic national dish.

One of the dishes for which we are famous the world over, bacon or ham and eggs may date from these times, for the peasant sometimes had bacon, and eggs were plentiful. We have traced no reference to the dish as we now

[1] *The Pleasaunt Poesye of Princelie Practise*, William Forrest, 1548 (*Tudor Economic Documents*, Vol. III, edited by R. H. Tawney and E. Power, 1924).
[2] *Churchyard's Challenge*, T. Churchyard, 1593.
[3] *A Compendyous Regyment, or a Dyetary of Helth*, Andrew Boorde, 1542.

D

know it, but Andrew Boorde speaks of 'coloppes and egges' and the doctor in *Piers Plowman* ate 'egges y-fryed with grece' on 'heighe dees'.[1]

§ 2 THE FOOD OF THE MANOR SERVANTS AND FARMERS

In the Middle Ages the manor servants appear to have lived largely on bread — less coarse than that eaten by the peasants — a good deal of meat, cheese, salt fish, herrings, ale, beer or cider. These are the foods mentioned in manorial records, such as that at Martham in Norfolk, in 1272, which Mr. H. S. Bennett quotes in his book on English manor life.[2] The servants on this estate ate beef, wheat and rye bread, pease-pottage, herrings, cod, cheese, and an occasional goose, and drank beer brewed on the estate.

A good description of the 'fermers dailie diet' is given in Thomas Tusser's doggerel verse.

> A Plot set downe, for fermers quiet,
>   as time requires, to frame his diet;
> With sometime fish, and sometime fast,
>   that household store, may longer last.

Lent.

> Let Lent well kept, offend not thee,
>   for March and Aprill breeders be,
> Spend herring first, saue saltfish last:
>   for saltfish is good, when Lent is past.

Easter.

> When Easter comes, who knowes not than,
>   that Veale and Bakon, is the man.
> And Martilmas beefe, doth beare good tack:
>   when countrie folk, doe dainties lack.

Midsomer.

> When Mackrell ceaseth from the seas,
>   John Baptist brings, grasse beefe and pease.

Mihelmas.

> Fresh herring plentie, Mihell brings,
>   with fatted Crones [mutton] and such old things.

Hallomas.

> All Saintes doe laie, for porke and souse: [pickled pork]
>   for sprats and spurlings [smelts], for their house.

[1] The old English word 'Coloppe' seems to have been used in the sixteenth century both for fried eggs and bacon and for slices of fried meat.
[2] *Life on the English Manor, 1100-1450*, H. S. Bennett, 1937.

Christmas.   At Christmas play, and make good cheere:
                    for Christmas comes but once a yeere.

           ·   ·   ·   ·   ·

          The land doth will, the Sea doth wish,
                    Spare sometimes flesh, and feede of fish:

          Where fish is scant, and fruite of trees:
                    Supplie that want, with butter and cheese.[1]

Brawn appears to have been a popular dish. It is mentioned by several writers, including Tusser.

          At Mihelmass safely, go stie up thy Bore,
          least straying abrode, ye doo see him no more:
          The sooner the better for Halontide nie,
          and sooner he brawneth, if hard he doo lie.[2]

Andrew Boorde says it was 'an vsual meate in wynter amonges Englysshe men'.[3]

The dishes of beef and mutton which came to the table of the prosperous yeomen, farmers and merchants of the sixteenth century established the reputation of England as a meat-eating nation. All the foreigners who visited this country were deeply impressed by the quality and variety of these meats.

   ... the English Cookes, in comparison with other Nations, are most commended for roasted meates.[4]

It was at this period that the beef, beer and bread of England became famous. 'Befe of Englande to Englyshemen whiche are in helthe, bryngeth stronge nouryshynge', wrote Sir Thomas Elyot in 1539.[5]

§3 THE FOOD OF THE WEALTHY COUNTRYMAN

The tables of the medieval nobleman were heavily laden with meat and fish: beef, mutton, pork, veal, game and venison, and carp, pike, eels, lampreys, etc. Their bread was fine wheaten manchet and they drank red and white French and German table wines, sweet wines from the Levant, ale,

---

[1] *Fiue hundred pointes of good Husbandrie*, Thomas Tusser, 1580.
[2] Ibid.
[3] *A Compendyous Regyment, or a Dyetary of Helth*, Andrew Boorde, 1542.
[4] *Fyne Moryson's Itinerary, 1617*, edited from *Holinshed's Chronicles*, by F. J. Furnivall, 1878
[5] *The Castel of Helth*, Sir Thomas Elyot, 1539.

beer and cider. The larder of one manor in the reign of Edward II held
'40 tunnes of wyn, 600 bacons, 80 carkasses of martilmasse beefe, 600
muttons and 10 tunnes of syder'. The household expenses of Richard de
Swinfield, Bishop of Hereford,[1] for the years 1289-90, include fresh and
salted meats, game, venison and wildfowl, and in addition to the common
vegetables such as onions, leeks and garlic, there is a reference, rather
exceptional in records of this date, to salted and pickled greens. These were
probably cabbages. The interesting fifteenth-century MS. by Gilbert
Kymer in the Sloane Collection mentions cabbages, lettuces, spinach and
beetroots as being boiled with meat. Occasionally they were eaten raw with
olive oil and spices, as a salad. Kymer questioned the propriety of this.[2]

Dried fruits, raisins, prunes, etc., are often mentioned. They came from
Spain and the Levant.

Nearly three hundred years later much the same stores were to be found
in the larders of the big houses. The household book for Lord Middleton's
establishment at Woollaton Hall, Nottinghamshire, for the years 1587-88
shows purchases of eggs, butter, ling (probably dried), saltfish (cod), stockfish (dried cod), white (pickled) herrings, red herrings, cheese, beef, bacon,
mutton, capons, hens, ducks, plovers, hernshaws, beer, vinegar, sugar,
pepper, prunes, currants and raisins.[3] No mention is made of fresh fruit or
vegetables but a single purchase of 2 lb. 1 oz. of 'marmelade' at 5s. 3d. shows
what a luxury such imported preserved fruits were. A considerable amount
of wine, both 'table' and 'sweet', was bought. In 1515 claret and sack cost
about 8d. and 'Malmyse' 1s. 4d. a gallon.

When 'Mr. Percyvall Wyllughby' dined at Woollaton the steward
recorded that he 'spente for him and his two men, viz: imprimis a quarter of
mutton, 16^{d}.; for a piece of beife, 8^{d}.; for butter, 6^{d}.; for bread, 6^{d}.'

§ 4 THE TOWNSMAN'S FOOD

Even in medieval times more fish and meat was eaten by the craftsmen
and workpeople in the towns than by the villagers. An Act passed in 1363
dealing with the food and apparel of the servants of noblemen, artisans and
tradesmen, orders that they be given meat or fish once a day and the offal of
other victuals, together with milk and cheese, according to their station.

During the early Tudor times the workpeople of the towns seem to have
lived well. It is doubtless this period Harrison had in mind when he spoke

[1] Camden Society Publication, No. 62, 1855.
[2] Cited in *Manners and Household Expenses of England in the thirteenth to fifteenth Centuries*,
Beriah Botfield, 1841, Roxburghe Club Publication.
[3] Report on MSS of Lord Middleton, Historical MSS Commission, 1911.

of the workmen as living on a great variety of meats, mutton, veal, lamb, pork, souse (pickled pork), brawn, bacon and 'foules of sundrie sorte', as well as cheese, butter, eggs and fruit. It certainly does not apply to the year in which his *Description of England* was published (1577) for this was a time of hardship for all except the wealthy. The Tudor townsman ate three meals a day. When times were good he ate as much meat as he could afford; when they were bad he fell back on salt fish, cheese and soups. Breakfast, taken rather early at about 6 or 7 o'clock, usually consisted of bread, salted or pickled herrings, cold meat, pottage, cheese and ale. The mid-day meal, which was often eaten at a tavern or bought at the cookshop and taken home, was roast meats, pies, stews or soups, bread, cheese, ale or beer. Early in the evening, at 5 or 6 p.m., came a supper of cold meats and cheese with bread and ale or perhaps a little wine.

The only vegetable used in quantity was the onion but cabbages were occasionally boiled with the meat or soup. Fresh fruit, shellfish and sweet pastries were occasional treats.

Before the middle of the sixteenth century food was cheap. One penny would buy two good-sized loaves of wheaten flour or nearly a pound of beef or cheese; a pound of butter or a chicken cost about 2d. while a fine large goose or capon could be had for 3d. or 4d.

Until prices began to mount about 1525 the townspeople could afford to live well but for the rest of the century the steadily rising prices, accompanied as they were by only a slight increase in wages, inevitably meant that the standard of living fell. The poorest wage-earners fared the worst because, as Thorold Rogers's analyses indicate, their wages scarcely changed during the hundred years from 1541-1642. The skilled artisans were not quite so badly affected for during that period their earnings rose by about 50 per cent. The average increase in the price of the chief foodstuffs was, however, of the order of 120 per cent. This meant that the poorer classes were able to afford less and less meat and milk and were forced to base their diet on bread, cheese and salt fish.

As early as 1390 the civic authorities of London bought quantities of corn to relieve the poor during a dearth. From that time onwards there are many records of the measures they and the authorities in other towns took to equalize the distribution of grain and to prevent profiteering. Large reserves of corn were held in the granaries built by the Corporations and the City Companies. The period of 1400 to 1600 marks the transition of the corn-trade from a small and localized affair, where one area might have an acute shortage while only twenty miles away supplies might be plentiful, to a commerce based on the corn-markets of the larger towns. A clear picture of the measures which were taken in the sixteenth century to obtain equitable distribution of corn and to prevent its waste at a time of dearth and high prices is given by the *Book of Orders* published in 1587.[1]

Some idea of the measures taken by the authorities to relieve corn shortages may be gathered from such facts as the following: In 1560, a time of dearth, the Grocers' Company paid the enormous sum of £400 for corn for the poor. This grain was sold at a reduced price at the market at Queenhythe. Prices were exceptionally high in 1587 when wheat rose to 64s. a quarter, remaining at about the same price until 1597. In 1595 the city fathers of Norwich spent £200 to obtain rye from Denmark so that it could be sold at the cheap rate of 4s. a bushel to the half starved poor. In London similar charitable steps were taken both by the civic authorities and by the City Companies.

The diets provided in charitable institutions in the sixteenth century were all of the meat, salt fish, cheese, beer and bread variety. Large quantities of pork, mutton, ribs of beef, barrels of herrings (salted or pickled), bread, rye flour and beer were ordered for the inmates of St Bartholomew's Hospital,[2] while the 'Annual Accompt' of Christ's Hospital makes frequent mention of mutton, 'Beof', 'whytinge', 'hearinge', 'playse' and other 'ffyshe'. Dr E. H. Pearce remarks, 'The modern Lawsonian must not be scandalized if the first item of all was "Beare, iij^li vj^s viij^d", [£3.6.8.] and if a mere trifle was spent on "Mylke" and "Butyer".'[3] In January 1554, however, they purchased 154 gallons of milk at 3d. a gallon.

Sir Frederic Eden[4] gives the 'Orders . . . for the House of Correction at Bury, Suffolk, Anno 1588.'

Item, It is ordered, that every person committed to the said house, shall have for theire dietts, theis portions of meate and drinke followinge, and not above, (viz). At every dynner and supper on the fleshe daies, bread made of rye, viij ounces troye waight, with a pynte of porredge, a quarter of a pound of fleshe, and a pinte of beare, of the rate of iijs. a barrell, every barrell to conteyne xxxvj. gallands; and on every fyshe daie at dynner and supper the like quantitie, made eyther of milk or pease or such lyke, and the thurd part of a pound of chese, or one good heringe, or twoe white or redd, accordinge as the keper of the house shall thinke meete.

Item, It is ordered, that such persons as will applie theire worke, shall have allowance of beare and a little bread between meales, as the keper of the house shall fynd that he doth deserve in his said work.

[1] *Evolution of the English Corn Market*, N. S. B. Gras, 1915.
[2] *The History of St. Bartholomew's Hospital*, Sir Norman Moore, 1918.
[3] *Annals of Christ's Hospital*, E. H. Pearce, 1901.
[4] *The State of the Poor*, Sir Frederic Eden, 1797.

Item, It is ordered, that they which will not worke shall have noe allowance but bread and beare onley, untill they will conforme themselves to worke.

The list of provisions to be taken on board a 'shippe of 200 tunnes ... to catch the Whale fish in Russia' in 1575 is instructive, including as it does, bread, 'cedar oile', bacon, 'hogsheds of beefe', salt, 'beanes and pease', salt fish and herring, wine and mustard seed.[1]

§5 THE FOOD OF THE WEALTHY CLASSES

Passing from what is known of the daily meals of the artisan to the food of the wealthy merchants and the great noblemen who possessed both town and country mansions, our first impression is of the extraordinary variety of their daily food. But on closer examination it appears that the majority of the sources of information refer to the menus of great feasts and elaborate meals provided in celebration of some special occasion, the details of which the chroniclers, one suspects, sometimes recorded with too lively an imagination. It would be misleading to attach importance to such feasts in a study of the national diet. Indeed, the menus are only of interest in bringing home to us the extravagance of the upper classes and the astonishing resources of their kitchens. An example may be given to illustrate the variety of the dishes and the curious conventions which determined the order in which they were presented at formal banquets in the fifteenth and sixteenth centuries. Three separate courses of meat were followed by three fish courses. Each of the six courses was brought to a close by a dish of pastry, a sweetmeat or a jelly, often elaborately devised and decorated, and known as a 'sotelte' [subtlety]. The occasion of the following banquet was the marriage of Henry IV and Joan of Navarre in 1403.[2]

First course
Fylettes in galentyne: — Vyand ryall: [a dish prepared with rice, spices, wine and honey] — Gross chare: [beef or mutton] — Sygnettes: — Capoun of haut grece: — Chewetys: [puddings] — A sotelte.

The seconde course
Venyson with fermente: — Gelye: — Porcellys: [young pigs] Conynge: [rabbits] — Bittore: [bittern] — Puleyng farcez: — Pertryche: — Leche fryez: [a sweet] — Brawne bruse: — A sotelte.

[1] *The Principall Navigations ... of the English Nation*, Richard Hakluyt, 1598-1600.
[2] *Antiquitates Culinariae*, Rev. Richard Warner, 1791.

The third course

Creme de almaundys: — Perys in syruppe: — Venison rosted: — Ryde:
— Woodecokke: — Plovere: — Rabettys: — Qualys: — Snytys: [snipe]
— Feldfare: — Crustade: — Sturgeon: — Frettoure: — A sotelte.

THE ORDER OF THE THREE COURSES OF FISH
The first course

Vyaund ryall: — Sew lumbarde: [a broth] — Salty fyshe: — Lampreys
powderyd: [highly spiced] — Pyke: — Breme: — Samoun rostyd: —
Crustade lumbarde: — A sotelte.

The seconde course

Purpayis [porpoise] en frumente: — Gely: — Breme: — Saumoun:—
Congre: — Gurnade: — Plays: — Lampreys in past: — Leche fryez: —
Panteryse coronys for a sotelte [the sweet was in the shape of a crowned
panther].

The third course

Creme of almaunds: — Perys in syrippe: — Tenche enbrace: — Troutez:
— Floundrys fryid: — Perchys: — Lamprey rosted: — Lochys and colys:
[two species of fish] — Sturjoun: — Crabbe and creveys: — Graspeys:
— Egle coronys: in sotelte [a sweet in the shape of a crowned eagle].

Reference to 'perys in syrippe' reminds us that almost the only way of
preserving fruit was to boil it in syrup and flavour it heavily with spices.
An interesting feature of medieval and early Tudor menus is the occurrence
of dishes prepared from porpoise, seal or whale meat. Such dishes appear to
have been by no means uncommon, but seem to have gone out of fashion
in the late sixteenth century.

The scale on which food was provided can be judged better if the number
of diners is known. Here is the kitchen list for a dinner of 50 people given
by the Salters' Company in 1506.[1]

36 Chickens	4 Gallons curds
1 Swan and 4 geese	1 ditto gooseberries
9 Rabbits	2 Dishes of butter
2 Rumps of beef tails	4 Breasts of Veal
6 Quails	Bacon
2 Ounces of pepper	3 Gallons and a half of
2 Ounces Clove and mace	Gascoyne wine
1½ Ounce Saffron	1 Bottle Muscadina
3 lb. Sugar	Cherries and Tarts

[1] *The History of the Twelve Great Livery Companies of London*, William Herbert, 1837.

2 lb. Raisons	Salt
1 lb. Dates	Verjuice and vinegar
½ hundred Eggs	1 Bushel and a half of meal.

This record mentions gooseberries and cherries but a striking feature of all such accounts is the scarcity of references to garden vegetables and fruits. Cabbages are sometimes mentioned but only for use in soups. The items for a sumptuous dinner given by the Brewers' Company in 1419 included 'cabboges to the potage'.[1] This is the only use suggested for 'caboges and whyte wortes' in fifteenth-century cookery books,[2] although John Parkinson writing at the beginning of the seventeenth century says they were sometimes dressed 'to delight a curious palate'.[3] In the 'Estymacion for the Kinges dietts and the Quenes, with other Nobles' in connection with the festivities at the Field of the Cloth of Gold in 1520, a long list of the food required is given, including 'bieffes', 'muttons', 'veales', 'hogges', 'fyshe, salt and fresshe', 'spices', 'pultrye', 'swete wynes', 'bere' and 'ipocras' [a spiced wine], but there is no mention of either fruit or vegetables.[4]

Salads consisting principally, as will be seen from the following fourteenth-century recipe, of onions and herbs, were fairly popular.[5]

Salat

Take Psel, Sawge, garlee, chibol'i, oynons, leek, borage, myn't poneet, fenel, and ton tressis [cresses], rew, rosemarye, purslayre, laue, and waische hem clene, pike hem, pluk he small wip phu [thine] hand and myng hem wel with rawe oile, lay on vyneg' and salt and sue it forth.

The Church vied with the Court and the Nobility in the luxurious magnificence of its banquets. When the 'reverende father in God' George Nevell, Archbishop of York and Chancellor of England, was enthroned in 1467 the kitchen provided amongst a seemingly endless list of beasts, birds and fish, the following items: 300 quarters of wheat, 300 tuns of ale, 100 tuns of wine, 1 pipe of hippocras, 105 oxen, 6 wild bulls, 1000 sheep, 304 calves, 304 pigs and 400 swans.[6] Even allowing for a stretch of imagination on the part of the chronicler, the quantities are enormous. Although such gargantuan meals marked special occasions there was a good deal of extravagance and luxury at the tables of the lords of Church and State. Archbishop Cranmer[7] was compelled to take steps to check the scandalous extravagance of the abbots and higher dignitaries of the Church in 1541, and he made it a rule

[1] Ibid.   [2] *Two Fifteenth Century Cookery Books*, Early English Text Society, 1888.
[3] *Paradisus Terristris*, John Parkinson, 1629.
[4] *The Rutland Papers* (Camden Society Publication, No. 21, 1842).
[5] *Foods*, Edward Smith, 3rd Edition, 1874 (Volume III of the International Scientific Series).
[6] *Antiquitates Culinariae*, Rev. Richard Warner, 1791.   [7] Ibid.

that an Archbishop must not have more than six flesh dishes — or six fish dishes on fast days — followed by not more than four 'second' dishes. With due regard for dignity a sliding scale was devised. Bishops were allowed five and three dishes respectively, deacons and archdeacons four and two, while minor orders had to be content with not more than three 'flesh' and two 'second' dishes. This, of course, referred to the mid-day meal which often began at 11 and lasted until 4 in the afternoon. Whether he expected the order to be obeyed we do not know but we are told that it 'was kept for two or three monethes, tyll by the disusing of certaine wylful persons it came to the olde-excesse'.

It seems always to have been a disheartening task trying to make people abstemious by law. Harrison recounts in his *Description of England* an effort to restrain high living in Scotland in 1433.

> In Scotland likewise they haue given themselues (of late yeares to speake of) vnto verie ample and large diet, wherein as for some respect nature dooth make it equall with vs; so otherwise they far exceed vs in ouer much and distemperate gormandize, and so ingrosse their bodies that diuerse of them doo oft become vnapt to anie other purpose than to spend their times in large tabling and bellie cheere... [However] a law was presentlie made there for the restreint of superfluous diet, amongest other things baked meats (dishes neuer before this mans [James I] daies seen in Scotland) where generallie so prouided for by vertue of this act, that it was not lawfull for ainie to eat of the same vnder the degree of a gentleman, and those onlie but on high and festiuall daies; but alas it was soone forgotten.

Sir Frederic Eden[1] mentions 'an ancient statute . . . against excess of diet (10 E. 3. st. 3) [which] remains unrepealed. It ordains, that no man shall be served at dinner or supper with more than two courses, except upon certain holidays therein specified, on which three courses are allowed'. A certain amount of valuable information has come down to us about the ordinary meals of the wealthy families and their dependants. Some of it is quite definite and informative. For example, 'A compendious recytation compiled of the order, rules, and constructione of the house of the righte excellent princesse Cicill, late mother unto the right noble prince kinge Edward IV'[2] lays down exact rules for the victualling of the household. The Head Officers alone were given breakfast and provided with wine. The rest of the staff were given large amounts of bread and ale, and their dinner and supper. On Sundays, Tuesdays and Thursdays dinner consisted of beef, mutton and

---

[1] *The State of the Poor*, Sir Frederic Eden, 1797.
[2] *Antiquitates Culinariae*, Rev. Richard Warner, 1791.

'one roste'; on Mondays and Wednesdays it was boiled beef and mutton, and on Fridays and fast days there was salt fish and two dishes of fresh fish. Supper was to be 'leyched beefe, and mutton roste' except on fish days.

Even more precise are the Ordinances of the Household of the 5th Earl of Northumberland, dated 1512.[1] For breakfast my lord and lady were served on fast days with 'Furste a loif of bred in trenchors, ij manchets, a quart of bere, a quart of wyne, ij peces of salt fysche, vj baconn'd [baked] herryng, iiij white [pickled] herryng or dysche of sproits' [sprats]. On 'Flesche days dayly throwte the Yere' the fish was replaced by 'half a chyne of mutton or ells a chyne of beif boiled'. It is interesting to compare these meals with those served in the 'Nurcy' of this house for 'my Lady Margaret and Maister Ingeram Percey'.

Braikfast on Fysche daies

Item, a manchet, a quart of bere, a dysche of butter, a pece of saltfish, a dysche of sproittes, or iij white herryng.

Braikfast on Flesche daies

Item, a manchet, one quart of bere, and iij muton bonys boyled.

For dinner and for supper the food is much the same; a quarter of salt salmon, a slice of turbot, a dish of smelts, a dish of fresh ling, a dish of mutton, a dish of salt bacon, but never any mention of fruit or vegetables.

The surprising variety of game which was used in the kitchens when a 'principall feeste' was being prepared is illustrated by a list taken from the records of the same household.

Cranys	Bustardes	Kyrlewes
Redeshankes	Great Byrdes	Wegions
Fesauntes	Hearonsewys	Dottrells
Sholardes	Bytters	Ternes
Pacokes	Reys	Smale Byrdes
Knottes		

Bread, meat, fish, wine and beer constituted the staple diet of the professional classes. On 'heighe dees' the 'doctour' in *Piers Plowman*:

> Drank wyn so faste.
> *Væ vobis qui potentes estis ad bibendum vinum!*
> He eet many sondry metes,
> Mortrews [soups] and puddynges,
> Wombe-cloutes [tripe] and wilde brawen,
> And egges, y-fryed with grece.

[1] *The Regulations and Establishment of the Household of Henry Algernon Percy, 5th Earl of Northumberland, 1512*, edited by T. P. (Thomas Percy, Bishop of Dromore), 1827.

There are two interesting academic records. One is the bill for a meal served in the fourteenth century at Alreton to the Warden and two Fellows of Merton College, with four servants, who halted there on a journey from Oxford to Durham.

bread 4d., beer 2d., wine 1¼d., meat 5½d., pottage ¼d.[1]

Two centuries later Thomas Cogan, who had been at Oriel College, Oxford, wrote a book 'for the Comfort of Students'.[2] In it he advises them to breakfast on milk, butter and eggs and refers to his own Oxford dinners of 'boyled beefe with pottage, bread and beere, and no more'.

From another source we learn that dinner in an Elizabethan home consisted of a 'piece of bief, a loyne of veale, 2 chickens, orenges and sauce'. For supper there was a 'shoulder of mutton, 2 rabbetts, pigs' pettie toes, cold bief and cheese'. This is one of the rare records which specifically mentions fruit. It was clearly a well-to-do household for apart from the number of meat dishes 'orenges' were an expensive luxury. Oranges were sometimes called 'portynggales' [Portuguese oranges] and under this name they appear on the menu of a banquet given by the Skinners' Company in 1560. Other interesting items among the sweetmeats were 'spyse-bred', 'comfets', 'sukett' [fruits preserved with sugar], 'marmelade' and 'cheres' and 'straberes'.[3] From the same source we learn of the sweetmeats served at a private dinner.

> The xij even was at Henley a-pon Temes a mastores Lentall wedow mad a soper for master John Venor and ys wyff, and I and dyver odur neybors; . . . the gentyll-woman had hordenyd a grett tabull of bankett, dyssys of spyssys and frut, as marmelad, gynbred, gele, comfett, suger plat, and dyver odur.

The sweets considered necessary for 'banketting on shipboord persons of credite' included:

Marmelade. ⎱
Sucket. ⎰   ⎰ Figs barrelled.
            ⎱ Raisins of the sunne.

Comfets of divers kind made of purpose by him that is most excellent, that shal not dissolve.

Prunes damaske. ⎱
Dried Peares. ⎰   ⎰ Walnuts.
            ⎱ Almonds.

Smalnuts.

Olives to make them taste their wine.

[1] *English Wayfaring Life in the Middle Ages*, T. Jusserand, translated from the French by L. T. Smith, 1920.
[2] *The Haven of Health*, Thomas Cogan, 1584.
[3] *Diary of Henry Machin, 1550-1563* (Camden Society Publication, No. 42, 1848).

The apple John that dureth two yeeres to make shew of our fruits.

Hullocke. } { Sacke.

Suger to use with their wine if they will.

The sweet oyle of Zante, and excellent French vinegar, and a fine kind of Bisket stieped in the same do make a banketting dish, and a little Sugar cast in it cooleth and comforteth, and refresheth the spirit of man.[1]

§ 6 'FYSSHE DAYES'

On 'fysshe dayes' appointed by the Church meat was replaced by salt fish of various kinds, herrings, salmon, eels, sprats, etc., and to a lesser extent by fresh fish. To eat flesh on a 'fysshe daye' was sometimes a serious offence.

The 18 day of March [1552] a wyfe of Hammersmith brought two pigges to London to a carpenter dwellinge in Smythfeild, which was taken contrary to a proclamation for eatinge of fleshe in Lent, and by iudgment of my Lord Mayor and Aldermen they did ryde on 2 horses with panelles of strawe about the markettes of the Citie, havinge eche of them a garland on theyr heades of the pyges pettie toes, and a pygge hanginge on ech of theyr breastes afore them.[2]

The 'fysshe dayes' assumed great importance in the second half of the sixteenth century. There were two major reasons. One was the desire to encourage ship-building and the training of mariners, the other — and it is the less generally recognized — was the dearth and high price of meat. Harrison refers to the introduction of 'fysshe dayes' not for 'religions sake or publike order' but 'to the end our numbers of cattell may be the better increased, and that abundance of fish which the sea yeeldeth, more generallie receiued. Beside this, there is the great consideration had in making of this law for the preseruation of the nauie, and maintenance of conuenient numbers of sea faring men, both which would otherwise greatlie decaie, if some meanes were not found whereby they might be increased'.[3]

Every effort was made to encourage or to enforce the consumption of fish. A typical proclamation, dated 1595, is described as 'very necessary to be placed in the houses of all men, especially common Victualers'. It enumerates the 'Benefits that growe to this Realm, by the observation of Fish Days:

[1] *The Principall Navigations . . . of the English Nation*, Richard Hakluyt, 1598-1600.
[2] *A Chronicle of England, 1485-1559*, Vol. II, Charles Wriothesley (Camden Society Publication, New Series, No. 20, 1877).
[3] *Description of England*, William Harrison, 1557.

with a reason and cause wherefore the Law in that behalf made, is ordained', and points out that 135,000 head of beef 'might be spared in a yeere, in the Cittie of London, by one dayes abstinence in a weeke'.

There is a document dated February 1563, annotated by William Cecil, which sets forth the arguments for increasing the number of fish days.

> Arguments to prove that it is necessary for the restoring of the Navye of England to have more fishe eaten and therfor one daye more in the weeke ordeyned to be a fissh daye, and that to be Wednesdaye, rather than any other.[1]

The report draws attention to the large amount of fish which was brought to England in foreign ships. An Act based on the proposals contained in this document was passed in the same year (5 Elizabeth, C. 5) and appears to have had an immediate effect in stimulating the fishing and ship-building industries.[2] The fine for non-observance of the Act was £3 or 'three months close imprisonment'. It was, however, possible to obtain a special licence to eat flesh on fish days.

> Lords of Parliament and their wives shall pay for a licence 26/8 yearly to the poor men's box in their parish, knights and their wives shall pay 13/4, persons of lesser degree, 6/8. Provided that no licence extend to the eating of beef at any time of the year nor to the eating of veal between Michaelmas and May 1st. Provided also that all persons whiche by reason of notorious sickness shalbee inforced for Recoverye of Helthe to eate Fleshe for the time of their sickness, shalbe sufficiently licensed by the Bishoppe of the Dyoces or by the Parson, Vicar or Curate of the Parishe where suche person shalbee sicke.

It apparently became increasingly difficult to enforce the observance of two fish days a week and the attempt seems to have been abandoned about 1585.

---

[1] S. P. D. Eliz., Vol. XXVII, No. 71 (*Tudor Economic Documents*, Vol. II, edited by R. H. Tawney and E. Power, 1924).
[2] *Statutes of the Realm*, Vol. IV, Pt. I, p. 422, ibid.

CHAPTER IV

DIET AND HEALTH

§ I THE HUMORAL DOCTRINE

ALL medical teaching during the Middle Ages and for several centuries afterwards was based on the Greek system built up on the teachings of Aristotle and Hippocrates, and extended in the second century A.D. by Galen. A curious blend of philosophy, observation and experience, its essential structure was so simple and logical that it dominated medical thought for the best part of two thousand years.[1] The fundamental principles of the natural world, or elements as they were often called, were air, fire, water and earth.

> The elements be those originall thynges vnmyxt and vncompounde, of whose temperance and myxture all other thynges, hauynge corporall substance, be compacte.[2]

Each element had its characteristic quality; earth was dry, water was moist, fire was hot and air was cold. A combination of two elements produced, by the blending of their qualities, a complexion, of which four were recognized and to each complexion there was an appropriate humour.

Complexion	Qualities	Humour
Sanguine	Hot and moist	Blood
Phlegmatic	Cold and moist	Phlegm
Choleric	Hot and dry	Yellow or green bile
Melancholic	Cold and dry	Black bile

The complexion determined the individual's appearance and characteristics; for example, one in whom heat and moisture had 'sovereignity', i.e. one of 'sanguine temperament', might be distinguished by the following signs:

> Carnosite or fleshynesse.
> The vaynes and arteries large.
> Heare plentie and redde
> The visage whyte and ruddy.
> Sleape moche.

---

[1] Readers who desire a more detailed account of these teachings are advised to consult Dr Charles Singer's scholarly volume, *A Short History of Medicine*, 1928.
[2] *The Castel of Helth*, Sir Thomas Elyot, 1539.

Dreames of blouddy thynges or thynges pleasaunt.
Pulse great and full.
Digestyon perfecte.
Angry shortly.
Siege, vryne, & sweate abundant.
Fallynge shortly into bledynge.
The vrine redde and grosse.[1]

The complexion could, however, be affected by an excess of another humour. Thus, a person of sanguine temperament would be rendered melancholic if anything occurred to cause an excess of black bile, which was thought to come from the spleen.

All foodstuffs were thought to be composed of the same four elements and their digestibility and nutritive value to be entirely determined by the related qualities. Lamb, for example, was very moist and phlegmatic; it was, therefore, regarded as unsuitable food for old men, whose stomachs were supposed to have already too much phlegm. The classification of foods might be extended by introducing degrees of the four qualities. Lettuce was cold and moist but cabbages were 'hote in the firste degree, and drye in the seconde'.[2]

Diets were prescribed on logical lines. Children were supposed to be by temperament phlegmatic, that is, moist and cold. Therefore, 'Chyldrene wold be nourysheth with meates and drynkes, whiche are moderarely hote and moyste, not withstandynge Galene dothe prohibite them the vse of wyne, bycause it moysteth and heateth to moche the bodye'.[3] As the child grew its temperament tended to become more sanguine or choleric. Therefore, 'Yonge men, excedyng the age of xiiii. yeres, shal eate meates more grosse of substance, colder and moyster: also salades of cold herbes, and to drynke seldome wyne, except it be alayd with water.'[4] In old age when the natural heat and strength of the body was declining, hot and moist meats were once again indicated.

On the same essentials the 'operations' were founded. Appetite was 'operated' by heat and dryness, digestion by heat and moisture, retention by coldness and dryness and expulsion by moisture and coldness.

Complications in so simple a system would seem unnecessary but there were many. There were, for example, the 'powers' or 'spirits' which included the 'animal', 'natural' and 'spiritual'. How deeply these teachings influenced everyday life can be appreciated from the fact that almost every essential term of the Hippocratic and Galenic systems has passed into our general speech.

[1] *The Castel of Helth*, Sir Thomas Elyot, 1539.
[2] Ibid.   [3] Ibid.   [4] Ibid.

§ 2 THE SCHOOL OF SALERNO AND THE 'REGIMEN SANITATIS SALERNI'

The Hippocratic and Galenic teachings survived the dissolution of the great Mediterranean Empires through their preservation at the very remarkable lay school of medicine which flourished at Salerno. Founded some time during the first five hundred years of the Christian era its importance grew until by A.D. 1000 it had become a centre of international reputation. It maintained its standing for another three hundred years but the middle of the twelfth century was its most distinguished period, when it produced many important medical writers. The most famous of the works of the Salerno school is the *Regimen Sanitatis Salerni*, which legend says was originally compiled for Robert, Duke of Normandy, eldest son of William the Conqueror. Tired of trying to keep order in his turbulent land the weak-willed young man gladly responded to the call of Pope Urban II for volunteers for the first Crusade. On the way to the Holy Land he spent several months of the winter of 1096 at Salerno and made an even longer stay on his return three years later. Many romantic tales are told of the second visit; how he came back to be cured of a poisoned wound and how his young wife saved his life by sucking out the poison, but the unromantic fact is that he wasted his time there in pleasant idleness while the crown of England slipped through his fingers. The belief that the *Regimen Sanitatis* was actually compiled for him rests mainly on dedications to *Francorum regi* and *Anglorum regi* which appear in some of the early manuscript and printed copies. Although the main substance of the *Regimen* is of earlier date, it is more than likely that contemporary manuscripts were inscribed in honour of the distinguished visitor and that this inscription passed into later copies.[1]

The *Regimen* was widely copied and translated during the next five centuries and, as usually happened in such cases, amendments, excisions and additions were made by the writers, so that surviving MSS show a great many differences. Some copies contain only 300 lines of the Latin verses, others more than 1000. Sir Norman Moore thought that the Schola Salernitata first became known in England about 1250;[2] its influence may be seen in the writings of Robert Grosseteste, Bishop of Lincoln (1235-53). The Latin manuscript versions of this work were the basis of medical practice in England, particularly in the monasteries, during the fourteenth and fifteenth centuries, and they provided the greater part of the material for the earliest English medical writings. The famous *Rosa Anglica* of John of Gaddesden — or *Rosa Medicinae* as he preferred to call it — an important medical treatise of the fourteenth century, was strongly influenced by the teachings

[1] *The History of the School of Salernum*, F. R. Packard and F. H. Garrison, 1922.
[2] *Glasgow Medical Journal*, 1908, Vol. LXIX.

of Salerno. Another important early English medical work printed by Caxton in the latter half of the fifteenth century is *The Gouernayle of Helthe: with The Medecyne of ye Stomacke*. The author is unknown but many of the stanzas — these early works were often written in verse in order to facilitate memorizing — are free translations of the *Regimen*.

A version of the *Regimen* which was widely used in the sixteenth century was the one prepared by Thomas Paynell, Canon of Merton Abbey. It gave the Latin text and an English translation of the Latin commentaries by the famous teacher of the School of Salerno, Arnaldus de Villa Nuova, which were added some time during the thirteenth century. A complete English version — if not the earliest certainly the one that had the widest popularity — was the translation prepared by Sir John Harington, whom Queen Elizabeth called 'that saucy poet, my godson'. It is from this version,[1] which has been edited by F. R. Packard and F. H. Garrison in *The History of the School of Salernum*, that we have taken the quotations which appear in the following pages.

It was undoubtedly through the influence of the *Regimen Sanitatis* and of the works based on it that the Hippocratic and, even more strikingly, the Galenic teachings became so firmly established in England, and indeed throughout Europe. Medical views on food and diet scarcely changed at all during the three centuries under discussion. They conformed almost without question to the orthodox doctrines of the original Greek school. A striking example is the teaching with regard to fruit.

Galen had regarded fruits with suspicion because they might give rise to fevers; he stated that his own father lived to a hundred years as the result of never eating them. The author of the fourteenth-century *Gouernayle of Helthe* gives the same advice: 'and fro frutis/hold thyn abstynence'. He adds that people who live long eat them sparingly. Two hundred years later the belief was still strong, although at least one author seems to have felt that some explanation of the immunity of our original parents from 'putrid fevers' was called for.

> Forasmoche as before that tyllage of corne was inuented, and that deuoryng of flesh and fyshe was of mankynde vsed, men undoubtedly lyued by fruites, & Nature was therwith contented & satisfied: but by chaunge of the diete of our progenitours, there is caused to be in our bodies such alteration from the nature, which was in men at the begynnyng, that nowe all fruites generally are noyfulle to man, and do ingender ylle humours, and be oftetymes the cause of putrified feuers, yf they be moche and contynually eaten.[2]

---

[1] *The Englishmans Doctor or The School of Salernum*, translated by Sir John Harington, 1608.
[2] *The Castel of Helth*, Sir Thomas Elyot, 1539.

Nevertheless, used in moderation, fruits, as cold and moist in various degrees, might be useful to 'represse the flame' of those 'which haue abundaince of choler'. In other words, suitable fruits could usefully be employed in the treatment of conditions marked by an excess of 'heat' and 'dryness' i.e. fevers. Peaches were regarded as among the less harmful.[1]

It is not difficult to understand how this fear arose. The summer was a time when there was a high incidence of infections and it is not surprising that the popular fancy saw a relation between the diarrhoeas and dysenteries of the hot months and the laxative effect of a liberal diet of fruit. Women nursing children were, in particular, warned that if they ate too much fruit the child might fall a victim to a 'grievous flux'. Probably this flux was infantile diarrhoea, a summer complaint which caused a fantastic child mortality in those days. There can be no doubt that this widespread belief greatly increased the likelihood of a scorbutic condition, a particularly serious matter for young children.

§3 VIEWS ON INFANT FEEDING

There was practically no alternative to breast feeding for infants, although doubtless many ineffectual efforts were made to give cows' or asses' milk. There is evidence that a cow's horn was sometimes used as a primitive feeding-bottle.

> Wherefore as it is agreing to nature, so it is also necessarye & comly for the own mother to nource the own child. Whiche yf it maye be done, it shal be most comendable and holsome, yf not ye must be well aduised in taking of a nource.[2]

Great care was taken in the choice of a wet nurse, in view of the widespread belief that the moral and spiritual character of the child would be influenced by the milk it imbibed. If the nurse was a dolt or a drunkard the child would certainly take after her; if there was a trace of blood in her milk the child might grow up to be a murderer. The nurse should therefore be carefully examined. When her moral qualities had been approved her milk should be examined. It must not be 'thicke and grosse, or to moch thinne or watrye, blackysshe or blewe, or enclynyng to rednesse or yelowe, all suche are unnaturall and euyll'.[3]

It is interesting that one authority, the famous writer Jacques Guillemeau,

[1] Ibid.
[2] *The Regiment of life . . . with the boke of children, newly corrected and enlarged*, by T. Phayre, 1550.
[3] Ibid.

surgeon to Henry IV of France, several of whose medical works were translated into English, recommended that wet nurses should be given plenty of fresh herb soups, made not from strong herbs likely to impart a flavour to the milk, but from lettuce, sorrel, parsley, borage, bugloss and succory, but 'shee shall refraine from all kind of raw fruits'.[1]

Guillemeau was in many ways a very shrewd observer. He devoted a great deal of attention to the curious cravings which so many women experience during pregnancy. For example, a common craving is for fresh fruit. Bosola tempted the Duchess of Malfi with 'apricocks' to discover if she were pregnant.[2] This craving has been interpreted as a physiological call for increased amounts of vitamin C. Again, there is often a craving for foods containing lime. Guillemeau recognized both types. '. . . we will. . . speake of that wherewith great-bellied Women are troubled, which is called Pica',[3] the name by which it is known today. He goes on to give a rational explanation in terms of the humoral theories.

> . . . the cause of this sicknesse . . . is, that the sides and tunicles of the stomacke . . . are infected, and stuffed with diuers excrements, and ill humours; and according to the qualitie they haue, the Woman with Child longeth after the like; As if Melancholie abound, not burn't or adust; she longeth after sharpe things, as Vinegar, Citrons, and Orenges: if the Melancholie be adust shee desireth Coles, Ashes and Plastering.

§ 4 THE FEEDING OF CHILDREN

If the child escaped falling a victim to the diseases which caused a very high rate of infant mortality it was fed after weaning very much as the modern child is, except that fruit was not permitted.

> The childe must bee nourished with milk only, till his foreteeth come forth both aboue, and beneath.[4]

After weaning children were given bread crusts and milk. Their 'temperament' or 'complexion' was thought to be hot and moist 'like unto yᵉ seed whereof they bee procreated',[5] so the coldness and moisture of milk needed

---

[1] *Child-Birth, or, The Happy Deliverie of Women . . . To Which is added, a Treatise of the diseases of Infants, and Young Children: With the Cure of them,* Jacques Guillemeau (English translation), 1612.

[2] *The Duchess of Malfi,* Act II, Scene 1, John Webster (1580-1625).

[3] *Child-Birth, or, The Happy Deliverie of Women,* Jacques Guillemeau (English translation), 1612.

[4] Ibid.

[5] *The Gouernment of Health,* William Bullein, 1595.

to be blended with the qualities of bread which tended to engender choler and melancholy. In other words, it was an attempt — and a curiously successful one — to construct a balanced diet, for modern knowledge has taught us that in almost all respects bread and milk is a well balanced diet. When the teeth appeared children might be given chicken bones to chew, while at fifteen months the flesh of capon or partridge in small quantities was recommended.

The growing child graduated naturally to the 'grosser meats' and so to the free choice of the adult man or woman, still guided, however, by reference to the complexion or character of the prevailing humour.

A recipe for a long life commends 'good aire', then 'diet, moderate eating of meate of good digestion, as all that haue pure white flesh, both of beastes and foules, and good bread of wheate, partly leauened. Eate no raw hearbs, purslem, lettis, young lettish or sorrel, except with vinegar'.

§ 5 VIEWS ON MILK

Milk was regarded as closely related to and derived from blood.

Milke is made of bloud twice concocted . . . For untill it come to the paps, or udder, it is plaine bloud: but afterward by the proper nature of the paps it is turned into milke.[1]

Modern physiology can add little to this statement.

It was thought to be composed of three substances, 'Creame, Whey and Cruds' [curds],[2] a division which represents the three most important components, fat, water-soluble constituents and the protein casein. Its high nutritive value was, of course, well known. 'A man may liue with milke only, and it wil serue instead of meat, and drinke, and medicine.'[3]

The different character and value of the milk of various species was recognized; woman's milk was held to be the best, followed by that of asses and goats, with lastly cows' milk.

> In great consumptions learn'd Physicions thinke,
> 'Tis good a *Goat* or *Camels* milke to drinke,
> *Cowes-milke* and *Sheepes* doe well, but yet an *Asses*
> Is best of all, and all the other passes.[4]

[1] *The Haven of Health*, Thomas Cogan, 1584.
[2] Ibid.
[3] *Sundrie new and Artificiall remedies against Famine*, Sir Hugh Platt, 1596.
[4] *The School of Salernum*, translated by Sir John Harington, 1608.

These views are very old. They are found in Gilbert Kymer's *Dietarium de Sanitatis custodia*. '*Lac vero mulerium est optimum genus lactis, deinde azinarum, deinde caprinum, deinde camellinum, deinde equarum, deinde raccinum, de hinc ovinum.*'[1] They were derived from Greek teachings. The milks of goats, sheep and camels are, indeed, highly nutritious by virtue of their large proportion of protein and fat, but the most digestible is that of the ass because the small amounts of these constituents make a soft, readily resolved curd in the stomach. Asses' milk is, therefore, particularly suitable for delicate digestions.

In an empirical way many important facts had been discovered about milk. It was rightly thought to be more nutritious in spring and summer than in winter. 'In sprynge tyme mylke is moost subtyll, and milke of yong beastes, is holsomer, than of olde.'[2] Here and there we find a word of warning to the effect that milk may cause ill-health, and if we try to imagine what the quality of much of the milk was, particularly that sold in the towns, it is soon apparent that there must have been a great deal of milk-borne infection. Erasmus, in his translation of Plutarch's *Gouernance of good healthe* (1530), wrote 'Concerning moystures, [it] is not mete to drynke mylke usually, but moderately to use it for a meate for it engendereth dyseases.'

Very considerable amounts of whey were drunk. It was regarded as a 'temperate drinke' and one which was 'both moyste and nourishing'.[3] It was also supposed to be very digestible, as indeed it is. 'Also by reason of the affinitie, whiche it hath with mylke, it is conuertible into bloudde and fleshe.'[4] On the other hand, Bullein and other authorities were inclined to think that it was sometimes unwholesome, particularly in winter, and that its laxative action might be harmful. Others again regarded this action as beneficial.

> *Whay*, though it be contemn'd, yet it is thought
> To scoure and cleanse, and purge in due degree.[5]

Both milk and whey were said to be moist and cold. They were, therefore, indicated for persons of a choleric or melancholic complexion. 'But it [milk] is especially good for them which be oppressed with melancholy, which is a common calamity of Students. And for this purpose it should be drunke in the morning.'[6]

---

[1] Cited in Botfield's *Manners and Household Expenses of England in the thirteenth to fifteenth Centuries*, 1841.
[2] *The Castel of Helth*, Sir Thomas Elyot, 1539.
[3] *The Breviary of Healthe*, Andrew Boorde, 1552.
[4] *The Castel of Helth*, Sir Thomas Elyot, 1539.
[5] *The School of Salernum*, translated by Sir John Harington, 1608.
[6] *The Haven of Health*, Thomas Cogan, 1584.

§ 6 CHEESE

Except to the wealthy man the wide range of cheeses was unknown. To most people there were only soft cheese, hard cheese, green cheese and spermyse. The first was what we call today cream cheese. Only the hard cheeses would keep for any length of time and in general character seem to have been of the Cheddar type; that is, the curd was prepared from renetted whole-milk and the cheese hardened by pressure. Hard cheese was a popular and relatively cheap food. 'Green' cheese was not, as one might imagine, a variety showing green markings, as, for example, Stilton, but a very new soft cheese. Spermyse was a cream cheese flavoured with herbs. The difference in digestibility of hard and soft cheese is so obvious that it is not surprising that it was frequently referred to. The sensations in the stomach after a meal of hard cheese suggested that heat was being released, so hard cheese was considered a hot and dry food, suitable for those of a phlegmatic complexion.

> For healthie men new *Cheese* be wholesome food,
> But for the weake and sickly 'tis not good,
> *Cheese* is an heauie meate, both grosse and cold
> And breedeth Costivesse both new and old.

> Cheese makes complaint that men on wrong suspitions,
> Do slander it, and say it doth such harme,
> That they conceale his many good conditions,
> That oft it helps a stomach cold to warme,
> How fasting 'tis prescrib'd by some Physicions,
> To those to whom the flux doth giue alarme:
> We see the better sort thereof doth eate,
> To make as 'twere a period of their meate;
> The poorer sort, when other meate is scant,
> For hunger eate it to releeue their want.[1]

§ 7 BUTTER

Butter was much more extensively used for cooking than as a table food. It was recommended for growing pains in children and for constipation.

> *Sweete-butter* wholesome is as some haue taught,
> To cleanse and purge some paines that inward be.[2]

> Now butter with a leaf of sage is good to purge the blood.[3]

[1] *The School of Salernum*, translated by Sir John Harington, 1608. [2] Ibid.
[3] *The Knight of the Burning Pestle*, Act IV, Scene v, Francis Beaumont (1584-1616) and John Fletcher (1579-1625).

The rancid state of the greater part that was sold would account for its reputation as a strong laxative.

It was usually made early in the summer and 'May butter' was regarded not only as the best but as the most wholesome. '. . . yet would I wish that such as have children to bring up, would not bee without May Butter in their houses'.[1] There is some confusion about the term 'May butter', for it is sometimes used of butter made at that time of the year, and sometimes of a curious product resembling the Indian *ghee*.

It is to bee made chiefly in May, or in the heate of the yeare, by setting Butter new made without salt, so much as you list in a platter, open to the Sunne in faire weather for certaine daies, untill it bee sufficiently clarified, and altered in colour, which wil be in twelve or fourteene daies, if it be faire Sunne shining.[2]

Such treatment would cause all the natural pigment (carotene) and the associated vitamin A to be destroyed by oxidation. A good deal of rancidity would also occur. It is difficult, therefore, to understand why such a product, all its vitamin A content gone and reeking of rancidity, should have been so highly recommended. Exposure to the sun's rays would tend to increase the amount of vitamin D present and it is possible that the beneficial effect of 'May butter', discovered empirically, was due to its antirachitic properties. This may explain why it was sometimes used in the spring to relieve pain in the joints.

§ 8 BREAD

Good wheaten bread, leavened and well baked, was regarded as a digestible and nutritious food. The heaviness of hot, unleavened or coarse breads was ascribed to their tendency to produce 'slymy humours' in the stomach. Very coarse breads were known to be poorly digested.

Browne bread . . . having moch branne . . . fylleth the belly with excrements, and shortly descendeth from the stomacke.[3]

Barley bread, for some unknown reason, had a reputation for curing gout, a disorder sometimes ascribed to gluttony and intemperance. The patient probably went on to a poor man's diet for a few days and felt all the better for it, for as Thomas Cogan remarked 'poor men seldome have it'.[4]

[1] *The Haven of Health*, Thomas Cogan, 1584.   [2] Ibid.   [3] Ibid.   [4] Ibid.

§ 9 MEAT

A few of the more indigestible meats were suspected of engendering evil humours although curiously enough pork was not among them, probably because Galen praised it. Andrew Boorde dared rather timidly to question this ruling, 'where-as Galen, with other auncyent and approbat doctours, doth prayse porke, I dare not say the contrarye agaynst them; but this I am sure of, I dyd neuer loue it: And in holy scrypture it is not praysed'.[1]

This whimsical writer, incidentally, gives a nice variant of a well-known saying: 'God may sende a man good meate, but the deuyll maye sende an euyll coke to dystrue it.'

A great deal of offal was eaten but on the whole this was not regarded favourably by the experts, who thought it tended to provoke 'euyl humours'. The spleen, rarely used as food nowadays, was thought to be particularly apt to upset the body because it was the reservoir of all black bile.

> The Splene or milt, maketh ill iuice . . . For it is the very place where melancholy is made.[2]

§ 10 THE PEASANT'S DIET: IMPORTANCE OF 'WHITE MEATS'

We have concluded that the medieval peasant's diet was of coarse 'black' bread, milk, cheese, eggs and occasionally bacon or fowl, supplemented by pulses, onions, leeks, parsnips, turnips and cabbages, and in summer such fruits as apples, plums, cherries and wild berries.

This must have been in most ways a good diet, though much would have depended on the amount of 'white meats' eaten by the peasant and his family. The proteins of milk, whey, cheese and eggs are of high biological value, that is they contain all the amino-acids essential for growth and maintenance. It has been found that these proteins of animal origin, when eaten with proteins of lower biological value, such as those of cereals and pulses, supplement the value of the latter, so that the resultant mixture has much the same protein value as that of the animal proteins alone. Diets composed of mixtures of animal and vegetable protein foods accord with modern nutritional instruction. If the amount of 'white meats' eaten was considerable, equivalent let us say to a pint of milk and some cheese and whey per day, the balance of the peasant's diet, with the possible exception of antiscorbutic foods, would have been excellent, far better indeed than in many of our modern diets (see Appendix A).

[1] *A Compendyous Regyment, or a Dyetary of Helth*, Andrew Boorde, 1542.
[2] *The Haven of Health*, Thomas Cogan, 1584.

It may be instructive at this point to give an illustration of the remarkable manner in which the development of growing children can be influenced by milk. The investigation was carried out between 1922 and 1925 by Dr Corry Mann on behalf of the Medical Research Council.[1] The results are relevant to the point we are now considering because the subjects of the study were boys living in an institution on a basic diet providing rather small proportions of animal protein and fat and insufficient green vegetables. Their meals gave them an average of about 18 g. of animal protein a day, out of a total of 63 g. Their ages ranged from 7 to 11 years, and their weights from 45 to 65 lb. The usual rate of growth in the institution was represented by a yearly average gain in weight of 3.85 lb. and in height of 1.84 inches.

When the amount of animal protein was raised to 33.5 g. daily by the addition of casein (the highly digestible and nutritious protein of milk), the amount of total protein being thereby increased to 79 g., the average response was 4.01 lb. in weight and 1.76 inches in height. The difference is scarcely significant. The first impression from this result might be that the boys were already getting sufficient protein in their diet.

A totally different response followed the addition of a pint of milk a day to the boys' food, an amount which actually provided about the same quantity of extra animal protein as had been given in the form of casein to the boys in the first group. The boys in the 'milk group' made an unexpectedly big gain in weight, averaging 6.98 lb., and grew no less than 2.63 inches during twelve months. Fortunately, the investigation did not stop at these two groups. Other groups of boys were given butter, margarine, watercress or extra sugar as supplements to the basic diet. The only group which showed an improvement approaching the response of the 'milk group' was that in which butter was the supplement.

The results, and also scrutiny of the constituents of the basic diet, suggest that the diet was lacking in calcium and in vitamin A, both of which are essential for growth. Both would have been supplied by the extra milk. Butter, but not margarine,[2] would have supplied extra vitamin A, but not calcium. In the more recent experiment conducted by Dr E. M. Widdowson and Professor R. A. McCance in Germany, milk did not have the growth-promoting effect demonstrated by the earlier work, the explanation probably being that the quality of the mixture of amino-acids and the calcium content of the diets of the German children studied were adequate.[3]

In passing it may be remarked that the striking result of the investigation by Dr Corry Mann finally convinced the experts that milk has a special

[1] *Medical Research Council, Special Report*, No. 105, 1926.
[2] Margarine was not then enriched by the addition of vitamins A and D.
[3] *Medical Research Council, Special Report*, No. 287, 1954.

value in the diet of young growing children which cannot be measured in terms of proteins, fats or calories. It was the foundation on which has been built the great national scheme for providing extra milk for children at school.

§ 11 VITAMIN C

It is not easy to decide whether or not the peasant's diet contained adequate supplies of vegetables. If they were common articles of diet, readily available, they may not always have been mentioned in written records — estimates of home production of such foods as vegetables are notoriously difficult to obtain. The importance of vegetables as antiscorbutics would, however, depend not only on the quantities and frequency of consumption but on the methods by which such vegetables as turnips, leeks and cabbages were cooked. Soups, which may or may not have contained vitamin C, were frequently served, but Miss Dorothy Hartley has provided some evidence that green vegetables were cooked quickly, shredded, in milk and butter, a method which would be likely to preserve vitamin C. Nevertheless, it seems likely that the winter diet of salt bacon, bread and peas gave little protection against scurvy, so that by the end of the winter most of the poor country people must have been in at least a pre-scorbutic condition. Some measure of protection might have been obtained in the summer from fruits as well as fresh vegetables, but it must not be forgotten that the peasant may have shared the popular superstition that fruit caused fevers.

Owing to the difficulty of estimating vegetable and fruit consumption these foods have not been included in the calculation given in Appendix A.

§ 12 VITAMIN A

When the peasant was unable to get milk and eggs there was a real danger that the shortage of animal fats meant a deficiency of the associated vitamins A and D. For the moment only vitamin A will be discussed because it will be more appropriate to deal with the antirachitic factor (vitamin D) when the question of rickets is being considered. Vitamin A, in the form of its precursor or provitamin A, β-carotene, is found in all green vetegables — more or less in proportion to their greenness — but these foods contain very little fat. A diet supplying little fat or only fat obtained from cereal foods which contain very little vitamin A, should, therefore, be supplemented either with green vegetables and salads, which provide the provitamin without much fat, or with animal fats. There are many races today living almost exclusively on vegetable foods whose people are virile and healthy. They obtain vitamin A almost entirely from vegetables.

If, however, as may have happened with the medieval peasant, insufficient green vegetables are eaten, a proper intake of animal fat becomes essential in order to ensure a sufficiency of the vitamin. It must be appreciated that vitamin A passes into milk or egg yolk only if the diet of the cow or hen contains ample supplies of this vitamin. If the supplies fall off the amount of vitamin found in the milk or eggs will decrease and may disappear entirely. Usually the vitamin A value of dairy produce is highest when the cows are out at pasture and the hens running loose on grass. Cows in stall in winter, fed on dried hay, concentrated cattle foods and roots, yield a milk which tends to become progressively poorer in vitamin A. This is one reason why conditions arising from vitamin A deficiency are more prevalent in the early spring.

Modern estimates of man's requirements for vitamin A indicate that about 2500 international units are necessary per day if the vitamin A comes from animal sources, but up to 7500 are needed if vegetables are the main source.[1] If we assume that a diet of bread, vegetable soup and an ounce or two of cheese was supplemented by a pint of summer milk, the daily intake of the peasant would have been about 2000 units. In winter, with little or no milk available, the most he would have been able to get in the other foods would have been about 1000 units daily. One important point must, however, be mentioned. The viscera of animals, particularly the liver and kidneys, are much richer in vitamin A than the flesh. Rabbits and other game, of which everything edible was eaten, would, therefore, have provided additional sources of the vitamin. The general impression we have formed is that the summer was a period when the poor country people were getting sufficient vitamin A. In winter the supply was greatly reduced and in consequence the reserves in the body would be depleted. Vitamin A can, however, be stored for many months in the liver, provided that it is healthy, and signs of deficiency do not develop rapidly.

The intake of vitamin D was at best small, judged by our modern standards. This was true of all classes of the community, and we shall discuss in another chapter the whole question of the vitamin D content of early English diets in relation to the incidence of rickets.

§ 13 HIGH-PROTEIN DIETS

Wealthy Englishmen lived on diets which were generously proportioned in respect to animal fat and protein. They thought nothing of eating two or

[1] *Medical Research Council, Special Report*, No. 264, 1949.

three pounds of meat or fish a day, an amount which would provide them with some 200-300 g. of animal protein. By our modern European standards these are very large amounts but not by comparison with those consumed by meat-eating peoples. The warriors of the Masai, an East African tribe, were reported by Dr J. B. Orr (now Lord Boyd Orr) and Dr J. L. Gilks to consume milk, flesh and blood equivalent to 300 g. of protein per day and to be fine vigorous specimens of manhood.[1] In our own latitudes there is the example of the tribesmen of the nomadic races of Central Europe who at the period of their great conquests were almost exclusively meat-eaters.

> The Tartars eat raw meat, and most commonly horse-flesh, drink milk and blood, as the Nomades of old ... They scoff at our Europeans for eating bread, which they call tops of weeds, and horse-meat, not fit for men; and yet Scaliger accounts them a sound and witty nation, living an hundred years.[2]

Even the European can quite soon and happily adapt himself to such a diet. Stefansson, the Arctic explorer, wishing to learn for himself the effects of the food of the Eskimos, whose customs he has so carefully studied, decided to live for a year on a typical Eskimo diet. Two of his friends volunteered to do the same and for twelve months they ate the large amounts of meat and fatty foods which this necessitated. They never experienced a moment's discomfort and, indeed, were remarkably fit during the whole period, an elaborate series of medical and physiological tests failing to reveal the slightest adverse effect.

An earlier experience is related by Hulderike Schnirdel who 'in twentie yeeres space from 1534 to 1554' visited South America.

> ... for this Nation and Countrie, by reason of the plenty of victuall, was also most fit, and commodious for us, especially when in foure whole yeares past, we had not seene a morsell of bread, living onely with fish and flesh, and oftentimes also in great penurie.[3]

It is difficult to form a true impression of the position with regard to vitamins A and D in the diet of the prosperous Englishman of the fourteenth-fifteenth centuries. On the other hand, there is little doubt that there was a good deal of under-nourishment in respect of vitamin C. Herb salads were probably the only source of the vitamin, for it seems likely that the educated classes accepted more generally than did the peasantry the belief that fruits were dangerous unless eaten in small amounts. Pre-scorbutic conditions

[1] *Medical Research Council, Special Report*, No. 155, 1931.
[2] *The Anatomy of Melancholy*, R. Burton, 1621.
[3] *Purchas His Pilgrimes*, S. Purchas, 1625-26.

must have been extremely common on a diet of bread, meat, fish and wine, and there may have been danger of deficiency of vitamins A and D, because little milk was drunk, eggs and butter were used chiefly in cooking and green vegetables were rarely seen on the rich man's table.

The artisans and tradespeople ate a great deal of meat by comparison with the country people. From a medical standpoint their diet was excellently balanced with regard to the main constituents, proteins, fats and carbohydrates. Its mineral composition, particularly calcium and iron was a good deal more satisfactory than that of many of our modern diets. (*See* Appendix A.) In fact, the only criticism that could be made would be with respect to the deficiency of antiscorbutic foods and a possible deficiency of vitamins A and D, particularly in the winter. It is very difficult to form an opinion about these last-mentioned substances. A wide variety of meat and fish was available, but it is possible to draw up a long list of such foods, mainly lean meat and fish, which could be eaten without materially adding to the intake of these vitamins. On the other hand, if a reasonable proportion of certain other meats such as liver, and fish such as herrings, was eaten the necessary requirements for both these vitamins might be covered.

§ 14 VITAMIN A DEFICIENCY

A mild degree of deprivation shows itself in a curious manner. The sufferer becomes what is known as 'night-blind'. Passing from a bright to a dim light he is for a time unable to see properly. It has been for centuries a very common disorder in the East, where the natives live on cereal diets of low vitamin A content. The defect is corrected with surprising rapidity by administration of vitamin A.

If a greater degree of vitamin A deficiency prevails other and more serious eye disorders may appear. The lids become swollen and sore and the surface of the eyeball dry. In chronic cases the dryness may be followed by ulceration of the cornea and the development of opaque areas. Unless treated such cases may become blind. This disorder, which is known as *xerophthalmia*, is common in Egypt, India, Ceylon, China and other countries where a cereal diet is not adequately reinforced by green vegetables or animal foods. It is curious that the natives of these countries did not discover empirically that it could be cured by certain foods.

The earliest references to the use of liver in the treatment of eye diseases is that found in the Egyptian medical treatise known as the *Ebers Papyrus*, now in the Leipzig Museum. The date is about 1600 B.C. The significance of the passage was first pointed out by van Leersum;[1] a literal translation

[1] *Nederlandsche Tijdschrift voor Geneeskunde*, 1924, Vol. III.

which Professor S. R. K. Glanville has kindly made for us reads as follows:

Another [pre- -ription] for the eyes: liver of ox roasted and pressed, give for it. Very excellent.

There is little doubt that the eye disease was the common *nyctalopia* or night-blindness. Hippocrates and Galen knew it well, the former advising ox-liver in honey as a remedy.[1] The same advice is found in certain Roman medical writings and definite proof that knowledge of this remedy was brought to Europe to is be found in a verse by the fourteenth-century Dutch poet, Jacob van Maerland.[2]

> He who can not see at night
> Must eat the liver of the goat
> Then he can see all right.

Xerophthalmia is rarely seen in Europe nowadays because vitamin A insufficiency is seldom as serious or as prolonged there as in these Eastern countries. It may, however, appear under abnormal economic conditions. During the war of 1914-18 Denmark was receiving such high prices for butter that it almost disappeared from the home markets. At that time margarine was not artificially fortified with vitamins, as it is today. The result was that the poor people were subjected to a greater degree of A deprivation than in normal times and hundreds of cases of xerophthalmia occurred, mostly in young children. All, except the advanced cases in which permanent damage to the eye had occurred, improved rapidly when butter or cod liver oil was administered. It was, in fact, the study of this outbreak which gave the first convincing proof that the disease is caused by vitamin A deficiency.

Long continued deprivation of vitamin A is dangerous in other ways for it leads to a weakening of the defences of the body against invasion by bacteria and other disease-producing organisms. One of the main defences against disease lies in the layer of cells covering all surfaces of the body; the skin, the mucous membrane of the nose and throat, the cells lining the digestive tract, and so on. It is this line of defence which becomes weakened when vitamin A is lacking. There is a tendency to localized infection, such as abcesses and ulcers, and when the deficiency is more marked, the skin may become thickened, rough and dry. The latter condition is common in the Far East, where it is sometimes known as 'toad-skin'.

[1] *Opera Medicorum Graecorum*, 1927, Vol. III, 4b, edited by C. G. Kühn. (We are indebted to Dr G. Logaras for a translation of the passage concerned.)

[2] This verse is cited in Dr M. van Andel's interesting survey of the history of night-blindness in the *Nederlandsche Tijdschrift voor Geneeskunde*, 1925. (We are grateful to M. G. van Eysselsteyn for a translation of this paper.)

We have not succeeded in tracing any descriptions of eye diseases resembling either xerophthalmia or night-blindness in English medical writings prior to 1600. Either the conditions were rare or they were confused with the many other disorders which affect the eyes. There are, however, many references to 'sore eyes', 'films over the eyes', 'dimness of vision', and although it is obvious that these terms must have covered a wide variety of common complaints it is significant that they seem to have been more common in the spring and that most of the remedies advised for their cure were preparations of fresh green herbs, which would, of course, have provided vitamin A. Fennel, rue and eyebright were all recommended; sometimes they were used in the form of a local application, at other times the expressed juice of the leaves was drunk in oil. It is interesting that liver was never suggested as a remedy.

Both xerophthalmia and night-blindness were, however, recognized in France in the late sixteenth century. The famous French clinician, Jacques Guillemeau, gave a remarkably true picture of xerophthalmia and of the condition of 'ceux qui ne voyent rien de nuict, que l'on peut nommer aueuglement de nuict'.[1] He knew the value of liver, for he advised, in addition to the inevitable bleeding, 'le foye de bouc rosti, estant salé & le manger'. Speaking of a related condition he said: 'Quand à la guarison, il faut auoir esgard, que le malade vse de bonnes viandes . . . si le mal est causé, pour la paucité & tenuité d'iceux.' It must be remembered that the standard of living at this period was, for all but the wealthy classes, a good deal lower in France than it was in England, and vitamin A deficiency may, therefore, have been more marked.

§ 15 STONE

There is another aspect of vitamin A deficiency to be considered. Stones in the bladder and urinary tract seem to have been very common in England centuries ago, the trouble usually being ascribed to gluttony and luxurious living. '[It] commeth of hote wines, spices, long banquets, repletions, fulnesse, costifenesse, warme keeping of the backe, salte meates, etc.' wrote William Bullein.[2] He certainly expressed the popular view but it is hardly a satisfactory explanation because quite young children often suffered from the stone. The cause of stones (calculi) in the urinary tract is still the subject of investigation but certain observations made during recent researches are of importance to our study. The experimental investigations of Osborne and Mendel in America, of Sir Robert McCarrison in India, and of a group

[1] *Traité des Maladies de l'œil*, Jacques Guillemeau, 1585.
[2] *The Gouernment of Health*, William Bullein, 1595.

of Dutch scientists at the University of Amsterdam, leave no doubt that faulty diet will produce calculi in animals. The dietary defects which appear to be concerned are a deficiency of vitamin A and an abnormally high intake of lime. When the balance of the diet is adjusted by increasing the amount of vitamin A, or in certain cases by adding phosphate, the incidence of stone is greatly reduced. Milk stands out pre-eminently as the best preventive food. It seems to be impossible to obtain conditions under which stone will form in the urinary tract if milk forms a reasonable part of the diet.

The primary defect appears to be the deficiency of vitamin A. Chronic shortage of this dietary component induces degenerative changes in the epithelium covering the papillae of the kidney, the little projections from which the urine flows to be collected in the pelvis of the kidney and thence passed by the ureters into the bladder. The areas which are thus affected tend to form minute plaques of calcified matter when the conditions are rendered favourable by a diet rich in lime. The plaques may break away and, either in the pelvis of the kidney or after passing into the bladder, serve as nuclei around which urinary salts tend to accumulate. A deposition which leads to the gradual growth of the stone is favoured if the urine is rich in calcium salts, a condition which usually prevails when the diet contains a great deal of lime. Infections of the bladder and urinary tract are apt to encourage the formation of stones. Here, again, vitamin A is concerned because the resistance to invasion by germs of the layer of cells lining that tract is markedly reduced when the supply of this vitamin is restricted.

Studies of human diets reveal interesting points in connection with the incidence of stone. The African negro rarely suffers from it. Dr Vermoolen traced only one case in over a million hospital admissions, whereas the white population of South Africa showed an incidence of 1 in 460 admissions.[1] The negro diets were found to be rich in vitamin A and relatively very poor in calcium. By comparison, the food of the white people was often rather deficient in A and usually richer in calcium.

When we turn to the food of the English people during the centuries we are considering, we find that both poor and rich were living on diets which by modern standards we would regard as rich in both calcium and phosphorus.[2] It is accepted today that the growing child needs 1.0-1.4 g. of calcium and the adult 0.8 g.

Medieval and Tudor diets, thanks to the large amount of wholemeal bread, cheese and meat which they contained, often provided as much as 1.5-2 g. of calcium. It might be expected that a lime intake of that order would be liable to cause stone-formation if associated with long-standing

[1] *Journal of the American Medical Association*, 1937, Vol. CIX.
[2] Analyses are given in Appendix A.

F

vitamin A deficiency. To what extent such deficiency conditions were common in medieval and Tudor England we have no means of telling, but we have already indicated that there is some evidence, although it is very slight, that a good many people did not get all the vitamin A they required.

It is certain that infections of the urinary tract were very much more common in those days than they are today. A considerable proportion was of venereal origin, but as none could be effectively treated there was every probability that once the infecting organisms gained entry they would maintain and extend their hold.

§ 16 THE VITAMIN B 'COMPLEX'

The large amount of wholemeal bread eaten by all classes must have given ample protection against most of the disorders of health which are associated with a deficiency of the dietary factors grouped together under the term 'vitamin B complex'. Nevertheless, a short account of these substances may be helpful, in view of the fact that we shall have occasion to discuss them in some detail later when we deal with the period in which white flour began to replace wholemeal in the national diet.

At first it was thought that there was only one 'vitamin B' and that the disease beri-beri was caused by lack of it. It soon became clear that vitamin B was not a single substance but contained at least two vitamins, one effective against beri-beri and one against pellagra. Both were soluble in water, but one was less stable to heat than the other. In 1927 the Accessory Food Factors Committee of the Medical Research Council recommended that the two should be named vitamin B_1 and vitamin B_2, the former being the heat-labile and the latter the heat-stable vitamin. Vitamin B_1 was the factor effective against beri-beri, but vitamin B_2 eventually proved to be a mixture of several vitamins, only one of which was effective against pellagra; this was subsequently shown to be nicotinic acid or its derivative nicotinamide. Some of the others were riboflavin (still sometimes named vitamin B_3), pyridoxin (or vitamin B_6) and pantothenic acid. The intermediate names B_3, B_4 and B_5 were used for substances thought to be necessary for rats or pigeons.

Vitamin B_1 (or Thiamine)

Many foods contain moderate amounts of vitamin B_1, but none has a very high concentration. The richest natural source is yeast. The germ of wheat and other cereals, as well as bran are good sources. Other good sources are peas, beans, egg-yolk, liver, kidney and pigmeat.

Vitamin B_1 is essential for the combustion (or oxidation) of carbohydrate in the body and thus for the release of energy. It plays a part in one of the enzyme systems of the body. It is a *coenzyme* and is necessary for the disposal and breakdown of *pyruvic acid*, which is formed during the metabolism of carbohydrates (starches and sugars). If vitamin B_1 is lacking these reactions are held up and pyruvic acid and also the closely related *lactic acid* accumulate. The symptoms of mild vitamin B_1 deficiency include loss of appetite, muscular weakness and certain forms of neuritis. Later come the nervous and other signs which together make the clinical picture of beri-beri, a condition which is practically unknown in Europe. Conditioned deficiency of vitamin B_1 may cause neuritis in chronic alcoholism, when the diet is usually poorly supplied with vitamins, in pregnancy, when the needs of vitamin B_1 and other vitamins increase and in cases of gastro-intestinal obstruction, when absorption may be poor. It is usual to express requirements of vitamin B_1 in terms of calorie or, preferably, non-fat calorie requirements.

Nicotinic acid (or Niacin) and its derivative Nicotinamide

The foodstuffs richest in nicotinic acid include yeast, meats, fish and other animal protein foods. The vitamin is not easily destroyed by heat and so is present in processed or cooked foods.

One of the amino-acids, tryptophan, is converted into nicotinamide in the body. The vitamin is active in the form of nicotinamide, to which nicotonic acid is also converted in the body.

Nicotinamide is active in two further enzyme systems which promote the oxidative processes of the body. They are specifically concerned with the transport of hydrogen atoms. Deficiency of nictotinamide causes a specific form of dermatitis, also diarrhoea and finally dementia, the so-called three Ds of pellagra, a condition which used to be extremely common in the maize-eating areas of the world. The complete reason for the association between maize and pellagra is not known. Partial explanations are that in maize nicotinamide occurs in a bound form, that maize is deficient in tryptophan, that it may contain an antivitamin and that diets based on maize are often short of animal protein foods (which would supply tryptophan). As maize was never the staple cereal in England it is unlikely that pellagra was ever common here though it has been suggested[1] that cases which were thought to have been leprosy were in fact pellagra.

Riboflavin

This is a yellow-coloured substance soluble in water and found in many foodstuffs including milk, eggs, liver, kidney, yeast, green vegetables and beer. It is not easily destroyed by heat alone but it is destroyed by heat and sunlight and is thus lost if milk is left in sunshine.

[1] *A History of Epidemics in Britain*, C. Creighton, 1891-94.

Like vitamin B_1 and nicotinamide, riboflavin is a coenzyme. It is concerned in the transport of hydrogen atoms in at least ten different chemical reactions.

The most marked symptom of lack of riboflavin is severe inflammation at the corners of the mouth and possibly of the tongue.

Pyridoxin (or vitamin B_6)

The richest sources of this vitamin are yeast, liver, pulses and high extraction cereals. It also has specific functions in the body which include some of the reactions involved in the metabolism of proteins and fats. Deficiency of pyridoxin causes characteristic changes in the skin.

Pantothenic acid

This is named after the Greek *pantothen*, indicating its widespread distribution. It is part of the enzyme system concerned in the oxidation of *pyruvic acid*. During the Spanish Civil War and the Second World War the 'burning foot' syndrome in man was reported, and was probably caused by deficiency of this vitamin.

§ 17 ERGOTISM

There is another disease of dietary origin of which we find no record in contemporary English writings although it affected most of northern Europe and was very well known in France and Germany. The condition is known today as ergotism and it results from eating rye which is heavily infected with a specific mould or fungus (*Claviceps purpurea*). In the ripe heads of the rye the ergot appears as a blackish, horn-like growth. If this growth is ground up with the grain there is danger of ergot poisoning. Consumption of such grain may cause one of two clearly differentiated forms of ergotism, known as the gangrenous and the convulsive type. In both forms the primary agent is a highly poisonous constituent of the ergot known as ergotoxin, but the symptoms and general history of the cases are so different that it is not surprising that they were for a long time regarded as different diseases.

The gangrenous form begins with an intense burning sensation and itching of the skin. This caused the ailment to be known in early times by a variety of names which suggested that the patient was suffering from an internal fire: *ignis sacer*, or Holy Fire, and St Anthony's Fire, were the commonest. As the disease progresses the burning sensation increases and the circulation of the extremities becomes impeded. This leads to gangrene, and toes, fingers and sometimes whole limbs are lost. The other form of ergot poisoning is characterized by severe convulsive fits, showing that the nervous system rather than the circulation is being disordered.

Rye was eaten quite extensively in England in medieval times, particularly by the poorer people, and yet we have been unable to trace any records of ergotism. It must surely have been noticed had there been any outbreaks, for the symptoms are so characteristic; when an outbreak did occur in Suffolk in the eighteenth century it attracted a good deal of attention. There are several possible explanations for this apparent freedom from the disease. One is that rye was seldom eaten alone. In the south it was mixed with barley or wheat, and in the north with barley or oats. This may have reduced the proportion of ergot in the bread to a comparatively harmless level. In most countries where rye is a staple cereal today the government has fixed a limit for contamination with ergot, beyond which the grain must not be used for human food.

Another possibility is that English rye was less heavily infected than the Continental variety. This is not likely since, although improved agricultural methods lessen the chances of a crop becoming infected, the practice of growing cereals was just as primitive in England at that date as it was in Germany or France. Moreover, and this is important, we do not hear of any outbreak of the disease following the purchase of large quantities of Continental rye for the use of the poor in times of scarcity of corn; in 1597 for example, very large amounts were imported from Germany and Poland.

Little significance can be attached to the remedies for 'St Anthony's Fire' given in the English herbals of the late sixteenth century, because these works were composed to a very large extent of extracts from Continental authors. It must be admitted that no satisfactory explanation has as yet been offered to account for the rarity, indeed one might almost say the non-existence, of ergotism in England. The most plausible is that the people were at no time wholly dependent on rye for a sufficient length of time for the disease to manifest itself.

§ 18 STARVATION

It is necessary to make brief reference to times of famine, because such occasions were by no means infrequent. If a failure of the harvest occurred inevitably hundreds starved, particularly in the countryside. In medieval times the distress was often so severe that England gained an unenviable reputation.

Tres plagae tribus regionibus appropriari solent — Anglorum fames, Gallorum ignis, Normanorum lepra.

The memory of some of these terrible times lived long; as late as the sixteenth century we find the famine of 1371 described as the 'grete dere yere'. Another bad year was 1383 when the harvests were very poor and the fruit crop was also affected. Many deaths were attributed to the starving people having fed on unripe or bad fruit.

When the main crops failed the poor man was forced to live on 'horsse corne, beanes, peason, otes, tares, & lintels'.[1] When times grew even worse, as for instance between 1437 and 1439, when there was a succession of wet summers and the harvests were ruined, the peasantry were reduced to eating such herbs and roots as they could gather in the hedgerows, and thousands died.

The resistance of the people as a whole must have been greatly impaired by such periods of privation, and it is not surprising to find that many of the bad outbreaks of disease, particularly of the plague, which was for a long time endemic in England after the first visitation in 1348-49, followed years of want. There was, for example, great mortality from plague for two or three years after the famine of 1371 and again in 1438 and 1439. The latter part of the sixteenth century also had several periods of serious shortage followed by bad outbreaks of the plague.

With the development of national life under the Tudors conditions tended to improve but even so there were many years of bad dearth, particularly towards the end of the fifteenth century and in the second half of the sixteenth century, when there must have been widespread malnutrition if not actual starvation.

The most usual reaction to shortage of food is decreased activity. Even a slight shortage leads to irritability, complaint and unrest; a severe shortage results in lack of initiative, apathy and an unwillingness to co-operate in any kind of activity, physical or mental. The body conserves itself to the greatest possible extent, but if the shortage continues long enough body weight is inevitably lost.

People dying of acute starvation seldom show any peculiar symptoms. There is increasing weakness and emaciation followed by overwhelming lethargy merging into a state of coma. If the shortage of food is less severe but more prolonged the decline is correspondingly slower and a condition known today as 'hunger-oedema' may appear. The limbs, and sometimes the whole body, swell as in dropsy, the circulation is impeded and death follows from failure of the heart.

[1] *A Description of England*, William Harrison, 1577.

PART TWO

THE SEVENTEENTH CENTURY

CHAPTER V

FOOD AND MEALS

§ I RISE OF THE GREAT ESTATES

THE seventeenth century saw another change in the English countryside, the establishment of country estates by those who had made fortunes out of the great trading ventures, of which the most famous and most remunerative was the East India Company, founded in 1600. These men invested a good deal of their newly gained wealth in land, spending money lavishly on their houses, gardens and farms. Davenant, a reliable observer, recorded that the rents of English farm lands increased threefold and the purchase of land doubled between the years 1600 and 1688.[1]

The country as a whole undoubtedly benefited. A much larger area came under the control of landowners who were receptive to new ideas and who had the capital to indulge them. The growth of farming as a great national concern is distinctly marked during these years of transition and change, and by nothing more clearly than by the readjustment of the balance between the production of wool and of corn which, it will be recalled, had become rather badly disturbed in Tudor times. The price of corn was unusually high when the century opened, partly as a result of a series of bad harvests but chiefly because the increasing demand of the growing population was having its effect. The high prices encouraged farmers to turn land over to corn and by 1620 increased production, favoured by good summers, had brought the price down to 27s. a quarter. Throughout the century the acreage under corn steadily increased, although owing to several periods of poor harvests there were rather disturbing fluctuations in its price. In such times the poor were badly hit, for with wheat at 50s. to 60s. a quarter, most other foods were proportionately dear. On the other hand, when in the good years corn was fetching only 27s. to 30s. and bread was cheap, the farmers were loud in their outcry that low prices meant ruin for them. The payment of a bounty of 5s. a quarter on all wheat exported when the price was below 48s. was legalized in 1673 and again in 1688, ostensibly to encourage tillage but in fact to give relief to the landed interests who were clamouring against the low prices.[2]

The much-needed readjustment between tillage and wool brought some-

---

[1] *Discourses on the Publick Revenues, and on the Trade of England, by the author of Ways and Means* [C. Davenant], 1698.
[2] For discussion of motives and effects see *The Corn Laws and Social England*, C. R. Fay, 1932.

what improved conditions to the villagers, because an increase in arable farming and in the number and size of estates meant more employment.

§ 2 IMPROVEMENT IN AGRICULTURAL METHODS

The general lines of agricultural practice did not change very greatly during the seventeenth century but there was a steady improvement, brought about by the efforts of the educated class of landowners and farmers, who were anxious to learn and to experiment. Many books on agriculture and gardening were published during this century, but from the historical point of view the most important are those of Gervase Markham, because they appeared at an early stage in the new development, were widely read, and full of useful information and sound advice. Markham was a too prolific writer, but one can forgive his constant repetition and shameless re-issuing of unsold books under a new title for the great influence his writings had on English agriculture. His most important work was *Markhams farewell to Husbandry or, The inriching of all sorts of Barren and Sterrill Grounds in one Kingdome, to be as fruitfull in all manner of Graine, Pulse, and Grasse as the best Grounds whatsouer*, which was published in 1620. It dealt fully and expertly not only with ploughing, sowing and harvesting, but with methods such as sanding, liming, marling and manuring, by which fertility of land could be increased. His stout advocacy of marling as a means of making poor soils fit to bear wheat had considerable influence at a time when the demand for corn was rapidly increasing, and it led to the reopening of many of the old marlpits.

The chief crops were much the same as those which had been grown for centuries past, but there was a steady increase in the acreage under wheat and a tendency for the cultivation of rye to decrease as the century progressed.

In the latter half of the century a few farmers began to experiment with two new crops, 'great clover' and turnips, which had been introduced from Holland. Interest in them had been aroused by Hartlib's publication in 1650 of Sir Richard Weston's *A Discourse of the Husbandrie used in Brabant and Flanders*. The innovation was encouraged by other agricultural experts, such as John Worlidge[1] and John Houghton,[2] and marks an important advance in English agricultural practice, because in time it led to a solution of the problem of keeping cattle in health throughout the winter. At first field crops such as turnips were used for feeding sheep, the flocks being folded on the land where the roots were growing, but towards the end of the

[1] *Systema Agriculturae*, John Worlidge, 1669.
[2] *A Collection of Letters for the Improvement of Husbandry and Trade*, John Houghton, 1681.

century the more progressive agriculturists began to show an interest in the Dutch practice, to which Sir Hugh Platt[1] had drawn attention some years earlier, of gathering roots and storing them during the winter packed in dry soil or sand.

An effort was made in 1664 to encourage the cultivation of potatoes. At this time they were grown in a few kitchen gardens but had not become at all generally popular as they had in Ireland, where they were rapidly becoming the staple food of the peasantry. In England times were bad for the poor; for nearly twenty years the harvests had been disappointing and corn had become scarce and dear. Rye, the alternative cereal, was also scarce and becoming unpopular, especially in the towns, where popular taste had turned towards the whiter wheaten breads. It seemed a peculiarly appropriate time to develop the cultivation of the potato. The scheme had the blessing of the newly founded Royal Society, and the Fellows were asked to plant the tubers in order to have a cheap food available for the necessitous poor.

A much more comprehensive scheme was put forward by John Forster in a quaint volume entitled *Englands Happiness Increased, or a Sure and Easie Remedy against all succeeding Dear Years; by A Plantation of the Roots called Potatoes* (1664). At that time four sorts of 'potatoes' were recognized in England, all of them having come originally from the New World. What were called 'Spanish potatoes', usually grown in rich men's gardens, seem to have been the sweet variety, batatas. The species referred to as 'Canadian potatoes', then steadily increasing in popularity, was the Jersualem artichoke of our modern gardens. The third and fourth kinds were referred to by Forster as 'Virginian' and 'Irish' respectively, and were differentiated by him because the former had purple and the latter white flowers; they were different varieties of the same species, *Solanum tuberosum*, the common potato of today. He recommended the latter because it grew so well in Ireland and had quite recently been introduced with success into the north of England.

> First if it shall please His Majesty to command, that there be brought out of *Ireland*, so many of the said Roots.

He pointed out how easily the tubers could be grown by the poor people so that when corn was dear they would have a good cheap substitute from which to prepare both bread and cakes 'at reasonable Rates'. He gave many recipes for making the latter, and strove to overcome the popular belief that potatoes were indigestible.

> But if any shall Object; That *this Bread is windy*, I answer; That it cannot be, for the Roots being first boyled, and then mingled with Flower, and afterwards baked, it is impossible they should be windy.

[1] *The Garden of Eden*, Sir Hugh Platt, 1653.

His enterprise and enthusiasm, however, had no reward and the scheme came to nothing in spite of his almost lyrical commendation of it.

> But when these Roots shall once come into use, People will live more happily and plentifully, Trading will flourish, and much Glory will redound to Almighty God, for discovering so profitable a Secret.

§3 THE POPULARITY OF GARDENS

The art of gardening developed rapidly in England during the seventeenth century, and fruit and vegetables, particularly the former, became available in greater variety and quantity than formerly. There is abundant evidence in contemporary diaries, estate accounts and pictures, that the gardens of the wealthy class were elaborately planned and well stocked. The pages of Evelyn's *Diary* alone are sufficient to show the size, beauty and wealth of the seventeenth-century country estates. Here is his description of an estate which Sir Robert Clayton had bought from a relative of his, Sir John Evelyn of Godstone, Surrey:

> It is such a solitude among hills as, being not above sixteen miles from London, seems almost incredible, the ways up to it are so winding and intricate. The gardens are large, and well-walled, and the husbandry part made very convenient and perfectly understood. The barns, the stacks of corn, the stalls for cattle, pigeon-house, etc. of most laudable example. Innumerable are the plantations of trees, especially walnuts. The orangery and gardens are very curious.[1]

Lady Clarendon's house at Swallowfield also earned his admiration.

> There is one orchard of 1000 golden, and other cider pippins; walks and groves of elms, limes, oaks, and other trees. The garden is so beset with all manner of sweet shrubs, that it perfumes the air. The distribution also of the quarters, walks, and parterres, is excellent. The nurseries, kitchen-garden full of the most desirable plants; two very noble orangeries well furnished; but, above all, the canal and fish ponds, the one fed with a white, the other with a black running water, fed by a quick and swift river, so well and plentifully stored with fish, that for pike, carp, bream, and tench, I never saw anything approaching it.[2]

[1] *Diary of John Evelyn*, October 12th, 1677, edited by William Bray, 1859.
[2] Ibid., October 22nd, 1685.

Glasshouses were becoming common features of such estates and were used for growing vines, peaches, nectarines and even orange and lemon trees. Artificial heating was being introduced.

> I went to see Mr. Watts, keeper of the Apothecaries' garden of simples at Chelsea ... What was very ingenious was the subterranean heat, conveyed by a stove under the conservatory, all vaulted with brick, so as he had the doors and windows open in the hardest frost, secluding only the snow.[1]

Many of the owners of these new estates were *parvenus* whose fortunes had been made by speculation in the soaring markets of the East Indian trade.

> I went to see Sir Josiah Child's prodigious cost in planting walnut-trees about his seat, and making fishponds, many miles in circuit, in Epping Forest, in a barren spot, as oftentimes these suddenly monied men for the most part seat themselves. He from a merchant's apprentice, and management of the East India Company's Stock, being arrived to an estate ('tis said) of £200,000.[2]

Such men imported a wealth of expensive wines, sub-tropical fruits, China oranges, French confectioneries, Westphalian hams and other luxuries from abroad, in addition to living in grand style on the produce of their own estates.

It is clear, however, from the many and full descriptions, that the gardens of these estates were primarily designed for beauty. Their owners took more interest in their long walks with tall clipped hedges, terraces, fountains, sunken Italian gardens, and pleasant shaded pavilions, than in their orchards or kitchen gardens. One of the most important books on English gardening, *Paradisus Terristris*, written in 1629 by John Parkinson, apothecary to James I and holder of the title *Botanicus Regius Primorius*, conferred on him by Charles I, is most instructive. Of a total of 612 pages no less than 459 deal with garden flowers. The remainder is divided into 77 pages on the care of orchards and 76 on the kitchen garden. Most of the plants which he mentions in the latter connection, and it must be borne in mind that his book was a comprehensive work of reference, are herbs. Apart from these he describes the cultivation and use of beet, endive, spinach, asparagus, cabbages, carrots, turnips, parsnips, radishes, potatoes, beans, peas, artichokes, cucumbers, melons and pumpkins. In spite of this list it is surprising how small a quantity of vegetables was grown even on large estates.[3] In a list of

[1] Ibid., August 7th, 1685.
[2] Ibid., March 16th, 1683.
[3] See, for example, the very full account of the Bedford Estate at Woburn which Miss Scott Thomson gives in *Life in a Noble Household, 1641-1700*, 1937.

purchases for the garden of Lord William Howard at Naworth the only vegetables mentioned are cabbages.

> 100 cabbish plantes   xijd.
> for cabbitch seede   xijd.[1]

Of the poorer classes in the country it is less easy to speak, for it is difficult to trace any records of the vegetables grown in their cottage gardens. It seems reasonably certain that the Tudor enclosures seldom deprived the cottager of his small plot, although they may have caused him to lose some of his common fields. Those who kept their employment and, therefore, their simple homes, were probably able to obtain seeds and plants without great difficulty. In popular books such as Culpeper's herbal *The English Physitian Enlarged* (1653) there are many references to cabbages, parsnips, carrots and other garden vegetables, which suggest that they were found in every type of garden. Potatoes, however, are not mentioned.

§ 4 MARKET GARDENS

An important development was the growth of market gardening. The raising of vegetables, especially lettuce and other salad plants, had for many years been a highly developed industry in Holland, the market gardens outside Amsterdam being already famous in the early fifteenth century.[2] When the knowledge and skill of the Dutch gardeners was brought to England towards the end of that century market gardens began to spring up on the outskirts of some of the large towns. Those supplying London were for the most part to the north and north-east. The produce was sold, as it had been for centuries, in the market near St Paul's, but during the disturbed years of the Civil War the stalls had gradually spread unheeded into the churchyard itself. Once again the Lord Mayor was obliged to take action to stop what had become a public nuisance, and in 1673 it was ordered that the sale of garden produce should be limited to certain streets.

> And for the ease and benefit of such of his Majesties Subjects . . . who have occasion to sell or by Rootes, Hearbs, Fruit or other garden Commodities, two places onely, namely, the streets called Alderman-bury and Broadstreet, London.

London was extending rapidly towards the west and a new fruit and vegetable market sprang up when the street traders found a convenient site

[1] *Selections from the Household Books of Lord William Howard* (Surtees Society Publication, No. 68, 1877).
[2] *Oud Nederlandsche Tuinkunst*, C. van Syfesteyn, S'Gravenhage, 1910.

for the sale of their produce in the Square at Covent Garden which Inigo
Jones had erected for the 4th Earl of Bedford about 1630. Some forty years
later the 5th Earl was granted letters patent licensing him to hold a market
'within the Piazza at Covent Garden'.

§5 MEAT

The meat problem had not altered very greatly. Only a few of the more
progressive farmers paid any attention to the quality of their stock or tried
to improve it by suitable breeding. For the greater part of the century the
approach of winter was still a time when old and weakly stock were slaughtered and the carcasses salted down or otherwise preserved.

We find in seventeenth-century writings many references to powdered
meat, usually beef. By this is meant meat preserved by powdering with dry
salt. Muffett says it was frequently used on board ship and in 'rich Farmers
houses, that keep beefe a whole twelve-month till they eat it'.[1]

> Memorandum that I powdered of the xxixl. aforsayd spent in meate
> the value of iijl.xjs; and yet ther was none, or very little left at Mid-
> sommer.[2]

It was a coarse food and probably used mainly for the labourers' meals.

> ... it is tough, hard, heavy, and of ill nourishment, requiring rather
> the stomach of another *Hercules* (who is said to have fed chiefly of
> Bulls flesh) then of any ordinary and common ploughman.[3]

It was only late in the century, when the value of turnips and other roots
began to be recognized, that there was any prospect of overcoming the
difficulties of the winter feeding of livestock, and the provision of ample
supplies of fresh meat during these months. Pigeons were still an important
stand-by in winter and every large house had its loft. They provided not
only food but valuable manure.

In Anno 1618

The Proffites of my pegion house Imprimis I iudge that the younge
pegions kild out of him were worth (for ye first flight was 34 dozens
worth — lijs) besides those let fly which was the last flight allmost

iiijl. xvs. [£4 15s. od.]

---

[1] *Healths Improvement*, Thomas Muffett, Corrected and Enlarged by Christopher Bennet,
1655.
[2] *Robert Loder's Farm Accounts, 1610-20* (Camden Society Publication, 3rd Series, No. 53,
1936).
[3] *Healths Improvement*, Thomas Muffett, 1655.

Item the dounge I value worth   xxxvs.
    Summa est   vjl. xs.[1] [£6 10s. 0d.]

Some agriculturists blamed the pigeons for the great waste of corn.

> The next great destroyers of Corne . . . are your Pygeons, which the
> wisdom of our nation, hath so well found out that they haue prouided
> many wholesome Lawes for the restraint of the great multiplicity
> thereof.[2]

§6 POACHING AND WILD GAME

The owners of the big estates and the prosperous farmers stocked their
larders almost entirely from their own lands. Almost every form of wild
life from small birds to deer was trapped or hunted; venison was one of the
most popular winter meats. There are indications that the prohibition of
poaching was less strictly enforced than it was in feudal times. It seems probable that the villagers were able to snare and trap with a certain amount of
freedom until the laws against poaching were tightened up about 1650.
Rabbits, not unnaturally, were the most popular catch.

> . . . *Connies*, which with us, above all nations is so common a meat.[3]

The various methods used for trapping and snaring are fully described by
Gervase Markham in a book called *Hungers Preuention: or, The Whole Arte
of Fowling by Water and Land* (1621), which he compiled especially for the
benefit of 'all the most worthy and noble Lords, Knights, Gentlemen and
Merchants, Counsellors and Aduenturers for the Blessed Plantation of
Virginia'. In spite of this flowery dedication there is no suggestion that the
pursuit of game was the exclusive privilege of the wealthy or landed classes.

§7 THE CONDITION OF THE POOR

The century opened with the country in a very depressed condition.
For at least twenty-five years it remained in this state; there were financial
troubles, a great deal of unemployment — in 1615 Sheffield had 725 'begging
pore' in a population of only 2207[4] — and distressing poverty, particularly in

[1] *Robert Loder's Farm Accounts, 1610-20* (Camden Society Publication, 3rd Series, No. 53,
1936).
[2] *Markhams farewell to Husbandry*, Gervase Markham, 1620.
[3] *Healths Improvement*, Thomas Muffett, 1655.
[4] *Social and Agrarian Background of the Pilgrim Fathers*, G. E. Fussell, *Agricultural History*,
1933, Vol. VII.

the towns. In the second half of the century the trade with the expanding markets in the New World and the East brought great wealth to the financiers and merchants, but it was slow to bring better conditions to the bulk of the population.

There was, however, an appreciable and much needed rise in wages during the century. Farm hands received from 6d. to 9d. a day — more in harvest time — early in the century;[1] by 1650 the usual wage was 1s. a day for the greater part of the year. In the towns the wages of the artisans rose in about the same proportion and many of them were getting as much as 2s. a day by the turn of the century. This contributed in some measure towards raising the standard of living but it had fallen to such a deplorably low level in late Tudor times that the conditions of life for the labouring classes were still fairly bad until well into the middle of the century.

John Evelyn, who made an extensive tour of the country in 1654, commented several times in his diary on the miserable condition of the villagers.

> Went to Uppingham, the shire-town of Rutland, pretty and well-built of stone, which is a rarity in that part of England, where most of the rural parishes are but of mud, and the people living as wretchedly as in the most impoverished parts of France, which they much resemble, being idle and sluttish. The country (especially in Leicestershire) much in common; the gentry free drinkers.[2]

It does not seem possible that these villagers were as well fed as their forefathers had been a century earlier. Conditions such as Evelyn and other writers of the period describe would have made it impossible for a large number of the farm labourers to keep their own cow; probably the only livestock they could afford was poultry, or occasionally a pig. Certainly milk became dearer in the south; about 1640 it ranged in price from 4d. to 6d. a gallon. In the north and in Wales, probably because the development and growth of great estates was much less marked there, milk seems to have been a good deal cheaper and there are many indications that the villagers of these regions were better off than those of the changing south and east.

It is reasonable to suppose that the consumption of 'white meats' by the poorer country people, which, as we have seen, declined rather sharply in late Tudor times, did not rise again significantly during the first half of the century. Most of these people seem to have lived on broth, prepared with beans and salted meat, bread, fish, cheese, a little bacon, and what they could trap or snare.

[1] *Robert Loder's Farm Accounts, 1610-20* (Camden Society Publication, 3rd Series, No. 53, 1936).
[2] August 7th, 1654.

G

Husbandmen, and such as labour, can eat fat bacon, salt gross meat, hard cheese &c. (*O dura messorum ilia!* [what tough insides have these mowers!], coarse bread at all times, go to bed and labour upon a full stomach, which to some idle persons would be present death.[1]

The seventeenth century saw some bad periods of dearth. Thorold Rogers, speaking of this period, says:

Nothing has struck me more in looking over the prices of corn in the seventeenth century, than the prolonged and serious dearths which mark it. I do not pretend that I have discovered in this record of 444 continuous harvests, anything which can indicate the cycle of the seasons. But I have never noticed in any earlier century such a continuity of dearth as from 1630 to 1637, from 1646 to 1651, from 1658 to 1661, and from 1693 to 1699, in each case inclusive.[2]

During such periods the poor people suffered severely from the dearness of food. About the middle of the century there was a particularly bad phase when beef, which had been as cheap as 2d. a pound, rose to 5d., and cheese became almost as dear. The poorer town dwellers lived largely on bread, salt or pickled herrings and cheese; now and again they could afford the cheaper meats such as sheep's heads or pigs' trotters, but for many in these bad times the words of Thomas Muffett, 'Bread and Cheese be the two targets against death,'[3] must have been all too true.

It is difficult to form a clear picture of the state of the lower classes during the latter part of the seventeenth century, although it seems to have become worse. There were good harvests from 1685 to 1691 when the price of corn remained low, averaging for this period 29s. 5d. a quarter, but there was a very bad spell from 1693 to the end of the century when there was scarcity all over England, and the price rose to 56s.;[4] 1693 was a particularly bad year, many people emigrating from the north of England and Scotland to Ireland and elsewhere. The wars with the Dutch and with France had gravely disturbed our trade and impoverished the exchequer. Prices were higher than they should have been owing to the debasing of the currency, although matters improved somewhat when the clipped coinage was called in in 1695 and a new issue appeared the following year, but prices did not fall appreciably until the good harvests which opened the eighteenth century brought plenty.

In a report drawn up by Locke for the Board of Trade in 1697 he had written regarding the labouring classes:

[1] *The Anatomy of Melancholy*, R. Burton, 1621.
[2] *History of Agriculture and Prices*, Vol. V, J. E. Thorold Rogers, 1866-87.
[3] *Healths Improvement*, Thomas Muffett, 1655.
[4] *A History of Prices*, Thomas Tooke, 1838-57.

What they [children under 3 years of age] can have at home from their parents is seldom more than bread and water, and that very scanty too.[1]

It was a period when the poor were helpless against the sharp reaction which the price of bread showed to a defective harvest. Gregory King revealed in his careful studies how disproportionate these rises usually were. If the harvest was one-tenth below expectation the price of corn rose three-tenths; if the yield was only half, bread might become as much as four and a half times as dear.[2] More than a century was to pass before the influence of over-seas production and international trade stabilized matters so as to lessen the extent of the fluctuations in the price of bread and wheat.

Soon after the middle of the century there appears to have been a fairly large importation of rice, probably as a result of the rise in the price of wheat. We have not been able to trace many references to its use but it is on record that the Committee of Christ's Hospital made inquiries whether they could safely instruct their Steward to replace cheese in the diet of the children by 'boyled Rice'. We do not know what the doctor and apothecary who were consulted reported, but in January 1689 'A meale of Rice once a week instead of Water-Gruell' was approved. The innovation was apparently a success for after six weeks' trial it was suggested that 'the children should have buttered wheate for dinners and abate one meale of Rice, it being cheaper & much wholsomer. Whereupon the Com[ee] are of opinion that they may have two meals of wheate in a weeke (except during Lent) & one of Rice and noe Water-gruel'.[3]

It is difficult to believe that the condition of the working people improved during the years of war, pestilence and dearth which the second half of the century brought, yet we find so shrewd an observer as Davenant writing in 1698:

> As to the Common People, there is no Country in the World where the Inferior Rank of Men were better cloath'd, and fed, and more at their ease, than in this Kingdom, nor consequently where they propagate faster.[4]

§8 THE FOOD OF THE LABOURING CLASSES

Bread, beef, beer and cheese are the foods mentioned over and over again in the contemporary accounts of working-class life and it seems clear,

[1] Cited by M. Dorothy George in *English Social Life in the Eighteenth Century*, 1923.
[2] *A History of Prices*, Thomas Tooke, 1838-57.
[3] *Annals of Christ's Hospital*, E. H. Pearce, 1901.
[4] *Discourses on the Publick Revenues, and on the Trade of England* [C. Davenant], 1698.

moreover, that the standard of living was judged to a considerable extent by the amount of meat eaten. When money was short or prices were high, meat had to give place to cheese or to thick broths prepared with dried peas and beans but in good times people wanted meat and still more meat. Garden vegetables, which were being grown in greater quantities by the cottagers, were rather despised by the townspeople, probably because being to some extent the standby of the country labourer when times were hard they came to be regarded as the food of poverty. Sir Ralph Verney reveals the contempt of the English maidservants for the 'potages' and 'legumes' which were the ordinary fare of the working people in France. His 'Luce' and 'Besse' demanded meat.

> I know noe English maids will ever bee content . . . to fare as thes [French] servants faire . . . Noe English maide will bee content with our diet and way of liveing . . . I rost but one night in a weeke for Suppers which were strainge in an English maide's oppinion.[1]

§9 'BRITAINE'S BUSSES'

An enlightening picture of the type of food thought proper for a working man in the early seventeenth century is provided by the details of an interesting project put forward by an anonymous writer in 1615 and recalling a similar proposal made by Robert Hitchcock in 1580 for 'the honour of the Prince, the greate profite of the publique state, relief of the poore, preseruation of the rich, reformation of Roges and Idle persones, and the wealthe of thousandes that knowe not how to liue'.[2] Speculation and trading ventures were all the rage and the author thought a scheme for catching Yarmouth herrings would prove a financial attraction. He set forth his plans in a tract entitled *Britaine's Busses or a Computation as well of the Charge of a Busse or Herring-Fishing Ship* (1615). It provides a very detailed account of the expense of fitting out such a boat for a 16-week fishing season, and estimates that each boat would bring in a profit of £600. It is interesting to note that the catch was to be sold in Continental ports and that the boat was to return loaded with pitch, hemp, flax or corn. For the crew of 15 men and a boy needed to man her the following stores were to be provided:

Beere. A gallon of beer a day 'which is the allowance made in the king's ships', which at 40/- a tun would cost £16.0.0. for the voyage.

Bisket. 1 lb. a day 'as in his Majesty's ships'; total cost, £10.13.4.

---

[1] *Memoirs of the Verney Family*, Vol. II, Frances P. Verney, 1892.
[2] *Tudor Economic Documents*, Vol. III, edited by R. H. Tawney and E. Power, 1924.

Oatmeale or Peaze. 1 gallon a day; cost at 4/- a bushel £2.16.0.

Bacon. '2 pounds of bacon for 4 meales in a weeke.' Total cost at 2/2d. a stone, £6.18.8.

Fresh fish. 'They may take, daily, out of the sea, as much fresh fish as they can eate.'

Butter. 'To allow every man and boy (to butter their fish, or otherwise to eate as they like,) a quarter of a pound of butter a day, that is for each person 28 pounds of butter, that is halfe a firkin of Suffolk butter'; total cost at 20/- a firkin £8.0.0.

Cheese. ½ lb. of Holland cheese a day at 23/4d. the 'hundred waight'; total cost, £9.6.8.

Vinegar. 3 pints a day among the 16 people; total cost £1.0.0.

In addition the following stores were taken:

	s.	d.
Aquivita, 4 gallons	12	0
Zantoyle, 2 gallons	12	0
Honny, 2 gallons	10	0
Sugar, 4 lb.	4	0
Nutmegge, ¼ lb.	1	0
Ginger, ½ lb.		6
Pepper, 1 lb.	2	0

Apart from the deficiency of fruit and vegetables, it is an excellent diet. An estimate of its food value, excluding fresh fish, is given in Appendix A.

§ 10 ARMY RATIONS

The rations of the Army at Tangier (1660-80) are thus described by Thacker:

> The private soldiers live there better than in any part of the world, for they have fresh and wholesome quarters with small gardens; Coals for dressing their provisions they have out of the stores, at the King's charges; Every Monday morning each man receives one piece of beef, one piece of pork, 7 lbs. of bread, a quart of pease, a pint of oatmeal besides butter and cheese, for his week's allowance.[1]

> In 1670 the ordinary allowance to a soldier in the field was two pounds of bread, one pound of meat or an equal weight of cheese, and one pottle of wine or two of beer.[2]

[1] R. Thacker, cited in *The History of the British Standing Army*, Clifford Walton, 1894.
[2] Ibid.

§ 11 HOSPITAL DIETS

The new diet table approved by the Governing Body of St Bartholomew's Hospital in April 1687 was as follows:[1]

Dyett Appointed

Sunday	10 ounces of Wheaten Bread
	6 ounces of Beefe boyled without bones
	1 pint and a halfe of Beef Broth
	1 pint of Ale Cawdell
	3 pints of 6 shilling Beere
Monday	10 ounces of Wheaten Bread
	1 pint of Milk Pottage
	6 ounces of Beefe
	1½ pints of Beefe Broth
	3 pints of Beere
Tuesday	10 ounces of Bread
	halfe a pound of Boyled Mutton
	3 pints of Mutton Broth
	3 pints of Beere
Wednesday	10 ounces of Bread
	4 ounces of Cheese
	2 ounces of Butter
	1 pint of Milk Pottage
	3 pints of Beere
Thursday	The same allowance as Sunday
	1 pint of Rice Milke
Friday	10 ounces of Bread
	1 pint of Sugar Soppes
	2 ounces of Cheese
	1 ounce of Butter
	1 pint of Water Gruell
	3 pints of Beere
Satturday	The same allowance as Wednesday

An analysis is included in Appendix A. As this shows it was not a bad diet apart from the lack of fruit and vegetables.

Of a somewhat similar character was the diet of the children of Christ's Hospital in 1678.[2]

[1] *The History of St Bartholomew's Hospital*, Vol. II, Sir Norman Moore, 1918.
[2] *Annals of Christ's Hospital*, E. H. Pearce, 1901.

§ 12 BUTTER IN THE TOWNS

There is evidence that the consumption of butter by the working people of the towns increased steadily during the seventeenth century. A great deal more cheese was also eaten. This is not surprising, because there was a very large increase in the number of milch cows as a result of the growth of the big estates. The change meant that there was less milk available as food in the country districts. The farmers found it paid them to make butter or cheese to sell to the nearby towns, and to use the whey or buttermilk for feeding pigs. It is clear, from the wording of the diet sheets quoted above, that butter was often eaten with bread and cheese by the poorer people; by the wealthy classes it was used almost exclusively for cooking.

§ 13 MEAT IN THE TOWNS

There was very little change in the meat markets during the century, except that much larger numbers of cattle came to the towns for slaughter as a result of the rapid growth of the big farming estates. The civic authorities did their best by constant inspection to prevent the sale of bad meat but the amount of illness and the number of deaths caused by food poisoning must have been appalling.

Much meat still went to the cookshops, those in London being for the most part in 'Cooks row' near the river. A French visitor, M. Masson, has left a good picture of such a cookshop.

> Generally, four Spits, one over another, carry round each five or six Pieces of Butcher's Meat, Beef, Mutton, Veal, Pork and Lamb; you have what Quantity you please cut off, fat, lean, much or little done; with this, a little Salt and Mustard upon the Side of a Plate, a Bottle of Beer and a Roll; and there is your whole Feast.[1]

He was deeply impressed by the large amount of meat eaten by the English, even by the poor people, and assured his readers that he had met people who rarely tasted bread, so much meat did they habitually consume.

§ 14 BREAD IN THE TOWNS

The townspeople had always demanded bread of better quality than that eaten in the country but the rise of the seventeenth century marks the period during which the working classes in the south gave up the dark rye and bran

[1] *M. Misson's Memoirs and Observations in his Travels over England,* translated from the French by Mr Ozell, 1719.

breads, except in times of shortage. The greater part of the bread sold in
London was made from 'white' wholemeal flours. Even the prisoners were
given bread of this quality, for the captured Dutch seamen lodged in Chelsea
College in 1665 complained to John Evelyn that it was too fine for their
taste and that they wished to have coarser loaves, more like those to which
they were accustomed in their own country. Throughout the century the
weight of loaves — '½d white lofe, penye white lofe, halfe peny wheaten
lofe'[1] — was regulated by the Assize of Bread.

§ 15 THE FOOD OF THE MIDDLE AND UPPER CLASSES

People with comfortable incomes fed well. Thomas Muffett quotes a
contemporary saying, 'The Spaniard eats, the German drinks, and the
English exceed in both.'[2]

Breakfast, still taken early by modern standards, from 6 to 7 o'clock,
consisted of cold meats, fish, cheese and ale or beer. Herrings, both salted
and dried, were a popular breakfast dish. Pepys gave his guests a New Year's
breakfast of a 'barrel of oysters, a dish of neats' tongues, and a dish of anchovies, wine of all sorts and Northdowne ale'.[3]

Dinner was the chief meal of the day and was usually eaten about midday,
although towards the end of the century there was a tendency to dine later
among the class that had taken to the new custom of drinking tea, coffee and
chocolate. The introduction of these beverages had a marked effect on the
habits of the leisured class who could afford to drink them, because it
favoured the development of social entertainment in which both sexes could
take part. They were in no small measure responsible for the alteration in
the times of meals, which can be traced in the late seventeenth century and
which continued in the eighteenth. A light breakfast of coffee or chocolate
and rolls became fashionable, and being taken rather late, about 9 or 10
o'clock, tended to put back the dinner hour.

From all accounts the main meal of the day was a formidable affair.

> The *English* eat a great deal at Dinner; they rest a while, and to it
> again, till they have quite stuff'd their Paunch. Their Supper is
> moderate: Gluttons at Noon, and abstinent at Night.[4]

Typical dishes were a 'hot shoulder of mutton', a 'good pie baked of a leg
of mutton', a 'cold chine of beef', a 'good dish of roasted chickens', eaten
with bread, cheese, ale or wine.

[1] *Assize of Bread*, 1608.
[2] *Healths Improvement*, Thomas Muffett, 1655.
[3] *The Diary of Samuel Pepys*, January 1st, 1661, edited by the Rev. J. Smith, 6th Edition, 1858.
[4] *M. Misson's Memoirs*, translated by Mr Ozell, 1719.

On special occasions the dinner consisted of several courses of meat. Pepys gave a dinner party on January 13th, 1663, for which 'my poor wife' had to rise at 5 in the morning to buy the provisions. The meal consisted of oysters, a hash of rabbits and lamb, a 'rare chine of beef', a 'great dish of roasted fowle', a tart, fruit and cheese. Oysters, sold in small barrels costing from 2s. to 3s. each, were a very popular dish. The tarts so often referred to were sometimes filled with fruit — gooseberries being particularly popular — and sometimes with meat.

Another of Pepy's special dinners, a postponed celebration of his being 'cut for the stone', gave him great satisfaction 'for that my dinner was great, and most neatly dressed by our own only mayde'.[1]

> We had a fricasee of rabbits, and chickens, a leg of mutton boiled, three carps in a dish, a great dish of a side of lamb, a dish of roasted pigeons, a dish of four lobsters, three tarts, a lamprey pie, a most rare pie, a dish of anchovies, good wine of several sorts, and all things mighty noble, and to my great content.

In the towns people often dined at the taverns which provided an 'ordinary', consisting usually of a hot meat dish, bread, cheese and ale. Such a meal 'hard by Temple-Gate' cost Pepys 10d.

The extent to which meat predominated in the diet of wealthy people can be judged from the record of a week's purchases of stores for the Woburn household of the Earl of Bedford in April 1654.[2]

	£	s.	d.
One bullock of 68 stone	—	—	—
2 sheep	—	—	—
1 calf	—	—	—
A quarter of mutton	—	4	6
A side of veal	—	7	6
10 stone 4 lb. of pork	—	19	3
1 pig	—	2	10
2 calves' heads	—	1	10
4 capons	—	8	6
12 pigeons	—	5	6
20 lb. of butter	—	10	0
Eggs	—	3	0
Crayfish	—	1	10
A peck and a half of apples	—	1	9

[1] April 4th, 1663.
[2] *Life in a Noble Household, 1641-1700*, G. Scott Thomson, 1937.

Bread	—	1	6
2 pecks oatmeal	—	2	8
Yeast	—	1	8
Six bushels of fine flour	—	—	—

Poultry, which in earlier times had been rather despised as the poor man's food, came to be regarded as a delicacy. Chickens became quite expensive, costing as much as 1s. 4d., compared with the mere 2d. or 4d. they had fetched a century earlier. Geese were dear for the times at 3s. each. To be able to afford poultry was beginning to be an indication that you had risen in the world. When Holdfast in *The City-Madam* enters with porters carrying market baskets full of provisions and is asked what he brings, he replies:

> The Cream of the market, provision enough
> To serve a garrison. I weep to think on't.
> When my Master got his wealth, his family fed
> On roots, and livers and necks of beef on Sundays.
> But now I fear it will be spent on pultry.
> Butchers meat will not go down.[1]

During the seventeenth century the order in which the courses were served was changed. In Tudor days fish usually came after meat but this was now often reversed and the sequence of soup, fish, meat with which we are familiar today became fashionable.

The preponderance of meat and fish in the diet of the upper classes can again be illustrated by records of the purchase of food. One such record concerns the wedding dinner of John Verney, for seven people, 'at the Rummer in Queen Street London'.[2]

	£	s.	d.
Beer-ayle	0	3	0
Wine	0	11	0
Orings	0	1	0
A dish of fish	1	0	0
2 Geese	0	8	6
4 fatt Chikens	0	8	0
2 Rabets	0	3	0
A dish of peese	0	6	0
8 hartey Chokes	0	5	0
A dish of Strabreys	0	6	0
A dish of Chereys	0	5	6

[1] *The City-Madam, a Comedie. As it was acted at the private House in Black Friars with great applause*, written by Philip Massinger, Gent, 1658.
[2] *Memoirs of the Verney Family*, Vol. IV, Margaret M. Verney, 1899.

Although this dinner took place in May the cost of fruit for seven people was quite considerable.

Another interesting record is the formidable list of purchases made for the Star Chamber early in the reign of James I.[1]

> The expenses of diett provided for the Kings Majesties most hon'ble privy Counsell at the Starchamber in Easter Trinity Mich. and Hilary termes in the twentieth yere of the rayne of our Sovereign Lord King James 1612.
>
> *Friday 22 May.*
>
> Imprimis in Bread 38s., in Beere 12s., in Ale 5s., in Flower 6s.
>
> Item in sweet Butter 2s. 6d., in old Linges 13s., in Greenfish 8s., in three great Pikes 17s., in two small Pikes 8s., in Carpes 18s., in eight Tenches 16s., in great Eales 6s., in six Breames 14s., in Knobbards 4s., in eighteen Flounders 7s., in Roches 14s., in Pearches 7s., in fower Troutes 12s., in eight Barbells 14s., in Chevons 4s., in three paire of Soales 8s., in Anchoves 3s. 4d., in Pickled Oysters 2s., in one firkin of Sturgeon 38s., in one fresh Salmon and ½ 38s., in one great Conger 14s. 4d., in two Birts and two Turbotts 18s., in three Mullets 8s., in one Dorie 4s., in fower great Lobsters 8s., in five Crabbes 11s., in fower long Oysters 10s., in six Plaice 9s., in Mackrells 7s., in two fresh Coddes 8s., in Whitings 8s., in Cocles and Prawnes 4s., in pound Butter 20s., in Creame 2s. 6d., in Eggs 8s., in Herbes 3s., in Apples 18d., in Quinces 6s. 8d., in Oringes and Lemons, 6s., in Rosewater and Barberies 2s.

This is a typical list of purchases for 'a fish day'. On other days meat was bought.

> *Tuesday 26 May.*
>
> Imprimis in Bread 38s. 6d., in Beare 12s., in Ale 5s., in Flower 6s.
>
> Item in thirtytwo stone of Beefe at 2s. 6d. the stone, in six Neets-tongues 10s., in fower Marrow-bones 2s., in three loynes fower legges three brests and two necks of Mutton 28s., in two loynes and two brests of Veale 12s., in one Lambe and ½ 15s., in eight Geese 18s. 8d., in three dozen and ½ of Chicken 42s., in twelve tame Pigeons 10s., in two Pheasants 20s., in six Hearons 20s., in one dozen of Quailes 16s., in eighteen Bucklinges 16s., in eighteen Rabbetts 16s., in Butter 20s., in Creame 2s. 6d., in Eggs 8s., in Herbes 3s., in Gooseberries for Tartes and Broth 8s., in Apples 18d., in Oringes and Lemons 8s., in Rose-water and Barberies 2s., in Portage 3s. 6d., in Boathire 4s.

[1] Record Office, Ref. E. 40755.

The distribution of the expenditure is illuminating. About £17 is spent on fish or meat; nearly £5 on bread and flour; £3 on dairy produce (it will be noticed that milk is not mentioned); 34s. on beer and ale; 6s. on herbs and 31s. 8d. on fruit. There is no mention of vegetables, unless these are included under herbs. Even so the amount is very small but it is more likely that dried herbs for broths are intended by this entry. It is interesting to note that gooseberries were sometimes used in broth. In a later record of purchases for the Star Chamber there stands the item 'potatoes, 3s.', but as the quantity is not stated we cannot say how expensive they were.

A good illustration of the best fare a ship could provide before the fresh provisions taken on board when she sailed had been exhausted is given in the *Diary of Henry Teonge*, who was 'Chaplain on Board His Majesty's Ships Assistance, Bristol, and Royal Oak, Anno 1675 to 1679'. They left England on June 30th, 1675, and on July 10th he notes in his diary:

> Wee are past the Rock of Lysbon... This day our noble Capt. feasted the officers of his small squadron with 4 dishes of meate, viz. 4 excellent henns and a peice of porke boyled, in a dish; a giggett of excellent mutton and turnips; a peice of beife of 8 ribbs, well seasoned and roasted; and a couple of very fatt greene geese; last of all, a great Chesshyre cheese:... His liquors were answerable; viz. Canary, Sherry, Renish, Clarett, white wine, syder, ale, beare, all of the best sort; and punch like [as plentiful as] ditch water.

§ 16 FRUIT AND VEGETABLES

It is not easy to get a clear picture of how popular fruit and vegetables had become. The rapid development of gardening must have made them available in larger quantities than ever before but judging from contemporary writings they were still little used. One searches the pages of that minute chronicler Pepys in vain so far as references to vegetables are concerned, and it seems that they were still employed more as ingredients for soups than as an accompaniment to meat. Later in the century, however, we begin to find references to their use in this latter fashion and the practice became widespread in eighteenth-century England. Misson is describing the last few years of the seventeenth century when he says:

> Another time they will have a Piece of boil'd Beef, and then they salt it some Days before-hand, and besiege it with five or six Heapes of Cabbage, Carrots, Turnips or some other Herbs or Roots, well pepper'd and salted and swimming in Butter.[1]

[1] *M. Misson's Memoirs*, translated by Mr Ozell, 1719.

The belief was widely held, at any rate in the earlier part of the century, that vegetables were 'windy' and unfit to be eaten except in broths, or occasionally, well seasoned with oil, in salads. Fruit was eaten more often than vegetables — we have already seen that the orchard developed earlier and more rapidly than the kitchen garden — but it was by no means common. Misson comments on the rarity of fruit as a dessert.

> The Desert they [the English] never dream of, unless it be a piece of Cheese. Fruit is brought only to the Tables of the Great, and of a small Number even among them.[1]

When fruit was eaten it was usually with the idea that it was useful to 'keep down the vapours'.

For the greater part of the year the price of fruit placed it beyond the reach of the ordinary purse, but it is surprising to find how expensive it sometimes was even at the season when one would have expected to find a glut in the markets. Purchases made in June 1663 for the household of the Earl of Bedford show that 8 lb. of cherries cost 5s. 4d., 2 quarts of gooseberries 6d., 3 bushels and a peck and a half of peas 9s. 4d. These would, of course, be prohibitive prices for a labourer earning only about 1s. a day or a skilled craftsman earning at the most 2s. There were some curious contrasts, asparagus being sometimes only 6d. a bundle while artichokes — presumably the 'globe' and not the 'Jerusalem' variety — were as much as $9\frac{1}{2}$d. each.[2] Another queer contrast, noted in 1662, is that lemons 'unwasht' were 3s. a dozen while oranges were 1s. each.[3] That these fruits were regarded as luxuries can be judged from the fact that when Edmund Verney went up to Trinity College, Oxford, in 1685, his father packed some in what appears to have been the equivalent of the schoolboy's tuckbox.

In yr trunk I Have putt for you
18 Sevill Oranges
6 Malaga Lemons
3 pounds of Brown Sugar
1 pound of white poudered sugar made up in quarters
1 lb. of Brown sugar Candy
$\frac{1}{4}$ of a lb. of white sugar candy
1 lb. of pickt Raisons, good for a Cough
4 Nuttmeggs.[4]

[1] Ibid.
[2] *Life in a Noble Household, 1641-1700*, G. Scott Thomson, 1937.
[3] *Memoirs of the Verney Family*, Vol. IV, Margaret M. Verney, 1899.
[4] Ibid.

§ 17 SUGAR AND SWEETMEATS

With the opening up of the trade with the East the price of sugar fell. At the beginning of the century it was about 1s. to 1s. 6d. a pound; by 1700 it had fallen to 6d. or less. This fall did much to popularize the serving of fruit tarts or puddings after the meat courses. We first find evidence of this practice at the tables of prosperous citizens about the middle of the century. Misson waxed quite lyrical about the English puddings, which he ascertained were made from 'Flower, Milk, Eggs, Butter, Sugar, Suet, Marrow, Raisins, &c. &c.'.

BLESSED BE HE THAT INVENTED PUDDING, for it is a Manna that hits the Palates of all Sortes of People.

He particularly mentions 'Christmas Pye', a forerunner of our Christmas pudding, which he says was 'eaten everywhere'.

It is a great Nostrum the composition of this Pasty; it is a most learned Mixture of Neats-tongues, Chicken, Eggs, Sugar, Raisins, Lemon and Orange Peel, various Kinds of Spicery, &c.[1]

§ 18 WINE, ALE AND BEER

During the seventeenth century important changes occurred in the consumption of liquors. In Tudor times a fair amount of wine was drunk, not only by the rich who could afford to buy good imported varieties but by the townsman who frequented the taverns and bought the cheap and frequently sophisticated stuff that went under the name of wine. The sale of these inferior wines seems to have declined during the latter part of the sixteenth century, for judging by early seventeenth-century writings the man in the street was for the most part a beer or ale drinker, except in the West Country where cider reigned supreme.

Wine	I, iouiall Wine, exhilirate the heart.
Beere	Marche-Beere is drinke for a king.
Ale	But Ale, bonny Ale, with spice and a tost,
	In the morning's a daintie thing.
Chorus	Then let vs be merry, wash sorrow away,
	Wine, Beere, and Ale shall be drunke to-day.
Wine	I, generous Wine, am for the Court.
Beere	The Citie calls for Beere.

[1] *M. Misson's Memoirs*, translated by Mr Ozell, 1719.

Ale	But Ale, bonny Ale, like a lord of the soyle,
	In the Countrey shall domineere.
Chorus	Then let vs be merry, wash sorrow away,
	Wine, Beere, and Ale shall be drunke to-day.[1]

The foreign trade in wine received a grievous blow when Cromwell passed the Navigation Act in 1651. This measure, planned to ruin the Dutch trade, refused admission to English ports of ships carrying goods of countries other than their own. It precipitated a war with the Dutch and gave the French wine trade a check from which it never fully recovered. Formerly practically all the wine from the Rhine and Moselle, and a considerable proportion of that from France, had been imported in Dutch ships. After the war was over any hope the merchants had of re-establishing the market for cheap French wines was dispelled by the heavy taxation of £4 a tun which was imposed by the Wine Act of 1688, a measure bitterly resented by the trade. The immediate effect of this taxation was to increase the consumption of beer and ale by the lower and middle classes and the consumption of Portuguese and sweet Levant wines by the wealthy classes, although if one can judge from the crop of books and pamphlets, mostly wisely anonymous, which appeared about this time and gave full instructions how to concoct wine from vinegar, 'clary juice', 'pippin syder' and 'blackberry water', some part of the trade hoped to be able to keep going without depending on foreign imports.[2]

In 1683 the importation of Portuguese wines was over 16,000 tuns while that of French wines had sunk to the almost incredibly low level of 65 gallons.[3] The French trade improved decidedly after the prohibition was relaxed in 1686 but was again badly hit by the famous Methuen Treaty with Portugal at the opening of the eighteenth century (1703), to which we shall refer later.

All wines, whether the French or German 'beverage' wines, or the sweeter sacks, Madeiras, Canary and Levant wines, were drunk from the wood; that is, they were stored in wooden casks and the bottles, fitted with a wooden peg, were filled just before being put on the table. Cork bark stoppers, which in time were adapted so as to provide a lasting seal to the bottle, were introduced in the late seventeenth century. From that time dates the custom of bottling and laying down special wines.[4]

[1] *Wine, Beere, and Ale, together by the Eares*, John Grove, 1629, quoted by Edward Smith in *Foods*, 3rd Edition, 1874.
[2] *The Art and Mystery of the Vintners and Wine Coopers*, 1692; *The Vintner's Mystery Displayed*, 1695 (?).
[3] *The Economic History of England*, Vol. II (*The Age of Mercantilism*), E. Lipson, 2nd Edition, 1934.
[4] *Bottlescrew Days*, André Simon, 1926.

Home-brewed beer was still drunk in the country, but it was going out of fashion in the towns, where most of it was made by the innkeepers. Each one had his own formula, as did every farmer in the country, so that it is not surprising that Misson should write 'There are a hundred and a hundred Sorts of Beer made in *England*'.[1] We can perhaps forgive a mere wine-drinking Frenchman for adding 'and some not bad'. Its strength varied from that of the strong beer which would soon put a man under the table to the light 'small beer', little stronger than a modern lager, which was the ordinary table drink even of young children. The allowance at Christ's Hospital at the end of the century was 30 barrels a week for 407 people, i.e. about 2½ gallons a head. It had the advantage of being a good deal safer and probably more palatable than most of the drinking water available.

Some people lamented the passing of the old English ale.

> *Beere*, is a Dutch boorish Liquor, a thing not knowne in *England*, till of late dayes an Alien to our Nation, till such times as Hops and Heresies came amongst us, it is a sawcy intruder in this Land.[2]

The food value of beer was far from negligible, for it seems probable that this 'small beer' had a calorific value of about 150-200 Cal. per pint. This meant that a young boy drinking about 3 pints a day would get some 500-600 Cal. towards his daily needs of about 2500. In addition to the calories provided by the alcohol and sugary substances, beer would have supplied a modest amount of calcium and appreciable quantities of ribo-flavin, nicotinic acid, pyridoxin, pantothenic acid and perhaps other vitamins. Vitamin B_1 is readily absorbed by the yeast during fermentation and is therefore poorly represented in the finished beer. The amount of riboflavin and nicotinic acid present appears to be directly related to the strength of the beer.[3][4] In any case an ample supply of the B vitamins would have been provided by the wholemeal bread still universally eaten. It is certain, how-ever, that home-brewed beer was a good, sound, healthful drink and one which could not possibly do any harm to children when drunk in reasonable amounts. Perhaps Molly and Ralph Verney, 'very ill of a feaver & pains with a short Cough very fast', were wise when they would not say where they felt their pains and refused to allow themselves to be 'blouded nor vomited' or to take anything but 'small Beare'.[5] One is glad to learn that they recovered, somewhat, apparently, to the discomfiture of the family physician.

[1] *M. Misson's Memoirs*, translated by Mr Ozell, 1719.
[2] *Ale Ale-vated into the Ale-titude*, John Taylor [The 'Water-Poet'], 1651.
[3] 'Unconsidered Trifles in our Diet', J. C. Drummond and T. Moran, *Nature* (1944), CLIII, 99.
[4] 'The Nutritive Value of Yeast, Beer, Wines and Spirits', H. J. Bunker, *Chemistry and Industry* (1947), No. 16, 204.
[5] *Memoirs of the Verney Family*, Vol. IV, Margaret M. Verney, 1899.

§ 19 THE RISE OF SPIRIT DRINKING

Although spirits were known in England in Tudor times they were not widely drunk. By the beginning of the seventeenth century a change was apparent. One finds more frequent references to 'aquavitae', which was a simple distilled spirit like a crude gin, and, rather surprisingly, one reference which suggests that Irish whiskey was quite a popular drink.

> The Irish Aquavitae, vulgarly called Vsquebagh, is held the best in the World of that kind; which is made also in *England*, but nothing so good as that which is brought out of *Ireland*. And the Vsquebagh is pre-ferred before our Aquavitae, because the mingling of Raysons, Fennell seede, & other things, mitigating the heate, & making the taste pleasant, makes it lesse inflame, & yet refresh the weake stomacke with moderate heate, & a good relish. These Drinkes the English-Irish drink largely, & in many families (especially at feasts) both men & women vse excesse therein.[1]

There certainly appears to have been a fairly considerable trade in 'Aqua-vitae'. The word was rather indiscriminately applied to any strong spirit distilled from fermented grain, or from less wholesome materials such as fermented fruit, wine lees, old cider, etc. There are references to the manu-facture of Aquavita in fifteenth-century London, but Queen Elizabeth granted the monopoly to prepare 'Aqua-Composita, Aqua Vitae, Vinegar and Alegar' to Richard Drake as a reward for his services under Sir Francis Drake. It may have lapsed after the outcry in Parliament in 1601 against the abuse of monopolies, but there was certainly a brisk trade in London in the early seventeenth century because in 1621 a petition was presented to Parlia-ment for the 'Releife of the distillers and sellers of Aqua-Vitae, Aqua Com-posita, and other stronge and hott waters'.[2] From this we learn that no less than two hundred establishments in the cities of London and Westminster depended for their livelihood on distilling these liquors.

In 1624 the Statute of Monopolies, the foundation of our modern Patent Law, was passed. Twelve years later a patent for distilling 'strong waters' was granted to Sir Theodore Mayerne and Thomas Cadman. They drew up the rules and regulations of the Distillers' Company, founded in 1638. There was certainly a need for some sort of control for Mayerne's description of the methods employed in preparing 'strong waters' shows that the practice of distilling beer dregs, rotten fruit, wine lees and other unsavoury raw materials was still widespread.[3]

[1] *Fyne Moryson's Itinerary, 1617*, edited from *Holinshed's Chronicles* by F. J. Furnivall, 1878.
[2] *Commons Debates*, W. Notestein, F. H. Relf and H. Simpson, 1935.
[3] *The Distiller of London*, Theodore Mayerne, 1639.

H

It has been suggested, and the suggestion seems a reasonable one, that the wars in the Low Countries at the end of the sixteenth century made our men familiar with gin. Certainly imports from Holland increased noticeably early in the seventeenth century. Genever, as it was called, soon became very popular and the amount imported towards the end of the century was as much as half a million gallons. After the expiration of the patent granted to Mayerne and Cadman the production of 'strong waters' was put on a firm basis by the Act of 1690 'whereas good and wholesome brandies, aqua-vitae and spirits may be drawn and made from malted corn'. This was another measure directed against the French. It is quite clear that the word 'brandy' was sometimes applied to spirituous liquors distilled from raw materials other than wine. This spirit, which in character must have resembled a crude, raw whisky or *schnapps*, came later to be known as 'British brandy', a name which survived until well into the eighteenth century. We have no idea to what extent the illegal production of crude 'aqua vitae' continued but it seems to have been considerable. The nature of much of the material produced must have been appalling and was doubtless responsible for much sickness and many deaths.

Another drink that acquired great popularity in the latter part of the seventeenth century was punch. For some obscure reason punch-drinking became closely associated with the Whigs, so much so that a true-blue Tory would not touch the beverage, but remained faithful to his sack and claret.[1]

Tea, Coffee and Chocolate

Tea, which before a century had passed was to become a national beverage, coffee and chocolate, were all introduced about the middle of this century. A Turkish merchant opened the first coffee house in London, in St Michael's Alley, in 1652. It immediately became popular and within a few years similar establishments had sprung up in every part of the town. Many of these coffee houses gained world-wide fame as the meeting place of literary, artistic or commercial circles. They were a striking feature of London life and Misson remarked on the large number he saw and recommended them as pleasant places in which to while away an hour or two.

> You have all Manner of News there: You have a good Fire, which you may sit by as long as you please: You have a Dish of Coffee; you meet your Friends for the Transaction of Business, and all for a Penny, if you don't care to spend more.[2]

[1] *The History of the Wine Trade in England*, André Simon, 1906.
[2] *M. Misson's Memoirs*, translated by Mr Ozell, 1719.

One of these houses, situated in Queen's Head Alley, is credited with the introduction of an 'excellent West Indian drink called Chocolate'. It soon became fashionable with the rich — it was the more expensive drink of the two — and was regarded as nutritious, and beneficial to the health. By the end of the century it was 'much used in *England*, as Diet and Phisick with the Gentry'.[1]

Tea was introduced about the same time as coffee, the first supplies being brought from China by the Dutch East India merchants. Some of it reached the London market, where it was sold for the remarkable price of £3 10s. a pound. The price dropped to about £2 in nine or ten years when, according to *Rugge's Diurnal*, 'Coffee, chocolate, and a new kind of drink called tea' were sold in every coffee house. A further reduction in price occurred when our own East India Company began to bring home supplies and by the end of the century, in spite of the heavy tax imposed in 1689, it could be bought for little more than 20s. a pound. The importation was then about 20,000 lb. a year. It did not, however, become cheap enough to be a general drink until well on into the next century.

Tea was then drunk in the Chinese fashion as a weak infusion without milk. Indeed, very little milk seems to have been drunk, if one can judge from the rarity with which it is mentioned in this connection. Whey, on the other hand, was quite popular. There were several 'whay-houses' in London and Pepys often patronized them, sometimes drinking 'a great deal of whay'. The belief was still current that it was more wholesome than milk.

§ 20 ADULTERATION OF FOOD

There appears to have been little appreciable improvement in the quality of the food offered for sale in the seventeenth-century shops and markets. Salting, pickling and drying were still the most commonly used methods for preserving food, although Robert Boyle gives an account of some successful experiments which were made in preserving meat during voyages to and from the East Indies.[2] The meat was roasted, cut in small pieces and packed closely in a cask, the air space being then wholly filled by pouring in melted butter. It was kept without developing taint during more than six months' voyage, much of it in a hot climate. Boyle stressed the importance of excluding the air. He himself tried preserving fresh meat by immersion in spirits of wine. The carcase of a puppy and several pieces of beef remained

[1] *The Manner of Making Coffee, Tea and Chocolate ... With their Vertues. Newly done out of French, and Spanish*, by John Chamberlayn, 1685.
[2] *Some Considerations touching the Usefulnesse of Experimental Naturall Philosophy*, R. Boyle, 1663-67.

unchanged for nearly two years. He thought it would be possible to render such meat edible by washing away the taste of alcohol with water but lack of time prevented his carrying the experiments further.

In the markets much that was sold as fresh meat must have been in a questionable condition, particularly in the hot months of the year. The municipalities and City Companies carried on their efforts to exercise some sort of control, as they had done in the past, by inspection of the markets and exercise of their powers of condemnation and confiscation, but the fines and other more drastic punishments they meted out to offenders were but a slight deterrent when fraud and adulteration were so likely to escape detection.

The weights of loaves, the dimensions of casks, the weights of cheese and butter and other matters of a like nature were still regulated by Assizes; reference has already been made to the Assize of Bread in 1608.

Not surprisingly sophistication was most rife where articles of high price were concerned. We have referred to the extensive trade in fabricated or adulterated wines, but tea also soon attracted the attention of the fakers. They sometimes used the crudest of methods, mixing dust, fine sand and floor sweepings, with the tea. Others were more cunning and made extensive use of cheap dried herbs or of a material known as *catechu* or *terra japonica*, which was prepared from the young leaves and shoots of an oriental climbing shrub, *Uncaria gambir*, and imparted a deceptively astringent flavour to the decoction. This addition was exceedingly difficult to detect for apart from tasting there was no known test for it, and even an expert palate might be deceived.

The opening up of trade with the Far East gave a great fillip to the markets dealings in drugs and spices. Prices were still in many cases high, so that there was a good deal of adulteration. During this century control of medicinal drugs passed out of the hands of the Grocers' Company. There had been many complaints about the system of 'garbelling' which they supervised and the protests grew to such an extent that in 1617 the charge of controlling the quality of these drugs was handed over to the Apothecaries, who separated from the 'Mistery of Grocers and Apothecaries' in that year.

§ 21 BIRTH OF MODERN SCIENCE

The helplessness of the authorities in the face of anything but the most obvious adulteration is not surprising. Nothing was known of the composition of food and drugs. There were no chemical tests of any value and such essential instruments as the balance, the microscope and even the hydrometer were in the earliest stages of their development. But there were indications that times were about to change. Throughout Europe there was a remarkable awakening of the spirit of scientific research. Men were refusing any longer to accept the orthodox teachings of the classical writers, which had seldom been questioned and rarely put to experimental test. Galileo's telescopes, primitive as they were, shattered the Aristotelian theory of the constitution of the heavens. The dissections and experiments of Fabricius of Aquapendente and our own William Harvey swept away views on the movement of the blood which had remained unchallenged since the time of Galen. The rudimentary microscopes of Malpighi at Bologna and of Antony van Leeuwenhoek at Delft revealed a world unsuspected by the ancients. Robert Boyle was laying the foundation of modern chemistry.

This remarkable burst of enthusiasm for scientific research and unfettered thought affected the greater part of Western Europe. In Italy there was founded, under the patronage of the wealthy Duke of Aquasparta, the first of the great academies of Science, the Academia dei Lincei (1609). About thirty-five years later a group of men in London interested in the study of natural phenomena banded themselves together under the title of 'The Invisible College' and began to hold meetings for scientific investigation and discussion. This coterie, meeting at first at Gresham College, then for a time at Oxford, and after the Restoration once again in London, founded the Royal Society, which received its charter from Charles II in the year 1662. In France a movement of almost identical character led to the foundation of the world-famous Academie des Sciences in 1666.

Strange new worlds were being revealed on every hand. There were new species of animals and plants and other curiosities from abroad to be examined. There were experiments to be made — 'and we to Gresham College, where we saw some experiments upon a hen, a dog, and a cat, of the Florence poyson. The first it made for a time drunk, but it come to itself again quickly; the second it made vomit mightily, but no other hurt. The third I did not stay to see the effect of it'.[1] There were lectures to be attended — 'And here a good lecture of Mr Hooke's about the trade of felt-making, very pretty'[2] — and practical projects to be considered — 'concerning planting his Majesty's Forest of Dean with oak, now so much exhausted of the choicest ship-timber in the world'.[3] Sometimes ambitious plans for investigations were made and one of these, elaborated in 1666 by the members of the Academie des Sciences in Paris, is of interest because, as part of a comprehensive study of the natural history of plants, it was proposed to make a

---

[1] *Diary of Samuel Pepys*, April 19th, 1665.
[2] Ibid., February 21st, 1666.
[3] *Diary of John Evelyn*, November 5th, 1662.

chemical study of their composition. The scheme, as a whole, came to nothing; even if it had been carried through it is doubtful whether any information of value about the composition of plant materials would have been obtained by applying the crude methods of lixiviation, extraction, distillation and calcination which were all that were then available. But the project illustrates the urge to investigate and experiment which was so apparent in the centres of learning in the middle of the seventeenth century.

In England an invention was described about this time which, although it was not much used until the following century, was suitable for the detection of what was then a very common form of adulteration, namely, the watering of milk, wine and other beverages. This was the hydrometer which Robert Boyle, 'that excellent and great virtuoso', as John Evelyn called him, referred to in 1663 as an 'Essay Instrument'[1] and which was fully described twelve years later.[2] This was probably the 'glass bubble, to try the strength of liquors with' which interested Pepys when he spent an amusing morning looking at the 'pretty things' which Mr Spong showed him and his wife in the 'bye place' in Southampton Market, 'with a good prospect of the fields'.[3]

[1] *Some Considerations touching the Usefulnesse of Experimental Naturall Philosophy*, Robert Boyle, 1663-67.
[2] *Philosophical Transactions of the Royal Society*, 1675, Vol. CXV.
[3] December 9th, 1668.

CHAPTER VI

DIET AND HEALTH

§ 1 CHANGES IN SCIENTIFIC THOUGHT

FOR the greater part of the century medical teaching remained under the influence of Galen, and diagnosis and treatment were still governed by the humoral system. Its phraseology had become a part of the general speech; John Evelyn, in the introduction to his Diary, refers to his father as a man of 'sanguine complexion, mixed with a dash of choler'. These beliefs were so tenaciously held that the freedom of thought of many who were entering the new field of experimental research was inhibited. Had Fabricius dared to make the logical deduction from his discovery of the valves of the veins in 1600, namely that they must serve to prevent the blood flowing in any direction but towards the heart, he could scarcely have failed to discover the circulation of the blood. But fourteen hundred years earlier the great Galen had laid it down that the blood ebbs and flows in the vessels and Fabricius hesitated to call such authority in question. Sixteen years later Harvey was bold enough to interpret his own observations without reference to the old theoretical teachings and established that the blood circulates in one direction only, though he did not publish until 1628.

No one had as yet performed any experiments which might throw light on the views Galen had expressed on the nature of food and digestion, and all the hoary old teachings still survived.

> *Galen* saith, that as the broth of a Hen bindeth the body, and the flesh loosneth the same; so contrariwise the broth of a Cock loosneth, and the flesh bindeth.[1]
>
> *Galen* saith that the flesh of a Hare prevents fatness, causeth sleep, and cleanseth the blood.[2]
>
> Galen numbreth it [deer's flesh] amongst hard, melancholique, and gross Meats.[3]

Three sorts of diet were recognized: a full diet, a moderate diet, and a thin or low diet.

> The first increaseth flesh, spirits, and humors, the second repaireth onely them that were lost, and the third lesseneth them all for a time to preserve life.[4]

[1] *Healths Improvement*, Thomas Muffett, 1655.   [2] Ibid.   [3] Ibid.   [4] Ibid.

In simple language this meant that the first was suitable for growing and strong, vigorous people, the second for middle age, and the third for old age or more particularly during illness.

Great stress was laid on the 'substance' of meats.

> In substance, such meats are generally commended, which are moist, easy of digestion, and not apt to engender wind, not fried, nor roasted, but sod (saith Valescus, Altomarus, Piso, etc.) hot and moist, and of good nourishment.[1]

'Substance' was a comprehensive term which covered all that we mean today when we speak of digestibility.

> Touching the difference of meats in substance: some are of thin and light substance, engendring thin and fine blood, fit for fine complexions, idle citizens, tender persons, and such as are upon recovery out of some great sickness: as chiken peepers, rabbet suckers, young pheasants, partridge, heath-poulse, godwits, all small birds being young, all little fishes of the river, the wings and livers of hens, cockchickens and partridges, eggs warm out of the hens belly, &c. Others are more gross, tough, and hard, agreeing chiefly to country persons and hard labourers: but secondarily to all that be strong of nature, given by trade or use to much exercise, and accustomed to feed upon them: as poudred beife, bacon, goose, swan, saltfish, ling, tunnis, salt samon, cucumbers, turneps, beans, hard peaze, hard cheese, brown and rye bread, &c. But meats of a middle substance are generally the best, & most properly to be called meats; engendring neither too fine nor too gross bloud.[2]

Lamb, pork, sturgeon, were meats 'hot in the first degree'; hare, roe-buck, turkey, were hot in the 'second'; onions, scallops and leeks in the 'third', and a few substances, 'skallions' and garlic among them, were so 'hot' that they came into a 'fourth' degree. Other meats were 'moist', 'dry' or 'cold' in differing degree, in strict conformity with the Galenic theory. So firmly were these humoral doctrines established that it was possible for a medical man, a leading authority on diet, to believe such fantastic nonsense as the following story.

> Yea, my self have known a young Maide, of an exceeding moist and cold complexion, whose meat for two years was chiefly pepper, wherewith another would have been consumed, though she was nourished: for it is hot in the third, and dry in the fourth degree.[3]

[1] *The Anatomy of Melancholy*, R. Burton, 1621.
[2] *Healths Improvement*, Thomas Muffett, 1655.
[3] Ibid.

Although most of the seventeenth-century works on food and diet reflect the Galenic teachings, there is traceable in some of them the influence of the school founded in the first half of the sixteenth century by a Swiss alchemist named Paracelsus, or to give him his full name, Phillipus Aureolus Theophrastus Bombastus von Hohenheim. He was a remarkable man if for no other reason than that he dared publicly to reject the greater part of the teachings of Galen; he is reputed to have burnt Galen's works at his inaugural lecture at Strasburg. The outraged Faculty hounded him out of the University and as a result of his heresies he was forced to lead a peripatetic existence, moving from town to town, writing and teaching, until he died at Salzburg in 1541.

A large amount of what he wrote is almost unintelligible, being simply a hotch-potch of alchemy, occultism and astrology, but in two directions his teachings had an effect on contemporary thought. He was the first to advocate the use of mineral remedies in medicine in place of those compounded solely from herbs, and he was the author of a curious theory of the constitution of the material world which gave great prominence to three essential elements, the *tria prima*, salt, sulphur and mercury. His influence and that of his disciples, who came to be known as the 'Iatro-chemists' or 'spagyrists', spread quite rapidly throughout Europe. For the most part it was retrograde and pernicious but fortunately before it became too powerful in England it was destroyed, almost at a single blow, by the convincing arguments and sound logic of Robert Boyle's *The Sceptical Chymist* (1661), which showed beyond all doubt that some of the accepted elements must be 'mixt Bodies'.

Boyle's chemical studies, which laid the foundation of our knowledge of acids, alkalies and salts, began to influence progressive medical thought towards the end of the century. It is seen clearly, for instance, in one important work published in 1689, Walter Harris's *De morbis acutis infantum*. Harris was one of the first to turn away from the humoral system and to substitute for it a primitive chemical conception of disease. He thought that all children's disorders were due to 'an Acid prevailing through the whole Habit' and prescribed 'testaceous powder' prepared from oyster and other shells, and various other alkaline remedies. Many sick children doubtless benefited by such simple treatment. Harris was, however, ahead of his time and the new chemistry did not have any marked effect on medicine until well into the next century.

§ 2 VIEWS ON MILK

Milk was still regarded as suitable only for young children and very old people. It was thought to be hurtful to young men because they were by nature choleric. It was liable to cause sore eyes, headaches, agues and rheums because it was 'full of vapours', convulsions and cramps because it 'led to repletion', 'resolution' or palsies because it was 'over moist', and stone and other obstructions because the 'cheesy part of it is very great'.[1]

Men still believed that character would be influenced by the milk drunk in youth.

> For as Lambs sucking she-goats bear coarse wool, and Kids sucking Ewes bear soft hair, so fine Children degenerate by gross womans milk, losing or lesning that excellency of nature, wit, and complexion, which from their Parents they first obtained.[2]

Very old people and invalids were thought to run the same risk, for it was by no means unusual to provide them with a wet nurse.

> What made Dr. *Cajus* in his last sickness so peevish and so full of frets at Cambridge, when he suckt one woman (whom I spare to name) froward of conditions and of bad diet; and contrariwise so quiet and well, when he suckt another of contrary disposition? verily the diversity of their milks and conditions, which being contrary one to the other, wrought also in him that sucked them contrary effects.[3]

Pepys heard this story (which refers to the founder of Caius College) from Dr Whistler during a merry evening at a tavern with some friends. Many other good stories were told and he remarks that:

> Their discourse was very fine: and if I should be put out of my office, I do take great content in the liberty I shall be at, of frequenting these gentlemen's company.[4]

Asses' milk still had a great reputation as an alternative to women's milk for children and invalids.

> Neither is womens Milk best onely for young and tender infants, but also for men and women of riper years, fallen by age or by sickness into compositions. Best I mean in the way of nourishment, for otherwise Asses Milk is best.[5]

Lady Gardiner wrote to Sir Ralph Verney during the trying time of the Buckingham election in 1685:

[1] *Healths Improvement*, Thomas Muffett, 1655.   [2] Ibid.   [3] Ibid.
[4] November 21st, 1667.
[5] *Healths Improvement*, Thomas Muffett, 1655.

... I am sur if you due not begin to take the asses milk quickly, you will have bot a short tim to take it.[1]

§ 3 FRUIT AND VEGETABLES

Vegetables, although they gradually became more popular as the century advanced, were not regarded with favour, because they were supposed to engender wind and melancholy.

> The same Crato will allow no roots at all to be eaten. Some approve of potatoes, parsnips, but all corrected for wind.[2]

Flatulence seems to have been a common affliction in those days but at any rate there was no lack of remedies; Burton gives a list of 64 herbs or simples for 'expelling the wind'.

Fruit was still regarded with suspicion as a result of the survival of the medieval belief that it caused fevers.

> In the afternoon had notice that my Lord Hinchingbroke is fallen ill, which I fear is with the fruit that I did give them on Saturday last at my house: so in the evening I went thither, and there found him very ill, and in great fear of the small-pox.[3]

§ 4 VIEWS ON DIGESTION

The digestion of food was little understood although the Galenic views were elaborated by an important contribution from the famous Belgian alchemist, Jan Baptist van Helmont. He postulated the theory that digestion resembled fermentation in being brought about by a ferment. The first digestion took place in the stomach — nothing was suspected of the digestive function of the saliva — through the agency of a ferment which, he thought, came from the spleen. It was known that the contents of the stomach were usually acid, and van Helmont thought that a second digestion occurred when the acid chyle passed from the stomach into the duodenum and became neutralized. The digested food was thought to pass through the walls of the intestines, like water through a pig's bladder, and to be converted into blood by another ferment in the liver.

[1] *Memoirs of the Verney Family*, Vol. IV, Margaret M. Verney, 1899.
[2] *The Anatomy of Melancholy*, R. Burton, 1621.
[3] *The Diary of Samuel Pepys*, August 12th, 1661.

In many ways van Helmont's guesses, for they were little more, were curiously near what we now believe to be the facts, but they attracted little attention at the time because of the obscure and pseudo-mystical style in which the original Latin publication of 1648 was written. The English translation which appeared in 1662 was more popular. About this time the view was gaining ground in England that the dissolution of meat in the stomach was due to the presence of acid. Boyle, however, was sceptical of this theory, for on examining the stomachs of certain fish in which partly digested food was present he was unable to detect any acidity.

> Yet I am loth, till I have perfected what I design in order to that enquiry, either to imbrace or reject the Opinion I finde so general among the Moderns, concerning the Solution of Meat in the Stomach by something of Acid.[1]

The older view that the heat of the body caused foods to become digested was more generally accepted.

> Digestion is performed by natural heat; for as the flame of a torch consumes oil, wax, tallow, so doth it alter and digest the nutritive matter. Indigestion is opposite unto it, for want of natural heat.[2]

After digestion the food was supposed to pass as chyle into the blood of the portal vein and so into the liver.

The urine and faeces were regarded as the means by which the impurities of the body and the undigested food were expelled but no other means of excretion was suspected until the discoveries of a pioneer investigator named Sanctorius, a professor at the famous University of Padua. The quaint woodcut in his *Medicina Statica* shows how he made the observations which led him to postulate an 'insensible perspiration' in order to explain the loss in weight which could not be accounted for by the ordinary excretions. After eating a meal he sat in the chair, suspended from one end of a yard-arm, and recorded his gradual fall in weight. He realized that the loss occurred through the mouth and the surface of the skin.

> Insensible perspiration, is either made by the Pores of the Body, which is all over Perspirable and covered with Skin like a Nett; or it is performed by Respiration through the Mouth, which usually in the space of one Day amounts to about the quantity of half a Pound, as may plainly be made to appear by breathing upon a Glass. (Aphorism V)

The large amount of 'insensible perspiration' surprised him.

[1] *Some Considerations touching the Usefulnesse of Experimental Naturall Philosophy*, R. Boyle, 1663-67.
[2] *The Anatomy of Melancholy*, R. Burton, 1621.

If eight Pounds of Meat and Drink are taken in one Day, the Quantity that usually goes off by Insensible Perspiration in that Time, is five Pounds. (Aphorism VI)[1]

He cannot be blamed for thinking that the lost weight was mainly moisture for nothing was known of the nature of air and gases until Boyle showed that they are material substances having weight. Indeed it was not until 1668 that Mayow proved that part of the air around us is necessary for respiration and even that important discovery attracted little attention for nearly a century.[2]

In the second half of the century there came a reaction against the lifeless, static condition of medical thought. The wisdom which lay behind the aphorisms of Hippocrates and this great master's insistence on careful study of the patient and his symptoms had in the passage of centuries become as obscured by convention and concern for orthodoxy as had the teachings of the founder of Christianity and his early disciples. Thomas Sydenham broke away from most of these conventions and tried to build up once again the method of diagnosis based on a close observation of symptoms. His remarkable work *The Method of Treating Fevers* (1666), appropriately dedicated to another revolutionary, Robert Boyle, may justly be regarded as one of the main foundations of modern clinical medicine.

It was by no means easy to throw over the old beliefs. Even Boyle, the leader of the new movement of scientific inquiry by experiment and deduction, cherished many of them. Sympathetic magic had survived from Greek times. The ancients thought that a 'milk-stone' worn by a woman would encourage a good flow of milk; Boyle strongly recommended the wearing of a blood-jasper to prevent haemorrhagic effusions. The Greeks thought that 'snake-stone' was a sovereign remedy for snake-bite; Boyle knew of a woman who had been cured of incontinence of urine by wearing a silver pipe.[3] Equally surprising was his faith in many of the unpleasant and often gruesome medical remedies of his day; powdered dried human excrement blown in the eyes to restore dim sight, woodlice crushed in white wine for ulcers of the breast, raspings of the skull of a dead man for convulsive fits, such were the remedies he offered with profound assurance to the 'poor Upholders of Families, who cannot find or Fee a Surgeon or a Doctor', so that they might be 'cheaply relieved without either of them'.[4] Little wonder that he held, with Paracelsus, 'that God hath created nothing so Vile, Despicable, Abject

---

[1] *Medicina Statica*, translated by John Quincy, 1712.
[2] *De Sal-Nitro, 1668*, included in *Tractatus quinque medico-physici*, 1674.
[3] *Some Considerations touching the Usefulnesse of Experimental Naturall Philosophy*, R. Boyle, 1663-67.
[4] *Medicinal Experiments; Or, a Collection of Choice and Safe Remedies*, R. Boyle, 1692-94.

or Filthy in the World, that may not make for the Health and Use of Man'.[1]
Some years later Campbell, speaking of the training of physicians and
chemists, commented cruelly but not altogether unfairly on this curious
strain of credulity in Boyle.

> Of this Truth the honourable Mr. *Boyle* is a recent Example, who,
> after a whole Life spent in the most laborious Chymical Researches, has
> enriched the World with no more Medicines than what may be pur-
> chased, and that too dear, for Twelve Pence . . . The honourable Mr.
> *Boyle* has writ much on this Subject, but he is voluminous; and it was
> the Misfortune of that truly great Man, that he was too Credulous, and
> took many Things upon the Relation of others not sufficiently war-
> rented by Experiments.[2]

§ 5 VITAMIN A DEFICIENCY

The herbals of the seventeenth century provide indirect evidence that
symptoms of vitamin A deficiency were common in England at this time.
There are so many references to the use of herbs such as fennel and parsley
for mists and films over the eyes that it is fair to assume that mild forms of
xerophthalmia and corneal opacities of dietary origin formed a significant
proportion of the very prevalent 'sore eyes'. The first reference we have
been able to trace in English medical works to the value of liver in eye
diseases is in Muffett's *Healths Improvement* (1655). Although liver, as a
food, was supposed to be 'hardly concocted' and 'of gross nourishment' it
was thought to be wholesome because it would 'please the taste, clear the eyesight, agree with the stomack, and encrease bloud'.

Walter Bayly, at one time physician to Queen Elizabeth, wrote a treatise
on the relation of diet to the state of the eyes, in which he classified a large
number of foods according to whether they benefited or impaired the sight.
Curiously enough, he thought butter harmful; indeed, he feared that all oils
except 'sallet oyle' did more harm than good. With regard to herbs, he said:

> Albeit few rawe herbes in common vse for sallets are commended,
> except fenell, eiebright, yoong sage, terragone.[3]

Peg, the daughter of Cary (Verney), Lady Gardiner, may have been

---

[1] *Some Considerations touching the Usefulnesse of Experimental Naturall Philosophy*, R. Boyle,
1663-67.
[2] *The London Tradesman*, R. Campbell, 1747.
[3] *A Briefe Treatise touching the preseruation of the eie sight, consisting partly in good order of diet,
and partly in vse of medicines*, W. Bayly, 1586.

suffering from xerophthalmia when with 'ill Eyelidds, & falling away of the haire, a spott on the pupill, & a corrupt fistula in the Corner of her Eye towards her Nose',[1] she was taken to 'Crick Kerne' to be examined by Daubeney Turberville, the 'famous oculist of Sarum'.[2]

It is by no means unlikely that the children of wealthy parents sometimes suffered from vitamin A deficiency; the two good sources of vitamin A, green vegetables and butter, were seldom eaten by this class. Even towards the end of the century, when the consumption of vegetables was steadily increasing, they were looked upon as poor men's food. Butter was eaten in large amounts only by the working classes; it was despised by the rich who thought it only fit to be used for cooking.

> Only I wonder with him, [Pliny] that *Africa*, and other Barbarous Countreys esteem it a Gentlemans dish, when here and in *Holland*, and in all the Northern Regions, it is the chief food of the poorer sort.[3]

Doctors disapproved of it except for growing children.

> It is also best for children whilst they are growing, and for old men when they are declining; but very unwholesome betwixt those two ages, because through the heat of young stomacks, it is forthwith converted into choler.[4]

It is interesting in the light of what has already been said about the relation of vitamin A deficiency to stone in the kidneys or bladder, conditions which were apparently quite common in seventeenth-century England especially among the wealthy classes, that Paracelsus stated that the Dutch were less troubled by stone than other nations because they ate more butter.[5] An old Dutch proverb, quoted by Thomas Muffett, says, 'Eat butter first, and eat it last, and live till a hundred years be past.' Muffett did not, however, agree with Paracelsus that the Dutch were less afflicted by the stone than the English.

> . . . the silly Alchymist was not a little mistaken, for no people in the world are more subject to that disease, as the number and excellency of stone-cutters in that Country may plainly prove.

But Muffett misses the point that it was the rich man who employed the stone-cutter and the poor man who ate the butter. Unfortunately we have no

---

[1] *Memoirs of the Verney Family*, Vol. IV, Margaret M. Verney, 1899.
[2] *A Vindication of Sugars*, F. Slare, 1715.
[3] *Healths Improvement*, Thomas Muffett, 1655.
[4] Ibid.
[5] *De Tartaro*, cited by Thomas Muffett in *Healths Improvement*, 1655.

reliable information with regard to the prevalence of the stone among the wealthy classes compared with the poor people, but one gets the impression that the former suffered more severely than the latter, and in view of the difference in their diets this may well have been so.

§ 6 'GREEN-SICKNESS'

The frequent references to 'green-sickness' in seventeenth-century literature, both medical and lay, suggest that it was a not uncommon condition. Burton classified it as one of the symptoms and signs of 'love-melancholy' — 'the green-sickness therefore often happeneth to young women'[1] — and pointed out that since the mind is distracting the spirits the liver is unable to play its part in turning the food into blood.

The condition, to which a later generation gave the name chlorosis, is an anaemia of dietary origin. It arises where there is insufficient iron in the food to provide for the formation of haemoglobin, the pigment responsible for the colour of the red blood cells and which plays an essential role in carrying oxygen from the lungs to all parts of the body. The 'green-sickness' was treated either with herbs or with iron preparations. Sydenham had great faith in chalybeate waters or steel, and treatment with iron in one form or another has survived down to the present day.

The diet of the time was, as has been shown, largely composed of bread, meat, fish and cheese. Milk, and therefore cheese, is a very poor source of iron. Wholemeal flour, rye and oatmeal contain about 3 mg. per 100 g. Meat is, generally speaking, rich in iron; beef and mutton contain 2-4 mg. and pork 1 mg. per 100 g. 'as purchased' (i.e. including the weight of bone and other inedible material). Liver and kidney are particularly rich with 13-14 mg. per 100 g. Fish is a poorer source, white fish containing about 0.5 mg. and herring about 1 mg. per 100 g. 'as purchased'. Green, but not root, vegetables are good sources and supply 0.5-1.0 mg. of iron per 100 g. 'as purchased': most dark green vegetables (except spinach in which the iron is not available) contain more than light green vegetables.

The body of an adult contains 4-5 g. of iron, which must be taken into the body with the food or fluid. It may be an intrinsic part of the food or it may have been picked up from iron manufacturing or kitchen utensils. The daily loss of iron, in the absence of haemorrhage, is very small — in the male about 1 mg. It is known that men can maintain normal haemoglobin on a diet containing 8 mg. daily whereas women of child-bearing age become anaemic on such a small intake. The mechanism of iron absorption is very

[1] *The Anatomy of Melancholy*, R. Burton, 1621.

delicate and is such that if iron is not needed it is not absorbed. On the other hand, in nutritional anaemia, after haemorrhage and in pregnancy it is readily absorbed from almost any source. Iron requirements of adults except pregnant and lactating women are usually placed at 12 mg. daily, and those of adolescents and pregnant and lactating women at 15 mg. daily.

A seventeenth-century diet based on wholemeal bread, with some meats and vegetables, should have provided this amount. It seems fair to conclude that chlorosis was not common among those who lived, as did the poorer country people, mainly on bread. Those who were better off, however, lived on diets in which meat, fish and cheese formed a much larger proportion of the meals than bread, and poultry, which contains less iron than 'red' meats, was becoming popular. It may well be that the chlorotic young women obtained less than their requirement from such diets.

An important aspect of this anaemia of dietary origin in women is that the deficiency tends to affect their children. During pregnancy, stores of iron are laid down in the liver of the developing child which are used for the manufacture of blood pigment not only before but *after* birth, for it is a curious fact that mothers' milk does not normally contain enough iron for the young child's needs. If the mother is anaemic during pregnancy the child starts life with deficient reserves and will itself soon become anaemic. Even in recent years this nutritional anaemia was very prevalent; Dr Helen MacKay held that it was 'the commonest form of anaemia in infants in this country'.[1] It can be cured by giving the child iron in an assimilable form, but it is no use giving the iron to the mother and expecting her milk to be enriched.

If nutritional anaemias were at all common in England centuries ago it is certain that there were related anaemias in infants. No treatment was available and it is probable that those who survived gradually recovered when they came to the age at which they could eat bread and other solid foods.

§7 CONSTIPATION

It is hard to decide whether constipation, or costiveness as it was then called, was a prevalent minor disorder at this period. Certainly the poorer people living on coarse wholemeal breads would scarcely have known what it was. The roughage of the bran would have kept their bowels working regularly so that two or even three motions would have been passed daily without effort. Constipation is almost unknown among peasants living on coarse cereal breads. Our own modern diets are so defective in roughage

[1] *Medical Research Council, Special Report*, No. 157, 1931.

I

and in the natural laxative and tonic substances present in wheat germ that our intestinal musculature has to some extent lost the tone which these constituents of the diet help to maintain. If we were to change over to such a coarse diet the immediate result would be a rather sharp attack of diarrhoea. Attempts to replace white flour breads by wholemeal in the diets of schools and institutions have usually had to be made very gradually in order that the muscles of the intestine might become adapted.

Although we can safely assume that the poor people were rarely troubled with constipation in the centuries before the introduction of white flour, we cannot be so definite about those who were better off. The wealthier classes ate very large amounts of meat and this, being almost wholly digested, would tend to cause sluggishness of the bowels. Most primitive meat-eating races are subject to constipation, which they sometimes relieve by a dose of partly rancid fat. It is interesting, therefore, to find that 'May butter' was used in sixteenth- and seventeenth-century England as an opening medicine.

It is necessary when reading contemporary works to differentiate between the use of purges and remedies for costiveness. The former were very extensively used but their object was to rid the system of 'ill vapours' or 'black melancholy'. In illness purges were the almost invariable accompaniment of the bleedings in which so much faith was placed, on the grounds that the poison or putrefactive vapours were being allowed to escape from the body. It is true that many of the purges in common use were laxatives such as senna or rhubarb, but others such as decoctions of fumitory, dandelion, succory or scurvy-grass, were at most mildly aperient, and probably any benefit they produced was due to their antiscorbutic action. It was this type of purge that was very commonly used in spring to 'cleanse the blood'. Actually, there are extraordinarily few references to the treatment of costiveness in medical books of this date and, although it is difficult to reach a definite conclusion, one is inclined to think that the population of England was a good deal less troubled by constipation than we are today.

CHAPTER VII

SCURVY

WE have already reached the conclusion that the winter diet of the medieval English peasant would have given little protection against scurvy, that in late winter and spring most of the poor country people must have been at least in a pre-scorbutic condition, and that the same must have applied to town-dwellers. There is evidence in support of the belief that pre-scorbutic conditions were common in sixteenth-century England in the frequent mention in contemporary herbals of remedies for making 'loose teeth' firm and for 'puryfying the blod in spryngtyme'. The majority of these remedies were fresh herbs or extracts prepared from them, fresh strawberry leaves, raw purslane, elecampane leaves, raw gooseberries, decoctions of bramble leaves, leaves in wine, etc. It is interesting that even as late as the first quarter of the twentieth century it was not unusual at least in the north of England to give blackcurrant tea (made from blackcurrant jam and hot water) as a cure for colds and sore throats; another remedy was turnip juice extracted by covering cut turnip with sugar and leaving overnight, and it was customary for all members of at least one family to drink a daily dose of 'spring medicine', a concoction made of lemons, sugar, a little Epsom salts and water, during the early months of the year as a 'blood cleanser'.

The most serious shortages of fresh foods occurred in the sixteenth century, however, among sailors on long voyages, and during military sieges. Under these conditions scurvy became a dreaded and much-described menace.

In his survey *A Treatise of the Scurvy* (1753) Lind classified three degrees of violence of scurvy stating firstly that sometimes it 'rages with great and diffusive virulence' citing as examples of this 'epidemic or universal calamity', seamen on long voyages, armies, closely besieged troops and occasionally whole countries such as Brabant in 1556 and Holland in 1562. Secondly 'where these causes are fixed and permanent, or almost always subsisting, it may be said to be an endemic or constant disease; as in Iceland, Groenland, Cronstadt, the northern part of Russia and in most northern countries as yet discovered in Europe, from the latitude 60 to the north pole'. He mentioned particularly the Low Countries, parts of Germany and Scandinavia. Thirdly he cited the places 'where these causes prevail less frequently, and are more peculiar to the circumstances of a few, it may there be said to be sporadic, or a disease only here and there to be met with; as in Great Britain and Ireland, several parts of Germany etc.'

A legend has come down through early Dutch writings that the Roman legions fell victims to scurvy when they crossed the Rhine and that the Frieslanders taught them how to cure the disease with certain herbs. If there is any truth in the story one of the herbs was probably scurvy grass (*Cochlearia officinalis* L.) which under the name *lepelbladen* (spoon leaves) seems to have been used in Holland for centuries as a household remedy against the disease.[1] The Dutch physician, Forestus, made a great reputation for himself about the middle of the sixteenth century by preparing an antidote called *syrupus sceleturbicus* which he concocted from *lepelbladen* and *becca-bunga* (*Veronica beccabunga*, L. (Brooklime)). He used it extensively in his own practice and sent supplies all over Flanders and Brabant but he admitted frankly that he did not discover the remedy himself, having compounded it as a result of information he had received from the country people. It is interesting to note, in passing, that the prevalence of scurvy in the low-lying parts of Flanders gave support to the belief that damp soils, fogs and sea mists played a part in causing the disease. There is no reason for thinking that the Dutch recognized as 'Schorbuck', 'Scorbuck' or 'Scorbuyt' anything but the advanced condition of ill-health which arises when the diet is devoid of vitamin C (*ascorbic acid*). They diagnosed as scurvy the swollen limbs, with dark discoloured blotches caused by haemorrhages under the skin, and the foul mouths, with swollen, ulcerated and bleeding gums.

All the evidence points to the English having learnt about scurvy from Dutch sailors, who apparently learnt by experience to carry antiscorbutics with them on their long voyages. Lind[2] coupled the growth of the disease with the great improvement in navigation and the discovery of the Indies and suggested that the 'first account of the disease at sea is to be met with' in the records of 'the voyage of Vasco de Gama, who first found out a passage by the Cape of Good Hope to the East Indies, in the year 1497; above a hundred of his men, out of a number of a hundred and sixty dying of this distemper'. He added: 'At that time, and for a considerable time afterwards it was a disease little known.' Fernandus Magellan, groping his way round the southernmost point of America in search of a western route to the Spice Islands, entered the Pacific Ocean on November 28th, 1520. He had been away from land for three months and twenty days, enduring great hardships, when his men began to fall sick.

... having in this time consumed all their Bisket and other Victuals, they fell into such necessitie, that they were inforced to eate the powder

---

[1] A comprehensive study of the history of scurvy in Holland is given in the paper by Dr M. A. van Andel, *Nederlandsche Tijdschrift voor Geneeskunde*, No. 31, 1927.
[2] *A Treatise of the Scurvy*, James Lind, 1753.

that remayned thereof, being now full of Wormes, and stinking like Pisse, by reason of the salt Water.

Another passage indicates scurvy.

By reason of this Famine, and the uncleane feeding, some of their gummes grew so over their teeth, that they died miserably for hunger.

Magellan did not recognize the disease that was decimating his men. He and they came from sunny Portugal where fruit was eaten all the year round, and this was a new affliction. So it was to Jacques Cartier, some months out from St Malo, exploring 'those partes of America, which lie to the West-wardes, and as it were, to the backside of Newfoundland', whose men began to sicken during the long winter at Stadacona in 1535. At first it was thought to be an infection contracted from the natives. The account of the outbreak and the accurate descriptions of the symptoms and of the prompt relief when a curative herb was found leave no doubt that it was scurvy.

In the moneth of December, wee understood that the pestilence was come among the people of Stadacona, in such sorte, that before we knew of it, according to their confession, there were dead above 50: . . . And albeit we had driven them from us, the said unknowen sicknes began to spread itselfe amongst us after the strangest sort that ever was eyther heard of or seene, insomuch as some did lose all their strength, and could not stand on their feete, then did their legges swel, their sinnowes shrinke as black as any cole. Others also had all their skins spotted with spots of blood of a purple coulour: then did it ascend up to their ankels, knees, thighes, shoulders, armes, and necke: their mouth became stincking, their gummes so rotten, that all the flesh did fall off, even to the rootes of the teeth, which did also almost all fall out. With such infection did this sicknesse spread it selfe in our three ships, that about the middle of February, of a hundreth and tenne personnes that we were, there were not tenne whole.

The captain commanded an image of Christ to be set up on a tree and everyone to prepare himself devoutly by prayer. We know that the first to die was Philip Rougemont and that the captain courageously decided to open the body in the hope that the true nature of the disease might be revealed. The rough and ready post-mortem carried out on the bleak, frozen shore told them nothing. The notes which have been preserved tell us that Philip died, far from his sunny Amboise, a victim of acute scurvy.

By mid-March there had been 25 deaths in the camp at Holy Cross

Then it pleased God to cast his pitifull eye upon us, and sent us knowledge of remedie of our healthes and recoverie.

The captain's shrewd observation also played a part. He noticed one day that a native whom he knew to have been grievously ill was cured; on questioning the man he learnt that in the spring the leaves of a certain tree were an effective remedy. He ordered branches of the tree, which 'is in their language called Ameda or Hanneda' (and which the sailors took to be sassafras) to be brought to him; the native women instructed the sailors how to make decoctions of the bark and leaves.

Our captain presently caused some of that drink to be made for his men to drink of it, but there was none durst tast of it, except one or two, who ventured the drinking of it, only to tast & prove it: the others seeing that did the like, and presently recovered their health, and were delivered of that sicknes.

Their enthusiasm then knew no bounds.

... it wrought so wel, that if all the phisicians of Mountpelier and Lovaine had bene there with all the drugs of Alexandria, they would not have done so much in one yere, as that tree did in sixe dayes.

It is sometimes stated, apparently on the authority of Lind,[1] that Cartier's men were saved by decoctions of spruce tips. The Indian names, *Hanneda* or *Ameda*, do not help us to identify the species, but it is almost certain that it was not the American spruce, *Picea nigra*. This is an evergreen fir and Cartier's notes particularly refer to the fact that the Indians had to wait for the leaves to appear in the spring. Moreover, it is unlikely that the men would have mistaken a spruce for sassafras. The tree was probably *Sassafras officinale*, which is native to that part of Canada.[2] It is none the less interesting that young pine needles provide an excellent antiscorbutic extract, and are used in the preparation of protective remedies for the children in the north of the Soviet Union, where they are in grave danger of developing 'sub-scurvy' during the long winter months.

The nature of the *Ameda* or *Hanneda* which cured Cartier's men becomes even more mysterious when we learn that in 1608 another French explorer wintered at Holy Cross, where he too saw many of his men fall sick. He recognized the symptoms as those of the unknown disease which Cartier had described, and hoped to be able to cure them by the same means. To his surprise the Indians professed to know nothing of *Ameda* or *Hanneda* and

[1] *A Treatise of the Scurvy*, James Lind, 1753.
[2] Information kindly supplied by Dr J. Gilmour, formerly Assistant Director of the Royal Botanic Gardens, Kew.

he lost forty men before the spring came and the survivors were able to cure themselves by making decoctions from other shoots and buds.

The Portuguese and Spanish explorers were soon followed by the Dutch and the English. Many of the expeditions must have been ravaged by scurvy for only the Dutchmen seem to have had any acquaintance with the disease or, rather, to have recognized it. The English medical works of this period make no reference to it. Andrew Boorde claimed that his *Breviary of Healthe* (1552) treated of 'all manner of sickness and diseases, which may be in man or woman' but scurvy was not one of them. Popular herbals and books of remedies and simples such as William Turner's *The Names of Herbes* (1548) and Sir Thomas Elyot's *Castel of Helth* (1539), pay little attention to anti-scorbutics. It is not certain where the sailors learned the value of fruit and salads but probably from the Dutch on the west coast of Africa. Being accustomed to treat it at home with simple herbs it would not have been long before the Dutchmen discovered that tropical fruits made a good substitute. It is clear that in the latter part of the sixteenth century the antiscorbutic value of herbs and fruits was beginning to be recognized in England. Gerard's *Herball* was published in 1597, and although it was compiled very largely from Continental sources there is evidence that the malady was by this time well known in England. Gerard described it very accurately.

> The gums are loosed, swolne and exulcerate; the mouth greeuously stinking; the thighes and legs are withall verie often full of blewe spots, not vnlike those that come of bruses: the face and the rest of the bodie is oftentimes of a pale colour; and the feete are swolne, as in the dropsie.

He added that the disease haunted camps; he doubtless had in mind the many occasions during the wars on the Continent on which it had ravaged the inhabitants of besieged cities.

Gerard recommended garden cresses as 'good against the disease which the Germaines call Scorbuck and Scorbuyt: in Latine *Scorbutus*: which we in England call the Scuruie, and Scurby, and vpon the Seas the Skyrby.' He also advised the use of winter cresses because 'This herbe helpeth the scuruie, being boiled among scuruie grasse, called in Latin cochlearia, causing it to worke the more effectually.'

The voyage of Sir John Hawkins's son, Sir Richard Hawkins, to the South Seas is important to us in attempting to trace the growth of knowledge in England regarding scurvy. In 1593 his ship the *Repentance* lay off the Royal Palace at Greenwich. 'The Queen's Majestie' was rowed out to inspect her and everything except the name received the royal approval. She was promptly renamed the *Daintie* and after provisioning at Plymouth with 'Beefe, Porke, Bisket and Sider', set sail for the South Seas. After leaving the

Canaries they came to within three or four degrees of the Equinoctial Line and within a few days scurvy had appeared.

> The signes to know this disease in the beginning are divers, by the swelling of the gummes, by denting of the flesh of the legges with a mans finger, the pit remaining without filling up in a good space: others show it by their lasinesse.

The last remark is important because the debility in the early stages of the disease, before recognizable symptoms had appeared, often led to confusion between cause and effect. Gerard expressed a popular opinion when he said that the disease attacked 'such as delight to sit still without labour and exercise of their bodies'. Hawkins, who thought that the primary cause was 'change of aire in untemperate climates' and that a diet of salt meat and insufficient exercise were contributory factors, recommended that the ships' company be kept 'occupied in some bodily exercise of worke'.

He had considerable experience, 'for in twentie yeeres (since I have used the Sea) I dare take upon me, to give account of ten thousand men consumed with this disease'. He held the view that prolonged exposure to sea air increased the tendency to develop scurvy. To counteract this exposure he ordered that the decks should be washed with vinegar and that tar should be burnt. He also recommended closing the pores of the skin. This he proposed to do by giving every man in the morning 'a bit of bread, and a draught of drinke, either Beere, or Wine mingled with water . . . that the poores of the bodie may be full, when the vapours of the Sea ascend up'.

In these early views of the English sailors is to be found the reason why 'sea scurvy' and 'land scurvy' came to be regarded as different diseases. Outbreaks were so much more frequent at sea and the symptoms were usually so much more severe that the acute form of the disorder came to be associated with sea air, sea salt and salted fish and meat. Sir Richard Hawkins knew of the curative action of 'sowre Oranges and Lemons' but he did not put them first on his list of antidotes.

> . . . the principall of all is the Ayre of the Land; for the Sea is naturall for Fishes, and the Land for men.

Nevertheless, he was glad to reach Santos where he was able to get fruit for his suffering men.

> This is a wonderfull secret of the power and wisdome of God, that hath hidden so great and unknowne vertue in this fruit, to be a certaine remedy for this infirmity.

An occasion on which a chance discovery of scurvy grass saved an expedition is told in the story of William Barent's voyage to find the North Passage in 1596. The ship was frozen into the ice in August of that year and a long and anxious winter was passed in a house which they built upon the ice floes. In spite of strict rationing their bread and beer were eventually exhausted and they had to keep themselves alive on the meat of the foxes and bears which they shot. Their privations lasted for months and there was a good deal of illness. On July 31st, 1597, nearly a year later, they sailed away and found land.

> . . . in this Iland wee found great store of Leple leaves, which served us exceeding well, and it seemed that God had purposely sent us thither: for as that wee had many sicke men, and most of us were so troubled with a scouring in our bodies, and were thereby become so weake, that wee could hardly row, but by meanes of those leaves we were healed thereof: for that as soone as we had eaten them, we were presently eased and healed, whereat wee could not choose but wonder, and therefore, wee gave God great thanks for that, and for many other his mercies shewed unto us, by his great and unexpected aide lent us, in that our dangerous Voyage: and so as I said before, wee eate them by whole handfuls together, because in Holland we had heard much spoken of their great force, and as then found it to be much more than we expected.

There is a marginal note to this account in *Purchas His Pilgrimes*: '*Scurvy-grasse, or Leple leaves cure their scowring and Scorbuticall infirmitie.*'

The discovery of the exceptionally high antiscorbutic power of oranges and lemons led to interesting developments. Efforts were made to preserve the juices so that they might be carried on long voyages. As most of these efforts depended on the preparation of syrups by the evaporation of the juice over an open fire it is probable that there were many disappointments. Gerard suggested in his *Herball* that sailors might use dried herbs and evaporated juices preserved in bottles 'with a narrowe mouth, full about to the necke, and the rest filled up with oliue oile, to keep it from putrefaction'. One voyage on which lemon juice was used, although whether it was preserved in this manner is not known, was the first English expedition to the East Indies which sailed under the command of Master James Lancaster on behalf of the newly formed East India Company. The four ships left Woolwich on February 13th, 1600, and after a slow voyage crossed the tropic of Capricorn on July 24th. They had last touched land, at the Canaries, on May 7th. August began with 'very many of our men . . . fallen sicke of the Scurvey in all our ships' but one ship, the Commander's, had surprisingly few cases.

And the reason why the General's men stood better in health then the men of other ships, was this: he brought to sea with him certaine Bottles of the Juice of Limons, which hee gave to each one, as long as it would last, three spoonfuls every morning fasting: not suffering them to eate any thing after it till noone. This Juice worketh much the better, if the partie keepe a short Dyet, and wholly refraine salt meate, which salt meate, and long being at the Sea is the only cause of the breeding of this Disease.

Impressed by the experiences of this voyage the East India Company arranged for a supply of lemon-water for all its ships.

Another voyage, commanded by William Keeling, set out in 1607 and returned in May 1610. With the help of the lemon-water and occasional supplies of fresh fruit they kept free of scurvy, but on the homeward voyage they met some Dutchmen less fortunate than themselves.

The eight and twentieth, in the morning, the wind being Westerly, and reasonable faire weather, we steered with the Dutch . . . He told us, that he had but eight or nine men standing, the rest sicke, and sixe and forty dead. A grievous chastisement unto them, and to us, a never sufficiently acknowledged mercy: that they who offered to spare me ten or twenty men, or more upon occasion, should so generally decay, and we lose no one, nay every one in good health.

At this time the Dutch Company was trying to supply their East Indiamen with fruit from special ships. They had also established a garden at the Cape to grow vegetables for sick sailors.

One fact which struck these early explorers, and it had a far-reaching influence on later views about scurvy, was that the sourer and more acid fruits seemed to be the best antiscorbutics. This gave rise to the belief that the curative virtues lay in the acidity and as fruit juices were difficult to keep in hot climates other acid drinks were used instead. Some people put their faith in vinegar, others in oil of vitriol (sulphuric acid). It is difficult to understand how these liquors maintained their reputation as efficient anti-scorbutics. Perhaps if the vinegar had come from a barrel of pickled herrings it might have contained a small amount of ascorbic acid but no explanation has yet accounted for the extraordinary reputation enjoyed by oil of vitriol for more than a hundred years. Sir Richard Hawkins thought it valuable, if less effective than fresh fruit.

The Oyle of Vitry is beneficiall for this disease: taking two drops of it.

There is not a single suggestion in these early records that the disease was caused by lack of fresh fruit or vegetables. It was always ascribed to the influence of sea air, to too much salt meat or to the change in the habits of life. The curative action of the antiscorbutics was in no way related to the primary cause of the trouble. This may appear strange to us who think so readily in terms of dietary deficiencies and their correction but we must not forget that in those days the cause of a disease and its cure were not necessarily associated in the minds of medical men. They were the days of absolute faith in the herbal. God had given man a herb to cure every ailment; scurvy grass was provided as a remedy against scurvy just as pimpernel was provided as a cure for the plague. It no more occurred to them that scurvy was due to a lack of scurvy grass, or similar herbs, than that a deficiency of pimpernel would bring about an outbreak of plague. The idea that illness could be related to a purely negative factor, the absence of something, remained unacceptable to the medical profession for some hundreds of years to come, and persisted even after the discovery of vitamins.

During the later part of the sixteenth and the opening of the seventeenth century scurvy undoubtedly attracted a great deal more attention in England than it had formerly done. In medical circles interest was stimulated by the works of such foreign authors as Wierus (1567), Forestus (1595), Eugalenus (1604) and Sennertus (1624),[1] which became known over here through the influence of the great Dutch medical schools, notably that at Leyden. They gave reasonably accurate pictures of the disease but offered no more satisfactory explanation of its appearance than 'overflowing of black bile', 'obstruction of the spleen' or 'corruption of the humours'. Sennertus wrote:

It is an evil occult quality, or disposition, impressed upon the whole body, chiefly the parts destined for nutrition, arising from gross melancholy or serous ichorous humour after a peculiar manner corrupted with lassitude and heaviness.[2]

Maynwaring, one of the earliest English writers on scurvy, commented 'this definition looks imperfect and unsatisfactory', but he himself offered sixteen theories to account for the origin of the disease, each one as obscure and meaningless as that of Sennertus.[3] The other English writers were little better. Willis, who gave a very complete description of the symptoms, thought the principal causes were unwholesome air and a 'vitiated texture of the blood'.[4] Gideon Harvey, physician to Charles II, caused some

[1] A useful early bibliography of writings on scurvy is given in Lind's *A Treatise of the Scurvy*, 1753.
[2] *De Scorbuto Tractatus*, D. Sennertus, 1624. (Translation given in *A Treatise of the Scurvy*, E. Maynwaring, 1665.)
[3] *A Treatise of the Scurvy*, E. Maynwaring, 1665.
[4] *Tractatus de Scorbuto*, T. Willis, 1667.

confusion by attempting to differentiate between mouth-scurvy, leg-scurvy, acid-scurvy, joint-scurvy, stomachic-scurvy, land-scurvy and sea-scurvy.[1] Harvey spoke of it as the 'Disease of London'. He thought it infective, its miasma being communicable by contact. Infants, he suggested, were liable to become scorbutic from being kissed by people suffering from the disease. Confusion with other skin diseases would account for this belief.

John Woodall, who was appointed surgeon to the East India Company in 1612, wrote a valuable book entitled *The Surgions Mate* (1612), in which he gave a full account of the diseases of seamen and the methods of treating them. Scurvy is one of the diseases he mentions.

> The cheefe cause whereof is the continuance of salt diet, either fish or flesh, as porke and the like, which is not be auoyded at sea, as I suppose by the wit of man: another cause, is want of sufficient nourishing food, and of sweete water, and also for want of *Aqua vitae*, wine, beere, or other good water to comfort and warm their stomackes, which by contrary windes men are too much incident vnto in long voiages how-souer the Marchants are carefull, prouident, and bountifull in that point.

Scurvy grass, horse radish, sorrel and similar herbs, were all, in his opinion, useful remedies, 'but marke how farre they extend only to the cure of those which liue at home, or else it may bee sayd, they also helpe some sea men returned from farre'. He did not know that Hudson's men, on their fateful voyage to find the North-West Passage in 1610, had once been saved by touching land where they were able to gather 'Sorell, and that which wee call Scurvy-grasse, in great abundance'.[2] In the case of sea scurvy Woodall put his faith in the curative action of the citrus fruits.

> And further experience teacheth which I haue oft found true, that where a disease most raineth, euen there God hath appointed the best remedies for the same grefe if it be his will that they should be dis-couered and vsed: and note for substance, the Lemmons, Limes, Tama-rinds, Oringes, and other choyce of good helpes in the Indies which you shall finde there doe farre exceed any that can be carried thither from England, and yet there is a good quantity of Iuice of Lemmons sent in each ship out of England by the great care of the Marchants, and intended onely for the releefe of euery poore man in his neede, which is an admirable comfort to poore men in that disease; also I finde we haue many good things that heale the Scuruy well at land, but the Sea

[1] *The Disease of London; or, a new discovery of the Scurvey*, Gideon Harvey, 1675.
[2] *Purchas His Pilgrimes*, S. Purchas, 1625-26.

Surgeon shall doe little good at Sea with them, neyther will they indure. The vse of the iuyce of Lemons is a precious medicine, and wel tried, being sound & good, let it haue the chiefe place for it will deserue it.

He also supported the seaman's belief that oil of vitriol was a good remedy.

... and in want of all these vse oyle of Vitrioll ... I can affirme that good oyle of Vitrioll is an especiall good medicine in the cure of Scuruy.

William Cockburn, physician to the Fleet at the end of the seventeenth century, was another who believed that sea scurvy was a distinct disease, primarily caused by over-indulgence in salt foods.

I think, I have said enough to explain the way how this sickness is produced with us, and to show that 'tis a necessary consequence of an idle life, and a feeding on *Salt Beefe* and *Pork*.[1]

'Honest Dr. Cockburn', as Swift called him, had an eye for publicity and the main chance. He quite unblushingly took for himself the credit of ascribing scurvy to salt food.

Dr. *Boerhaave*, the famous and learned Professor of the Practice of Physick, in the University of *Leyden*, has not concealed his Esteem of my Performance, but has taught publicly, in his Schools, my Doctrine of the Scurvy.[2]

He spoke of an outbreak which occurred in 1695 in the ships which had been moored in Torbay for a month, during which time the men had not been allowed to land. He urged the Commander, Lord Berkeley, to put the sick men ashore but was met with the objection that if this were done they might take the opportunity to desert. The men, however, became so ill that finally more than a hundred gaunt skeletons, scarcely able to move, were rowed to land where they were able to get carrots and turnips and 'other Green Trade'. Within a week they were crawling about and soon all but two or three were fit to return for duty.[3]

The French physician, Chameau, who lived in England for some time, was greatly impressed by the prevalence of scurvy in this country.[4] It was apparently but little known in France for an outbreak in Paris in 1699

---

[1] *An Account of The Nature, Causes, Symptoms and Cure of the Distempers that are incident to Seafaring People*, William Cockburn, 1696.
[2] *Sea Diseases*, William Cockburn, 3rd Edition, 1736.
[3] Ibid.
[4] *Traité du Scorbut*, Chameau, 1683.

attracted a good deal of attention.[1] It is difficult to say whether this merely indicates that the doctors had learnt to recognize the disease but it certainly seems the most probable explanation, for there is no evidence that less fruit and vegetables were eaten; indeed, as we have seen, there are reasons for thinking that the reverse was the case. The seventeenth-century doctor may, of course, have diagnosed scurvy simply to be in the fashion. Thomas Sydenham hinted that this was so, for he observed that the two great subterfuges of the ignorant physicians of his time were 'malignity and the scurvy', which they blamed for disorders and symptoms 'often owing to their own ill-management'. One wonders what he would have said if he could have seen the advertisement which John Pechey, M.D., brazenly attached to his translation of Sydenham's works which appeared in 1696, seven years after the latter's death.

> Excellent purging Pills prepared by *John Pechey . . . Basing-Lane, London.* They cure the Scurvy, the most reigning Disease in this Kingdom . . . The Price of each Box is one Shilling Sixpence with Directions for use.

There was considerable confusion between the forms of scurvy seen at sea and on land. Most people believed they were distinct diseases, probably because at sea the symptoms appeared rather suddenly and were usually much more severe. One reason for this was that once the fresh provisions were exhausted the sailors were living on a diet almost completely devoid of the antiscorbutic vitamin. On land few except the very poor or those in prison suffered so severe a deprivation. Their diets were rarely wholly deficient in vitamin C and the onset of the disease was, therefore, more insidious and the symptoms less clearly marked. It is now known that severe injury increases the body's utilization of vitamin C. Thus, another reason for the severity of scurvy at sea may have been that the hard conditions of life there — the fatigue and exposure to cold and injury — increased the sailor's requirements for the vitamin.

The most popular remedies were oranges, lemons and oil of vitriol at sea, and scurvy grass, brooklime or cresses on land. Parsley, chervill, lettuce, purslane, winter rocket and strawberries were all recomemnded as 'good to fasten loose teeth and to heal spungy, foul Gums'.[2] Robert Boyle gave a recipe based on an infusion of barley and lemon rind, which he recommended for 'scorbutick cholick',[3] but scurvy grass was the remedy most widely used. Judging by an entry in the household books of Lord William

---

[1] *A Relation of Some Strange and Wonderful effects of Scurvy, which happened at Paris in the year 1699,* Poupart.
[2] *The English Physitian Enlarged,* Nicholas Culpeper, 1653.
[3] *Medicinal Experiments: Or, a Collection of Choice and Safe Remedies,* R. Boyle, 1692-94.

Howard (1612-33),[1] 'Skirvie grasse for my Lady ij^s' it was by no means inexpensive. The most popular method of administration was in ale. Dr Parry's recipe was as follows:

> Of the juyce of scouruy-grasse one pint; of the iuyce of water-cresses as much; of the iuyce of succory, half a pint; of the iuyce of fumitory, half a pint; proportion to one gallon of ale; they must be all tunned vp togither.[2]

Scurvy grass ale was usually recommended in the spring, a time when scorbutic symptoms would have been at their worst. An item in the accounts of the Woburn household of the Earl of Bedford (1653) concerns the payment of 4d. to John Morrice for 'scurvy-grass, or gittings, to put in the children's ale'.[3] It is significant that the date is April. In 1678 the patients in St Bartholomew's Hospital were given scurvy grass ale, provided it was ordered by the doctor and entered in the apothecary's book.[4] A translation of Moellenbrock's book on this herb appeared in England in 1676.[5]

> 'Tis a Treatise of Scurvy Grass, a Plant that grows very plentifully in our Country, a sign, as the Author assureth us, that the Scurvy, in which disease it is particularly advantagious, is but too frequent amongst us, which our own experience doth sadly confirm.

It is interesting to note that the author thought the curative action of scurvy grass, although 'occult and secret, as almost all modern Physitians do agree', to be due to a 'volatile salt of a certain bitterish Taste', which counteracted the 'gross and fixed salt' in which the 'scorbutick humour abounds'. A plausible theory had been evolved regarding the cause of the disease. Salt foods loaded the blood with a 'fixed' salt, which required for its dispersal the administration of a 'volatile salt'. The uses to which scurvy grass was put are well illustrated by the following quotations from Moellenbrock's book.

> ... take of Scurvy-Grass very small cut or minced, and adde of juice of Lemmons or sowre Orenges, and so you will have a Sawce pleasant to the taste, and effectual against the Scurvy, for these kind of Sawces are mighty advantagious in the Scurvy, insomuch that the people of *Norway* are preserved from this Disease by the use of them, as is attested by *Gr. Horst*.

[1] *Selections from the Household Books of Lord William Howard* (Surtees Society Publication, No. 68, 1877).
[2] *Diary of John Manningham, 1602-3* (Camden Society Publication No. 99, 1868).
[3] *Life in a Noble Household, 1641-1700*, G. Scott Thomson, 1937.
[4] *History of St Bartholomew's Hospital*, Sir Norman Moore, 1918.
[5] *Cochlearia Curiosa; or the Curiosities of Scurvygrass*, written in Latine by Dr Andreas Valentinus Molimbrochius, Englished by Tho. Sherley, M.D., 1676.

And again:

The leaves of the new Scurvygrass are to be boiled in Milk, or, if they be troubled also with a fever and heat, then boil them in buttermilk, also in Whey, Wine, Ale, Beer, or Water, and let the Decoction be drank several dayes together, if the leaves of Scurvygrass be used by themselves, they ought not to be boiled long ... lest the volatile Salt do quite vanish away.

CHAPTER VIII

RICKETS

§ 1 GROWTH OF BONES

THE bones of an infant are soft and pliable, but during the period of growth they become gradually hardened by the deposition of mineral material which is almost entirely composed of calcium phosphate. This substance is also responsible for the hardness of teeth. It is deposited in soft matrix structures as a result of precipitation brought about by interaction of compounds of calcium and phosphoric acid which are present in the blood. The process by which this precipitation is controlled so that it occurs only at sites of ossifica-tion and not all over the body is extraordinarily interesting. It can best be explained by first describing a simple chemical experiment. Sodium phos-phate and calcium chloride are white solids which dissolve very readily in water to form clear solutions. If a few drops of one are added to the other a white precipitate of calcium phosphate is formed *unless* the original solu-tions were exceedingly dilute. The reaction can be represented as follows:

sodium phosphate + calcium chloride =
(soluble)   (soluble)

calcium phosphate + sodium chloride
(insoluble)   (soluble)

There is a critical strength of the solutions at which on mixing the first signs of a precipitation occur. Solutions that are more dilute remain clear in-definitely when they are mixed. They can, however, be made to deposit calcium phosphate in solid form by the simple procedure of adding a minute amount of a *stronger* solution of *either* component. It is not sufficient to add more of the original solutions, it is necessary to raise the *concentration* either of the calcium or of the phosphate.

The blood of normal individuals contains both soluble calcium com-pounds and phosphates but the amounts which are present in forms capable of reacting according to the simple equation given above are insufficient to permit the deposition of calcium phosphate. In other words, the critical concentration has not been reached. Obviously, this is the only possible state of affairs; otherwise solid calcium phosphate would be deposited in every part of the body and would soon lead to extensive calcification.

What is needed, therefore, to bring about deposition of solid calcium phosphate in the bones and teeth of a normal infant is a *local* increase at those sites of the concentration either of reacting calcium compounds or phosphates, or both. Such an increase does, in fact, occur. It is brought about by the action of one of those substances known as the enzymes, which are the agents by which the cells of the body carry out all manner of chemical changes, and which seem to have a constitution intermediate between the non-living proteins and the living viruses. The enzyme in question, known as bone-phosphatase, is found at the centres at which bone formation is required and it brings about the necessary changes in the local conditions by converting a phosphate in the blood which does not react with soluble calcium salts into one that does. The increase in the local concentration of phosphate is then sufficient to cause precipitation of calcium phosphate. In this manner the tooth or developing bone becomes gradually ossified and hardened. But conditions are not always like this. Sometimes, for example, the amounts of calcium and/or phosphate in the blood become raised beyond the critical concentrations required for precipitation. Over-activity of the parathyroid gland or very excessive treatment with vitamin D have such an effect and raise the concentration of calcium in the blood from the normal level of about 10 mg. per 100 c.c. to as much as 15 mg. per 100 c.c. This may result, as one would expect, in more generalized deposition of calcium phosphate. In the very early days of enthusiasm for vitamin D therapy, before it was known that heavy dosage had this undesirable effect, several cases occurred of calcium deposits forming in the kidneys and other organs of young children as the result of such treatment.

On the other hand, there are conditions in which there is less calcium and/or phosphate in the blood than there should be. One of these conditions is known as rickets. The amount of phosphates in the blood of a rachitic child is low. Sometimes the amount of calcium may be subnormal. This means that even with the supplementary action of the enzyme operating at the sites of bone formation there may be insufficient calcium and phosphates in reactive forms to provide for normal deposition. Such is the case in rickets and it explains why the bone is soft and apt to bend under pressure. Rickets is a reflection of disordered metabolism of calcuim and phosphorus, and as soon as means are found to raise the amounts of these substances in the blood to a normal level the formation of bone proceeds regularly once again.

In studying rickets, therefore, we have to focus our attention, not on the bones which show the obvious defects, but on the task of finding out why the blood contains too little of the soluble bone-forming salts. It has already been stated that these are originally derived from the food and it would be reasonable, therefore, to think that the amounts in the blood depend solely on the amounts in the diet. To some extent this is true, but the relationship is by no means a simple one. The calcium and phosphates must be absorbed from the digestive tract before they can enter the blood stream and the extent to which they are so absorbed is determined not only by the amounts in the food but also by the *ratio* between these amounts. At one year a child should be getting about 1 g. of calcium a day and about half to three-quarters of this amount of phosphorous. The demand for calcium rises to 1.2 to 1.3 g. at puberty (and the desirable calcium/phosphorous ratio falls), amounts of calcium which can be supplied by 1½ to 2 pints of milk. There are all sorts of complications which make the assessment of these requirements difficult. One is the fact that both calcium and phosphorus, but more particularly the latter, occur in foods in many different forms, some of which are more assimilable than others. Cereals, for example, contain a compound known as phytin which, although very rich in phosphorus, yields little to the body during digestion. Another is the part played by vitamin D.

§ 2 THE ANTIRACHITIC VITAMINS

About a century ago medical men in Europe began to appreciate the value of cod liver oil in curing rickets. The reason for its curative effect was not known, although it was the subject of much speculation, until Professor (later Sir) Edward Mellanby made his pioneer investigations on the part played by diet in the causation of the disease. Earlier investigators had suspected that improper feeding was responsible, but they had laid the blame on such faults as too little lime or too much starchy food. Mellanby's experiments showed that one of the vitamins is necessary for the formation of healthy bones and teeth and that this substance accounts for the curative action of cod liver oil.

For a time his views seemed to be in conflict with those of another school, which held that lack of fresh air and sunlight, and other defective hygienic surroundings, were primary factors in the production of the disorder. These two opinions, which at one time appeared to be irreconcilable, were correlated by the remarkable discovery that the short wave-length rays of the sun, the ultra-violet rays which cause tanning, produce a vitamin D in the superficial layers of the skin. A rachitic child can be treated equally well, therefore, by administering vitamin D directly in the form of a fish liver oil, or by giving sunlight treatment or ultra-violet therapy, thereby enabling the body to form its own vitamin.

For some time after the recognition that the beneficial effect of cod liver oil in rickets is due to vitamin D it was thought that there was only one such vitamin and that there was no better source. Subsequently it was discovered that the liver oils extracted from certain other species of fish are very much more potent than cod liver oil, and that there are at least three different vitamins of the D type. It is not important to discuss the latter discovery because the individual vitamins are very closely related and can be probably regarded as having the same physiological action. Some fish liver oils are very much richer in vitamin D than cod liver oil. The following list shows the range of potencies that are encountered.

Liver Oil	International units (i.u.) Vitamin D per g.
Cod	50-200
Halibut	1000-4000
Sea bass	4000-5000
Sword fish	4000-10,000
Yellow-fin tunny	13,000-45,000
Striped tunny	220,000-250,000

By the side of the potencies of ordinary natural foods which contain vitamin D (butter, 0.1-1.0; egg yolk, 1.5-5.0 i.u. per g.) some of these figures appear almost fantastic. They raise the interesting question why there should be such relatively enormous stores of vitamin D in the liver of some fish and little in the liver of mammals. No answer to this question has yet been found. It is known, however, that in any one species of fish the stores of vitamin D increase with age.

Modern research has shown that the administration of a vitamin D increases the amount of calcium, and possibly also that of phosphates, absorbed from the digestive tract and retained in the body. Its intervention is, therefore, particularly helpful in all cases in which defective absorption is suspected and, conversely, is least needed when absorption of bone-forming salts is good. A child needs relatively a large dose of vitamin D when its diet is poor in lime and/or phosphate or when the calcium/phosphorus ratio is faulty; it needs very much less when its food is rich in these constituents and the proportion between them is favourable to good absorption.

Mothers' milk contains a good deal less calcium and phosphorus than cows' milk. In spite of this it is very rare to detect any trace of rickets in an infant fed at the breast of a well-nourished woman. This means that the utilization of the bone-forming elements of mothers' milk is usually excellent. So far as we know this is due to the calcium being present in a very readily assimilable form and to the fact that the calcium/phosphorus ratio (about 2) is ideal. Vitamin D seems to come into the picture to a relatively unimportant extent because very little is found in human milk; Drummond and his colleagues found a range of values from 2-9 i.u. per 100 g. of milk, with a mean value of

3.5. This means that the unsupplemented intake of an infant is often less than 20 units a day and seldom rises above double that figure. During recent years the requirement of infants and young children has usually been set at 400-800 i.u. of vitamin D daily, a quantity which has been given, and sometimes exceeded, in the form of cod liver oil or other fish liver oils and dried milk fortified with additional vitamin D. Very recently a new condition has been reported though never in wholly breast-fed infants — idiopathic hypercalcaemia, a condition causing loss of appetite, vomiting, constipation, failure of growth, listlessness, mental retardation, increased retention of calcium and phosphorus, calcification of parts of the kidney and sometimes death. At the time of writing consideration is being paid to the dangers of excessive amounts of calcium and vitamin D in the diets of infants, particularly those who are artificially fed, though these factors are unlikely to provide the complete answer to the problems raised by this type of abnormal metabolism of calcium and phosphorus.

§ 3 RICKETS IN ENGLAND

As we shall see later the worst period in English history, so far as rickets is concerned, was during the rapid industrialization of the towns which occurred in the 'forties of the nineteenth century. The disease had, however, been prevalent for at least two centuries. Some authorities believe that this was why it came to be generally known on the Continent as 'The English Disease' (*Die englische Krankheit*), although others favour the view, and it seems the more plausible one, that it arose from the fact that English medical writers were the first to recognize and describe the disorder and its symptoms. The most important of these works appeared in 1645 and 1650 respectively and both authors assured their readers that the disease was a new one, having made its appearance in England some twenty years or so previously. Does this mean that rickets was almost unknown in pre-Stuart England and that Whistler's and Glisson's accounts of it were something quite new to the doctors abroad? This is a question which it is very difficult to answer. There is one piece of evidence which is sometimes brought forward to show that rickets was common in the Low Countries and north Germany in the fifteenth and sixteenth centuries. It is derived from a study of the paintings of that period, most of them, of course, of religious subjects, in which many of the infants are depicted showing the characteristic bent limbs, swollen abdomen and square head of the rachitic state.[1] This may mean that the

[1] 'Evidence of Rickets prior to 1650', J. A. Foote, *American Journal of the Diseases of Children*, 1927, Vol. XXXIV.

disease was so prevalent that an artist quite naturally painted a young child showing these abnormalities. On the other hand, it must not be forgotten that at that period the Flemish school was inclined towards conventionalism and that there was a great deal of copying, particularly of human figures. If rickets was as common in Flanders and north Germany as our first impression of these pictures might lead us to think, it is rather surprising that, after the publication of the descriptions of the disease by Whistler and Glisson, the Dutch and German medical men — the former among the best in Europe in the seventeenth century — did not immediately recognize its prevalence in their own countries.

The evidence is not sufficient for us to assume that rickets was common in north-western Europe before it was recognized in our own country although, as we shall see, it is likely that it was known. The history of its recognition is an interesting one but complicated, as so many scientific discussions are, by rival claims regarding priority, although in this case they were made not by the original writers themselves but have been since advanced by commentators. It will be best, perhaps, if the known facts be treated chronologically. So far as we have been able to discover, the first mention of the disease by the name of rickets is in a Bill of Mortality for the City of London, dated 1634. It must have been a fairly well-known condition by then because these Bills were compiled by the Parish Clerks from lists furnished every Tuesday by the 'Searchers', whose duty it was to inspect the dead and register the cause of death.

> The *Searchers* hereupon (who are antient Matrons sworn to their Office) repair to the place, where the dead Corps lies, and by view of the same, and by other enquiries, they examine by what *Disease* or *Casualty* the Corps died.[1]

We are not at the moment concerned with the unreliability of the lists drawn up by these searchers, who were seldom able to diagnose the cause of death except in such obvious conditions as plague. What does impress us is that in 1634 a condition known as rickets was sufficiently well known to be one of the recognized causes to which death was attributed; 14 were recorded in that year.

The next important date is 1645 when a young English doctor, Daniel Whistler, who entered the University of Leyden in 1642, was awarded the degree of Doctor of Medicine there for a Thesis entitled *De Morbo puerili Anglorum, quam patrio idumate indigenae vocant* 'The Rickets'. The record in the University archives reads:

[1] *Natural and Political Observations . . . upon the Bills of Mortality*, by John Graunt, Citizen of London, 1662.

Ex Actis Senatus Anni 1645 rectore Polyandro Octob. 17. Concessus est Danieli Whistler ad disputandum privatim pro supremo in Medicina gradu dies ejusden mensus ad.

October 18. Virus et dignus Daniel Whistler cui supremus in Medicina conferatur gradus quem illicontucit D, Weurnius (Med. Prof.).[1]

This work gives a good general account of the disease. It is true that it does not compare in depth and detail with that which Glisson published five years later, and which has for long been accepted as the first description of the disease, but it certainly gives most of the fundamental observations.

The more famous Glisson was a Dorsetshire man born, it is thought, in 1597, who studied at Cambridge, where he took his M.D. in 1634. He appears to have stayed at Cambridge, where he was appointed Regius Professor of Physic in 1636, until about 1640 when he moved to Colchester and started in practice. He was there during the siege in 1648, but appears to have left shortly afterwards to settle in London.

The classic work which carries his name, *De Rachitide sive Morbo Puerili qui vulgo* The Rickets *dicitur*, published in 1650, resulted from the deliberations of a group of members of the College of Physicians, and we are led to understand from the introduction that of eight interested doctors three, Dr G. Bate, Dr A. Regemorter and Francis Glisson, were most concerned. It is also quite clear that Glisson contributed so much more to the compilation of the information than any of his colleagues that they willingly allowed the book to appear with his name as author. There is a remark in the introduction which indicates that the self-appointed Committee (the archives of the Royal College of Physicians contain no reference to the inquiry being carried out officially under their auspices) had been working for five years, that is, since 1645, the very year in which Whistler's Thesis appeared. Sir Norman Moore interpreted this coincidence as evidence that young Whistler had learnt of the project and tried 'to utilize an imperfect knowledge of the well known but not yet printed discovery of a great scientific investigator'.[2] It is difficult to understand why this biographer reached such a conclusion. Whistler was a native of Walthamstow and must have known London in his youth before he went to Oxford to study medicine. It is more than likely that he had seen plenty of rickets and that he knew it to be one of the diseases into which deaths recorded in the Bills of Mortality were classified. It must also be borne in mind that Whistler was residing in Leyden for the best part of the two years before his Thesis was published in 1645 and that it is,

---

[1] We are greatly indebted to Professor Dr L. Knappert for searching the records on our behalf and providing this and other extracts from the *Albo Studiosorum* of Leyden University.

[2] *Dictionary of National Biography*, Article on Francis Glisson.

therefore, unlikely that he heard more than a rumour or two, if anything at all, about the project of Glisson and his colleagues.

A rather curious point, which weighs in Whistler's favour, is the strange similarity of the titles of the two books. It is inconceivable that Glisson's committee had decided on the title of their publication five years before it appeared: there is not sufficient evidence to justify the charge of plagiarism which Sir Norman Moore brought against Whistler.[1] On the other hand, it is difficult to dispel the suspicion that Glisson's interest in a disease which he seems to have known in his native Dorset when a young man was aroused by the publication of the Leyden Thesis in 1645.

If there were reasons for believing that Whistler stole his ideas from the group of people headed by Glisson it is surprising that no charge was brought against him in *De Rachitide*: there is no reference in its pages to the Leyden Thesis. Even if this be overlooked — for, after all, the latter was a foreign publication — it is less easy to explain why Glisson makes no reference to another description of rickets which appeared in London a year before his own work. In 1630, two brothers, Arnold and Gerard Boate,[2] graduated in medicine at Leyden. They were the sons of a Dutch physician who had come to London in 1625 and died there shortly afterwards. His sons practised here with considerable success, for one, Gerard, became Physician in Ordinary to Charles I, while his brother Arnold moved to Dublin and became private physician to Robert Sydney, Earl of Leicester, later establishing a flourishing practice there. Arnold wrote a textbook entitled *Observationes medicae de affectibus omissis* which he published in London in 1649. In the twelfth chapter, under the heading *Tabes Pectorea*, he gave a short but concise account of rickets which, he stated was quite common both in England and Ireland. It is not reasonable, in the face of these facts, to preserve for Glisson the pre-eminent position he has held for so long as the first person to give the English medical profession a clear description of rickets. Whistler and Boate, and particularly Whistler, must be given a share of that honour. It is beside the point to contrast Glisson's subsequent career, in which he proved himself to be a born investigator, with that of Whistler who spent his time building up a fashionable practice in London and trying to climb the social ladder.

It is curious how often the clues seem to lead us back to Leyden, at that time one of the most famous of the medical schools of Europe. Whistler was there, three of Glisson's collaborators, Regemorter (1635), Paget (1639) and Wright (1642), took degrees there, and Arnold Boate graduated

---

[1] It is clear that Dr G. F. Still, an eminent authority on the history of pediatrics, shares the view that neither Whistler nor Boate has had sufficient credit given them in this matter. Cf. *The History of Pediatrics*, 1931.

[2] The name is given variously as Boate, Boot, de Boot and Bootius.

there in 1630. Is this mere coincidence, or does it mean that those who studied at Leyden about that time learnt of a disease in which the legs of young children were bent by pressure or by walking too soon and that when they returned to England they recognized the condition in a more severe form as that popularly known as rickets? Further research is needed to throw light on this interesting question, but meanwhile, it is worth mentioning that two famous Dutch physicians, Petrus Forestus (1522-97) and Johan van Beverwyck (1594-1647) refer in their writings to the risk of causing young children's legs to bend if they are allowed to walk too soon. This may mean that rickets was known in Holland in the sixteenth century.

The origin of the word rickets is obscure. The derivation which Glisson seemed to favour was from the Greek word for a spine ῥάχις, which became converted into the word ῥαχῖτις, and so to rickets. There is no doubt that the Greek physicians knew of bone deformities such as a crooked spine and bow-legs. They were clearly described both by Soranus of Ephesus and by the omniscient Galen, but there is no evidence that any word which might be regarded as the origin of the word rickets was applied to those conditions. Whistler suggested it might have arisen from the word *rucket*, stated to be a Dorset dialect word meaning to breathe with difficulty, which is probably a form of the word *ruckle*, of Scandinavian origin, meaning to make a rattling noise in the throat. This is not convincing. An alternative speculation is based on early English words, *wrick, wrikken*, meaning to twist or sprain. The question remains an open one, except that the evidence leads one to think that the word has a long but unknown English history. Not the least puzzling of many strange points regarding the early history of rickets is the fact that we find the word being used in 1634 as if it were generally known and yet no trace of it is found in earlier writings. Whatever the origin of the word, the medical profession decided to call it *rachitis*, much to the disgust of stout old Nicholas Culpeper, who never lost an opportunity of baiting the pompous College of Physicians for obscuring their wisdom or their ignorance by using the classic tongues. They were scarcely less angry when he translated Glisson's *De Rachitide* into English in 1651 than when earlier he had infuriated them by translating their Pharmacopœia 'very filthily into English', so giving the ordinary person a large amount of information which had previously been available only to those who could read Latin. In his widely read *The English Physitian Enlarged* which he published in 1653 Culpeper recommended 'Down' or 'Cotton-Thistle' for rickets, and having Glisson's recent book in mind, he says it is good for 'Children that have the Rickets, or rather (as the Colledg of Physitians wil have it) the *Rachites*, for which name for the Disease, they have (in a particular Treatise lately set forth by them) Learnedly Disputed, and put forth to publick view, that the

World may see they took much pains to little purpose'. And later 'about which name they have quarrel'd sufficiently'.

The early references to rickets all indicate that it had first attracted attention about 1620. It is also suggested that it first appeared in the west, in Dorset and Somerset, and then gradually spread east and north. To what extent people merely passed on the views of Glisson is uncertain, but at least one non-medical writer stated before *De Rachitide* was published that the disease appeared early in the century. He was a well-known divine named Thomas Fuller, who compiled a series of tracts published in 1649, entitled *Good Thoughts in Bad Times, Together with Good Thoughts in Worse Times.* It is most unlikely that he knew of Whistler's Thesis or of Arnold Boate's book, although it is just possible, since he lived in London, that he may have heard something of the deliberations of Glisson and his colleagues. At any rate, in Section XX on 'Meditation on The Times', he says:

> There is a *disease* of *Infants* (and an *Infant-disease*, having scarcely as yet gotten a proper *name* in *Latin*) called the *Rickets*, Wherein the *Head* waxeth too *great*, whil'st the *Legs*, and *lower parts* wain too *Little.* A *woman* in the *West* hath happily *healed* many, by cauterizing the *Vein* behind the Ear. How proper the *Remedy* for the *Malady* I engage not, *experience* of times outdoing *Art*, whil'st we behold the Cure easily effected, and the natural Cause thereof hardly assigned.

This gives him an excellent opening to inquire 'have not many now *adayes* the same *sickness* in their souls?' and to point a moral to those whose heads are swollen but whose spiritual understanding is weak.

One thing is certain, the malady was widespread at this time. Arnold Boate, writing in 1649, was emphatic that it was common not only in England but also in Ireland. He could at any rate speak with authority of Dublin, and it was certainly his opinion that his brother expressed in his well-known *Ireland's Natural History* published posthumously in 1652; Gerard had not visited Ireland when the volume was compiled in 1645.

> Amongst the reigning diseases of Ireland the Rickets also may with good reason be reckoned, a disease peculiar to young children, and so well known to everybody in England, as it is needless to give any description of it.

It is very puzzling. The doctors seem to have been satisfied that the disease first appeared in the early part of the century. Yet it was already called by a name which suggests a long popular usage and an Anglo-Saxon origin, and by 1652 it is supposed to be so common and well known that no description of it is thought necessary in a book intended not for the medical man but for the general reader.

What is the explanation? Rickets must have occurred in England before the early seventeenth century. There were many periods of dearth when thousands upon thousands were half-starved and when every type of nutritional disorder must have been rife. Unfortunately we have no evidence to show the extent to which rickets occurred in these earlier times. It is, however, by no means surprising that the disease became noticeably prevalent at the time of the terrible depression and poverty in the last decade or two of the Tudors. We have seen that 'white meats', which had been for centuries an important part of the food of the poorer country folk, had become scarce and dear, at any rate in the south. This had the effect of reducing both the calcium and the phosphorus intake, but more particularly the former. A diet consisting of $1\frac{1}{2}$ pints of milk, $1\frac{1}{2}$ lb. of bread and 1 lb. of dried peas (which can be taken as a fair estimate of a peasant diet providing about 3000 Cal.), would have supplied nearly 2 g. of calcium and 3 g. of phosphorus (Ca/P ratio 1:1.5). When milk was unobtainable and the 3000 Cal. had to be made up by eating more bread, the calcium intake would have been reduced to perhaps 0.5 g. while the phosphorus would not have been much affected. Apart from any question of the intake of vitamin D, such a reduction in the daily amount of calcium would make one suspect that a rise in the incidence of rickets might have occurred. Imbalance between calcium and phosphorus in either direction can cause rickets in animals, a situation that can be combated by vitamin D or sunlight or ultraviolet light. The mechanism of the calcification process is still not fully understood, though it is known that the concentrations of calcium and phosphorus in the serum have an influence on the process, and that vitamin D regulates these concentrations.

There are good reasons for believing that a woman living on a diet so poor in calcium would be unable to provide her child with milk fully enriched with bone-forming materials. The consequences might not be obvious until quite late in the nursing period or, indeed, they might not cause trouble until the child began to live on the defective diet of its parents. Glisson commented particularly on the frequency with which the disease appeared in children of from 9 to 18 months, which is the age at which one would expect the highest incidence in a community living on diets poor in calcium and having low calcium/phosphorus ratios.

In this connection it is important to remember that the only food many of the infants got at weaning was a thin slop made with flour and diluted cows' milk or whey. Glisson has recorded that he found more cases of rickets in the cradles of the rich than of the poor. At first sight it appears unlikely that this was a fact and one is inclined to think that he may have looked more carefully for the disease among the wealthy than among the poor. It must be remembered, however, that rich people frequently employed wet-nurses chosen from the poorer country folk and that they were quite as ignorant as the poor regarding the right type of diet for the child at weaning. The peasant's child usually got cows' milk in one form or another at this time, if any was available, because it was a convenient food. The educated classes, on the other hand, were influenced by the medical view that milk was only appropriate to infancy and old age and should be discarded soon after weaning. Very young children were, therefore, often put on to bread, soups and thin gruels. It may have been such a diet that produced the rickets from which little John Verney was probably suffering when his mother sent a letter of home news to her husband in August 1647.

> I must give thee some account of our own babyes heare. For Jack his leggs are most miserable, crooked as ever I saw any child's, and yett thank god he goes very strongly, and is very strayte in his body as any child can bee; and is a very fine child all but his legges, and truly I think would be much finer if we had him in ordering, for they lett him eate anythinge he hath a mind toe, and he keepes a very ill diett.

To which Sir Ralph replied:

> . . . truly the Crookednesse of his Leggs grieves my very Hart, aske some advise about it at London, but doe not Tamper with him.[1]

A year later Dr Denton said of the boy that 'His swelled leggs and great belly looks so like a dropsy. . . it argues a very weake liver.'[2] In the light of recent work on kwashiorkor and other forms of protein malnutrition in infants Dr Denton's report makes one wonder whether this boy was suffering from such a condition. Insufficient protein, particularly if it is of low biological value, on weaning leads *inter alia* to enlarged and fatty livers, macrocytic anaemia, changes in pigmentation of hair and skin, oedema and often a reduction in the proportion of albumin in the serum.[3] Dr Denton's remark about 'a very weake liver' is particularly interesting.

This family seems to have suffered rather severely from what was probably rickets, although the possibility of tubercular trouble cannot be ruled out in the case of the boy Mun, who was sent to Utrecht to be 'straightened' by Dr Skatt, a Dutch consultant, who had a great reputation for curing

---

[1] *Memoirs of the Verney Family*, Vol. II, Frances P. Verney, 1892.
[2] Ibid., Vol. III, Margaret M. Verney, 1894.
[3] See, for example, *Kwashiorkor*, H. C. Trowell, J. N. P. Davies and R. F. A. Dean, 1954, and *Protein Malnutrition*, Proceedings of a Conference in Jamaica (1953). Sponsored jointly by Food and Agriculture Organization of the United Nations, World Health Organization and Josiah Macy Jnr. Foundation, New York, 1955.

'crooked children'. His treatment was to strap the wretched lad in a corselet of iron and leather and to release the fastenings only once a week to permit him to change his shirt. When his father asked that he might be permitted to change it twice weekly the learned doctor replied that as he had 2000 patients to look after he could not possibly spare the time to give such special attention to one of them.

Glisson regarded diet in relation to rickets solely from the standpoint of the humoral doctrines. The disease, he held, was a 'cold distemper' arising from the 'penury and paucity' of the spirits and from their 'stupefaction'. It was aggravated by cold and moist air and, therefore, following the same line of thought, he condemned 'cold and moist' meats. This was in one respect an unfortunate judgment for his ban extendended to fish, which were then thought to be particularly 'cold and moist'. The commonest and cheapest fish of those days was herring which, whether salted or pickled, would have provided a valuable supply of vitamin D. Glisson also condemned over-eating, again on humoral grounds.

> ... for too liberal feeding doth overwhelm and choak the heat, and therefore must needs accumulate many crude and raw humours.[1]

Later in the century Dr Walter Harris seems to have suspected that the condition of the mother might be related to the appearance of rickets in the infant, for he remarked that it was particularly likely to occur if she suffered from 'indigested food' or 'gripes'.[2]

There is no indication in the writings of Whistler, Boate or Glisson that the disease could be cured by dietary means. There is, however, a reference in a letter written by Sir Thomas Browne in 1672 which suggests that a simple remedy, ravens' liver, was used by the country people near Norwich.

> Many are killed for their Livers, in order to the cure of the Rickets.[3]

The interest of this quotation lies in the probability that he is referring to an old household custom in that part of the country, which, in turn, indicates that the disorder had been known there for much more than a generation or two. It is a strange fact that the large modern literature on the distribution of vitamin D in animal foods does not contain a single reference to the amount present in any bird liver. Fish livers are for the most part rich, whereas mammals store very little of this vitamin in their livers. Whether ravens'

---

[1] *A Treatise of the Rickets ... published in Latin by Francis Glisson, Enlarged, Corrected, and very much amended throughout the whol Book* by Nich. Culpeper, Gent, Student in Physick and Astrology; living in Spittlefields, neer London, 1651.

[2] *An Exact Enquiry into, and Cure of the Acute Diseases of Infants*, Walter Harris, 1689 Englished by W. C.[ockburn], 1693.

[3] W. J. Rutherford, *British Journal of Children's Diseases*, 1935, Vol. XXXII.

livers are or are not worthy of the old belief to which Sir Thomas referred cannot, therefore, be decided until tests have been made.

Throughout the early literature on rickets we find the idea that the liver is involved. Doubtless it arose from the swollen abdomen so often seen in badly rachitic children. Physical examination of the abdomen was very primitive in those days and a distention was nine times out of ten put down to liver trouble; it was the first thought that came to Dr Denton when he examined the Verney child. The earliest seventeenth-century Bills of Mortality for London do not mention rickets but we find a heading 'Liver-grown', which in later years is bracketed together with rickets, while after 1634 they are listed separately. Capt. John Graunt, one of the founders of the study of vital statistics, tried to determine from these Bills what was the relation between the two conditions and their relative incidence, but careful as was his analysis his conclusions are quite valueless because of the ignorance of the 'Searchers' who decided upon and recorded the cause of death.[1] How worthless are the lists of the Bills of Mortality except for readily identifiable diseases such as the plague, can be judged from the later records of rickets. Some four to five hundred deaths a year were attributed to the disease in the period 1658-60 when it was certainly prevalent. In the prosperous years about 1725-50, when the standard of living rose the incidence according to these lists fell to about 30-50 a year. When, however, we come to the dearth and starvation at the end of the eighteenth century we find only about three or four deaths a year recorded, while after 1810, when the rickets was rife among the poor of the industrial towns, no mention is made of it.

§4 FORMATION OF TEETH

It seems certain that the calcification of teeth occurs by a process similar in character to that which leads to the mineralization of bone. Certainly Lady Mellanby, who made experimental studies on teeth parallel with her husband's investigations on rickets, showed that young animals deprived of sufficient vitamin D grow teeth which are abnormal in structure and imperfectly calcified. The abnormalities range from the worst conditions, in which the tooth is misshapen, discoloured and obviously defective, to those which are so slight that careful microscopic study is needed to reveal them. She drew particular attention to the less obvious defects because she thought they were usually unsuspected or ignored and yet just as likely to lead to tooth decay as the grosser faults: microscopic fissures harbour bacteria and food residues and eventually give rise to cavities. Lady Mellanby, having

[1] *Natural and Political Observations . . . upon the Bills of Mortality*, John Graunt, 1662.

satisfied herself that the whole range of defects she had detected in experimental animals is commonly found in children's teeth, planned and supervised an extensive investigation to ascertain whether the addition of vitamin
D in the form of cod liver oil to the diet of young school children would
arrest the spread of dental caries. Taken as a whole the results were encouraging. Over the whole spell of about seven years the vitamin D
therapy significantly reduced the spread of caries in teeth developing during
the progress of the test, but it produced less effect than had been expected on
teeth erupted before treatment began.[1]

§ 5 DENTAL CARIES

Ever since Miller[2] showed that certain bacteria growing in solutions of
starch and sugars produce acidic substances which can dissolve the enamel
of teeth, many dentists have considered that this provides a satisfactory
explanation of ordinary dental caries. According to them food residues collect round the teeth, particularly in the crevices between them and at the
margins of the gums — and it must be remembered that this is where caries
usually starts — and become fermented by bacteria, with the production of
acids which slowly erode the hard enamel surface. An obvious objection to
this very simple theory is that it does not account for the perfect teeth which
are found in many native races whose diet is rich in starchy foods and who
pay little or no attention to the cleanliness of their mouths. The West
Indian native under his natural conditions has excellent teeth, although from
the time he is a little child he loves to chew and suck sugar-cane. Almost
invariably when these people come into the towns and adopt the living habits
of the white man their teeth, or, at any rate, those of their children, decay. If
one makes a compilation of the distribution of dental caries related to changes
in diet the most striking correlation appears where modern white flour and
sugar are concerned. Time and time again examples will be found of communities in which the teeth were generally excellent so long as the people
lived on natural unrefined foodstuffs. Soon after the introduction of the
highly milled modern type of white flour caries appeared.

One such isolated community is of particular interest because the state of
the teeth has been kept under expert observation during a period when the
character of the diet has changed. It is the small population of the remote
island of Tristan da Cunha. When H.M.S. *Carlisle*, surveying the Southern
Atlantic, called in 1932, the ship's surgeon took the opportunity to examine

[1] *Medical Research Council, Special Report,* No. 159, 1931; No. 211, 1936.
[2] W. D. Miller, *Dental Cosmos,* 1905, Vol. XLVII.

the teeth of the 162 inhabitants. They were remarkably good, 83 per cent being entirely free from caries, with not a single bad tooth in any child under five years of age. At that time the diet was essentially the same as it had been for many years, potatoes, fish, eggs, a little milk and vegetables, with hardly any cereals. Only when a ship called, a rare event, was there an opportunity to obtain a little white flour and sugar. Breast feeding was universal and toothbrushes were unknown.[1] H.M.S. *Carlisle* paid another visit to the island in 1937 and the teeth were again examined. Caries was more apparent than it had been five years before; indeed, the spread was rather alarming. In so short a space of time the percentage of persons with wholly sound teeth had dropped to 50 per cent. Moreover, the striking fact was revealed that the young children were most affected and mainly responsible for the rise in the figures of incidence. There was only one change in the mode of living of the islanders with which the deterioration of the teeth can be correlated. It had been exceptional for the island to be visited more than once a year by a passing vessel. Between the middle of 1933 and early 1937 no less than ten ships called, and the people had quantities of white flour and sugar such as they had never seen before; incidentally, they had also received their first toothbrushes.[2] The teeth of the islanders have been examined on several other occasions during the last thirty years. Royal Naval dental officers took part in the two surveys already mentioned, a third in 1952, and another in 1955, and the results of these four surveys were compared in the report of the last one.[3] The percentage of persons entirely free from caries and extractions had fallen from the 83 per cent of 1932 and the 50 per cent of 1937 to 22 per cent in 1952 and, even further, to 12 per cent in 1955. The percentage with healthy gums had decreased steeply from 96 in 1932 to 69 in 1937, more slowly to 58 in 1952 and then more sharply again to 48 in 1955. Although the basic diet in 1955 was still stated to be potatoes and fish, the dietary pattern had been changed fundamentally by the opportunity of buying processed and refined foods from the Tristan Development Company's Canteen. In the first half of 1955, quantities of foods were purchased which would have been equivalent if expressed per head per week to roughly $4\frac{1}{2}$ lb. of flour (including small quantities of biscuits and rice) and 2 lb. of sugar and jam (including a little canned fruit and sweets), as well as about a third of a can of milk.

Lady Mellanby was certainly right in thinking that there is need for vitamin D in infancy and childhood to help to form the substance of sound teeth but one does not find a good correlation between vitamin D intake and

---

[1] W. E. A. Sampson, *British Dental Journal* (1932), LIII ,397.
[2] H. N. V. Barnes, *British Dental Journal* (1937), LXIII, 86.
[3] E. W. King-Turner and P. Davies, *British Dental Journal* (1956), CI, 262.

the distribution of caries in world populations. Nowhere is caries more rife than in New Zealand, a country of exceptionally high average standard of living, with a large *per caput* consumption of butter and where the atmosphere is for a good part of the year clear and sunny: the consumption of sugar, sweets, cake and biscuits is exceptionally high. One observer who has studied caries both in New Zealand and Great Britain found more sets of sound teeth among the slum children of Birmingham than in well-to-do and middle-class families in New Zealand.[1] The Maoris, however, are immune so long as they keep to their native diets. When they come to the towns and adopt the white man's mode of living their teeth deteriorate.

It is a striking fact that meat-eating races very rarely show carious teeth. The teeth of the carnivorous Masai warriors were perfect, even if their oral hygiene left much to be desired, whereas those of their sickly neighbours, the Akikuyu, who lived almost exclusively on millet, maize, sweet potatoes and yams, were rather badly affected.[2] This was probably related to the calcium and phosphorus contents of their respective diets, for whereas the former is rich in both and reasonably well balanced (estimated male intake, 2.94 g. calcium, 4.36 g. phosphorus) that of the latter is calcium-poor and exceptionally badly proportioned (estimated male intake, 0.28 g. calcium, 3.0 g. phosphorus).

It is impossible to draw definite conclusions on the causes and prevention of dental caries, though there is no doubt that there is a strong association between diet and tooth decay. The subject was recently reviewed for the National Research Council of the United States of America,[3] and some of the more important conclusions reached are: Poorly formed and poorly calcified teeth seem to be more susceptible to caries than normal teeth. Vitamin D supplements reduce caries activity if the diet is short of this vitamin. There is no evidence of an increased tooth decay in vitamin C deficiency, though shortage of this vitamin causes impairment of the supporting structures of the teeth, and consequent loss of teeth and gum infections. (This observation accords with the old records on scurvy.) There is no incontrovertible evidence that diets partially deficient in calcium or phosphorus or both result in increased caries, but the ability to utilize and retain calcium and phosphorus seems to be important. It is not known whether there is a relationship between the sugar and refined carbohydrate content of an adequate diet and susceptibility to dental caries, though in many countries where sugar supplies

[1] Personal information from Dr E. M. Wilkins.
[2] *The Physique and Health of Two African Tribes*, J. B. Orr and J. L. Gilks, Medical Research Council, Report No. 155, 1931.
[3] *A Survey of the Literature of Dental Caries*, G. Toverud, S. B. Finn, G. J. Cox, C. F. Bodecker and J. H. Shaw, Publication 225. National Academy of Sciences — National Research Council, Washington D.C., 1952.

L

were restricted during World Wars I and II there were reductions in the incidence of tooth decay, which did not reach its lowest point until sugar had been restricted for six or more years. Fluorine in moderate amounts affords a significant degree of protection against caries.

§6 STATE OF EARLY ENGLISH TEETH

Perfection in teeth is by no means common today in civilized communities but it is very often seen among native races. Each jaw carries a set of perfectly aligned and formed teeth and if the individual is in the thirties or older it will be seen that the surfaces are worn down with chewing. This attrition causes a reaction in the healthy tooth by which more hard bony material, secondary dentine, is constantly being laid down to protect and to prevent exposure of the soft interior. In this manner a hard surface is maintained which does not crack or wear thin. In the jaws of an old person the grinding teeth may be worn down almost level with the gums, the surfaces looking like polished ivory. We can get a little evidence about the state of the teeth in England at different periods by examining skulls which can be dated with some certainty, but, unfortunately, there is not a great deal of this material available. The task is made more difficult by the fact that teeth readily drop out of the skull in the course of time. It is important, therefore, in examining the jaws of old skulls to note whether gaps represent teeth lost during or after life. They are quite easy to distinguish, because when a tooth is lost during lifetime the bone of the jaw gradually grows and covers over the socket. An open socket in an old skull or jawbone means, therefore, that the tooth was either lost very shortly before death or that it dropped out afterwards.

The vaults of St Leonard's Church, Hythe, have given us material representing the population of that seaport between the approximate dates 1250 to 1650. The examination of 199 complete palates showed that approximately half had not lost a single tooth before death and most of the mature jaws showed the polished surfaces of well-worn teeth. Carious cavities were present in some of the teeth but a statistical examination of the jaws for this defect was not made.[1] The general statement is permissible that it was a good deal less prevalent than it is today. The evidence becomes a little clearer when we reach the seventeenth-century material because some of it can be dated with more certainty. A collection of mandibles from a burial ground in Farringdon Street showed that 26 per cent of the males and 14.5

---

[1] We are greatly indebted to Dr G. M. Morant, formerly of the Galton Laboratory, University College, for this information and for assistance in tracing evidence on the state of English teeth.

per cent of the females had lost no teeth before death. It will be seen that the percentage is lower than that shown by the Hythe skulls and compares unfavourably with the high figures (80.6 per cent for males and 72.2 per cent for females) which examination of the Australian aborigines reveals. Loss of teeth before death does not necessarily mean caries. We have already mentioned the prevalence of scurvy and of the less obvious pre-scorbutic conditions in England during these centuries. It is not surprising, therefore, to find numerous references to loosened teeth in contemporary medical books. Other dental troubles are seldom mentioned but now and again one comes across a remedy to be inserted in a hollow tooth to relieve the pain. One passage taken from Paul Hentzner's account of his visit to England in 1598 suggests that bad teeth were fairly common at that time among those who could afford to indulge a taste for sweetmeats. He gives a good description of the visit of Queen Elizabeth to the Royal Palace of Greenwich, when he had a close view of her. He remarks on her hooked nose, her narrow hips and, particularly, on her black teeth, with the comment that it was a 'defect the English seem subject to, from their too great use of sugar'.[1] It rather looks as if this was a popular view, even at this date, and that it had arisen from the observation that the rich suffered more than the poor and that an obvious difference between their diets was the relatively large amount of sweetmeats which the former could afford.

> The immoderate vse thereof, and also of sweet confections and sugar-plummes, heateth the blood . . . rotteth the teeth, maketh them look blacke.[2]

The only quantitative information we have about the incidence of caries is that derived by Sir Frank Colyer from the study of material dug up from a burial ground in the City of London, most of which dates from the seventeenth and early eighteenth centuries.[3] He estimated that the skulls had originally held just over 6800 teeth, of which nearly 3500 were *in situ*, while another 2500 had been lost after death. This shows that about 15 per cent of the teeth had been lost during life. Of the surviving teeth some 10 per cent were carious, but this figure is not a true indication of the distribution because of 103 bad teeth in skulls with mandibles attached no less than 50 were present in 4 specimens. It is not easy to compare these figures with modern estimates, because the latter are based almost exclusively on the examination of young children, but they indicate very strongly that caries was much less common in the seventeeth century than it is today, when it is

---

[1] *A Journey into England*, 1598, Paul Hentzner, translated by Horace Walpole, 1757.
[2] KΛINIKH, *Or The Diet of the Diseased*, James Hart, 1633.
[3] *Dental Record*, 1922, Vol. XLII.

quite usual to find 60 per cent or more of the teeth of the children of poorly nourished families affected with caries.

Glisson seems to have been the first to suggest that the teeth might be affected by conditions which produce rickets. He thought that the distortion and the swellings of the bones which develop in bad rickets were due to unequal nutrition of the bones.

> For they spring from the unequal nourishment of the parts which is a Symptom of the first essence of this Disease.[1]

He was very near to the truth but it was many years before anyone followed up the clue.

§7 RELATION OF STATURE TO BONE GROWTH

Our height is determined almost entirely by the extent to which the long bones of our limbs grow before they become fully calcified. The deposition of hard mineral salts does not take place uniformly throughout such bones in the early stages of growth. If it did we should find that our bones, and therefore our limbs, ceased to grow in length quite early in youth. The rounded ends of the long bones, which form the units of the joints, consist of hard caps, which begin to calcify quite early in life, but which are not firmly united to the shaft of the bone itself until maturity is reached. During growth there is a narrow zone just behind each of these terminal caps and separating it from the main part of the shaft which has already become hardened. This zone consists of uncalcified bone-matrix and grows lengthwise. As new matrix is formed part of that next to the shaft calcifies and so the length of the bone slowly increases. Sooner or later, however, some influence, the nature of which is as yet unknown, causes the intermediate zone to ossify. When this occurs growth is retarded and it ultimately ceases when complete calcification of the intermediate zone firmly unites the cap to the shaft. It was Stephen Hales, Vicar of Teddington and friend of Horace Walpole, who first demonstrated these facts about the growth of long bones.

> As I was assured by the following Experiment, *viz.* I took a half-grown Chick, whose leg-bone was then two inches long; and with a sharp-pointed iron, at half an inch distance, I pierced two small holes thro' the middle of the scaly covering of the leg and shin-bone; two months after I killed the Chick, and upon laying the bone bare, I found on it obscure remains of the two marks I had made at the same

[1] *A Treatise of the Rickets ... by Francis Glisson, Enlarged ... by Nich. Culpeper, 1651.*

distance of half an inch: So that part of the bone had not at all distended lengthwise, since the last time I had marked it: notwithstanding the bone was in that time grown an inch more in length, which growth was mostly at the upper end of the bone, where a wonderful provision is made for its growth at the joining of its head to the shank.[1]

Although we do not know what mechanism comes into play in normal conditions to cause the cessation of growth in man we do know that two of the ductless glands, the pituitary which lies underneath the centre of the brain, and the parathyroids which are found in the neck in close proximity to the thyroid, can affect the growth of bone. Over-activity of the pituitary may cause unusual growth in the long bones and 'giantism' while a deficiency is the chief cause of 'dwarfism'. To what extent the small stature of the African pigmy tribes is due to an unusual glandular balance is not known.

Defective diet is often responsible for short stature. When growth is retarded by vitamin or mineral deficiencies during childhood the long bones usually become wholly calcified before a normal height for the age is reached. Nothing can be done about such cases once the calcification of the bones is complete. Drill and exercises may teach them to stand more erect, but their true height remains unchanged. On the other hand, a great deal can be done to stimulate growth in ill-nourished individuals before the age at which the bones become fully hardened. In such cases good food or making good the deficiencies of their ordinary diet will usually produce a surprising spurt of growth.

There is ample evidence in support of the view that improvements in diet and standard of living, hygiene and medical care increase speed of growth, but no adequate data to show whether speed of growth influences final height or merely the age at which maximum height is reached.

There is a popular belief that we are today taller, on the average, than were the men who repelled the Armada or fought the Dutch. It seems to be based on the statement that suits of armour of these periods would be found too small for the average man today — though a suit of armour which Henry VIII carried was built for a man of 5 ft. 10 in. A possible explanation is that small suits of armour take up less storage space than large ones and have been kept preferentially for exhibition. Measurements of the leg bones from seventeenth-century burial grounds, for example, those of the population of Hythe between 1250 and 1650, and those given by a few estimates of the stature in man in pre-historic England suggest an average adult male height of about 5 ft. 6 in. The most recent large-scale report for Great Britain gives for 1943 an average height for men of about 5 ft. 7 in. at 20-25 years,

[1] *Statical Essays*, Stephen Hales, 3rd Edition, 1738.

falling to 5 ft. 5 in. to 6 in. at 60 to 70 years.[1] This does not suggest any marked change over the centuries, though differences depending on social class, place of origin and mortality rates have been frequently reported. In a recent review[2] the conclusion is reached that in Britain our information is inadequate to show whether the mean maximum stature of the population has increased over the last century or not, though the authors do cite records from Sweden and Denmark which support the view that mean maximum height in those countries has risen with improved social conditions.

[1] 'Weight and Height of a Population in 1943', W. F. F. Kemsley, *Annals of Eugenics* (1950), XV, 161.
[2] 'Secular Changes in the Height of British Adults', A. W. Boyne and I. Leitch, *Nutrition Abstracts and Reviews* (1954), XXIV, 255.

PART THREE

THE EIGHTEENTH CENTURY

CHAPTER IX

RISE OF ENGLISH AGRICULTURE

§1 A CENTURY OF CONTRAST

WHEN Queen Anne came to the throne the long struggle for the supremacy of the seas which we had waged with varying success since the pioneer days of Drake and Hawkins was nearly over. The once great power of Portugal and Spain was little more than a memory. The French were badly crippled after the treaty of Utrecht in 1713. The Dutch were being outmanœuvred and outrivalled on every trade route. Everywhere overseas our merchants were in the ascendancy; at home our industries were developing rapidly. For the first fifty years of the century fortune smiled on most of the people of England.

In the whole half century the years of wet summers, droughts and bad harvests can be counted on the fingers of one hand. Corn was cheap, the average price over the whole period being about 33s. a quarter, and the cost of living in relation to wages was favourable to a steady rise in the general standard of living. All the staple foods were plentiful and cheap. The wages of labourers and the less highly skilled workmen ranged from 7s. to 9s. a week during the first half of the century.[1] Although they were very little higher than they had been nearly a century before they represented a greatly increased purchasing power because of the fall in price of the principal food-stuffs. Meat, which had been 5d. or 6d. a pound, could be bought for 2d. or 3d., cheese was seldom more than 2d. a pound, a chicken cost about 3d., a rabbit 4d., butter was cheap at 5d. or 6d. a pound and a penny bought a large wheaten loaf.[2] A rise in the standard of living of the working people was favoured not only by the cheapness of food but by the appearance on the market of the products of the new industries, many of which, such as cheap fabrics and candles, were within the reach of their purses. Only one class of the community did not fare well in the early years of the century, the smaller tenant farmers. They were feeling the effects of a rather long period of low returns and many of them fell on very bad times and were forced to give up their farms.

The condition of the people generally steadily improved during the first half of the century. There was plenty of work both on the land and in the

[1] *A History of Prices*, Thomas Tooke, 1838-57.
[2] *A Collection of Bills, Accounts and Inventories*, edited by J. O. Halliwell, 1852.

towns, where the new industries were developing apace; indeed, there were times when labour was scarce in the countryside because of the steady drift to the towns. The improvement in the conditions of living of the country people was particularly striking. They were assured of work and with food so cheap they were able to buy meat several times a week. Once again the villagers, or at any rate a considerable proportion of them, were able to keep a cow, a pig or two, and a few ducks or chickens. To some extent 'white meats' came back to their tables. They were, too, more fortunate than the town workers in possessing gardens in which they could cultivate a variety of vegetables unknown to the peasants of an earlier generation. The towns-man did not, in fact, envy the villagers' 'white meats' and vegetables; he felt himself to be far superior because his wages allowed him to buy surprisingly large amounts of butcher's meat.

The turn of the century saw England a contented and prosperous or, as one contemporary writer expressed it, an 'opulent' country.[1] The picture changed soon after the accession of George III. The rapid growth of popu-lation was beginning to make heavy demands on the production of corn. The expansion of agriculture might for a time have relieved the situation had it not been for a disastrous sequence of wet seasons and bad harvests extend-ing from 1764 to 1775. Naturally the price of wheat soared and the prices of other foodstuffs tended to follow suit. In 1765 there was a grave dearth. In 1776 the quartern loaf touched the unprecedented figure of 1s. 6d.[2] The position was made worse by the many bad harvests experienced at this time on the Continent. This explains why the suspension of the duty on imported corn, as for example in 1772, did so little to ameliorate the state of affairs. Things went rapidly from bad to worse. The wars with America and France and the apprehension regarding the financial security of the country all tended to keep prices high. The good harvests of 1778-79 might have brought improvement had it not been for the unhappy chance that the price of silver had fallen sharply as a result of developments in the American mines about 1770. In 1793 there were poor crops and an acute financial crisis. Two years later the position was even worse and when the century closed a large proportion of the population was facing dearth, depression and distress. The only prosperous people at this period were the big farmers and the great landowners, who were reaping the benefits of the abnormally high prices.

We learn from Arthur Young's accounts of his tours in 1768 to 1771 that the price of many staple foods had risen sharply after the turn of the century. About 1770 the cheaper meats cost from 3½d.-4½d. a pound, cheese was about

---

[1] *Characteristics of the Present Political State of Great Britain*, R. Wallace, 1758.
[2] *A History of Prices*, Thomas Tooke, 1838-57.

the same price, butter from 6d.-8d. a pound and milk cost ½d. a pint. In the large towns prices were higher. In London, for example, meat cost 4d.-5d. a pound, while not many miles away it could be bought for 3½d.-4d. Again, the Londoner had to pay 8d. a pound or more for his butter.

The series of County Surveys made by the Board of Agriculture in 1793-94 show that prices had continued to rise, although the difference between the average figures for the ordinary foodstuffs at this time and those of twenty years previously are not so striking as one would expect from the outcry which was heard all over the country against the dearness of food. On the other hand, there is evidence that many of the staple foods were dearer than the county reports indicate, at any rate in the manufacturing towns. Trussler goes out of his way to draw attention to the serious rise in prices which he noted between the appearance in 1787 of the first edition of his book *The Way to be Rich and Respectable, addressed to Men of Small Fortune,* and the second edition of 1796. During these nine years the quartern loaf had risen from 7½d. to 1s. 1½d., sugar from 10d. to 1s. 2d. a pound, butter from 9d. to 1s. 2d. a pound and meat had reached the high figure of 8d. a pound.

The poor people did not get much sympathy in their distress. Many of the wealthy classes shared the views expressed by Arthur Young.

> Some years ago, they could buy bread and beer, and cheese, &c. &c. much cheaper than they can *at present,* while their earnings were the same. What was the effect of such cheapness? If the present *dearness* is so afflicting, sure the former good times were attended with no trifling effects? Instead of laying up three or four pounds; they then, doubtless, saved twice as much! No such matter; whatever was gained by such cheapness, was constantly expended by the husband in a proportionable quantity of idleness and ale, and by the wife in that of tea.[1]

Many of the landowners looked upon the village ale-houses as nothing more nor less than a nuisance.

> Those only ought to be suffered that are absolutely necessary for the accommodation of travellers.[2]

§ 2 THE AGRICULTURAL REVOLUTION

A remarkable agricultural revolution occurred in the eighteenth century, the influence of which on our history was quite as great as that of the

[1] *The Farmer's Letters to the People of England,* Arthur Young, 3rd Edition, 1771.
[2] *General View of Agriculture (County of Gloucester),* G. Turner, 1794.

industrial revolution which was so striking a feature of this period. The movements were, of course, related. The rapid growth of the towns and of the population and the rising prosperity during the first half of the century enormously increased the demand for food, and particularly for wheat and fresh meat. The poorer people were no longer content to eat dark rye breads and salt meat. They had formed a taste for fine wheaten loaves and fresh meat.

> The ploughman, the shepherd, the hedger and ditcher, all eat a white bread as is commonly made in London, which occasions the great consumption of wheat.[1]

Arthur Young commented disgustedly that 'Rye and barley-bread, at present, are looked upon with a sort of horror, even by poor cottagers.'[2]

The farmers increased the land under wheat and the size of their herds and flocks. After 1750, when prices began to rise, there was an even greater inducement for them to increase both land and cattle. This was largely responsible for the wave of 'enclosing' which swept England under the Georges, and which shattered once and for all the simple economic structure of English village life.

§ 3 ENCLOSURES

The amount of land enclosed in the first fifty years of the century was not large. In the twelve years of Queen Anne's reign only about 15,000 acres, covered by two Acts of Enclosure, were taken. It was very different after the middle of the century. While George III was on the throne more than three million acres were filched from the people. The villagers were helpless. It is true that they had the right to lodge an objection to a proposed enclosure and that there were certain rights of appeal, but of what value were such rights when it was possible, at any rate before 1774, for a landowner who wished to acquire more land to submit a petition for its enclosure, to have it made the subject of a Bill and to get it legalized before his neighbours, rich or poor, had heard a word about it? Even when an appeal was lodged, and there are many of these pitiful petitions on record, the childlike pleas and arguments of the simple country people stood no chance against the wiles and artifices of the lawyers representing a governing class cynically indifferent to the rights of the poor man.

A typical appeal is that made by a Northamptonshire community in 1797.

---

[1] *The Gentleman's Magazine*, 1776.
[2] *The Farmer's Letters to the People of England*, Arthur Young, 3rd Edition, 1771.

... the Petitioners beg Leave to represent to the House that, under Pretence of improving Lands in the said Parish, the Cottagers and other Persons entitled to Right of Common on the Lands intended to be inclosed, will be deprived of an inestimable Privilege, which they now enjoy, of turning a certain number of their Cows, Calves, and Sheep, on and over the said lands; a Privilege that enables them not only to maintain themselves and their Families in the Depth of Winter, when they cannot, even for their Money, obtain from the Occupiers of other Lands the smallest Portion of Milk or Whey for such necessary Purpose, but, in addition to this, they can now supply the Grazier with young or lean Stock at a reasonable Price to fatten and bring to Market at a more moderate Rate for general Consumption, which they conceive to be the most rational and effectual Way of establishing Public Plenty and Cheapness of Provision; and they further conceive, that a more ruinous Effect of this Inclosure will be the almost total Depopulation of their Town, now filled with bold and hardy Husbandmen.[1]

It was indeed a rare event for the land to be saved for those who lived by it and whose forefathers had tilled it for centuries past. But while many who had the welfare of the poor at heart deplored the change, it was not only the greedy landowners and complaisant lawyers who furthered the movement. Many saw in it a change for the better so far as the good of the country as a whole was concerned and not a few felt that the clear need for greater agricultural production could only be met by an expansion of the estates farmed by men with capital and enterprise.

Sir John Sinclair, first President of the Board of Agriculture, who made sincere if laboured efforts to improve farming practice in England, expressed this point of view in a speech made to members of the Board.

The idea of having lands in common, it has been justly remarked, is to be derived from that barbarous state of society, when men were strangers to any higher occupations than those of hunters or shepherds, or had only just tasted the advantages to be reaped from the cultivation of the earth.[2]

Even Arthur Young thought that the small, inefficient farmer should be eliminated. In Yorkshire he noted that 'the farmers are a poor wretched set of people' and that their husbandry was 'universally bad'. He added:

If it be demanded, how such ill courses are to be stopped: I answer, Raise their rents. First with moderation; and if that does not bring

[1] *Journal of the House of Commons*, June 19th, 1797.
[2] *Address to the Members of the Board of Agriculture on the Cultivation and Improvement of the Waste Lands of this Kingdom*, 1795.

forth industry, double them: But if you would have a vigorous culture go forwards, throw 15 or 20 of these farms into one, as fast as the present occupiers drop off. This is the only means in such cases to improve husbandry, and consequently to promote population.[1]

In another outburst in favour of driving the inefficient farmer out of business by ruthlessly raising his rent, Young said:

> He [the landlord] need not say in an arbitrary manner, *You shall pay me so much more rent, or quit;* but make it conditional, *You shall pay me 2s. an acre more than at present, till I ride over your farm, and find not an anthill left.*[2]

How successful such methods proved can be judged by reading some of the County Surveys published by the Board of Agriculture. The report on the County of Dorset drawn up by John Claridge states that the situation of the poor labourer is very bad since the large farms have swallowed up the smaller ones. It was true that, apart from often being unable to afford to make changes, the villagers and small farmers were backward in their outlook and reluctant to adopt the new agricultural methods which were coming into use. The majority of the big landowners, on the other hand, were progressively minded and anxious to get better yields of crops and improved breeds of cattle. From this point of view the Georgian enclosures must be regarded as beneficial to the development of English agriculture, but they brought desolation to the villages. Everything was lost, the arable land, the grazing for the cottagers' cows, the scrub where they collected their winter fuel, sometimes even their little garden plots.

There was a striking depopulation of the villages, the most important cause being the attraction of the towns where the growth of industry was calling for more and yet more labour. Another cause was the distress and unrest resulting from the enclosures. The terrible depression of the countryside has been immortalized by Oliver Goldsmith in the *Deserted Village*, in which he described what he himself had seen.

> I have taken all possible pains in my country excursions, for these four or five years past, to be certain of what I allege, and ... all my views and inquiries have led me to believe those miseries real, which I here attempt to display.[3]

---

[1] *A Six Months Tour through the North of England*, Arthur Young, 2nd Edition, 1771.
[2] *The Farmer's Tour through the East of England*, Arthur Young, 1771.
[3] *Deserted Village*, Oliver Goldsmith, 1769 (Dedication to Sir Joshua Reynolds).

§ 4 EXPERIMENTAL AGRICULTURE

This period marks the turning point of English agriculture. In scarcely more than a century farming methods advanced from a state little less primitive than that of the Middle Ages to something not greatly inferior to those in use today. There is hardly a year that is not marked by a useful invention, the introduction of a new crop, an improved method of cultivation or the breeding of a more valuable strain of livestock. It was a remarkable period of agricultural enterprise, linked for ever with the names of Jethro Tull, Charles ('Turnip') Townshend, Coke of Norfolk, Bakewell and Arthur Young, to mention a few of the more outstanding.

Of considerable importance was the influence of an organization founded in 1754 under the name of the Society for the Encouragement of Arts, Manufactures and Commerce, better known today as the Royal Society of Arts. Although an interest in agriculture was not contemplated when the Society was first founded it developed so rapidly that within ten years it overshadowed every other activity. Widespread interest was aroused by the articles in *Museum Rusticum et Commercial* (1764-66) and by Robert Dossie's *Memoirs of Agriculture and other Oeconomical Arts* (1768-82), periodicals in which the Society published their communications before the appearance of their own journal. In addition to publishing this information the Society sponsored innumerable experiments with new crops, land drainage and schemes for afforestation; the latter was then very much in the air owing to a fear that the timber for the Navy was running short. Valuable prizes were offered to the winners of competitions for the design of drills, reapers and other machines.

At the same period there was a steady flow of information from the pen of Arthur Young. The volumes in which he described farming practice in various parts of England provided a wealth of valuable advice for the progressive farmer.[1] In 1784 he began to publish his famous *Annals of Agriculture*, which had a wide circulation. Of the 46 volumes which appeared before failing eyesight forced him to cease publication in 1809, more than a quarter were written by Young himself. It was undoubtedly as a result of his activities that the Government were induced to take an active part in fostering agriculture. In the face of considerable opposition the Board of Agriculture was established in 1793 with Sir John Sinclair as President. Arthur Young was appointed Secretary at a salary of £400 a year.

---

[1] *A Six Weeks Tour through the Southern Counties of England and Wales*, 1768; *A Six Months Tour through the North of England*, 1769; *The Farmer's Tour through the East of England*, 1771.

§ 5 RISE OF WHEAT

The most striking feature of agricultural development in the eighteenth century was the enormous increase of the acreage under wheat.[1] Early in the century the south of England grew about 60 per cent wheat, 20 per cent barley and 20 per cent rye; the north roughly a third each of wheat, rye and oats. By 1750 little rye was grown in the south and the percentage of wheat had risen to 75. At the end of the century the south grew 80 per cent wheat and 20 per cent barley; the north 50 per cent wheat and about 25 per cent each of barley and oats.

One of the most unexpected changes was the amount of wheat grown in East Anglia, where for centuries the light soil had been held to be unsuitable for this crop. Thomas Coke was largely responsible for this conversion. When he succeeded to Holkham in 1776 not only was there no wheat grown from there to King's Lynn but the farmers were convinced that it was impossible to grow it. Ten thousand quarters were imported annually to Wells. By the end of the century, largely as a result of Coke's enterprise and tireless efforts, this part of Norfolk was beginning to be known as the 'Granary of England'.[2]

In spite of increased acreage under wheat and enlarged yields, the population was increasing so rapidly by the end of the eighteenth century that supplies did not keep pace with the numbers to be fed and England ceased to be a wheat-exporting country. It has been estimated[3] that at the end of the century the average consumption of wheat per head was about two-thirds that at the beginning.

§ 6 TURNIPS

It has already been stated that turnips were grown as a root crop in the latter part of the seventeenth century, sheep being folded on to the land on which they were growing. The popularity of the roots grew rapidly in the eighteenth century. Defoe remarked, during his tour of England in 1722, on the extent of their cultivation and their suitability for fattening cattle.[4] It did not take agriculturists long to realize that they would make excellent winter fodder for cattle. Jethro Tull (1674-1741), who devised the first practicable field drill, is sometimes given the credit for being the first man to

---

[1] The subject is very fully discussed by Sir William Ashley in his interesting monograph *The Bread of Our Forefathers*, 1928.
[2] *Coke of Norfolk and his Friends*, A. M. W. Stirling, 1908.
[3] *The History and Social Influence of the Potato*, R. N. Salaman, 1949.
[4] *A Tour thro' the Whole Island of Great Britain*, Daniel Defoe, 1724-27.

advocate their use in this manner, but it seems that his interest was more closely connected with their value as a field crop for sheep. One of the earliest references in English agricultural literature to the use of turnips as a winter food for cattle is in William Ellis's *The Practical Farmer or the Hertfordshire Husbandman* (1732). He speaks of the value of hay, grains and malt dust and says 'raw turnips, chopt or whole, are given by some'. It had for many years been the practice in Holland to store roots as winter food for beasts.

> We usually feed cattle with straw in racks in the yard, or turn them to the fields ... But in *Holland* they do thus: ... for the winter-provision. They lay in not only *Hay*, but also grain, which they buy in summer and bury in the ground; and also *Rape-seed*-cakes, and sow *Turnips* not only for themselves but for their cows also. They slice the *Turnips* and their tops, and with *Rapeseed*-cakes and grain, they make meshes for their cows, and give it them warm, which the cows will slop up like hogs; and by this means they give much milk.[1]

For a long time turnips were the only roots grown in England for cattle feeding. They seemed to provide a complete solution of 'a WINTER PABULUM (as it was called by the gentleman who set on foot this matter) for CATTLE'.[2]

§ 7 OILCAKE

Another discovery, made by the Dutch farmers, was that cattle would eat and thrive on the residues left after the oil had been expressed from crushed rape seed. The oil was prepared in Holland in considerable quantities at that time for use as an illuminant. The attention of the English farmers was drawn to the value of this 'cake' in an early number of the *Museum Rusticum et Commercial*. The advantages of the new type of food were so obvious that others of the same nature were sought. In 1783 the Society of Arts offered a prize for a method of extracting the oil from cottonseed in such a way that a press-cake suitable for the winter feeding of cattle would be left. Not long afterwards linseed 'cake' was tried and proved to be a success. By the end of the century a considerable number of farmers were using these 'concentrates'.[3]

[1] *A Treatise concerning the Husbandry and Natural History of England*, Sir Richard Weston, 1742.
[2] *Memoirs of Agriculture and other Oeconomical Arts*, Robert Dossie, 1768.
[3] *Annals of Agriculture*, Arthur Young, 1794.

M

§ 8 SWEDES, BEETS, ETC.

The popularity of the turnip paved the way for other root crops. The swede, or as it was at first called the 'turnip-rooted cabbage', was brought to England from Holland in 1755 and quickly became popular. The mangel wurzel did not appear until twenty years later and it is interesting that a mistranslation of its original German name was partly responsible for its introduction. This cultivated variety of the sea-beet (*Beta maritima*) had been grown in north Germany and Holland for a century or more under the name *mangold-wurzel* or, as we should call it, beet-root. Its cultivation spread to northern France where in the terrible 'eighties it was often the only food the half-starved peasants could get. Confusion between the German words *mangold* (beet) and *mangel* (dearth) led to the root being given what was thought to be the French equivalent of the original name, i.e. *racine de disette*. During the periods of dearth in England in the latter part of the eighteenth century it was suggested that this crop should be grown in order to provide cheap food for the hungry people. At a meeting of the Society of Arts in 1787 a letter on the virtues of the *racine de disette* was read by Boothby Parkyns and seeds were distributed by Sir R. Jebb.[1] The general impression was that the roots were unpalatable and more suited for feeding animals than men. Even with farmers they did not immediately become popular — probably the false name was partly responsible — but early in the nineteenth century they were being grown fairly extensively for cattle.[2]

§ 9 POTATOES

The potato did not win popularity in England as easily as it did in Ireland, where by the end of the seventeenth century it had become the staple food of the peasantry. At the beginning of the eighteenth century it was rarely found in England (apart from certain districts in the north-west where its cultivation had spread as a result of contact with Ireland) outside the gardens of big houses. Several popular books on gardening published at this period make no reference to the common potato,[3] but a little later R. Bradley in his *General Treatise of Husbandry and Gardening* (1726) drew attention to the merits of the tubers and wondered at the scant use made of them.

---

[1] *Journal of the Society of Arts*, 1787, Vol. II.
[2] *The History of the Royal Society of Arts*, Sir H. Trueman Wood, 1913.
[3] *The Compleat Gard'ner*, M. de la Quintinye, abridged and improved by G. London and H. Wise, 2nd Edition, 1699; *The Retir'd Gardener*, G. London and H. Wise, revised by Joseph Carpenter, 1717.

And considering how much Profit they bring to a Family, I wonder they are not more generally propagated in the poorer parts of our Country.

Twenty years later the same writer remarked:

... they are cultivated pretty plentifully about *London*, but are not I think got enough into the Notion of our Country People, considering their Profit.[1]

Salaman[2] has shown that potato cultivation developed much more rapidly north than south of the Coal Line and was firmly established in the north by 1770. Elsewhere the potato was regarded with much prejudice, white bread being commonly considered a greatly superior food.

It is odd how great a prejudice there was against potatoes in southern England. It took Coke more than seven years to satisfy the slow-moving East Anglian farmers by his own experiments that the Norfolk soil was eminently suited to their cultivation.[3] Probably it was the demonstration of their value in fattening cattle which finally won over the majority of the farmers, and once again we have to thank Arthur Young, who had been greatly impressed on his Irish tour by the way in which the peasants fattened their hogs on half-boiled potatoes, using the smaller ones, together with cabbage leaves and hay, as winter food for their cows.[4]

In 1794 the weather was disastrous and the country suffered one of the worst harvests ever recorded with the result that the price of wheat rocketed. The quartern loaf having cost 4½d. to 6d. between 1750 and 1764, rose to 7d. or 8d. between 1765 and 1794 and then to 12¼d. in 1795, 13d. in 1799, 14¾d. in 1801 and 17d. (the highest price ever recorded in this country) in 1812.[5] The newly created Board of Agriculture was not altogether unprepared for this crisis, Sir John Sinclair and his energetic Secretary, Arthur Young, having had a survey made of the agricultural and industrial state of the country. This and other activities culminated in 1795 in the issue of a series of well-informed articles on the potato[6] and in considerable efforts to persuade the people to substitute potatoes for bread,[7] efforts which seem to have been received by the population in much the same way as were their counterparts in the Second World War.

[1] *A Dictionary of Plants*, R. Bradley, 1747.
[2] *The History and Social Influence of the Potato*, R. N. Salaman, 1949.
[3] *Coke of Norfolk and his Friends*, A. M. W. Stirling, 1908.
[4] *A Tour in Ireland made in the Years 1776-7 and 1768*, Arthur Young, 1780.
[5] *The History and Social Influence of the Potato*, R. N. Salaman, 1949.
[6] Ibid.
[7] *Report of Committee of the Board of Agriculture concerning the Cultivation and Use of Potatoes*, 1795.

§ 10 CLOVER AND CABBAGES

Clover, sanfoin and similar crops gained steadily in popularity throughout the century, as their value in feeding cattle became recognized. In 1771 Young spoke of clover as 'one of the pillars of good husbandry', at the same time remarking that 'it has not been able to make its way through all the counties'.[1]

The use of cabbages as a field crop for feeding cattle seems to have spread southwards from Scotland and the north of England. Young commented very favourably on the crops of the 'great *Scotch* cabbage' he had seen in Yorkshire and other northern counties,[2] and he did much by his writing to encourage its introduction in the south. By the end of the century cabbages were grown in practically every part of England.

§ 11 MARKET GARDENING

The variety of vegetables which had been introduced into England in the seventeenth century together with the rapid growth and prosperity of the towns in the eighteenth century favoured the development of market gardening. There is ample evidence that a rapid expansion of this branch of gardening took place during the century under review. It started in the south and was particularly noticeable in the multiplication of market gardens in the vicinity of the quickly growing London. As late as 1742 the ignorance of the art of gardening in the north and west was a matter for comment.

> I could instance divers other places both in the North and West of *England*, where the name of Gardening and Howing is scarcely known; in which places a few Gardeners might have saved the lives of many poor people, who starved these dear years.[3]

But it is equally clear that vegetables had not long been grown in the south.

> Some old men in *Surrey*, where it flourishes very much at present, report. That they knew the first Gardeners that came into those parts, to plant *Cabbages* and *Cauli-flowers*, and to sow *Turnips, Carrots* and *Parsnips*; to sow Raith (or early ripe) *Rape, Pease*; all which at that

---

[1] *The Farmer's Tour through the East of England,* Arthur Young, 1771.
[2] *A Six Months Tour through the North of England,* Arthur Young, 2nd Edition, 1771.
[3] *A Treatise concerning the Husbandry and Natural History of England,* Sir Richard Weston, 1742.

time were great rarities, we having few or none in *England*, but what came from *Holland* or *Flanders*.[1]

Before long, however, every large town had its belt of gardens which supplied the markets with vegetables and fruit. Young described those at Lewisham and Blackheath which supplied the market in Spitalfields. Peas, beans, potatoes, carrots, celery, cabbages, cauliflowers and savoys were among the vegetables grown. To the east of London, at Wanstead and Ilford, there were farms, rented for the most part by Irishmen, which specialized in potatoes. Apparently it was the Irish who started the cultivation of potatoes for the London markets.

It was once very common to have all the potatoe-grounds belonging to them, but of late the farmers have got pretty much into the culture themselves.[2]

Arthur Young was impressed with the novel idea of growing garden vegetables as field crops. He mentioned Mr 'Scroope' [Scrope] of Danby, who drilled single rows of onions, 'endiff', beans, cos-lettuce, cauliflowers and carrots, 'a proof, says this gentleman, that garden-stuff may be cultivated to a greater perfection in the fields than in the garden'.[3]

It is interesting that the surveyor for the County of Lancashire thought that the excellent vegetable market at Liverpool had developed as a result of the influx in 1756 of French Canadians, who demanded cheap vegetables for their soups. In 1793 potatoes were sold there for about 6d. a peck and carrots for 2s. 6d. to 3s. a hundredweight.

The London markets received large supplies of fruit from the Kentish orchards which expanded rapidly during this century. The produce was sold to London factors and transported by water. In 1794 apples fetched from 7s. to 8s. a sack, while filberts cost from 16s. to as much as 42s. a 'hundred' of 104 pounds.[4] Some of the fruit was sold to local 'higglers' who did a good business at the new watering places in the Isle of Thanet. There were many complaints about the high cost of provisions in these towns 'in the bathing season, owing to the great influx of company'.[5]

Another interesting development of market gardening which occurred late in the century was the introduction of rhubarb. The Society of Arts presented a number of prizes and medals to encourage its cultivation.

[1] Ibid.
[2] *A Six Weeks Tour through the Southern Counties of England and Wales*, Arthur Young, 3rd Edition, 1772.
[3] *A Six Months Tour through the North of England*, Arthur Young, 2nd Edition, 1771.
[4] *A General View of the Agriculture of the County of Kent*, John Boys, 1794.
[5] Ibid.

§ 12 LIVESTOCK

The advances in animal husbandry during this century were almost as striking as those made in arable farming. The turning point was the solution of the problem of keeping livestock in health throughout the winter. When it was no longer necessary to thin out the herds by slaughtering in the late autumn, and when there was a reasonable chance that a valuable animal would survive the winter without degenerating into a physical wreck, it was worth while to spend money on improving the breeds. At this time English agriculture became famous for the enormous prices paid for pedigree animals, a development which is associated with the name of Bakewell.

CHAPTER X

EIGHTEENTH-CENTURY FOOD

§ 1 FOOD IN THE TOWNS

THE rapid growth of the towns revealed the defects of the existing means of transport. Food was required by the townspeople on a scale which would not have been credited a century before. In the early years the roads throughout the country were in a terrible condition. Few of them were better than deeply rutted tracks, ankle deep in dust in summer and veritable bogs in winter. Over such roads the food came slowly to the towns, the grain in creaking carts dragged by labouring teams, the cattle driven stage by stage, day by day, over distances of a hundred miles or more. The London meat markets received regular supplies by road from as far afield as N. Wales and Yorkshire, and even poultry was brought to London on foot from Norfolk and Suffolk.[1] The turn of the century saw some improvement, the Turnpike Acts of George III's reign enabling a good many of the main roads to be put into a state of repair and, incidentally, providing a considerable amount of employment. Arthur Young, however, seems to have been but little impressed by the result of these activities; a few stretches, he noted, had a good surface, but 'as to all the rest, it is prostitution of language to call them turnpikes; I rank them nearly in the same class, with the dark lanes from *Billericay* to *Tilbury* fort'.[2]

It is not surprising, therefore, that food was often unfit for consumption when it did at length reach the towns; Defoe speaks of the consignments of 'stinking' fish which had been brought by road from the east coast.[3] About the middle of the century an attempt was made by an enterprising individual called Blake to set up in Broadway, Westminster, a market for fresh fish, which was to be kept supplied from the coast by a speedy system of specially designed 'land carriages'. Ostensibly his aim was to break the ring of fishmongers who were suspected of keeping up the price of fish. By harping on this aspect of the scheme he succeeded in obtaining enthusiastic backing from the Society of Arts and later from the Government. His supporters even went so far as to put through a Bill reducing the toll charges on the carriage of fresh fish. It does not appear that the scheme benefited anyone

[1] *A Tour thro' the Whole Island of Great Britain*, Daniel Defoe, 1724-27.
[2] *A Six Weeks Tour through the Southern Counties of England and Wales*, Arthur Young, 3rd Edition, 1772.
[3] *A Tour thro' the Whole Island of Great Britain*, Daniel Defoe, 1724-27.

except Blake; he received a gold medal inscribed 'Fish Monopoly Restrained' from the Society of Arts, and, it is suspected, something a good deal more substantial out of the sums of money, running into several thousands of pounds, granted him for the development of his schemes by Parliament and the Society.[1]

Arthur Young was very scornful about the 'land-carriage fish-scheme'.

> Of what good was the lowering the price of fish at *London*? Did the *Spittlefields* manufacturers [workmen] eat one pound the more? No, but the nobility, gentry, merchants, and tradesmen; and let me add the country gentlemen; who came to town to spend their rents, in the vain frippery of the capital, purchased it the cheaper.[2]

The transport problem was eased in the second half of the century by the considerable construction of canals, which provided a much more rapid form of transit than the roads. There is a suggestion of a modern advertisement for air travel in the arguments in their favour brought forward by a supporter of the project, launched in 1758, for the construction of the Duke of Bridge-water's Navigable Canal. Speaking of the wonderful system of canals in Holland he says:

> An inhabitant of Rotterdam may hereby breakfast at Delft or the Hague, and dine at Leyden; he may sup at Amsterdam, and return home again before night.[3]

There is indisputable evidence that a marked deterioration occurred in the eighteenth century in the quality of many foodstuffs, particularly those likely to be bought by the poorer people. It can to some extent be ascribed to the rapid commercialization of the trade in food which developed with the growth of the towns, and for this reason it was noticeable even in the first half of the century when the country as a whole was prosperous. It became much more striking, and its effects much more serious, when the dearth and high prices of the second fifty years brought greater temptation to the unscrupulous.

§ 2 DETERIORATION IN THE QUALITY OF BREAD

The inhabitants of the towns, with the exception of those in the north, would eat nothing but fine wheaten bread.

[1] *The History of the Royal Society of Arts*, Sir H. Trueman Wood, 1913.
[2] *The Farmer's Letters to the People of England*, Arthur Young, 3rd Edition, 1771.
[3] *The History of Inland Navigation*, John Phillips, 1792.

They eat no Bread of Wheat and Rye, but as our Steward says, as white as any Curd.[1]

This change of taste had important consequences in the latter half of the century, when there were several periods of shortage of corn, because the townspeople were reluctant to accept inferior grades of bread. A French visitor, M. Grosley, was greatly impressed by the fine quality of the bread sold in London at a time of serious shortage.[2]

On three occasions, from 1756-58, 1772-74 and 1795-1800, Parliament authorized the sale of a 'Standard' bread, stamped with a capital S, which contained a higher proportion of bran, and was therefore darker in colour, than the ordinary white wheaten bread. It was usually 1d. cheaper than the wheaten loaf, but it was by no means popular;[3] nor did the people take at all kindly to the admixture of rye, barley, oats and potatoes with wheaten flour which the serious scarcity of the late 'nineties sometimes made necessary.[4]

The public demand for white flour was undoubtedly responsible for the great increase in the addition of alum to bread, for this chemical has the effect of increasing the size and at the same time improving the texture and colour of a loaf baked from inferior flour. Nothing could have been more suitable for the millers and bakers. The public suspected, however, that other materials were being employed for 'improving' the quality of bread, and not unnaturally they thought of chalk, whiting and similar substances.[5]

Matters came to a head during the years of shortage 1756-58. An anonymous pamphlet was published in 1757 entitled *Poison Detected: or Frightful Truths: and Alarming to the British Metropolis*. It dealt mainly with the adulteration of bread but it also drew attention to the colouring of tea with copperas, the sophistication of wine and the use of acids or other unwholesome materials in the preparation of beer. As regards bread and the alleged practices of the millers it was indeed a hair-raising document. Alum, 'a very powerful stringent and styptic, occasioning heat and costiveness', was the least harmful of the ingredients which, it was asserted, were commonly added to flour to 'improve' the quality of the bread. The author, who hid his identity under the *nom de plume* 'My friend, a Physician', claimed to have himself seen 'lime and chalk in the proportion of one to six' extracted from bread. Nor was this the worst.

[1] *The Rake's Progress, or the Humours of Drury Lane, a complete Key to the eight prints of Mr. Hogarth*, 1753.
[2] *A Tour to London*, M. Grosley, translated by T. Nugent, 1772.
[3] The public dislike of Standard bread in the eighteenth century may be compared with their descendants' disapproval of 'war bread' in 1918 and the outcry against national bread when it first appeared in the Second World War.
[4] *A Friendly Address to the Poor of Great Britain in the Present Scarcity of Wheaten Bread*, T. Tapwell, 1796; *Tracts on Scarcity*, 1792-1800, British Museum.
[5] Chalk (*creta praeparata*) is now added to all flour at the rate of 14 oz. per 280 lb. flour as part of the Government's nutritional policy to increase the calcium content of the diet.

Nor are alum, lime and chalk the only pernicious mixtures employed by the artifices of the bakers to abuse the people with; there is another ingredient, which is more shocking to the heart, and if possible more hurtful to the health of mankind: it must stagger human belief; I shall only just mention it, to make it abhorred. It is averred by very credible authority, that sacks of unground bones are not unfrequently used by some of the bakers amongst their other impurities, to increase the quantity, and injure the quality of flour and bread. The charnel houses of the dead are raked to add filthiness to the food of the living.

Was it surprising, he added, that the children of the cities were for the most part 'pale, puny, lingering and sickly?'

There is evidence from Dr Filby's studies[1] that the author of this pamphlet was Dr Peter Markham, who later openly took part in the controversy.

Meanwhile the charges against the millers and bakers were repeated and elaborated in *The Nature of Bread, Honestly and Dishonestly Made*, written in the same year by another doctor, Joseph Manning, M.D. He described the detection of chalk and bone-ash in the sediment deposited when bread was stirred up with water, and hinted at the extensive use of even more sinister ingredients than those previously described, including one 'that the Physician will know what he means, when he says its Quality is Suffocation'. He would not describe it more fully lest it teach those 'who with sufficient Wickedness are deficient in Knowledge'. He stated, however, that he had actually separated it from bread and that he might 'produce it before those who have Authority to punish'. It seems certain that he was hinting at the use of white lead.

The millers and bakers were not long in putting up a spirited counter-attack. 'Sampson Syllogism, a Baker' led off with his *Modest Apology in Defence of the Bakers* (1758), an amusing satire on the arguments which Markham and Manning had employed. The author of *Poison Detected* had rather laboriously proved, to his own satisfaction, that the population of London had fallen from nearly two million souls 'a few years ago' to less than a million as a result of the loss of life consequent on eating adulterated breads. 'Sampson Syllogism' pointed out that this was all to the good: with fewer people there would be less illness, less vice and more employment. Whiting, ground bones and alum would, therefore, benefit mankind and actually alleviate famine by reducing over-eating.

A more serious counter-attack came from the pen of a Bristol writer, Emmanuel Collins. The title, *Lying Detected; or, some of the Most* frightful *Untruths that ever alarmed the British Metropolis* (1758) is an obvious parody

[1] *A History of Food Adulteration and Analysis*, F. A. Filby, 1934.

of Markham's work. Collins started by saying that surely adding bones to bread is an old-established custom.

> Fe, Fa, Fum.
> I smell the Breath of an English Man,
>   Be he alive, or be he dead,
> I'll grind his Bones to make my Bread.

He adds:

> Can any Thing be plainer than this now! You see that Bones were not only human Food, but brave, stout, strong Food, even the Food of Giants.

But he soon passed to a more serious vein. The Law stands ready. If Dr Manning knows that the millers use these dreadful ingredients why does he not charge them openly?

> If this be true, if you can prove this, as you say you easily can, why don't you do your County Justice by bringing these *Miscreants* to the Bar? Convict but one Man and we will believe all you have said; but till you have done that, we shall place you in very unhappy light.

Nevertheless the charges were repeated in a publication entitled *Syhoroc* signed by Peter Markham, which gives an account of 'ten ingredients' used by the millers; only six are mentioned in *Poison Detected*. The descriptions of the four new substances are as vague as were Manning's; for example, he speaks of 'an alcali of a very firy exalted violence'. Markham alleged that these harmful substances had been found in sackfuls by the indignant mobs who broke into the premises of millers suspected of using them. A more plausible story is that of the merchant whose sales of alum rose by over a ton during a period when bread was dear.

It is a relief to turn from these biased and distorted views to a publication called *An Essay on Bread; wherein the Bakers and Millers are vindicated from the Aspersions contained in Two Pamphlets*, written by 'H. Jackson, Chemist' in 1758. It is a remarkable little volume of fifty-five pages which deals in a judicial manner with the evidence for and against the bakers and millers and describes tests for the adulteration of bread and other foodstuffs. It marks the beginning of our modern knowledge of the chemical detection of food adulteration.

Jackson showed how fantastic were many of the charges brought against the millers and bakers. Their use of alum he wisely did not attempt to deny; it would have been useless to do so, for there is no doubt that it was widely employed in the towns. But, as he pointed out, it was most unlikely that the trade would use whiting, chalk or bone-ash, for not only were they very easy of detection, but, an even more convincing argument, they actually reduced the size and impaired the texture of loaves; it was a fallacy to suppose that bread could be made whiter by their use. He was withering about Manning's vague references to the use of sinister poisons.

Unfortunately Jackson's honest examination of the matter did not stop the scandal. A shocked public firmly believed that their flour was mixed with dead men's bones and that the millers and bakers were a set of rascals. The controversy dragged on for some fifty years or more and much the same charges were being brought against the millers and bakers in the early part of the nineteenth century. Smollett's Matthew Bramble says:

> The bread I eat in London is a deleterious paste, mixed up with chalk, alum, and bone-ashes; insipid to the taste and destructive to the constitution. The good people are not ignorant of this adulteration; but they prefer it to wholesome bread, because it is whiter than the meal of corn. Thus they sacrifice their taste and their health, and the lives of their tender infants, to a most absurd gratification of a misjudging eye; and the miller or the baker, is obliged to poison them and their families, in order to live by his profession.[1]

§ 3 MEAT

The towns required large quantities of meat. The beasts came slowly by road, being sold from fair to fair, until at last they reached the butchers. Whereas in the past there had been a falling off both in quantity and quality during the winter owing to the difficulties of feeding, in the eighteenth century it became increasingly easy for the markets to get supplies throughout the year. Moreover, the introduction of turnips and cabbages had made it possible for beasts to be specially fattened for sale in the towns.

In London the important meat markets were those of St James's, Clare Market, Newgate and Leadenhall.[2] It has been estimated that for the first fifty years of the century something like seventy-five or eighty thousand head of cattle came annually to the London markets by road and that the number was nearer a hundred thousand as the century closed.[3] Professor Skreel has traced the journey of cattle coming from Anglesey to London; they were made to swim across the Menai Straits and then driven to Abergele Fair. From there their purchasers drove them to Barnet Fair where they were re-sold and kept in the vicinity of London until they were sufficiently fattened for the city markets.[4]

[1] *The Expedition of Humphrey Clinker*, T. Smollett, 1771.
[2] *The London Adviser and Guide*, Rev. Dr Trusler, 1786.
[3] *Eighteenth Century Traffic in Livestock*, G. E. Fussell, *Economic History*, 1936, Vol. III.
[4] *Transactions of the Royal Historical Society*, 1926, 4th Series, IX.

It is difficult to say whether these markets were an improvement on those of the previous century. Probably, as in earlier days, a good deal of the meat was tainted before it was sold. M. Grosley, a French visitor, was disappointed by the quality of the meat sold in the London shops, which apparently had a great reputation abroad. He thought it inferior, on the whole, to that sold in Paris.[1] Matthew Bramble was disgusted by the mutton sold in St James's Market.

> ... which, in fact, is neither lamb nor mutton, but something betwixt the two, gorged in the rank fens of Lincoln and Essex, pale, coarse, and frouzy.[2]

And there is a slightly sinister implication behind Dr Trusler's advice to 'Young People' on their behaviour at table; they are warned to refrain from 'smelling to the meat whilst on the fork'.[3]

Poultry was also dealt with by the meat markets. It was now fully established as a luxury and enormous numbers of hens were fattened for the table by feeding them in coops, a practice which Smollett condemned.

> ... the poultry is all rotten, in consequence of a fever occasioned by the infamous practice of sewing up the gut, that they may be the sooner fattened in coops, in consequence of this cruel retention.[4]

§4 FISH

This century saw the rise of the great fish market at Billingsgate. From earliest times fish had been sold in the streets in the vicinity but in 1699 the site was declared a 'free and open market'. Larger quantities of 'fresh' fish were sold than formerly, some of it having been brought seventy or a hundred miles by road from the coast. It was often in such a state when it arrived that, as Smollett says, it would have turned a 'Dutchman's stomach, even if his nose was not saluted in every alley with the sweet flavour of "fresh" mackerel, selling by retail'.[5] It was probably because mackerel went bad so quickly that it was permitted to 'cry' it in the streets on Sundays before 9 a.m. and after 4 p.m. This order also applied to milk.[6]

Oysters were still plentiful and not too expensive; in 1701 200 could be

---

[1] *A Tour to London*, M. Grosley, translated by T. Nugent, 1772.
[2] *The Expedition of Humphrey Clinker*, T. Smollett, 1771.
[3] *The Honours of the Table for the Use of Young People*, Rev. Dr Trusler, 1788.
[4] *The Expedition of Humphrey Clinker*, T. Smollett, 1771.
[5] Ibid.
[6] *The London Adviser and Guide*, Rev. Dr Trusler, 1786.

bought for 4s.[1] In London they were sold, together with gilt gingerbread, from hucksters' barrows in the streets.[2] If we can believe Smollett they were sometimes given the green colour which appealed to the connoisseur by keeping them for some days in 'slime-pits' covered with 'vitriolic scum'.[3]

§5 VEGETABLES AND FRUIT

If one can generalize from conditions in the London markets the quality of the garden produce offered for sale in the towns was far from good. There is a hint in Arthur Young's *Six Weeks Tour through the Southern Counties of England and Wales* that the barges which took vegetables to the London market returned laden with the contents of the London cess-pools. Certainly the market gardens around the metropolis took large quantities of excrement and 'night-soil' from the city. Trusler warns 'persons used to the country' that they 'will not relish the vegetables and fruit generally sold in London'.[4] Much of the produce was sold in the streets from barrows, and he advised people who wanted good fruit and vegetables to make their own arrangement with a market gardener or to go to Covent Garden where although the prices might be high the quality was on the whole satisfactory. Oranges, lemons and other fruits were sold in the streets from 'moveable shops that run upon wheels, attended by ill-looking Fellows'.[5] It is not surprising that Matthew Bramble felt a bit squeamish about the wares of the coster-mongers.

> It was but yesterday that I saw a dirty barrow-bunter in the street, cleaning her dusty fruit with her own spittle; and who knows but some fine lady of St. James's parish might admit into her delicate mouth those very cherries which had been rolled and moistened between the filthy, and perhaps ulcerated, chops of a St. Giles's huckster?[6]

During this century the London markets, and to a certain extent those of the other big towns, began to receive increasingly large supplies of fruit from foreign sources. Regular shipments of 'Lisbon, China Oranges and Sower Oranges' and lemons were landed. They were not particularly cheap, the price being about 2d. to 3d. each early in the century and somewhat higher later on.[7] The West Indies began to send limes, which proved

[1] *A Collection of Bills, Accounts, and Inventories, 1650-1750*, edited by J. O. Halliwell, 1852.
[2] *The London Spy, by the Author of A Trip to Jamaica* [Edward Ward], 1703.
[3] *The Expedition of Humphrey Clinker*, T. Smollett, 1771.
[4] *The London Adviser and Guide*, Rev. Dr Trusler, 1786.
[5] *The London Spy* [E. Ward], 1703.
[6] *The Expedition of Humphrey Clinker*, T. Smollett, 1771.
[7] *A Collection of Bills, Accounts and Inventories, 1650-1750*, edited by J. O. Halliwell, 1852.

popular as an ingredient for punch, and bananas, which were seldom eaten raw, being usually baked in tarts or boiled in dumplings.[1]

Vegetables came almost entirely from the market gardens which formed a ring round most of the towns. There is little doubt that the common vegetables were very cheap in the first half of the century. Potatoes could be bought in London for 4d.-6d. a peck,[2] and a cabbage for a halfpenny. Tucker remarked in 1748, just before the period of rising prices, 'But the Price of Garden Stuff is prodigiously sunk to what it was in former Times'. He doubted whether 'any Town of note... can now vie with the Common Markets of *London* in that *Respect*'.[3]

Prices rose after 1750 but in 1770 it was still possible to buy a large white-heart cabbage 'dressed', in Spitalfields Market, for 1¼d. or 1½d.[4] Potatoes seem to have been about 7d. a peck; later they probably became more expensive but records of prices are lacking.

Grosley did not think very highly of the English vegetables. As a Frenchman they struck him as expensive and of indifferent quality.

> All that grow in the country about London, cabbage, radishes, and spinnage, being impregnated with the smoke of sea-coal, which fills the atmosphere of that town, have a very disagreeable taste... I ate nothing good of this sort in London, but some asparagus.[5]

§6 DAIRY PRODUCE

The supply of milk to the towns was almost indescribably bad. Some of it came from farms in the vicinity and this was probably tolerable, although by the time it was retailed much of it must have been nearly sour and in a condition which would have driven a modern dairy bacteriologist frantic. The greater proportion was provided by cows kept in the towns; the wretched beasts were herded together in dark sheds or hovels, standing ankle deep in filth and fed on little besides hay and brewers' grains. Some-times the cows were driven round the streets, the milk being sold straight from the udder. This way of buying milk was popular in the West End of London because it lessened the risk of getting watered milk, which was almost inevitable if one dealt with the milk-women.[6] The best milk in London was

[1] *English Society in the 18th Century*, J. B. Botsford, 1924.
[2] *A Collection of Bills, Accounts and Inventories, 1650-1750*, edited by J. O. Halliwell, 1852.
[3] *Tracts on Political and Commercial Subjects*, J. Tucker, 3rd Edition, 1776.
[4] *A Six Weeks Tour through the Southern Counties of England and Wales*, Arthur Young, 3rd Edition, 1772.
[5] *A Tour to London*, M. Grosley, translated by T. Nugent, 1772.
[6] *The London Adviser and Guide*, Rev. Dr Trusler, 1786.

that obtained direct from the cows grazing in St James's Park, which was usually drunk on the spot.[1] Asses' milk still had a great reputation as a food for invalids and young children, and London was not unfamiliar with the sight of these animals being driven from door to door and stopping at intervals to be milked.[2]

The quality of the milk hawked in the streets of London must have been appalling and there is no reason to think that Smollett was exaggerating when he wrote:

> But the milk itself should not pass unanalysed, the produce of faded cabbage-leaves and sour draff, lowered with hot water, frothed with bruised snails; carried through the streets in open pails, exposed to foul rinsings discharged from doors and windows, spittle, snot, and tobacco quids, from foot-passengers; overflowings from mud carts, spatterings from coach-wheels, dirt and trash chucked into it by roguish boys for the joke's sake; the spewings of infants, who have slabbered in the tin-measure, which is thrown back in that condition among the milk, for the benefit of the next customer; and, finally, the vermin that drops from the rags of the nasty drab that vends this precious mixture, under the respectable denomination of milkmaid.[3]

The report on the County of Lancashire which John Holt drew up at the request of the Board of Agriculture contains an account of the new 'lactometer' invented by Mr Dicas which it was proposed to use for 'determining the goodness of milk'. This was the prototype of the lactometer used in every dairy today to determine the specific gravity of milk.

In London milk was fairly cheap in the first half of the century, at about a penny a quart, but the price rose later until in 1780 it was as much as 3½d. or 4d. It was always a good deal cheaper in the north of England than in the south. Whey and buttermilk were popular drinks, both being sold in the streets of London. Bristol received large quantities of buttermilk in barrels from South Wales; it cost about a halfpenny a quart.

The rise of the gentleman farmer enormously increased the production of milk in the country. As there was in most cases a very small local market for the milk most of it was converted into cheese and butter, the buttermilk and whey being used for feeding pigs.[4] The butter and cheese were sent to the towns and the consumption of both rose sharply during the century, particularly during the first fifty years. London got most of its butter from

[1] *A Journey to England*, C. P. Moritz, 1782, cited in *The British Tourists; or Traveller's Pocket Companion*, W. Mavor, 1798-1800.
[2] *Eighteenth Century London*, R. Bayne-Powell, 1937.
[3] *The Expedition of Humphrey Clinker*, T. Smollett, 1771.
[4] *Eighteenth Century Milk*, G. E. Fussell, *Economic History*, 1937, Vol. III.

Yorkshire and East Anglia. Young estimated the amount from these areas at 210,000 firkins in 1786, i.e. just over 5000 tons. Most of it came by sea and was sold by the butter merchants of Clare Market. The cheaper grades were not infrequently rancid and Smollett speaks of 'butter served out by the gill, that tasted like train-oil thickened with salt'.[1] The Londoner had a particular fancy for butter made in the vicinity of Epping and 'Epping-butter' commanded a good price. In the latter half of the century the home production was insufficient for the demand and considerable quantities were imported from Ireland.

A very large amount of cheese came to London from Cheshire and the cheesemongers of London formed a combine which ran a fleet of no less than sixteen ships between London and Liverpool. The organization had factors all over the West Country and maintained warehouses at Chester.[2]

It was during this century that the townsman, and particularly the Londoner, came to know the many different types of cheese produced in various parts of the country. Formerly they had only been known locally or to the wealthy man who could afford to have them specially sent to him. With improved sea and road transport, but more particularly after the canals had simplified the movement of perishable foods, these cheeses began to appear in the shops of all the principal towns. By the end of the century it is quite common to find references to Gloucester, Double Gloucester, Cheddar, Wiltshire and Stilton cheeses, which a generation before had been little known a hundred miles outside their own locality. Cheshire cheese was, towards the end of the century, often coloured artificially with 'Spanish Arnotta' (*anatto*).[3]

§7 THE ADULTERATION AND CONTAMINATION OF FOODS

The pioneer food adulteration studies of the chemist Jackson[4] showed that a great deal of vinegar was adulterated or faked. Vitriolic acid (sulphuric acid) was the most common substitute for the natural preparation and dilute solutions of oil of vitriol coloured with burnt sugar or infusions of oak-chips were widely sold as vinegar. Jackson devised a test of a roughly quantitative nature for the detection of sulphuric acid in vinegar.

In 1755 a pamphlet by an anonymous author was published, called *Serious Reflections on the Dangers Attending the Use of Copper Vessels*. It pointed out that copper from cooking vessels was often dissolved by the

[1] *The Adventures of Roderick Random*, T. Smollett, 1748.
[2] 'The London Cheesemonger of the 18th Century', G. E. Fussell, *Economic Journal*, 1928.
[3] *A General View of the Agriculture of the County Palatine of Chester*, Thomas Wedge, 1794.
[4] *An Essay on Bread*, H. Jackson, 1758.

N

acid juices of fruits and vegetables, and by butter. This the author rightly regarded as highly dangerous.

> The matter, which Copper throws out, is Verdigrease, a rank caustic Salt; in plain Terms, a Poison!

A much more serious matter was the addition of copper salts to improve the colour of green vegetables, an obnoxious practice to which Jackson drew attention.

> The prodigious Consumption of Pickles in the Navy, as well as in private Families, has induc'd the Wholesale Dealers to give them an enticing Green Colour by various fraudulent Arts; Verdigrease and Blue Vitriol [copper sulphate] are previously dissolv'd by some, for this Purpose.[1]

He also maintained that cooks were in the habit of pickling vinegar in copper vessels in order that a green colour might be imparted to the vegetables.

He employed a simple test to detect dissolved copper by putting a knife-blade into the pickles and looking for the reddish deposit of metallic copper. Falconer later made a series of experiments and by using the ironwire test he showed that certain vegetables, of which cabbage was one, were more prone to become contaminated by being cooked in copper or brass pans than others. Fruit juices, especially lemon juice, dissolved quite large amounts of the metal.[2] Jackson, who was a very careful observer, warned those who wished to make pickles not to employ glazed earthenware vessels because of the possibility of lead being dissolved from the glazing.

§8 SPIRITS, WINE AND BEER

There was a great deal of heavy drinking among all classes of the community in the eighteenth century, particularly in London and other rising centres of industry. The chief cause of the trouble was the unrestricted sale of cheap 'gin' and other forms of raw, crude spirit. During the first fifty or sixty years things came to such a pass that there were not a few level-headed people who feared that the social structure of the country was being undermined.

The sale of ale and beer had long been under control. As far back as the reign of Edward VI it had been made illegal to sell these drinks except at licensed houses and in 1700 there was in force an Act of Charles I which

[1] Ibid.
[2] *Observations and Experiments on the Poison of Copper*, William Falconer, 1774.

inflicted a penalty of 20s. for selling ale, beer, perry or cider except at such places. There was no such restriction on the sale of spirits, and as the duty on these drinks was a mere 2d. a gallon they were absurdly cheap. Before the century was very old gin-shops were springing up in every part of London, and, what was even worse, it was possible to buy 'gin' at hundreds and hundreds of 'dives' and cellars in all the back streets and alleys. As in the prohibition days in Chicago or New York, it was only necessary to take a few steps to find a convenient 'speakeasy'. It has been stated that about 1750 every fourth or fifth house in some of the worst areas, such as the slums of St Giles, sold 'gin'.

It has been estimated that the consumption of real gin, that is spirit on which duty had been paid and which was probably more or less drinkable, rose from half a million gallons in 1700 to more than five million gallons in 1735, when the authorities began to take steps to check the evil. It is impossible to form any estimate of the enormous consumption of illicit liquor, much of which was terrible stuff, distilled from any rubbish that would ferment.

Driven by a rising tide of protest to do something the Government raised the taxation on spirits in 1736. It was a half-measure and did little more than arouse widespread wrath leading to rioting; a mob smashed the windows of the house of Sir Joseph Jekyll, who was held responsible. By the middle of the century gin-drinking was causing untold misery and ill-health and thousands of deaths. The terrible picture which Hogarth's 'Gin Lane' reveals is no exaggeration in the light of what contemporary writers have said. Henry Fielding's words can be taken as an example.

> The drunkenness I here intend is that acquired by the strongest intoxicating liquors, and particularly by that poison called *gin*: which I have great reason to think, is the principal sustenance (if it may be so called) of more than a hundred thousand people in this metropolis. Many of these wretches there are who swallow pints of this poison within the twenty-four hours: the dreadful effects of which I have the misfortune every day to see, and to smell too.[1]

It was in this year, 1751, that the authorities took more drastic measures to check the evil. Taxation was raised, this time substantially, and some efforts were made to suppress the preparation and sale of illicit spirits. It is possible to get an idea of the sort of stuff which the less reputable gin shops sold by glancing at some of the recipes which were published quite openly. Here is one, by no means one of the worst.

[1] *An Enquiry into the Causes of the late Increase of Robbers, etc.*, H. Fielding, 1751.

Oil of vitriol [sulphuric acid]
Oil of almonds
Oil of turpentine
Spirits of wine
Lump sugar
Lime water
Rose water
Alum
Salt of tartar.[1]

The increased taxation and the other measures did something to check the growth of the evil.

The custom of the common peoples' drinking great quantities of a most inflammatory and *poisonous* liquor, certainly created an incredible devastation amongst the children of the Poor till the hand of Providence interposed, by the instrumentality of His Majesty's ministers, to avert the dreadful progress of it.[2]

It was, however, the sharp rise in the price of grain and other fermentable material that ultimately brought about a big reduction in the preparation of cheap spirits. The public, of necessity, returned to beer and other cheaper and healthier drinks.

Beer, commonly call'd Porter, is almost become the universal Cordial of the Populace, especially since the necessary Period of prohibiting the Corn-Distillery; the Suppression presently advanc'd the Price of that common Poison Gin, to near three times its former Price, and the Consumption of Beer has kept Pace with such advance.[3]

One of the most striking changes of the time was the rapid rise in the consumption of tea by all classes, both in town and country. The growing popularity of tea was a source of considerable anxiety to the brewers who were obliged, in order to compete with it, to brew weaker beer and to keep their prices as low as possible.

A few Years ago, a *Winchester* Quart of old sound Porter, would yield near six Ounces of good proof Spirits by a Careful Distillation; but the Beer brew'd lately, will not yield four Ounces of the same Proof: whether this be owing to the Avarice of the Brewer, or the Quality or Scarcity of the Malt, is not very pertinent to the Subject.[4]

[1] *The Publican's Daily Companion*, P. Boyle (undated, probably 1794).
[2] *A Candid Historical Account of the Hospital for the Reception of Exposed and Deserted Young Children*, by Airon [Jonas Hanway], 1759.
[3] *An Essay on Bread*, H. Jackson, 1758.   [4] Ibid.

Much of the small beer, that is the table beer drunk at every meal, had an alcohol content as low as 2-3 per cent, whereas that of beer brewed in the preceding century rarely fell below 4-5 per cent.

It is interesting to note that, in spite of the competition first from gin and then from tea, many of the large breweries which have since become world-famous date from this period.

> Mr. Meux, of Liquorpond-St, can shew twenty-four tuns; containing in all, thirty-five thousand barrels ... Other great breweries possess corresponding grandeur.[1]

The practice of brewing at this period is very fully described in a book entitled *The London and Country Brewer* which first appeared in 1738 and proved so popular that several editions were brought out before 1800. The anonymous author, who stated that he had been '*formerly concerned in a Publick Brewhouse*', claimed to have written it for the enlightenment of a public which had for a long time past 'suffered great Prejudices from un-wholsome and unpleasant Beers and Ales, by the Badness of Malts, Under-boiling of Worts, Mixing injurious Ingredients, the Unskilfulness of the Brewers'. He is revealing on the subject of the variety of undesirable ingredients used by unscrupulous brewers. '*Coculus India Berry*', that is the seeds of *Cocculus indicus*, a poisonous drug used in Italian medicine, was apparently quite extensively employed to impart a bitter flavour and a 'heady' character to weak beers. The stupefying effect it produced was due to the action of a poisonous compound, *picrotoxin*. Coriander seeds, less harmful than cocculus, were often relied on to give flavour to thin or 'off beers', and capsicum (red pepper) was added to give the mixture 'strength' and 'bite'.[2]

Some of these additions were prohibited by Acts of Parliament passed in the reign of George III but it is doubtful whether such measures did much to check the adulteration of beer. The small brewers were probably the worst offenders and the temptation to water, to brew 'thin', or to adulterate was greatest towards the end of the century when the price of corn was so high. Complaints about the quality of the beer brewed at this time were frequent and widespread. Five bushels of malt were made to serve where eight had formerly been used; 'thin' beers were 'bittered' with the 'baneful drug' (*Cocculus indicus*); tobacco and liquorice were used to give a dark, rich colour. These were some of the charges brought against the brewers.[3]

[1] *A Tour of London*, Thomas Pennant, 1780, cited in *The British Tourists; or Traveller's Pocket Companion*, W. Mavor, 1798-1800.
[2] *The Publican's Daily Companion*, P. Boyle, 1794 (?).
[3] *The Crying Frauds of London Markets proving their Deadly Influence upon the Two Pillars of Life Bread and Porter*, by the Author of the *Cutting Butchers Appeal*, 1795.

It is possible by reading a book of the type of *The London and Country Brewer* to get a clear idea of how great an element of chance there was in brewing at this date. The practice was carried out by rule of thumb methods and the brewers were at a loss to explain why one brew kept quite well while another turned acid, cloudy or 'ropy'. They were, of course, entirely ignorant of the fact that these changes were due to the growth of organisms, and all kinds of recipes were suggested for preventing and curing these 'diseased' beers. Some of them could scarcely be regarded as innocuous. 'An ounce of Allum very fine' mixed with 'two Handfuls of Horse-bean Flour' would 'cure a Butt of fox'd, or ropy Drink'. One addition suggested for 'curing' cloudy beer, 'Chemical Oil of Sulphur', is interesting because the sulphites which would have been present in this preparation would have had a marked bactericidal action.

What were known as 'Balls' were extensively used to preserve beer in casks. There are many recipes for making them and one recommended by the author of *The London and Country Brewer* can be given as an example.

> Alabaster, or Marble calcined to a Powder, two Pounds. Oyster-shells, a little calcined and freed from their brown, or dirt-coloured Outside, one Pound. Pure fat Chalk, well dried, one Pound. Horse-bean Flour, first freed from the Hulls, one Pound. Red Saunders, four Ounces. Grains of Paradise, half an Ounce. Florentine Orrice-root, half an Ounce. Coriander-seeds, a quarter of an Ounce. Cloves, in number, six. Hops, half an Ounce. The best Staple incised Isinglass, two Ounces. The first Runnings of the Molosses or Treacle, two Pounds.

Six dried 'Balls' were dropped into each barrel and well stirred in. The calcined marble, shells and chalk served to neutralize acidity as it developed, the bean-flour and isinglass helped to clear or 'fine' the beer, carrying down impurities to form a sludge at the bottom of the cask, while the coriander, orris-root, cloves, etc., imparted a flavour which would help to mask the earthy taste caused by the addition of so much lime.

The use of too much isinglass and flour was, however, apt to cause beer to go 'flat', so some brewers added what were known as 'headings'. A popular one was 'green vitriol commonly called copperas or salt of Iron'.[1] Another was a mixture of alum and copperas. They were guaranteed to produce a 'Head like a Collyflower'.[2] The chemist Jackson, who roundly denounced the addition of 'alkaline salts, soaplese and calcarious salts' for reducing the acidity of beers, described a useful and simple test for detecting the addition

---

[1] *Every Man his Own Brewer*, Samuel Child (undated, probably 1795-1800).
[2] *An Essay on Bread*, H. Jackson, 1758.

of copperas. A decoction of galls was added to the beer; if a black colour was produced the sample was known to be adulterated.[1]

Cider was still popular, particularly in the West Country, but it fell under a cloud following the revelation that it might be responsible for lead poisoning if, as often happened, it came in contact with the metal. A distinguished medical man, Sir George Baker, himself a Devonian, drew attention to the danger of using lead pipes and vessels in the preparation of cider and thereby brought upon himself the charge of being a disloyal son of his native county. Jackson also stressed the risk of poisoning from particles of lead dissolved in cider which had been stored in vessels made from this metal.

Powdered calcined alabaster or marble dust was sometimes added to cider to reduce its acidity but this was a relatively innocuous method of making it less sharp in taste. Other methods were more dangerous and one which, it is true, was more widely practised on the Continent than in England, included the addition of 'sugar of lead'. This substance is highly poisonous but it has a distinctly sweet taste which would to some extent counteract the sharpness of an acid cider or wine. It had been found by experience that when these liquids were stored in leaden or pewter vessels they tended to become considerably sweeter.

There is abundant evidence that the cheaper wines were grossly adulterated and that there was considerable manufacture of faked wines. Smollett, through the mouthpiece of Matthew Bramble, condemned:

> ... the intoxicating potion sold for wine ... a vile, unpalatable, and pernicious sophistication, balderdashed with cider, corn-spirit, and the juice of sloes.[2]

The methods for preparing these crude mixtures were frankly described in a book called *The Retail Compounder and Publicans Friend* by John Hardy (undated, probably 1794). Colour was provided by burnt sugar, sassafras, logwood, cochineal, turnsole, blackberry juice, etc., flavouring by orange peel and *terra japonica*, sweetness by sugar, and astringency by hops or oak-chips. Anything from a Malmsey to a hock could be compounded on the basis of a thin solution of spirit of wine. A good deal of the latter was prepared by fermenting molasses, imported from the West Indies. Crude wines were 'molified' by adding alum and rendered less sour by plaster of Paris and chalk.[3]

Thomas Pennant has left a description of a large factory for faking wines of a better class, which was owned by Mr Mark Beaufroy and situated near

[1] Ibid.
[2] *The Expedition of Humphrey Clinker*, T. Smollett, 1771.
[3] *Valuable Secrets Concerning the Arts and Trades*, Anonymous, 1795.

the Cuper's gardens, a recreation place of ill-fame on the south side of the Thames. The raw material employed was dried grapes or raisins and the process consisted in soaking them and then allowing the juice to ferment. The faking came in when 'by a wonderous magic' the product of the fermentation was skilfully converted into 'almost every species of white wine'. One of the tuns at this factory held no less than 56,749 gallons and was, therefore, more capacious than the famous 'Tun of Heidelberg'.[1]

The most dangerous form of sophistication was the addition of lead. Sometimes, as we have already said, 'sugar of lead' was added for the purpose of sweetening a sour wine, and one book recommended the addition of a pint of good wine vinegar saturated with litharge (lead oxide) to each hogshead of wine.[2] Lead preparations were also believed to be helpful in clearing a muddy white wine.[3] The merchants claimed that no trace of metal passed into the wine but they were soon proved wrong when the first reliable chemical tests were devised.[4] It then became clear that the worst fears of Dr Richard Mead,[5] Sir George Baker, and others who had drawn attention to the grave risk of lead poisoning were justified, and that many deaths must have resulted from this cause.

Very large quantities of wine, both good and indifferent, were imported and it is interesting to note in the lists of this period a number of wines which are rarely met with in England today. The Portuguese table wines, Bucellas, Colares and Calcevella,[6] for example, were quite extensively drunk although we are told now that they will not travel. Other names unfamiliar today are Sheraaz, Lunel, Zante and Lissa.

Brandy, which came into use in England in the seventeenth century, became a favourite drink with the middle and upper classes and was consumed by them in large quantities. The Hon. John Byng noted in his diary:

> ... I give sufficient encouragement to the French, by a consumption of their Brandy, of which I commonly call for a Pint per Diem.[7]

The annual importation, legal or illegal, from France was considerable but a great deal of the faked spirit still widely known as 'British Brandy' was sold. Byng protested at this stuff being offered to him in a country inn.

[1] *A Tour of London*, T. Pennant, 1780, cited in *The British Tourists*, W. Mavor, 1798-1800.
[2] *Valuable Secrets Concerning the Arts and Trades*, Anonymous, 1795.
[3] *The Art of Making Wines from Fruit, Flowers, and Herbs*, W. Graham, 1770.
[4] *Description of a Portable Chest of Chemistry*, J. F. A. Göttling, 1791.
[5] *A Mechanical Effect of Poisons*, Dr R. Mead, 1702.
[6] This is probably a corruption of Carcavellos, one of the well-known wine-growing districts of Portugal.
[7] *The Torrington Diaries*, Vol. IV, 1781-94, edited by C. Bruyn Andrew, 1938.

I must send decent liquor to these inns, else when I am tired, and faint, I am forc'd to drink British spirits call'd brandy — or medicated sloe juice call'd port.[1]

Rum, imported in large quantities from the West Indies, was also very popular. Faked rum was made from cheap spirit coloured and flavoured with molasses.

The control of the strength of alcoholic liquor was greatly simplified by the invention of a practical form of hydrometer by an instrument maker called Clarke.[2] It was similar in form to the hydrometer in use today but was made of copper. The stem bore three marks, one representing the depth to which the instrument would sink in 'proof' spirit and the other two one-tenth above and one-tenth under 'proof' respectively. Other forms of hydrometer were soon devised, that of Dicas (1780) attracting most attention. The invention was a very important one and most of the books on brewing and the wine trade published late in the century refer to the use of one or other form of hydrometer.

§9 TEA

No change in the habits of the English is more striking than the adoption of tea-drinking by all classes. Tea had been steadily becoming cheaper towards the end of the seventeenth century as imports from the East increased, and the trade expanded enormously after 1700. In that year about 20,000 lb. was imported; within ten years this figure was trebled. In 1715 the market was flooded with Chinese green tea and in 1760 duty was paid on over five million pounds. By the end of the century the amount imported was over twenty million pounds, that is, about 2 lb. per head of the population. In addition to these official figures we have to allow for the amount which was brought into the country as a result of a brisk smuggling trade with France. It was estimated that in 1766 as much reached England illegally as came through the proper channels.

This change in habit surprised everybody and disturbed not a few. Some people feared that tea would supplant ale and beer. In 1744 Duncan Forbes wrote:

But when the opening a Trade with the *East-Indies* . . . brought the Price of Tea . . . so low, that the *meanest* labouring Man could compass the Purchase of it; — when the Connection which the Dealers in this Country had with many *Scotsmen* in the Service of the *Swedish* Com-

[1] Ibid.   [2] *Philosophical Transactions of the Royal Society, 1729-30*, Vol. XXXVI.

pany at *Gottenburg*, introduced the common Use of that Drug amongst the *lowest* of the People; — when *Sugar*, the inseparable Companion of *Tea*, came to be in the Possession of the very *poorest* Housewife, where formerly it had been a great Rarity, — and thereby was *at hand*, to mix with Water and Brandy, or Rum; — and when Tea and Punch became thus the *Diet* and *Debauch* of all the *Beer* and *Ale* Drinkers, the effects were very *suddenly* and very *severely* felt.[1]

Eden writes in much the same terms:

Any person who will give himself the trouble of stepping into the cottages of Middlesex and Surrey at meal-times, will find, that, in poor families, tea is not only the usual beverage in the morning and evening, but is generally drank in large quantities at dinner. Whether this exotic is more palatable or more nutritious than home-raised barley converted into broth, I leave to Medical Gentlemen to determine.[2]

The amount spent on tea by working-class families was considerable. The family budgets given by Eden show that it was not uncommon for two pounds a year to be so spent when the total income was only a matter of forty pounds a year, and Arthur Young expresses surprise that the inmates of the Nacton House of Industry, who were allowed to spend 2d. out of every shilling they earned on food, almost invariably bought tea and sugar with this money.[3]

Many people thought the increasing use of this 'deleterious produce of China'[4] was undesirable but some writers went so far as to express the view that it was a pernicious drug. One of the most vehement attacks came from Jonas Hanway. 'When will this evil stop?' he asked, after pointing out that no less than four million pounds had been imported a year or so before he wrote. 'Your very *Chambermaids* have lost their bloom, I suppose by *sipping tea*.' And after an equally violent attack on gin he added 'What an *army* has *gin* and *tea* destroyed!'[5]

There were others who believed that tea, being an infusion of a herb, possessed medicinal value.

. . . and with drinking of Tea only, and regular living, the Distemper of England [Scurvy] occasioned by our too much feeding upon Flesh, may be cured.[6]

[1] *Some Considerations on the Present State of Scotland*, Duncan Forbes, 1744.
[2] *The State of the Poor*, Sir Frederic Eden, 1797.
[3] *The Farmer's Tour through the East of England*, Arthur Young, 1771.
[4] *The State of the Poor*, Sir Frederic Eden, 1797.
[5] *An Essay on Tea*, by Mr Hxxxxx, 1757.
[6] *A Treatise on the Inherent Qualities of the Tea-Herb*, J. N. Pechlinus, from the Latin, by a Gentleman of Cambridge, 2nd Edition, 1750.

Enterprising individuals seized the opportunity of making money out of a gullible public by selling them the essential medicinal essence of tea and Mr Lawrence, at his Toy Shop, at the Sign of the Griffin in Poultry, offered a 'Chimical Quintessence of Bohee-tea, and Cocoa Nuts, wherein the Volatile Salt, oil and spirit of them both, are chymically extracted and united'.[1]

The consumption of sugar rose as the habit of tea-drinking spread. It had ceased to be a luxury as the trade with the West Indies developed and ordinary white sugar candy cost about 6½d. a pound in the first half of the century, refined varieties being about 2d. a pound dearer. The price rose a little after 1750. Later in the century attention was drawn to the possibility of preparing sugar from roots such as carrots and beets. The first reports came from the Continent, where successful extractions had been made by Marggraf and by Achard. These were only small-scale experiments but in 1798 it was announced that Professor Klaproth had succeeded with a large-scale extraction. The discovery aroused little interest in England outside the pages of the scientific journals.[2]

The popularity of tea brought about a sharp decline in the sale of coffee, cocoa and chocolate, all of which were a great deal more expensive than tea, and towards the end of the century many of the once famous coffee houses had disappeared.

[1] Advertisement in *The Tatler*, No. 97, 1709.
[2] *Journal of Natural Philosophy and the Arts*, edited by William Nicholson, 1797-1802.

CHAPTER XI

EIGHTEENTH-CENTURY MEALS

§ 1 THE FOOD OF THE COUNTRY PEOPLE

As has been seen, the condition of the labouring classes in the villages tended to improve steadily when prices were low during the first fifty years of the eighteenth century. Although in the south the staple diet was bread, butter and cheese, there were few who could not afford meat once or twice a week. In the north they ate less meat but drank more milk. In the south the cottage gardens provided cabbages, carrots, onions and other vegetables for soups and savoury stews, whereas in the north the potato was rapidly becoming the most important garden product. The contrast became greater in the second half of the century, because the effects of enclosure were much more marked in the south and because the potato gave the poorer people of the north a measure of protection against the shortage of corn which affected the whole country. Eden was impressed by the remarkable difference between the diets of the village labourers in the north and those in the south, when he made his survey in 1795.[1] In the south he found them living almost exclusively on bread and cheese. By that time their condition had deteriorated to such an extent that they were lucky if they had meat once a week, and when they did they usually had to send it to the baker to be cooked owing to their own lack of fuel. In the north and north-west even the poorest labourer enjoyed a variety of food unknown to those in the south. From the standpoint of nutrition the important difference was that the poor people in the north and in Wales were still able to get plenty of milk and vegetables. As Eden said:

> It is not to be expected that milk should ever form a considerable part of the diet of labourers in the South of England, until the practice of keeping cows becomes more general among cottagers than it is at present... In the vicinity of large towns, the value of grass land is much too high to enable labourers to rent it to advantage.[2]

It was of course the system of enclosures that had taken away their pasturage and the land where they collected the fuel for cooking their hot meals. Describing the village families he saw at Cobham in Kent, Eden says:

---

[1] *The State of the Poor*, Sir Frederic Eden, 1797.
[2] Ibid.

The usual diet of labourers is, bread, butter, cheese, pickled pork, and a little butcher's meat . . . milk is very scarce.[1]

Young, in discussing the rise in the cost of provisions which occurred after 1750, indignantly rejected the suggestion that it was due to the small farmers being swallowed up by the large landowners. He added:

Of what benefit would it be to manufacturers, and the labouring poor in general, to have chickens sold at market 19 *per cent* (the rise talked of in provisions) cheaper than they are at present? Or would you have a poor man able to buy a fat fowl for 2d. as he might have done some hundred years ago? . . . all those who chuse to eat such food, must take care that they can afford it; and if they go without, and eat mutton instead of it, I desire to know of what consequence it is to the public?[2]

The 'manufacturers' of which he spoke were the new class of factory worker. They were, according to Young, the cause of all the trouble.

Sober and industrious workmen, of any sort, *never* riot.[3]

But the rioting over the price of provisions, he added, was the work of idle 'manufacturers'.

In all occupations, there will be idle, drunken, unsettled, and disorderly persons; a few of these getting together, and talking over the *dearness of provisions*, (which presently becomes a cant term among them) inflame each other.

The contrast between the north and the south of England late in the century can best be illustrated by taking two of the typical family budgets which Eden compiled. The first represents the amount spent on food during one year by a labourer, with a wife and four children, living at Streatley in Berkshire. The total family income — the wife and two of the children also worked on the farm — was £46 a year. The second budget is that of a labourer, his wife, and three children, living at Kendal in Westmorland and having a yearly income of just under £30.

The Streatley family estimated their weekly consumption of food as follows:

[1] Ibid.
[2] *The Farmer's Letters to the People of England*, Arthur Young, 3rd Edition, 1771.
[3] *A Six Weeks Tour through the Southern Counties of England and Wales*, Arthur Young, 3rd Edition, 1772.

8 half peck loaves
2 lb. cheese
2 lb. butter
2 lb. sugar
2 oz. tea
½ oz. oatmeal
½ lb. bacon [usually boiled]
2d. worth of milk [probably about 2 pints]

It is stated that they rarely ate meat and could seldom afford potatoes. The cost of their food amounted to over £52 a year, a sum already greater than their income and revealing the effect of the high prices in the south towards the end of the century.

The family in Westmorland spent the following sum in one year:

	£	s.	d.
75 stone of oatmeal, at 2/4d. the stone	8	15	0
Butchers' meat [probably about 5d. a lb.]		5	0
Milk [probably 1½d. a quart]	5	0	0
Tea and sugar	1	12	0
Potatoes [probably 3d. for 4 quarters]	2	12	0
Butter, 40 lb. at 9d. a lb.	1	10	0
Treacle		8	0
	£20	2	0[1]

It is clear from these two budgets that living was much cheaper in the north than in the south. The contrast in the amount of milk is particularly striking. There seems to have been any amount available in the north at about 1½d. a quart; in the south the villagers had not only lost their own grazing land but practically all the milk produced on the large farms was converted into butter or cheese and the whey or buttermilk used for feeding pigs. Jonas Hanway, the reformer, said of the poor of Stevenage in 1767:

The food of the poor is *good bread*, cheese, pease, and turnips in winter, with a little pork or other meat, when they can afford it; but from the high price of meat, it has not lately been within their reach. As to milk, they have hardly sufficient for their use.[2]

Potatoes had by this time become a great standby in the north.

[1] *The State of the Poor*, Sir Frederic Eden, 1797.
[2] *Letters on the Importance of the Rising Generation*, Jonas Hanway, 1767.

No vegetable is, or ever was, applied to such a variety of uses in the North of England as the potatoe; it is a constant standing dish, at every meal, breakfast excepted.[1]

In the south, being grown only on big estates or in market gardens for the supply of big towns, it was less widely distributed, although Eden speaks of it as 'a principal article in large families'.[2]

The two budgets quoted above show another difference between the diets of the north and the south, and that is the large amount of oatmeal eaten by the northerners. At this time wheat was still little known in the far north and north-west and oatmeal remained the staple cereal of the poor people. It was the principal ingredient of the famous 'Hasty Pudding', a kind of porridge eaten with butter, milk or treacle. Sometimes the oatmeal was boiled with the milk or baked into a form of oatcake. In the south wheaten loaves were eaten everywhere; rye bread and mixed flours of wheat and rye had almost disappeared.

The diet of the working people in the north was very similar to that of the Scotch and Irish labourers. Matthew Bramble wrote of the former:

> The countrypeople of N. Britain live chiefly on oatmeal and milk, cheese, butter and some garden stuff, with, now and then, a pickled herring, by way of delicacy, but fresh meat they seldom or never taste.[3]

Arthur Young gives a like picture of the Irish peasant. He describes a family, consisting of a man, his wife and four children, who ate 18 stone (252 lb.) of potatoes and 40 lb. of oatmeal in a week together with milk and an occasional salted herring.[4] For the majority of these people meat was a luxury which came their way but a few times in the year, and then usually at some feast or junketing. Catharine Hutton has left an amusing account of a village wedding in the north of Wales which shows the forty guests sitting outside the bridegroom's house being served with relays of helpings from five rounds of beef and 'bags of peas and mountains of cabbage'. No less than forty quarters of malt had been brewed for the occasion and the meal was finished off with a 'dessert of bread, butter and cheese'.[5]

From the wealth of information in Eden's great survey we can take another interesting budget. This represents the expenditure of a labourer living at Epsom, with his wife and eight children, on a yearly income of £45-50, which was by no means bad for the times. He was fortunate in

---

[1] *The State of the Poor*, Sir Frederic Eden, 1797.
[2] Ibid.
[3] *The Expedition of Humphrey Clinker*, T. Smollett, 1771.
[4] *A Tour in Ireland made in the Years 1776-7 and 1778*, Arthur Young, 1780.
[5] *Reminiscences of a Gentlewoman of the Last Century*, edited by Mrs C. H. Beale, 1891.

having a small garden and being able to fatten a pig every year. His weekly
purchases were estimated as follows:

> 13 quartern loaves
> One joint of meat (i.e. about 12 lb. [4/-], for Sunday)
> 1½ lb. butter
> 1½ lb. cheese
> Tea and 2 lb. sugar
> Small beer, 1½d a day.[1]

The mention of beer is worthy of note as it is seldom met with in the
estimates quoted by Eden. Tea and sugar, on the other hand, are almost
universal. We shall refer to this again later, but in the meantime we may note
what Eden says:

> They [farm labourers] seldom, however, can afford to purchase beer,
> and in its place, have very generally in this part of the country, sub-
> stituted tea at every meal.

It must not be forgotten, in considering the food of the villager of these
times, that his opportunities for adding to the larder by trapping or snaring
were much more restricted than they had been a century or so before. The
Game Laws were rigorously enforced and landowners protected their preserves with man-traps and spring-guns. In the more remote parts of the
north and west and in Scotland, however, it was a different matter and Eden
mentions the crofters' venison — 'for there is no restraint, but 'tis every man's
own that can kill it' — and salmon. Elsewhere the severe punishment meted
out to anyone convicted of poaching was a sufficient deterrent to most
country people, for it was by no means uncommon for a magistrate to order
a man so convicted to be transported for life, but nevertheless it did not put
an end to the practice; skilled rascals used to make a good living by poaching
birds, fish and sometimes even venison, and it was common knowledge that
the shops in the towns were to no small extent stocked by this means.

§2 THE FOOD OF THE COUNTRY GENTLEMAN

The big landowners lived exceedingly well. Their farms, orchards and
kitchen gardens supplied them with a wealth of food to which they added
costly wines and other luxuries from abroad. There is such an excellent
picture of the style in which they lived in a letter from Matthew Bramble to
Dr Lewis that it deserves to be quoted in full:

[1] *The State of the Poor*, Sir Frederic Eden, 1797.

At Brambleton Hall ... I drink the virgin lymph, pure and crystalline as it gushes from the rock, or the sparkling beverage home-brewed from malt of my own making; or I indulge with cider, which my own orchard affords; or with claret of the best growth, imported for my own use, by a correspondent on whose integrity I can depend: my bread is sweet and nourishing, made from my own wheat, ground in my own mill, and baked in my own oven; my table is, in a great measure, furnished from my own ground; my five-year-old mutton, fed on the fragrant herbage of the mountains, that might vie with venison in juice and flavour; my delicious veal, fattened with nothing but the mother's milk, that fills the dish with gravy; my poultry from the barn door, that never knew confinement but when they were at roost; my rabbits panting from the warren; my game fresh from the moors; my trout and salmon struggling from the stream; oysters from their native banks; and herrings, with other sea-fish, I can eat in four hours after they are taken. My salads, roots, and pot-herbs, my own garden yields in plenty and perfection; the produce of the natural soil, prepared by moderate cultivation. The same soil affords all the different fruits which England may call her own so that my dessert is every day fresh-gathered from the tree; my dairy flows with nectareous tides of milk and cream, from whence we derive abundance of excellent butter, curds, and cheese; and the refuse fattens my pigs, that are destined for hams and bacon.[1]

Breakfast, usually a light meal of tea, coffee or chocolate, with rusks or cakes, was taken at 9 or 10 o'clock and was followed an hour or so later by a glass of sherry and a biscuit. In the early part of the century dinner was eaten about 2 p.m. but the hour tended to get later and later until by about 1780 it was not uncommon for the squire and his guests to sit down to their chief meal at 3 or even 4 in the afternoon.

The following description of what appears to have been a quite ordinary dinner is taken from Catharine Hutton's letters:

A little before three, we sat down to dinner, which consisted of three boiled chickens at top, a very fine haunch of venison at bottom; ham on one side, a flour pudding on the other, and beans in the middle. After the cloth was removed, we had gooseberries, and a remarkably fine dish of apricots.[2]

It was by no means an unusual dinner that the Rev. James Woodforde gave to Mrs Farr on April 19th, 1768:

[1] *The Expedition of Humphrey Clinker*, T. Smollett, 1771.
[2] *Reminiscences of a Gentlewoman of the Last Century*, edited by Mrs C. H. Beale, 1891.

O

A roasted Shoulder of Mutton and a plum Pudding — Veal Cutlets, Frill'd Potatoes, cold Tongue, Ham and cold roast Beef, and eggs in their shells. Punch, Wine, Beer and Cyder for drinking.[1]

It was a very different matter when he gave an 'elegant' dinner, as he did to a party of friends on April 20th, 1774.

The first course was, part of a large Cod, a Chine of Mutton, some Soup, a Chicken Pye, Puddings and Roots, etc. Second course, Pidgeons and Asparagus. A Fillet of Veal with Mushrooms and high Sauce with it, rosted Sweetbreads, hot Lobster, Apricot Tart and in the Middle a Pyramid of Syllabubs and Jellies. We had Dessert of Fruit after Dinner, and Madeira, White Port and red to drink as Wine.

It seems unnecessary for him to add 'We were all very cheerful and merry'. Sometimes the country gentry followed the town fashion of drinking tea at 5 or 6 o'clock, but more often they sat over their dinner for several hours. Supper, which usually consisted of a variety of cold meats, was seldom eaten before 10 p.m. These people were prodigious meat eaters and consumed correspondingly small amounts of bread. Parson Woodforde's household consisted of three men, three women and a boy; these seven people, five of them at least engaged in manual work, consumed a mere thirteen pounds of flour a week, an amount which would have lasted a labourer's family of the same size little more than a day.

§3 FOUR-BOTTLE MEN

The eighteenth century, particularly the second half, was an age of heavy eating and heavy drinking both in town and country, but it is more particularly the hunting squire who has become famous as the 'four-bottle man'. He drank chiefly claret, burgundy or Rhenish with his dinner, and port, Madeira or some other 'sweet' wine with the dessert. The famous Methuen Treaty of 1703, designed to draw Portugal away from the influence of France and to damage the latter's trade, imposed the excessively heavy duty of £55 a tun on all French wines. As the duty on Portuguese wines at that time was £7 a tun an immense fillip was given to the trade with Oporto and Lisbon, which took in return large shipments of dried and salted fish.

In the seventeenth century a large proportion of the Portuguese wines imported into England consisted of ordinary *vin du pays* such as Colares and Bucellas, but with the growth of the wine trade with England and its demand

[1] *The Diary of a Country Parson, The Reverend James Woodforde, 1758-1781*, edited by J. Beresford, 1924-29.

for sweet dessert wines more and more port came to be shipped. The fortification of port, which consists of adding extra spirit at an appropriate stage of the fermentation in order to retard the process, gave a drink which by its strength and sweetness appealed to the English taste. In consequence, sack, a kind of sweet sherry, which had been the popular sweet wine of the seventeenth century, almost disappeared. The practice of keeping wine in bottles laid on their sides dates from about the last quarter of the eighteenth century when the cylindrical bottles and the form of cork in use today were first introduced.[1]

A prodigious quantity of port was drunk by the country gentlemen in the second half of the eighteenth century and the stories of three- and four-bottle men are quite authentic. The bottles in use then held the same amount of liquor as our modern ones and the wine was the same strength (approximately 20 per cent alcohol by volume) but although many of these men finished the evening under the table or met later retribution in the form of chronic gout there is little doubt that it was the long hours spent over their port that enabled them to drink these enormous quantities. As André Simon has put it 'the all-important factor is TIME: it's wonderful what one can do — given time to do it!'[2]

§ 4 THE MEALS OF THE WEALTHY TOWN-DWELLERS

For the rich the century was one of extravagant living. It was marked quite early by a tendency for the times of meals to get later and later and by the growing popularity of French and Italian cooking. There was undoubtedly an enormous amount of gluttony and over-eating not only among the very rich but also among the prosperous merchants and the professional classes. The heavy jowls and fat paunches in the drawings by Hogarth, Rowlandson and other contemporary artists tell a tale of good living and heavy drinking.

In the early part of the century the leisured classes took a late breakfast, about 10 or 11 o'clock, of tea or chocolate with bread and butter or toast. An hour or so later they met at a coffee-house for coffee or chocolate. Dinner took place at 5 or 6 p.m. and supper was customarily eaten so late that, as one writer expressed it, the meal was 'now in Danger of being entirely confounded and lost in Breakfast'.[3] How greatly the hours had changed can

[1] Information kindly supplied by Mr Bruce Todd of Messrs. Findlater, Mackie, Todd & Co. Ltd. at whose offices in Wigmore Street may be seen an interesting collection of English wine bottles, formerly the property of M. André Simon.

[2] Private communication from M. Simon. We are also indebted for a great deal of our information on this subject to M. Simon's interesting book *Bottlescrew Days* (1926).

[3] The *Tatler*, December 12th, 1710.

be appreciated from the fact that the Oxford Colleges, which kept to the old customs, still dined at 11 in the morning and supped at 6. Later in the century there was a definite swing back to a more natural division of the day. Dinner was put back to 2 or 3 p.m. and supper to 7 or 8.

It was at this period that 'afternoon tea', taken at about 5 o'clock, began to become popular, and the bread and butter and buttered toast of England to acquire a great reputation. Here are tributes from two appreciative foreigners:

> The Butter and Tea which the Londoners live upon from morning until three or four in the afternoon, occasions the chief consumption of bread, which is cut in slices, and so thin, that it does as much honour to the address of the person that cut it, as to the sharpness of the knife.[1]

> The slices of bread and butter, which they give you with your tea, are as thin as poppy-leaves — But there is another kind of bread and butter usually eaten with tea, which is toasted by the fire, and is incomparably good. This is called toast.[2]

There are several striking features in eighteenth-century menus, including the influence of French cooking, the variety and richness of the sweets and the growing use of vegetables and fruit. Many people deplored our adopting the Continental type of cookery and Steele, writing in an early number of the *Tatler*,[3] pleaded for a return to the diet of our forefathers, the beef and mutton on which we had won the battles of Crécy and Agincourt. Among the many protests against the highly seasoned French dishes was one from Robert Campbell, author of *The London Tradesman* (1747), from which this extract is taken:

> In the Days of good Queen *Elizabeth*, when mighty Roast Beef was the *Englishman's* Food; our Cookery was plain and simple as our Manners; it was not then a Science or Mistery, and required no Conjuration to please the Palates of our greatest Men. But we have of late Years refined ourselves out of that simple Taste, and conformed our Palates to Meats and Drinks dressed after the *French* Fashion: The natural Taste of Fish or Flesh is become nauseous to our fashionable Stomach; we abhor that any thing should appear at our Tables in its native Properties; all the Earth, from both the Poles, the most distant and different Climates, must be ransacked for Spices, Pickles and Sauces, not to relish but to disguise our Food. Fish, when it has passed the Hands

[1] *A Tour to London*, M. Grosley, translated by T. Nugent, 1772.
[2] *A Journey to England*, C. P. Moritz, 1782, cited in *The British Tourists*, W. Mavor, 1798–1800.
[3] March 21st, 1710.

of a *French* Cook, is no more Fish; it has neither the Taste, Smell, nor Appearance of Fish. It, and every Thing else, is dressed in Masquerade, seasoned with slow Poisons, and every Dish pregnant with nothing, but the Seeds of Diseases both chronick and acute. This depraved Taste of spoiling wholesome Dyet, by costly and pernicious Sauces, and absurd Mixtures, does not confine itself to the Tables of the Great; but the Contagion is become epidemical; Poor and Rich live as if they were of a different Species of Beings from their Ancestors, and observe a Regimen of Diet, calculated not to supply the Wants of Nature, but to oppress her Faculties, disturb her Operations, and load her with, till now, unheard of Maladies.

A contemporary print showing St George holding aloft a spear with a large sirloin impaled on it bears the following verses:

> Behold your Saint with Gorgeous English Fare,
>   Noble Sirloin, Rich Pudding and Strong Beer.
> For you my Hearts of Oak, for your Regale,
>   Here's good old English Stingo Mild and Stale.

The cookery books of the period show how richly served were the tables of the rich. The recipes which Mrs Glasse prepared are suited to an age when a quart of the best cream, the yolks of two dozen eggs and a quart of the best Madeira were incidental items on the kitchen list.[1]

Vegetables and fruit were eaten at practically every meal, the latter both as dessert and for a 'sweet', in the form of stewed fruit dishes, pies, tarts, etc. Sugar became an essential ingredient in cooking and a book such as Mrs Glasse's *The Compleat Confectioner* (1770), dealing as it did almost entirely with sweetmeats and sweet dishes, was an innovation. Perhaps her most famous recipe was her 'Everlasting Syllabub'.

> Take three pints of the thickest and sweetest cream you can get, a pint of rhenish, half a pint of sack, three lemons, near a pound of double-refined sugar, beat and sift the sugar and put it to your cream, grate off the yellow rind of three lemons, put that in, and squeeze the juice of three lemons into your wine; put that to your cream, beat all together with a whisk just half an hour, then take it up all together with a spoon, and fill your glasses.

It may be interesting, as an indication of the change in character of the menu for a formal banquet over two centuries to compare the accounts of

---

[1] *The Art of Cookery Made Plain and Easy*, by a Lady, 1747. (This book went through many editions, the later ones of which bore the name, Mrs H. Glasse.)

some of the festival dinners of the Butchers' Company.[1] The list of food provided for the 'Election Dinner' in 1546 is given as:

'brede'	18d
'alle'	12d
'lownys of welle'	2/10d
'abreste of welle'	10d
4 qrs. of 'coollys'	20d
3 'rompys of beff'	12d
2 'rybbes of brawne'	4/4d
'wynne'	3/4d
1 lb. of sugar	12d
'spyeses'	2/-
'rootes'	1d
a 'pottell of wynnegar'	8d
'sawltte'	1d
6 lbs. of butter	12d
6 'knockettes of weelles'	2/4d

It is a typical dinner of the period, before vegetables had become common and when fruit was seldom served at table. The 'rootes' were probably cabbages or carrots for flavouring the soup. Seventy years later the cook provided:

beef . . . 6 surloynes, 3 ribbs, and 8 stone for the poore,	£3/19/8
one kilderkine of ale and 1 kilderkine of bere	12/-
strewings oatmeall and onions	2/9
oringado biskett and arman-paste	2/6
12 Marybones oringes and lemans	5/-
pipkins, rosemary and varges	8d
a hundred of egges	4/-
Barberryes	12d

By this time fruit was becoming popular but vegetables were still a rarity.

A complete change is shown by the menu for the Lord Mayor's Day Dinner in 1774.

[1] *The History of the Butcher's Company*, A. Pearce, 1929.

Five hams, about 20 lbs. each.
Fourteen boyl'd fowls.
Twenty-six roast fowls.
Three boyl'd turkies and oysters.
Three roast turkies.
Three geese.
Twenty-four ducks.
Eight mince pyes and ten marrow puddings for
the Company.

.   .   .   .

3 lbs. of Epping butter.
2 lbs. of Gloucester and 2 lbs. of Cheshire cheese.
Twenty-one quartern loaves and twenty-one
quartern bricks.
Eighteen gallon cask small beer.
Three loaves of sugar.
Eighteen bunches of sprouts.
Sage and onions.
Some beetroot and one bunch of carrots.
Two bunches of turnips.
One dozen sticks of horseradish to be scraped.

.   .   .   .

Five dozen of red port.
Three dozen of white.
Six gallons of brandy to be made into Punch.
Two hundred and fifty lemons.
Two bushels of golden pippins.

There is here a variety of vegetables, even if the amount be small. It will
also be noted that Epping butter is specially mentioned and that the cheeses
are referred to by name.

One effect of the influence of French fashions on London society was a
marked improvement in table manners. By all accounts it was about time.
Ward was probably not exaggerating very much when he wrote his description of a Lord Mayor's Banquet early in the century.

Then each tuck'd his Napkin up under his Chin.
That his Holiday-Band might be kept very clean;
And Pin'd up his Sleeves to his Elbows, because
They should not hang down and be Greas'd in the Sauce.
Then all went to work, with such rending and tearing,
Like a Kennel of Hounds on a Quarter of Carri'n.

When done with the Flesh, they claw'd off the Fish,
With one Hand at Mouth, and th' other in th' Dish.
When their Stomachs were Cloy'd, what their Bellies Denied,
Each clap'd in his Pocket to give to his Bride;
With a *Cheese-cake* and *Custard* for my little *Johnny*,
And a Handful of *Sweet-Meats* for poor Daughter *Nanny*.[1]

Books on table deportment became popular; amongst other things they
deplored the habit of scratching the body or spitting when at table.[2]

§ 5   THE MEALS OF THE ARTISAN AND WORKING CLASSES

During the first half of the century the artisans and labourers in the towns
lived well.

> ... in a word the working manufacturing people of England eat the
> fat, drink the sweet, live better and fare batter, than the working poor
> of any other nation.[3]

They breakfasted early on bread, butter, cold meats and cheese (of which
they ate enormous quantities), and beer, although as the century progressed
tea began to replace the latter. Dinner, at noon, was the chief meal of the
day. It was often eaten at a tavern or bought at a cookshop and usually
consisted of meat and vegetables followed by cheese. The poorer people
frequented the 'dives' in the back streets.

> He accordingly conducted us to a certain lane, where stopping, he bade
> us observe him and do as he did; and, walking a few paces, dived into
> a cellar, and disappeared in an instant. I followed his example, and
> descending very successfully, found myself in the middle of a cook's
> shop, almost suffocated with the steams of boiled beef, and surrounded
> by a company of hackney coachmen, chairmen, draymen, and a few
> footmen out of place, or on board wages, who sat eating shin of beef,
> tripe, cowheel, or sausages, at separate boards, covered with cloths
> which turned my stomach.[4]

Their dinner of shin of beef, small beer and bread cost them twopence halfpenny each.

[1] *O Raree Show, O Pretty Show, or the City Feast*, by the Author of *The London Spy* [Edward
Ward], 1704.
[2] *The Honours of the Table for the Use of Young People*, Rev. Dr Trusler, 1788.
[3] *The Complete English Tradesman*, Daniel Defoe, 1726.
[4] *The Adventures of Roderick Random*, T. Smollett, 1748.

Vegetables were now in daily use, potatoes being the most popular in the north and cabbages, carrots, turnips and sprouts in the south. Whereas in earlier centuries descriptions of meals usually referred simply to a chine of beef, a loin of veal or a saddle of mutton, with no mention of vegetables, eighteenth-century menus speak of a 'calves head with cabbage' or a 'large need's tongue with greens'.[1]

Fetch your Mistriss and I three hap'worth of boild Beef, see first they make good Weight and then stand hard for a bit of Carrot.[2]

It was a centuries-old custom for the Thames watermen to 'attack each other with scoffs and scurrilous language'[3] as they passed on their way but it was indeed a sign of the changing habits when they taunted a boatload of Lambeth gardeners with being

You . . . who can't afford Butter to your Cabbage, or Bacon to your Sprouts.[4]

The meals served in the inns and taverns show how common fruit and vegetables were in this century. *The Torrington Diaries* afford ample illustration of this.[5]

Bedford, June 1st, 1789. My Host, of the true fat Breed, said Dinner was just ready, and instantly brought in a Roasted Fillet of Mutton (a joint not very common) with Cabbage, Cucumbers, and Sallad; and upon this, and Cheese, I fared very well.

For Dinner	10
Brandy	6
Hay and Corn	4
Servants	4
	2 0

Très bonne Marché.

Grantham, June 7th, 1789. — . . . She [the landlady] almost instantly returned . . . placing before us a Round of Beef boil'd, a Leg of Mutton roasted, with Greens, a Rice Pudding, and a Gooseberry-Pie.

Sometimes the traveller was lucky.

[1] *The London Spy* [E. Ward], 1703.
[2] Ibid.
[3] *A Tour to London,* M. Grosley, translated by T. Nugent, 1772.
[4] *The London Spy* [E. Ward], 1703.
[5] *The Torrington Diaries,* Vol. IV, 1781-94, edited by C. Bruyn Andrew, 1938.

Southwell, June 8th, 1789. — . . . put up at the Saracens-Head Inn . . . where, to my great contentment, I was instantly Served . . . with Cold Beef, Cold Veal and Gooseberry Tart.

And sometimes he was not.

Wellwyn, May 20th, 1789. — Mrs. S. Talk'd about Mutton chops: but I stuck to my demand of cold meat, with a gooseberry tart; and was right, for she instantly produced a cold Tongue, and a cold Fillet of Veal: as for her old fusty tart of last years fruit, I open'd the Lid, and closed it tightly down for the next Comer. No Tricks upon Travellers.

Dover, September 22nd, 1790. — Never did I Enter a more dirty, noisy, or more imposing Inn than this York House; for we were charged most exorbitantly, for wine not drinkable, for musty Fowls, and stinking Partridges; never did I leave an Inn with greater Pleasure.

The London Spy gives a nauseating picture of the cheap cookshops in the vicinity of Smithfield.

We soon deliver'd our squeamish Stomachs from the Surfeiting Fumes, that arose from their Rotten-Roasted Diet, which made the Street stink like a *Hampshire* Farmers Yard, when Singeing of a Bacon-Hog.[1]

Charles Moritz, an observant Swiss visitor, had a poor opinion of the ordinary Englishman's midday meal, which according to him usually consisted of

. . . a piece of half-boiled or half-roasted meat; and a few cabbage-leaves, boiled in plain water; on which they pour a sauce made of flour and butter, the usual method of dressing vegetables in England.[2]

This must surely be the forerunner of the boiled cabbage which has made the meals in our hotels and boarding-houses a byword the world over. Many years later a great lover of England complained, 'They have only three vegetables, and two of them are cabbage.'[3]

Moritz also expressed himself freely about English coffee; he might have been describing the fluid served in many a modern English café.

I would always advise those who wish to drink coffee in England to mention beforehand, how many cups are to be made with half an

[1] *The London Spy* [E. Ward], 1703.
[2] *A Journey to England,* C. P. Moritz, 1782, cited in *The British Tourists,* W. Mavor, 1798-1860.
[3] *Life and Letters of Walter H. Page,* edited by B. J. Hendrick, 1924.

ounce, or else the people will probably bring them a prodigious quantity of brown fluid.[1]

§ 6 THE FOOD OF THE PEOPLE IN POVERTY AND DEARTH

The poorer people knew hard times in the second half of the century. The barest necessities of life became scarce and dear and the widespread distress and discontent culminated on many occasions in riots and lawlessness. Many suggestions were put forward for relieving the shortage; the coast fisheries should be utilized to a greater degree, dried fish should be imported from Newfoundland, cheap rice could be brought from Carolina.[2] The Government did sometimes take action, usually as the result of considerable pressure and after quite unnecessary delay. Carolina rice was allowed into the country duty-free in 1796 but it proved no more popular than the maize which was introduced in 1795 as a cheap substitute for wheat.

Undoubtedly much of the discontent was due to the fact that the working people, particularly those in the towns, had become accustomed to plenty of butter, cheese and good butchers' meat during the more prosperous early days of the century. Josiah Tucker, who wrote on economic subjects, deplored this taste for the more expensive kinds of meat, which with the turn of the tide of prosperity could not be gratified.

The Palates of the Poor are become *Nice* and *Sickly* . . . They are not able to purchase *Dainties*; and they cannot *touch* what is *coarse* and *ordinary* . . . hence it is, that the great Dealers in Flesh-meat in *Southwark* and *White-Chapel* have justly complained of late Years that they can have no Purchasers for the coarser Parts of Meat, which used formerly to be Sold to the Poor at Low Price, but must now be buried, or thrown upon a Dunghill.[3]

During the lean years Jonas Hanway was at great pains to prove that considerably less meat need be eaten if vegetables were added to the meal.

With the addition of legumens, roots, and vegetables, *five pounds* weight of meat will go as far as we generally make *ten* or *fifteen*, and

[1] *A Journey to England*, C. P. Moritz, 1782, cited in *The British Tourists*, W. Mavor, 1798-1800.
[2] *Letters on the Importance of the Rising Generation*, Jonas Hanway, 1767.
[3] *An Impartial Inquiry into the Benefits and Damages Arising to the Nation from the present very great Use of Low-priced Spirituous Liquors*, by J. T. of Bristol, 1751.

the consumer will be more free of the scurvy, and not less fit for the laborious offices of life.[1]

He proposed a recipe for a dish which, he asserted, would provide food 'for five stout men, or ten common persons, including women and children'.

> 1 lb. lean beef
> 1 pint of split peas
> 12 ounces mealy potatoes
> 3 ounces of ground rice
> 3 large leeks
> 2 heads of 'salary' and salt
> 9 pints of water.[2]

At a generous estimate this dish would provide 3500 Cal., which is less than *one* 'stout man' would require for a day's manual labour. Hanway had no patience with the working-class demand for butter, which he considered an unnecessary luxury for them and liable to upset their digestions.

> Not many years since, it [butter] was deemed an article of luxury; it was not common to *domestic* servants in families of rank; but now, if the *laboring* part of mankind are not supplied with it at 6d. or 8d. a pound, they think the *times* are very hard.[3]

§7 DIETS IN WORKHOUSES AND INSTITUTIONS

It seems likely that the inmates of the workhouses were fairly well fed in the early part of the century. In 1714 a prominent citizen of Bristol, Mr Cary, reported as follows:

> ... [we] appointed their diets to be made up of such provisions as were very wholesome, afforded good nourishment, and were not costly in price, (viz.) beef, pease, potatoes, broath, pease-porridge, milk-porridge, bread and cheese, good beer, (such as we drank at our own tables,) cabbage, carrots, turnips, &c. in which we took the advice of our physician, and bought the best of every sort. They had three meals every day: and, as I remember, it stood us, (with soap to wash,) in about 16d. *per* week for each of the 100 girls. We soon found the effect of their change of living. Nature, being well supported, threw

---

[1] *Letters on the Importance of the Rising Generation*, Jonas Hanway, 1767.
[2] Ibid.   [3] Ibid.

out a great deal of foulness, so that we had generally 20 down at a time, in the meazles, smallpox, and other distempers; but by the care of our physician, and the blessing of God on his endeavours, we never buried but two, though we have had seldom less than 100 in the house at any time.[1]

At Bedford early in the century the workhouse food was, as Eden thought, 'better than the most industrious labourer, either then or at present, could afford himself at his own habitation'. The weekly diet is given below.

	Breakfast	Dinner	Supper
Sunday	Bread and cheese	Boiled beef and suet pudding	Bread and cheese
Monday	Broth	Cold meat left on Sunday	The same
Tuesday	Bread and cheese	Boiled beef, and a little mutton and suet pudding	The same
Wednesday	The same as Monday	The same as Monday	The same
Thursday	The same as Tuesday	The same as Tuesday	The same
Friday	The same as Monday	The same as Monday	The same
Saturday	Bread and cheese	Hasty-pudding, or milk-porridge	Broth, or bread and cheese

An attached note says:

Their bread is wheat dressed down, and made into large household loaves by a woman in the house. Their drink is beer, turned in from the public brew-house at three half-pence per gallon. The overseers do sometimes put a cow upon the common for them; and that nothing may be wasted or lost, they have a pig or two bought in, to live upon their wash, and dregs, and fragments; which, when well grown, is fed and killed for the house. They have also a little garden for herbs, onions.

At Heckingham, in Norfolk, in 1794, Eden found the diet to be as follows:

[1] *The State of the Poor*, Sir Frederic Eden, 1797.

	Breakfast	Dinner	Supper
Sunday	Bread and cheese, and butter, or treacle	Dumplins, butcher's meat and bread	Bread and cheese, or butter
Monday	The same as Sunday	Broth and bread	Ditto
Tuesday	Milk and water gruel, and bread	Baked suet puddings	Ditto
Wednesday	The same as Sunday	Dumplins and milk broth; or milk and water-gruel	Ditto
Thursday	The same as Tuesday	The same as Sunday	Ditto
Friday	The same as Sunday	The same as Monday	Ditto
Saturday	The same as Tuesday	Bread and cheese, or butter	Ditto

Eden added a note:

The men are, each, allowed a pint of beer at every meal, except when they have broth, or gruel. Women, with children at the breast, have the same allowance. Others have two-thirds of a pint.

There are many similar records in the pages of Eden's survey. They show that the diet in the southern workhouses and institutions was nearly always composed of bread, meat, cheese and beer. In the north, surprisingly large quantities of milk were given to the paupers and they received a regular ration of potatoes. What is even more surprising is that the diets seem to have remained unchanged even during the hard times at the close of the century. The inmates of Carlisle workhouse, for example, received a fairly liberal diet in 1793, a year of bad harvest and serious financial crisis. Their breakfast consisted of 'Hasty-pudding' with milk or beer. For dinner they were given meat three times a week, with potatoes and milk or bread and milk on the other four days. For supper there was bread and cheese or broth. Beer was served at most of the meals.

One might suspect that the inmates did not always get the food set out on the diet sheets, but Eden, who was a careful recorder, gave no hint of this.

It is unlikely, however, that his statement about one house of industry where a pauper was 'allowed to eat until he is satisfied' could have been generally applied. The food was often qualitatively good but insufficient in amount.

The amount of milk given to the poor in the north is astonishing. The year 1795 was one of the worst of a bad period, but the authorities of Liverpool workhouse, with approximately a thousand inmates to feed, purchased 3640 gallons of skimmed milk and the same quantity of fresh milk in a single week. The weekly provision of 1500 lb. of potatoes and 384 lb. of turnips is also in sharp contrast with the south where it seems to have been almost unheard of for vegetables to be provided in 'houses of industry'.

§ 8 DIETS IN ORPHANAGES AND SCHOOLS

There is scant mention of vegetables in the diet sheet adopted for the children of the Foundling Hospital on November 17th, 1747.[1]

In the Pork Season

	Breakfast	Dinner	Supper
Sunday	Broth	Roast Pork	Bread
Monday	Gruell	Potatoes	Milk & Bread
Tuesday	Milk Porridge	Boiled Mutton	Bread
Wednesday	Broth	Rice Milk	Bread & Cheese
Thursday	Gruell	Boiled Pork	Bread
Friday	Milk Porridge	Dumplins	Milk & Bread
Saturday	Gruell	Hasty Puddings	Bread & Cheese

In the other Season

	Breakfast	Dinner	Supper
Sunday	Broth	Roast Beef	Bread
Monday	Gruell	Potatoes	Milk & Bread
Tuesday	Milk Porridge	Boiled Beef	Bread
Wednesday	Broth	Rice Puddings	Bread & Cheese
Thursday	Gruell	Boiled Mutton	Bread
Friday	Broth	Sewett Puddings	Milk & Bread
Saturday	Gruell	Hasty Puddings	Bread & Cheese

RESOLVED

'That on the 17th of October yearly the Children in this Hospital have a Holiday and Roast Beef and Plumb-Pudding for Dinner being the Date of the Charter.'

[1] The History of the Foundling Hospital, R. H. Nichols and F. A. Wray, 1935.

Mention of 'Plumb-Pudding' reminds us that it was only towards the end of the century that the practice of including meat among the ingredients was discontinued. Recipes in the middle of the century always included a 'leg or shin of beef'.[1] By the end of the century the Foundling Hospital recipe has quite a modern ring about it.

> 1 cwt. Plums, 40 pounds suet, 20 gallons milk, 25 pounds sugar, 2 pounds allspice, 2 pounds ginger, 4 bushels of flour.[2]

The diet adopted for the staff of the Hospital in 1747 contained plenty of vegetables, in marked contrast to the one for the children quoted above.

> That the Diet to be used in this Hospital shall be as follows Viz[t] Upon Sundays Roast Beef, Mondays Stew'd Beef with Turneps and Carrotts, Tuesdays Roast Mutton, Wednesdays Boil'd Beef with Greens or Roots, or Pork with Pease Pudding in Winter, or Shoulders of Veal in Summer, Thursdays Stew'd Beef with Turneps and Carrotts, Fridays Roast Mutton, and Saturdays Boiled Beef with Greens or Roots, or Pork with Pease Pudding in Winter and Shoulders of Veal in Summer. And that the Proportion of the said Diet be at present Regulated at a Pound for each Head a Day one with other. And, That the Breakfasts and Suppers be Milk, Milk Porridge, Rice Milk or Bread and Cheese.[3]

A few years later, in 1762, vegetables were added to the children's meals.

	Breakfast	Dinner	Supper
Sunday	Bread and Butter	Roast Beef and Greens	Milk Porridge
Monday	Gruel	Potatoes or Parsnips mashed with Milk	Bread and Butter
Tuesday	Milk Porridge	Boiled Beef and Greens	Broth
Wednesday	Bread and Milk	Stewed Shins of Beef and Broth with herbs and roots	Milk Porridge
Thursday	Gruel	Mutton and Greens	Broth

[1] *The Art of Cookery Made Plain and Easy*, by a Lady, 1747.
[2] *The History of the Foundling Hospital*, R. H. Nichols and F. A. Wray, 1935.
[3] Ibid.

Friday	Milk Porridge	As Wednesday	Bread and Cheese
Saturday	Bread and Milk	Rice Pudding	Gruel[1]

The rising prices of the latter half of the century compelled the Governing Committee to seek cheaper forms of food. They tried the new cereal Carolina rice, which was not particularly popular, but it is rather unexpected to find that 'Eight boys who have a natural Aversion to eating of Rice Pudding' were permitted instead to have 'a pudding made of half flour and half ground rice'. In 1782 a proposal to reduce the meat rations and substitute suet puddings was rejected on the advice of Dr Watson who insisted on the beneficial effect of meat. In 1796, owing to the shortage of bread, the whole institution was put on to 'Standard White Bread' and flour puddings were discontinued.

There are many interesting records of the food purchased for the boys of Christ's Hospital.[2] The chief purchases in 1704 consisted of bread, cheese, butter, beef, oatmeal and dried pease. There is no mention of vegetables but the boys got more than a quart of small beer a day. In 1721 the Governors realized that the 'Dyett from Thursday Noon to Sunday Noon was only Bread Butter and Cheese Pease Porridge and Water gruell' and they approved the addition of 'Leggs and Lynns of Mutton Boyled'.[3]

Charles Lamb has left a famous description of the food at Christ's Hospital while he was a pupil there (1782-89).

... while we were battening upon our quarter of a penny loaf — our *crug* — moistened with attenuated small beer, in wooden piggins, smacking of the pitched leathern jack it was poured from. Our Monday's milk porritch, blue and tasteless, and the pease soup of Saturday, coarse and choking ... The Wednesday's mess of millet, somewhat less repugnant (we had three banyan to four meat days in the week) ... our *half-pickled* Sundays, or *quite fresh* boiled beef on Thursdays (strong as *caro equina*), with detestable marigolds floating in the pail to poison the broth — our scanty mutton scrags on Fridays — and rather more savoury, but grudging portions of the same flesh, rotten-roasted or rare, on the Tuesdays (the only dish which excited our appetites, and disappointed our stomachs, in almost equal proportions).[4]

'Banyan days' were apparently days on which no meat was eaten. Smollett

---

[1] Ibid.
[2] *The Schoolboy, A Study of His Nutrition, Physical Development and Health*, G. E. Friend, 1935.
[3] *Annals of Christ's Hospital*, E. H. Pearce, 1901.
[4] *The Essays of Elia*, Charles Lamb, 1823.

P

says, 'they take their denomination from a sect of devotees in some parts of the East Indies who never taste flesh'.[1]

We shall deal later with the fact that many of these institutional dinners were scorbutic but meanwhile it is noteworthy that scurvy did afflict the boys of Christ's Hospital around this date and that on the recommendation of Dr Richard Budd, Physician-Apothecary to the School, potatoes were introduced into the diet in 1770 to counteract the disease. Later in the century, when there was a shortage of potatoes, the disease reappeared.

It can be seen from Jonas Hanway's remarks that the diets in even the better class of schools were composed largely of gruel, pease puddings and other starchy foods. Speaking of Winchester, he says:

> In respect to their *diet*; as they are seldom glutted with *quantity*, the *quality* becomes the less material; and yet, to indulge my concern for their welfare, I must observe that farinaceous foods, which are generally esteemed the *best*, or rather the *cheapest* for them, being preferred after the usual manner of schools, are not so wholesome as common bread if rightly prepared.[2]

He advocated the introduction of broth made from beef or mutton, and good vegetables.

§9 DIET IN PRISONS

There are few grimmer pictures than that of an eighteenth-century prison. The conditions were appalling. The prisoners, half-starved and clad in verminous rags, were herded together in filthy and insanitary surroundings. For the greater part of the century all the food they received from the authorities was an allowance of bread and since this was usually given on a money basis the daily loaf grew smaller and smaller as the price of bread rose.

> I often weighed the bread in different prisons, and found the penny loaf seven ounces and a half to eight and a half, the other loaves in proportion. It is probable that when this allowance was fixed by its value, near double the quantity that the money will now purchase, might be bought for it: yet the allowance continues unaltered: and it is not uncommon to see the whole purchase, especially of the smaller sums, eaten at breakfast; which is sometimes the case when they

---

[1] *The Adventures of Roderick Random*, T. Smollett, 1748.
[2] *A Journal of Eight Days Journey*, by Mr Hxxxxx, 1757.

receive their pittance but once in two days: and then on the following day they must fast.[1]

At no time adequate, the bread, reduced in this manner, meant starvation and starve the prisoner did unless he could afford to buy food from the jailer or was strong enough to seize it from another unfortunate sufferer.

Everyone on entering prison was expected to pay 'garnish' to the jailer. It was partly a bribe, to ensure somewhat milder treatment, and partly to treat the other prisoners to drink. The author of *The London Spy* speaks of the half-starved creatures in the prison of the King's Ward who

> ... came hovering round us, like so many *Canibals*, with such devour-
> ing *Countenances*, as if a Man had been but a Morsel with 'em, all
> crying out *Garnish, Garnish.*[2]

The jailers made large profits by selling intoxicating liquors to the wretched prisoners. William Smith, one of the first to try to bring medical care to the prisoners, has left an account of this trade, which was mostly in cheap and injurious substitutes for gin.

> There have been no less than 30 gin-shops at one time in the King's
> Bench, and I have been credibly informed by very attentive observers
> that upwards of two hogsheads or 120 gallons of gin, which they call
> by various names, as vinegar, gossip, crank, mexico, sky-blue, etc. sold
> weekly, besides other spirits in proportion. The beer consumed upon
> an average amounts, by calculation, to eight butts a week; and from the
> 26th of June till the last clearance took place, 24 butts a week were
> drunk.[3]

This recalls the indignation of the turnkey of Clerkenwell prison when Humphrey Clinker attempted to convert his fellow prisoners.

> Rabbit him, the tap will be ruined. We han't sold a cask of beer, nor
> a dozen of wine, since he paid his garnish; the gentlemen get drunk
> with nothing but your damned religion.[4]

Properly supplied with 'garnish' the jailer would supply the prisoner with extra food or look the other way when it was brought in from outside by his friends. It was a recognized thing for the leader of a gang or a well-known 'fence' to keep his associates in prison supplied with food and drink to the best of his ability. Such food could be cooked at one of the prison

[1] *The State of the Prisons in England and Wales*, John Howard, 1777.
[2] *The London Spy* [E. Ward], 1703.
[3] *State of the Gaols in London, Westminster, and Borough of Southwark*, William Smith, 1776.
[4] *The Expedition of Humphrey Clinker*, T. Smollett, 1771.

kitchens. Few prisoners, however, were able to afford extra rations and they were obliged, therefore, to subsist on bread and water. It is scarcely surprising that every kind of disease was rife and that scurvy was one of the most common complaints. Smith, who was an authority on diet, made a strong appeal for better food.

> There is then a constant and necessary waste in the body to preserve life and health, but that waste must be made up by a fresh supply of food to support the animal spirits and the vital principle of life, otherwise the person dies of inanition and putrefaction. And if that supply be too small, and not proportioned to the necessary waste, then the principle of animation becomes feeble, and the person droops, and becomes ill, and has more or less a tendency to putridity, which is the case of prisoners in gaol; therefore a proper allowance of bread, oatmeal, rice, codfish, cheese, apples, turnips, potatoes, etc. clean and well-dressed, should be allowed, and all flesh-meat totally forbid, especially to felons.[1]

He also advised the abolition of the sale of alcoholic liquors.

Howard made much the same recommendations.

> Those who drink only water, and have no nutritious liquor, ought to have at least a pound and a half of bread every day. The bread should be one day old, and then honestly weighed to them. If once a week (suppose on Sunday) some of the coarser pieces of beef were boiled in the copper, and half a pound of the meat without bone given to each prisoner, with a quart of the broth, this *Sunday dinner* might be made an encouragement to peaceable and orderly behaviour: the turbulent and refractory should not have it.

>   .   .   .   .

> I have before said, that I am no advocate for luxury in prisons; for I would have no meat diet for criminals in houses of correction, or at most, only on Sundays. Yet I would plead that they should have, at least, a pound and a half of good household bread a day, and a quart of good beer; besides twice a day a quart of warm soup made from pease, rice, milk or barley. For a change they might sometimes have turnips, carrots, or potatoes. It may be said this diet will starve those who work in houses of correction; but I am persuaded of the contrary, by what I have seen abroad, in the galleys, in the houses of correction, and among the most robust labourers.[2]

---

[1] *State of the Gaols in London*, etc., William Smith, 1776.
[2] *The State of the Prisons in England and Wales*, John Howard, 1777.

One need not be surprised at the callousness of the public with regard to the sufferings of prisoners when it was accepted even by those who wished to reform the system that restricted diet should form part of the punishment of a criminal. Contemporary ideas are summed up in the title of one of Jonas Hanway's pamphlets.

> *Solitude in Imprisonment with proper profitable Labour and a Spare Diet as the Most humane and effectual Means of bringing Malefactors who have forfeited their Lives and are subject to Transportation to a right Sense of their Condition.* (1776).

The naval prisoners in the hulks at Woolwich, who were chained in pairs, were little better off although their ration contained a certain amount of meat.

> They eat in messes; each mess, which consists of six convicts, has an allowance of half a bullock's head, four pounds of biscuit, and broth thickened with bread and oat-meal, every twenty-four hours. Sometimes, though rarely, they have hearts and shins of beef. They calculate, but with what degree of exactness I cannot take upon me to say, that from three ounces to half a pound and upwards of meat come to each man's share daily . . . Their flesh-meat, as they inform me, is not at all times sweet, but even green with rottenness. The biscuit, which is the only bread they have, is made of the third or coarsest part of the flour and is very unwholesome.[1]

It is scarcely surprising that 'Most of them complain of a diarrhoea; few are free from scorbutic blotches'. It would seem that they would have been better off if they had fallen into the hands of the French and been incarcerated at Calais. According to Howard, the prisoners there received a pound and a half of bread and three-quarters of a pound of meat on six days of the week, four ounces of butter and six of cheese on the seventh, half a pound of dried peas or beans four days a week and a quart and a half (Paris measure) of beer or three-quarters of a quart of wine daily.

[1] *State of the Gaols in London*, etc., William Smith, 1776.

CHAPTER XII

VIEWS ON DIET

§ 1 COMPOSITION OF FOODS

THE eighteenth century saw a complete change in ideas on food and nutrition. It was caused by the discoveries made by the experimentalists who were building the new chemistry and physiology which brought such discomfiture to the old guard, who still clung to the outworn conceptions of the material world derived from metaphysical speculation. But the old ideas could not long survive the positive proof that the very elements, or essential principles, air, water, salt, etc., upon which the whole philosophical structure was based, are not elementary at all but can be resolved into more simple and therefore more elementary units. Robert Boyle's attack on the old ideas of the elements[1] was carried further by the results of Joseph Black's experiments. These results were published in Latin in 1754 and a year later an English translation appeared.[2] They had far-reaching effects not only on chemistry but on medicine as well. Before Black's observations became known it was thought that there was one material substance, 'air'. It was recognized that its character might be changed by different conditions but it would still remain 'air'. The seventeenth-century doctor in speaking of 'mephitic air' or 'tainted air' had in mind 'air' which had acquired certain undesirable properties by contact with damp ground or putrefying material. He did not suspect that there are other 'airs', or gases as they are called today, which might be responsible for the obviously changed character of the atmosphere. Black showed conclusively that 'fixed air' (carbon dioxide) is quite distinct from ordinary 'air'.

Then came Priestley's discovery of yet another 'air';[3] 'dephlogisticated air' he called it, and he detected it as the respirable constituent of the atmosphere. We know it today as oxygen. Mayow's work of a century earlier had indicated the existence of this substance but it had long been forgotten. Even more shattering than the conclusive proof that there are several airs was the revelation by Cavendish in 1781 that water is a compound of two 'airs', 'dephlogisticated air' (oxygen) and 'inflammable air' (hydrogen), for of all the elements water had come to occupy the pre-eminent position. In-

[1] *The Sceptical Chymist*, R. Boyle, 1661.
[2] *Dissertatio de humore acido e cibo orto ex de Magnesia*, Joseph Black, 1754. (*Experiments on Magnesia alba, Quicklime and other Alcaline Substances*, 1755.)
[3] *Experiments and Observations on Different Kinds of Air*, J. Priestley, 1774-86.

deed, there were many who thought it was the one fundamental element or principle of nature, since van Helmont had shown that a young plant would grow in a tub full of soil to a fair-sized tree with the addition of nothing but water, there being afterwards no demonstrable loss in the weight of the soil.

It is not surprising that the old beliefs began rapidly to crumble under a succession of such heavy blows. For a time the position was very confused but gradually there emerged the new ideas regarding the character of the elements and the nature of chemical substances which form the foundations of our modern teaching. The atomic theory, which has provided the essential structure of our chemical theories for more than a hundred years, came into being soon after the eighteenth century had closed.

But while the development of the new ideas gave scientists a clearer picture of the true nature of simple chemical substances such as water, salt, nitre or chalk, it did not materially assist those who were interested in the nature and function of foods. The reason was that nobody at that time suspected how very complex and labile are the majority of the chemical compounds which make up our foods, and how involved and delicately balanced are the changes which they undergo during digestion and assimilation. Ignorance of this led to the publication of a great deal of misleading and valueless information. The point can be illustrated in a very simple manner. One of the commonest chemical procedures of the period was distillation. Material was placed in a retort which was heated in a furnace in such a manner that volatile products could be trapped and condensed in a suitable receiving vessel. On rare occasions this crude method yielded results of value. For example, a volatile acid (benzoic acid), which is a constituent of gum benzoin, was discovered in this way. Usually, however, the excessive heat of the furnace caused such extensive decomposition in the retort that none of the products isolated had any real relation to the composition of the original material. This fact, however, being unsuspected, the eighteenth-century chemists proceeded to make their deductions about the composition of the material from an inspection of the products of distillation.

These were broadly divided into the watery, oily and saline fractions. In addition they used to examine the carbonized and partly incinerated residue left behind in the retort. The watery distillate attracted a good deal of attention because its smell, taste and other characters differed so greatly when different foods were examined. It was not appreciated that these peculiarities were usually due to volatile products of decomposition. It was supposed that they represented some characteristic quality of the foodstuff itself. The aqueous fraction of the distillate was for this reason termed the 'phlegm', and it is important to note that the name implied an intrinsic relationship with the material from which it was derived.

The curious blending of the old and the new ideas which can be traced in this period of transition can be illustrated by quotations from Louis Lemery's book on diet which, although originally published in France, enjoyed a considerable success in England.[1] Strawberries, which had been classified as moist in the second degree and cold in the third, he described as containing 'much phlegm, and essential Salt, and a small Quantity of fine Oil'. Reverting to the humoral doctrines, however, he added that they are suitable for 'Young people that are of a choleric and sanguine complection'. Onions are described as 'hot' but the newer knowledge enabled Lemery to state that 'they contain much volatile Acid Salt, and an indifferent Quantity of Oil'. As food they were recommended as particularly suitable 'for those who abound in gross and viscous Humours'.

Perhaps the most important change in ideas about foods and their nutritional value came from the gradual development of the views regarding the nature of 'salts'. Apart from its popular significance the word salt had meant little more than the semi-mystical element of the Paracelsian system until late in the seventeenth century when scientists began to use it rather generally for substances of a saline appearance which were either obtained from natural sources or produced in their laboratories. It began to be apparent that there are many 'salts', not one 'salt', just as later it was shown that there are many 'airs' and not one 'air'.

The earliest classification of the salts was based on the fact that some change the colour of tinctures prepared from plants — a popular one was made from violets — and that others reverse the colour change. The use of these primitive indicators of acidity or alkalinity gave a rough and ready means of differentiating between 'acid salts' and 'alkaline salts', as Boyle originally called them. Less clearly defined were the 'volatile salts', found in the distillate after material had been heated in a retort.

The study of the nature of these salts had a far-reaching effect on the development of chemical thought during the eighteenth century. We are not concerned with this but it is of great importance for us to trace its influence on the ideas with regard to the function of food and the causes of disease. Acids and acid salts are usually sharp or bitter to the palate while many of the alkaline ones have an unpleasant caustic quality. When they mutually neutralize one another, however, the resulting salt is often relatively bland and innocuous. The idea therefore took root that the health of the body was governed by a balance between acidity and alkalinity. Many plausible arguments were adduced in support of this theory. Foods came to be classified according to whether their influence was acid (*acescent*) or alkaline (*alkalescent*). All meats were placed in the second category on the

[1] *A Treatise of all Sorts of Food*, Louis Lemery, translated by D. Hay, 1745.

ground that they were prone to undergo putrefaction. This may seem a curious view but it must be remembered that until late in the eighteenth century most people regarded the breakdown of meat in the stomach as a process essentially akin to that which occurs when it putrefies on keeping. It was known that alkaline substances (ammonia, etc.) are formed when meat putrefies; meat, therefore, must be a food with an alkaline tendency. The same simple type of argument placed all the fruits and most of the vegetables in the 'acid' class of food.

The basic idea was novel and plausible and was supported by what appeared to be convincing arguments. One example will serve. Scurvy had long been regarded as a 'putrid fever'. It was known to be associated with the excessive consumption of salt meats and curable by the administration of fruit and vegetables. What more acceptable, then, than the hypothesis that a disease caused by the excessive 'alkalescence' or putrefactive tendency of a meat diet would be cured when a proper balance, a readjustment to neutrality, was brought about by appropriate treatment with 'acescent' fruits?

> ... scurvy, ferocity, fœtor, leprosy and every kind of alkaline corruptions, all which evils are cured by change of diet, and the exclusive use of acid vegetables.[1]

It seems likely that it was these new ideas on the role of fruit and vegetables which led to the centuries-old theory that they were liable to cause fevers being gradually discarded, although early in the century medical writers were expressing the belief that they had 'evil pernicious qualities'.[2] After 1750, however, the medical profession came slowly round to the view that they were necessary for health.

> Ripe fruits, in moderate quantity, are wholesome; and, contrary to the vulgar prejudice, tend rather to prevent than to induce bowel complaints.[3]

It is perhaps not without interest to point out that there is, in fact, a scientific basis for a theory of 'neutralization' between meat and fruit, but it involves a reversal of the roles given to them by the eighteenth-century scientists. The proteins of meat contain considerable amounts of sulphur and phosphorus in different forms, most of which become oxidized in the body to yield sulphuric and phosphoric acid respectively. Meat is, therefore, in the old parlance, 'acescent', not 'alkalescent'. Basic (alkaline) material is

---

[1] *First lines of Physiology*, Albrecht von Haller, translated from the Latin, 1779.
[2] *The Sea-Surgeon or the Guinea-Man's Vade-Mecum*, T. Aubrey, 1729.
[3] *The Soldier's Friend; or the Means of Preserving the Health of Military Men*, W. Blair, 1798.

needed to neutralize the sulphuric and phosphoric acid and it has to be obtained ultimately from other foods. Many fruits, although they are deceptively acid in taste, are in fact potential sources of alkali suitable for neutralizing acids. This is because some of the acids they contain (e.g. citric and malic) are completely oxidized in the body to carbon dioxide which is expelled from the lungs. The alkaline or basic constituents, such as soda, potash or lime remain in the blood, however, and are available for neutralizing acids produced by the assimilation of other foods.

Reverting to the eighteenth-century theories about 'acescence' and 'alkalescence', we find that they were adopted with alacrity and enthusiasm by a medical profession which had been a bit discouraged by the alarming disintegration of its age-old beliefs. Within a very short time every symptom, every disease, every food was being discussed in terms of acescence or alkalescence. An early reference to the theory is to be found in Dr John Arbuthnot's *Essay Concerning the Nature of Aliments* (1731).

> Acrimony in the Blood it self is commonly of three Sorts according to the Nature of the Salts in which it resides; Acid, Alkaline or Muriatick.

'Muriatick' salt was common sea-salt and was much involved, as will be shown later, in discussions on the cause of scurvy.

A few years later another writer gave a classification of the foods which was wider than that based solely on the salts.

> Most Sorts of Food or Aliment may be reduced to one or other of the following Classes; *viz*; 1. The SALINE. 2. The ACID and ASESCENT. 3. The ALKALESCENT. 4. The VISCOUS and GLUTINOUS. 5. The OLEAGINOUS. 6. The ACRID AROMATICK. 7. The SPIRITUOUS. And, 8. The AQUEOUS.[1]

This list is of particular interest because it differentiates between the 'viscous and glutinous' components, the 'oleaginous' and the salts. To some extent it foreshadows our modern categories, the proteins, fats and mineral salts.

All the important eighteenth-century writers on food and diet based their views on the current hypothesis of the antagonism and mutual neutralization of 'acescence' and 'alkalescence'.

> When a person attempts to live upon flesh meat alone, though it be fresh, his appetite becomes keener, and even ravenous; and nature will crave for some acids and vegetables to correct the alkaline acrimony of the blood. And when he lives upon vegetables alone, whereby the

[1] *A Treatise on the Various Kinds and Qualities of Foods*, William Forster, 1738.

stomach will contract an acid tendency, he will find a craving for animal food to temperate the acidities.[1]

Eggs and cheese were grouped together with the meats as 'putrescible' or 'alkalescent' foods, although cheese, together with fish, was regarded as less endowed with this quality than red meats such as beef and mutton. Milk, however, although an animal food, was thought to be rather more acescent than alkalescent, a view certainly derived from the well-known tendency of milk to turn sour or acid.

This theory seemed compatible with the recognized value of milk in illness and convalescence.

In all putrid diseases of the chronical kind, consumptions, etc. vegetable or milk diet, which is only one degree removed from a vegetable state, is very proper.[2]

Fruits and vegetables, as has already been stated, were held to be 'acescent' although cabbage, for reasons which will perhaps be obvious, was relegated to the 'putrescent' or 'alkalescent' class.

How were these new ideas reconciled with the old belief that fruit was a cause of disease? Obviously, since neutralization of an acid by an alkali required careful adjustment it was merely a question of maintaining an appropriate balance between the alkalescent meats and the acescent plant foods. Excess of either would be liable to upset the proper functioning of the body and produce a diseased condition. Cucumbers, for example, were thought to produce cholera and diarrhoea; a poor person, therefore, who ate little meat would be wise to abstain from them, but for those who habitually ate too much flesh they were valuable in 'allaying the heat of meat'. This was the opinion of the great medical teacher, William Cullen, whose writings show clearly the transition from the humoral doctrine to the new ideas which were derived from contemporary chemistry. Sometimes he relapsed into pure Galenism.

The PLUMB is most refrigerant, and liable to ferment and produce *cholera, diarrhoea*, &c.[3]

In eighteenth-century medical writings there is sometimes more than a mere modification of the Galenic teaching about the dangers of eating fruit; we find the first definite statements that fruit may be more beneficial than harmful. William Smith, a leading authority on diet, advanced the revolutionary idea that it was 'the lightest, most wholesome food we can eat'. He

[1] *A Sure Guide in Sickness and Health*, W. Smith, 1776.   [2] Ibid.
[3] *Lectures on the Materia Medica*, William Cullen, 1773.

actually advised a liberal consumption of fruit, even in summer, as a preventive measure against certain diseases, pointing out that the country people in southern Europe suffered no more from fevers than did the English, in spite of the large amounts they habitually ate.

There was some difference of opinion about the nutritive value of fruit. Some people thought it was determined by two factors, the quality of acescence and the quantity of sugar, while others, regarding sugar as an acescent food, thought it was merely a question of how much sugar it contained.

The medical profession was expected to pronounce an opinion on the food value of sugar during this century, since it became a cheap and common household commodity. They were, as usual, divided. Some doctors feared that it was unwholesome by virtue of its strong 'acescence', and the old idea that it might cause decay of the teeth appeared in a new light. Perhaps, they surmised, it was the acid which corroded the surface of the enamel. The modern theory relating caries to the fermentation of sugars and starches on the surface of the teeth is clearly foreshadowed by an eighteenth-century suggestion.

> ... it may, perhaps, by what adheres of it about them, turning acid, corrode them.[1]

The writer, William Cullen, continues the argument along very much the same lines as are followed in dental circles today. If this view is entertained, he says, it becomes difficult to understand why the people in Mediterranean countries have such good teeth since they eat liberally of sweet raisins, a foodstuff even more 'acescent' than sugar.

A vigorous defence in favour of sugar was put forward. Fred. Slare ridiculed the idea that it contained a 'secret acid' which caused scurvy and other disorders. That its character is 'pleasant, soft and balmy' rather than 'acrimonious' could, he argued, be proved by blowing some into a person's eye. Far from aggravating acidity it relieved it. Did it not reduce the acidity of fruits? Was it not, in fact, a preservative?

> That which preserves Apples and Plumbs,
> Will also preserve Liver and Lungs.[2]

As a final argument he quoted the case of the 'Great Duke of Beaufort' who died at the age of seventy with all his teeth firm and the viscera of a man of twenty, in spite of having eaten a pound of sugar a day for the greater part of his life.

[1] *Lectures on the Materia Medica*, William Cullen, 1773.
[2] *A Vindication of Sugars against the Charge of Dr. Willis, other Physicians and Common Prejudices*, Fred. Slare, 1715.

Butter, which as we have seen had not been regarded too favourably in the past, was still looked upon with some suspicion by eighteenth-century dietary experts. It was rather widely regarded as unsuitable for children; it was thought that it choked the 'Glans and Capillaries', and caused children to grow 'weakly, corpulent, big-belly'd, very subject to breakings-out, and to breed Lice'.[1]

§2 VIEWS ON DIGESTION

In the early part of the eighteenth century the views on digestion were very confused and ill-defined. The most popular theory was that it was a kind of fermentation, comparable if not actually identical with one of the three recognized types of fermentation, the spirituous, the acetous and the putrefactive. This rough and ready classification was based on the three obvious changes which fresh foods tend to undergo on keeping; some ferment to produce alcoholic fluids, some turn sour and acquire acidity, while others become putrescent. There was another belief, which was sometimes found as a distinct hypothesis and sometimes in conjunction with the fermentation theory, which held that food was broken down in the stomach and intestines by a process of attrition due to the churning movement of these organs. Yet another popular idea saw digestion as a process of solution effected by an unknown agent, much in the same manner as chalk is dissolved in acids. In this connection the question of the existence of an acid in the stomach continued to attract a good deal of attention.

The first fallacy to be disposed of was the idea that food 'putrefied' in the stomach. That this was not so was shown by the ingenious experiments carried out by a French scientist, de Reaumur, whose name is perpetuated by one of the thermometric scales. The experiments were carried out on a young kite, a bird which habitually ejects undigested food from its crop. He fed the bird with small metal tubes, open at both ends, containing fragments of food. Later, when they were vomited, he examined the contents. He found that meat was softened and partly dissolved after a few hours in the digestive tract of the bird, but that far from being 'putrid' it was quite sweet. There was no evidence whatever of a 'putrefactive' fermentation.[2]

Later, similar information was published in two independent papers which appeared in the same year (1777), one at Edinburgh and the other at Pavia. The latter, which attracted considerable interest in western Europe, brought its author, l'Abbé Spallanzani, widespread fame and earned him an honoured

[1] *A Treatise on the Various Kinds and Qualities of Foods*, William Forster, 1738.
[2] *Sur la Digestion des Oiseaux*, de Reaumur, 1752.

place in the history of physiology. The other, for no very clear reason, passed almost unnoticed and its existence is only known today to a very few physiologists.

Stevens used for his experiments, he says, 'a Hussar, a man of weak understanding, who gained a miserable livelihood, by swallowing stones for the amusement of the common people, at the imminent hazard of his life'.[1] Following the lines of de Reaumur's experiment he got the man to swallow perforated silver spheres containing weighed amounts of different foods. After remaining a certain time in the stomach the contents of the spheres were examined. Stevens found that beef and fish lost weight and became softened in quite a short time and that they were completely dissolved in 36 hours. Like de Reaumur, he was satisfied that putrefaction was not a part of the digestion of food in the stomach.

He made similar experiments on dogs to which he gave food in ivory spheres, and noticed with some surprise that the spheres, as well as the meat inside, were attacked. His most remarkable achievement was to effect the digestion of meat outside the body. This he did by placing it in a phial containing gastric juice obtained from a dog. The phial was then incubated at blood heat in a sand furnace. The fragment of meat dissolved completely in eight hours and did not putrefy as did the other pieces which were merely placed in water.

Convinced by these experiments that digestion is not a form of putrefaction, he turned his attention to the other theories. He rejected the idea that food is simply broken down by a process of attrition and was finally led to a conclusion which brought the truth a good deal nearer.

Digestion is not the effect of heat, trituration, putrefaction or fermentation alone, but of a powerful solvent secreted by the coats of the stomach, which converts the aliment into a fluid resembling blood.

Lazzaro Spallanzani experimented along almost identical lines, first on a variety of birds and animals and then, somewhat timorously, on himself.[1] He was afraid the little containers would remain inside him, but comforting himself with the reflection that cherry stones usually reappear, and taking the precaution of putting the food into linen bags instead of metal containers, he finally took the risk. Most of his findings confirmed those of de Reaumur and Stevens.

During this century the important part played by the bile (long thought to be nothing more than an excretory product) and the pancreatic juice in

[1] An English version of Stevens's work is given as an appendix to the English edition of Spallanzani's *Dissertation relating to the Natural History of Animals and Vegetables*, 1784.

[2] *Expériences sur la Digestion de l'Homme*, par l'Abbé Spallanzani. *Avec des Considérations, etc.*, par Jean Senebier, 1783.

bringing about the emulsification of the food began to be realized, though scientists had no idea that the chemical character of foods was modified during digestion. Digestion was thought to be simply a matter of reducing the food to a sufficiently fine state of division or emulsification to permit of absorption. The disappearance of the milky chyle from the interior of the bowel was known to occur through the agency of the innumerable villi which line the surface of the small intestine. It was also known that the absorbed chyle passes into the lacteals and thence into the blood. The general view was that the food absorbed in the form of chyle soon became converted into blood but that it might sometimes be separated again from the blood. There was a popular theory that the breast was a mechanism for separating chyle from the blood, so enabling the child to get almost untouched the digested food absorbed by the mother.[1] It was a simple idea based on nothing more than the superficial resemblance between milk and chyle.

Nothing was known of the way in which the organs and tissues of the body are nourished. It was generally accepted that the nourishment came from the blood but there was complete ignorance both as to the nature of the nutrients and how they reached their destination. The two most popular theories differed in that one visualized a direct nourishment from the blood while the other postulated the distribution of a nutritive principle by way of the nerves; a survival of the old Greek teaching of the transmission of the 'vital spirit' by means of the ramifications of the nervous system. These two theories are well illustrated by quotations from contemporary writers.

> A gelatinous juice is conveyed from the aliments, through the arteries, to all parts of the body, and exudes into the cellular texture every where.[2]
>
> ... the cortical part of the brain, or common origin of the nerves, is a secretory organ, in which the gluten of the blood, being freed from all saline matter before adhering to it, becomes fit for the nourishment of the solids, and being poured in a sufficiently diluted state upon the organ of the nerves, it is filtrated along the fibres of these, and is thus conveyed to every staminal fibre of the system.[3]

There was, too, considerable speculation regarding the nature of the mechanism by which the warmth of the body is maintained. Most physiologists accepted the old explanation that heat is generated by the friction caused by the blood moving in the vessels. In 1777, however, Adair Craw-

---

[1] *First Lines of Physiology*, Albrecht von Haller, translated from the Latin, 1779.
[2] Ibid.
[3] *The Works of William Cullen*, edited by John Thomson, 1827.

ford advanced an ingenious theory; the inspired air, he said, brought an 'elementary fire' to the lungs whence it entered the blood. During circulation this was given off as heat, the blood taking in exchange an 'inflammable principle', which in turn was expelled by the lungs when more 'elementary fire' was absorbed. One can trace in this theory the germ of the modern view regarding the exchange of oxygen and carbon dioxide in the lungs, but it gave no real clue to the origin of the body's warmth. The problem was solved by the brilliant investigations of the French scientists Lavoisier and Laplace. Employing, almost for the first time in the history of physiology, the precise methods of weighing and measuring provided by the new chemistry and physics, they showed that the amount of heat given out is proportional to the quantity of carbon converted into carbon dioxide in the body and that the phenomenon of respiration is essentially the same as that of combustion. By 1790 the foundations of our modern knowledge were firmly established.

Lavoisier thought the products of the digestion of food were absorbed into the blood and carried to the lungs, where they became oxidized by the oxygen of the respired air, the carbon and hydrogen of these products being thereby converted to carbon dioxide and water with liberation of heat. Only in thinking that the combustion occurred in the lungs, from which the heat was carried away by the blood stream, did Lavoisier and his colleagues go astray.[1]

The records of revolutionary tribunals throughout the centuries contain few more terrible words than those uttered by Coffinhal when he condemned Lavoisier and twenty-seven other members of the hated Ferme-Générale to the guillotine: '*La République n'a pas besoin de savants*'.

§5 THE EXPERIMENTS OF WILLIAM STARK[2]

In 1770 there died in London a young medical man, not thirty years of age, who, had he lived, would probably have earned for himself a world-wide reputation in experimental dietetics. William Stark was a graduate of Glasgow, where he probably came under the influence of William Cullen. After taking his doctorate at Leyden he came to London, about 1765, to continue his anatomical studies under John Hunter. While engaged on these his interest was diverted to the study of the function of foods as the result of a chance conversation with Benjamin Franklin, who was at that time in

[1] *La Transpiration des Animeaux*, par Seguin et Lavoisier, 1790.
[2] For a fuller account of this remarkable young man see the authors' note, 'An Eighteenth Century Experiment in Nutrition', by J. C. Drummond and Anne Wilbraham, *Lancet* (1935), ii, 459.

ANDREW BOORDE
(*By permission of the British Museum*)

A THIRTEENTH-CENTURY MINIATURE
showing an infant being fed from a cow's horn
(*By permission of the Wellcome Historical Medical Museum*)

SANCTORIUS

He is shown seated in the chair attached to a yard-arm by
which he recorded his changes of weight after eating

VIRGIN AND CHILD
(Hans Bergmaier, Nuremberg, 1500?)
This picture shows a typically rachitic infant
(*By permission of the American Medical Association*)

BROADSHEET SATIRIZING THE INTRODUCTION OF
FRENCH COOKING

(By permission of the British Museum)

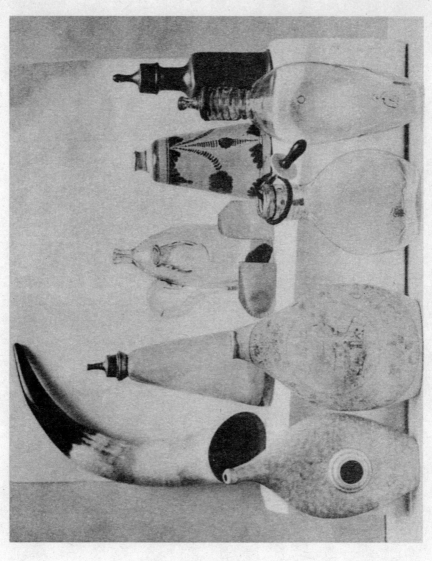

THE EVOLUTION OF THE FEEDING-BOTTLE

(*From the collection in the Wellcome Historical Medical Museum*)

ACCUM LECTURING AT THE SURREY INSTITUTION

(By permission of Mr R. B. Pilcher, Registrar of the Institute of Chemistry)

FRONTISPIECE TO 'THE FAMILY ORACLE OF HEALTH'

Dr Kitchiner is about to be arrested for eating live oysters and thereby contravening
Martin's Bill for the Prevention of Cruelty to Animals

London on one of his political missions and who continued to preach, even if he no longer practised, the doctrine of the simple life that he so strongly supported in his apprentice days.

Stark consulted his colleagues, among them Sir John Pringle, and decided as a result of his inquiries that there was much to be learned about food and that the best means of getting the information he wanted would be by experimenting on himself.

> ... and I confess it will afford me a singular pleasure if I can prove by experiment, that a pleasant and varied diet is equally conducive to health, with a more strict and simple one; at the same time, I shall endeavour to keep my mind unbiassed in my search after truth, and, if a simple diet seems the most healthy, I shall not hesitate to declare it.[1]

He began his experiments on June 12th, 1769, by attempting to live on bread and water with an occasional allowance of sugar. He persisted with this diet for ten weeks and by the beginning of August was complaining of swollen and bleeding gums and sore nostrils, obvious although apparently unrecognized scorbutic symptoms. These symptoms continued until early September when, feeling rather ill, he relaxed the rigour of his self-imposed restrictions and 'lived freely on animal food, milk, and wine; . . . when I felt myself quite recovered'.

Stark next tried to live on bread and cooked meats. As his gums remained in good condition on this diet he decided to find out whether the symptoms he had previously noted were due to the bread and water or to the sugar; sugar was thought by some to cause scurvy and other skin eruptions. He satisfied himself, however, by living for five days on bread, water and sugar, that the latter substance was not to blame for his symptoms.

Late in November he began a period in which his diet was composed solely of puddings. From his description of how he made them they must have been peculiarly unappetizing mixtures. In about a month's time the symptoms of scurvy had returned, but they cleared up to some extent when on Boxing Day he broke his hard and fast rules and enjoyed half a pint of black currants. His next experiment was on the relative value of fat and lean meat and he planned to follow this by a study of the effects of fresh fruit and vegetables. Had he done so his by then chronic scurvy would have been cured, but for some reason he changed his mind and went on to a diet of honey puddings and Cheshire cheese. He developed an intestinal disorder, the scorbutic symptoms became worse, and he died on February 23rd, 1770, a true martyr to science.

It is impossible to say if Stark realized he was suffering from scurvy.

[1] *The Works of the late William Stark, M.D.*, edited by J. C. Smyth, 1788.

Q

Probably he did not at first, but the notes in his meticulously kept journal suggest that towards the end it had begun to dawn upon him that his symptoms might be scorbutic. He consulted Sir John Pringle, at that time a recognized authority on the disease, who advised him to omit salt from his diet, advice which he took without bringing about any noticeable amelioration of his symptoms.

Stark's experiments did not add very much to the knowledge of the nutritive value of foodstuffs because insufficient information was available to allow his findings to be interpreted. He could not think of bread as a mixture of such 'principles' as starch, protein, salts and vitamins; to him it could only be bread. But his records reveal unusual powers of observation and a desire for investigation in advance of his time.

§ 4 THE FEEDING OF INFANTS

There is a good deal of information about contemporary views on the rearing of young children in the writings and records relating to the foundation of the Foundling Hospital by Thomas Coram in 1739. In the first place there is the clear picture of a terrible mortality among infants and young children. A baby born in one of the big towns had about one chance in three of reaching the age of a year and the odds that it would die before it was five were about the same. Under the insanitary conditions prevailing in the poorer parts of the towns or wherever large numbers of people were herded together, as in the workhouses, the mortality was even greater. Hanway gives a grim picture of the fate of infants handed over to the tender mercies of parish nurses; in one parish only 11 children out of 174 survived two months, in another out of a total of 3000 no less than 2960 died before reaching the age when they could be placed as apprentices.[1]

The mortality among infants was in no small measure due to the heavy spirit-drinking in the towns, particularly in the first half of the century. Wet-nurses were all too often gin-tipplers and the practice of giving spirits to babies to quieten them was very general. Forster speaks of the 'mad and imprudent Fondness of many Mothers, who do often permit their Infants to sip up Ale, Wine, and other Strong and Spirituous Liquors'.[2]

It must not be forgotten in considering the rearing of young children during this century that industrialization had begun and that hundreds of women were working long hours in the factories under fearful conditions. In the

---

[1] *Letters on the Importance of the Rising Generation*, Jonas Hanway, 1767.
[2] *A Compendious Discourse of the Diseases of Children, Taken chiefly from Harris's Incomparable Treatise. With the Author's Own Practice*, William Forster, 1738.

second half of the century the dearth and high price of food added to their misery. It is, therefore, not surprising that the appalling infant mortality was forced on the public's notice and that eventually something had to be done about the thousands of abandoned children.

Not until the eighteenth century do we find attention being paid to the artificial feeding of infants. It is impossible to say whether this was a consequence of industrialization, whether it means that wet-nurses were more difficult to find or regarded with more suspicion, or whether people generally were more concerned than they had been over the mortality among the very young. The hire of a wet-nurse in London was at least 4s. a week.[1] The old belief survived and was widely held that undesirable moral characteristics might be imbibed with the nurse's milk unless she were chosen with the greatest care.

The Governors of the Foundling Hospital had to face some of these difficulties in the early days of their activities. A Report from the General Committee to the Court in 1740 contains the following paragraphs:

> We having next considered of the best method to bring up Young Children, submit to You, if it is not most advisable to apply to the College of Physicians for their opinion upon the following Questions Viz[t]

> First, Whether it will be most prudent for the Governors to endeavour to provide Wet Nurses for all the Children they take in? or whether it will not be better to bring up by hand all such as will feed, and suckle only those that will not?

> Second, How Long ought a Child to continue to Suck?

> Third, The Committee has been informed, that it is a very frequent if not Universal Custom among Nurses, to give Opiates to quiet the Children, when restless; they therefore desire the Opinion of the College, whether that Custom is pernicious and ought to be prevented?[2]

Apparently, the Governors decided to rear some infants in the Hospital itself but to send a good many others out to wet-nurses in various parts of the country, where they would be kept until they were five years old. This farming-out of children became a terrible scandal, few surviving more than a few months 'care' by their foster-mothers, even if they ever reached their destination, for as often as not they were entrusted to any rogue who offered to take them.

[1] *The London Adviser and Guide*, Rev. Dr Trusler, 1786.
[2] *The History of the Foundling Hospital*, R. H. Nichols and F. A. Wray, 1935.

There is no record that the Hospital tried artificial feeding, so perhaps the College of Physicians reported adversely on that point. They may well have done so, for it seems certain that the feeding of infants on cows' or asses' milk was not widely practised in England before the middle of the eighteenth century, though there is evidence that very primitive devices for giving milk to infants were used in medieval and even earlier times.

It is clear from an inspection of the collection of early feeding bottles in the Wellcome Historical Medical Museum that the modern pattern has evolved from the spouted invalid feeding-cup, which has itself retained its shape almost unchanged from Greek and Roman times. Some of the earliest forms are of pewter and in shape rather like a beer tankard, with a lid and a long tapering spout. It seems that they were sometimes used with the end of the finger of an old glove tied over the end of the spout so as to make something resembling a teat. George Armstrong, who founded the first Dispensary for Sick Children in London in 1769, stated:

> There are two ways of feeding children who are bred up by the hand; the one is by means of a horn, and the other is with a boat or spoon.[1]

He referred to the use of a 'teat' made from the finger of a glove as if it were quite an innovation. The whole contraption was called a 'bubby-pot'.[2] The 'boat' seems to have been a later pattern of feeding-bottle. Most of those in the Wellcome Collection are made of earthenware, and have a hole at each end, one to be covered by the finger or thumb so as to regulate the flow of milk, while to the other was attached a 'teat' of linen or thin leather. Occasionally, a small piece of sponge was used as a teat or was placed inside the glove-finger.

That earnest reformer, Hanway, was a strong advocate of artificial feeding, chiefly because he thought the low standard of morality among wet-nurses contributed in no small measure to the alarming spread of vice, by imparting evil qualities with their milk. He had been assured by a correspondent in France that not only the spread of godlessness but also the terrible infant mortality in that country were due to a large extent to 'mercenary nurses, libertinism and bad diet'. Hanway added, 'This author expects no speedy reformation and therefore recommends the feeding of infants with the *milk of animals*, which he says is the constant custom in the *North*.'[3]

Considerable use was made of paps prepared from flour or bread with water or milk. Sometimes rice flour or arrowroot was used. When sweetened or slightly spiced they were still often called by the sixteenth-century

---

[1] *An Account of the Diseases most incident to Children from their Birth till the Age of Puberty*, G. Armstrong, 1772.
[2] *The History of Pediatrics*, G. F. Still, 1931.
[3] *A Journal of Eight Days Journey*, by Mr Hxxxxx, 1757.

name of *panadas*. They were most frequently used during weaning or for young children. Still, in his most interesting *History of Pediatrics* (1931) refers to the use in Germany in the eighteenth century of 'sucking-bags'. These were linen bags, rather like a jelly-bag, through which soft *panadas* could be squeezed to give a very soft pap for the child. It is not known whether they were used in England to any extent. If they were they must have been responsible for as many deaths as were the linen 'teats' and sponges, veritable breeding grounds for bacteria, which were attached to the primitive feeding-bottles.

A number of the leading medical men disapproved of feeding 'pap' to very young children as a substitute for the breast. Forster, for example, held the view that infants invariably did badly when given 'Milk-Pottage, boiled till it be almost as gluttinous as syzing'.[1]

He expressed surprise that Dr Harris did not condemn it in his well-known book, which was still regarded as one of the most authoritative works on the rearing of children. Its popularity had been increased by the publication in 1693 of an English translation from the Latin by the famous naval surgeon William Cockburn.[2] Moss also condemned the usual type of 'bread-pap', which was all too often made with water, and he advocated the use of milk and a little finely broken up floury potato.[3] Hanway was another who thought 'flour-pap' very bad for babies "tho it may serve as a medicine, where none better can be had, used with great caution it may stop a purging'.[4]

Sir William Fordyce, an eminent physician, who held very advanced views on the rearing of children, believed that much of the high infant mortality rate was due to improper diet; incidentally he was one of the few doctors who deplored 'hotbed chambers and nurseries'.

> ... they are fed on meat before they have got their teeth, and what is, if possible, still worse, on biscuits not fermented, or buttered rolls, or tough muffins floated in oiled butter, or calves-feet jellies, or strong broths, yet more calculated to load all their powers of digestion.[5]

Another question that worried the doctors was the tendency for cows' milk to cause indigestion. Fresh cows' milk tends to form a much denser clot in the stomach than does human milk. This, not infrequently, gives rise to digestive disorders. The difficulty can be overcome to some extent by

---

[1] *A Compendious Discourse of the Diseases of Children*, William Forster, 1738.
[2] *Tractatus de Morbis acutis Infantus*, Walter Harris, 1689. (*An Exact Inquiry into and Cure of the Acute Diseases of Infants*, Englished by W. C.[ockburn], 1693.)
[3] *An Essay on the Management, Nursing and Diseases of Children*, W. Moss, 1781.
[4] *An Essay on Tea*, by Mr Hxxxxx, 1757.
[5] *A New Inquiry into the Causes, Symptoms and Cure, of Putrid and Inflammatory Fevers*, Sir William Fordyce, 1773.

'humanizing' the milk. By that is meant altering its composition so as more nearly to approach the natural food.

	COW'S MILK per cent	HUMAN MILK per cent
Protein	3.5	1.5
Milk sugar	4.5	6.5
Fat	4.0	3.5
Mineral salts	0.7	0.2

This can be done, as the above figures indicate, by suitable dilution with water and addition of milk sugar (lactose) and cream fat.

Another method of preventing heavy curd formation is to add a small proportion, 1 grain to a fluid ounce of milk, of sodium citrate. This reduces the amount of calcium which is present in the milk in a form in which it influences the texture of the curd. 'Citrated' cows' milk therefore forms a soft, digestible curd in the stomach.

All this was unknown in the eighteenth century, but it had been discovered in an empirical way that acid milks — and it must be remembered that a great deal of the cows' milk then sold in the towns was near curdling point owing to acid produced by bacteria — were particularly liable to cause stomach disorders in infants. Some experts advised adding the alkaline 'testaceous powders' which William Harris had made so popular in the previous century. These mostly consisted of ground-up calcined oyster shells and were formed, therefore, of lime. They could have done little harm and might sometimes have done good. Armstrong's remedy for acid milks was rather more drastic. He advised adding a piece of 'Castille' soap, the size of a filbert, to half a pint of milk to aid digestion.[1] This would certainly have supplied alkali, because such soaps are alkaline, but one wonders what happened to the babies who were so treated.

We have to thank the General Committee of the Foundling Hospital for placing on record a very remarkable expression of opinion about the rearing of infants and young children. The eminent physician William Cadogan had written to one of the Governors setting out his views at some length. His letter was brought to the attention of the General Committee who were so impressed that they ordered it to be published.[2] It is not surprising that the document made an impression; what is surprising is that the Governors should have been so sympathetic to ideas which, to the majority of them, must have appeared revolutionary. At a time when babies were heavily swaddled to keep them from chills and to straighten their limbs, and when

[1] *An Account of the Diseases most incident to Children*, G. Armstrong, 1772.
[2] *Essay on Nursing and Management of Children*, W. Cadogan, 1750.

the leading physicians of the day advised that they be kept from direct sunshine lest the light damage their eyes,[1] Cadogan insisted that they were not 'hot-bed plants' and that the lighter and looser their clothing the better they would be. He even dared to suggest that deformities were more likely to be caused than cured by binding and swaddling.

He then turned to the feeding of children which, he insisted, was 'of much Greater Importance to them than their Cloathing'. Heaping heresy on heresy, he completely rejected the old belief that fruit and vegetables are dangerous for children.

> I am sure all these things are wholesome and good for them.

As soon as they were able to live on bread and butter and a little meat he wanted them to have raw, baked or stewed fruit and 'all the produce of the kitchen garden'.

Cadogan was a remarkable man and nearly two centuries ahead of his time. He seems also to have been modest, judging by the concluding lines of his delightful essay.

> These few loose Thoughts on the Subject of nursing Children, I send you for your private Satisfaction, if they be lucky enough to give you any.

[1] *Dissertation sur l'Education physique des Enfants*, M. Ballexserd, 1762.

CHAPTER XIII

DIET AND HEALTH

§ I GENERAL CONSIDERATIONS

IT is a remarkable fact that the second half of the eighteenth century saw a striking improvement in the general health of the people in spite of the declining standard of living among a large section. Although food was cheap before 1750 and most people fed amply and well it was not a healthy half century, at least in the towns. There is a rather general impression that the high death-rate was due in no small measure to excessive spirit-drinking. Whether that view be accepted or not it is certainly true that an improvement occurred about the time that the heavy taxes on spirits were imposed.

The very marked increase in the population which occurred in the last twenty-five years of the century was due to a declining death-rate rather than to a mounting birth-rate. That this should have been so at a time when the price of so many foods was high and when there was so much hardship and want among the poor is surprising, but before unreservedly accepting the view that it was mainly the decline in gin-drinking or the improvement of sanitary conditions that bettered the general health of the population, we must remember that in this century potatoes and other vegetables became more general items of diet among all classes of the population. It is not easy to say how great an influence this had on the nation's health for we do not know how the consumption of potatoes and the cheaper green vegetables such as cabbage, was affected by the rise in price of the staple foods in the second half of the century.

The information about the fluctuations in the price of vegetables is very scanty. We know from John Holt's survey that in 1794 the farmers in the vicinity of Liverpool could only get 2s. 6d. to 3s. a hundredweight for carrots.[1] About 1770, potatoes could be bought for 4d. to 6d. a peck and cabbages, in the London markets at any rate, for 1d. to 1½d. each. Twenty-five years later potatoes were still relatively cheap in the north-west, if one can judge from the fact that large quantities were used to feed the paupers in Liverpool workhouse.[2] In Bristol, in 1795, they were no more than 6d. a peck as compared with 5d. a peck in 1771; a labourer in Bristol earning only £24 a year could afford two pecks a week for himself, his wife and two children.[3]

[1] *A General View of Agriculture in the County of Lancashire*, John Holt, 1794.
[2] *The State of the Poor*, Sir Frederic Eden, 1797.   [3] Ibid.

On the basis of this meagre information we are tempted to think that the price of garden produce did not increase in proportion to the rise in the price of bread and meat but we are unable to say whether the poor people were able to afford to buy it in view of the enormous increase in the cost of the staple foods. It is tantalizing to be unable to trace this information, which might enable us to say whether the fall in the death-rate was to some extent a result of the increased consumption of certain of the protective food factors provided by vegetables. It is certain that milk became dear and scarce in the towns in the south and that the price of butter rose to a level which put it beyond the reach of many of the labouring classes, so that in respect to the protective substances provided by these two foods the poor people were a great deal worse off in the last fifty years of the century.

§2 EYE DISEASES

The rise in prices which caused milk, butter and perhaps also green garden vegetables to be expensive for the poor people of the towns might well have caused widespread vitamin A deficiency, but there is no means of telling whether it did. The medical textbooks of the day make no mention of the eye diseases which are now recognized as being of dietary origin. We have only been able to trace one reference to a condition resembling xerophthalmia. Sir Hans Sloane, speaking of a certain medicine, said that it

> ... has cured many, whose eyes were covered with opake *films*, and *cicatrices* left by inflammations and apostems of the cornea; which, though they happen to persons of all conditions, yet are more common among the poorer sort of people.[1]

Cullen makes a passing reference to the belief that rice is bad for the eyes; he had probably heard of the prevalence of eye diseases among the rice-eating populations of the East which are prone to vitamin A deficiency conditions. He comforted himself with the reflection that since the inhabitants of Carolina are immune in this respect it must be attributed to the excessive sunshine in the East.[2]

One of Gilbert Blane's junior naval surgeons reported cases of night blindness in one of His Majesty's ships on the Barbados Station. It is clear that he was mystified by the condition.

[1] *An Account of a Most Efficacious Medicine for Soreness, Weakness, and Several Other Distempers of the Eyes*, Sir Hans Sloane, 1762.
[2] *Lectures on the Materia Medica*, William Cullen, 1773.

Four patients have last month complained of an almost total blindness
towards evening ... Two of them had the scurvy in a high degree
... I am not well acquainted with the nature or cure of this disease,
which I believe is called Nyctalopia, by some systematic writers ...
I can form no probable conjecture concerning the cause of this disease.[1]

Blane himself says that the troops at the siege of Gibraltar were severely
afflicted by a similar complaint. He was inclined to regard it as one of the
manifestations of scurvy.

§3 AN OUTBREAK OF ERGOTISM

It is curious that England, which seems to have escaped ergotism throughout the centuries when her poor people were eating a good deal of rye,
should have experienced an outbreak when this cereal had almost ceased to
be used for breadmaking. It occurred at the little village of Wattisham in
Suffolk in 1762. The family most seriously affected was that of John Down-
ing, 'a poor labouring man'. The whole family was attacked by an acute
form of the gangrenous type of ergotism, mortification causing the loss of a
foot or limb in the case of the mother and five of the children. Perhaps the
most interesting feature of this outbreak is the fact that it was traced to the
consumption not of infected rye but of an unsound lot of the previous year's
wheat which a farmer had threshed separately and sold cheaply because of its
poor quality. The local surgeon, Dr Wollaston, and the parson, the Rev. J.
Bones, have left very full notes of this tragedy.[2] They suspected that it
might have been caused by *Raphania*, as ergotism was then called, but were
satisfied that this could not be the case when they found that no rye-bread
had been eaten. They were unaware of the fact that infection of wheat with
ergot has been known to occur.

The diet of this Suffolk labouring family, living 'as do the other poor',
consisted of dried pease, pickled pork, bread, cheese, milk and small beer.

§4 GLUTTONY

A word must be said about the gross over-indulgence of the eighteenth-
century Englishman. The rich at all times, the poor when they could, were
intemperate in meat and drink to an extent which made the English notorious
all over Europe. The swollen limbs, bulging cheeks and pendulous paunches

---

[1] *Observations on the Diseases Incident to Seamen*, Sir Gilbert Blane, 1785.
[2] *Philosophical Transactions of the Royal Society*, 1762, Vol. LII.

which nearly every artist and cartoonist of the time depicted tell their own story.

Many writers deplored these intemperate habits, among them Joseph Addison.

It is said of Diogenes that meeting a young Man who was going to a Feast, he took him from the street and carried him on to his Friends, as one who was running into imminent danger, had he not prevented him. What would that Philosopher have said had he been present at the Gluttony of a modern Meal? Would he not have thought the Master of a Family mad, and have begged his Servants to tie down his Hands, had he seen him devour Fowl, Fish and Flesh; swallow Oil and Vinegar, Wines and Spices; throw down Sallads of twenty different Herbs, Sauces of an hundred Ingredients, Confections and Fruits of numberless Sweets and Flavours? What unnatural Motions and Counterferments must such a Medley of Intemperance produce in the Body? For my part, when I behold a fashionable Table set out in all its Magnificance, I fancy that I see Gouts and Dropsies, Fevers and Lethargies, with other innumerable Distempers lying in Ambuscade among the Dishes.[1]

The medical profession joined in the protests.

'Tis amazing how the voluptuous and lazy people of delicate constitutions should think themselves able to carry off such loads of high-seasoned food and inflammatory liquors without injury and pain.[2]

The large quantities of meat eaten came in for particular censure. Indeed, meat was often held responsible for the prevailing corpulency.

Now, as animal food is easier converted, and also longer retained in the system, and as it contains a greater proportion of oil, it will afford both kinds of nutriment more copiously than vegetables. A proof that corpulency is produced most by animal foods is, that in England there are more fat people than in any country of twice the bulk in the world.[3]

One writer suggested as a corrective the consumption of a proportionate amount of vegetables.

A large quantity of vegetables should be constantly mixed with animal food, to take off its putrescency, and to prevent it from corrupting while

[1] Article by Joseph Addison in the *Spectator*, October 13th, 1711.
[2] *Lectures on the Materia Medica*, William Cullen, 1773.
[3] Ibid.

it continues in the stomach . . . In short we should eat in great moderation, and make vegetables the principal part of our food.[1]

It was an appropriate age in which to draw attention to the writings of
Luigi Cornaro, a sixteenth-century nobleman of Padua, who, suffering
severely from gout and the consequences of luxurious living, decided at the
age of forty to follow the advice of his physicians and live the 'simple life'.
He is reputed to have lived to become a centenarian by restricting his diet to
12 oz. of solid food and 14 oz. of wine a day. Translations of his works had
a considerable vogue in England in the eighteenth century.

Doctors frequently reported instances of men and women who had
benefited by adopting a sparse diet. There was the much quoted case of Mr
Thomas Wood, 'a Miller of Billericay in the County of Essex', which was
reported to the College of Physicians in 1771 by Sir George Baker. In his
forty-fourth year he had been troubled by disturbed sleep, heartburn, sickness and pain in the bowels. In August 1764 his friend, the Rev. Mr Powley,
'recommended him an exact regimen: and pointed out the life of Cornaro as
a book likely to suggest to him a salutary course of living'.[2] He started by
cutting down the amount of animal food he ate and found that his health
was vastly improved. He then gave up alcohol, next cheese, and finally he
ceased to eat flesh of any kind. On a simple diet of puddings made from sea-
biscuits, skimmed milk and eggs, his health was fully returned.

Excessive meat-eating was regarded by many doctors as the chief cause of
gout,[3] a complaint which afflicted a large proportion of the leisured classes.
Haygarth, commenting on the good health of the inhabitants of Chester,
remarked that in spite of enjoying the 'elegant refinements of life' they suffered, as a consequence, nothing more serious than gout.[4] Contemporary
accounts of the disease show that in recognizing its association with good
living and lack of exercise, the existence of inheritable predisposition (the
gouty diathesis), and the value of a light milk diet and certain spa waters in
treatment, the doctors of those days knew as much about the disease as the
medical profession today.

§ 5 THE AMOUNT OF FOOD REQUIRED

It was not until the very end of the eighteenth century that the researches
of Lavoisier and his colleagues laid the foundations of the knowledge which

---

[1] *A Sure Guide in Sickness and Health*, W. Smith, 1776.
[2] *Collection of Medical Tracts by Sir George Baker*, published by His Son, 1818.
[3] *A Dissertation on the Gout*, William Cadogan, 1771.
[4] 'Observations on the Population and Diseases of Chester in the Year 1774', J. Haygarth,
Philosophical Transactions of the Royal Society, 1778, Vol. LXVIII.

we use today in calculating the food requirements of an individual. They showed that the utilization of food in the body is a process comparable with the burning of carbonaceous matter such as coal or a candle. Equally important was their proof that there is a *quantitative* relation between the amount of food combusted in the body, the respired oxygen utilized in effecting that combustion and the amounts of carbon dioxide and water expired. It is a result of this discovery and the developments which followed it that the food requirements of a man or woman can be calculated.

The Calorie, which is usually used as a measure of the energy value of a diet, is a unit of heat, like the therm which is the unit employed for measuring the energy value of the domestic gas supply. Energy from food is used by the body for two main purposes: to maintain the processes of living, such as the circulation of blood, breathing and the maintenance of body temperature, and to perform muscular activity which may range from such light activity as sitting in a relaxed position to such heavy work as carrying a load uphill. The amount of energy used by an individual depends on the total amount of his or her living tissues, which decrease slightly with increasing age. Activity also decreases as the individual becomes older. In general men are larger than women and thus need a greater supply of energy from foods. Children, though smaller, are more active and thus require relatively more, though absolutely less, calories than their elders.

The energy requirement of a young man of moderate activity in a country like Great Britain is about 3200 Cal. daily and of a young woman, also fairly active, about 2300 Cal.[1] Elderly men require 2000-2500 Cal. and elderly women probably less than 2000 Cal. daily. Labourers engaged in heavy manual work may need 4000-5000 Cal. daily, but intakes of this order are not often observed, at least under modern conditions of life. Mental activity does not add to energy requirements. If the amount of food eaten provides more calories than are expended the surplus is converted into fat. Thus a common cause of obesity is failure, as an individual grows older, to adjust food intake to fit reduced activity. Appetite is not always a good indicator of need. It has been observed that sedentary workers are often more likely to be obese than manual workers.[2]

[1] *Report of Second Committee on Calorie Requirements*, Food and Agriculture Organization o the United Nations. Rome, in the press.
[2] 'The Physiological Basis of Obesity and Leanness', J. Mayer, *Nutrition Abstracts and Reviews* (1955), XXV, 597, 871.

§6 EIGHTEENTH-CENTURY ESTIMATES OF FOOD REQUIREMENTS

Two hundred years ago the doctors who advised on diet had little more to go on than their own speculations or observations and what they had learned by hearsay. When they cited the example of Cornaro, who was reputed to have regained his health and to have lived for over sixty years on a diet of 12 oz. of solid food a day, they had no idea that such a diet, providing at most 1300 Cal., or more probably, if vegetables formed any significant proportion, about 800, would have led to debility and ill-health if persisted in for any length of time. The Germans were restricted to diets of 1500-1700 Cal. a day for a long period during the blockade in 1916-17 and records show that many people lost 25-35 lb. in weight in the course of seven or eight months.

There is a good illustration of this point in the history of William Stark, to which we have already referred. He describes himself as a young man of 29 years of age, weighing 12 stone 3 lb. It is clear from his diary that he led a quiet and sedentary life. He began his experiment by eating about 20 oz. of bread a day, which would have given him roughly 1400 Cal. The records show that, as one would expect, he lost weight. Later he ate 30 oz. a day (2100 Cal.) and still lost weight, although not as much as before. When he increased his consumption to 38 oz. (2600 Cal.) his weight remained even. His intake and output of energy were then about balanced. For a man of his size and age this must have meant a very sedentary existence.

One well-known authority, George Cheyne, gave a definite ruling on this point. He estimated the amount of food needed by a 'man of an Ordinary Stature, following no laborious Employment, in due *Plight*, *Health*, and Vigour; to wit, 8 Ounces of Flesh Meat, 12 of Bread, or vegetable Food, and about a Pint of Wine or other generous Liquor'.[1] This was under-estimated. Such a diet, providing less than 2000 Cal. daily would in fact not supply the requirements of a woman of average size and little activity.

Reference has already been made to Hanway's recipe for a cheap soup which, he claimed, would provide nourishment for 'five stout men, or ten common persons', but which, in reality, would only have supplied sufficient calories for one person living a sedentary life. Arthur Young thought Hanway had rather under-estimated the amount that would be needed, 'but as I think the quantity small I have allowed two penny-worth of it'. This concession would have provided each of the 'five stout men' with 1100 Cal.; i.e. to get their daily requirement of say, 3500-4000 Cal. they would each have needed well over two pounds of bread in addition.

[1] *An Essay of Health and Long Life*, George Cheyne, 1724.

Young offered alternative 'messes for a stout man', planned so that the expenditure over a week should not exceed 3d. a day.

		Approximate calories a day
2 *days*	2 lb. bread 4 oz. cheese 1 quart beer	3100
2 *days*	rice pudding (½ lb. rice) 2 quarts skim milk sugar (1 oz.?)	1600
2 *days*	¼ lb. fat meat 2 lb. potatoes 2 oz. cheese 1 quart beer	1700
1 *day*	three messes of soup	?

These figures are only approximate but they show how low were the estimates of the well-meaning eighteenth-century experts. Unless these people had had one and a half pounds of bread on at least five days out of seven in addition to the above diet, they would have been quite literally half-starved.

There were few enough people in the latter half of the eighteenth century who had any regard for the sufferings of the poor but of those who had many seemed to be obsessed with the idea that all the troubles of the needy would vanish if only they would learn to make nourishing soups. It does not seem to have occurred to them that most of the poor could not afford fuel and in consequence seldom tasted hot food. The end of the century saw the start of the charity soup-kitchens which in the course of the next fifty years were to form so strong an association in the minds of the poor between soup and pauperism that to this day it is not a popular dish in England.

Count Rumford, the famous American scientist, unwittingly did the poor of Europe a great disservice when he published an account of how he had effected economies, while in the service of the Elector of Bavaria, in feeding the poor of Munich. His writings on the subject attracted widespread attention. He claimed that the paupers in the House of Industry at Munich were adequately nourished for the infinitesimal cost of two farthings a day, the diet consisting of seven ounces of rye bread and a helping of soup prepared from peas, barley and bread cuttings. From the quantities he gives it is a simple matter to calculate that the diet would have provided rather less than 1000 Cal. Men and women could not have lived for any length of time on such a diet and at the same time performed the manual work which the House of Industry demanded.

Unquestionably a large number of the paupers in public institutions in England were undernourished, partly as a result of ignorance and partly from callous indifference. The food in the workhouses varied so far as qualitative considerations were concerned but it was seldom adequate in amount. For example, the rations provided in 1782 for the poor of one parish were, qualitatively, reasonably good, consisting as they did of bread, cheese, pease, broths, a 'bowl of vegetables' twice a week, meat twice a week, and milk five days a week as well as beer. Nevertheless, the amount provided for a grown man gave only about 2000 Cal. a day, which would have meant a steady loss of weight. For 'working children' even smaller quantities of food were provided, the daily calorific intake being of the order of 1500-1800. This would have meant real starvation because, although it is often not fully appreciated even today, and was certainly unsuspected two hundred years ago, an active, growing boy of 14 or 15 needs as much food as a fully-grown man. To scale down the food in proportion to the age is, therefore, physiologically unjustifiable. If food has to be 'burnt' to provide energy for work it cannot be used for building new tissues. It goes without saying, therefore, that the 'working children', in spite of their 'bowls of vegetables' and milk, were stunted and malnourished by the quantitative inadequacy of their diet.

CHAPTER XIV

SCURVY

THE introduction of garden vegetables into the diets of all classes should have reduced the incidence of the chronic scorbutic conditions to which the Englishman of earlier centuries had been a victim. There can be little doubt that this was so, although it is difficult to trace any really satisfactory evidence on this point. Dr Macbride says it was a rare disease in Dublin,[1] which was probably true at a time when potatoes were the staple food of the working people. On the other hand there is a suggestion in an essay by Bissett that 'land-scurvy' was rather common at this time.[2] An advertisement in an early number of the *Tatler* states that 'The Only True Purging Essential Salt of Scurvy-Grass', sold by Mr Harisson at the White Hart in Poultry, is an infallible cure for 'the reigning disease'.[3] More convincing is Dr Cheyne's assurance in 1724 that 'The *Scurvy* is a kind of Catholick [universally prevalent] Distemper here in Britain'.[4]

From, say, 1720 to 1760, when the common garden vegetables and fruit were comparatively cheap and plentiful, we have traced little information that gives us any clue to the incidence of scorbutic conditions. There is a hint in Hanway's *Essay on Tea* (1757) that loose teeth and sore gums were still fairly general.

If we drank less tea, and used gentle *acids* for the gums and teeth, particularly *sour oranges*, though we had a less number of *French dentists*, I fancy this *essential* part of beauty would be much *better* preserved.

Lind also gives a few hints in *A Treatise of the Scurvy*. He observed, for example, that outbreaks of scurvy at sea occurred more quickly if the voyage started in the late spring than in the late summer and autumn. This suggests that summer fruits and vegetables provided some protection not found in the winter and spring diet. He made another interesting observation that there was a difference in the incidence of scurvy between the officers and 'common seamen' suggesting that the upper social classes were in the better state of protection against scurvy. He wrote:

[1] *Experimental Essays (IV. On the Scurvy)*, D. Macbride, 2nd Edition, 1767.
[2] *Medical Essays and Observations*, Charles Bissett, 1766.
[3] November 1st, 1710.
[4] *An Essay of Health and Long Life*, George Cheyne, 1724.

In an epidemic scurvy at sea, the indisposition attacks, in a regular order, such people as are predisposed to it by manifest causes. It is for a long time confined first to the common seamen; and though the officers servants are at such times often afflicted with it . . . ; yet it is but rare to see this disease in an officer, nay even a petty officer.

Lind's observations on the length of time required on a scorbutic diet before signs of scurvy appear are in such accord with recent observations[1] [2] that it is of interest to quote one example.

. . . for there are persons everywhere, who, from choice, eat few or no green vegetables; and some countries are deprived of the use of them for five or six months of the year; as is the case of many parts of the highlands of Scotland, Newfoundland etc., where, however, scurvy is not a usual malady.

These observations suggest that at some seasons of the year and among the favoured classes the English eighteenth-century diet provided several months' protection against scurvy.

An overwhelming mass of literature dealing with 'sea-scurvy' appeared during the century. A few of the works are outstanding and deserve to be ranked as classics. One, which most certainly merits the title, seems to have attracted little attention at the time. It is a slender little volume of 85 pages, published in Leyden in 1734 by Johannes Bachstrom, M.D. With a few clear arguments and examples the author demolished all the complicated differentiations between land-scurvy, sea-scurvy and all the other forms of scurvy that had been 'discovered' and showed that there is, in truth, only one disease meriting this name. He was equally clear and definite about its primary cause, which he held to be a deficiency of fresh vegetables in the diet.

Causam veram et primarium Scorbuti nullam aliam esse, quam abstinentiam diuturniorem a quocunque genere recentium vegetabilium.[3]

It was Bachstrom who coined the word 'antiscorbutic', and he excluded from his list of such remedies everything except fresh herbs, fruits and berries. There is wisdom in every line of his book. Seamen, he said, would do better to lay up a store of vegetables than of meat. Besieged troops should plant seeds of antiscorbutic plants on the ramparts. Everyone should eat as much vegetable food as possible in order to keep healthy.

To what extent Bachstrom's views came to be known in England before

---

[1] J. H. Crandon, C. C. Lund and D. B. Dill, *New England Journal of Medicine* (1940), CCXXIII, 353.
[2] *Medical Research Council, Special Report*, No. 280, 1953.
[3] *Observationes circa Scorbutum*, J. Bachstrom, 1734.

Lind drew attention to them in 1753 is uncertain. They do not appear to
have made much impression on the medical profession which, for the greater
part of the century continued to argue and wrangle over the cause and
character of the disease. A number of the leading authorities clung to the
view that salt and salted foods were chiefly responsible. The influential
Cullen, for one, upheld this theory.[1] The idea that it was infective gradually
lost ground, although many people, no doubt, would have endorsed Smollett's view that to bathe at Bath was to run the risk of catching the 'King's
Evil, the Scurvy, the Cancer, and the Pox'.[2]

There was a suspicion in some minds that the quality of the salt used for
preserving food might be of importance. A certain Thomas Lowndes, a
native of Middlewich, brought to the notice of the Admiralty a process for
making and purifying salt. Most of the salt used in England at that time was
'Bay-salt' made in France and northern Spain by the evaporation of sea-
water by the sun. Lowndes gives an unpleasant account of its manufacture
and alleges that it was often contaminated with filth arising from 'putrified
human bodies and dead fish'. Having seen the method which the Dutch
used to refine salt, and observing that their salted herrings kept much better
than those preserved with 'Bay-salt', he suggested that he should be allowed
to submit samples of his purified product for the approval of the College of
Physicians before asking the Admiralty to use it in the preparation of salt
foods for the Navy.[3] It must be remembered that scurvy was still regarded
as a 'putrid fever'; the implication was that the purified salt by making the
meat less putrescible would be healthier for the sailors. His product was
given a trial and a few years later Dr Mead expressed the opinion that it was
in fact healthier for the men because it was 'land' salt and not 'sea' salt. It
need hardly be explained that he was an adherent of the old theory that
scurvy was related to some intangible property of the sea itself which was
communicated to sea-air and sea-salt. Associated with that view was the
belief that something emanating from the land was curative. Dr Mead stated
categorically that the vapour of cold earth would cure scurvy and asserted
that patients responded promptly if they were held over a hole in the
ground after a slice of turf had been removed.[4]

A remarkable instance of faith in this remedy is to be found in the *Private
Sea Journals of Admiral Sir Thomas Pasley*. The record of his voyages gives
a good picture of the ravages of scurvy at that period. With half the crew of
his 28-gun frigate *Sybil* down with the disease he wrote despairingly:

[1] *A Treatise of the Materia Medica*, William Cullen, 1789.
[2] *The Expedition of Humphrey Clinker*, T. Smollett, 1771.
[3] *Brine-Salt Improved or the Method of Making Salt from Brine, that shall be as good or better
than French Bay-Salt*, T. Lowndes, 1746.
[4] *A Discourse on the Scurvy*, R. Mead, 1749.

Of all disorders this at Sea is the worst; once taken, no shadow of hopes of their recovery and returning to their duty, till Land Air and Vegetable Refreshments can be procured.[1]

On a later voyage in H.M.S. *Jupiter* he noted in his diary 'the very Earth is the first of cures for the Scurvey'. This apparently gave him an idea for curing his stricken men. He had been in the habit of growing salads in boxes of earth which stood on deck. Why should he not use the earth itself as a remedy? In his own words:

To day my Garden (which it has been my Practice to raise daily Sallad in) I have given up, and Buried as many Men in it as possible, greatly to their Satisfaction. They are happy and seem to have faith in it. So have I, not for an absolute cure on board, but as putting an undoubted check to the Scurvey's progress — God Grant it!

Apparently the men improved under this curious treatment.

... the Men who were carried and lifted in and out of it, incapable of moving a Limb, walked of themselves to day — wonderful effect.

What caused the temporary alleviation, for such is all it could have been, is difficult to say. Perhaps the faith he and his men had in their new remedy.

Scurvy was a grim spectre feared by the commander of every ship undertaking a long voyage. During the Seven Years War 185,000 men were raised for 'sea-service', of whom no less than 130,000 died from disease. One doctor held that 'two-thirds of this number may be safely charged to the account of diseases which take their rise from putrefaction'.[2]

Anson gives a terrible picture of the crew of H.M.S. *Centurion*, stricken with scurvy on the long voyage to Juan Fernandez.

In this desponding condition, with a crazy ship, a great scarcity of fresh water, and a crew so universally diseased, that there were not above ten fore-mast men in a watch capable of doing duty and some of these lame and unable to go aloft.[3]

The rations in the Navy at this period (1745) were as follows:[4]

[1] *Private Sea Journals, 1778-1782, Kept by Admiral Sir Thomas Pasley*, edited by R. M. S. Pasley, 1931.
[2] *Experimental Essays (IV. On the Scurvy)*, D. Macbride, 2nd Edition, 1767.
[3] *A Voyage round the World (1740-1744)*, G. Anson, 1748.
[4] *Admiralty Regulations*, 1745.

	Biscuits lb.	Beer gal.	Beef lb.	Pork lb.	Pease pints	Oatmeal pints	Butter oz.	Cheese oz.
Sundays & Thursdays	1	1		1	½			
Mondays	1	1				1	2	4
Tuesdays & Saturdays	1	1	2					
Wednesdays & Fridays	1	1			½	1	2	4

The allowances were, on paper, liberal, equivalent to over 5000 Cal. a day (see Appendix A), but in practice the amounts were usually cut by the purser as one means of covering the heavy wastage. In 1776 the pursers petitioned successfully for an allowance of one-eighth to cover this loss 'of Bread by its breaking, and turning to Dust: of butter, by that part next to the Firkin being not fit to be issued: of Cheese, by its Decaying with Mold and Rottenness, and being eaten with Mites, and other insects: of Peas, Oatmeal and Flower, by their being eaten by Cockroches, Weavels and other Vermin'.[1]

This passage gives a glimpse of the quality of most of the food served out to the sailors. Much of it was so bad that it could not be eaten; the salt meat was often so hard that the men carved snuff-boxes and other trinkets from it. The quality of the food was one of the chief causes of the mutiny of 1797. The pathetic yet dignified petition which the discontented men addressed to the Admiralty asked, amongst other things, that 'our provisions be raised to the weight of sixteen ounces to the pound, and of better quality'.[2]

No account of life at sea in the eighteenth century would be complete without a picture of the almost indescribable conditions in the ships engaged in the slave-trade or in transporting convicts. Aubrey tells how the wretched negroes, packed so close together below decks that they could scarcely breathe, much less move, were fed on rotten grain boiled into a stew with a few decayed herrings. Concerned about his losses — 'what a Devil makes these plaguey Toads dye so fast' — he pleaded with his company for a little palm oil, to which the natives were accustomed, and which he thought might save valuable lives.[3]

It appears that his reports made some impression for in 1786 Trotter described the feeding of cargoes of slaves from the Guinea Coast on a diet of boiled beans, rice and Indian corn, mixed with palm oil. Scurvy broke out during the six months they were waiting to collect a full cargo and by

[1] *The Case of the Pursers of His Majesty's Navy*, 1776.
[2] *The Floating Republic*, G. E. Mainwaring and B. Dobrée, 1935.
[3] *The Sea-Surgeon or the Guinea-Man's Vade-Mecum*, T. Aubrey, 1729.

the time they reached Antigua there were 300 cases. There, however, they
were able to buy lemons and limes cheaply and the trouble soon disappeared.[1]

The convict ships, conditions aboard which beggar description, were
seldom long without a visitation of the disease. On one occasion the half-
starved wretches in the 'hulks' at Woolwich were kept for six months
(October 1794-April 1795) without fresh food of any kind; it is small
wonder that scurvy mercifully thinned their ranks.[2]

The Dutch East India Company seem to have been a little more considerate, or at any rate more concerned for the safe arrival of their cargoes, for
acting on the advice of one of their surgeons who advised radical changes
affecting the hygiene of the slave ships, they made efforts to improve the
diet, providing yams, potatoes and even lemons.

Before 1757 no provision of antiscorbutics was made in the Navy other
than the useless 'elixir of vitriol' which formed part of the surgeon's stores
and which, incidentally, was the choice of the College of Physicians. In
that year the Admiralty issued additional regulations regarding diet, including one dealing with vegetables.

> And whereas some of the eldest pursers of the Royal Navy at some
> Time since presented a Memorial in behalf of themselves, and the rest of
> their Brethren, representing that it had been their constant Practice, as
> often as their respective Ships were victualled with Fresh Meat, to
> boil such a Quantity of Greens and Roots with it, as to give sufficient
> Satisfaction to the Men; and that, to give them no Room to murmur on
> Account of their Saving of Pease by boiling with Fresh Meat, to boil
> Pease for their Mondays Dinners, besides the allowed Oatmeal for
> Breakfasts; and proposing, if the Greens and Roots furnished by them
> should be judged sufficient for the Men, to increase the same to any
> Quantity that should be prescribed; all Commanders are to take
> Care, that their respective Pursers do comply with what is contained in
> the said Memorial, by furnishing a sufficient Quantity of Roots and
> Greens to Seamen, with their Fresh Meat; or to report to us, if they
> fail therein.[3]

It seems certain that this instruction was often disregarded, particularly in
home ports where the health of the men would be of little concern to an
indifferent commander. The Seamen's Petition of 1797 asked that no flour
should be served in ports under the British flag and that 'there might be

---

[1] *Observations on the Scurvy with a Review of the Theories lately advanced on that Disease*,
T. Trotter, 1786.
[2] *Medicina Nautica; an Essay on the Diseases of Seamen*, T. Trotter, 1797.
[3] *Admiralty Regulations*, 1757.

granted a sufficient quantity of vegetables . . . which we greviously complain and lay under the want of'.[1]

In 1753 James Lind published his classic work *A Treatise of the Scurvy*, the most comprehensive study of the disease that has ever been written.[2] In the first place he gave a full account of much that had previously been written on the subject and discussed the multitude of theories which had been advanced. He examined each one with shrewd common sense against the background of his own experience as a naval surgeon. He dismissed the idea that salt was the cause of the disease and pointed out that the men working in the Polish mines did not suffer from it, nor did the sailors who, firmly believing in its curative powers, used to drink salt water.[3] The German troops in Hungary, moreover, who ate no salt had suffered severely from the disease.

Lind believed that exposure to damp, cold and bad air together with confinement, lack of exercise, fatigue, anxiety and infection were important factors in the genesis of scurvy. This view is in line with modern observations, though the precise part 'stress' plays in increasing utilization of ascorbic acid is not known. It is known, however, that the body is depleted of ascorbic acid under the stress of severe injury or various kinds of infection.

We have already mentioned the irregularity with which the symptoms appeared. Gilbert Blane some years later found the right answer when he suggested that the previous diet of the men was responsible. The freedom from scurvy of part of Lord Hood's fleet he ascribed to

> . . . the previous refreshments; for we have seen, that, in a passage of seven weeks from Jamaica to New York, the fleet was greatly affected with scurvy in consequence of not having had the advantage of fresh meat and vegetables when last in port.[4]

Lind was clearly impressed by Bachstrom's views and made a number of investigations into the respective merits of the many antiscorbutics then fashionable. He had no great opinion of the 'magazine of spinach' recommended by the College of Physicians and agreed with Cockburn 'that no moisture whatever could restore the natural juices of the plant lost by evaporation'. He was, of course, quite right; at that time no satisfactory method of drying vegetables so as to preserve their antiscorbutic virtues had

---

[1] *The Floating Republic*, G. E. Mainwaring and B. Dobrée, 1935.
[2] In 1953 the (British) Nutrition Society celebrated this with a Lind Bicentenary Symposium, the proceedings of which have been published in *Proceedings of the Nutrition Society* (1953), XII, 201-356, and the Treatise was reprinted with additional notes at the University Press, Edinburgh.
[3] J. Wilkinson, the author of *Tutamen Nauticum, or, the Seamen's Preservation from Shipwreck, Disease and other Calamities incident to Mariners* (1763), firmly believed that sea water cured scurvy: '*it restores that stiptic balsam to the blood of which it was deprived by the disease*'.
[4] *Observations on the Diseases Incident to Seamen*, Sir Gilbert Blane, 1785.

been discovered. One observant student of scurvy, the Viennese physician Mertens, noted that cooked vegetables afforded less protection than fresh. He ascribed the loss to the release of some of the 'fixed air' by ebullition.[1]

This idea, of course, sprang from the current views about the protective acidity of vegetables. Many people thought that any form of acid would counteract the harmful 'alkalescence' of meat and that 'fixed air' (carbon dioxide) was, therefore, an antiscorbutic. Thomas Beddoes, a great admirer of the new chemical work of Black, Priestley and Lavoisier, expressed the opinion that scurvy was largely due to a lack of oxygen, which at that time was thought to be supplied by acids.[2] (Lavoisier originally gave the name *oxygène* to his *principe acidifiant*.) The dark colour of the blood in advanced cases of scurvy strengthened this view. Thomas Trotter, another naval surgeon, agreed with Beddoes, although he did not think that better ventilation would provide the necessary oxygen; acids alone, he maintained, would do this.[3]

Throughout the eighteenth century there was a good deal of controversy about the best type of antiscorbutic. Some authorities held that the mineral acids, oil of vitriol, etc., or acids such as citric acid and vinegar, were as good as fresh vegetables. Others found the former useless. Each doctor produced an apparently convincing series of records of cases cured by his own particular method, but few of them attempted a comparative trial. Lind was one of those who did.

On the 20th of May 1747, I selected twelve patients in the scurvy, on board the 'Salisbury' at sea. Their cases were as similar as I could have them ... They lay together in one place ... and had one diet common to all ... Two of these were ordered each a quart of cyder a-day. Two others took twenty-five drops of *elixir vitriol*, three times a day, upon an empty stomach ... Two others took two spoonfuls of vinegar three times a day ... Two of the worst patients were put under a course of sea-water. Of this they drank half a pint every day ... Two others had each two oranges and one lemon given them every day ... The two remaining patients, took the bigness of a nutmeg three times a day of an electary recommended by an hospital-surgeon, made of garlic, mustard-seed, horse-raddish, balsam of *Peru*, and gum myrrh, using for common drink barley water boiled with tamarinds.[4]

[1] *Observations on the Scurvy*, Mertens, 1778.
[2] *Observations on the Nature and Cure of Calculus, Sea-Scurvy, Consumption, Catarrh and Fever*, T. Beddoes, 1793.
[3] *Medicina Nautica; an Essay on the Diseases of Seamen*, T. Trotter, 1797.
[4] *A Treatise of the Scurvy*, James Lind, 1753.

The lucky men who got the oranges and lemons were restored to health in six days. The ones receiving cider improved slowly but all the other treatments proved disappointing.

Such evidence, backed as it was by Lind's comprehensive review of the opinions of the earlier authorities who had found oranges and lemons the best antiscorbutics, should have impressed the Admiralty authorities. Perhaps it did, but with considerations of expense uppermost in their minds they paid more attention to the cheaper alternatives, which may explain why they listened so attentively to the views of Dr Macbride. He was a supporter of the view that 'fixed air' (carbon dioxide) bore a close relationship to scurvy and worked out an elaborate argument, which we need not follow, by which he satisfied himself that materials that were prone to undergo fermentation with the production of 'fixed air' must be the best antiscorbutics. On these grounds he suggested that the sailors should be given more sugar, molasses and, most important of all, wort, the infusion of malt which forms the first stage in the preparation of beer.[1]

Orders were given in 1762 that wort was to be tried as an antiscorbutic in the hospitals at Portsmouth and Plymouth. The trial was a failure because the doctors did not like to forbid the sick men to have fresh vegetables as well. A certain Dr Huxham, however, reported that the remedy 'had very bad effects'. The Admiralty then gave instructions that it was to be tried out at sea 'where no temptations of fresh vegetables would offer to make the men uneasy'.[2] In 1766 Macbride was still waiting for reports on this new trial; he suspected, rightly no doubt, that the orders had been disregarded. However, his patience was rewarded in the end for Captain Cook took a considerable quantity of wort on his second voyage in 1772 and wrote to Sir John Pringle on his return:

> This is without doubt one of the best antiscorbutic sea-medicines yet found out ... but I am not altogether of opinion, that it will cure it [scurvy] in an advanced state at sea.[3]

Sir John Pringle communicated the information to the Royal Society in March 1776 and in the following November he gave a lecture on the best means of preserving the health of seamen, after announcing that the Society had awarded the Copley Medal to Cook for his discoveries. His address, a rather pompous affair in which he clung tenaciously to the old beliefs in salt food as a primary cause of 'sea-scurvy', did much to mislead people regarding the antiscorbutic properties of wort, for he laid particular stress on Cook's

[1] *Experimental Essays (IV. On the Scurvy)*, D. Macbride, 2nd Edition, 1767.   [2] Ibid.
[3] *A Discourse upon some late Improvements of the Means for Preserving the Health of Mariners, Delivered at the Anniversary Meeting of the Royal Society, November 30th, 1776*, by Sir John Pringle, Baronet, President.

remark that it was 'one of the best antiscorbutic sea-medicines yet found out'.

It is difficult to explain why Cook thought 'Sweetwort' so beneficial. It is clear from his account of this voyage that many antiscorbutics were tried. The ships carried as part of their original stores *sauerkraut*, which the Dutch Navy used extensively and which the Admiralty was at that time investigating. Cook found it 'highly antiscorbutic' and ordered a pound per man to be served out twice a week and sometimes more often. Later, when outbreaks of scurvy appeared, he tried 'marmalade of carrots', 'Rob of lemons', oranges, celery and scurvy-grass. Moreover, whenever they touched land fruit and vegetables were bought. It was the fact that Cook returned from this three years' voyage having lost only one man from disease — and that not scurvy — that made such a sensation in naval circles. But why, when so wide a range of antiscorbutics had been used the chief credit should have been given to the 'Sweetwort' is difficult to understand.

Cook's faith in the efficacy of oranges and lemons seems to have been shaken by the disappointing results obtained with 'Rob', an evaporated or inspissated juice which, according to Trotter, was taken on the voyage on Lind's recommendation.[1]

> I entirely agree with you, that the dearness of the Rob of lemons and oranges will hinder them from being furnished in large quantities, but I do not think this is so necessary; for though they may assist other things, I have no great opinion of them alone.[2]

It was, of course, disconcerting to find, as so many of these explorers did, that the antiscorbutic potency of fruit and vegetables disappeared when they were dried. Had the vitamin been unaffected by such treatment the problem of supplying seamen with a cheap antiscorbutic, such as the 'inspissated juice of turnips' recommended by Wilkinson,[3] would long before have been solved. If, as is probable, Cook prepared the wort from the malt taken with him on the voyage there can be no doubt that its content of antiscorbutic vitamin was negligible, for the heating to which the grain is subjected in the 'kilning' of malt destroys all antiscorbutic properties.

It is true that vitamin C is formed during the germination of the grain. Lind was well aware of the beneficial properties of young wheat.

> An antiscorbutic inferior to none is the juice of tender sprouting tops of green wheat, in the months of May and June.[4]

[1] *Observations on the Scurvy*, T. Trotter, 1786.
[2] *Letter from Captain Cook to Sir John Pringle*, July 7th, 1776, cited in Pringle's address to the Royal Society, November 30th, 1776.
[3] *Tutamen Nauticum*, J. Wilkinson, 1763.
[4] *A Treatise of the Scurvy*, James Lind, 1753.

Germinated beans have on more than one occasion been used as an emergency remedy for outbreaks of scurvy, for example, when the disease appeared
among the Serbian soldiers in 1917.[1]

Shortly after Cook's return from his second voyage the ships of the Royal
Navy were supplied with 'essence of malt', or malt extract as it is called today.
The reports on it were conflicting. Blane, off Antigua in 1780, spoke rather
well of it;[2] Pasley, commanding the *Jupiter*, whose crew was stricken with
scurvy, found it of little use.

> They have daily one Pint of Wine, one Pint of Beer and as much of
> the Essence of Malt made into Wort as they chose to drink. In no
> other Ship can they have so many antiscorbutics — yet all does not
> even cheque that Horrid disorder.[3]

The Admiralty was at this time also experimenting with two other antiscorbutics, molasses, which Macbride had so strongly recommended, and
sauerkraut upon which Cook had reported favourably. Lind favoured the
latter, 'after the fashion of the Dutch Navy', but it seems that a large proportion of the supplies sent to H.M. ships was badly pickled and soon decomposed.[4]

Another antiscorbutic in which some people had faith was spruce-beer.
Lind drew attention to the age-old custom of treating scurvy in northern
Russia and Sweden with decoctions of young pine shoots. Extracts of the
fresh young shoots would certainly have had a beneficial effect but such
evidence as we have regarding the method of making 'spruce-beer' indicates
that its ascorbic acid content would have been nil, since old, dried material
was generally used.

> Dry spruce, if boiled in water about one hour and a half, will make
> good *Chowder-beer* ... the spruce may be kept in any dry place good,
> for two or three years after cut.[5]

A few years later H.M. ships carried stores of 'essence of spruce', presumably
a concentrated extract of the dried material, which as an antiscorbutic would
have been quite useless.

In 1795 after endless discussions and, let it be noted, nearly two hundred

---

[1] H. W. Wiltshire, *Lancet* (1918), ii.
[2] *A Short Account of the Most Effectual Means of Preserving the Health of Seamen*, Sir Gilbert
Blane, 1780.
[3] *Private Sea Journals, 1778-1782, Kept by Admiral Sir Thomas Pasley*, edited by R. M. S.
Pasley, 1931.
[4] *Observations on the Scurvy*, T. Trotter, 1786.
[5] *Experimental Essays (IV. On the Scurvy)*, D. Macbride, 2nd Edition, 1767.

years after Captain Lancaster had proved its value on the long voyage to the Indies, the Admiralty decided on the recommendation of Sir Gilbert Blane and Dr Blair to adopt lemon juice as the principal antiscorbutic. The allowance was fixed at one ounce, together with an ounce and a half of sugar, and the ration was usually issued after the sixth week at sea. The result was dramatic. In 1760 there had been 1754 cases of scurvy in the Naval Hospital at Haslar; in 1806 there was one.

CHAPTER XV

RICKETS

It is interesting that eighteenth-century literature gives very little information about the prevalence of rickets. The century was so sharply divided into periods of relative prosperity and depression that one would expect to find clear evidence that the disease began to be less common in the years of plenty before 1750, and that it again became the scourge of the poor in the latter half of the century, when prices rose and times were hard. Buer remarks that 'rickets seems to have been very prevalent in London in the seventeenth and early eighteenth centuries but to have decreased rapidly during the second half of the eighteenth century',[1] which is scarcely what one would have expected. The chief authority for his statement seems to be Thomas Bateman's work on the *Diseases of London* (1819). So far as rickets is concerned this is valueless, for it is a study based largely on the Bills of Mortality which, as we have shown, are worthless except for the records of clearly identifiable diseases such as plague. Miss Dorothy George has also made the mistake of accepting these figures as evidence of the prevalence of rickets and scurvy in the eighteenth century.[2]

Bateman noted in his book that the disease was 'no longer fatal', which statement, again, is based on nothing more than the fact that the Bills of Mortality had for some years previously given only a few deaths from rickets. Buer's view that the disease declined during the second half of the century, owing to the increased consumption of garden vegetables, is misleading but excusable, for it was put forward at a time (1926) when differentiation between the vitamins A and D was not clear. Green vegetables serve as a source of A but not of D.

It seems reasonable to think that the incidence of rickets, which was high in the towns (at any rate in the south) in the seventeenth century, declined somewhat during the first half of the eighteenth century. It is true that living conditions in the poorer parts of the towns were still indescribably bad but, on the other hand, the cheapness of butter and cheese gave a measure of protection against the types of dietary deficiency which tend to cause rickets. The disappearance of milk, whether whole, skimmed or even whey, as an everyday article of diet among the poorer people in the south was, we

[1] *Health, Wealth and Population in the Early Days of the Industrial Revolution*, M. C. Buer, 1926.
[2] *London Life in the Eighteenth Century*, M. D. George, 1925.

believe, largely responsible for the appearance in the early seventeenth century of rickets on such a scale as to attract widespread attention. The change
disturbed the highly satisfactory calcium/phosphorus balance of a diet based
on wholemeal bread and milk, in which the requirements for vitamin D were
at their lowest. Without milk the diet, consisting chiefly of bread, tended to
have too low a calcium/phosphorus ratio for optimum calcification. More
vitamin D would, therefore, be required to improve absorption of the lime
salts. This could not easily be obtained during the period of high prices in the
seventeenth century, but it may have been available in the first half of the
eighteenth century when butter cost only 5d. or 6d. a pound. With the hard
times of the second half of the eighteenth century the price of butter rose
rather steeply. At 8d. a pound it was beyond the reach of the poor.

These considerations indicate that the second half of the eighteenth
century must have seen an increase in the incidence of rickets in the larger
towns. William Farrer, writing in 1773, refers to 'the unhappy progress the
Rickets has of late years made among us',[1] but he then goes on to destroy all
our theories by remarking that it appears to be more common among the
rich than the poor. This he attributed to the widespread custom of rearing
the child by a wet-nurse. The medical profession seems to have been
divided in its opinion. Robertson and Black, both writing in the second half
of the century, suggest respectively that the disease was uncommon,[2] and
that it was on the decline.[3] If, as seems almost certain, their opinions were
based on the Bills of Mortality they can be disregarded. Most convincing of
all is Fordyce's statement, which seems to be founded on his own observations and which refers specifically to the poor.

> ... there must be very near twenty thousand children in London and
> Westminster, and their suburbs, ill at this moment of the Hectic fever,
> attended with tun-bellies, swelled wrists and ancles, or crooked limbs.[4]

Probably more than one disorder was covered by his description but there is
no doubt that florid rickets formed a good proportion. He challenged those
who doubted his statement to 'examine the public charity-schools and workhouses, the purlieus of St. Giles's and Drury-Lane, and satisfy yourselves'.

Ideas about its causes were very confused. Fordyce attributed the 'hectic
fever' he described to 'impure air and bad diet'. Cullen, an enthusiastic
supporter of the new ideas of acescence and alkalescence, was inclined to
think that it might be caused by too great acidity arising from the consump-

---

[1] *A particular account of the Rickets in Children*, W. Farrer, 1773.
[2] *De Rachitide*, W. Robertson, 1766.
[3] *A Historical Sketch of Medicine and Surgery from their origin to the Present Time*, W. Black, 1782.
[4] *A New Inquiry into the Causes ... of Fevers*, Sir William Fordyce, 1773.

tion of milk and farinaceous foods, but he had to admit that many children were reared successfully on such a diet.[1] An inherited tendency was acknowledged by most authorities — it is true that an inherited predisposition to the disease is traceable in some cases — while another school of thought held that it was linked with a 'scrofulous or venereal taint' in the parents.[2] The idea that a 'venereal stigma' was concerned was very widely held although Cullen did not support it.

In a vague sort of way improper diet was suspected of being a cause of the disease. William Forster was one who thought that injudicious feeding played a part in bringing about a rachitic condition. The wrong type of food would, he felt certain, favour the development of 'a Big-Belly, the most convenient Thing in Nature for producing the Rickets or King's Evil'.[3]

The beginnings of modern views on the nature of rickets are traceable in a paper which a French scientist, Citoyen Bonhomme, read before the *Société Nationale de Médecine* in 1793.[4] It had not long been known that the greater part of the bone mineral is calcium phosphate and the fact that the hard substance of bone dissolves in acid led Bonhomme to think that the development of an acid in the body was responsible for the softness of the bones in rickets. In this he was wrong, but he came very near the truth when he expressed the opinion that a deficiency of phosphates might lead to defective bone formation.

> La nature du vice rachitique dépend, d'une part, du développement d'un acide dont la nature est voisine de celle des acides végétaux, et particulièrement de l'acide oxalique, de l'autre, de défaut d'acide phosphorique dont la combinaison avec le terre calcaire animale forme la basse naturelle des os et leur donne leur solidité.

It was, of course, easy for him to link up his ideas with the popular views on acescence and this he did, advising alkaline lotions as treatment. Among the experiments he carried out were some on growing chickens, in which he demonstrated that the addition of calcium phosphate to certain diets increased the deposition of bone minerals in the limbs.

Bonhomme was far ahead of his day in his ideas on the calcium balance in the body. He realized that the demands of lactation may cause a drainage of that element from the bones of the mother.

> Si l'on considère qu'a l'époque de la grossesse et de l'accouchement il se fait dans toutes les jointures des os de la mère un ramollissement... que

[1] *The Works of William Cullen*, edited by John Thomson, 1827.
[2] *Encyclopaedia Britannica*, 3rd Edition, 1797, see Rickets.
[3] *A Compendious Discourse of the Diseases of Children*, William Forster, 1738.
[4] *Annales de Chimie*, August 1793.

les fractures des os qui surviennent dans tems sont plus qu'en aucun autre
lentes à se reunir par le cal, que c'est dans le tems même de ce ramollisse-
ment que le lait se charge du phosphate calcaire, qu'il perd à mesure que
l'enfant, ainsi que la mère, s'eloignent du moment de la naissance.[1]

These interesting views came to the attention of scientists in England in
the form of a long abstract published in William Nicholson's *Journal of
Natural Philosophy, Chemistry and the Arts*,[2] but they do not appear to have
made a very great impression.

In general, treatment consisted of tonics, remedial exercises and the wearing of supports for the weakened limbs. It does not appear to have been at
all uncommon for children to wear supports and stays such as Mrs Parsons,
'Stay-maker, at the Golden Acorn, James' Street, Covent Garden', made for
'Misses that are crooked, or inclined to be so, either by falls, rickets, sickness,
etc.'[3] Advertisements such as this suggest that bone deformities due to
rickets, tubercle and other causes were fairly common among the class of
people who could afford to pay for these contraptions.

Some authorities thought that improved diet would benefit the rickety
child, but they had no very definite ideas as to what type of food would be
most suitable. Cullen, who was almost as vague about the treatment of
rickets as about its cause, refused to commit himself.

> There is no doubt that a certain diet may contribute to the same end,
> but what may be the most eligible, I dare not determine ... I cannot
> find any reason to believe that strong beer can ever be a proper remedy.[4]

Cod liver oil first came into use in clinical medicine in England in the
eighteenth century. Such oils, extracted from fish livers by heat or pressure,
had probably been used as household remedies in the fishing villages along
the northern European coastline since time immemorial. In Iceland the
poor people had for centuries eaten a mixture of mutton tallow and fish liver
oil which they called *broedingur* and which was highly valued for its health-
giving properties.[5] Very large quantities of oil were prepared by primitive
means from fish livers in these northern countries and sold in the markets at
Bergen and Hamburg.

> Having taken them [fish] they plucke out the bones, and lay up their
> bowels, and make Fat or Oyle of them.[6]

[1] Ibid. [2] Vol. I, 1794.
[3] *The General Advertiser*, February 11th, 1748.
[4] *The Works of William Cullen*, edited by John Thomson, 1827.
[5] Information supplied by Dr T. Thorbjarnarson.
[6] *Life and Manners of the Icelanders* (1563); *Purchas His Pilgrimes*, S. Purchas, 1625-26.

These dark-coloured, evil-smelling oils, known as train-oils, from a corruption of the old German word *träne* (a tear), were used extensively throughout Europe for illumination and in dressing leather. Newfoundland was one of the chief exporters of these oils, though what proportion were prepared from blubber and what proportion from fish livers it is hard to say. Percival, however, says that cod liver oil formed 'a considerable article of merchandize' in the eighteenth-century trade with Newfoundland.[1]

It is not easy to say what led to this remedy gaining a reputation in England as a treatment for bone affections but it must be borne in mind that rubbing with oil is one of the oldest methods of treating a painful joint or limb. It was probably found by people living on the coast that fish liver oils were superior to any other for this purpose. The fishermen of the Western Isles of Scotland had for centuries past regarded the oil extracted from fish livers as a valuable remedy for rickets and bone affections.[2] They sometimes rubbed it on the affected limbs and sometimes swallowed it.

The first recorded clinical trial of cod liver oil in England was carried out at the Manchester Infirmary by Dr Kay and Dr Darbey. The circumstances are set forth in a letter from Robert Darbey to Dr Percival, dated February 12th, 1782.

> For several years after I came to the infirmary, I observed that many poor patients, who were received into the infirmary for the chronic rheumatism, after several weeks trial of a variety of remedies, were discharged with little or no relief . . . About ten years since, an accidental circumstance discovered to us a remedy, which has been used with the greatest success, for the above complaint, but is very little known, in any county, except Lancashire; It is the cod, or ling liver oil.[3]

The infirmary doctors were so pleased with the results they obtained that no less than fifty or sixty gallons were prescribed annually in spite of the fact that the smell and taste were so repulsive that many patients could not stomach it.

The investigations of the new remedy at Manchester are important because they are based on the oral administration of the oil. The results would, therefore, have been very impressive, for any cases which would be benefited by the vitamins of cod liver oil would respond much more rapidly to internal administration than to treatment by inunction, absorption through the skin being a slow process.

[1] 'Observations on the Medicinal Uses of the Oleum Jecoris Aselli or Cod Liver Oil', *London Medical Journal*, Vol. III, reprinted in *Essays Medical, Philosophical, and Experimental*, Vol. II, T. Percival, 4th Edition, 1789.
[2] *Encyclopaedia Britannica*, 3rd Edition, 1797, see Rickets.
[3] *Essays Medical, Philosophical, and Experimental*, Vol. II, T. Percival, 4th Edition, 1789.

S

It is not surprising that some of the patients found it difficult to swallow the oil for it was made by the primitive method of allowing the livers to soften by putrefaction until the oil rose to the surface and could be skimmed off. The smell was so revolting that 'train-oil' was unpopular even as an illuminant. One of the many prizes offered by the Society of Arts was for the 'edulcoration' of this oil. Heat-treatment was among the processes suggested but it was thought to be impracticable for it 'added an empyreumatic smell to the putrid foeter, which was very little diminished'.[1] Dark, evil-smelling blubber and nauseating oils of this type continued in use in medicine until the latter part of the nineteenth century when they were gradually displaced by the more palatable and cleaner oils prepared by steaming the fresh livers.

It will be noted that cod liver oil was first employed by English physicians as a cure for 'rheumatism', a word which was indiscriminately applied to many painful conditions of the joints or limbs. Many cases so described were, of course, of a type which would not directly benefit from the administration of the vitamins A and D in fish liver oils. On the other hand, there were plenty of disorders such as rickets, tuberculous joint affections, adult rickets in nursing women, etc., which would be relieved by this treatment and it is easy to understand that the remedy quickly gained a considerable reputation. We get a glimpse of its use in an ordinary household from Parson Woodforde's Diary.

> Mr Thorne sent Nancy over to day some Cod's Liver Oil about a Quarter of a Pint, for her to make use of about her stiff arm and lame knee — she began it this Evening on her arm only — Pray God! send thy blessing upon it for her good.[2]

[1] *History of the Royal Society of Arts*, Sir H. Trueman Wood, 1913.
[2] *Diary of a Country Parson, The Rev. James Woodforde, 1758-1781*, edited by J. Beresford, 1924-29.

PART FOUR

THE NINETEENTH CENTURY

CHAPTER XVI

INDUSTRY AND AGRICULTURE

THE opening of the nineteenth century was a depressing time for all except the landowners, big farmers and manufacturers. To the ill effects of war and financial and trade disturbances were added the grave consequences of another sequence of indifferent harvests; in 1812 the country came very near real famine. A bumper crop in 1813 brought the price of wheat down, but when this was followed by a second good harvest the farmers protested that cheap corn would ruin agriculture and the Corn Law of 1815 was passed to placate them. This measure hit the poor very severely, keeping up the price of wheat by authorizing the suspension of imported grain when the price fell below 80s. a quarter.

The Peace of 1815 found England in a thoroughly exhausted condition, with distress and discontent rife among the labouring classes and even spreading to the middle class which, with the rapid growth of industrialization, was beginning to form a distinct and important stratum in English town life. Peace brought no more than transient relief. There was a sharp fall in prices but it was offset by a considerable increase in unemployment, and once again the fates were cruel. Three short harvests (1817-19) caused dearth and distress with widespread rioting, culminating in the tragedy of Peterloo.

One does not have to look far to find evidence that during the first twenty-five years of the nineteenth century the condition of the poorer people, both in town and country, went from bad to worse. Thousands driven to desperation by their terrible struggle for existence faced the horrors of the long voyage to Australia rather than endure the misery at home. Many writers could be quoted but few of them were so concerned at the depth of the misery and degradation of the poor as Cobbett. Speaking of Cricklade he said:

> The labourers seem miserably poor. Their dwellings are little better than pig-beds, and their looks indicate that their food is not nearly equal to that of a pig. Their wretched hovels are stuck upon little bits of ground *on the road side*, where the space has been wider than the road demanded. In many places they have not two rods to a hovel ... Yesterday morning was a sharp frost; and this had set the poor creatures to digging up their little plats of potatoes. In my whole life I never saw

human wretchedness equal to this: no, not even amongst the free
negroes in America.[1]

It must be remembered that during these early years of the nineteenth
century the poor countryman was still being victimized by the Enclosure
Acts. The small farms were being swallowed up by the big estates and many
a cottage with its little garden plot was ruthlessly 'liquidated'. In 1822
Cobbett said:

> ... here [Windsor Forest] are new enclosures without end ... The
> farm-houses have long been growing fewer and fewer; the labourers'
> houses fewer and fewer; and it is manifest to every man who has eyes to
> see with, that the villages are regularly wasting away ... The farm-
> houses are not so many as they were forty years ago by three-fourths.[2]

It was becoming very rare to find, as he did in the Forest of Dean, a village
community with a little land of its own.

> Every cottage has a pig, or two. These graze in the forest ... Some
> of these foresters keep cows, and all of them have bits of ground,
> cribbed, of course, at different times, from the forest ... I saw several
> wheat stubbles from 40 rods to 10 rods. I asked one man how much
> wheat he had from about 10 rods. He said more than two bushels.
> Here is bread for three weeks, or more, perhaps; and a winter's straw
> for the pig besides.[3]

Those who championed the cause of the poor against the high prices and
dearth of food and who agitated for measures which would bring more than
temporary relief, were not slow to make capital out of the plight of the
villagers and cottagers. When it was already too late even Government
circles began to be alarmed at the loss of the cottagers' land. In 1801 Sir John
Sinclair presented a Report to his Board on the subject of enclosures. He
drew particular attention to Arthur Young's mention of certain landlords in
Rutland and Lincolnshire who had given sufficient land to industrious
labourers to enable them to grow most of their own food and to keep a cow.
Sinclair envisaged a plot of three acres and suggested a system of cultivation
involving potatoes, winter tares, barley, oats, wheat, clover and rye-grass.
The produce of this plot together with a cow, some pigs and poultry, would
support a man and his family. The report led to nothing more concrete than
an unsuccessful attempt by the fiery Chartist, Feargus O'Connor, to establish a colony (O'Connorville) near Rickmansworth based on the formula,
which had become a slogan of this movement, 'three acres and a cow'.

[1] *Rural Rides*, November 7th, 1821, William Cobbet, 1830 (1853 Edition).
[2] Ibid., October 31st, 1822.   [3] Ibid., November 14th, 1821.

In spite of the high cost of living the wages of farm labourers had scarcely risen during the first quarter of the century. Cobbett says the ordinary wage was 8s. to 12s. a week in 1822. This means that in the fifty or more years since Arthur Young made his tour agricultural wages had risen 1s. to 2s. a week, largely as a result of the shortage of labour. After peace was signed in 1815, however, unemployment increased and by 1825 wages were on the down grade, the fall continuing steadily for more than twenty years. The hardships caused widespread unrest. In 1830 and again in 1831 there were many outbreaks of disorder and incendiarism which were dealt with by the Government in ruthless fashion. The demand for 2s. 6d. a day for agricultural workers was ignored. In 1844 a *Times* correspondent confirmed from his own observations Engels's statement that the wages of farm hands had fallen as low as 6s. to 8s. a week. It is not surprising to find that this period is marked by a startling increase in the expenditure on poor relief. As one cynic remarked: 'If God punished men for crimes as man punishes men for poverty, then woe to the sons of Adam!'

Confirmation that such conditions persisted, at least in some rural areas until the eighteen-eighties, is to be found in the first part, *Lark Rise*, of Flora Thompson's trilogy. From this one learns that in a hamlet in Oxfordshire the labourers' wage at that time was 10s. a week, of which 1s. to 2s. 6d. went to house rent. Every house had a good vegetable garden and there were allotments for all. Vegetables and potatoes were grown in abundance and a great variety, including salad vegetables, were eaten in their season. Each cottage kept a pig, which during its lifetime was an important member of the family and at its death a scene of rejoicing, for its meat provided bacon for the winter or longer. Fresh meat was a luxury only seen in a few cottages on Sunday, when sixpennyworth of pieces would be bought to make a meat pudding, or occasionally a small roast would be cooked on a spit, as a pot-roast or as a 'toad' encased in a suet crust and boiled. On ordinary days at 'tea' which was taken in the evening a boiled fruit, current or jam pudding would precede the bacon and vegetables to take the edge off the appetite. But 'at a pig feast there would be no sweet pudding, for that could be had any day, and who wanted sweet things when there was plenty of meat to be had!'[1] Bread had to be bought and was a heavy item of expenditure. It formed the main part of all meals but 'tea' and was eaten with any relish that happened to be available, for example, mustard, black treacle or brown sugar. Flour for the daily pudding and an occasional plain cake could be laid in without any cash outlay, by gleaning the wheat fields after harvest. Fresh butter was too costly for general use. Margarine, called 'butterine', was on the market, but was little used, as most people preferred lard, especially when it was home-

[1] *Lark Rise to Candleford*, Flora Thompson, 1945.

made and flavoured with rosemary leaves. Milk was a rare luxury, and when available, was hand-skimmed. Nevertheless, it was cheap at a penny a jug or can, irrespective of size. When eggs were plentiful they sold at twenty a shilling.

Nothing that Cobbett had to say about the misery in the villages is as dreadful as Engels's description of the state of the wretched factory operatives. His account of the slums of Manchester and other manufacturing towns and of the conditions which the workers had to endure in the factories and in their own miserable hovels is stark horror. Here is a picture of a 'rookery'.

> It is a disorderly collection of tall, three or four-storied houses with narrow, crooked, filthy streets ... The houses are occupied from cellar to garret, filthy within and without, and their appearance is such that no human being could possibly wish to live in them. But all this is nothing in comparison with the dwellings in the narrow courts and alleys between the streets, entered by covered passages between the houses, in which the filth and tottering ruin surpass all description. Scarcely a whole window-pane can be found, the walls are crumbling, door-posts and window-frames loose and broken ... Heaps of garbage and ashes lie in all directions, and the foul liquids emptied before the doors gather in stinking pools.[1]

Dickens's description of 'the neighbourhood beyond Dockhead in the Borough of Southwark' is as grim as anything Engels ever wrote.

> ... a maze of close, narrow, and muddy streets ... tottering house-fronts, projecting over the pavement, dismantled walls that seem to totter as he passes, chimneys half crushed half hesitating to fall ... Crazy wooden galleries common to the backs of half-a-dozen houses, with holes from which to look upon the slime beneath; windows, broken and patched, with poles thrust out, on which to dry the linen that is never there; rooms so small, so filthy, so confined, that the air would seem too tainted even for the dirt and squalor which they shelter; wooden chambers thrusting themselves out above the mud, and threatening to fall in—as some have done; dirt-besmeared walls and decaying foundations; every repulsive lineament of poverty, every loathsome indication of filth, rot, and garbage.[2]

Engels was writing at a time when wages touched the lowest level of the century, just before the crisis of 1846-47. The steady fall which had occurred — actually it was greater in proportion in the country than in most

---

[1] *The Condition of the Working-Class in England in 1844*, F. Engels, 1892 (First English Edition).
[2] *Oliver Twist*, Charles Dickens, 1838.

towns — hit the farm hand and the factory worker cruelly. There were several periods of high prices when the staple foods were dear and scarce, and the struggle for existence was not made easier by all the visible signs of wealth which industrial prosperity was bringing to the rising middle class.

At this time the only ray of hope was the first sign of a growing public conscience over the terrible conditions under which the poor were forced to live. The period has to its credit a number of humanitarian measures which, although long overdue, brought some relief and a promise of a more tolerable future. One of the first was Peel's revision of the Criminal Law in 1819 when no less than one hundred crimes were removed from the list of those punishable by death. Not long before, a poor wretch who attempted to impersonate an out-patient at an infirmary had been convicted of fraud and hanged. In 1833 came the first Factory Act for improving the terrible conditions of child labour in the factories. It made it illegal to employ a child under nine years of age and limited the working hours for a child under thirteen to eight a day. Even this produced an outcry on the part of many of the manufacturers, some of whom asserted that the wretched children enjoyed their factory lives. Dr Andrew Ure, a humourless old hypocrite, said he had seen the 'lively elves' in the factories, happy, cheerful and alert and 'enjoying the mobility natural to their age'.[1] He pooh-poohed the idea that their health was undermined. More convincing, however, is Engels's description of the 'hollow-eyed ghosts' riddled with scrofula and rickets.

The appalling growth of pauperism and of the expenditure necessary to deal with it did at last arouse the Government. A Royal Commission was appointed and in 1832 reported that the pernicious system of giving outdoor relief in money or kind to able-bodied men should be abolished. This Speenhamland system, named after the village in which it was first introduced in 1795, had been a direct inducement to employers, particularly farmers, to pay low wages. The Poor Law Amendment Act of 1834 paved the way for a more rational treatment of the age-old problem of pauperism.

Things came to a head in 1845 when, with wages at the lowest level they had touched for over a century, the food situation became desperate for the very poor as a result of a widespread invasion of 'potato disease' in conjunction with a poor corn harvest. England has never been nearer to revolution. The fungus (*Phytophtora infestans*), however, did what twenty years of bitter agitation had failed to do; it brought about the repeal of the Corn Laws in 1846. Although the next two years were ones of uncertainty and financial instability the fall in the price of bread and most other staple commodities checked the wave of revolution which had threatened to engulf England.

[1] *The Philosophy of Manufactures*, Andrew Ure, 1835.

For the next twenty years there was an amazing development of England's industrial and commercial enterprises, associated, as might be expected, with a further period of migration to the towns. This migration was of such magnitude that it considerably handicapped the efforts which the civic and municipal authorities were beginning to make to improve housing, sanitation and other matters involving public health. But there is no doubt that during this era of industrial expansion and prosperity the condition of the working classes gradually improved. As Engels said, 'The truth is this; that during the period of England's industrial monopoly the English working class have, to a certain extent, shared in the benefits of monopoly.'[1] Wages tended to rise and food to become cheaper. By 1868 the average wage for a farm labourer was 12s. 6d. a week, that of the town labourer about 18s.; the more skilled workmen, bricklayers, carpenters, etc., could earn from £1 to 32s. weekly.[2]

From about 1870 the condition of the working class has tended to improve steadily in spite of setbacks at recurring periods of industrial depression.

The nineteenth century marks the beginning of the modern period of scientific agriculture. The remarkable progress in practical farming which the eighteenth century had seen had been made largely as a result of rough-and-ready empirical methods and much hit-or-miss experimentation. There was little or no scientific basis and nothing was known of the principles involved. The fundamental questions of agriculture, soil fertility and manuring, were not clearly revealed as scientific problems until the new chemistry was born at the end of the century. There was vision, however, in the words of Francis Home who in 1755 was invited by the Edinburgh Society 'to try how far chymistry will go in settling the principles of agriculture'.[3] He found that certain salts, nitre (potassium nitrate), Epsom salts (sodium sulphate) and vitriolic tartar (potassium sulphate), brought about increased growth, and wrote, 'The more they [farmers] know of the effects of different bodies on plants the greater chance they have to discover the nourishment of plants.' Later in the century the Earl of Dundonald made an important contribution to the subject by pointing out the value of alkaline phosphates and of humus.[4]

The new chemistry soon made its influence felt in the more progressive agricultural circles. For the first time it was recognized that the chemical composition of the soil determines plant growth and that the salts found in plants are actually derived from the ground. The pioneer investigator in

[1] *The Condition of the Working-Class in England in 1844*, F. Engels, 1892.
[2] *Journal of the Society of Arts*, 1868, Vol. XVI.
[3] *The Principles of Agriculture and Vegetation*, F. Home, 1756.
[4] *A Treatise showing the Intimate Connection that Subsists between Agriculture and Chemistry*, Earl of Dundonald, 1795.

this field was the Swiss chemist, Théodore de Saussure, whose clean-cut experiments and logical deductions carried conviction.[1] The new outlook was presented to English agriculturists by Sir Humphrey Davy who for ten years, from 1802 to 1812, delivered annually a course of lectures on 'Agricultural Chemistry' for the Board of Agriculture. The lectures appeared in book form in 1813.[2] Davy showed the importance of analysing soil in order to ascertain what mineral nutrients were present and described methods for their detection. Lime, carbonates, silica, magnesia, aluminia and iron oxide were among the salts to which he drew attention.

An example of the application of the new chemical methods of analysis occurs in a report on the subject of Dutch farming which Sir John Sinclair presented to the Board of Agriculture in 1815.[3] In Holland they were still well ahead of us, in spite of the great strides made by English farming since 1750, and Sinclair noticed that Dutch crops of clover seldom failed whereas those at home frequently deteriorated year by year. He found that the Dutchmen laid great stress on the use of certain types of ashes for land to be put under clover. Sinclair asked Brande, who had followed Davy as Professor of Chemistry at the Royal Institution, to analyse a sample. The report stated that the material contained 'siliceous earth, 32 parts; calcium sulphate, 12; sodium sulphate and chloride, 6; carbonate of lime, 40; oxide of iron, 3', and thereby gave the clue to the valuable manuring properties of the 'Dutch ashes'.

The memorable year in the history of agriculture is 1840. Three years earlier the Committee of the Section of Chemistry at the seventh meeting of the British Association had recorded the following resolution:

> Professor Liebig was requested to prepare a Report on the present state of our knowledge in regard to Isomeric Bodies. He was also requested to prepare a Report on the State of Organic Chemistry and Organic Analysis.[4]

Liebig, at that time Professor of Chemistry at Giessen, appears to have taken a very broad view of the request for in 1840 he published his famous work, which, as the preface says, was his report to the British Association. An English translation appeared in the same year.[5]

---

[1] *Récherches chimiques sur la Végétation*, T. de Saussure, 1804.
[2] *Elements of Agricultural Chemistry in a Course of Lectures for the Board of Agriculture*, Sir Humphrey Davy, 1813.
[3] *Hints regarding the Agricultural State of the Netherlands compared with that of Great Britain*, Sir J. Sinclair, 1815.
[4] *Report of Liverpool Meeting of the British Association*, 1837.
[5] *Chemistry in its Applications to Agriculture and Physiology*, J. v. Liebig, 1840.

The effect on scientific thought of this remarkable work was revolutionary. Liebig completely shattered the old idea that plants derived a large proportion of their organic substance directly from the humus of the soil and showed that the chief if not the sole source of carbon was the inexhaustible supplies of carbon dioxide in the atmosphere. Nitrogen he found was usually absorbed by the roots as ammonia and he made clear the function of lime in regulating the acidity of soils. His researches laid the foundation of the practice of artificial manuring. Liebig, who had strongly developed commercial instincts — he was at one time or another connected with projects for marketing a meat-extract, an infant and invalid food, a baking powder and other similar ventures — actually attempted to put on the market a 'chemical manure'. Much to his disappointment and somewhat to his discomfiture it was a failure, for although it contained some valuable salts (potassium and phosphates) he had not then realized that a source of nitrogen, such as ammonia, was essential.

It is probable that Liebig's views would have made little more than a superficial impression on practical agriculture in England had it not been for the enterprise of a young man who inherited a considerable estate in Hertfordshire about the time that the famous book was published. John Lawes decided to use some of the fields of his new Rothamsted home to test on a practical scale the manuring processes which the German chemist was advocating. Lacking himself the chemical knowledge required to make the necessary analyses of soils and foodstuffs, he engaged as an assistant young Joseph Gilbert, who had been trained in the laboratory at Giessen. For over forty years these two worked in collaboration in a series of practical investigations on manuring, crop yields and food values, which have since become world famous, and which laid the foundations of the Rothamsted Experimental Station. It is true that for a long time their researches failed to influence the great body of farmers in England, for with the exception of a very small minority of progressively-minded men the farming community was deeply suspicious of the new developments and resentful of scientific intrusion. In the long run, however, the influence of the Rothamsted experiments began to make itself felt. Even the most conservative farmer could not long remain indifferent to the fact that by supplementing an appropriate mineral fertilizer with 86 lb. of artificial nitrogenous manure per acre more than double the crop of wheat was produced.

Progress was also made in animal husbandry. Particularly important was the general adoption of 'cakes' and other 'concentrates' for winter feeding. The by-products of the mills crushing oil from imported cottonseed, linseed and other cheap oilseeds from overseas were found to be of great value as winter foods and eventually came to be extensively used, although in parts of England it was some time before the farmers could be persuaded to make use of them. In 1875 one of the successful candidates for Lord Leicester's prize for an essay on 'improvements in agriculture during the past twenty years' drew attention to the fact that only a couple of decades before cattle in the Eastern Counties were brought into open yards in winter and kept exposed to the inclemency of the weather 'with as much flesh on their bones as the pasture — without much assistance from cake — and the flies allowed them to gain during the summer'. There they were expected to fatten 'on the few roots grown on the farm ... and straw, or at best hay, with comparatively little cake or artificial food'.[1]

It was an ironic fact that the enormous practical value of the new scientific knowledge really began to be appreciated in the late 'seventies, by which time the tide of England's agricultural prosperity had turned as a result of the heavy imports of grain from abroad. Free Trade and the demand for cheap food gave the death-blow to an English agriculture based on wheat. There were serious crises for farmers in the 'seventies. Within fifty years the greater part of the food came from abroad, and most of the population was dependent on the food that it bought.

[1] *Lord Leicester's Prize Essay on Agriculture*, No. 1 by Mr A. J. Smith, and No. 2 by Mr J. Danby, 1875.

CHAPTER XVII

QUALITY OF FOOD

§ 1 FOOD SUPPLY

An inevitable consequence of the increasing dependence on purchased food, and in the latter half of the century on imported food, was that the diet of the vast majority of the people tended to become uniform in town and country and in north and south. This transition was, of course, accelerated by the development of the methods of transport. In the early part of the century many of the roads were still in a very bad condition. In 1802 the Society of Arts offered a gold medal and a prize of fifty guineas for a cheap method of clearing dust and mud from the turnpike roads. A few years later McAdam introduced his method of surfacing roads with a layer of granite lumps and chips. He was rewarded in 1827 by a parliamentary grant of £10,000 and the post of Surveyor-General of the Metropolitan roads.

The next big advance in the history of transport was the advent of the railway. By 1845 there were already 50 lines covering over 1700 miles, although to reach this impressive total it was necessary to include a line of 24 miles operated by horses and several 'stationary', i.e. cable, lines. Nevertheless a new era had dawned which had a profound influence on all questions concerning the transport of food. Some of these questions began to assume a major importance. The growth in size and complexity of the food industry, for we can now fairly refer to it in this manner, meant that foodstuffs were being handled, transported and stored in far larger quantities than ever before. This enormously increased the difficulties of those engaged in the wholesale trade because the liability to deterioration was much greater when large consignments were concerned. It must be borne in mind that nothing was known of the reason for foods going rancid or mouldy, the view generally held being that the cause of all decomposition was contact with the air.

As an example of the changed conditions, we can take the case of wheat. In the underground state it will keep unharmed for a long time if the conditions of temperature, humidity, ventilation, etc., are carefully controlled. Such conditions are maintained with great care in a modern silo, but a century or so ago all that the farmers and distributors had to guide them was a certain rough-and-ready knowledge, gained in an empirical way. Much more serious difficulties were encountered with the ground grain. The germ of wheat is rich in oil and contains an agent, one of the enzymes, the function of which is to break down the fat when the young embryonic plant begins to develop during germination. As long as the seed is dry and dormant the enzyme is inactive. It only begins to act on the oil when the natural process of absorbing water preparatory to germination occurs or when the grain is crushed. The crushed germ very quickly turns rancid; in warm weather the oil is unpleasantly so in a few days, which is why wholemeal flour tends to acquire a sour or tallowy smell on keeping.

In earlier times this did not greatly affect the miller, whose trade was a purely local one. His corn was ground and the flour sold as it was required. It was a very different matter when the towns grew to such a size that the chief trade was in flour rather than in unground corn and when large stocks had to be held. Not only was there then a greater likelihood of rancidity during storage or transport but there was also a much greater susceptibility to attack by weevils and other damaging insects.

§ 2 FOOD ADULTERATION

At no period have contemporary records shown the merchants to be guilty of such flagrant adulteration as between 1800 and 1850. It may be that one is misled into thinking sophistication was more rife and more blatant than in the previous century because of the larger amount of information available and because the rapid growth of analytical chemistry led to so many revelations. It is, however, certain that food adulteration was practised on an almost incredible scale for more than half a century.

In 1820 a German Jew, born in Bückeburg in 1769, made a considerable sensation by ruthlessly exposing the character and extent of this food-faking. His family name was originally Marcus, that of Accum being adopted by his father when he embraced Christianity. He may have acquired his early chemical training in the apothecary's shop of Brande in Hanover, for in 1793 he came to London and entered the Brande Pharmacy in Arlington Street. Brande was at that time apothecary to George III as both King of Hanover and of Great Britain.

Accum came to the attention of Nicholson the well-known chemical experimentalist and writer who gave him facilities to gain greater chemical experience. His first published work, which showed an interest in the purity of druggists' materials, was a paper in Nicholson's *Journal of Natural Philosophy, Chemistry and the Arts*, which appeared in 1798. In 1800 he established a chemical laboratory at 11 Old Compton Street, where he soon built up a flourishing practice as a consultant and gained a considerable reputation as a teacher and lecturer. The latter was recognized by his appointment as 'chemical operator' at the Royal Institution, where he frequently acted as assistant to Davy, and as Professor of Chemistry at the Surrey Institution in Blackfriars Bridge Road.

Accum was undoubtedly a remarkably versatile man, but of all his many interests, such as the manufacture and use of coal gas, mineralogy, the development of beet-sugar, analysis of drugs, the one which occupied the greatest part of his time was the chemical examination of foods. He was a prolific writer on this subject and his books on *Culinary Chemistry*, on brewing and on bread-making, remained the standard works on these subjects for many years. It was, however, his book on food adulteration, published in 1820, that brought him fame.[1] The very appearance of the book attracted attention. The stiff blue-grey cover carried the suggestive design of a spider in its web about to devour a fly, surrounded by a pattern of intertwined serpents, with a skull and crossbones at the top. Underneath was the quotation, 'There is DEATH in the Pot. 2 *Kings*. C.4. V.40.'

Many of the adulterations to which Accum drew attention had been practised for a great number of years, e.g. the addition of alum to bread, of copperas to beer and of capiscum to mustard, but his denunciations were far more alarming than those of his predecessors because they were supported by chemical analysis. It is clear that alum was extensively used in all the town bakeries. According to Accum it was necessary to add as much as three to four ounces to a sack of flour to improve the colour of some of the inferior grades.

He revealed all the tricks of the trade with regard to faked wine, pointing out that much of it was made from spoiled cider, that artificial colouring was widely used and that even the 'crusting' of old port was imitated by lining the bottles with a layer of 'supertartrate of potash'.

When he described the illicit methods of many London brewers — they were still using the poisonous drug *Cocculus indicus* and other harmful or noxious substances on a considerable scale — he had the courage to publish a list of the druggists and grocers who had been convicted of selling much material to the brewers, and another of the publicans recently fined for adulterating beer. This caused a tremendous outcry. It was bad enough that the sins of Hannah Spencer, who had been fined £150 for using salt of steel and molasses in making beer, or of Josiah Nibbs of Tooting, who had paid £300 for being found in possession of 12 lb. of *Cocculus indicus* as well as large amounts of Spanish juice (liquorice), should be set out in the *Minutes of the House of Commons Committee on the Price and Quality of Beer*, but few people saw that official report. Accum's book, in which they were reprinted, sold out in a month and ran through four editions in two years.

[1] *Treatise on the Adulterations of Food and Culinary Poisons*, F. Accum, 1820.

The brewers were furious. So were those people whom he accused by name of collecting and drying blackthorn leaves to make artificial tea, of selling spurious coffee and of faking gin and other spirituous liquors. He described cases in which Gloucester cheese had been coloured with red lead, cream thickened with arrowroot and flour, and the bright colours of London confectionery obtained by the use of the highly poisonous salts of copper and lead. As the *Literary Gazette* put it:

> It is so horribly pleasant to reflect how we are in this way beswindled, betrayed, dedrugged, and be-devilled, that we are almost angry with Mr. Accum for the great service he has done the community by opening our eyes, at the risk of shutting our mouths for ever.[1]

Accum was subjected to a violent and bitter campaign of abuse on the part of those whom he had so ruthlessly exposed. Unfortunately, he himself gave them the opportunity for an ample revenge. The authorities of the Royal Institution discovered that someone was in the habit of removing leaves from certain books in their library. Suspicion fell on Accum. A warrant was applied for and his rooms were searched. It was claimed that a number of the missing pages were found there and he was accordingly charged with theft. The case was dismissed on the grounds that the leaves separated from the books were only waste paper and that Accum had not stolen a sufficient quantity of waste paper to form the basis of a charge. This suggests that the magistrate thought the whole affair rather trivial and had it not been for the hatred with which Accum was regarded in certain circles it is probable that the matter would have ended there. As it was, the authorities of the Royal Institution were persuaded to institute proceedings against him on a charge of mutilating the books. Many of those who had a high regard for Accum and his scientific reputation fought to get the prosecution dropped, while his enemies took the opportunity to heap calumny on him and to press for the case to be carried forward. Poor Accum, his great reputation crashing about him, driven to desperation by the worry of the whole affair, finally decided the matter by failing to appear when the case came up for trial. He forfeited his bail and a few months later returned to his native Germany, an embittered and disillusioned man.

The truth of the affair, which reflects little credit on the authorities of the Royal Institution, will probably never be known. It seems likely that Accum was guilty, but that does not absolve those who were instrumental in bringing the case from a charge of vindictive persecution. It is this clear determination to ruin him that strongly suggests the influence of those who

---

[1] Cited by C. A. Browne in 'The Life and Chemical Services of Frederick Accum', *Journal of Chemical Education*, November 1928, Vol. II, No. 11.

bore him a bitter grudge for his exposure of their nefarious practices. Perhaps the most serious consequence of Accum's public disgrace was the loss of confidence in what he had written and it is certain that his enemies did everything in their power to foster the belief that he had grossly exaggerated the extent to which adulteration was practised. They were successful in inducing the public to cease worrying about the state of affairs and by 1824 the alarm had almost died down.

Within a few years, however, it was raised again by the publication of a booklet entitled *Deadly Adulteration and Slow Poisoning; or Disease and Death in the Pot and Bottle.* The anonymous author, who called himself 'An Enemy of Fraud and Villany', dedicated his book to the Duke of Wellington and called upon his adminstration to take steps to protect the public against the widespread 'blood-empoisoning and life-destroying adulteration'. The date of publication is probably 1830. It was clearly based on Accum's book, but it differs from that work in that many of the allegations were made without substantial evidence. It is written in the ironical and slightly irresponsible style of many of the eighteenth-century pamphlets and for this reason it has been compared unfavourably with Accum's more balanced book. The anonymity of the author, together with a suspicion that he had indulged in a good deal of exaggeration, tended to lessen the impression which he had doubtless hoped to make. The *Lancet*, for example, thought the author a 'well-meaning individual, but of that class of exaggerating alarmist' who write in a 'tone of half-mad honesty'.[1]

Nevertheless, adulteration appears still to have been widely practised. Even the allegation that highly poisonous mineral products were used to colour confectionery seems to have been substantiated, for in 1824 a Mr Tatham of Golden Square informed the magistrate at Marlborough Street that his family and a party of friends had been taken ill after eating coloured 'wafer cakes' bought from 'a respectable shop'. The cakes were analysed by the family doctor, Mr Shelton, who reported that they contained verdigris and sugar of lead.[2]

Nearly twenty years passed before there was another scare. In 1848 John Mitchell claimed that matters were in precisely the same state as when Accum's book was published. He repeated most of the original charges — alum and ammonium carbonate in bread, lead in cider and wine, plaster of Paris and pipeclay in flour, flour and chalk in milk — and this time the alarm did not subside.[3] In 1850 Wakley, the editor of the *Lancet*, announced that an Analytical and Sanitary Commission had been appointed to inquire into

[1] *Lancet*, 1830, Vol. XV.
[2] *The Family Oracle of Health, Economy, Medicine, and Good Living*, Vol. I, 1824.
[3] *Treatise on the Falsification of Food and the Chemical Means employed to detect them*, J. Mitchell, 1848.

and report on the quality of the 'solids and fluids consumed by all classes of the public'. Only two commissioners were appointed, Dr Hassall who was responsible for the chemical analyses, and Dr Letheby, a recognized authority on diet.

Wakley was determined from the outset to take a strong line.

> We re-enter upon the labour (which we actually commenced in 1831) with a full sense of the responsibilities it involves, and a full determination to cope with them, come in what shape they may, satisfactorily and successfully.[1]

Under the motto 'Forewarned, forearmed' the first article, dealing with the adulteration of coffee, appeared in 1851. Following Accum's courageous lead the editor printed the names and addresses of those merchants whose products were found to be adulterated. There was, of course, another outcry particularly since it transpired that some of the accused had purchased their supplies in perfectly good faith. The reception by the press, however, was cordial, *Punch* in particular lending enthusiastic support.

THE LANCET'S DETECTIVE FORCE

Our contemporary the *Lancet* has conferred a great boon on the public by establishing a new order of constabulary, which may be called the Scientific Detective Police. The function of these detectives is to investigate and expose the fraudulent adulteration of articles of food practised by a set of scoundrels under the names of grocers and other tradesmen. In his researches into this rascality, the *Lancet's* policeman is assisted by a microscope, which, in throwing light on the fraud in question, exerts a power far superior to that of the common bull's eye. By the help of this instrument, an immense quantity of villainous stuff has been discovered in coffee, arrowroot, and other substances sold for nutriment, and some of them, 'particularly recommended to invalids'. The *Lancet* seconds the exertions of its intelligent officer by spiritedly publishing the addresses of the rogues at whose swindling establishments the samples of rubbish were purchased. If any of the knaves thus pilloried in the *Lancet*, abetted by a disreputable attorney and a dishonest barrister, endeavour to avenge themselves through the technicalities of the law, *Punch* hopes they will meet with twelve true men in the

[1] *Lancet* (1851), i.

jury-box who will scout both them and their legal accomplices out of court.[1]

Punch went even further and published a series of articles entitled 'Sermons to Tradesmen' which were as outspoken as anything Accum had written. In 'A Gossip by Way of Preface', which was the first of these articles, there are scathing descriptions of the 'imps' who infest the food trade.

> Imps of all trades were there. The Baker-Imp who grinds his alum to make his bread; and selling the staff of life, makes the staff carry a mischievous weapon for the bowels of him who trusts to it.
> The Grocer-Imp who enriches his chocolate with brick-dust; and with a morning draught conveys the materials of a vault.
> The Milk-man Imp with chalk against customer, and chalk inside him.
> The Confection-Imp, who paints Twelfth Cakes with emerald green (a beautiful change for coppers, in an arsenite development) and — especially in holiday times — plays HEROD among the innocents.
> The Publican-Imp, whose head of beer is green copperas — whose ale is sharpened with the fiery edges of vitriol, and whose grains-of-paradise are gifts of the serpent.[2]

For four years article followed article in the columns of the *Lancet*. Hassall's analytical methods were greatly in advance of anything previously known. It was he who first demonstrated the value of the microscope in detecting adulteration and he made extensive use of this new method. In 1855 the whole of his work was published in book form.[3] His disturbing revelations made a deep impression on the public mind, and were not allowed to pass off without action being taken. The articles in the *Lancet* led to the appointment in 1855 of a Select Parliamentary Commission to consider the question of food adulteration. As a result of the evidence they collected, which fully bore out the allegations of the *Lancet* commission, the first Food and Drugs Act of 1860 was passed.

It was a well-intentioned measure, by which county authorities were given powers to appoint analysts to control the quality of foods, but unfortunately it was administered in so half-hearted a fashion that it very soon became a dead letter. It seems likely that there was some truth in the assertion that 'thanks to trade opposition in and out of Parliament, some six or seven only [analysts] appear to have been appointed, of which four were allowed to do

---

[1] *Punch*, 1851, Vol. XX.   [2] Ibid.
[3] *Food and its Adulteration*, A. H. Hassall, 1855.

nothing at all; two of them had a few samples submitted to them at first, and at first only'.[1] The only analyst who stood out for his rights and insisted on taking some steps to stop the scandalous state of affairs was old Dr Cameron of Dublin. In 1862 he examined 2600 samples of food, proved 1500 of them to be adulterated and succeeded in securing 342 convictions. In that year there had been under 300 analytical examinations in the whole of England.

In 1872 the Act was drastically amended. All counties and boroughs maintaining police forces were supposed to appoint an analyst, and a large proportion of them did so. From that time dates the beginning of the suppression of the food adulterator.

A clear picture of the improvement effected by 1875 is given by Lascelles Scott in the *Journal of the Society of Arts* for that year.[2] Many of the analysts were slack, not a few were incompetent, perhaps some were not above suspicion on other grounds, but the tide had turned and England was soon to look back with wonder on the days when it was possible for a confectioner to escape with a fine of 6d. for colouring cakes yellow with lead chromate.

§ 5 BREAD

As we have shown, bread was very frequently adulterated during the first fifty or sixty years of the century, the use of alum or 'stuff', a mixture of alum and salt, being general, at any rate in the towns. The early volumes of the *Lancet* show that the medical profession was seriously disturbed by the practice. In 1829 an editorial article in that journal suggested that the evil might be mitigated by a heavy tax on alum. Many doctors wrote to say that country people who enjoyed perfect health on home-baked bread and home-brewed beer were afflicted with chronic dyspepsia when they came to the towns and lived on alum-whitened bread and adulterated beer. The *Lancet* deprecated the craving of the poor people for white bread, remarking that the housewife was partly to blame for the adulteration with her 'Lord, baker, how brown your bread is to-day!'

In 1851 Hassall examined loaves purchased at random in various parts of London and found that every one contained alum. He also reported that the League Bread Company, which claimed that its products were of 'perfect purity, being warranted free from alum', was in fact supplying the public with loaves containing considerable quantities of that chemical. Hassall deplored the fact that he was unable to find a single baker who could supply bread free from alum, although there was a Statute on the books which punished this adulteration by a fine not exceeding £20.

[1] *Journal of the Society of Arts*, 1875, Vol. XXIV.   [2] Ibid.

It is not surprising that in the years of want much bread was baked with flour of very inferior quality, often mixed with potato flour, barley, bran and other products which darkened the loaf. Count Rumford could not understand why there was such a strong prejudice in England against dark bread.[1] He failed to understand the dislike of rye bread, which formed the staple food in many European countries. He was one of many writers who suggested that the poor people should be fed on this type of bread in times of want.[2] The poor, however, had other ideas and remained supremely indifferent to the argument that black bread was more wholesome than white, an argument based on the fact that the famous French physiologist, Magendie, had found a few years previously that dogs lived for a long time in good health when fed on coarse dark bread or soldier's biscuit and water, but declined and died in less than two months if the bread was made from a high grade of white wheaten flour.

About 1860 an interesting proposition was being examined in France, which attracted some attention among scientists in London. A well-known French food chemist, Mège-Mouries, the inventor of margarine, devised a machine for removing the husks of wheat, or decortication as it was called, so that the whole grain could be ground into a wholemeal flour almost entirely devoid of bran. He claimed that nearly 90 per cent of the grain could be obtained as flour and that it was, therefore, a very economical process. The flour was a little dark in colour but contained all the nutritive value of the wheat. The Society of Arts investigated the matter carefully but made no move to popularize the new type of flour in England. Apparently the scheme came to nothing.

One effect of the charges against the millers was to arouse interest in the use of hand mills suitable for grinding corn at home. The Society of Arts had for many years offered a prize to inventors of a simple, efficient mill of this type. A portable form used by the French soldiers in the Russian campaign was brought to the notice of the Society by Sir John Sinclair and favourably mentioned in the *Journal* for 1817, but it does not appear that this or any similar machine was ever widely used. This was probably because they would have produced a coarse wholemeal flour which would have been difficult, in an ordinary household, to sift in order to remove the bran.

About the middle of the century important developments occurred in the milling industry. One was the introduction of silk gauze for sifting or 'bolting' the flour, in place of the woollen or linen fabrics previously used. This enabled a better separation of the finer particles of the bran to be made. The

[1] *Essay on Food, particularly on Feeding the Poor*, Count Rumford, edited by Sir Richard Musgrave, 1847.
[2] *The Necessity of Brown Bread for Digestion, Nourishment and Sound Health, and the Injurious Effects of White Bread*, D. Carr, 1847.

innovation was, however, of minor importance compared with the introduction of the 'roller' mill. Mills of this type, in which the grain is crushed
between rollers instead of being ground between flat stones, had been tried
out at least a hundred years earlier but none had proved really practicable.
A north Lancashire ironmonger, Wilkinson by name, took out a patent for
iron rollers in 1753. This was followed by a number of similar devices, of
which the first to be used with any marked success was one constructed in
Budapest by a Swiss engineer named Sulzberger, in the early 'forties of the
next century.

Most of these early mills had rollers of chilled iron, which it was found
difficult to keep in a serviceable condition. The introduction of porcelain
rollers about 1870 gave a great fillip to the movement. Two years later a
roller mill was opened in Glasgow by a German miller, Oscar Oerle. It was
successful but did not arouse much interest. Meanwhile, the new process had
been rapidly developed in Budapest and Vienna and when in 1877 a party of
British millers visited these cities they were profoundly impressed by the
possibilities of the new development. In 1878 Radford of Liverpool was
operating a roller mill with a capacity of 3000 sacks a week, and within a very
few years so many new mills had been set up that the new method had almost
superseded the age-old process of stone-grinding.[1]

There were many reasons for this rapid change-over. Roller mills were
quicker, their upkeep was less, and it was much easier to control the degree
of milling. Last, but by no means least, the new method enabled the greater
part of the germ to be separated. In stone-grinding the germ was ground up
with the flour; under the rollers it was flattened into a minute flake which
could be sifted off with the bran. This meant that the flour would keep
better, the danger of deterioration by rancidity being almost entirely
eliminated. It also meant that the miller was more easily able to satisfy the
demand for white bread, because the greyish-yellow colour of the germ was
removed. What was not appreciated at the time was that in removing the
germ all the highly nutritious food substances it contained were also being
eliminated.

The actual yield of white flour was of course smaller than formerly but
the miller found a good market for the by-products as foodstuffs for agricultural purposes. For the higher grades of domestic flour the degree of 'extraction', that is the percentage of flour from wheat, fell from about 75-80
per cent with stone-grinding to about 70-73 per cent with the roller mills.
The proportion of the various products in two actual millings were found
to be as follows:

[1] *The History of Corn Milling*, R. Bennet and J. Elton, 1898.

STONE-GRINDING		ROLLER-MILLING	
Percentage yield		*Percentage yield*	
Flour	79	Flour	73
		'Sharps'	14
Middlings	11	Bran	12
Bran	10	Germ	1

The most important changes in the nutritive value of flour caused by this alteration in milling technique were reductions of the vitamin B_1 content to about one-third and of iron to just over one-half of their previous values. The nicotinic acid was reduced by about one-third.

The growing demand for whiteness in bread and flour was not satisfied by the products of the roller mills. The flour thus produced had in many cases a very pale cream colour, due to the presence of traces of natural yellow pigments. It had been known for some time that the colour of flour tends to lighten on storage and exposure to air owing, as is now known, to oxidative destruction of the pigment. About the middle of the nineteenth century attempts were made to accelerate the bleaching process by artificial means. Primitive oxidation methods, such as exposing the flour to the fumes of burning sulphur or resin or to currents of air or ozone, were the subjects of numerous patents from about 1860 onwards. None of them appears to have been of practical value, for Jago's classic work on the chemistry of bread-making, published in 1886, makes no reference to them.[1] The first successful method was that involving the use of nitrogen peroxide which formed the subject of a patent taken out by John and Sidney Andrews in 1901. Later, chlorine, chlorine dioxide, nitrogen trichloride (agene) and other chemical bleaching and improving agents were introduced. In 1946 the late Sir Edward Mellanby showed that a diet composed largely of agenized flour caused running fits in dogs. Workers at the Cereals Research Station at St Albans subsequently identified and isolated the toxic factor, methionine sulphoximine, which is formed by the action of nitrogen trichloride on the amino-acid, methionine, of the flour protein gluten. In spite of extensive investigations on both sides of the Atlantic agene has not been shown to have toxic effects on man. Nevertheless in view of its deleterious effects on dogs and certain other animal species its use in the United Kingdom has been banned since the beginning of 1956. Chlorine dioxide, which produces no such toxic effects as nitrogen trichloride, is probably most extensively used in its place. The use of flour improvers and bleachers has recently been fully discussed.[2]

---

[1] *The Chemistry of Wheat, Flour and Bread, and Technology of Breadmaking*, W. Jago, 1886.
[2] *Bread*, Lord Horder, Sir Charles Dodds and T. Moran, 1954.

The craze for whiter and still whiter flour has long been an obsession with the milling trade. Whereas in the past they could claim that their efforts were being made to satisfy a public demand it appears more likely that at the present time it is increased competition in the face of a slowly declining consumption that urges them on.

The decline in the consumption of bread and flour to which we have referred is an interesting phenomenon which began to be evident in Great Britain and the United States late in the nineteenth century and which is now so clearly marked that it is causing the milling and baking industries considerable concern. It seems to be related to a rising standard of living for the falling curve representing bread and flour is complementary to the rising curve for sugar and sweetmeats. It is also related to a rise in the consumption of meat. These relationships reflect the fact that bread is the staple food of poverty and that people eat much less of it when they can afford to buy meat and to indulge in the type of dish with which sugar is eaten.

Before leaving the subject of bread it should be mentioned that yeast began to displace 'leaven' about the middle of the nineteenth century. At first brewers' yeasts, or those grown in potato mash, were employed but later the special high-fermenting types of yeast developed on the Continent, and which were marketed in compressed form, became more popular. These latter were the forerunners of our modern bakery yeasts.

Self-raising flours, which contain a mineral mixture of a carbonate and an acid salt which liberates carbon dioxide on the addition of moisture and so 'raises' the dough, seem to have first been used successfully about 1846. The *Lancet* for that year mentions them as an interesting new invention. Late in the century considerable interest was aroused by a process invented by a certain Dr Dauglish in which dough was charged with carbonic acid gas by mixing it in sealed chambers containing the gas under pressure. The bread came to be known as 'aerated bread' and it was claimed that it was more hygienically made than when yeast was used.

§ 4 MILK

The quality of the milk supplied to the towns was unbelievably bad until well after the middle of the century, when the influence of Hassall's report and the activities of the public health authorities began to effect a change for the better. An undated publication calling attention to the disgraceful condition of the London milk supply was written by a certain H. Hodson Rugg. His description of the half-underground dens and cellars in which the cows were kept for the greater part of the year, standing knee-deep in filth, with little or no ventilation and with hay, brewers' grains and turnips as their only food, shows that the state of affairs about 1845, when the book was probably written, was as bad as it had been in the eighteenth century.[1] His assertion that it was difficult to find a sample of London milk which would fail to show the presence of blood or pus when examined under the microscope was fully supported by Hassall's investigations.

In 1847 the *Lancet* strongly condemned the unhygienic character of the milk supply of London and pointed out that doctors were beginning to believe that it was responsible for a good deal of scrofula.[2] It was just as bad in other large towns. Ure said that he could not recommend milk as a substitute for tea in the diet of the Manchester factory workers because of its bad quality.[3] It is not suprising that many of the cattle were diseased and the milk heavily infected before it was drawn from the udder. Here is a description of the condition of the cow-sheds in Golden Square.

> Forty cows are kept in them, two in each seven feet of space. There is no ventilation, save by the unceiled tile roof, through which the ammoniacal vapours escape . . . Besides the animals, there is at one end a large tank for grains, a storeplace for turnips and hay, and between them a receptacle into which the liquid manure drains, and the solid is heaped . . . the stench thence arising, [is] insufferable.[4]

It was the practice of these town cow-keepers to bring the animals into their sheds as soon as they had calved and to milk them until they ran dry, when they were sold. Up to the early 'thirties there were still a few cow-houses in London run on these primitive lines. In 1895 about one-third of the 2 million gallons consumed each year in Newcastle-upon-Tyne was produced in 73 cow-houses within the city and even as late as 1931 10 per cent of 112 samples of milk tested were adulterated.[5]

London did not get all its milk from the town dairies. The development of the railways made it possible to bring country milk up to the capital. There was very little such traffic in 1850 but by 1853 the quantity arriving annually by rail, mostly by the Eastern Counties Railway, was not far short of half a million gallons. The production in London itself at this time was estimated at about 45 million gallons, but this is clearly a gross over-estimate if it be true that the number of cows then housed in the metropolitan area was only 24,000.[6]

[1] *Observations on London Milk, showing its Unhealthy Character*, H. Hodson Rugg (undated).
[2] *Lancet* (1847), ii.
[3] *The Philosophy of Manufactures*, Andrew Ure, 1835.
[4] *An Address to the Inhabitants of St. James's Westminster*, by A Retired Churchwarden [Hon. F. Byng], 1847.
[5] *A Thousand Families in Newcastle-upon-Tyne*, James Spence, W. S. Walton, F. J. W. Miller and S. D. M. Court, 1954.
[6] *Dairy Farming*, J. P. Shelden, 1870 (?).

In 1863 cattle plague, or *rinderpest*, attacked a large number of the cows in England. The epidemic was not at first serious but later it became very severe. The years 1865-67 are memorable for the losses caused by this disease. The mortality in the crowded, unhygienic city cow-houses was, as would be expected, particularly heavy. In many cases the whole stock was lost. After such losses many of the cow-sheds were never filled again and the towns became increasingly dependent on milk brought in from the country districts. By 1866 over two million gallons were arriving annually in London by rail.

Watering the milk or removing the fat were very common practices. The crafty milkman had discovered that by decreasing the specific gravity by adding water, and then removing some of the fat, which is lighter than water, the gravity could be brought back again within the normal range. Detection by means of the lactometer was thus frustrated. It was not until chemical means of estimating the true amount of fat were introduced that this clever fraud was countered.

The normal range of fat in cows' milk can be taken as between 2.5 to 4.5 per cent. Breed, time of milking, stage of lactation and many other factors influence the amount. For mixed milk, however, a narrower variation with a mean of about 3.65 per cent is usual. Typical London milks analysed in 1865 by Voelcker gave a mean value of 2.17 per cent. Some were as low as 1.75 per cent; this was almost certainly due to watering.

It cannot be said that the bacteriological knowledge which resulted from Pasteur's pioneer studies had much influence on the handling of milk until nearly the end of the century. The great French scientist had shown that micro-organisms which cause disease and those which are responsible for fermentation and putrefactive changes are destroyed when fluids are heated to a temperature of about 145° F. This process, known today as pasteurization, was first used in the dairy industry about 1890, more as a means of increasing the 'life' of the milk than to kill the germs likely to cause harm to the consumer. For example, milk reaching a town in the late afternoon after a long railway journey would probably turn sour before it could be distributed next morning. Pasteurization was found to retard this by killing the bacteria which produce acid. It was a few years later, about 1896, that it began to be appreciated that pasteurization also provided a valuable protection against milk-borne disease.

§5 CONDENSED AND DRIED MILKS

Although early attempts had been made to prepare concentrated milk by evaporating part of the water, most of these efforts were failures because the heating was done over an open fire. This caused the milk to turn brown and to acquire a taste and smell which were extremely unpalatable. Just over a century ago an Englishman, Newton, took out a patent (1835, No. 6787) for the concentration of milk by indirect heating with steam and acceleration of the evaporation by blowing a current of air through the liquid. By using 'gentle warmth' he was able to prevent some of the undesirable changes occurring during concentration and succeeded in producing a 'honey-like mass' which kept 'fairly well' in pots. It is interesting to note that he added sugar before concentrating. There is no record of the process ever being tried out on a commercial scale.

Seven years later came the first reports of the preparation of a dried milk.[1] It had been made by a Russian chemist, Dr Dichort, by evaporation at gentle heat. The fine powder was packed in cans and was found to dissolve in warm water, even after long storage, to form a 'reconstituted' milk. No further information about this product has been traced.

In 1847 Grimwade took out patent No. 11,703 for evaporated milk. He used steam-jacketed pans and assisted concentration by partial vacuum. The condensed milk was sent out in bottles closed with waxed caps. When the Government inquiry into the deterioration of preserved meats was held in 1852 one of the witnesses, Edward Moore of Ranton Abbey, told the Committee that he prepared annually 50,000 pint and half-pint tins of condensed milk. He stated that it was used by 'Government Arctic Expeditions'. It seems likely that it was milk evaporated by Newton's or Grimwade's method and canned by Golder's process. The manufacturers claimed that it kept well.[2]

In 1855 Grimwade took out a patent (No. 2430) for drying milk in powder form. After neutralizing the free acidity of the milk by the addition of sodium carbonate — in those days most of the milk was acid by the time it had been kept for a few hours — it was evaporated in vacuum pans until a dough-like mass was produced. This was taken out of the pans, mixed with sugar and pressed into thin ribbons between rollers. These were then dried and powered.

These pioneers were up against a great many difficulties, two of them particularly causing endless trouble. One was that the prolonged heating converted some of the milk constituents, namely protein and calcium salts, into insoluble forms. On reconstitution with water this material formed a sediment which the consumer usually disliked and sometimes suspected. The other difficulty was the liability of the final product to decompose on storage. We now know that this was due to the survival of heat-resistant

---

[1] *Lancet* (1842), i; (1843), i.
[2] *Report on Preserved Meats* (*Navy*), 1852.

micro-organisms — thermophilic bacteria as they are called — which sub-sequently developed and caused deterioration. The problems caused by these germs have been solved in recent times.

Considerable improvements on the technical side of milk condensing were the basis of the famous Borden patent, applied for in the United States in 1853 but not granted until 1856 (No. 15,553). This was the key patent to all the processes used in America for many years to come and to those used by the Anglo-Swiss Company, later Nestlé's, which began operations at a fac-tory at Cham on Lake Zug in Switzerland in 1866. The 'tin-boxes' used for packing the finished product were partially evacuated by an air-pump before being hermetically sealed.

Most of this condensed milk was sweetened by the addition of sugar before concentration, one of the advantages of this method being that the contents of the tin kept much better, because a high concentration of sugar inhibits bacterial growth. Any heat-resistant germs which survived the heating of the milk during manufacture would, therefore, be much less likely to develop in 'sweetened' condensed milk than in milk to which sugar had not been added. For more than twenty years unsweetened condensed milk was a source of trouble to the manufacturers. In time, however, it was realized that adequate sterilization of the contents of the tin by heat would render them stable, and the greatest of their worries was overcome. At this time a great deal of skimmed milk was condensed. Condensing provided a valu-able means of disposing of a product of the butter-factories which otherwise often went to waste.

The modern type of milk powders came into use soon after 1902, when Just in the United States and Hatmaker in England patented a process for rapidly drying a very thin film of milk on heated rotating drums. The film is spread on the drum at one point of the rotation and before a cycle is com-pleted a knife-edge scrapes the tissue-thin sheet of dried milk from the surface. This is powdered and packed. Later processes are based on the method of spraying partially concentrated milk into heated chambers. These products, owing to the shortened times of heating, are very nearly completely soluble in water, and are thus great improvements on the earlier types which often left a considerable insoluble sediment.

§ 6 BUTTER

We have already stated that much of the butter sold in the eighteenth century was rancid. It was little better in the first half of the nineteenth century. Hassall gives a revealing account of the quality of the butter sold in London and of the extensive practice of incorporating as much water as it would hold. Some of the cheaper blends of imported 'Hollands' butter known to the 'trade' as *Bosh* were found to contain as much as 33 per cent of water. He reprinted in his book a letter the *Lancet* had received from a 'Student', which revealed the methods by which inferior or rancid butter was 'reconstituted' and sold as best 'Epping butter'. The 'Student', who was lodging at the house of a 'butterman', woke up at three o'clock one morning and hearing the family astir he descended and found them making 'Epping butter'. Cheap Irish salted butter, probably badly rancid, was well washed with water. This removed salt, acid and the unpleasant odour. It was then washed with milk and a small quantity of sugar added. The butterman, who had the reputation of getting his 'Epping Butter' from one of the best dairies in the neighbourhood, admitted to a profit of at least 100 per cent. The practice was apparently common.

The cattle plague which raged from 1863 to 1867 caused a shortage of butter. In 1864 the price rose to 1s. or 1s. 2d. a pound and later it touched the very high figure of 2s. It is not surprising, therefore, that as one article remarked, 'Substitutes have been much spoken of'.[1]

§ 7 MARGARINE

In the late 'sixties a French food technologist, Mège-Mouries, was experimenting, at the request of the Victualling Department of the French Navy, with the object of making a cheap substitute for butter. He had observed that cow's milk contained fat even when the animals were so badly fed that they were losing weight. From this he reasoned that their body-fat was being transported either to the stomach or to the udder and there converted into milk-fat.

On this simple assumption he took beef-suet, chopped it into small pieces, suspended it in slightly alkaline water at blood heat and added ground-up sheep's stomach. This resulted in the fat being liberated from the suet by the partial digestion of the connective tissue in which it was held. The fat floated to the top after a few hours and Mège-Mouries was quite satisfied at first that he had actually made butter by a reproduction of the natural process. When, however, he separated and cooled the fat he found that it was too solid at ordinary temperatures. He therefore pressed it between warmed plates so that the more liquid fraction ran out and could be collected. This fraction melted at about the same temperature as butter.[2]

Actually he had done nothing more than separate the softer fats of the

---

[1] *Journal of the Society of Arts*, 1864, Vol. XII.   [2] Ibid., 1872, Vol. XX.

suet, a process which could have been done much more simply by gentle warmth and pressure. The artificial 'digestion' was really unnecessary. The oily fraction which escaped when the fat was pressed between hot plates was called *oleine*, while the solid which remained behind was termed *stearine* or *margarine*. The name margarine was at that time used by chemists for one of the natural components of animal fat.

Mège-Mouriès was disappointed with the flavour of his first preparations. They lacked the true flavour of butter. Suspecting that the udder played a part he carried out further experiments, in which the fat was digested with chopped cows' udder and a little warm milk. The product which he separated resembled butter more closely and he was satisfied.

Mège-Mouriès's process was patented in England in 1869. In 1870 he won the award offered by Napoleon III for an edible substitute for butter and a factory at Poissy was put at his disposal. Manufacture of oleomargarine or butterine as it came to be called was on the point of beginning when the Franco-Prussian War broke out. Immediately after the war, however, Pellerin, who had bought the patent rights, got the factory going, although another temporary setback was caused by the Paris Council of Hygiene's hesitation to permit it to be sold for human consumption. Their opposition was withdrawn in 1873 but it was ruled that the material must not be sold under the name of butter.

Meanwhile the proprietors of the big American stockyards had not been slow to recognize the importance of the discovery. They soon found that the minced stomach and udder were unnecessary and that a product resembling butter could be made by melting out the softer part of the caul-fat of oxen and shaking it while warm with milk. *The Times* was rather shocked at the success of one manufacturer, Mr Parof of New York.

> Margarine may have the consistence, but can never possess the flavour of butter which depends on small quantities of butyric, capric and caproic acids; very similar operations are being conducted in England, the raw material being the fat of horses obtained from the knackers. If this be the only obstacle, there is little doubt that the ingenious gentlemen who have manufactured jargonet-pear flavour from fusel oil will procure caproic acid to order. Judging from the recent 'butter controversy' among chymists, chymical tests for purity of butter have failed us, and there is now no obstacle to the success of Mr Parof in driving genuine butter out of the market.[1]

Stories soon began to circulate to the effect that all kinds of undesirable fats were being secretly converted into 'spurious butter'. *The Times* felt

[1] September 4th, 1873.

that it had to intervene when it heard on good authority that men were col-lecting refuse fat from the Thames mud to be made into 'mild Dorset'. They sent an investigator down the river. Four boatloads of men were found sal-vaging lumps of fatty refuse near the outfall of the North Metropolitan Sewer, but on further inquiry it was ascertained that this unsavoury material was destined to be made into cheap candles.[1]

In the same year over a million pounds of 'butterine' were imported into England from the United States. Holland was also producing 'butterine' and exporting it to us; there were more than fifty Dutch factories producing the substance by 1880. Production in England was very backward and on a small scale until the firm of Otto Monsted erected an up-to-date factory at Godley in Cheshire in 1889:[2]

Margarine had a hard fight to overcome the popular prejudices of the early years. It was bought by the poor people because it was cheap but for a long time it was unpopular on account of its texture and rather insipid flavour. In spite of this the sales rose steadily and considerable alarm was caused among the butter merchants. Fears that 'butterine' was being ex-tensively used for adulterating genuine butter were widespread and not without good cause, for the practice was by no means uncommon. This led to the passing of the Margarine Act of 1887 which clearly defined 'butter' and 'margarine' and made admixture illegal.

Soon after 1890 important modifications of the manufacturing process were introduced. It was found possible to blend beef-fat with certain veget-able oils, such as those expressed from ground-nuts (monkey-nuts) and palm kernels, so as to obtain a mixture which would have about the same melting point as butter. This made margarine even cheaper than it had been before. The quality was often very variable until the rise of the big manufacturing concerns in the early part of the twentieth century. They realized that if margarine was to become a serious competitor to butter it must be manu-factured under hygienic conditions and from materials of the very best quality. Enormous sums of money were spent in building up-to-date factories and in investigations on how to make the product more closely resemble butter. One of the most important advances was made when it was found that by thoroughly emulsifying the fat mixture with skimmed milk instead of merely agitating them together and then separating, much in the same way as in making butter, the final product had a better 'texture' and a more pronounced butter flavour. Another development was when Storch introduced the use of selected strains of 'starters', cultures of micro-organisms

---

[1] December 16th, 1876.
[2] Information kindly supplied by Mr C. F. Butler, Secretary of the Margarine Manufacturers' Association.

similar to those which are extensively used in 'ripening' cream before the separation of butter, and which produce the substances responsible for the distinctive and delicate smell of butter.

The manufacture of margarine from purely vegetable oil mixtures did not reach any considerable scale until after 1910, when it became possible by chemical treatment with hydrogen to 'harden' liquid oils. 'Hardened' oils then replaced beef 'oleo' at any rate in the preparation of the cheaper brands. 'Vitaminized' margarines were introduced in the 'twenties. They represent a very important advance, and are made by incorporating with the fat small quantities of concentrated preparations of vitamins A and D. The amount which it is necessary to add is so small that the flavour of the final product is unimpaired. Moreover, it can be done economically, so that the price is not significantly raised. This is a remarkable achievement of applied science and represents years of costly and patient research on the part of the firms concerned.

§ 8 MEAT AND FISH

There were many important changes in the character of the meat and fish supply during this century, particularly in the towns, although most of them were not noticeable until about 1850. When Engels wrote about the condition of the towns in 1844 it is obvious that the state of the meat markets in the poorer parts of the manufacturing centres was little better than in medieval times.[1] An occasional prosecution had little effect in checking the widespread sale of tainted meat and stinking fish. Matters began to improve when the public generally and the municipal authorities in particular learnt to appreciate the importance of hygienic precautions. Some of the revelations of the experts caused considerable alarm. For instance, Professor Gamgee reported to the Privy Council in 1863 that more than one-fifth of the meat sold in the markets came from diseased cattle.

Even this was not the worst feature because about this time it became known that disease and death could result from the eating of certain forms of diseased meat. Dr Thudichum described in a lecture before the Society of Arts how certain parasitic worms, *trichina* and *cysticerus*, could be passed on to people who had eaten infected pork and ham which had been insufficiently cooked. Such revelations led to a much more strict and skilled inspection of the meat markets by the municipal authorities.

An important development affecting the character of the meat supply, particularly in the poorer markets, was the introduction of cheap tinned meats and the importation of 'frozen' meat a few years later.

[1] *The Condition of the Working-Class in England in 1844*, F. Engels, 1892.

A serious attempt was made about 1867, probably as a result of the rise in the price of meat owing to the cattle epidemic, to introduce horse-flesh, or *chevaline* as its sponsors preferred to call it, to the British public. The project was launched as a result of the success of a similar scheme in Paris. The consumption of horseflesh had been officially advocated there at the time of the dearth of the late eighteenth century and, doubtless, was consumed in large quantities by the half-starved poor, but there does not seem to have been any attempt to organize a recognized trade until 1864. In that year a group of interested people made plans to open shops for the exclusive sale of horsemeat. They held a much-advertised *Banquet hippophagique* in 1865, at which most of the dishes were prepared from horseflesh, and a little later the first *Boucherie hippophagique* was opened. In 1867 a correspondent of the *Medical Times and Circular* reported that several such shops were doing a good trade and that some customers preferred the meat to beef. It is not surprising, therefore, that an attempt was made to launch a similar enterprise in England at a time when ordinary butcher's meat was very dear. In 1868 a certain Mr Bicknell gave a lecture before the Society of Arts and loudly praised the merits of *chevaline*.[1] In the same year an imposing, and also much publicized, dinner was held at the Langham Hotel, under the auspices of the 'Society for the Propagation of Horse Flesh as an Article of Food'.[2]

During the first part of the century the condition of the meat sold to the poor people was only equalled by that of the fish, even the pickled herrings offered for sale in the poorer districts being often partly decomposed owing to faulty preparation. The Society of Arts did what it could to improve the quality of this cheap and valuable food by offering premiums for preservation by the superior 'Dutch method'. After the turn of the century the state of affairs began steadily to improve. The introduction of steam transport made an enormous difference, particularly in the latter part of the century when steam trawlers began to replace the old sailing boats, and to bring home the harvest of new fishing grounds. The rich banks of the North Sea had scarcely been touched until the invention of the trawl enabled them to be swept. The catches were brought back to port packed in ice, most of which was brought to the English fishing ports by Norwegian or Icelandic ships, until the introduction of efficient ice-making machinery rendered this source of supply unnecessary.

The transport of fish in ice had been successfully carried out as early as 1820, by George Dempster, a London fishmonger.[3] In those days it was a very costly procedure and he employed it solely to bring to London the best

---

[1] *Journal of the Society of Arts*, 1868, Vol. XVI.
[2] *Foods*, Edward Smith, 3rd Edition, 1874.
[3] *The Family Oracle of Health*, Vol. I, 1824.

Scotch salmon, for which he could ask a high price. When ice became cheaper, and more particularly with the improvement in railroad communications, fresh sea fish began to appear in large quantities in the markets of inland towns. It is from this period (about 1850) that we can date the decline in popularity of salted and pickled herrings, for so many centuries one of the chief foods of the inland population.

The end of the century saw two other important developments, the introduction of the relatively fast 'deep-sea' trawler, capable of making a voyage to Iceland or the White Sea, and considerable improvements in the design and operation of trawls, which enabled fishing to be carried out at much greater depths than formerly.

An unimportant but interesting change which occurred about 1850 was that oysters quite suddenly became scarce and expensive. They had for centuries been so cheap that they were within the reach of all but the very poorest. At the beginning of the nineteenth century they were even associated with poverty, for as Sam Weller put it:

> ... poverty and oysters always seem to go together ... the poorer a place is, the greater call there seems to be for oysters ... here's a oyster stall to every half-dozen houses [in Whitechapel]. The street's lined vith 'em. Blessed if I don't think that ven a man's wery poor, he rushes out of his lodgings, and eats oysters in reg'lar desperation.[1]

As late as 1840 they cost only 4d. a dozen but within a very few years they were so dear as to be a luxury only the wealthy could afford. There is little doubt that the cause of this rise in price was reckless dredging of the natural beds as a result of increasing demand from the rapidly expanding towns. Had it not been that something was known by this time of the breeding habits of oysters, and of methods of cultivating them artificially, the mollusc might have become almost extinct in English waters. One of the first projects for preparing artificial beds was put forward in 1865 by the South of England Oyster Company, which proposed to operate off Hayling Island. The plans were based on those which had been successfully employed by the French at Arcachon since 1830.

§9 WATER SUPPLY

Passing reference must be made to the vast improvement which took place in the nineteenth century in the character of the town water supplies. Sanitation was extremely primitive during the first half of the century, few

[1] *The Pickwick Papers*, Charles Dickens, 1837.

houses being equipped with anything but a cesspool. The problem of the disposal of sewage became acute with a rapid growth of the towns at the end of the eighteenth century. Various suggestions were put forward for dealing with it, the most widely adopted being the 'privy-bucket' system, which entailed frequent emptying and removal of the contents, a troublesome and rather expensive process. Water-closets were still uncommon when Queen Victoria was crowned. By the middle of the century London had nearly 250,000 cesspools, Birmingham was spending over £5,000 a year in emptying 'privy-pails', and in Manchester not one house in twenty had a water-closet.

The value as manure of the contents of the privies was constantly being stressed by the scientists — it was stated that the amount available in Birmingham in one year was worth £100,000 to the farmers — but the difficulty was to find an economical method of transporting it to the country. It was all very well to say that the 'chamber-pot is a penny savings bank' but when it came to collecting the contents by house-to-house visits and transporting them in carboys to distant farms the cost was found to be prohibitive. Sir William Worsley's proposal, put forward in 1857, to construct a gigantic cesspool at Greenwich Marshes to hold the contents of the London privies until the turn of the tide carried them down the river, serves to remind us that there were still experts who saw no objection, apart from the nuisance of the smell, to the contamination of river water with sewage. As it was, the river received a great deal of sewage before it reached Westminster and in hot weather the smell was sometimes so bad as to make it questionable whether Parliament could continue to sit.[1] Many of the intakes of water for drinking purposes higher up the river were not far removed from the local sewer outfalls.

In 1837 the scientist and engineer, Chadwick, pressed for the appointment of a sanitary commission. He and the Unitarian minister-cum-medical man, Southwood Smith, had for some time previously been gravely concerned at the obvious effects of bad sanitation on the health of the people in the larger towns. The Commission was appointed in 1839 and their work led to the publication in 1842 of the Parliamentary Report on the Sanitary Condition of the Labouring Population of Great Britain. This, in turn, gave birth six years later to the 'General Board of Health', the forerunner of the present Ministry of Health.

Just over a hundred years ago, in 1845, Playfair reported on the sanitary condition of Buckingham Palace in such strong terms that the Government did not dare to publish his findings. He reported that a great main sewer ran through the courtyard, the connections with the Palace itself being

---

[1] *Memoirs of an Ex-Minister*, The Earl of Malmesbury, 1884 (Diary for June 23rd, 1858).

untrapped. A room in the basement painted freshly with white lead paint was blackened by the next morning owing to putrefactive gases. The kitchens were fitted with charcoal fires with no flues, the fumes going straight up to the Royal nurseries.[1]

At about the same time investigations during one of the terrible outbreaks of cholera experienced by Victorian England gave the clue that the disease might be contracted from contaminated drinking water. This had the effect of focusing attention on the question of the purity of the water supply. Chemical analysis revealed that putrescible organic matter, or more frequently products arising from the decay of animal and vegetable debris (e.g. ammonia), can find their way into well-water by percolation through the soil. Sir Edward Frankland, whose name is honoured as a pioneer in this field, laid the foundations of modern methods of water analysis. In 1859 he and Hoffmann reported on methods for deodorizing the raw sewage which went into the Thames and caused the river to be 'black and stinking'. In 1865 he was asked to make the monthly analyses of Metropolitan drinking water, previously made by Hoffmann. He was also responsible for most of the investigations carried out by the Rivers Pollution Commission, which published six valuable reports between 1868 and 1874.

By this date, however, an even graver menace than the contamination of water by the products of animal and vegetable decay — 'the soakings of graveyards' as Letheby had called them[2] — had appeared. People were beginning to think in terms of the microscopic bodies discovered by Pasteur which appeared to be responsible for so many infective diseases. The cholera epidemic of 1847-49 had drawn attention to water as a source of the infection; when the epidemic flared up again in 1853 and 1865 some people suspected that the *animacules* carried by contaminated water were responsible. It was about this time that 'charcoal-filters' for purifying the domestic water supply became popular.

The second half of the century saw a great improvement in the sanitary conditions of the towns. For this we have to thank not only the pioneers, Southwood Smith, Chadwick and Frankland, but a very remarkable man, Sir John Simon, who was appointed Medical Officer for London in 1848. This was the second appointment of its kind in the country, Liverpool being the first city to take such a progressive step. Simon was largely responsible for abolishing cesspool drainage and the unhygienic 'privy-bucket' system and for substituting enclosed sewers. Partly as a result of his efforts the annual death rate in London fell from about 26 per thousand in the year of his appointment to less than 21 per thousand when the century closed.

[1] *Memoirs and Correspondence of Lord Playfair*, Wemyss Reid, 1899.
[2] *Report on the Sanitary State of the City of London*, W. Letheby, 1861.

(The science of vital statistics really began with William Heberden's studies, published in 1801,[1] but there was little accurate material to handle until after the passing of the Births and Deaths Registration Act in 1838.)

No small proportion of the improvement in health was due to a safer water supply. It is not often appreciated that before 1850 a large proportion of the inhabitants of towns drew their drinking water from wells, many of which were liable to surface drainage contamination. Comparatively few houses had their own domestic supply and even those that had were sometimes limited to a few hours' supply a day. In London there existed many water companies, some providing a supply which might from the nature of its source be regarded as reasonably pure, others supplying their customers with water which could scarcely have escaped contamination with sewage. Writing of the 'Refreshments at the Great Exhibition of 1851', *Punch* said:

> The contractor is bound to supply, gratis, pure water in glasses to all visitors demanding it; but the Committee must have forgotten, that whoever can produce in London a glass of water fit to drink, will contribute the rarest and most universally useful article in the whole Exhibition.[2]

Soon after this date, however, a marked improvement was seen both in respect to the increased distribution of water and to its purity. The efficient scientific control of London's water supply dates from 1902, when the Metropolitan Water Board bought up all the old water supply companies.

---

[1] *Observations on the Increase and Decrease of Different Diseases and Particularly of the Plague,* W. Heberden, 1801.
[2] *Punch,* 1851, Vol. XX.

CHAPTER XVIII

PRESERVATION OF FOOD

§1 EARLY METHODS

MANY factors influenced and stimulated the search for new and more effective methods not only for the prevention of decay but for the preservation, to as great an extent as possible, of the natural freshness of foods. In the first place sea transport was expanding in every direction, making it desirable that a better diet than salt pork and sea biscuit should be available on long voyages. Then again, the rapid growth of the town populations and the demand for cheap food turned people's attention to the possibility of importing perishable food, such as meat, from abroad. They looked in the first instance to Australia and America, where by the middle of the century such vast herds of sheep and cattle were being reared that local values had dropped to a few shillings.

The art of preserving perishable foods was little more advanced than it had been two or three hundred years earlier. This is clearly shown by Sir John Sinclair's review of the subject in 1807. He summarized eight methods for keeping food fresh: by drying in the sun, the use of artificial heat, pickling, salting, covering with melted butter, the addition of sugar, by keeping it cold with ice, and finally by the use of charcoal.[1] All these methods are obvious enough except the last, and this becomes intelligible when it is remembered that charcoal absorbs many bad odours and that the removal of the smell of putrescence was at that time thought to be equivalent to preservation.

When the century opened it was universally believed that contact with air caused putrefaction. This centuries-old belief had only been slightly modified by Gay Lussac's theory that it was the oxygen in the air that was the harmful agent. The basic idea behind every suggeston for the preservation of food was, therefore, the exclusion of air.

The oldest form of preservation, drying, which it was believed expelled the air from the interior of the food, was still the subject of considerable research. Dr Hassall, of *Lancet* fame, took out a patent for manufacturing a dried preparation called 'meat flour'. It is not known whether it was ever made on a commercial scale, but when the representative of an Australian company brought a similar preparation (made by drying beef on steam-

[1] *The Code of Health and Longevity*, Sir John Sinclair, 1807.

heated, tinned-iron plates) to the attention of the Food Committee of the Society of Arts in 1868 there was a sharp reminder from Hassall's solicitor that to import such material into England would be an infringement of his client's patent.[1] Edward Smith speaks of large quantities of dried beef being imported from Germany. It was known as 'Hamburg beef' and was sold very cheaply in the towns.[2] None of these types of dried meat, however, gained the approval of the Food Committee of the Society of Arts, nor does it appear that such material ever became popular.

Another age-old process, that of salting, was employed extensively in an effort to bring the produce of the ranches of Australia and America to the English market. Before canning was established on a large scale in the U.S.A., Cincinnati and Chicago, then engaged in a cut-throat struggle for supremacy as the meat market of the New World, exported large quantities of salted beef and pickled pork to England. Australia also sent a certain amount. They were inferior, coarse-textured products, which were sold only in the poorer parts of the towns, for about 4d.-5d. a pound. This cheap meat was, however, particularly acceptable in the years 1865-67, when the ravages of the cattle plague caused a sharp rise in the price of home-produced meat and cheese.

In 1807 Plowden took out a patent (No. 3051) for preserving 'meat and other comestible substances' by encrusting them with a special medium made from thick gravy. Here, once again, is the idea of excluding air. Ten years later Granholm patented the use of hot fat or 'a strong hot animal jelly' for the same purpose (Patent No. 4150, 1817). There is no record of either of these preparations being manufactured on a commercial scale but Professor Redwood's scheme for coating fresh meat with melted paraffin wax proved a failure.[3]

§ 2 DRIED VEGETABLES

The first patent for drying vegetables was taken out by Graefer in 1780 (No. 1275). He immersed green vegetables in boiling salt water for one minute and then hung them on lines in a heated room to dry. Of greater importance was the process patented by Edwards in 1840 (No. 8597), which was operated commercially for many years to produce dried vegetables, mainly potatoes. The latter were boiled until the skins cracked when they were put into perforated cylinders and pressed through small holes. The

[1] *Journal of the Society of Arts*, 1868, Vol. XVI.
[2] *Foods*, Edward Smith, 3rd Edition, 1874.
[3] *Journal of the Society of Arts*, 1866, Vol. XIV; *Foods*, E. Smith, 3rd Edition, 1874.

fine threads of pulp were then dried on steam-heated tables. They were used to some extent for provisioning ships and supplies were sent out to the Crimea, but their flavour and rather dark colour made them unpopular.

More popular were the vegetables dried by the French process of Etienne Masson (Patent No. 13,338, 1850). In this method they were dehydrated on wicker trays by a current of warm air (75°-145° F.), the removal of the water being accelerated by the use either of dehydrating chemicals such as lime or calcium chloride or by a partial vacuum. The dried vegetables were finally compressed into hard cakes, usually provided with a groove so that they could conveniently be broken into portions, wrapped in tinfoil and packed in air-tight tins. Devaux operated this patent in England and sold his products mainly for ships' stores.

A great improvement in the quality of dried vegetables was made when Buchanan introduced a method by which the moisture was removed at low temperature. The products were much more palatable than those which had been more drastically treated. In 1871 a recommendation was made to the Board of Trade that 'preserved vegetables' should be substituted for 'compressed vegetables' in the list of stores to be carried by merchant ships under the Act of 1867.[1]

§ 3 DRIED SOUPS

Captain Cook took cases of 'portable soup' with him on his voyage round the world in 1772. Mixed with pease flour he found it a valuable food for sick sailors. Sir John Pringle described its manufacture.

> ... having by long boiling evaporated the most putrescent parts of the meat [it] is reduced to the consistence of a glue, which in effect it is, and will like other glues, in a dry place, keep sound for years together.[2]

For a good many years it formed part of the stores of H.M. ships.

Part of a cake of this 'portable soup' obtained from the Royal United Services Institution Museum and believed to be of those taken by Cook in 1772, was examined in 1938. It was a flat cake, 110 by 70 mm., greyish-white in colour and stamped with a broad arrow. In appearance it was, as Pringle said, just like a slab of glue. Analysis showed that it did not appear to have undergone any marked change in over 160 years.[3] It was probably made by evaporating a clarified broth to dryness.

---

[1] *Journal of the Society of Arts,* 1871, Vol. XIX.
[2] *A Discourse upon some late Improvements of the Means of Preserving the Health of Mariners,* Sir John Pringle, 1776.
[3] J. C. Drummond and T. Macara, *Chemistry and Industry* (1938), LVII, 828.

'Portable soup' was gradually dropped from the list of ships' stores when tinned meats came into favour about 1820. A patent for producing other types of dried foods, including soup, was taken out in 1847 by Davidson and Symington (No. 11,947) and 'Symington's Desiccated Soups' acquired a considerable reputation in the latter part of the nineteenth century.

§ 4 PRESERVED MEAT

Several attempts were made to impregnate fresh meat with sulphites, either by exposing it to the vapour of burning sulphur or by soaking it in solutions of calcium or zinc sulphite. One curious proposal came from a Dr Estor. He devised a pastille which on being ignited gave off first sulphur dioxide gas and then chlorine. These pastilles were burnt in the room containing the meat, the room remaining unopened until the food was required.[1]

The Society of Arts investigated a number of such proposals but judged none of them to be entirely satisfactory. Actually one such process was used commercially for a number of years in Australia. In 1871 the Victoria Meat Preserving Company was sending over beef and mutton which had been soaked in calcium sulphite and then packed in casks filled with melted butter. It was not popular with the working classes but was used a good deal for charity meals and soup kitchens.[2]

Another patent (No. 7036, 1836) illustrates the primitive devices to which these early pioneers resorted in order to try to overcome the tendency of meat to putrefy. It proposed that fresh meat should be placed in cans with a solution of salt and nitre and the air replaced by carbon dioxide. Before the tin was closed a bag of iron filings was to be placed inside to absorb the oxygen and a small piece of calcined charcoal to absorb any offensive smell which might develop. Many other projects were advanced for replacing the air in tins by inert gases such as carbon dioxide and nitrogen.

Another suggestion which attracted attention was that of Professor Gamgee, a distinguished physiologist, who believed that meat would keep fresh if air were expelled from the tissues before death by killing the animals with carbon dioxide. Although the Society of Arts' Journals for the years 1860-70 contain many references to this theory it does not appear to have led to any practical scheme. This is hardly surprising, as it would certainly have failed.

More successful was the proposal made by Morgan in 1864. He opened the animals immediately after death and infused directly into one of the

[1] *Journal of the Society of Arts*, 1868, Vol. XVI. [2] Ibid. 1871, Vol. XIX.

major veins a preservative fluid containing salt, sugar, nitre (this was afterwards replaced by phosphoric acid), and a small amount of spice. The idea was not a new one for a patent (No. 6711) was granted in 1834 to a certain D. R. Long by which an 'antiputrescent solution' containing salt, saltpetre, spices and vinegar was injected into the veins by a force-pump. Morgan's system, as it came to be called, was tried out at Paysandu in Uruguay with some success. In 1865 nearly half a million pounds of beef and mutton were prepared in this manner and exported from Montevideo to Liverpool. When freshly prepared it was quite edible but rather coarse. It sold for about 4d. a pound. It was not popular, however, for it tended to turn 'rusty' or rancid on keeping.

A brief reference must be made to a proposal put forward by Admiral Belcher for preserving meat in sugar or treacle. He persuaded the Admiralty to have a large quantity prep___d for his Arctic expedition in 1852, and stated on his return that it had remained in excellent condition. For a number of years this irrepressible and rather tiresome old man continued to press the claims of his method, which he held to be superior to all others, but no one paid very much attention to him.

§ 5 CANNING

One of the great achievements of the century in respect to food was the succesful development of canning. The pioneer was a Frenchman, Nicholas Appert, who, as the eighteenth century drew to its troubled close, worked out a method for preserving foods in glass bottles by subjecting them to heat. The four stages of his process were set out by him as follows:

1ᵉ. A renfermer dans les bouteilles ou bocaux les substances que l'on veut conserver;
2ᵉ. A boucher ces différents vases avec la plus grande attention; car, c'est principalement de l'opération du bouchage que dépend le succès;
3ᵉ. A soumettre ces substances ainsi renfermées, à l'action de l'eau bouillante d'un bain-marie, pendant plus ou moins de temps, selon leur nature et de la manière que je l'indiquerai pour chaque espèce ... de comestible;
4ᵉ. A retirer les bouteilles du bain-marie au temps prescrit.

It is interesting to note that although his stout glass bottles were filled and closed before they were heated he adhered to the view that contact with the air was the cause of putrefaction. Appert bottled all types of food, meat, fruit, vegetables and even milk. They were sampled by the French Navy in 1806 and proved so good that he was awarded a prize of 12,000 francs. In

1810 he published his famous book *Le Livre de tous les Ménages ou l'Art de Conserver pendant Plusieurs Années Toutes les Substances Animales et Végétales*.

In 1807 a somewhat similar process was used by an Englishman, Thomas Saddington, for preserving fruit. The fruit was put into wide-mouthed jars with loosely fitting stoppers. The bottles were then stood in a bath and heated to 160°-170° F. for about an hour, after which they were filled to the brim with hot water and tightly closed. Saddington was awarded a prize of five guineas for his invention by the Society of Arts.[1]

Bryan Donkin, a partner in the firm of John Hall, founder in 1785 of the Dartford Iron Works, realized that Appert's discovery would be very valuable to his firm if tinned iron containers could be used instead of glass jars. Experiments were made, of which many were failures, but about 1812 the project looked so promising that a factory for the preparation of canned foods was established at Blue Anchor Road, Bermondsey. Whether or not Donkin and his associates acquired the existing patent rights of de Heine (No. 3310, 1810) or of Durand (No. 3372, 1810) covering the use of iron or metal containers for preserving foods is not known. Samples of the new products were sent to the authorities of the Army and Navy. A brochure issued by the firm of Donkin and Hall in 1817 quotes flattering testimonials received in 1813 and 1814 from such people as Lord Wellesley, Admiral Cochrane and Sir Joseph Banks.[2]

The Navy took supplies of the 'preserved provisions' to form part of the medical stores for issue to sick men, the idea apparently being that as the contents of the tins looked fresh their antiscorbutic virtues would be unimpaired. Ross took some of the canisters with him to the Far North in 1814 and found that the foods were liked by his men. The Russian explorer, von Kotzebue, also found them excellent when he took them on his expedition to find the North West Passage in 1815. The contents of all the canisters were found to be in good condition when he opened them, whereas the preserved food — presumably dried — which the Economic Society of St Petersburg had advised him to take went bad. Subsequent Arctic expeditions came to rely more and more on Donkin, Hall and Gamble's tinned foods.

In 1818 the Admiralty purchases over a period of nine months amounted to 46,000 lb. packed in 23,779 canisters. There was a wide variety of contents including corned beef, boiled beef, carrots, boiled mutton, mutton and vegetables, veal and soup. They gained an excellent reputation but it seems clear from contemporary records that they were seldom eaten except at sea. They were, of course, more expensive than fresh food. Two of the tins

---

[1] *Transactions of the Society of Arts*, 1807, Vol. XXVI.
[2] *Official Reports and Letters relative to Donkin, Hall and Gamble's Preserved Provisions*, 1817.

were opened in 1938 and the contents, in one roast veal and in the other carrots, were found to be in perfect condition except that rather a large quantity of tin had become dissolved through long contact with the acid juices.[1]

Here is Captain Basil Hall's explanation of the popularity among sailors of tinned meats and other tinned provisions.

> It is really astonishing how good the preserved milk is ... you must, on examining the prices, bear in mind that meat thus preserved *eats* nothing, nor *drinks* — it is not apt to die — does not tumble overboard or get its legs broken or its flesh worn off its bones by tumbling about the ship in bad weather — it takes no care in the keeping — it is always ready, may be eaten hot or cold, and this enables you to toss into a boat as many days provisions as you require — it is not exposed to the vicissitudes of markets nor is it scourged up to a monstrous price as at St Helena, because there is no alternative. Besides these advantages it enables one to indulge in a number of luxuries which no care or *expense* could procure.[2]

In 1831 Admiralty Regulations ordered that all H.M. ships should carry preserved provisions as part of their store of 'medical comforts'.

By this date the original manufacturers were meeting competition. Morrisons were followed by Cooper, Cooper by Hogarth, and in 1841 a certain Stephen Goldner took out a patent (No. 873). Gamble and most of those who followed him preserved their foods by placing them in tinned wrought-iron canisters containing 2 to 6 lb., after which the lid was soldered on, leaving a small vent-hole open. The tins were all but immersed in a bath of hot water and heated, with the object of expelling the air. When this was judged to have been done the small vent-hole was closed by a dab of solder. Goldner improved on this method by using a 'chemical bath', consisting of a solution of calcium chloride, by which temperatures considerably higher than that of boiling water could be obtained. This, he thought, would more effectively expel the air and ensure better keeping qualities, although complaints of preserved food deteriorating on storage were few and far between. Gamble actually employed a 'stability test', very similar to that used by canning firms today, which soon reveals if the contents of the tin are not sterile.

> ... the cases thus hermetically sealed are exposed in a *test-chamber*, for at least a month, to a temperature above what they are ever likely

[1] 'The Examination of some Tinned Foods of Historic Interest', J. C. Drummond, W. R. Lewis, T. Macara, G. S. Wilson and H. L. Shipp, *Chemistry and Industry* (1938), LVII, 808, 827, 828, 834 and 914.

[2] *Encyclopaedia Britannica*, 7th Edition, 1841, Article on Food.

to encounter, from 90 to 110° F. If the process has failed, putrefaction takes place and gas is evolved, which in the course of time will bulge out both the ends of the case, so as to render them convex instead of concave. But the contents of whatever cases stand this test will infallibly keep perfectly sweet and good in any climate for any length of time.[1]

By 1845 Goldner was contracting on a large scale for the Admiralty and when in 1847 it was decided that as these meats were proving so valuable a food for men at sea preserved beef should be made part of the ordinary ration, he was well on the road to becoming a very wealthy man. But the storm clouds were gathering. There had been a few complaints from victualling yards that preserved meats, particularly those manufactured by Goldner, were not keeping properly. The number of these complaints began to increase very rapidly and the state of affairs soon became serious. Goldner had a factory at Galatz in Moldavia and it was suspected that he was allowing putrid meat to be canned there. The most damaging rumours began to circulate: tins had been found to contain sheeps' intestines; Franklin's expedition to the Pole would have survived had it not been that the tins he took were filled with putrid meat, and so on. In 1850 no less than 111,108 lb. of Goldner's meat had been condemned at one yard alone.

In desperation Goldner's partner, Samuel Ritchie, wrote to the Commissioners of the Admiralty.

Sir,

Understanding that the Lords Commissioners of the Admiralty have applied to other houses for the terms upon which they will supply the preserved provisions required for the use of the expedition proceeding to the Arctic Regions I take the liberty of once more entreating their Lordships to be allowed to compete with them for the supply of the whole or a portion of the order — that an opportunity may be afforded me of wiping off the disgrace under which I at present labour, the result of a combination of the most unfortunate circumstances against me — I have had the honour of supplying the Navy for the last 10 years and not until the last few months have any material complaints been urged against my goods. This, I confidently hope will be a sufficient excuse for thus imploring one more trial before I am entirely cut off.

The greatest possible care shall be taken in the preparation of the articles and my factory shall be open at all times for the inspection of any persons their Lordships may appoint during the progress of the work.

p. pro S. Goldner.
Samuel Ritchie.

[1] *Encyclopaedia Britannica*, 7th Edition, 1841, Article on Food.

This letter, now in the Record Office, bears in the handwriting of the Commissioner the one word 'Decline'.

The scandal finally grew to such dimensions that a Select Committee was appointed to hold an inquiry. They listened to a great deal of evidence and did, in fact, succeed in tracking down the chief cause of the trouble. Originally, preserved foods had been prepared in canisters of 2 to 6 lb. capacity. As the scale of the contracts grew there was a natural tendency to make larger 'packs'. The Committee ascertained that it was the contents of the larger canisters, those holding 9 to 14 lb., which most frequently went bad. One of their recommendations was that in future the largest size should be 6 lb. Another was that the Admiralty should establish their own canning factory. This was done, in 1856, at Deptford.

It is easy from our modern knowledge of the conditions necessary for sterilization to explain why Goldner's meat went bad. The large canisters were insufficiently heated for bacteria in the centre of the pack to be killed. These developed on storage and caused the meat to putrefy.

At this very time Pasteur was engaged on the experiments which revealed the part played by micro-organisms not only in disease but in fermentation and putrefaction. In a few years the news of his discoveries reached England and made a profound impression in scientific circles. One of the first references to these experiments and to their significance in problems of food preservation was made by Calvert in 1864, in the course of his Cantor Lectures before the Society of Arts.[1] He compromised between the old and the new ideas in his description of the methods of preservation as being dependent for success on the 'exclusion of air *and* cryptogamic sporules'. There was actually a good deal of discussion whether the germs were primarily responsible for the deterioration or whether they would only grow if air were present. Even after most people had accepted Pasteur's view that the micro-organisms must be killed by heat, at least one manufacturer of tinned foods continued not only to heat his canisters in a hot bath but also to extract as much air as possible by means of a vacuum pump.

The revelations of the Government inquiry in 1852 did a great deal of harm to an industry which was just getting into its stride and for some years the public regarded tinned meat with suspicion. By the 'sixties the position had changed. The scare had almost died down when the rise in the price of fresh meat caused by the cattle epidemic of 1863-67 stimulated the demand for cheap substitutes. A canning factory had been opened in Australia in 1847 by Henry Dangar and his brother William but they exported little of their produce to England until about 1866. Other factories were then opened and at once proved successful. They exported chiefly 'boiled mutton', which

[1] *Journal of the Society of Arts*, 1864, Vol. XII.

was in great demand in the Midlands, although not very popular in the rest of England. Later, tinned beef as well as mutton was sent over from Australia and found a ready sale in the cheaper markets at prices ranging from 5d. to 7d. a pound, or about half the price of butchers' meat. How rapidly the trade developed can be judged from the mere 16,000 lb. imported in 1866, compared with the impressive figure of 22 million lb., which was the amount brought over five years later. America did not start exporting her tinned meat to England until the early 'seventies.

Generally speaking tinned meats were rather unpopular although they were so cheap. The well-meaning people who would have liked to have seen the poor making greater use of them complained that 'the dislike of the working-classes of England to Australian and other tinned meats was more truly referrible [sic] to ignorance than to prejudice'.[1] This comment was hardly fair because it is certain that a large proportion of the material which came on to the market was unappetizing, coarse-grained and fatty. The public did not like it for they still had vivid memories of the 1852 inquiry. From this time dates the unfortunate belief that canned foods are peculiarly liable to cause food poisoning, a belief which is wholly unjustified today.

A correspondent has very kindly given us her own recollections of Australian tinned meat in 1874.

It was in *big*, thick, clumsy red tins and was very cheap . . . I have a vivid recollection of the unappetizing look of the contents — a large lump of coarse-grained lean meat inclined to separate into coarse fibres, a large lump of unpleasant looking fat on one side of it — and an irregular hollow partly filled with watery fluid.

What the general public thought of canned meats in the 'sixties can be judged from the name given by the Navy to the products produced by the newly established canning factory at the Victualling Yard at Deptford. They called this meat 'Sweet Fanny Adams', an expression which will be familiar to many who served in the First World War but who may be unaware of its origin. The name has been immortalized as a result of a notorious murder which took place in 1867, when a woman named Fanny Adams was killed at Alton in Hampshire, her body afterwards being hacked into small pieces. Her murderer, Frederick Baker, was hanged in Winchester Gaol on Christmas Eve of that year. The morbid humour of the sailors at Portsmouth soon traced a connection between this murder and the canned meat being turned out at the factory at Deptford.[2] It is one of the few cases where the victim rather than the murderer has achieved immortality.

---

[1] *Journal of the Society of Arts*, 1872, Vol. XX.
[2] *The Mariner's Mirror*, 1937, Vol. XXIII, No. 4.

§ 6 REFRIGERATED MEAT

The imports of Australian and American salted and tinned meat fell off rapidly towards the end of the century as a result of the development of refrigeration, although America began exporting tinned vegetables, mainly tomatoes, to England about 1880, and tinned fruits soon afterwards.

The difference in price between fresh meat in Australia or America and in England was a big stimulus to the efforts to find a way of transporting supplies without having recourse to canning which, as we have shown, did not produce a good quality of material. Many proposals were put forward for shipping live cattle but the difficulties were almost insurmountable until the length of the voyage had been reduced by improvements in ship design, and it was not until the early 'seventies that they were brought from America in appreciable numbers.

It was natural that attention should be turned to the possibility of shipping meat in a frozen or chilled condition. For a long time the chief obstacle in the way of this method was the excessive cost of ice. An enterprising American is said to have found it worth while to take cargoes of ice from Boston to the Cape in order to bring back grapes in a fresh condition.[1] About this date (1865) experiments were being made in America with a view to keeping perishable goods fresh with ice during railroad transport. Primitive refrigeration-vans were actually in use in 1868.

No serious development along these lines could, however, take place until some means of providing reasonably cheap ice was available. The first step towards solving this problem dates from 1850 when James Harrison, a Scottish emigrant to Australia, designed the first practical if not very efficient ice-making machine. It was based on the invention of Jacob Perkins in 1834 (Pat. No. 6662) and produced a fall in temperature by the evaporation of ether, the liquid ether being then regenerated by compression in another part of the apparatus. While working to increase the efficiency of this type of machine Harrison was outstripped in 1860 by the French engineer, Carré, who discovered that compressed ammonia gas was a cheaper and more effective refrigerant. In the following year a plant working along these lines and capable of turning out 8000 pounds of ice a day was erected at Darling Harbour, Sydney.

Both Harrison and Carré were a long way from solving the problem of how to transport meat in perfect condition over the 13,000 miles which separate England and Australia. They still had to find how best to pack the meat, whether as whole carcasses or in joints; whether the meat should be packed in ice or stored in cooled vessels or chambers, and whether it

[1] *Journal of the Society of Arts*, 1865, Vol. XIV.

X

would be possible to install a refrigeration plant on board. In 1872 Harrison thought success was in sight. He exhibited an 'ice-house' at the Melbourne Exhibition in which he kept sides of beef and carcasses of sheep in good condition for several months. Some of the meat was eaten at a public luncheon held in Melbourne in 1873 and was stated to be in excellent condition. This luncheon was a prelude to the voyage to England of S.S. *Norfolk*, carrying twenty tons of mutton and beef, frozen and packed in tanks kept cold with ice and salt. There was great excitement over this venture, and considerable publicity was given to the arrival of the ship in the Thames in October. Unfortunately it proved a sad fiasco. During the voyage through the tropics the ice had melted and the meat gone bad. Long before the English Channel was reached most of it had been thrown overboard and the little that survived the three months' voyage was uneatable.

Harrison was completely crushed by his failure. He retired to England and made no further efforts to complete the task on which he had spent more than a quarter of a century of hard and persevering endeavour. But there were others to carry on the work. The Darling Harbour ice-making venture had been largely the result of the enterprise of a Lancashire business man, Thomas Mort, who came to Australia from Bolton in 1838. He enlisted the help of an able engineer called Nicolle and together they planned to place meat in chambers cooled not by direct contact with ice but by pipes circulating cold brine. At a meeting held in the Sydney Exchange on February 4th, 1868, 300 gentlemen heard Mr Mort speak of his plans to ship meat to England in this manner.[1] Optimistically, he announced 'if you are ready with the meat, we are ready with the freezing apparatus'. There does not seem to have been any response to this challenge, which was probably just as well for Mr Mort, for even nine years later, after further expenditure of effort and money, the venture failed. It was in 1876 that Mort and Nicolle, again confident of success, chartered the S.S. *Northam* and fitted her with a brine pipe-cooled chamber to carry frozen meat. Just as she was on the point of sailing it was found that the pipe system was faulty and the cargo of meat had to be withdrawn.

There had apparently been more successful attempts because there is a record that the Meat Sub-Committee of the Food Committee of the Society of Arts, answering an objection brought forward by Professor Gamgee against the principle of refrigeration, reported that:

> No opinion, however, can override facts, and these we have before us, already fully confirmed by the safe arrival of three cargoes of meat.[2]

[1] *Journal of the Society of Arts*, 1869, Vol. XVII.　　　[2] Ibid., 1872, Vol. XX.

We have been unable to trace any further information about these cargoes but it seems probable that they came from the United States.

By this date experiments on refrigeration were being conducted in several countries, notably in the Argentine at the centre of the cattle trade on the River Plate. There a French engineer named Charles Tellier did a great deal to overcome the practical difficulties of the existing methods. After several unsuccessful attempts, the S.S. *Frigorifique*, fitted with one of his machines, sailed from Buenos Aires with a cargo of frozen meat. The voyage to Rouen took over three months and some of the meat was found on arrival to be stained or unappetizing in appearance. Other pieces, however, were in quite good condition. The *Frigorifique* was followed in 1877 by the S.S. *Paraguay*. She too brought a cargo of meat from the Argentine to France but it arrived in far better condition than that of the *Frigorifique*.

On February 2nd, 1880, the S.S. *Strathleven* arrived at London with a cargo of 40 tons of Australian beef and mutton in her refrigerating chambers, and practically all of it in excellent condition. It was sold at Smithfield at prices averaging 5½d. a lb.; in Melbourne the fresh meat had been sold for as little as 1½d. to 2d. a lb.[1] The problem had been solved after thirty years of heart-breaking effort and a vast expenditure of money. At times people must have felt that Edward Smith was unduly optimistic when he wrote:

> We need not despair of seeing the time when the whole carcass of an animal will be imported in a state fit to be cut up in our shops for immediate sale.[2]

§ 7 CHEMICAL PRESERVATION

Apart from salt, nitre and vinegar, which had been in use for centuries and which Pavy described as 'chemical agents', in his treatment of the subject of food preservation in 1875, chemical preservatives were unknown until quite late in the century. They were a natural consequence of the increasing interest in Pasteur's germ theories of disease and putrefaction. Just as the idea of antisepsis dominated surgery before that of asepsis, so the idea of preventing germs growing in foods by adding chemicals guided food preservation until it became recognized that it was far better to exclude organisms or kill them by heat. Lister operated on his patients in a mist of carbolic acid spray; when people began to appreciate that food went bad,

[1] For a great deal of the information contained in this section we are indebted to J. T. Critchell and J. Raymond's authoritative book *The History of the Frozen Meat Trade*, 1912.
[2] *Foods*, E. Smith, 3rd Edition, 1874.

not because it came into contact with air but because it was contaminated with bacteria and moulds, they followed the same line of thought and proceeded to add disinfectants to their milk or meat. Obviously, since carbolic acid is a very strong poison, they could not closely follow the surgeons, but they did choose many chemicals which we now know to be undesirable constituents of food. It was about 1880 that preservatives began to come into use and it is not surprising that as they proved so extraordinarily effective they soon became widely employed. Formalin (formaldehyde) was found to prevent milk going sour; borates and salicylates would keep cream sweet; sulphites preserved meat and fruit materials for quite a long time. These chemicals were often added quite indiscriminately and there was undoubtedly a very great deal of misuse. By 1899 the medical profession and the public generally were much alarmed, for there were real fears that some of these chemicals were actually harmful to health; the use of formalin for keeping milk fresh caused particular concern because this substance was recognized as an irritant likely to cause inflammation of the stomach. As a result of widespread uneasiness the Government appointed a Committee of the Local Government Board in 1899 to inquire into the use of preservatives and colouring matters used by the food industry. Their report appeared in 1901. It was followed by legislation which, among other prohibitions, forbade the use of formalin or any form of preservative in milk. It also laid down the quantities of certain preservatives which were to be permitted. One of these was boric acid, which could be added to cream (0.25 per cent) and to butter and margarine (0.5 per cent).

Many of the milk dealers protested loudly that the public could no longer expect sweet milk if they were prevented from using preservatives. It was well, however, that the Government disregarded them for the prohibition forced a number of the less progressive dairymen to follow the few who were struggling to improve the quality of their milk by eliminating as far as possible contamination with dirt and filth. The movement towards a cleaner milk supply which one or two pioneers in the milk industry began about this time received an immense stimulus from the prohibition of the use of preservatives. It is interesting, therefore, that exactly the same arguments were raised by many of those dealing in cream, butter or margarine, when a Committee of the Ministry of Health re-examined the question of food preservatives in 1924. Once again their protests were ignored and regulations were approved suppressing entirely the use of borates. The effect of this has been, not, as many of the cream and butter merchants predicted, to eliminate fresh cream from the towns, but greatly to improve the quality of that which is sold.

CHAPTER XIX

FOOD OF THE PEOPLE

§ 1 THE POOR MAN'S FOOD

THE staple food of the working man was still bread. Often in the hard times, particularly early in the century, it was all he got, unless he was lucky enough to be a countryman with a small plot in which vegetables could be grown or a pig reared. It seems to have been exceptional to find conditions as good as those observed by Cobbett at Singleton in Sussex in 1823.

> There is an appearance of comfort about the dwellings of the labourers, all along here, that is very pleasant to behold. The gardens are neat, and full of vegetables of the best kinds. I see very few of 'Ireland's lazy root'; [potatoes] . . . A young man . . . came running to me with his vituals in his hand; and, I was glad to see that his food consisted of a good lump of household bread and not a very small piece of *bacon* . . . I saw, and with great delight, a pig at almost every labourer's house . . . What sort of *breakfast* would this man have had in a mess of *cold potatoes?*[1]

Some writers in the early part of the century would have us believe that the countryman's diet usually consisted of bread, potatoes, vegetables and bacon.

> The diet of persons who live in the country is, in general, more wholesome than that of those who inhabit towns. A large portion of it consists of fresh vegetables and milk, which, though not excluded from the food of those who live in towns, are enjoyed in much greater plenty and higher perfection in rural situations.[2]

This may have been the superficial impression of the town-dweller but there is a greater weight of evidence in support of Cobbett's view that such cases were exceptional.

> Here and there a labourer's house buried in the woods . . . I stopped at a little house, and asked the woman, who looked very clean and nice, whether she would let us dine with her . . . She said they had a bit of

[1] *Rural Rides*, August 2nd, 1823, William Cobbett, 1830.
[2] *The Family Oracle of Health*, Vol. V, 1827.

327

bacon and a pudding and some cabbage; but that she had not much bread in the house ... we left her, quite convinced that my old observation is true, that people in the woodland countries are best off, and that it is absolutely impossible to reduce them to that state of starvation in which they are in the corn-growing part of the kingdom.[1]

In general, the poor country people were living at that time on bread alone and only rarely could afford meat or beer. Milk very seldom came their way except in the outlying districts of the north and west, or in Scotland.

> I asked a man who was hedging on the side of the road, how much he got a day. He said, 1s. 6d.: and he told me that the *allowed* wages was 7d. a day for the man *and a gallon loaf a week for the rest of his family*; that is to say, one pound and two and a quarter ounces of bread for each of them; and nothing more! And this, observe, is one-third short of the bread allowance of gaols.[2]

The poor people were somewhat better off in the second half of the century when conditions began to improve. The labourer was able to eat vegetables more frequently and to afford meat for his Sunday dinner. Edward Smith, who had studied the diets of the poorer people, said in 1864 that most farm labourers enjoyed one hot meal a week.[3]

In the same year a Committee appointed to report on the state of the prisons was asked by the Home Secretary to consider the diet of prisoners in the light of the meals required by a free labourer. Their reply is interesting.

> It is extremely difficult to ascertain what the ordinary food of free labourers is. Even if the inquiry was limited to that class of free labourers which is known to be the worst fed, namely, agricultural labourers, the true facts of the case would not be readily obtained. And even if it were to appear that, as a class, their food was badly chosen, badly cooked, and insufficient in quantity ... it would not be incumbent upon us in framing dietaries for prisoners, to imitate their bad example, or to conform ourselves to their exceptional circumstances.[4]

Letheby's estimate of the food of 'a labourer' appears to be hopelessly inaccurate. He pictured such a man as eating during the course of one week, 20 lb. of bread, 6 lb. meat, 3 lb. fat, 12 oz. cheese, 4 oz. butter, 1 oz.

[1] *Rural Rides*, November 13th, 1825, William Cobbett, 1830.
[2] Ibid., November 12th, 1825.
[3] *The Present State of the Dietary Question*, E. Smith, 1864.
[4] *Parliamentary Papers*, 1864, xlix.

tea, 4 oz. coffee, 8 oz. cocoa, 2½ gallons beer and 4 lb. vegetables.[1] There can have been very few labourers who fed as well as that.

It is interesting to note that the diet of the farm hands in some parts of Scotland and the far north of England had not changed for centuries. They still lived principally on oatmeal, milk and vegetable broths. This was due, in no small measure, to the survival of the primitive system, of providing the men working on the estate with food in part payment of their wages. As a result the Scottish labourers were men of much finer physique than the Southerners. Frank Buckland, at one time medical officer to the Guards, described the weedy condition of the English recruits compared with the hardy and well built men from the Scottish farms. The Irish appeared to be strong and fit when they joined the colours but their health often broke down on the Army diet of bread, meat and potatoes.[2]

During the first half of the century the diet of the poor people in the towns was bad. The greater part of their nourishment came from bread, potatoes and strong tea.

We are sorry to remark also, notwithstanding all we have so often said in favour of tea, that the use of it with bread and butter, as the almost *sole* food of the working classes in manufacturing towns, is a leading cause of the extension of scrofula among the mass of their population; and it hence becomes a question whether sobriety, which the introduction of tea has promoted, compensates for the loss of vigour of constitution and power of body, which have followed its use, by that class of the community.[3]

The consumption of tea was by this time enormous and later it increased still more. By 1871 it was nearly four pounds per head of the population. One expert put his finger on a very real danger of excessive tea-drinking. It was not, he said, that he feared the effects of its stimulating action or of the tannin, but he recognized that the consumption of large volumes of hot fluid tended to reduce the intake of other and more nutritious foods.[4] The poor people found they could enjoy a quite deceptive feeling of warmth after drinking hot tea, whereas, in fact, a glass of cold beer would have given them far more real food.

Engels described the diet of the poorest classes in the Northern manufacturing towns in 1844.

Descending gradually, we find the animal food reduced to a small bit of bacon cut up with the potatoes; lower still, even this disappears, and

[1] *Lectures on the Economy of Food*, W. Letheby, 1857.
[2] Discussion on Edward Smith's Lecture on Diet, *Journal of the Society of Arts*, 1863, Vol. XII.
[3] *The Family Oracle of Health*, Vol. II, 1824.
[4] *A Treatise on Food and Dietetics* W. Pavy, 1875.

there remain only bread, cheese, porridge, and potatoes, until on the lowest round of the ladder, among the Irish, potatoes form the sole food.[1]

Combe says that in 1842 many of the poor townspeople were living entirely on potatoes and porridge.[2] Generally speaking, their main standby was bread. Very little meat was eaten, for it was far too dear.

We have already described the state of the meat sold in the cheapest shops and the adulterated condition of the bread. Even the potatoes were often rotten. Engels draws a grim picture of the poor people of London collecting potato parings, rotten vegetables and vegetable refuse to eke out their miserable diet.

The potato meant a great deal to the poor people of the towns at this period, which was why the devastating epidemic of potato disease in 1845-46 had such terrible consequences. Not only were there sporadic outbreaks of scurvy but thousands of people were brought to the verge of starvation. Famine decimated Ireland, where potatoes had been for more than two centuries the staple diet of the peasants. Almost every type of deficiency disease afflicted these wretched people, thousands dying from scurvy and a dropsical condition that is clearly recognizable as hunger-oedema.

> ... and to this I may add the aged, who, with the young ... are almost without exception swollen and ripening for the grave.[3]

Many well-meaning people became concerned at the signs of under-nourishment they saw on all sides. Few of them, however, had any better suggestion for its alleviation than Count Rumford's famous soup. Sir Richard Musgrave republished Rumford's essay on feeding the poor during the potato famine in Ireland in 1847. He knew nothing, of course, of the dietary inadequacy of these soups, and was probably unaware that Millbank penitentiary had experimented with Rumford's 'scheme of economy' in 1823. The prisoners, who had formerly enjoyed a diet consisting of 20 oz. bread, 1 lb. of potatoes, 3½ oz. meat, 2 pints of gruel and 1 pint of broth daily, were drastically reduced to 21 oz. bread, 1 pint of gruel and about 2 pints of a broth made with two ox-heads for every 220 persons. It is small wonder that the prisoners went sick with 'sea-scurvy, bloody-flux, and weakness of sight'.[4] Out of a total of 850 prisoners 200 were taken ill and 37 died.

---

[1] *The Condition of the Working-Class in England in 1844*, F. Engels, 1892.
[2] *The Physiology of Digestion*, A. Combe, 4th Edition, 1842.
[3] Letter from the Rev. Traill Hall, February 1847, quoted in Creighton's *History of Epidemics in Britain*, 1891-94.
[4] *The Family Oracle of Health*, Vol. I, 1824.

In 1835, one of the worst periods of the century, Andrew Ure wrote his *Philosophy of Manufactures*, in which he asserted that the Glasgow operatives ate meat several times a week and implied that most of their ills were due to indolence or alcohol. The book is full of such deliberate and wicked misstatements and clearly reflects the fear that many of the governing classes then felt lest the discontent of the half-starved workpeople should ever bring about an organized movement to demand higher wages and better conditions. Ure had no patience with the doctors who ascribed the sickness of the workers to inadequate diet and bad factory conditions. Gastric complaints, which according to Dr Kay, were very common among the Manchester factory hands, were not, Ure would have us believe, due to a poverty diet but to their reprehensible liking for bad bacon. What, he asked, could be done with people who, when a considerate employer improved the ventilation of the factory, were so ungrateful as to demand higher wages on the grounds that their appetites had increased? His remedy was to instruct the working people of England to be more temperate and to live humbly on simple stews and vegetables as the French peasant did.

There was a tendency for the diet of the townspeople to improve somewhat after 1860 when the influence of rising wages and of a fall in the price of some of the staple foods began to be felt. But is is, nevertheless, true that bread remained the chief food of the poor people. In 1892 it was found that the children of Bethnal Green were nourished almost entirely on bread, 83 per cent having no other solid food for seventeen out of twenty-one meals in the week. There was an unfortunate setback to the improvement in 1865 when the cattle plague swept the country and forced up the price of meat and dairy produce. On the other hand, this disaster gave such a fillip to the production of canned meats in Australia that it was not long before these forms of beef and mutton were obtainable more cheaply than fresh meat. Cheap imported bacon, mainly American, was sold in the industrial towns at this time. It was coarse, very fat, and not particularly appetizing, but it was often the only meat the factory hands could afford before the canned meats came on the market.

Very little fresh milk was bought by these people, as it was much too dear for the majority of them. Some authorities deplored this fact for they felt that the children of the poorer classes were stunted in growth because of the lack of milk in their diet. Dr Wilson, for example, speaking at the Domestic Economy Congress in 1877, called for cheaper milk for the poor children.[1] He had found that factory children between the ages of 12 and 14 who were given milk at breakfast and supper, grew four times as fast as when

---

[1] *Journal of the Society of Arts*, 1877, Vol. XXV.

they drank coffee or tea, 'a fact which proves incontestably that milk is essential to the healthy nutrition of the young'.

There was, however, another side to the picture. The quality of the milk sold in the towns was, until very late in the century, appallingly bad. It was for the most part heavily contaminated with germs and a frequent source of infections and epidemics. Apart from serious outbreaks of typhoid and dysentery caused by infected milk, the majority of the cases of tubercular glands and joint affections, which were very common in Victorian days, were caused by infection with a strain of the tubercle bacillus derived from cows (bovine tuberculosis) and conveyed in milk. An increased consumption of unheated milk by children would, therefore, have resulted in an increased incidence of disease. It was not until the 'nineties that people began to recognize that a measure of protection against infection by milk can be obtained by boiling it.

The last quarter of the century saw a rapid increase in the sales of cheap condensed milks in the poorer districts of the towns. Although all forms were not the most suitable food for young children they had at least the merit of being sterile, all the germs being destroyed during the process of condensing and tinning.

A food bought in surprisingly large amounts by the poor, particularly in the north, was treacle. It was very cheap and became popular because it gave flavour and sweetness to porridge and puddings. It was a thick, dark brown substance; the refining process in which charcoal is used to decolorize it and convert it into the crystal clear 'golden syrup' we know today was not introduced until about 1880. Edward Smith's records of the diets of the Lancashire operatives in 1864 show that they lived largely on bread, oatmeal, bacon, a very little butter, treacle, and tea and coffee.[1] Cheap jams made their appearance on the market in the 'eighties and immediately became very popular. Most of them contained very little of the fruit they were alleged to be made from and were simply concoctions made from the cheapest fruit or vegetable pulp obtainable, coloured and flavoured as required. Their sweetness made them very popular with poor families; bread and jam became the chief food of poor children for two meals out of three.

While the poor people existed on these cheap, monotonous and defective diets the skilled workmen, with their better pay, were able to afford more meat and a variety of vegetables. In the first half of the century it was still a common practice to send the joints round to the baker's shop to be cooked. Even the cookshops supplying a whole meal were still flourishing.

Here's your mother been and bought at the cook's shop, besides

[1] *Journal of the Society of Arts*, 1864, Vol. XIII.

pease pudding, a whole knuckle of a lovely roast leg of pork, with lots of crackling left upon it, and with seasoning, gravy, and mustard quite unlimited.[1]

On working days the artisans and lower middle classes often ate their midday meal at a tavern or a cheap eating-house where an 'ordinary' of hot meat, vegetables, bread, cheese and beer cost from 6d. to 1s. Some of these places were none too attractive.

> I have dined at eating-houses, the effluvia of which, steaming up through the iron gratings made me qualmish before eating, and ill all the day after ... I have groped my way down hypocausts in Fleet Street, and dined in cavern-like taverns, wishing myself a thousand miles away the moment the eternal joint was uncovered.[2]

In the evening they would return home to a meal of cold meat, or a veal and ham pie, or a dish of stewed eels or pickled salmon, washed down by the bottled beer with which the larger towns had become familiar in the first half of the century. The bottling of beer, which was first successfully carried out about 1736, was originally intended to supply 'pale ale' for export to India, but soon after 1800 it developed into a flourishing home trade.[3] Before the heavy taxation imposed by Gladstone in 1861, spirits were still sufficiently cheap for the working classes to be able to indulge in them; gin and water, and brandy and water were the favourite drinks.

Perhaps it was this fairly comfortably off artisan class of which Kitchiner was thinking when he planned a 'family economy' for 'moderate persons in a frugal family'.[4] He estimated the amount required per person per week as follows:

Meat	6 pounds, weight (undressed)
Bread	4 pounds (quartern loaf)
Butter	½ pound
Tea	2 ounces
Sugar	½ pound
Beer (Porter)	1 pint per day (see Appendix A)

The proportion of bread to meat is instructive.

This estimate is taken from that curious compendium of information, *The Family Oracle of Health*, edited by A. F. Crell and W. M. Wallace,

[1] *The Haunted Man (Christmas Tales)*, Charles Dickens, 1848.
[2] *The Memoirs of a Stomach, Written by Himself, That All who Eat May Read*, edited by a *Minister of the Interior*, 4th Edition, 1853.
[3] We are indebted for this information to Mr D. Burrell, Secretary to Messrs Bass, Ratcliff and Gretton of Burton-on-Trent.
[4] *The Family Oracle of Health*, Vol. I, 1824.

assisted by a 'Committee of Scientific Gentlemen'. Their efforts were dedicated to 'the Scientific Amateurs of Good Living, who enjoy Prime Dinners, and jollify over Claret and Glenlyvet at Ambrose's, Edinburgh'. It is a mine of amusing and instructive information about the first quarter of the nineteenth century. Another estimate from this source gives the 'ordinary people's consumption' per day.

Bread	¾-1 lb.
Meat	¾-1¼ lb.
Vegetables (greens)	¼-¾ lb.
Butter	½-1 lb.
Beer	1 pt. to 1 qt.[1]

The higher figures are probably over-estimated in the case of meat and butter, for a pound of butter alone gives 3500 Cal., which is more energy than an 'ordinary person' doing a light day's work requires in 24 hours.

English domestic cooking has never stood in high repute, except perhaps in so far as roast meats are concerned. Its reputation appears to have declined during the nineteenth century, probably because when we acquired from the Continent the knowledge how to grow garden vegetables we did not trouble to learn how to cook them properly. It is one of the major tragedies of English domestic life. It is possible that the high cost of living in the latter half of the eighteenth century can to some extent be blamed, because butter was dear. By the time that it became reasonably cheap again the custom of ruining good vegetables by boiling them was established.

> The English system of cooking it would be impertinent for me to describe; but still when I think of that huge round of par-boiled ox flesh, with sodden dumplings, floating in a saline, greasy mixture, surrounded by carrots looking red with disgust, and turnips pale with dismay, I cannot help a sort of inward shudder, and making comparisons unfavourable to English gastronomy.[2]

In France there was a centuries-old tradition of domestic cooking which was scarcely disturbed by the years of dearth at the end of the eighteenth century. It is significant that English literature of the nineteenth century has produced nothing in any way comparable with Brillat-Savarin's classic of gastronomy *Physiologie du Goût*, which became so popular that it ran rapidly through several editions.

Perhaps the nearest approach to it is *The Cook's Oracle*, written by the versatile and slightly eccentric Dr Kitchiner. He considered 'the ART of

---

[1] *The Family Oracle of Health*, Vol. I, 1824.
[2] *The Memoirs of a Stomach, edited by a Minister of the Interior*, 4th Edition, 1853.

COOKERY, not merely as a mechanical operation, fit only for working COOKS — but as the Analeptic part of the Art of Physic'.[1] This dilettante was in the habit of cooking all his own food himself and under the guidance of Mr Osborne, cook to Sir Joseph Banks, he became an expert. *The Cook's Oracle* gives not only a large number of recipes, all of which had been tried out in his own kitchen, but an interesting list of 250 books on food and cookery, covering three centuries, most of which the author claims to have read. Kitchiner was also the anonymous author of an amusing little book, *Peptic Precepts*, which had a considerable sale, and he was one of the leading lights of the Committee who edited *The Family Oracle of Health*.

§ 2 THE RICH MAN'S DIET

There were few notable changes during the century, but one striking fact which emerges is the growth in popularity of what has come to be known as the 'typical English breakfast'. While a few of the more leisured people were content with a cup of coffee or tea and rolls or toast, and some of the more old-fashioned remained faithful to the eighteenth-century breakfast of cold meat, cheese and beer, the majority adopted the three- or four-course meal of porridge, fish, bacon and eggs, toast and marmalade, which maintained its popularity for a century but which today has been abandoned in favour of a lighter and simpler type of meal.

Another change was the alteration in the hours of meals. In the late eighteenth century fashionable people ate their dinner at 5 or 6 o'clock, but in the nineteenth century 7 o'clock was the more usual hour. It was this change that led to the disappearance of the old 'supper' and to the custom of eating luncheon in the middle of the day. In the early part of the century this was often quite a light repast, perhaps nothing more than a glass of wine and a biscuit, but it gradually took the form of the meal we know today. The late evening 'supper' of the eighteenth century was replaced by tea or coffee and cakes, with possibly cold punch or light wine for the men, served at about 9.30 or 10.

The regime recommended in 1824 by *The Family Oracle of Health* (Vol. II) as 'Beauty Training for Ladies' is reminiscent of eighteenth-century rather than nineteenth-century customs.

Before breakfast you must walk ... from half a mile to three miles ... and if you botanize by the way it will be of immense advantage. The ... breakfast itself — not later than eight o'clock — ought, in rigid

[1] *The Cook's Oracle. Actual Experiments instituted in the Kitchen of a Physician*, Dr Kitchiner, 3rd Edition, 1821.

training, to consist of plain biscuit (not bread), broiled beef steaks or mutton chops, under-done, without any fat, and half a pint of bottled ale — the genuine Scots ale is the best. Our fair readers will not demur to this, when they are told that this was the regular breakfast of Queen Elizabeth, and Lady Jane Grey. But should it be found too strong fare at the commencement, we permit, instead of the ale, one small breakfast cup — not more — of good strong black tea or of coffee — weak tea or coffee is always bad for the nerves as well as the complexion. If tea or coffee is taken, the half pint of ale is to be used three hours after breakfast with a biscuit, on returning from your second walk, which must be as long as the first ... dinner at two, the same as breakfast; no vegetables, boiled meat, nor made-dishes being permitted, much less fruits, sweet things, or pastry. Those who are very delicate may begin with a bit of broiled chicken or turkey, but the steaks and chops must always be the chief part of your food. A mealy potatoe, or a little boiled rice, may now and then be permitted, but no other vegetable ... supper at seven or eight as most convenient, at which we allow you tea or coffee, if you have had none to breakfast; if you have, you must take your half pint of mild ale, and a bit of cold fowl, or cold roast mutton or beef, but no fat. Butter, cream, milk, cheese, and fish, are prohibited. You may take an egg occasionally with a biscuit.

The diet suggested was thoroughly badly balanced. The exclusion of dairy produce and green vegetables would undoubtedly have led to vitamin A deficiency, while the restrictions with regard to vegetables and the absence of fruit would have produced a mild form of scurvy.

Here is an estimate of the annual expenses of a well-to-do family in 1824:

This family consists of two, and occasionally three, in the parlour, and two maids, and a man servant, who have a dinner party of a dozen once a month, and where there is always plenty of good provisions, but no affectation of profusion.[1]

Meat	£65
Fish and poultry	25
Bread	18
Butter and cheese	25
Milk	7
Vegetables and fruit	20
Tea and sugar	15
Table ale	25

[1] *The Family Oracle of Health*, Vol. II, 1824.

The relatively high expenditure on fruit and vegetables is particularly interesting.

This table can usefully be compared with estimates given for the weekly expenditure of a comfortably off man with a wife and child and two maids, and of an artisan with a wife and two children to be supported on the modest sum of a guinea a week.

Income — £300 a year 4 adults, 1 child		Income — £54 10s. 0d. a year 2 adults, 2 children
Bread	5/-	4/-
Meat	9/-	3/-
Cheese, butter, ham	4/6	1/3 (inc. eggs)
Milk and cream	2/-	6d. (milk only)
Vegetables and fruit	4/-	1/-
Fish	5/-	—
Groceries	11/-	1/6
Beer	9/-	1/3

The French fashion in the arrangement of the courses at dinner, adopted by the wealthy classes in the eighteenth century, remained popular throughout the following century. One connoisseur held that: 'It is a bad dinner when there are not at least five varieties: a substantial dish of fish, one of meat, one of game, one of poultry and, above all, a ragout with truffles ... They form the absolute minimum and *sine qua non* of a dinner for one person.'[1] A sweet course of pies, tarts, or puddings was usually served as well. Christmas pudding was by this time exclusively a 'sweet', meat no longer forming a part of its composition. The French *Almanach des Gourmands* had the temerity to describe it as 'Mélange indigeste et bizarre plutôt qu'une préparation savante et salubre.'[2]

The custom of taking an aperitif before dinner appears to have been introduced into England early in the nineteenth century. *The Family Oracle of Health* drew attention to the 'northern custom of whet-cup or *coup d'avant*'. It was doubtless referring to the old Russian and Scandinavian custom of drinking vodka or aquavite before meals, but the variant recommended by this journal was 'a large glass of rum, brandy, or bitters'. This, it was stated, would be a good English drink, certainly more than a Frenchman could stand up to — 'it would infallibly crisp his stomach' — but all such delicate creatures could have recourse to a 'large glass of a cold infusion of camomile, quassia, or any other good bitter'. Perhaps it is not inappropriate at this juncture to give the recipe recommended by the same journal for the 'morning after'.

[1] Ibid.   [2] Ibid., Vol. I, 1824.

Feaster's morning Draught

Take two drachms of Rochelle salts,
   one ounce of infusion of senna,
   one teaspoonful of compound tincture of cardamoms,
   and (*if you can get it*) a small wine glass of Ratafia of Eau de
   Cologne.

Mix, for a draught; and during the morning (after your coffee, of
course), take an occasional glass of *strong* ginger beer. It will also be
of great advantage to sit in a snug fauteuil before a good fire, with your
feet in carpet shoes, planted comfortably on the hobs. This position
tends to keep the head *erect*, which is of the utmost importance, while
the warmth of the feet draws the superabundance of blood downwards
from the brain, and consequently renders the nerves strong, the
spirits light, and the whole man cheerful and buoyant.[1]

The young man-about-town could, of course, take the precaution of
swallowing a spoonful of olive oil before starting out for an evening's
revelry. This is an old and very sound prophylactic measure. Sir Hugh
Platt recommended it in his *Jewell House of Art and Nature* (1594).

Drinke first a good large Draught of Sallet Oyle, for that will float
vpon the Wine which you shall drinke, and supresse the spirits from
ascending into the braine.

The presence of fat in the stomach delays absorption from that organ, so
that although in the long run the same amount of alcohol passes into the
blood the process does not occur as quickly as when no fat is present.
What produces intoxication is not so much the total amount of alcohol taken,
although obviously this is a factor, as the rate at which it passes into the
blood. It is the concentration in the blood that matters. Alcohol differs from
nearly all the other narcotic drugs in being also a food which can be oxidized
in the body to provide energy as sugars or fats are oxidized. When alcohol
passed slowly into the blood, as for example when light alcoholic drinks
are taken, it is oxidized almost as fast as it is absorbed so that it does not
accumulate to a sufficient extent appreciably to influence the nervous system.
When, on the other hand, there is a rapid absorption following the consumption of a considerable amount of strong spirits or cocktails, the tissues
cannot deal with it rapidly enough to prevent such an accumulation, with
the result that the brain is affected, just as it would be by an anaesthetic
such as ether, only not so rapidly. Anything that delays the rate of absorption
from the stomach reduces the effect of alcohol. That is why a few biscuits

[1] *The Family Oracle of Health*, Vol. I, 1824.

or an olive or two are helpful as well as pleasant accompaniments of cocktails. It is a custom derived from the very old Russian habit of eating *ʒakushki* with vodka before meals. Most of these little 'snacks', caviare, anchovies, olives, etc., are both salty and oily; the salt stimulates thirst and appetite, while the oil retards absorption and reduces the chances of too rapid intoxication. The rate of oxidation of alcohol is such that alcohol can be utilized to provide heat equivalent to about half the basal metabolism. Thus the speed of drinking has a decisive bearing on its effects.

A question that the scientist has not yet adequately answered is why mixing drinks can have such devastating effects. There is a great deal of truth in the old German proverb:

> Wein auf Bier rat'ich dir —
> Bier auf Wein lass hubsch sein.
>
> Wine upon beer is very good cheer.
> Beer upon wine, then you'll repine.

The Englishman could supply an equally true tag about the order in which it is advisable to take whisky and beer.

The fashions in wine changed a little in the nineteenth century. The taxes on alcoholic beverages which Gladstone imposed in 1861 helped to bring French wines back to favour. They were based on strength, which meant that the 'fortified' wines like port paid a heavier duty than the lighter table wines. Champagne, which was first introduced into England about 1650 and which remained something of a rarity for nearly a century, began to become popular with the wealthy. An innovation was the introduction of artificial 'soda-water' and, later, other aerated drinks, prepared by charging liquids with carbon dioxide under pressure. The famous divine and chemist, Joseph Priestley, had been one of the first to experiment with such liquors, and he was a strong supporter of Dr MacBride, who held that 'fixed air' (carbon dioxide) was a powerful preventive of putrefaction. Priestley succeeded in charging water with the gas and was convinced that his 'carbonated water' was a medicinal preparation of the highest value.

> I can make better than you import, and what cost you five shillings will not cost me a penny. I might have turned quack.

What 'you import', was evidently 'Pyrmont water', a German natural gaseous medicinal water which was much esteemed in the eighteenth century, but which was very expensive.

Soda-water was first made commercially in England about 1790 and soon became a popular drink, particularly as a corrective for what is known today as a 'hang-over'. A few medical men feared that it caused indigestion by inflating the stomach.

Early in the century a number of new fruits were introduced. North Carolina sent the tomato or 'love-apple', considered by some authorities to be violently aphrodisiac. It was grown, at first, more as a decoration than for eating but by 1880 it was being offered for sale in most of the fruit markets, although for a time there was a curious aversion to it on the grounds of its unusual colour. Vegetable marrows and pumpkins, although the latter never became popular, were also introduced at the beginning of the nineteenth century.

§3 FOOD IN SCHOOLS

The descriptions of the conditions prevailing in many private schools during the nineteenth century made terrible reading. The children were often half-starved. This was not entirely due to ignorance of the fact that growing children need far more food than their size would suggest; there was a general indifference to their welfare which strikes us today as appalling. Moreover, matters were all too often made worse by the widely held view that short commons and hard fare were good discipline for rebellious youth. Mrs Gaskell tells of the half-starved Brontë girls being lectured, when they pleaded for more to eat, on the sin of caring for carnal things and of pampering greedy appetites.[1] One is reminded of earlier views on 'original sin'.

> Iniquity is connatural to Infants, and they are more prone to Evil than to Good, we must not therefore indulge them too much.[2]

Dickens was not exaggerating when he wrote of Dotheboys Hall.

> Into these bowls, Mrs. Squeers ... poured a brown composition, which looked like diluted pin-cushions without the covers, and was called porridge. A minute wedge of brown bread was inserted into each bowl ... At one o'clock the boys having previously had their appetites thoroughly taken away by stirabout and potatoes, sat down in the kitchen to some hard salt beef.[3]

Small wonder that the wretched boys were like children from a famine area.

> Pale and haggard faces, lank and bony figures, children with the countenances of old men, deformities with irons upon their limbs, boys of stunted growth, and others whose long meagre legs would hardly bear their stooping bodies.[4]

[1] Life of Charlotte Brontë, E. C. Caskell, 1857.
[2] A General Treatise of the Diseases of Infants and Children, J. Pechey, 1697.
[3] Nicholas Nickleby, Charles Dickens, 1839.   [4] Ibid.

Even at the more expensive schools conditions were often nearly as bad. Commenting on the prevalence of curvature of the spine among young girls attending private schools, Dr Hale Thompson drew attention not only to their ill-chosen diet, consisting mainly of porridge, bread, meat and boiled potatoes, but also to the character of their day's work. The girls rose at 6 and did preparation until 8, when they breakfasted on porridge, bread and tea. At 8.30 preparation was resumed until school began at 9, lessons continuing without a break until 1. For half an hour they were free to leave the classrooms but were not allowed to go out of doors. Dinner, consisting of boiled or roast meat, or boiled fish, and potatoes, with perhaps a suet or rice pudding to follow, occupied half an hour, and was followed by another three hours of school. Tea and bread were served at 5; at 6, if it were fine, the girls took an hour's walk, otherwise they stayed indoors and read.[1] Not until late in the century did the more progressive heads of schools begin to realize that it was unreasonable and unwise to expect a child to rise at 6 and to do two hours' brain work on an empty stomach.

The most serious defect of school diets of the time was the paucity of fruit and vegetables. The former was regarded as an unnecessary luxury and the latter, unless very cheap, might well be replaced by bread. Henry Field's report on the diet of the boys at Christ's Hospital in 1813 supports this view.

> Their diet is plain and simple; the allowance of bread is very ample and of the best quality; that of animal food is in quantity moderate, and of culinary vegetables but small; but the great quantity of bread allowed to them renders the latter less necessary, and thus, without material inconvenience, they are dispensed with.[2]

It is hardly surprising that in 1816 the boys at this school were suffering from mild scurvy.

In 1834 the *Lancet* severely criticized the food at Christ's Hospital. The Governors resented this attitude.

> The care and attention of the Governors to the health and comfort of the children cannot be too much eulogised . . . particularly as regards the diet, which had always been sufficiently wholesome and good, with however a very small proportion of vegetable food.[3]

Nevertheless, they consented to make certain improvements.

[1] *Lancet*, 1839.
[2] *The London Medical Repository*, 1813, cited by G. E. Friend in *The Schoolboy, A Study of his Nutrition, Physical Development and Health*, 1935.
[3] *The History of Christ's Hospital*, J. I. Wilson, 1824.

... the dietary, a matter of prime importance, has been amended beyond all fair exception.

A comparison of the old and new dietaries does not indicate much improvement, except that the amount of potatoes was raised from one to two pounds a week and vegetable soup was provided twice a week. Against this there was the reduction of the weekly allowance of butter from 4½ ounces to 1½ ounces, which meant that the total calorific intake was reduced from 2050 to 1950, and the supply of vitamin A considerably curtailed.[1]

Even at many of the expensive public schools the diet was inadequate and monotonous; a breakfast of porridge and bread and butter, with beer or tea; meat and a few potatoes, followed by a stodgy pudding or cheese for dinner; and supper which was usually a repetition of breakfast. It was conditions such as these which favoured the growth of the 'tuck-box' or 'tuck-shop' system; a system which has been condemned, and rightly so, in modern times, but which must often have been the schoolboy's salvation in the days when it was almost his only chance during term-time of getting the fruit and the extra calories he needed.

[1] *The Schoolboy, A Study of his Nutrition, Physical Development, and Health*, G. E. Friend 1935.

CHAPTER XX

RISE OF THE SCIENCE OF NUTRITION

§ 1 FOOD REQUIREMENTS

DURING the early years of the nineteenth century the old ideas about the antagonism of alkalescence and acescence dominated the views of the function of foods. Even the humoral theories were by no means dead, if one can judge from the popularity of such a work as Nisbet's *Practical Treatise on Diet* published in 1801. It required time for people's minds to become amenable to the new discipline which the exact and quantitative studies of pioneers such as Lavoisier demanded. It was still a credulous age. Earlier centuries had produced many stories of people living for long periods without food yet remaining in good health, but few were as strange as that which startled England in 1809. A woman called Ann Moore gained considerable notoriety by claiming that she had eaten nothing for five years, having lost all desire for food after a long illness. Many people firmly believed in the 'Fasting Woman of Tutbury'.

> Though her bodily strength was represented as somewhat impaired, and her person was described as exhibiting several marked proofs of prolonged abstinence; yet her countenance was said to retain the appearance of health; her mental faculties were admitted to be entire; her memory was even stated to be increasingly strong.[1]

The lady in question completely deceived her own medical man and the local parson. Possibly because 'her piety was held up as extremely edifying' they fully believed her when, 'a large Bible . . . before her', she told visitors that not only had she eaten and drunk nothing all that time but that there had been no need to attend to the calls of nature. Unfortunately, she had not reckoned with the advances of science. Alexander Henderson, a doctor of the new school, went to see her. He first noted that 'some bustle was heard in the upper story, as if preparation had been making for our reception'. Then after one look at her moist skin he realized that she was perspiring in the usual way. This daily loss he estimated from her stature to be about 60 fluid ounces. Clearly, he argued, this could not have gone on day by day without rapid desiccation occurring. To strengthen this scientific demonstration of her fraud he thought it worth recording that chance contact

---

[1] *An Examination of the Imposture of Ann Moore*, A. Henderson, 1813.

of his foot with an earthenware vessel hidden under the bed left him in no doubt that her kidneys were functioning very much as other people's.

It is all very well for us to smile at the credulity of those who believed such fantastic stories, but it must be borne in mind that there was no suspicion that energy can neither be created nor destroyed and it did not seem impossible that a peculiarly constituted individual might be able to survive for very long periods without food or drink.

Nothing at all was known of the essential food requirements of man. The only basis for making estimates was knowledge of the amounts of food which people consumed. When, therefore, it came to deciding the diets for soldiers, sailors, or the inmates of gaols and institutions, rough-and-ready calculations were made on this basis, usually with a very keen eye to economy.

The ration for the Navy in 1811, for example, provided at a cost of 1s. 3¾d. a head per day, did not give the men anything like enough food for their needs.

Bread	16 ounces	Butter	⅞ ounce
Beef	4½ ounces	Sugar	⅞ ounce
Pork	2¼ ounces	Cheese	1¾ ounces
Flour	3 ounces	Beer	1 quart
Suet	¼ ounce		

In addition there were small quantities of pease, oatmeal, raisins and vinegar.

This diet (analysed in Appendix A) provided about 80 g. of protein, 100 g. of fat and 2900 Cal. daily. This is a good deal less than the quantities which should be provided according to modern views, for a man doing a hard day's work needs about 4000 Cal. of which about 12 per cent should be derived from protein and up to 35 per cent from fat. The same was true of the Army, for which the ordinary daily ration was 1 lb. of bread and 1 lb. of meat. The men were underfed and therefore obliged to supplement their rations as best they could from their own pockets.

§ 2 CLASSIFICATION OF FOODS

When the century opened the foods were classified according to a simple system based on obvious characteristics. As set out in a popular book on diet, written by Dr Paris in 1826, the sub-division was as follows:[1]

[1] *A Treatise on Diet*, J. A. Paris, 1826.

CLASS	NAME	EXAMPLES
1	FIBRINOUS	Flesh and blood of animals.
2	ALBUMINOUS	Eggs and certain other animal matter.
3	GELATINOUS	Flesh of very young animals, certain fish, calf's foot.
4	FATTY AND OILY	Animal fats, butter, fatty flesh of pork, ducks, etc.
5	CASEOUS	Milk and cheese.
6	FARINACEOUS	Cereals.
7	MUCILAGINOUS	Carrots, roots, cabbage.
8	SWEET	Sugar and sweet fruits.
9	ACIDULOUS	Acescent fruits, e.g. oranges and sour apples.

Such a classification meant very little, but it was not long before the beginnings of a more rational system began to be recognized. They are first traceable in the writings of the famous French physiologist, François Magendie. He tried the experiment of feeding dogs exclusively on one type of food. Those that he fed on fresh meat lived in good health but others to which he gave only sugar or starch, or fat, lost weight and became ill. Other experiments of the same character led him to conclude that foods containing nitrogen, or as he termed them, 'azotised foods', are essential for health. He had discovered that proteins are necessary for maintaining body weight.

It is interesting to note that some of the symptoms shown by the dogs which did not thrive in Magendie's experiments are recognizable today as due to vitamin deficiencies. He noticed, for example, that the dogs fed exclusively on bread developed sore eyes and opacities of the cornea. This was almost certainly xerophthalmia resulting from vitamin A deficiency. Again, the animals he tried to keep alive on boiled egg-white suffered from sore skin and loss of hair. This is recognizable today as one of the conditions of dermatitis attributable to lack of constituents of the vitamin B group. Magendie may, perhaps, be numbered with the pioneers of experimental vitamin research.

His work attracted widespread interest in England. It stimulated the anatomist and surgeon, Astley Cooper, to perform experiments to ascertain the relative digestibility of different foods. In these he examined the contents of dogs' stomachs at intervals, after giving different types of meats, and found considerable differences between the times required for their solution. From the results he drew up a table of the time required for the digestion of the commoner meats. Rather surprisingly, he found pork to be one of the most digestible.[1] A contemporary comment runs: 'We here see Sir Astley in a more favourable light than in his observations on Mr. Earle; and trying to

[1] *Encyclopaedia Britannica*, Edition 1818, Article on Diet.

discover, like a genuine philosopher, the digestible properties of food.'[1] The allusion refers to an unseemly struggle to snatch students which was carried on for several years between Barts and Guys with no small amount of personal invective and abuse.

It is clear that the trend of inquiry at this date was in the direction of finding to what could be attributed the differences between the nutritional value of foods. A primitive attempt to draw up a list of foods in the order of their nutritive value was given in a curious tract published in London in 1812. The author, who, incidentally, invented the word nutriology, placed butter at the head of the list with a value of 4000. Animal fat and cheese were rated at 2000; beans and peas at 900; fruits 250-500, and cabbages and greens at only 100-150. The figures, which did not refer to any known unit such as the modern calorie, were arrived at largely by empirical methods and guesswork. It is, therefore, interesting that they are not greatly at variance with the relative calorific values given in modern tables.

Magendie's work was the sure foundation on which the great chemist Liebig built. The German work began to attract attention in England about 1840, but a sensation was caused when two years later Lyon Playfair, who had studied with Liebig at Giessen and who returned to England fired with missionary zeal for his teacher's revolutionary ideas, communicated a short report outlining new theories of the function of foods to the members of the Section of Chemistry at the Glasgow meeting of the British Association.

Shortly afterwards the English translation of Liebig's book appeared giving a full account of these theories. It was then fully realized how great an advance had been made and what remarkable results were accruing from the application of chemical analysis to the problems of physiology and nutrition. Not only did he make the first accurate analyses of the composition of foodstuffs, he applied the information to the quantitative study of the function of foods.

> When a lean goose, weighing 4 lb. gains, in 36 days, during which it has been fed with 24 lb. of maize, 5 lb. in weight, and yields $3\frac{1}{2}$ lb. of pure fat, this fat cannot have been contained in the food, ready formed, because maize does not contain the thousandth part of its weight of fat, or of any substance resembling fat.[2]

> How clear are now to us the relations of the different articles of food to the objects which they serve in the body, since organic chemistry was applied to the investigation per *quantitative* method of research.[3]

[1] *The Family Oracle of Health*, Vol. I, 1824.
[2] *Animal Chemistry or Organic Chemistry in its Application to Physiology and Pathology*, J. v. Liebig, edited from the Author's Manuscript by William Gregory, 1842.
[3] Ibid.

Liebig constructed his main theory on the differentiation which Magendie had made between the nitrogenous and the non-nitrogenous foods. The former he regarded as essentially flesh-formers and, for this reason, he termed them the 'plastic elements of nutrition'. The non-nitrogenous foods he believed to be the chief source of animal heat and energy. Containing carbon, hydrogen and oxygen, they were, he rightly thought, the chief fuel of the body because they were 'burnt' or oxidized to carbon dioxide and water. These he termed the 'respiratory elements of nutrition'. Here is one of his classifications:

Plastic elements of nutrition	Respiratory elements of nutrition
Vegetable fibrine	Fat
Vegetable albumen	Starch
Vegetable casein	Gum
Animal flesh	Cane sugar
Animal blood	Grape sugar
	Milk sugar
	Pectin
	Wine, beer and spirits

Liebig's views prompted the first scientific quantitative studies of English diets. It is not surprising that these were based on estimations of the amount of carbon and nitrogen in the different foods, for the former was regarded as a measure of the energy or heat-producing value while the latter was believed to indicate blood-forming power, and, therefore, tissue-forming power; it was Liebig's view that the nitrogenous constituents of foods, the vegetable and animal fibrines and albumens, or proteins as we call them today, were directly converted into blood after digestion and then, later, became transformed into flesh.

Before passing on to describe how Liebig's ideas led to a more thorough and more profitable study of the food requirements of man than had ever before been possible, it may be interesting to refer briefly to another event that occurred at that historic meeting of the British Association in Glasgow in 1840, and which also had reference to a subject of nutritional interest.

Some little stir had been caused in medical circles a few years previously by the accounts published in America of a remarkable series of experiments on digestion in the human stomach which a certain Dr Beaumont had been able to make on the person of an individual named Alexis St Martin, who had a hole in his abdominal wall communicating directly with the interior of his stomach. The Section of Medicine of the British Association voted at their meeting a grant of no less than £200 for the purpose of making a study of the chemistry of digestion, reserving part of the money for the purpose of bringing this unique physiological freak to England for further examination.

Alexis St Martin was a young French-Canadian trapper who in June 1822 had been accidentally wounded by the discharge of a shot gun at close range. A terrible wound was caused involving both the chest and abdomen. He came under the care of a Dr Beaumont, at that time medical officer at the trading post of Fort Mackinac, who did not think his patient could possibly recover. Much to everyone's surprise, however, the extensive injuries gradually healed, although nearly a year elapsed before the man could leave his bed, and the healing process never became quite complete. By a curious chance the edges of a wound that had perforated the stomach became united with those of the wound in the abdominal wall in such a manner that a permanent opening, or fistula, was left, communicating with the interior of the stomach.

Young Beaumont realized that he had a case providing a unique opportunity for studying digestion, because it was possible actually to see what was happening to food inside the stomach. He therefore persuaded the convalescent trapper to come to his home, where during nearly two years he carefully nursed him back to full health. He then bound the young man by articles of contract, which are still preserved, to remain with him for the purposes of study. By these documents St Martin agreed to 'go or travel or reside in any part of the world' with Dr Beaumont and 'to submit, to assist and to promote by all means in his power such philosophical experiments as the said William shall direct or cause to be made on or in the stomach of him, the said Alexis, either through and by means of the aperture or opening thereto in the side of him'.[1]

Beaumont's book records the results of 238 experiments, all of which were carried out before the end of 1833.[2] Subsequently St Martin joined the U.S. Army for a time and then seems to have lost touch with Dr Beaumont. Many attempts were made to persuade him to submit to further study — he had earned the title of 'the man with a lid on his stomach' — but he did not respond to the offers. There is correspondence extant showing that the invitation from London was received but there is no record that he ever left America.[3] Later in life he seems to have earned a fairly comfortable livelihood by exhibiting his fistula at medical societies and hospitals, and he died in 1880 at the advanced age of 83. His relatives, devout Catholics, were so afraid his

[1] *Biographical Essay on W. Beaumont*, Sir W. Osler, 1929. (Preface to facsimile of the original edition of Beaumont's 1833 book published in Boston in 1929, on the occasion of the 13th International Physiological Congress.)

[2] *Experiments and Observations in the Gastric Juice and the Physiology of Digestion*, W. Beaumont, 1833.

[3] *Lancet*, September 28th, 1840.

body would be seized by interested parties, that they would not permit it to be buried until decomposition was well advanced, and even then insisted on it being interred at an unusual depth.

The value of Beaumont's observations on digestion in St Martin's stomach lies in the extent to which they dispelled the confusion of ideas about what did actually occur. The old theories that foods were digested by one or other of the processes of putrefaction, trituration, fermentation or maceration, were proved to be entirely wrong. Up to this time so conflicting had expert opinions been that many agreed with the famous Hunter.

> Some Physiologists will have it that the Stomach is a Mill: — others, that it is a fermenting Vat; — others, again, that it is a Stew-pan; — but in my view of the matter, it is neither a Mill, a fermenting Vat, nor a Stew-pan — but a STOMACH, gentlemen, a STOMACH.[1]

Beaumont's studies showed that solution of meat foods occurs as the result of a chemical process brought about by an agent in the gastric juice, which he was able to prove also contains hydrochloric acid. It is out of place here to speak of Beaumont's remarkable studies of the secretion of gastric juice, in which he actually watched it being poured into the stomach from the openings of the tiny glands in the mucous lining. Suffice it to say that he observed that both its amount and its character were influenced by the type of food, by mental disturbances, and by fasting, and that with these researches he laid the foundations for the work of the great Russian physiologist Pavlov seventy years later.

§ 3 THE VALUE OF NITROGENOUS FOODS

Liebig's early work laid the foundations of the knowledge of the nutritive value of the proteins. He discovered three of these nitrogen-rich substances in vegetable foods, a gluten or vegetable fibrine, a coagulable protein in roots and green vegetables which he called vegetable albumen, and a vegetable casein, so named because it was thrown out of solution by acids in a manner similar to the casein of milk. His chemical analysis of these compounds led him to think that they all contained the same proportions of carbon and nitrogen, and from this and other similarities, he concluded that they were identical in composition. It was not an original idea. In 1837 another German chemist, Mulder, had deduced from his analyses of similar materials that there was one complex, nitrogen-containing component of all living matter, both plant and animal, which was of fundamental importance. It was

---

[1] MS. notes of Hunter's Lectures, cited by J. A. Paris in *A Treatise on Diet*, 1827.

he who coined the name *proteine* (Greek — I take first place). This name came to be used in a much wider sense when it was discovered that there are many different proteins present in animal and plant foods.

Liebig believed from the results of his chemical analyses that the proteins of milk, eggs, meat and other animal foods, with the one exception of gelatin, were identical in composition with the proteins of plants. On this evidence he taught that herbivorous animals build up their tissues directly from the proteins of plant foods, they being first converted into blood proteins and then into those of the muscles and other organs. It was a very simple theory and it dominated opinions on nutrition for nearly fifty years. Since all proteins contained, according to his analyses, the same proportion of nitrogen, it is understandable that estimations of the amount of nitrogen in foods came to be employed as a method of assessing their 'tissue-forming' value.

The outstanding anomaly was gelatin, which, being rich in nitrogen, seemed to belong to the protein class. Once again Magendie led the way. His discoveries resulted from an investigation promoted by the Académie française to ascertain 'whether it was possible economically to extract from bones an aliment which alone or mixed with other substances could take the place of meat'. Magendie's earlier experiments had taught him that foods containing nitrogen are essential for life. He was, therefore, surprised to find that dogs fed on gelatin, which contains as much nitrogen as meat, rapidly lost weight and became ill. Other dogs obtaining the same amount of nitrogen in the form of meat lived in good health. Clearly, therefore, all 'azotised foods' were not identical so far as flesh-forming properties were concerned. Magendie's experiments were soon supported by the experience of a Frenchman who tried to live on gelatin as the sole source of 'azotised' food. In spite of taking as much as 800 grains of nitrogen in that form he lost two pounds weight in six days and felt not only hungry but ill.

Reviewing his analytical figures, Liebig found that there was slightly more nitrogen and a little less carbon in gelatin than in fibrin or albumen. This gave him the opportunity to suggest that gelatin is not an ordinary protein and that one would not expect it to form blood and flesh. He hinted that its role might be to form the soft matrix of bones and the gelatinous parts of tendons.

It was an explanation that served for the time being. Indeed, no better was offered until the cause of the nutritive deficiences of gelatin were discovered early in the next century. Nevertheless, it was rather disturbing for those who were attempting to follow Liebig's lead and estimate the 'tissue-forming' value of diets in terms of their nitrogen contents to be forced to admit that one important nitrogen containing constituent of meat foods had no 'tissue-forming' value.

They were soon to have other worries. Early in the nineteenth century books on food, particularly cookery books, frequently referred to a substance called osmazome. The name was applied to the appetizing, thick brown material which appears when meat is roasted and which, together with exuded juices, forms natural gravy. This 'sapid and odoriferous principle' of meat[1] came to be regarded as a food component of no little importance. Apart from the fact that it promoted appetite by its smell and flavour it gave the impression of being nutritious because it was very rich in nitrogen. The question naturally arose whether it was a 'body-builder' or not. Before long the question of the nutritive value of osmazome came to be linked with the study of the food value of soups and meat extracts.

When flesh is boiled in water the proteins coagulate and so remain undissolved. If the clear watery broth is examined, however, it will be found that it contains quite an appreciable amount of nitrogen. Liebig discovered that this nitrogen is present partly as gelatin and partly in the form of compounds quite distinct in character from the proteins which form the bulk of the residue of the cooked meat. Had these nitrogen-containing compounds of which one was thought to be osmazome, any nutritive value?

One thing appeared certain to Liebig, that there must be something highly nutritious in broth because such people as the French peasants developed a good physique and lived healthy lives on simple diets of broth, potatoes and bread. Gelatin could apparently be ruled out, for Liebig accepted the view that, by itself, it possessed no 'tissue-forming' potentiality. Curiously enough, the fallacy that a soup which sets to a jelly on cooling is particularly nutritious is still quite widely held.

Finally, he came round to the view that the nitrogenous constituents of broth, including osmazome, do not contribute to the formation of tissues. He did not, on the other hand, dismiss them as worthless, because he was inclined to think that they sometimes exerted a stimulant action on appetite and on general tone which might prove beneficial. He came to the conclusion that the nutritive value of clear broths must be attributable to the mineral salts extracted from the meat.

> It cannot, therefore, be maintained that the loss of nutritive value in lixiviated flesh is caused by the removal of the soluble organic constituents of the juice; and we must consequently look for the cause of this phenomenon in the incombustible constituents of the soup or the juice of the flesh.[2]

These investigations led to the commercial exploitation of 'extract of meat'.

---

[1] *The Physiology of Digestion*, A. Combe, 4th Edition, 1842.
[2] *Familiar Letters on Chemistry*, J. v. Liebig, 4th Edition, 1858.

During the 'fifties, when the over-production of meat in South America and Australia was already becoming an embarrassment to the ranch owners, Liebig decided there was an opening for such a preparation. A process of manufacture was described by Liebig in 1847 but manufacture of the extract did not begin until seventeen years later when a factory was opened at Fray Bentos in Uruguay.

The appearance of 'Liebig's *Extractum Carnis*' on the market created a good deal of stir. The claim that 1 lb. contained the concentrated 'essence' of 36 lb. of meat and provided 'the basis for 128 men', naturally made a deep impression at a time when meat was dear and when it was by no means generally appreciated, even in medical circles, that clear soups were devoid of 'body-forming' qualities. Many people accepted the implication in the advertised claims that the meat extract provided the essential nutritive principles of meat in highly concentrated form.

Soon, however, adverse reports were coming in. One, which carried a good deal of weight, came from a committee of experts appointed by the Society of Arts in 1866 to 'enquire and report respecting the Food of the People'. It was their considered opinion that meat extracts of this type were not foodstuffs in the ordinary sense but that they might be regarded as 'nerve-stimulants'.[1] As the eminent physician and dietitian, Pavy, remarked, 'the fact that from thirty-four pounds of meat only one pound of extract is obtained, shows how completely the substance of the meat which constitutes its real nutritional portion must be excluded'.[2]

Liebig was very much annoyed by the attacks on his extract; he was particularly bitter about those who ignored his own claim that it provided the essential mineral salts of meat. Later in life, having this matter in mind, he wrote:

> The word of a wise man teaches me that if a person once does a thing which is good for the world, the world takes pains to see that that person does not do it a second time.[3]

During recent years it has been shown that meat extracts contain appreciable quantities of riboflavin and nicotinic acid[4] and that gelatin if suitably supplemented by other proteins, such as those of wheat, is useful for body-building purposes.[5]

---

[1] *Journal of the Society of Arts*, 1866, Vol. XV.
[2] *Digestion, its Disorders and Treatment*, F. W. Pavy, 1867.
[3] Cited by Graham Lusk in *A History of Metabolism* (undated, probably 1922).
[4] 'Nicotinic acid and riboflavin in beef extracts and corned beef', R. G. Booth and E. C. Barton-Wright, *Lancet* (1944), i, 565.
[5] 'Nutritive Value of Vegetable Protein and its Enhancement by Admixture', Harriette Chick, *Brit. J. Nutr.* (1951), V, 261.

§4 NITROGENOUS FOODS AND MUSCULAR WORK

For centuries past there has been a popular belief that violent muscular exercise calls for a large amount of meat foods. In the 'fifties of last century it seemed that scientific justification for this view had been found. Liebig was entirely to blame. He postulated the theory that when exercise is taken the substance of the muscles is used up. Very hard work would, therefore, make a serious call on the actual material of the muscles which would have to be made good from the proteins of the food.

> All experience proves, that this conversion of living muscular substance into compounds destitute of vitality is accelerated or retarded according to the amount of force employed to produce motion.[1]

There were few at that time who dared to challenge the opinion of the great Liebig, but one Englishman had the temerity to do so. Dr Edward Smith was deeply interested in the practical aspect of dietetics and particularly in the question of the amount of food needed by different types of individuals. In order to gain information on this question he carried out at Coldbathfields Penitentiary a very careful investigation of the food eaten by the prisoners, paying particular attention to the amount of nitrogen they obtained in their diet and the amount they excreted. Much to his surprise he found that the latter quantity had no relation whatever to the amount of muscular work the men performed. It was related solely to the amount of nitrogen in the food. Unfortunately, his observations attracted little attention at a time when few would listen to anyone but Liebig or his mouthpiece in England, Lyon Playfair.

In was not until 1889 that a convincing experiment made by two Zürich scientists, Fick and Wislicenus, showed that Smith had been right and Liebig wrong. The experiment consisted in climbing the Faulhorn, a peak of 6500 feet in the Bernese Oberland, while living on a diet containing no nitrogenous foods. The two men found that they excreted no more nitrogen during and immediately after this heavy exercise than when they were resting quietly. Their work led to the modern view, which is that the muscle is a machine that oxidizes carbohydrate, and performs its work by virtue of the energy which these oxidations make available.

Only in starvation is the actual substance of the muscles used up to some extent, but this occurs whether exercise is taken or not, and simply means that the body is living as best it can on its own reserves.

[1] *Animal Chemistry*, J. v. Liebig, Edited by William Gregory, 1842.

§ 5 DIET AND ATHLETICS

These remarks on the relation of diet to muscular exercise make it not inappropriate to refer to nineteenth-century ideas on the most suitable food for an athlete. The use of special diets in training seems to have been a natural development of the marked growth of interest in sport which began to be apparent in England towards the end of the eighteenth century. There are few references to it in books on diet until early in the next century, when mention is made of the foods which should be selected by pugilists, runners and jockeys.

A period of training for an athlete in those days always began with a series of good strong purges in order to clear away 'all the noxious matter he may have had in his stomach and intestines'.[1] After that a special diet was indicated. Nearly all experts advised a great deal of red meat, preferably underdone, and without any seasoning or sauces. Veal, lamb, poultry, fish, cheese, vegetables, milk, butter, pastry and puddings were all condemned, so the diet was essentially one of red meat and bread, which, all agreed, must be stale. Mild beer was regarded as a more suitable drink than wine.[2]

Captain Robert Barclay, the famous athlete, who gained considerable fame by walking 1000 miles in 1000 successive hours in 1809, lived during this period almost entirely on beef or mutton, consuming from five to six pounds daily.[3] This amount of meat alone would have provided him with well over 5000 Cal. daily; bread and other foods probably accounted for another 1000, giving in all over 6000. He was one of many who advocated a heavy meat diet for all athletes.

The exclusion of veal and fatty meats, pastry, new bread and cheese, was advocated on the grounds of their indigestibility, while milk, eggs and butter were thought insufficiently stimulating. Opinion was divided on the question of vegetables. According to Maclaren,[4] the Oxford crew in the 'sixties trained on a diet of underdone beef or mutton, bread, tea and beer, with a little jelly or watercress as a treat at the evening meal. Instructions were given that no vegetables were to be eaten. Cambridge, on the other hand, suffered no restrictions regarding potatoes, greens, or even fruit. From 1861 to 1869 there was an unbroken succession of Oxford victories. So much for vitamins in athletics!

The athlete's faith in a diet of underdone meat and other protein foods has survived to the present day. A study of the diets consumed by the competitors in the Berlin Olympic games in 1936 revealed that every man out of the

---

[1] *The Code of Health and Longevity*, 4th Edition, Sir J. Sinclair, 1818.
[2] *Peptic Precepts*, 3rd Edition, Anon., 1822.
[3] *Pedestrianism*, by the Author of *The History of Aberdeen* [W. Thom], 1813.
[4] *Training in Theory and Practice*, A. Maclaren, 1866.

4700 present, except a team of 8 vegetarians whose achievements are unfortunately not recorded, had a very large intake not only of protein but also of calories.[1] The average was 320 g. protein, 270 g. fat and 850 g. of carbohydrate, giving the surprisingly high calorific value of over 7000, that is, more than twice the ordinary individual's requirement. The heavyweight champions ate as much as 2¼ lb. of meat a day and often took, in addition, a quart of milk and 3 or 4 eggs. Apart from the vegetarians, the Japanese were the smallest meat-eaters, for they ate a mere pound and a half of lightly grilled beefsteak daily.

So far as we are aware there is no scientific foundation for the popular belief that an athlete needs a great deal of meat. He requires plenty of food providing energy and naturally it should be in a highly digestible and assimilable form. The idea that he must have large quantities of underdone red meats is an old one that has been passed on by generation after generation of trainers and which probably originated from the same type of primitive belief that led men to swallow powdered lions' teeth to make them strong.

A dose of glucose or cane-sugar is sometimes taken by athletes just before a burst of very violent effort, such, for example, as the 100 or 220 yards race. This practice is physiologically sound. The chief foodstuffs used by the muscles in work is glucose and it is not unreasonable to think that an increased efficiency over a short period might be favoured by increasing the amount of this sugar available for it is very rapidly absorbed and assimilated.

§ 6 EVALUATION OF HUMAN DIETS

Out of Liebig's classic work came the first scientific method of assessing quantitatively the nutritive values of diets. Such a method was sorely needed and the need was widely recognized. An article in the *Lancet* had called for the application to the problems of human food requirements of the 'elements of weight, and time, and number' so that there might come into existence a new branch of the science which had already been called by Count Rumford 'The Science of Nutrition'.

The new method was based on the improved methods of chemical analysis. With these it was possible to determine exactly how much carbon and nitrogen are lost by the body in respiration and excretion every twenty-four hours. Another series of analyses of mixture of foods would supply those amounts of carbon and nitrogen; it should be remembered that carbon was regarded as a measure of the heat-forming, and nitrogen as a measure of

[1] P. Schenck, *Münchner Medizinischer Wochenschrift*, 1936, Vol. LXXXIII.

the body-forming, value of the foods. For a number of years a great deal of attention was paid to the carbon and nitrogen content of foods and diets. The quantities were expressed in our own measures because the metric system had not then come into general use in scientific circles in England.

A lecture which Dr Lyon Playfair gave before the Royal Institution in 1853 reviewed the whole question and revealed how little was really known about the quantitative aspect of the requirements of man. He presented a large number of analyses and computations showing how much carbonaceous and nitrogenous foods different types of individuals ordinarily consumed but he certainly shared the view expressed by Sharpey, the father of English physiology, that 'we are sorely in want of trustworthy data to show the absolute quantities of carbon and nitrogen indispensable for health under different circumstances'. Here are a few of Playfair's estimates:

	Weight per week oz.	Nitrogenous ingredients oz.	Non-nitrogenous ingredients oz.	Carbon oz.	Ratio heat-givers to flesh-formers
English soldier	378	36.15	127.18	71.68	3.66
English sailor	302	34.82	102.89	70.55	3.70
Christ's Hospital	216	17.16	61.27	39.18	4.21
English prisons (Class II males)	206.5	15.28	111.85	59.23	7.13

One thing these early studies did was to reveal the uselessness of the old method of measuring the total quantity of food without any knowledge of its composition. Even John Dalton, who gave chemists their fundamental Atomic Theory, had attempted not long before to decide what food a man required by weighing and measuring very exactly all that he himself ate over a period of several days.[1] His record is perhaps of greater interest in showing the type of foods, particularly the large amount of milk, consumed by a young man of the professional class at the end of the eighteenth century, than in the information it gives about the requirements of the 'average man'.

Dr Letheby, who was associated with Hassall in the work of the *Lancet's* Analytical and Sanitary Commission, also made considerable contributions to the quantitative study of diets. A lecture he gave before the Society of Arts in 1857 contains the beginnings of our modern system of presenting food analyses.[2] He gave a list of foods showing the relative proportions of fibrin (protein), fat, 'carbonaceous matter' (starchy foods) and salts they each contained. Here are a few of his estimates of ordinary diets:

[1] 'A Series of Experiments on the Quantity of Food Taken by a Person in Health', etc., John Dalton, *Memoirs of the Literary and Philosophical Society of Manchester*, Vol. V, 1831.
[2] 'The Economy of Food', W. Letheby, *Journal of the Society of Arts*, 1857, Vol. V.

Diet	Daily allowance oz.		Respiratory elements oz.	Plastic elements oz.
Army	bread	24		
	meat	12	19.4	4.8
	potatoes	16		
Yorkshire labourer	bread	40		
	meat	19		
	potatoes	4	42.2	8.8
	milk	30		
	butter	7		
Prison (punishment diet)	bread	16	19.4	4.8

All these experts were concerned with one main question. How much food does man require to supply his physiological requirements? Letheby attempted to derive an estimate from the scanty information available at the time and suggested that an adult doing a moderate day's work needed foods supplying 12.7 oz. of carbon and 0.3 oz. of nitrogen. These amounts he calculated would be supplied by 20 oz. of bread, 12 oz. of meat and 8 oz. of butter (which would provide something over 4000 Cal.).

§ 7 ENERGY VALUE OF FOODS

Although Lavoisier had proved before the century opened that the combustion of food in the body is the source of animal heat, it was not until two Englishmen, Groves and Joule, had established that energy in the form of heat and energy expended as mechanical work are interconvertible that people began to grasp the significance of the energy value of foods.

It must be borne in mind that it was difficult for these early pioneers to form an impression of how the foods are 'burnt' or undergo combustion in the body. They had no idea of the complex mechanisms so extensively studied today, by which the organic constituents of foods are oxidized and it is not surprising that they thought in terms of simple oxidations which they could carry out in the chemical laboratory. Thus, for example, sugar is oxidized by treating it with a powerful chemical oxidizing agent such as potassium chlorate. If the oxidation is complete the carbon of the sugar is oxidized to carbon dioxide and the hydrogen to water, that is, to exactly the same products as are formed in the animal organism. Both oxidations proceed without the visible signs of combustion, so that to speak of foods being 'burnt' in the body is perhaps misleading.

Ideas on combustion were so primitive in the early nineteenth century that there were not a few educated people who believed that death sometimes occurred as a result of spontaneous combustion. Liebig devoted a whole chapter of his fascinating series of *Letters on Chemistry* to repudiating the belief that a person could suddenly burst into flames and be consumed without leaving any trace other than a greasy stain or a small pile of cinders.[1] Most of the stories related to heavy drinkers and they were invariably recounted by someone who knew someone who had actually seen the tragedy. There was never any lack of circumstantial detail, the pale blue light flickering round the victim's lips, the burst of flame, the failure of every effort to extinguish it and then, the pathetic little spot of grease or a few cinders, never by any chance a charred corpse or a blackened skeleton. What gave substance to such fables was the well-known fact that a bunch of oily rags or a pile of hay sometimes ignites by virtue of the heat generated by atmospheric oxidation.

Professor Frankland, the eminent chemist who did much pioneer work on the purification of London's water supply, made the first attempts to ascertain by experiment what are the energy values of foodstuffs. To do this he oxidized weighed samples of foods by means of potassium chlorate, carrying out the process in an enclosed vessel immersed in water. By measuring the rise in temperature of the water which resulted from the liberation of heat by the oxidation it was possible to calculate the value of the food as a source of energy in the body, the conversion of heat units to units of work being based on the fact, but recently discovered, that the heat required to raise the temperature of 1 lb. of water 1 degree Fahrenheit was equivalent to the work performed when 772 lb. is raised to a height of one foot. We can illustrate his findings by the results obtained for a typical protein, carbohydrate and fat.

Food	Degree F. rise in temperature of 1 lb. of water	Equivalent in work expressed as foot-pounds
10 grains of meat	13.12	10,128
10 grains of lump sugar	8.61	6,647
10 grains of butter	18.68	14,421

From such figures Letheby calculated that his diet of 20 oz. of bread, 12 oz. of meat and 8 oz. of butter would provide a man with energy equivalent to fourteen million foot-pounds. It seemed to him a very large amount to be liberated in the body, and after remarking that the hardest day's work

[1] *Familiar Letters on Chemistry*, J. v. Liebig, 4th Edition, 1858.

of a criminal in the treadmill demanded an expenditure of not more than two million foot-pounds, he said:

> It is clear that a large amount of motive force is otherwise disposed of than in the outward manifestations of work.

He surmised that some of the surplus was dissipated as heat while, doubtless, some was required for the work of the internal organs and for 'exercise of the brain'. It may be remarked, in passing, that the most careful modern investigations have failed to show that the human brain expends more energy when engaged in concentrated work than when, comparatively speaking, it is resting. As a student once naively put it in an oral examination, 'Brain workers do not require food'.

§ 8 RESPIRATION CHAMBERS

Quite early in the century the Académie des Sciences in Paris offered a prize for the best thesis on the subject of the origin of animal heat. It was awarded in 1823 to a young scientist named Despretz, but there was little to choose between his essay and that of the runner-up, Dulong. Both had made experimental studies and both had employed essentially the same procedure, which consisted in placing a small animal in a chamber so constructed that one could measure the heat produced, either directly by recording the rise in temperature of surrounding water or indirectly by measuring how much carbon dioxide was produced by respiration and then calculating how much heat its formation by the oxidation of the carbon represented. The value of the method was placed beyond all doubt a few years later when the results of experiments by two other Frenchmen, Regnault and Reiset, became known.

One of Liebig's students had the idea of constructing a similar chamber but large enough to hold a man and to provide space for him to move about and to carry out simple exercises if required. The chamber was to be enclosed except for two pipes, one admitting air and the other carrying away the products of respiration. The latter was so arranged that samples of the emergent gas could be analysed to ascertain the amount of carbon dioxide and water vapour it contained. In this manner it was possible, knowing the rate of flow of air through the apparatus, to determine exactly how much oxygen was used up and how much carbon dioxide and water were given off by the individual inside the chamber. The heavy cost of constructing the chamber was borne by Maximilian II of Bavaria and soon after its installation the first really accurate information about the energy requirements of man were being obtained.

It is unnecessary to give any detailed account of the researches of Voit and Pettenkofer, but it is important to refer to one outcome of their experiments, namely, the first scientific assessment of the food required by the normal adult. Before setting this out, however, it is necessary to remark that as a result of this Continental work it ceased to be customary in England to estimate the energy value of diets in terms of foot-pounds. Instead the calorie, a unit of the metric system, was adopted. The calorie is the amount of heat required to raise the temperature of one gram of water one degree Centigrade. Actually, for convenience, we use another 'calorie' in computing diets. The latter is often referred to merely as the Calorie, occasionally as the 'large calorie', but its correct name is the 'kilogram-calorie' because it corresponds to 1000 ordinary calories. Using the 'large calorie' does away with the necessity of expressing the calorie value of diets in figures running into millions.

Here is the diet which Voit and his colleague put forward as representing the needs of an ordinary man occupied during eight hours of the day in light work. For purposes of comparison we give estimates which also attracted attention at that time but which were based on less accurate data.

	Protein g.	Fat g.	Carbohydrate g.	Calories
Voit and Pettenkofer	118	56	500	3055
Moleschott	130	40	550	3160
Playfair	119	51	531	3140
Ranke	100	100	250	2355

From this it was a simple matter to carry the investigations further; to find that a day of hard physical work demanded, not extra protein as Liebig had imagined but more Calories, 4500 or perhaps as much as 5000; to discover a fact that had been responsible for an immense amount of hardship to children, namely that a boy of six requires at least half as much food as a fully grown man, while one of fourteen may need as much; to show that the expenditure of energy for adults is proportional to the area of the surface of their body or, for most practical purposes, to their weight. These, and a hundred other new facts of vital importance to human nutrition were revealed by the pioneer experiments in the Munich laboratory and later by other workers elsewhere: Rubner in Marburg, and Atwater and Lusk in the United States.

§ 9 THEORIES REGARDING THE ESSENTIALS OF DIET, 1891

As the century drew to a close the orthodox teaching on man's need for food could be expressed in the following manner. There were five *proximate principles* of foods. Three, proteins, fats and carbohydrates, were organic, and two, salts and water, were inorganic.[1] The proteins were nitrogenous compounds which served, after digestion, to supply the material from which the growing animal formed new tissues or the adult replaced 'wear and tear'. They could also serve to supply energy by oxidation if they were not used for tissue-building. The carbohydrates and fats were mainly of use as sources of energy; they were the fuel for the adipose tissue. The mineral salts comprised calcium and phosphoric acid, used for hardening bones and teeth, sodium and chlorides needed for the blood, iron to form red blood pigment, iodine for the functioning of the thyroid, and, less important, potassium and magnesium.

To this list some authorities added a category of 'accessories', in which were placed condiments, alcohol, caffeine, etc., which might influence nutrition by promoting appetite or stimulating the body in some other manner. By most these were regarded as useful rather than essential constituents of the diet, although there were some who held that without flavouring principles food would be so unpalatable that it would not be eaten in amounts sufficient to maintain health; in that sense these 'accessories' could be regarded as 'essentials'.

It will be observed that this scheme makes no mention of any such food substance as the curative antiscorbutic principle of fresh fruits, in spite of the hundreds of years of experience of the disease. The nutrition experts were so busy at the end of the century amassing quantitative data about the need for protein and calories that they seem to have had little or no time for any wider problems. Nevertheless, the vitamins were very nearly discovered in 1881. It was a logical deduction from the theory about the proximate principles, protein, fat, carbohydrate and salts, that an appropriate mixture of these should provide everything necessary for life. In an article which Voit wrote for a widely read textbook of physiology, he suggested that experiments of this character might be undertaken, but he was careful to point out that it would be advisable to use 'pure protein, fat, sugar, starch and mineral constituents'[2] instead of ordinary foods.

He seems to have suspected that there might be other substances in natural foods which play a necessary part and which could only be excluded by subjecting the recognized food components to adequate purification. After

---

[1] *Kirke's Handbook of Physiology*, 14th Edition, W. D. Halliburton, 1891.
[2] *Hermann's Handbuch der Physiologie*, 1881, Vol. VI, 'Author's translation'.

consideration of the matter, however, he rejected the idea of such experiments as being impracticable, on the grounds that any such food mixture would be so tasteless that no animal, much less a man, would eat it.

The problem was, however, attacked and, in fact, along almost the lines Voit had suggested, but with a different object. There was a good deal of interest about that time in the function in the body of the various mineral salts derived from the food. Professor Bunge, of the University of Basle, was particularly interested in this subject, and he encouraged a young Russian assistant, N. Lunin, to attempt to rear young mice on food mixtures which had been so purified that they contained very small residual traces of mineral salts. Not surprisingly, he found that they survived a very short time. He then tried the effect of adding various salts and observed that although the mice were able to live a little longer they did not thrive. Finally he added the whole of the mineral ash of milk, thinking that by so doing he would be supplying all the necessary minerals. To his surprise the results were no better. This was indeed astonishing, because he had taken great pains to compound his mixture of purified protein, fat, carbohydrate, so that it reproduced, as he thought, the composition of milk itself. Side by side with these cages of mice were others containing animals fed on milk itself. These animals flourished. The experiment was repeated and the same result was obtained.

> It is a noteworthy fact, although animals can live on milk alone, yet if all the constituents of milk which according to the present teaching of physiology are necessary for the maintenance of the organism be mixed together, the animals rapidly die. Cannot cane sugar take the place of sugar of milk? Or are the inorganic constituents of milk chemically combined and only assimilable in this combination? . . . Or does milk contain, in addition to protein, fat, carbohydrates, other organic substances, which are also indispensable to the maintenance of life?[1]

The writer adds, 'It would be worth while to continue the experiment'. Unfortunately he did not do so, or at any rate there is no record of any further experiments. He was on the very threshold of the discovery of the vitamins, for it was by almost identical experiments that twenty-five years later Pekelharing and Stepp and Hopkins independently got evidence of the existence of a new class of dietary essential.

[1] *Textbook of Physiological and Pathological Chemistry*, G. Bunge, 1890.

CHAPTER XXI

DIETS IN NINETEENTH-CENTURY INSTITUTIONS

§ 1 WORKHOUSES

It is hard to get a clear picture of the diet given to the inmates of pauper institutions before the passing in 1834 of the Poor Law Amendment Act. Some of them appear to have provided fairly liberal diets of bread, meat, pease-soup, suet dumplings and, sometimes, vegetables once or twice a week. Small beer was the usual drink. The weekly fare of the institution of the parish of St Anne's, Westminster, in 1823, can be taken as an example of this type of regime.

Sunday   7 oz. boiled beef or mutton, with vegetables. 1 pt. broth, 13 oz. bread and 2 pt. beer.

Monday   1 pt. milk pottage, 3 oz. butter, 3 oz. cheese, 13 oz. bread, 2 pt. beer.

Tuesday   7 oz. boiled beef or mutton, with vegetables. 1 pt. broth, 13 oz. bread and 2 pt. beer.

Wednesday 1 pt. pease soup. 13 oz. bread, 2 pt. beer.

Thursday   7 oz. boiled beef or mutton, with vegetables. 1 pt. broth, 13 oz. bread, and 2 pt. beer.

Friday   3 oz. butter, 3 oz. cheese, 1 pt. rice milk, 13 oz. bread and 2 pt. beer.

Saturday   1 pt. milk pottage, 12 oz. suet pudding, 13 oz. bread and 2 pt. beer.

Other records show that similar diets were by no means uncommon.

The Act of 1834 made a great change. The Commissioners on whose report the measure was based had throughout their deliberations kept prominently before them the need for drastic economy. Expenditure on relief had been mounting alarmingly under the old system, which had grown out of the Speenhamland practice of giving money to those in need of assistance. As the Commissioners had recommended that the paupers should be housed and fed in return for work done they were by no means disposed to be generous in respect to food, which was why they insisted that many of the diets provided in existing institutions were quite unnecessarily liberal — indeed, almost luxurious. This attitude led them to disregard the doctors who warned them that the health of the inmates might suffer if their diets were drastically reduced. They lent a much more attentive ear to Chadwick, the sanitary engineer, who informed them that the death rate was lowest in gaols where the prisoners were kept on a 'low diet', and in those days a 'low diet' was indeed 'low'. The Commissioners were supported by the politicians. Lord Radnor stated in a House of Lords Debate that a great deal of illness in the Dudley workhouse had been attributable to 'dyspepsia due to overfeeding'. Fortunately we have a record of the food in this institution. The inmates were getting rather less than 2000 Cal. a day, or two-thirds of their requirements. The *Lancet*, a youthfully outspoken and revolutionary journal, remarked caustically that no one had ever before suspected that such a diet would produce the fatal consequence of plethora.[1]

In the records of an age characterized by much smug hypocrisy on the part of the wealthy and well-fed governing classes, there is nothing so revolting as the frequency with which the opinion was expressed that the ills of the under-dog were due solely to his gross greed and extravagance.

> It was their high wages which enabled them . . . to pamper themselves into nervous ailments, by a diet too rich and exciting for their indoor employment.[2]

The *Lancet* played a big part in fighting the proposals to give a 'low diet' to paupers in the new workhouses. Lord Radnor had ventured the opinion in the House of Lords that the effect of withdrawing meat from the diet would be 'altogether miraculous'. The *Lancet* scathingly replied that doubtless the noble Lord would also 'rejoice to see the benefits which would result by reducing the wages of a labourer with a big family to 7/- a week'. The scorn poured by the *Lancet* on those who ignored medical opinion regarding these diets was only equalled by the disgust which it expressed about the official indifference of the College of Physicians and the College of Surgeons: 'If that sated Vampire flap its wings, the effort is never to arouse or invigorate.'

Whatever may have been the truth about the feeding of paupers in the institutions which existed before 1834, there is no doubt whatever that for a good many years after that date the inmates were half-starved on diets composed largely of bread, gruel and thin unnourishing soups. It was bad enough for adults, but young boys and girls were also sent to these dismal places. Oliver Twist was only nine when he was sent to a workhouse.

> The room in which the boys were fed, was a large stone hall, with a copper at one end: out of which the master . . . ladled the gruel at meal-

---

[1] *Lancet*, February 24th, 1838.
[2] *The Philosophy of Manufactures*, A. Ure, 1835.

times. Of this festive composition each boy had one porringer, and no more — except on occasions of great public rejoicing, when he had two ounces and a quarter of bread besides. The bowls never wanted washing. The boys polished them with their spoons till they shone again; and when they had performed this operation (which never took very long, the spoons being nearly as large as the bowls), they would sit staring at the copper, with such eager eyes, as if they could have devoured the very bricks of which it was composed; employing themselves, meanwhile, in sucking their fingers most assiduously, with the view of catching up any stray splashes of gruel that might have been cast thereon. Boys have generally excellent appetites. Oliver Twist and his companions suffered the tortures of slow starvation for three months.[1]

The plight of these children was not entirely due to the heartlessness of the Government or the callousness of the workhouse Masters, most of whom, it is true, were ignorant, dishonest and sadistic brutes. Ignorance of the fact that young children need much more food than their size leads one to think was in part responsible.

It is probable that during the first half of the century the inmates of charitable institutions in the north of England fared better than those in the south. Potatoes and other vegetables figure more prominently in their diet sheets and milk was an important item. Up to the turn of the century these foods were probably more easily obtained in the north than in the south. The following dietary was in use in 1839 at the Northern Counties Institution for the Deaf and Dumb, at Newcastle-upon-Tyne.

BREAKFAST — AT EIGHT A.M.

Sunday	Bread and Tea.
Monday Wednesday Friday	Milk Pottage and Bread.
Tuesday Thursday Saturday	A Pint of New Milk with Bread.

DINNER — AT ONE P.M.

Sunday	Meat Pudding, and Potatoes.
Monday	Soup, with Bread.
Tuesday	Beef and Potatoes.

[1] *Oliver Twist*, Charles Dickens, 1838.

Wednesday   Boiled Rice (sweetened), and Bread and Cheese.
Thursday   Boiled Mutton and Potatoes.
Friday   Mutton Broth, with Vegetables and Bread.
Saturday   Irish Stew.

SUPPER — AT HALF-PAST FIVE P.M.

Bread and Milk every Evening, except Sunday, when Coffee is given instead of Milk.

§ 2 PRISON DIETS

The conditions in English prisons in the early part of the nineteenth century almost baffle description, but of all the hardships the prisoners had to suffer none was worse than the inadequacy and the dreadful quality of the food. It was very rare to find such a prison as the Gloucester County Gaol, where the diet was passably good, at all events on paper. There prisoners were given 1½ lb. of bread and 1½ oz. of oatmeal for gruel every day. In addition there was ¾ lb. of beef and 1 lb. of potatoes for dinner on Sundays and Thursdays, thick pease soup on Mondays and Fridays, 1½ oz. of rice and 1½ oz. of oatmeal on Wednesdays, and 2 lb. of potatoes and ¼ lb. of cheese on the remaining days.[1] (See Appendix A.)

In most gaols, however, the diet was composed chiefly of bread and thin gruel or broths and the inmates were indeed lucky if once or twice in a week they got a small piece of meat or cheese. It is not surprising that a large proportion of the prisoners in these gaols fell sick on these diets and that outbreaks of scurvy, dysentery and other epidemics were common, particularly when potatoes were not included.[2] There are most instructive records for Millbank penitentiary for this period.

Before 1822 the diet was reasonably good. Male prisoners were given bread and gruel for breakfast and supper, and for dinner 6 oz. of beef with potatoes on four days in the week, and vegetable soup on the other three. The quantities provided about 115 g. of protein, of which 15 to 20 g. was of animal origin, and nearly 3500 Cal. daily. The fairly liberal allowance of potatoes (1 lb. daily) and other vegetables provided adequate protection against scurvy. In the summer of 1822 the authorities, apparently at the instigation of Sir James McGrigor, decided that the diet was too liberal and cut out both the meat and potatoes. The new diet adopted for male prisoners was as follows:

[1] *The Gaol of the City of Bristol compared with what a gaol ought to be, by a citizen, with an Appendix giving a brief account of the Panopticon, or prison upon a new plan proposed by the Government, 1815.* (Jeremy Bentham.)
[2] *Report of the Committee of Aldermen appointed to visit several gaols in England, 1816.*

In the morning   ¾ lb. Bread and 1 pt. Gruel for the Males; 9 oz. Bread and ¾ pt. Gruel for the Females.

At Noon   ¾ lb. Bread and 1 pt. Soup for the Males; 9 oz. Bread and ¾ pt. Soup for the Females.

In the Evening   1 pt. Soup for the Males and ¾ pt. for the Females.[1]

At a generous estimate this gave the men 2000 Cal. daily. There was very little nourishment in the soup, as the following recipe shows.

> The Soup to be made with ox-heads, in lieu of other Meat, in the proportion of 1 ox-head for about 100 Male Prisoners, and the same for about 120 Female Prisoners, and to be thickened with Vegetables and Pease, or Barley, either weekly or daily as may be found most convenient.

Although the Committee could 'at their discretion' substitute 1 lb. of potatoes for ½ lb. of bread, as a precaution against scurvy, it seems that the order was seldom if ever given.

In the late autumn of 1822 the health of the prisoners began to decline and by February of the following year scurvy was causing trouble. In one fortnight the number of cases among about 850 prisoners increased from 53 to 118. When one of the medical officers, Dr Roget, made an inspection two months later he found no less than 448 prisoners with scorbutic symptoms visible on their limbs. In addition, nearly 150 were suffering from dysentery. Dr Latham, who had been called in in March to give medical assistance, gave it as his opinion that the principal cause of the sickness was 'deficient quantity of nutrition in the diet ordered in July last'. On his instructions the prisoners were given 4 oz. of solid meat, 8 oz. of rice and 3 oranges a day. He also advised that the men should be given good white bread instead of coarse brown loaves. This, he thought, would benefit the severe diarrhoea from which so many of the prisoners were suffering.[2]

The scurvy soon cleared up after this change of diet, and subsequently, as a result of the inquiries made by the Select Committee appointed in 1824 to consider this serious outbreak of disease, the prisoners were given 6 oz. of meat, potatoes instead of gruel for dinner, and a quarter of a pint of milk mixed with an equal quantity of water and flour.

The point that must be stressed is that the selection of these diets was largely a question of guesswork. Latham thought, and he was right, that the prisoners were underfed and needed antiscorbutics, but other experts giving evidence at the inquiry did not share this view. Hutchinson, the penitentiary doctor, was one of them. He believed the sickness to have been caused by the diet being so 'full' that it made the inmates lethargic.

[1] *Report from the Select Committee on the State of the Penitentiary at Millbank,* 1824.
[2] *An Account of the Disease lately Prevalent at the General Penitentiary,* P. M. Latham, 1825.

In 1835 the scandalous state of affairs in prisons all over the country led to the appointment of a Committee of the House of Lords, but the recommendations which resulted from their deliberations did not bring about any significant improvement in the prisoners' diet. In 1842, Peel's Home Secretary, Sir James Graham, instructed his inspectors to make a survey covering this question, and on receiving their reports he proceeded to draw up a group of rations for the different categories of prisoners. In doing this he was guided by a 'principle' which is set out below and which was an entirely new aspect of prison treatment.

'The principle' which we are of opinion ought to be acted on in framing a scale of prison diet, and that which we have endeavoured to carry into effect as far as possible in the annexed scale, is that that quantity of food should be given in all cases which is sufficient and not more than sufficient, to maintain health and strength, at the least possible cost; and that, whilst due care should be exercised to prevent extravagance or luxury in a prison, the diet ought not to be made an instrument of punishment . . . We are of opinion that there ought to be three meals each day in prison, and that at least two of the three should be hot.[1]

Considerable stress was laid on the desirability of giving prisoners a greater proportion of *solid* food, for in the opinion of the experts much of the illness which had decimated prison populations had been caused by too much 'slops', such as gruel and broths. The diets finally adopted are given below.

I. WITHOUT HARD LABOUR (per week)

	CLASS I Less than 7 days	CLASS II 7 days to 21	CLASS III 21 days to 4 months	CLASS IV More than 4 months
Bread	112	168	140	168
Potatoes	—	—	64	32
Meat	—	—	6	12
Total solid food	112	168	210	212
	pints	pints	pints	pints
Soup	—	—	2	3
Gruel	14	14	14	14
Cocoa	—	—	—	—
Total liquid food	14	14	16	17

[1] *Home Secretary's Circular*, January 24th, 1843.

II. WITH HARD LABOUR (per week)

	CLASS II 7 to 21 days	CLASS III 21 days to 6 weeks	CLASS IV 6 weeks to 4 months	CLASS V More than 4 months
Bread	168	140	168	154
Potatoes	—	64	32	112
Meat	—	6	12	16
Total solid food	168	210	212	282
	pints	pints	pints	pints
Soup	1	2	3	3
Gruel	14	14	14	11
Cocoa	—	—	—	3
Total liquid food	15	16	17	17

The diets were generally regarded with approval as representing a great advance. In actual fact the total amount of solid food had not been appreciably raised, except in the case of the long term sentences.

One important innovation was the provision of potatoes. It was promptly followed by the disappearance of scurvy from the gaols. On the other hand, the diets were seriously inadequate. It was partial starvation for a fully grown man to live for three weeks on 1 lb. of bread and 2 pints of thin gruel daily, providing less than 1500 Cal. Sir James Graham and his advisers did not know this, nor did they suspect that the loss of weight and weakness shown by convicts forced to carry out hard labour on a diet providing only 2000 Cal., two-thirds of what we regard as necessary for an individual doing a light day's work, was due to underfeeding. They thought the decline was an inevitable result of confinement. It must also be borne in mind that, lacking any accurate information about the food requirements of man and being forced to base their rations largely on guesswork, the authorities not only kept a sharp eye on expense but were also influenced to no little extent by the prevailing view that to show liberality in the provision of food would inevitably provoke an outburst of crime. Mr Merry, a visiting Justice of the model prison at Reading, clearly expressed this widely held fear.

If they wished imprisonment to deter from crime, they must cease to supply an excessive diet as to afford temptation to a poor man to commit crime in order to get into prison.[1]

[1] Quoted by E. Smith, *Journal of the Society of Arts*, 1864, Vol. XII.

Apparently the prisoners themselves preferred the quality of the new diets but were doubtful whether they were getting more than they had formerly received.

There is evidence to show that it was not long before the new diets were disregarded by many of the prison authorities. The meat, in particular, was often dispensed with. On some occasions when potatoes were not given, as for example during the time of the famine in 1845-46, there were bad recurrences of scurvy. Within a few years conditions seem to have deteriorated and in 1863 the House of Lords, responding to a widespread feeling of uneasiness, appointed another Committee to look into the matter. This time it was possible to call in scientific advice about the amount of food needed by prisoners and the Committee started well by inviting Dr Edward Smith to guide them.

He was able to give them the latest information available, having just completed a very careful investigation on the feeding of the prisoners in the well-known penitentiary in Coldbathfields. Apparently this investigation had been undertaken at the request of a Committee of the British Association. There he had weighed and measured the food and drink consumed by individual prisoners, and had also weighed and analysed their excreta so as to determine how much of the nitrogen derived from their food was lost from the body every day. From these investigations he had formed a good idea of the amounts of carbonaceous and nitrogenous foods needed. For example, from experiments on himself he had ascertained that the amount of carbon dioxide exhaled from the lungs was just under 5 grains per minute during sleep, nearly 26 grains when walking at a speed of 3 miles an hour, and no less than 45 grains when working at the treadmill. This taught him that the amount of carbonaceous food burnt in the body is increased considerably by exercise. He had already reported to the British Association Committee that 'the food supplied to the convict scale is so totally unequal to the wants of the system, that it can only be regarded as an instrument of punishment'. This Committee fully supported his contention and added the comment that 'a diet of bread and water or bread and gruel cannot be enforced without doing severe injury to the prisoner's health'.[1]

One of the most interesting observations Smith made during this practical study of prison diets concerned the nutritive value of skimmed milk.

> The effect of milk in arresting loss of weight was most striking, and in a degree far beyond that of the relation of its nutritive elements to the waste of the system. Thus the addition ... of only ¼ pt. of skimmed milk, containing not more than 7 grains of nitrogen, to the daily

[1] *British Association Report*, 1861.

dietary, resulted in a reduction in the extra diets (used only for cases losing weight) of 22.55 per cent in 1853.

To one accustomed to think of nutritional problems in terms of Liebig's views on the function of the nitrogenous 'plastic elements of nutrition' it was puzzling to find that a food so poor in nitrogen apparently had so marked an effect on weight.

The House of Lords Committee had been instructed by the Home Secretary to bear in mind the desirability that prison diets should not contrast favourably with the meals of a free labourer. They were inclined to think that Sir James Graham's 1843 diets for Classes I and II were a hardship, but, on the other hand, they rather frowned on the cocoa provided in Class v as an unjustifiable luxury.

Smith prepared a great deal of informative evidence for this Committee, most of it based on the new ideas regarding man's need for carbon and nitrogen. He was satisfied that it was impossible for a man to do hard labour at the crankwheel or treadmill on an intake of just over 4800 grains of carbon. A man's health would soon fail if he were made to do heavy work on the treadmill on a diet providing only 3150 Cal., whereas the higher figures represent energy intakes which would permit a reasonable amount of that labour.

Unfortunately, the Committee did not pay much attention to Smith's valuable advice. They were inclined to be suspicious of the new scientific outlook and to doubt whether science could really throw light on such a question as man's need for food. He could not convince them that the loss of weight in prison meant that the prisoners were underfed or ill. They preferred to keep to the old view that it was an inevitable consequence of confinement. So in spite of all Smith's proffered help they set to work and drew up a series of diets by the age-old method of guesswork.

DIETARY PROPOSED BY SELECT COMMITTEE[1]

			CLASS I oz.	CLASS II oz.	CLASS III oz.	CLASS IV oz.	CLASS V oz.
Breakfast	Every day	Bread	6	6	8	8	8
		Gruel	—	1 pt.	1 pt.	1 pt.	1 pt.
Supper	Every day	Bread	6	6	6	8	8
		Gruel	—	—	1 pt.	1 pt.	1 pt.

[1] *Parliamentary Papers*, 1864, xlix, 618.

			CLASS I oz.	CLASS II oz.	CLASS III oz.	CLASS IV oz.	CLASS V oz.
Dinner	Sundays	Bread	8	8	10	10	12
		Cheese	—	1	2	3	3
	Mondays	Bread	6	6	4	4	4
	Wednesdays	Potatoes	—	—	12	16	16
	Fridays	Suet Pudding	—	—	8	12	12
		Indian Meal Pudding	6	8	—	—	—
	Tuesdays	Bread	6	6	8	8	8
	Thursdays	Potatoes	8	12	8	8	16
	Saturdays	Soup	—	—	¾ pt.	1 pt.	1 pt.

Food of female prisoners apportioned on the principle of deducting 1-16th from weight of man to, and deducting ¼ from, articles of food served in solid form.

Hard labour men to receive extra cheese, gruel, and meat.

Smith was afraid that the new diets would mean that the prisoners got even less nourishment than under the old scheme, but more by luck than by any judgment on the part of the Committee, they were a slight improvement so far as protein and calories were concerned.

	SMITH'S ESTIMATES[1]		OUR CALCULATIONS	
	grains carbon	grains nitrogen	Cal.	g. protein
1843				
Class III diet	4200	189	2100	70
1864				
Class III diet	3500	126	2450	80

In the sense that none of the diets came anywhere near the level of intake of 'ordinary working people', Smith was justified in remarking that 'the late enquiry has left the whole question practically as I found it'.[2] These intakes Smith assessed as follows:

	Grains per day	
	carbon	nitrogen
Farm labourer	6470	300
Yorkshire labourer	11,590	570
Lancashire operatives	5900	185-250

[1] *Journal of the Society of Arts*, 1864, Vol. XII.   [2] Ibid.

CHAPTER XXII

DETERIORATION OF PHYSIQUE

§ I THE FEEDING OF CHILDREN

THE nineteenth century saw a marked decline, particularly noticeable among the working people of the towns, in breast-feeding of children. It also occurred to no inconsiderable extent among the more prosperous classes of the community. There were many causes. An important one affecting the poorer people was the increasing employment of women in factories. It also seems probable that the hard conditions of life, particularly during the bad periods, were responsible for a great many women being unable to nourish their children naturally. In former times most of these infants would have died, but as the nineteenth century passed an increasing proportion was successfully reared by artificial means. The century is also marked by a steady rise in the proportion of mothers in comfortable circumstances who from disinclination or inability to feed their children at the breast attempted to rear them by the bottle in preference to handing them over to a wet-nurse. The latter went steadily out of fashion as the century progressed, in spite of the doctors who still advocated breast-feeding as the only really satisfactory means of bringing up a child.

It was not long before the new method of chemical analysis were applied to the study of the composition of milk. Then it began to be apparent why milks of different species have different nutritive qualities. The new discoveries were so welcome that not infrequently enthusiasm for them led people astray. In 1842, for example, a French scientist, l'Heritier, reported that he had analysed the milk of a blonde woman and that of a brunette and found the latter to be the more nutritious. Many people accepted his conclusion without question, although it was based on nothing more substantial than a single and rather crude analysis of each type of milk. Even the eminent London physician Pavy, who was a leading expert on diet and much more scientifically minded than the majority of his profession, believed it.

When the century opened the death-rate among children, especially in the towns, was still very high. Dr Davis writing in 1817 said there was practically no medical attention at that time for mothers and young children; many hospitals would not admit a child under the age of two. Davis carefully recorded the fate of the children born to mothers who had attended his 'Universal Dispensary for Children' over a period of 15 years; 178 out of 413 (about 43 per cent) died under the age of 12.[1] He regarded improper feeding after weaning as the chief cause of the high mortality. Many of them, according to him, were given bad potatoes and half-cooked vegetables by their ignorant and poverty-stricken mothers.

Until quite late in the century, when condensed milks became of importance in the feeding of infants, the substitutes for mothers' milk were much the same as those used in the latter part of the eighteenth century. Contemporary practices about 1839 are fully described by Dr Andrew Ure. The most popular food was cows' milk and water. If this did not agree with the infant, skimmed milk with a little arrowroot, or diluted with barley water, was often tried. Ure was a staunch believer in the feeding bottle.

> In rearing by hand, the liquid food ought to be sucked out of one of the flattened glass bottles made on purpose; to the mouth of which is to be attached an artificial teat, made of softened parchment or washleather, inclosing a small conical piece of sponge.[2]

He drew attention to the need for keeping the bottle sweet and clean, but as absolutely nothing was then known of sterilization it is difficult not to believe that it, or more particularly the 'teat', was more often than not a death-trap. The Lancet for 1838 provides grim evidence of this. It reported that one of the French hospitals had tried the new method for feeding its orphan infants; 'all those who are received are nourished by hand through a suckling-bottle.'[3] Of 382 infants fed in this manner, 297 (about 78 per cent) died before they were a year old. Apparently the French hospital authorities thought this rather encouraging. The industrial use of rubber dates from about the middle of the century. It was in 1856 that an 'india-rubber valve' for use as an attachment to feeding-bottles was patented by V. Scully and B. J. Heywood (No. 115). This was the prototype of the modern teat.

Another cause of infant mortality was the widespread custom among the poor of giving infants spirits, beer or nostrums containing opiates, to keep them quiet.[4] It is clear from medical writings that this habit was still very prevalent over much of the country. The doctors also condemned another practice, namely, that of chewing food before putting it in the baby's mouth. It seems to have been suspected, fifty years before the germ theory of

---

[1] *A Cursory Enquiry into some of the Principal Causes of Mortality among Children*, J. B. Davies, 1817.
[2] *A Practical Compendium of the Materia Medica . . . adapted to the Treatment of the Diseases of Infancy and Childhood*, Andrew Ure, Enlarged Edition, 1839.
[3] *Lancet*, 1838.
[4] *The Family Oracle of Health*, Vol. I, 1824.

infection, that it might be a means of communicating disease.[1] This practice is still commonly reported from primitive communities.

In the earlier part of the century asses' milk was still in some demand both as a substitute for mothers' milk in rearing infants and for invalids. That curious compendium, *The Family Oracle of Health*, gave a revolting recipe for preparing an 'artificial asses milk' to be used in cases of consumption.

> Bruise eighteen garden snails, with
>   one ounce of hartshorn shavings,
>   one ounce of eryngo-root,
>   one ounce of pearl-barley. Boil these in
>   six pints of water down to half the quantity. Add
>   one ounce and a half of syrup of tolu.
>
> Take four ounces, morning and evening, mixed with four ounces of fresh milk from the cow. The snails may be omitted, or their use concealed from the patient.[2]

Liebig's researches on the chemistry of foods had both a direct and an indirect influence on the artificial feeding of children. Indirect, by virtue of the new views on the need for carbon, nitrogen and other nutritive principles to which his work gave rise, and direct, because he himself devised and marketed a patent infant food. He was the first to point out that a substitute for mothers' milk should have a composition as nearly identical with that milk as possible. This immediately revealed the defects of many of the mixtures, such as diluted milk and arrowroot, then in vogue. He emphasized the importance of the nitrogenous constituents of the diet for the building up of the tissues of a growing child.

> A deficiency of elements productive of warmth can be made up by a surplus of ingredients producing blood; but then this surplus loses its faculty of increasing corporeal weight. Elements producing warmth are unable to produce blood; if the surplus exceeds the just proportion, it loses its efficacy.[3]

With these ideas in mind he devised a formula for a 'perfect' infant food. It was a mixture of wheat flour, cows' milk and malt-flour, cooked with a little bicarbonate of potash, which he added to reduce the 'acidity' of the wheat and malt flour, Magendie having shown that wheat contains an 'acid phosphate' which requires alkali for its neutralization. Actually the idea was

[1] Ibid., Vol. IV, 1826.
[2] Ibid., Vol. I, 1824.
[3] *A Food for Infants: A complete substitute for that provided by Nature*, J. v. Liebig, 1867.

not entirely novel, because in 1862 an Englishman named Ridge had taken out a patent (No. 2891) for preparing infants' food from cooked flour to which sugar and bicarbonate of potash were added. It was sold as a powder and was entirely farinaceous. Such foods Liebig rightly condemned as unsuitable for infants and for this reason he included milk in his own formula.

The preparation of Liebig's food was commercialized in England by 'Liebig's Registered Concentrated Milk Co. Ltd.' of Tichborne Street, Regents Quadrant, who held a patent taken out with Liebig's approval by the Baroness Leisner-Ebersberg. They undertook to deliver the liquid 'milk' ready for use, at the price of 6d. a quart, which was only a 'trifle' higher than that of ordinary milk. Later, when the sale of this failed to come up to expectation, a dried preparation of somewhat similar type but containing less milk and some pea flour was manufactured. This, too, seems to have been a failure. Liebig was considerably annoyed by the doctors who reported that his food was indigestible or who doubted whether it was the counterpart of mothers' milk. In one statement he quoted the opinion of Dr Hecker, a German Court physician and Director of a large lying-in hospital. There is a typically Teutonic mentality behind the argument.

> For instance, if we were to say that this preparation does not agree with new-born babes, such a statement could not be supported on theoretical grounds, since *in the food they get the very same ingredients as in mothers' milk*. As therefore this milk agrees with them, I cannot understand why they should be unable to digest Liebig's Food.[1]

Ridge's and Liebig's foods were the forerunners of a large number of proprietary preparations for infants which appeared on the market during the next twenty years or so. A large proportion of them were preponderantly farinaceous, that is, they consisted of flour, starch, malted flour and similar materials. They were responsible for an appalling amount of sickness and malnourishment because they were deficient not only in protein and fat, but in most of the vitamins. The children of the more prosperous classes were most affected by these badly compounded preparations, for they were too expensive for the working people. The trouble was that children fed on these foods, which were usually, it is true, mixed with a certain amount of milk, grew in a deceptively encouraging manner. Indeed, they usually put on weight too well. At two or three years they were overweight for their age but pale, fat and, flabby. Almost invariably they developed mild rickets, usually undetected, and in later life their teeth were affected.

Another serious deficiency of these infant foods, which was not recognized

---

[1] *A Food for Infants*, J. v. Liebig, 1867.

at the time, was of vitamin C. They were undoubtedly responsible for a very large amount of scurvy or prescorbutic disorders, the existence of which was not suspected until the last quarter of the century when two London physicians, W. B. Cheadle and Thomas Barlow, revealed the fact. Cheadle was a firm believer in the need for a properly balanced mixture of proteins, fats and carbohydrates in the young child's diet. It was he, more than anyone else, who directed the attention of doctors to the harmful effects of too large a proportion of carbohydrates and especially of too much starch.

He was convinced that the prevalence of rickets was due largely to the increasing use of artificial infant foods rich in starch or malted flour.[1] In 1878 he reported the occurrence of scorbutic symptoms in children already showing rickets as the result of improper feeding,[2] and there was no doubt in his own mind that they were due to lack of 'an essential factor' in the food. Five years later Barlow published a paper, now regarded as a classic in the literature on scurvy, in which convincing proof was given that infants may suffer from this disease.[3] This was regarded at that time as a new and very important discovery, though Glisson had given a good description of the condition, which came to be known in England as infantile scurvy and abroad as Barlow's disease, in his original work on rickets published in 1650.

About 1870 condensed milk in tins came on the market in considerable amounts and it was a cheap food its consumption rapidly increased. It was used in large quantities for feeding infants and young children. The cheapest variety, and therefore the one purchased in the largest quantities by the poorer people, was made by evaporating skimmed milk to which a considerable proportion of sugar had been added. It was, therefore, almost devoid of fat and of the vitamins A and D associated with the fat. The doctors soon began to suspect that it was not such a good food as it was supposed to be.

In 1875 Dr Daly wrote to the *Lancet* pointing out that while children grew fat on this milk and 'looked well', he had reasons for thinking that their vitality was reduced 'below par to a very dangerous degree'. He drew particular attention to the frequency with which they showed the characteristic symptoms of rickets. There was soon a great deal of uneasiness about the nutritive value of these condensed skimmed milks, and in 1894 the whole question was fully discussed by the Select Committee on Food Products Adulteration. Shortly afterwards legislation was introduced making it compulsory for containers of this type of condensed skimmed milk to

---

[1] *The Artificial Feeding and Food Disorders of Infants*, W. B. Cheadle, 1889.
[2] *Lancet* (1878), ii.
[3] *Medical and Chirurgical Transactions*, 1883, Vol. LXVI; also *Lancet* (1894), ii.

carry a label clearly stating its character and that it was not suitable for feeding infants and young children.

Unfortunately, as a report published seventeen years later showed, this precaution did not have the full effect that was desired.[1] It was discovered that partly from poverty and partly from ignorance many mothers were continuing to use this type of condensed milk as food for their babies. Inquiries showed that many women had no idea that the designation 'machine-skimmed', which the label had to bear, implied impoverishment.

The discovery, or rather the rediscovery, of 'infantile scurvy' by Cheadle and Barlow was a very important event and was responsible for saving many young lives. It came at a time when there was a craze among educated people for sterilization. Pasteur's ideas on the role of micro-organisms in the causation of disease were spreading fast and people saw infection at every turn. Water must be boiled, milk must be 'scalded' and, most important of all, no precaution could be too great to ensure that baby's food was 'sterilized'. It is for this reason that so many cases of scurvy occurred, particularly among the infants and young children of wealthy people, in the last decade or so of the century. It is an interesting fact that it is rare to find scorbutic symptoms, even of the mildest character, in an infant fed at the breast. If the mother is well nourished they are never seen, because woman's milk contains up to 3 mg. of ascorbic acid per oz., depending on the character of her diet. In a study made in Reading and Shoreditch during the Second World War the ascorbic acid content of samples of human milk from 1499 women showed that there were considerable variations between individuals and for the same woman at different times. There were marked seasonal variations, from 0.6 mg. per oz. in the early spring of 1942-43 to 1.3 in the summer of 1943-44.[2] Cows' milk is much less rich in vitamin C, there being seldom as much as 0.6 mg. per oz. and often only half that amount. A child reared on raw cows' milk requires, therefore, extra vitamin, which in modern practice is usually given in the form of orange, or other fruit juice. Cows' milk, at its best a very poor antiscorbutic, suffers a considerable loss on boiling, the values falling to as low as 0.25-0.1 mg. per oz.

Although Cheadle had no suspicion of the existence of an antiscorbutic vitamin he did deduce from his own observations that the boiling of milk caused a marked loss of such antiscorbutic properties as it possessed in the raw state.[3] It was he who first advocated the use of fruit juice in the nursery

[1] 'Report on Condensed Milks, with special reference to their use as Infants' Foods', F. J. H. Coutts, Local Government Board Report, New Series, No. 56, 1911.

[2] 'Human Milk', S. K. Kon and E. H. Mawson, Medical Research Council, Special Report Series, No. 269, 1950.

[3] The Artificial Feeding and Food Disorders of Infants, W. B. Cheadle, 1889.

and thus put an end to some of the worries of Mayfair and Belgravia, where such elaborate precautions were being taken to protect the babies from typhoid and other infectious diseases.

The widespread adoption of 'patent' foods and condensed milks for the artificial rearing of infants and young children was also responsible for much 'infantile scurvy', for these foods were almost completely deficient in anti-scorbutic vitamin. In one investigation of 379 cases no less than 214 were traced to the use of proprietary infant foods.[1]

It is interesting that the age-old belief that fruit and vegetables are bad for children lingered on almost to the end of the century. It was finally killed by the demonstration that the 'summer diarrhoeas' and similar complaints, which had always been attributed to the 'corrupting influence' of fruit, were diseases of bacterial origin.

§ 2 RICKETS

As we have already stated there is surprisingly little information about the prevalence of rickets in England in the eighteenth century, in spite of the probability that it became very common in the larger towns in the second half, when industrialization was rapidly spreading and when the standard of living was falling. When we come to the first half of the nineteenth century we are left in no doubt. There is clear evidence that the disease was rife in all the poorer parts of the towns. It is a surprising fact, however, that this is much more strikingly revealed by the writings of those who were concerned about the terrible conditions under which the poor lived than by the medical literature. The doctors seem to have been curiously little interested. There is an occasional casual reference to the inadvisability of letting a child walk too soon or to the necessity for good nursing if rickets is to be avoided, but there is little indication that the profession recognized that the disorder was fast becoming a national scourge. Indeed, in the very early part of the century a good many of its members seem to have comforted themselves by accepting the figures of the Bills of Mortality as evidence that the disease had almost disappeared.[2] For thirty years or more after the *Lancet* was founded in 1823 its pages contain but rare references to rickets, and this at a time of almost unprecedented malnutrition. It is true that there are many articles dealing with the prevalence of bent limbs and curved spines in northern manufacturing towns but it is seldom suggested that rickets was responsible. The explanation usually given was

[1] Cited by L. E. Holt in *The Diseases of Infancy and Childhood*, 1900.
[2] *The Family Oracle of Health*, Vol. IV, 1826.

that it was due to long hours of standing in the factories. In 1841, for example, several letters were written to the Editor drawing attention to curious cases of softening of the bones leading to distortion without fracture. Most of these correspondents had observed that it was nearly always the poor children who were affected, but it did not seem to occur to them that it might be a condition related to rickets. Others noted that a large proportion of poor working-class women suffered from a malformed pelvis or bad curvature of the spine, but this, again, was put down to long hours of factory work. The same cause was blamed for the anaemic and menstrual disturbances from which so many of them suffered. Remedial exercises were suggested, to harden the bones. 'Invalids have soft bones, soldiers have hard ones'.[1]

It must not be thought that all these common deformities were due to rickets. Tubercular infection was rife among the ill fed poor and a great many cripples owed their misfortune to this. A very considerable proportion of this type of tubercular trouble was due to infected milk; the conditions under which cows were then kept made it highly probable that every drop was heavily charged with the organisms responsible for bovine tuberculosis, which is now recognized as being communicable to man. These bone conditions were often referred to as caries. The use of the word in reference to bad teeth did not become general until quite late in the century.

It is not until well after the turn of the century that we find evidence that the English medical man was beginning to get a clearer picture of rickets and to realize how prevalent it was. Probably this was to some extent due to the fact that its ravages were by then so apparent that he had to take notice. Also, scientific investigations into the nature and cause of the disease were beginning to be made, although as most of these were in Continental centres the English general practitioner did not hear much about them.

By 1870 it was admitted that a proportion as high as one-third of the poor children of cities such as London and Manchester were suffering from obvious rickets.[2] It is important to remember that such estimates were based on easily recognizable symptoms, bent limbs, rickety chest, etc., and that had there been available modern methods of diagnosis by X-rays, which detect much earlier stages and milder forms of the disease, the proportion would have been far higher. Uneasiness about the situation led the Medical Congress of 1884 to promote a survey of the distribution of rickety children. Their report, published in 1889, left no doubt of the ravages of the disease.

[1] *The Family Oracle of Health*, Vol. I, 1824.
[2] Gee, *St Bartholomew's Hospital Report*, 1868, Vol. IV; Ritchie, *Medical Times and Gazette*, 1871, Vol. IV.

In some areas, such as the Clyde district, almost every child was found to be affected. A map of its distribution over the whole of England was a map showing the density of the industrial population.

For the greater part of the century the doctors had no clear ideas on the causation of the disease. Inherited tendencies, syphilis, overwork, bad houses, faulty diet and a hundred and one other possible causes were blamed. Gradually, however, two of these, faulty diet and bad living conditions, began to attract more attention than the others. Those who thought that diet was at fault had, between them, a wide range of theories. One of the most important observations, made by a good many clinicians, was that young children artificially fed on starchy foods, such as arrowroot, were particularly liable to develop rickets. Children reared in this fashion often grew well, in the sense that they put on weight, but as we have remarked they were pale, fat and flabby, and before long showed signs of rickets. There was considerable discussion as to whether this was due to too high a proportion of starch in the diet, or to too little fat, or both, or whether Garrod was right in thinking that milk supplied some essential mineral salts which these starchy foods lacked.[1]

Another and more obvious line of thought drew attention to the possibility that the defective bone formation was due to insufficiency of calcium in the diet. A young French orthopaedic surgeon, Jules Guerin, had made rather a stir in this field by his discovery that puppies fed solely on meat developed what appeared to be rickets, whereas other animals of the same litter which continued to suckle the bitch grew good firm legs.[2] The *Lancet* reported this discovery, which was rather generally believed to be explicable in terms of calcium (lime) deficiency. It was a somewhat disconcerting fact, however, that medication with materials providing extra calcium failed time and time again to give the results that might have been expected. This fact seemed completely at variance with the conception of the disease as being due to a simple deficiency of calcium.

Those who saw the disorder as a consequence of a disturbed balance between carbohydrate and fat were on firmer ground. They could not, it is true, give a satisfactory explanation why an undue proportion of starch or a deficiency of animal fat should affect the deposition of mineral matter in developing bone, but they did produce very convincing evidence that such a correlation had been demonstrated. Cheadle was the leading supporter of this view. Malhygiene as a factor he dismissed, for he had seen far too many cases in families of the well-to-do, where the infant was brought up under excellent conditions of sanitation, ventilation and light and warmth.

[1] *Lectures on Chemistry of Pathology and Therapeutics*, A. B. Garrod, 1848.
[2] J. Guerin, *Gazette Médicale*, 1838, Vol. XVI.

'The only constant factor, always present, is the food factor.' He was convinced that the 'food factor' was not deficiency of lime because he had found that many infants developed rickets when living on food which should have provided ample supplies of this substance. He regarded the 'food factor' as being an excess of carbohydrate. Protection could, he thought, be given by animal fats and, although much less effectively, by animal protein.[1] There was some controversy as to why a diet unduly rich in farinaceous food should cause rickets. The most popular explanation, based on pure speculation, was that carbohydrates tended to produce acids in the body — lactic acid was uppermost in most people's minds — and that they dissolved lime out of the developing bones.

The strongest evidence the supporters of the 'food-factor' school could produce was the remarkable effects which cod liver oil was found to have when given to children suffering from rickets.

§ 3 COD LIVER OIL AND RICKETS

Cod liver oil had been used, at any rate in Manchester, in the late eighteenth century for the treatment of rheumatism and other bone affections, though it is fairly certain that the enterprise of the Manchester physicians was not followed up. The early part of the nineteenth century contains very few references to the clinical use of this remedy. It was a very different matter on the Continent. It appears that a German physician named Schenk had learnt of the remarkable results which Kay and his colleagues had obtained, and had tried it in his own practice. In 1822 he published a paper in the German medical press giving an enthusiastic account of his experience and followed it up with a series of publications of a similar kind. The German medical profession showed great interest in the new remedy and soon it was being extensively used, not only for the treatment of rheumatism, which is what Schenk first used it for, but also for rickets. The French followed, and then, in 1841, came a publication in England which woke up our own Faculty. The author was an enterprising English medical man, John Bennett, who after graduating in Edinburgh, had studied both in Paris, where he founded the Paris Medical Society, and in Germany. It seems certain that during these four years (1837-41) on the Continent he gained his knowledge of the medicinal virtues of cod liver oil.

On his return to England he wrote his famous *Treatise on the Oleum Jecoris Aselli*. He stated in the preface that he was 'not aware that it [cod liver oil] is prescribed to any extent in Great Britain'. He described how

---

[1] *The Artificial Feeding and Food Disorders of Infants*, W. B. Cheadle, 1889.

extensively and successfully it was employed in Germany for the treatment of both rheumatism and rickets. According to him it was so generally used there that its remarkable beneficial effects no longer excited curiosity. In 1849 there appeared an English translation of another informative book on cod liver oil, written by the Dutch physician de Jongh.[1] Although its contents were very similar to those of Bennett's monograph, the book served to strengthen the impression that a new therapeutic agent of extraordinary value had been discovered. For the next few months the *Lancet* and other medical papers published much about the merits of cod liver oil. They were followed by an experiment which has become world-famous in the history of rickets.

The authorities of the London Zoological Society had for some time been worried at their failure to rear lion and bear cubs. In spite of all their precautions the young developed severe rickets and then declined and died. Their troubles came to the ear of Bland Sutton, who had been greatly interested in the developments which seemed to indicate that faulty diet was the most probable cause of rickets. He made inquiries and found that the diet of the animals in question consisted of nothing but raw lean meat. This he judged to be deficient both in calcium and in animal fat and, therefore, quite likely in his opinion to be the cause of the poor bone development. On his advice the young cubs were given crushed bone, milk and cod liver oil in addition to their meat. The result was astounding. In three months there was no sign of the disease. The cubs grew up to be strong healthy adults, an event unique in the history of the Society to that time.[2] This triumphant vindication of the main theory of the 'food-factor' school made a tremendous sensation and, incidentally, gave cod liver oil immense advertisement. The popularity of this therapeutic agent was increased not only by this evidence of its nutritive properties but, and this was by no means unimportant for the patients, by the introduction of much purer grades of oil. This was primarily the result of an invention by a Scarborough man, Charles Fox, who discovered in 1848 that fresh cod livers when cooked in steam-jacketed vessels exude an almost colourless oil with a slightly fishy taste, a product contrasting strongly with the dark brown, foul-smelling products that had formerly been prepared by allowing the livers to putrefy. In the following year Fox was sent by the London firm of Langton and Scott to operate his process in Newfoundland, and some five years later the Norwegians were using a similar process at Romsdal, one of the centres of their great cod fishing industry.

[1] *The Three Kinds of Cod Liver Oil*, L. J. de Jongh, translated from the German by E. Carey, 1849.
[2] Bland Sutton, *Journal of Comparative Medicine and Surgery*, 1889, Vol. X.

One puzzle was why cod liver oil was so much more effective in the treatment of rickets than other animal fats. Many regarded it as a specific. Trousseau, the famous French clinician, had discovered in 1849[1] that it was many times more antirachitic than butter and other doctors had confirmed his finding. Looking for an explanation they seized on Hupfer de l'Orme's discovery in 1836 that cod liver oil differs from other animal oils in containing a minute amount of iodine. He himself had already suggested that this might account for the remarkable therapeutic value of the oil.[2]

For the rest of the century the 'iodine-theory', as it may be called, was generally accepted, in spite of the fact that it was shown that iodine added to other oils did not confer on them the qualities of the natural cod liver oil. It was not until 1912 that Williams showed that there is no correlation between the amount of iodine in cod liver oils and their therapeutic value. Williams substituted an alternative theory attributing the medicinal properties to the peculiar character of the fatty acids present in liver oils,[3] but although this enjoyed a good deal of popularity for some ten years or so, it rapidly lost support after the discovery of vitamins A and D and of their relation to growth and rickets respectively.

It is not surprising that the possibility of other fish liver oils possessing therapeutic value aroused interest after cod liver oil re-established its reputation in England.[4] In 1855 the *Lancet* drew attention to the possibilities of using shark liver oil, but the extraordinary potency of the liver oils of such fish as the halibut and tunny was unsuspected until quite recently. Perhaps this is understandable. Cod liver is exceedingly rich in fat (30-50 per cent), whereas most of the livers which yield the very potent oils contain a much smaller proportion (2-8 per cent). When substitutes for cod liver oil were sought it was natural to turn to those, like the shark, which also have a large amount of oil stored in the liver.

§ 4 COD LIVER OIL AND TUBERCULOSIS

Tuberculosis in all its forms was rampant in English towns during the nineteenth century. The rapid decline in its prevalence and virulence dates only from about 1910. Under the conditions of town life in the worst period of industrialization the incidence of tubercular infection was appalling. Phthisis and tubercular joints and glands were the commonest forms, the last two forming a very high proportion of the cases which the medical

---

[1] Trousseau and Lesegue, *Archives Generales de Médecine*, 1849, Vol. XIX.
[2] Hupfer de l'Orme, *Hufeland's Journal*, 1836, Vol. VIII.
[3] Williams, *British Medical Journal* (1912), ii.
[4] Paper by Bagot, and discussion, *London Journal of Medicine*, 1850, Vol. II.

profession at that time called scrofula. This is no place to discuss the sources of infection and its spread, but it is appropriate to mention that the susceptibility of the poorer people must have been greatly increased over a considerable part of the country by malnourishment.

The use of cod liver oil in England for the treatment of tubercular disorders, particularly phthisis, dates from the publication of John Bennett's book in 1841, and that of de Jongh in 1849. The first extensive clinical trials were made by Dr C. J. Blasius Williams, physician to University College Hospital, London. He was a founder of the Brompton Hospital for Consumption, and introduced the new treatment there. The results were good. He wrote extensively on the subject as a result of finding that the oil exerted so remarkably beneficial an effect in many cases, particularly with regard to increasing weight. His opinion was that 'pure fresh Oil from the Livers of the Cod, is more beneficial in the treatment of Pulmonary Consumption than any agent, dietetic, or regimenal, that has yet been employed'.[1] Unfortunately, he was rather a pompous, egotistical man — his nickname at U.C.H. was 'the cocksure physician' — and he angered Bennett by not giving him what he regarded as due credit for his early work on the use of the oil in the treatment of phthisis. For some years they conducted a wordy and rather acrimonious polemic in the medical press.

§ 5 TEETH

The general state of the teeth deteriorated badly during the course of the nineteenth century. Quite early it was noticed that bad teeth were becoming much more common,[2] while in the last twenty-five years the spread of caries became alarming. Throughout the century we find the popular view accepted that acids formed from food held in the crevices between the teeth was responsible for the erosion of the enamel and the formation of carious cavities. Every expert focused his attention on 'the effect of chemical action on the surfaces'.[3]

The old idea that sugar was harmful had many supporters, although there were those who recognized that it could not be the whole story because of the immunity from caries of certain native races, such as the West Indians, who habitually ate considerable quantities.[4]

The nineteenth century saw the adoption of the toothbrush, called at

[1] *London Journal of Medicine*, 1850, Vol. II.
[2] *The Family Oracle of Health*, Vol. IV, 1826.
[3] 'Lectures on Bones and Teeth', Mr Lawrence, *Lancet*, 1830.
[4] *A Practical Compendium of the Materia Medica . . . adapted to the Treatment of the Diseases of Infancy and Childhood*, Andrew Ure, Enlarged Edition, 1839.

first 'tooth-preservers', and tooth powders, although not every dentist approved of them. The author of an article on the care of the teeth which appeared in *The Family Oracle of Health* in 1824 was scornful of the idea that bad teeth were caused by insufficient cleaning. He pointed to the fact that many savage tribes have perfect teeth but do not know any form of brush. He advised his readers, if they insisted on cleaning their teeth, not to use one of the new-fangled brushes but to stick to the old-fashioned 'Lady Morgan's Toothbrush', made by pounding the root of a marsh-mallow plant to a bunch of soft fibres. This seems to refer to an old country device similar to that which some native tribes employ. We have not traced an earlier reference to its use in England.

Another view about toothbrushes is taken from the homely little volume *Peptic Precepts* published anonymously early in the century.

> The TEETH *should be cleaned after every meal* with a 'TOOTH PRE-SERVER', (i.e. a very soft brush) and then rinced with tepid water — *never neglect this at night;* — nothing destroys the Teeth so fast as suffering food to stick between them — those who observe this rule, will seldom have any occasion for *Dentifrices* — *Essences of Ivory* — *Indurating Liquid Enamels, etc.* But it is the rage just now with some Dentists, to recommend Brushes so hard, that they fetch Blood like a Lancet wherever they touch; — instead of '*Teeth Preservers*' these should rather be termed '*Gum Bleeders*'.[1]

The earliest forms of cleaning material for the teeth were fine powders of which plaster was the commonest. An alkaline tendency was favoured in the belief that the harmful acids would thereby be neutralized. Tooth pastes are quite a modern invention.

The fear of acids causing erosion of the surface of the tooth led some doctors to distrust acid fruits. Others condemned the use of toothpicks by young children for fear of chipping the enamel. A third theory, which seems to have originated with the German physician, Hufeland, was that hot food or drink should not be taken soon after cold, or *vice versa*, in case the sudden expansion or contraction of the enamel should produce fissures.[2]

It is scarcely surprising that the century saw a deterioration of the teeth of the population. As we have seen, the diets of the people, particularly in the towns, tended to become poorer in bone-forming elements, mainly as a result of the decline in the consumption of milk which had been proceeding since about 1750, and, later, as a consequence of the introduction of the

[1] *The Art of Invigorating and Prolonging Life . . . and Peptic Precepts*, 3rd Edition Enlarged, 1822.
[2] *The Family Oracle of Health*, Vol. I, 1824.

cheaper forms of condensed milk. To these causes must be added the decline in breast-feeding, and, perhaps most important of all, the corresponding increase in the artificial rearing of children, or, what is really more significant, the increasing proportion of children surviving that critical period. Some of the doctors were alarmed.

> Thousands of sickly parents are begetting sickly children with sickly teeth, and instead of feeding them with such food as is calculated to counterbalance the inherited predisposition, are doing just the opposite.[1]

These unfortunate people, however, rarely knew what foods were needed and probably could not afford them when they did. They did not suspect that condensed milks differed in nutritive value, and that to feed their children on the cheaper brands prepared from unsupplemented skimmed milk was to make it almost certain that they would suffer from rickets and bad teeth. It must also be remembered that the poorer people rarely saw a doctor unless they were so gravely ill that they had to go to hospital. By the end of the century the state of the teeth of the nation as a whole was appalling. One result was a great increase in the use of false teeth, called at first 'Patent Masticators'. Those who could not enjoy solid food because of bad teeth or the lack of them were assured that with the assistance of Mr Palmer, Cutler, in St James's Street, they would be able to 'Masticate, Denticate, Chump, Grind, and Swallow' with the best.[2] Bad teeth were one of the chief causes of the startlingly high proportion of rejections (40 per cent) which so alarmed the Army authorities when recruits presented themselves for service in the South African War.

§ 6 VITAMIN A DEFICIENCY

Vitamin A deficiency must have been very prevalent in England in the nineteenth century, particularly in the towns. The children were the worst sufferers because they were so often reared on diets that contained amounts of the vitamin far below those required for growth and health. In this connection one thinks particularly of the hundreds of thousands of babies who managed to survive being reared on vitamin-deficient patent foods and condensed milks. We know the growth of these generations was stunted, but the evidence that they showed other and more characteristic signs of vitamin A deficiency is remarkably slight. One can only conclude that night-blindness, opacities of the cornea and other defects of the eye attribut-

[1] *The Teeth and how to save them*, L. P. Meredith, 1872.
[2] *Peptic Precepts*, Anon., 3rd Edition, 1822.

2B

able to lack of vitamin A, were common but still unrecognized by the medical profession. One of the most distinguished ophthalmologists of the first half of the century, Mr Green, made no reference to any of these conditions when he gave a comprehensive course of lectures on diseases of the eye at St Thomas's Hospital in 1824.[1] This is rather curious because across the Channel the situation was quite different. Bennett describes in his book on cod liver oil how he learnt in Paris to treat xerosis of the cornea with that remedy, although he reveals that it was usually applied externally rather than given by the mouth.[2] At least one prominent French doctor was also treating night-blindness with the oil.[3] This is not surprising, for the physicians in France had recognized these eye diseases and used liver as a remedy as far back as the sixteenth century. It is much more remarkable that our own profession had remained so backward.

One significant reference suggests that xerophthalmia was common in Ireland, as it might well have been, at the time of the great famine. Sir John Forbes was very much struck by the prevalence of ophthalmia, more particularly in the Union Houses. He formed the opinion that it was to a large extent due to 'insufficient nourishment'.[4]

§7 EFFECTS OF THE INTRODUCTION OF 'ROLLER-MILL' WHITE BREAD

By 1890 the change in the character of the national diet which attended the displacement of the centuries-old process of grinding flour between stones by roller mills was complete. At that time the annual national consumption of flour was about 280 lb. per head. The change in flour composition meant a reduction of about 0.7 mg. of vitamin B_1, about 4 mg. of nicotinic acid and 3 to 4 mg. of iron a day. The magnitude of these changes may be judged by the comparison with requirements of these nutrients. On a 3000 Cal. diet 1.2 mg. of vitamin B_1 and 12 mg. of nicotinic acid are required daily. An adult's requirement for iron is about 12 mg. daily. Thus the change in flour milling technique could have made a material difference to the adequacy of the diet, the significance of the change depending on the composition of the rest of the diet.

The poor were most affected because they depended to a greater extent

---

[1] *Lancet*, 1824.

[2] *Treatise on Oleum Jecoris Aselli*, J. H. Bennett, 1841.

[3] Cited in *Die Vitamine und ihre Klinische Anwendung* by W. Stepp, J. Kuhnau and H. Schroeder, 1936.

[4] Cited by Dr Carpenter in his discussion of Dr Letheby's lecture on the *Economy of Food*, delivered before the Society of Arts on March 18th, 1857.

than the rich on bread and could not afford to buy other foods which might have readjusted the balance. The gravely deficient 'poverty diet' of England which persisted throughout the 'thirties dated from about 1890 and was responsible in the last decade of the nineteenth century for a marked deficiency in the physique and physical efficiency of much of the community.

The dietary deficiencies caused by the introduction of roller-milled white flour were not so serious as to cause beri-beri though they may have been responsible for much nutritional anaemia. It is almost certain that the health of the people was adversely affected but impossible to prove the truth of this statement. Unfortunately it takes a long time to discover what minor ills and ailments have their origin in relatively mild dietary deficiencies.

In 1931 an experiment[1] was started in an attempt to throw light on the effects of life-long subsistence on diets providing less 'vitamin B' than is required for full physiological needs. The results were most illuminating. Over 1000 young rats — a species which has digestive systems and nutritional needs comparable with those of man — were divided into two groups. One group was fed on what was thought to be a complete diet, while the other received a food mixture resembling the 'poverty diet' of the 'thirties which was chosen to be somewhat deficient in the B vitamins. It was, in effect, a comparison of the nutritive value of wholemeal and unfortified white breads. The rats were observed during the whole of their lives and a very thorough post-mortem examination was made on every animal at death. It was found that those fed on the deficient diet were stunted, failed to propagate in a normal manner, and tended to contract illnesses and die at an unusually early age. What was unexpected was the observation that a very large proportion of their ill-health was traceable to disorders of the stomach and digestive tract. Infections of the lungs, disorders of the blood system, kidney affections, glandular defects, skin complaints, even cancer, affected both groups to about the same extent. When, however, it came to the incidence of dilated stomachs, ulcers, inflamed conditions of the caecum (an organ that corresponds to the appendix in man) and related conditions, it was found to be much greater in the badly nourished colony than in the other group.

It would be easy to assume from these results that the prevalence today of appendicitis and stomach or duodenal ulcers is due in large measure to defective diets, but we are not justified in accepting such a view without more evidence. Unfortunately, we shall never know how common these complaints were a few generations ago. Their diagnosis was in its infancy and surgical treatment was almost unknown until the end of last century,

[1] J. C. Drummond, A. Z. Baker, M. D. Wright, P. M. Marrian and E. M. Singer, *Journal of Hygiene* (1938), XXXVIII, 356.

when developments in aseptic technique made it possible for the first time to undertake abdominal operations with a fair chance of success.

The loss of the germ and some of the bran from the flour reduced significantly the intake of iron. A person living largely on bread, as many of the poor were forced to do, could easily obtain all the iron they required for blood-formation from 1½ lb. of wholemeal bread, but the same amount of white bread provided just about half the estimated requirements of an adult. This was one reason why anaemias of dietary origin became much more prevalent in the latter part of the century, although they had been distressingly common among the very poor ever since industrialization began.

Doctor after doctor writing to the medical press commented on their prevalence. The majority of cases were due simply to deficiency of iron in the food, and iron medication was the usual treatment given to the few who troubled or could afford to consult a doctor. The poorer women just became steadily more anaemic until at an early age their health was gravely undermined. Their waxen, sickly, greenish faces were one of the commonest sights in the streets of the large towns in Victorian days. There must also have been a very great deal of infantile anaemia. The children were born iron-deficient, for their mothers could not possibly provide from their own starved bodies enough iron to furnish the reserves with which the normal child should start life. It was in 1889 that the Swiss physiologist Bunge discovered that the child is born with a reserve of iron stored in its liver to provide material for the formation of haemoglobin during the period of suckling when, no matter how well nourished the mother, it cannot get sufficient from the milk.[1] Infantile anaemia played no small part in causing the decline in physique which occurred among the industrial population of England in the nineteenth century.

§ 8 SCURVY

When the eighteenth century closed it seemed that the problem of scurvy had been solved, at any rate so far as its cure was concerned. The disease was still regarded by most of the medical profession as essentially one associated with a sea-faring life.

During the first thirty years of the nineteenth century many notable voyages were made without a single man falling ill with scurvy. Particularly interesting are the Arctic voyages under pioneers such as Ross and Parry, most of which were undertaken with the object of finding the North-West

---

[1] *Text-book of Physiological and Pathological Chemistry*, G. Bunge, translated from the 2nd German Edition by L. C. Woolridge, 1890.

Passage. On Ross's first voyage in 1818 supplies of Donkin and Hall's preserved provisions were taken. It is clear that he regarded these as valuable antiscorbutics because after the stock of fresh vegetables was exhausted he gave orders that the men should be issued with 'a certain proportion of preserved meat and soup, in lieu of a part of the salt provision, in order to prevent the scurvy'. H.M.S. *Isabella* and H.M.S. *Alexander* returned the following year with a clean bill of health so far as scurvy was concerned. It seems certain that this experience made a great impression on Parry who had been a Lieutenant in H.M.S. *Alexander*. It is not surprising, therefore, that when he was given command of the next expedition he arranged to take a considerable amount of these canned meats and vegetables in H.M.S. *Hecla* and H.M.S. *Gripper*. It is curious that these foods earned so high a reputation as antiscorbutics, because Ross's men had received a regular issue of preserved lemon juice as well as other antiscorbutics almost throughout the voyage. The effect of these, particularly the juice, seems to have been passed over in the enthusiasm for the novel form of foods, which by their apparent freshness must have been a very welcome change from the salt tack and biscuit of the ordinary daily ration, even although the men got no more than one pound of preserved meat and one pound of vegetable soup a week.[1]

It is recorded that for Parry's three Arctic voyages in 1819 (*Hecla* and *Gripper*), 1824 and 1825 (*Hecla* and *Fury*), the ships were provided with 'all the antiscorbutics in the medical stores ... preserved vegetable soups, lemon juice, pickles, preserved currants and gooseberries, spruce beer, etc.' Yet it was Donkin and Hall's tinned foods that acquired the greatest merit.[2]

It is unlikely that these preserved foods possessed any appreciable antiscorbutic power, for the rather crude method of canning then would almost certainly have caused destruction of all or the greater part of any ascorbic acid they originally contained. There is little doubt, therefore, that Ross and Parry ought to have thanked the lemon juice rather than Messrs Donkin and Hall for the good health of their men.

It is interesting that Parry was another officer who made a practice on his expeditions of raising mustard and cress in boxes of earth. A correspondent writing to *The Times* has described how he had come across a copy of *The Memoirs of Rear Admiral Sir W. Edward Parry* which had at one time been in the possession of the wife of Admiral Coote, a friend of the explorer. Between the pages he found a pressed plant of cress, brown with age but complete with leaves, stalk and root. It was carefully fastened to

[1] *A Voyage of Discovery* (*Baffin's Bay*), John Ross, 1819.
[2] *Journal of a Voyage for the Discovery of a North West Passage from the Atlantic to the Pacific*, W. E. Parry, 1821; *A Second Voyage, etc.*, 1824; *A Third Voyage, etc.*, 1825.

a slip of notepaper on which was written in Lady Coote's handwriting: 'Cress found in the *Fury's* Garden, at Winter Island, on the return of the Expedition there in 1823, after an absence of fourteen months.'[1]

Most of the lemon juice issued to H.M. ships at this time was preserved by adding 25 per cent of rum, which by its alcohol content would tend to suppress the growth of organisms and keep it from going bad. Sometimes extra sugar was also added. Apparently the method did not always work satisfactorily because from time to time there were complaints of the juice deteriorating. This may have been due to insufficient rum having been added.

Captain Bagnold tried to interest the Admiralty in a modification of Appert's process, which he believed would be much more trustworthy. He proposed to boil the strained juice for an hour and a half, to pour the hot fluid into bottles, leaving a very small space, just sufficient to hold the cork, and then to stopper tightly and cement over the outside of the cork. He was following the current idea that one must exclude air, but if properly carried out, his process was a simple sterilization. The only drawback would have been that so long a boiling would have destroyed part of the vitamin C. He claimed that the bottled juice kept unchanged in a hot climate for two years, but it is not known whether it was ever used on any scale by H.M. ships.[2]

It seems true that at this time scurvy had become a rare disease in the Navy. Dr Elliotson lecturing on the disease at St Thomas's Hospital in 1830 stated that cases were very seldom seen. He mentioned a well-known surgeon who a short time before had diagnosed cancer of the gums in a man who really had scurvy, because he was unfamiliar with the symptoms of the latter disease.

> Now all these blunders arise from a case of scurvy being so exceedingly rare — so rare, that many even in the Navy have never seen a case.[3]

It seems probable that cases of scurvy on land were also uncommon at this time. In 1839 a case of scurvy in the same hospital aroused widespread interest. The man rapidly recovered on being given lemon juice and vegetables. There was still a good deal of discussion on the old question whether citric acid, the natural acid of lemon and lime juice, was an antiscorbutic or not. The idea that all acids were of value had gradually lost ground and it is rare to find mention of the old 'elixir of vitriol' in nineteenth-century writings. It was a different matter with citric acid, about which

[1] *The Times*, February 23rd, 1938.
[2] *Transactions of the Society of Arts*, 1827, Vol. XLV.
[3] *Lancet* (1831), i.

opinion was sharply divided. Marshall Hall, lecturing to his students in 1838, claimed that it gave better cures than any form of fresh fruit.[1] Billings taught that it was useless compared with lemon juice.[2] Although it is not an anti-scorbutic at all, the controversy dragged on for a number of years before the subject ceased to have any interest.

But if all was well in H.M. ships, it was far from being the same in all our vessels. Some of the mercantile marine ships carried antiscorbutics but others did not, with the result that scurvy was by no means unknown in trading vessels, or in the terrible convict ships which conveyed prisoners to penal settlements in the early part of the century. Ullathorne gives a horrifying picture of the conditions under which as many as 6000 convicts a year were transported to places like Van Diemen's Land. Their diet was mainly coarse bread and water with thin soups, and any misbehaviour was punished if not always with lashes, at least with solitary confinement for a week or more on nothing but half a loaf of black bread a day and water. Scurvy freed many a poor soul from his sufferings on these dreadful voyages.

Revelations of the extent to which scurvy was affecting the crews of trading vessels on long voyages led to a clause being inserted in the Merchant Shipping Act of 1854 which laid down that antiscorbutics must form part of the stores of all ships likely to be away from port for longer than ten days. Lime juice or lemon juice were specifically mentioned but it is interesting that the old views still survived, for it was suggested that sugar or vinegar might be served out as substitutes. In a later Act (1894) the instructions were more explicit and only lime or lemon juice were mentioned. The ration was then fixed at one ounce a day, to be issued to all members of the crew after the ship had been at sea for ten days. It appears that lime juice, which was usually preserved by adding 10-20 per cent of rum, was more frequently carried than lemon juice. In many American ports our seamen were, and still are, known as 'limers' or 'limeys' as a result of these Board of Trade regulations. One ounce of lemon juice would have given about 10 mg. and the same amount of lime juice a mere 4 or 5 mg. Such doses were probably sufficient to prevent the appearance of recognizable scurvy. In 1927 the Board authorized the Masters of ships to issue concentrated fruit (orange) juice as an antiscorbutic,[3] which in the amount suggested, half a fluid ounce daily, would provide 30-50 mg. of ascorbic acid daily.

It is interesting, particularly in relation to such questions as the diets of the poor and of the inmates of prisons and other institutions, that the value of the potato as an antiscorbutic food was fully recognized about 1840. The medical profession could not have been surprised, therefore, when there was

[1] Ibid., 1838. [2] Ibid., 1832.
[3] *Board of Trade Circular*, No. 91, 1927.

a sudden and alarming increase in the prevalence of scurvy among the poor when the potato crops failed disastrously in 1845 and the subsequent years. The disease became widespread in Ireland and all too common in England. It was responsible for a great deal of suffering and misery, although in England most of the cases appear to have been of a milder character than those which used to occur at sea.

The disease was still rare in the Navy in 1850 when Captain Alexander Armstrong took H.M.S. *Investigator* to the Arctic. This voyage is an important one because, following a number of complaints about the quality of the lemon juice purchased in the Mediterranean, the Admiralty had made arrangements to press fresh fruit at the victualling yard at Deptford and to supply Armstrong with the product preserved in two different fashions. One kind was preserved by the addition of 10 per cent of brandy, whereas the other was boiled, poured hot into bottles and a layer of olive oil added to exclude all air before sealing. This voyage of H.M.S. *Investigator* lasted two years and three months. Not a single case of scurvy occurred. It was the longest period that an expedition had ever been immune from the disease. Armstrong compared the protective action of the two kinds of preserved lemon juice but did not observe any difference.[1]

Twenty-five years later, this officer, then Sir Alexander Armstrong, was Medical Director General of the Navy. He had the task of organizing the expedition which Sir George Nares was to command (H.M.S. *Alert* and H.M.S. *Discovery*) in a search for the North Pole. He was so impressed by his own experience with lemon juice that he ordered ample supplies for the new venture. Nares sailed in May 1875. Eight months later cases of scurvy began to appear. It is significant of the changed outlook of naval surgeons that they were not even recognized as scurvy at first, so long had the Navy been immune and so great was the faith in the juice which was issued to the men every day. Nevertheless, it was scurvy, and the expedition suffered badly before it got back to England towards the end of 1876.

This unexpected experience shook people's faith in 'lime juice', particularly as the House of Commons had published in 1872 rather disturbing information about numerous outbreaks of scurvy in the mercantile marine which indicated that this antiscorbutic was not as certain a protective agent as had been imagined.[2] The reference to 'lime juice' instead of 'lemon juice' brings us to a perplexing problem, which was not elucidated until 1918, when Mrs Henderson Smith made an historical research into the matter.[3]

It appears that about 1866 when there was still some trouble over the

---

[1] *Observations on Naval Hygiene and Scurvy*, A. Armstrong, 1858.
[2] Reported in the *Journal of the Society of Arts*, 1872, Vol. XX.
[3] *Lancet* (1918), ii.

supply of lemons and lemon juice from the Mediterranean, the Admiralty began to place contracts in the West Indies for the supply of lime juice. No one suspected for a moment that there would be any difference between two fruits so very similar. Indeed, it is quite plain in reading Armstrong's book published in 1858 that he thought them identical; he refers to lemon juice and lime juice quite indiscriminately. Armstrong's opinion was undoubtedly taken by the Admiralty authorities before the change was made, and probably he would have favoured buying lime juice from one of our own colonies rather than lemon juice from the Mediterranean. It is, however, known that he took *lemon juice* on the Arctic expedition that remained free from scurvy for over two years. It is also certain that Nares, twenty-five years later, was issued with *lime juice*. Long after those days it was discovered that the juice of the lemon (*Citrus limonum*) is from two to three times richer in the anti-scorbutic vitamin than that of the lime (*Citrus acida*).

Unfortunately, this fact was not discovered until nearly half a century later, and ignorance of it led to a most confusing state of affairs. Expeditions set out relying on 'lime juice', which was soon the name by which all juice carried in ships was known, whether it was lime or lemon, only to find that the men fell ill with scurvy. Some Arctic explorers refused to take the juice, being convinced from experience that fresh meat was a safer protective food.

Here we have another complication in the story of scurvy, because it takes us back to the old view that it is caused by salt meat. Explorers had often noticed that scorbutic symptoms would clear up if fresh food in the shape of bear or seal meat could be obtained. The cure was attributed to the meat being fresh, which was indeed true. Ross's men suffered from scurvy during their long stay in the Arctic in 1829-31, but it disappeared as soon as a little fresh meat was available.[1] Black was particularly scornful of lime juice and put his trust in fresh meat. He claimed that if the sailors would only eat like the Eskimoes, 'They will bid defiance to the scurvy. They will not ask for lime juice from the West Indies, nor repine after the water-cresses of Hertfordshire.'[2]

The explanation is that fresh meats contain appreciable, if small, amounts of the anti-scorbutic vitamin, but that this virtue is readily lost on cooking, canning or pickling.

No discussion of scurvy in the nineteenth century is complete without a reference to the Crimean War. At the opening of the campaign the rations of the British troops were, on paper, 1½ lb. of bread or 1 lb. of biscuit and 1 lb. of fresh or salt meat a day. Apart from any question of vitamins this was inadequate. It supplied scarcely 2500 Cal., when 3500-4500 were needed.

[1] *Voyage of Discovery in Search of a North-West Passage (1829-1833)*, Sir J. Ross.
[2] *Scurvy in High Latitudes*, P. Black, 1876.

It is not surprising that the health of the men soon began to suffer. Lord Raglan, finding the French troops in much better condition than his own, thought at first that it might be explained by the fact that their ration contained coffee, rice and sugar. He, therefore, ordered the issue of 1 oz. of coffee, and 1¾ oz. of sugar, and a little later, an extra 2 oz. of rice or Scotch barley and an additional ½ lb. of meat. By this addition he brought the calorific intake up to about 3200. What Lord Raglan did not realize was that the French soldiers made use of every available scrap of vegetables in the locality of their camps and thus kept themselves in better health than the British. By October of the first year of the war scurvy was ravaging our ranks. Lord Raglan tried to get fresh vegetables sent from Varna but the transport was in a chaotic state and it proved impracticable. Then, on the advice of Dr Andrew Smith, he applied to the Authorities at home for supplies of lime juice. Twenty thousand pounds reached the base at Balaclava in December 1854 and there it stayed, for the duration of the campaign.

> A more unaccountable, and still more unfortunate, failure to apply to the use of the Army Stores of which it stood in most urgent need occurred in regard to lime-juice.[1]

At the base camp were also dumped supplies of 'Edwardes dried potatoes' and dried carrots, which were sent out on the advice of the Medical Department who thought they would be valuable antiscorbutic foods as well as welcome ingredients for soups.

Florence Nightingale's outspoken evidence before the Commission of Enquiry into the mismanagement of the Commissariat during this tragic campaign suggested that scurvy had occasioned more loss of life among the British forces than any other cause. She wrote that, of 1200 sick men who arrived at Scutari in one consignment on January 2nd, 1855, 85 per cent were cases of acute scurvy.[2]

§9 VEGETARIAN DIET

From very ancient times there have been advocates of a vegetarian diet. Behind nearly all the early writings on the subject one can clearly trace the belief, and it is one which has survived until recent times, that the eating of meat arouses and stimulates animal passions and that it is, therefore, antagon-

---

[1] *Report of the Commission of Enquiry into the Supplies of the British Army in the Crimea*, 1856.
[2] For more information on the condition of the men see *Florence Nightingale*, Cecil Woodham Smith, 1950. For more detailed information on the food supply of the troops see *Soyer's Culinary Campaign* written by Alexis Soyer after his return from the Crimea in 1857 and *Portrait of a Chef*, Helen Morris, 1938.

istic to the development of spiritual and philosophic thought. This was certainly one of the motives that actuated those who began early in the nineteenth century the first clearly marked vegetarian movement in England, but it is also possible to trace in the writings at this time the influence of a reaction, particularly in intellectual circles, against the gross over-eating of the well-to-do in the previous century. There were not a few who thought with Shelley that vegetable diet produced 'Health and Virtue', while animal food encouraged 'Disease, Superstition and Crime'.

One of the first important books on the subject was the Rev. William Metcalfe's *Abstinence from the Flesh of Animals* (1821). The authors of books such as this had no difficulty in putting together what appeared to be a convincing case. They could point, on the one hand, to the many native races that thrive on purely vegetarian or 'lacto-vegetarian' diets, or give, on the other hand, example after example of those who claimed that they had regained health and strength on changing from a mixed to a vegetarian regimen. Old Dr Cheyne, for instance, was a much quoted case. It is reputed that he weighed thirty-two stone and was so unwieldly that patients had to come to his carriage when he went his rounds at Bath, for the simple reason that once he had been got into it, only another Herculean effort would get him out of it again. He brought himself back to a more reasonable weight and a greatly improved state of health by living for several months on a very light diet of vegetables and milk.

The vegetarian movement gained impetus from two men, Sylvester Graham in the United States, and a London physician named Lambe. Graham wrote extensively on food and digestion, but he is remembered more for his fierce advocacy of wholemeal wheaten bread, not that made from the ordinary stone-ground flour, but from one containing every scrap of the grain, including all the bran. A coarse grade of wholemeal flour is still sold in the United States under the name of 'Graham flour'.

Graham was an ardent vegetarian, and some of his many arguments in support of his beliefs were based on what he regarded as scientific evidence:

> ... a single pound of rice, absolutely contains more nutritious matter than two pounds and a half of the best butchers' meat: and three pounds of good wheat bread contain more than six pounds of flesh: and three pounds of potatoes, more than two pounds of flesh ... Incredible as this may at first appear ... yet a reference to facts in the history of the human species, will abundantly prove the correctness of what is here stated.[1]

Some excuse may be found for mis-statements of this kind, for the

[1] *Lectures on the Science of Human Life*, Sylvester Graham, 1839.

technique of food analysis was at that time very primitive, but it is difficult
to be so tolerant of arguments which reveal the worst side of the bigoted
food-faddist.

> The enormous wickedness and atrocious violence and outrages of
> mankind immediately preceding the flood, strongly indicate, if they do
> not prove an excessive indulgence in animal food.[1]

Lambe, who was greatly influenced by Graham, was a convert to vegetarianism because of his firm conviction that he had regained health and vigour
after years of bad health by giving up meat in 1806. Like many others who
have had the same experience he jumped to the conclusion that all the ills of
the body are due to eating animal food. He was quite certain that a vegetarian diet would cure all diseases, even including cancer. His views were, on the
whole, coldly received by the medical profession, although the great John
Abernethy was rather interested in them: this famous Bart's surgeon was
himself a very strong advocate of the view that most diseases arise from over-
eating and excessive drinking. Much of his reputation was built up as a result
of enforcing more temperate habits on his patients.

Outside medical circles Lambe's views made more appeal and in 1847
a group of enthusiasts launched the Vegetarian Society of England. The
new venture did not make much headway at first, but within twenty years or
so it had a fair number of supporters.

In passing it may be mentioned that Lambe, before his conversion to
vegetarianism, had done a valuable service in drawing attention to the large
number of cases of lead poisoning which were attributable to the use of leaden
vessels, pumps and pipes for storing or conveying drinking water.[2] Lambe
was so concerned with the potential dangers of the London water supply
that he made all his patients drink distilled water. He probably saved many
lives as a result, not because it was free from lead but because it was free from
infection.

The medical profession as a whole ridiculed the new ideas on vegetarianism. Within a few years Liebig had pronounced his views on muscular work
and these, since they laid great stress on the utilization of the muscle substance itself during exercise, greatly strengthened the opposition of the
doctors. Liebig was wrong, as it transpired, but it took many years to dis-
lodge the popular impression that meat food was essential to rebuild the
muscle tissue lost when exercise was taken.

The movement aroused considerable amusement on the Continent.

---

[1] *Lectures on the Science of Human Life*, Sylvester Graham, 1839.
[2] *Researches into the Properties of Spring Water, with Medical Cautions against the use of Lead*,
W. Lambe, 1803.

Cependant en Angleterre, ce pays des exentricités, ou l'on voit une belle et progressive civilisation marche dans presque toutes les directions avec quelque accompagnement de barbarie, une secte nombreuse tend à exclure la chair des animaux du régime alimentaire de la population; elle prêche d'example et fait quelques prosélytes.[1]

In considering the nutritional adequacy of vegetarian diets one must distinguish between those of lacto-ovo-vegetarians who eat milk and eggs as well as vegetable foods and of vegans who eschew milk and eggs as well as meat, poultry, game and fish. The lacto-ovo-vegetarian diet can be excellent and has been shown[2] to support equally satisfactory health, physique, blood pressure and blood composition as a meat diet in adolescents, adult men and pregnant and non-pregnant women.

The vegan diet, on the other hand, has been shown to be short of protein — with no animal protein it is difficult, though not impossible, to achieve suitable mixtures of amino-acids for adequate growth[3] — and of vitamin B_{12}, the most recently discovered vitamin. The latter shortage is particularly serious if associated with insufficient protein and may lead to sub-acute combined degeneration of the spinal cord as well as a poor rate of growth.[4] Vitamin B_{12} is probably part of at least one enzyme necessary for metabolic reductions and is involved in the metabolism of fat, protein, carbohydrate and, with another vitamin, folic acid, of nucleic acids. Thus, the metabolism of all major nutritional elements may become deranged in vitamin B_{12} deficiency. It is not surprising, therefore, that it is necessary for growth, the prevention of certain sorts of anaemia, including pernicious anaemia, and the prevention of degeneration of nerve cells, particularly of the spinal cord.[5] In pernicious anaemia the vitamin B_{12} in the food is not available for absorption through lack of a factor (the intrinsic factor of Castle) in the gastric juice. Patients are now treated by injections of vitamin B_{12}.

§ 10 FRUIT 'CURES'

One form of vegetarian diet that comes into prominence from time to times is the 'fruit cure'. There was a craze at one period in the 'nineties for

[1] *Substances Alimentaires*, C. Payen, 4th Edition, 1865.
[2] M. G. Hardinge and F. J. Stare, *J. Clin. Nutr.* (1954), II, 73.
[3] (a) 'Studies on the Nutritive Value of Bread and on the Effect of Variations in the Extraction Rate of Flour on the Growth of Undernourished Children', E. M. Widdowson and R. A. McCance, *Medical Research Council, Special Report*, No. 287, 1954.
(b) 'Plant Proteins in Child Feeding', R. F. A. Dean, *Medical Research Council, Special Report*, No. 279, 1953.
[4] 'Human Dietary Deficiency of Vitamin B_{12}', F. Wokes, J. Badenoch and H. M. Sinclair, *Amer. J. Clin. Nutr.* (1955), III, 375.
[5] 'Vitamin B_{12}', E. Lester Smith, *Brit. Med. Bulletin* (1956), XII, 52.

the 'grape cure'. More recently an 'orange cure' gained some notoriety. The essential features of these 'cures' are a drastic reduction in the amount of ordinary foods and the relatively large amount of fruit eaten. Sometimes, the 'solid' food is reduced to one or two rusks a day. A diet of this character with, say, ten oranges a day would provide a calorie intake of about a third of that required by an adult for an ordinary day's activities. Therefore, unless the individual keeps very quiet in bed this amount of energy would be a good deal less than the body's needs. It follows that the body's stores of fat are utilized to make good the balance and weight is lost rather rapidly if any appreciable amount of exercise is taken. Such a diet also provides a considerably higher intake of vitamin C than does the ordinary diet of the fairly well-to-do family. Here is the explanation why people feel so much better for a short spell, say two or three weeks, of a 'cure' of this type. It would be a good deal better for these people if they would adopt a simple and more rational diet in their everyday life, so that the need for a 'cure' would not arise, but many of them are obliged by the conventions of their social life to face a succession of elaborate meals and highly seasoned dishes.

§ 11 BANTING'S DIET

In every age there have been waves of enthusiasm for the teachings of those who have advocated simple diets as a means of regaining health. None made a greater sensation than that started by a certain William Banting when he published *A Letter on Corpulence addressed to the Public* in 1863. It told his own story. He had been so obese that it was exceedingly difficult for him to go up and down stairs. Doctor after doctor had been consulted but none had been able to reduce his weight until, much to the patient's surprise, he was advised to give up milk, butter, sugar and potatoes. He thereupon adopted a diet consisting essentially of meat, fish and fruit. His breakfast consisted of about 4 oz. of meat, fish or bacon and not more than an ounce of toast. For dinner he was allowed rather more meat, fruit and vegetables (other than potatoes) and again about an ounce of toast. For tea he could take a rusk and a little fruit, and at supper about 4 oz. of meat or fish was all he was permitted. He drank tea without milk and several glasses daily of sherry or claret. On this restricted diet he lost two stone and a half in weight in a little over nine months and, to his great delight, enjoyed better health than ever before. Banting's name has passed into everyday use in connection with slimming measures.

PART FIVE

THE TWENTIETH CENTURY

CHAPTER XXIII

THE TURN OF THE TIDE

§ 1 THE DIET IN 1900

THE close of Queen Victoria's reign marked the end of an epoch. Her life had seen a great Empire consolidated, vast national wealth built up and Britain's prestige raised to a level it had never before attained. What had been the cost? By most people it was counted in terms of the handful of casualties and the comparatively insignificant financial outlay on the campaigns which had opened up new lands and new trade routes, bringing us untold riches. Few troubled to look deeper. Few realized that the country had paid and was still paying heavily for its remarkable commercial and industrial expansion in the marked deterioration of physique and health which the appalling conditions of labour had brought about. It is no exaggeration to say that the opening of the twentieth century saw malnutrition more rife in England than it had been since the great dearths of medieval and Tudor times.[1] Apart from a handful of social workers there were few who showed any real concern at the terrible distress in the working-class districts. The apathy and callous indifference of the general public was clearly revealed when Seebohm Rowntree published in 1900 his study of the conditions under which the poor were living in the City of York.[2] His book, now a classic in the literature of social economy, should have caused a nation-wide outcry. In fact, its terrible revelations aroused but little interest and were forgotten by most people within a month or two. Sometimes it comes as a rude shock to realize how great is the inertia to be overcome before the public conscience can be awakened in the matter of social reforms.

It is not surprising that this pioneer paid most attention to housing and sanitation. It was a time when the science of domestic hygiene was making rapid strides. A great deal had been learnt of the need for pure water supply and efficient drainage. By contrast, little was known about the influence of

[1] It is interesting to compare this statement with the conclusions reached in 'Seven Centuries of the Prices of Consumables, compared with Builders' Wage-rates', by E. H. Phelps Brown and Sheila V. Hopkins (*Economica*, November 1956, p. 296); the equivalent of the wage rate in terms of consumables was higher between 1380 and 1510 than at any other time until the late nineteenth century. It fell again to something lower than the fifteenth-century level in the early twentieth century and has since risen to an entirely new region. It reached particularly low levels at the end of the the sixteenth century and again at the end of the eighteenth century. Cf. pages 49, 51, 88, 172, 173, 279 to 284.
[2] *Poverty, A Study in Town Life*, B. Seebohm Rowntree, 1900.

bad diet on health. Nevertheless, Rowntree did draw attention to the inadequacy of the diet of the poor families he had studied. Most of them lived practically entirely on bread — and it must be remembered that all of it was white bread — while many of them did not even get enough food to satisfy their hunger. In nine cases out of ten sheer poverty was the cause.

Perhaps it was too much to expect that Government circles would be disturbed by his exposures. They certainly showed no concern at the time and maintained an attitude of indifference until, about a year later, their complacency suffered a rude shock. The cause of the flutter in Whitehall was a memorandum from Sir William Taylor, Director General of the Army Medical Service, in which he reported that the Inspector of Recruiting was having the greatest difficulty in obtaining sufficient men of satisfactory physique for service in the South African War. The rejections in some areas were as high as 60 per cent and over the whole country nearly 40 per cent. The chief grounds were bad teeth, heart affections, poor sight or hearing, and deformities.

> The public which had rejoiced vicariously in the triumphs of the football field and cycle track, were discouraged to learn that of those who wished to serve their country in her day of trial a startling number were found physically unfit to carry a rifle.[1]

So serious was the shortage that it was found necessary in 1902 to reduce the minimum height for recruits for the infantry to 5 ft.; it had already, in 1883, been lowered from 5 ft. 6 in. to 5 ft. 3 in.

Rather shaken, Whitehall thought it might be advisable to hold an inquiry into the matter, but before taking this step decided first to consult the Royal College of Surgeons and the Royal College of Physicians. After long deliberation the replies of these august bodies were received. Both expressed the view that the Director General of Medical Services had not made out a case for believing that any deterioration of physique had occurred. The College of Physicians rather reluctantly approved the proposal for an investigation, pointing out, however, that unless it was made with the greatest care it might lead to quite erroneous conclusions. The College of Surgeons was more definite and was of opinion that an inquiry would serve no useful purpose. An Inter-Departmental Committee was, however, appointed and in due course the usual bulky Blue Books appeared.[2]

The inquiry had opened its proceedings on the note that even if the finding that 40–50 per cent of men volunteering for army service were physically unfit did not necessarily mean that the national physique had deterior-

---

[1] *Physical Deterioration, its Causes and Cure*, A. Watt Smyth, 1907.
[2] *Report of the Inter-Departmental Committee on Physical Deterioration*, 1904.

ated, it was a state of affairs so serious that it called for immediate attention. It was certainly a broader outlook than the doctors had taken.

The Committee had not sat long before it was obvious that nothing that Rowntree had said was in the least exaggerated. Witness after witness described the fearful conditions under which the poor were living and working. 'Back-to-back' houses with unpaved courts receiving the contents of the 'midden-privies' and saturated with excrement and filth; half-starved children in ragged clothing with pitiable, pallid faces and deformed limbs; areas with an infant mortality of nearly 250 per 1000; parents trying to rear large families on little more than bread and tea; these, and a hundred other tragic facts, were once again made public.

It was not surprising to learn that boys of 10 to 12 at private schools were on the average 5 inches taller than those in council schools. How could the mothers in these poverty-stricken areas produce healthy children? Here is the description of young girl factory hands which one of H.M. Inspectors of Factories (Mr Wilson) gave the Committee.

> The girls exhibit the same shortness of stature, the same miserable development, and they possess the same sallow cheeks and carious teeth. I have also observed that at an age when girls brought up under wholesome conditions usually possess a luxuriant growth of hair, these girls have a scanty crop which, when tied back, is simply a wisp or 'rat's-tail'.

The Committee made a comprehensive survey of the possible causes of the poor physique and the ill-health of the labouring population of the towns. It is understandable that they tended to give greater attention to such factors as overcrowding, bad sanitation, alcoholism, factory conditions, ignorance, etc., than to what was by far the most important cause, semi-starvation due to sheer poverty. To most people at the time defective diet seemed a less obvious cause than the other conditions. Certainly medical opinion tended to encourage this view. The doctors were completely obsessed with the quantitative outlook on dietary problems. Every problem was regarded in the light of the amount of protein needed or the total number of calories thought to be necessary. When, therefore, it was shown that the labourers in Edinburgh ate meals providing on an average 112 g. of protein and 3220 Cal. daily, it was concluded that their diet was not seriously defective by comparison with their estimated needs of 125 g. of protein and 3500 Cal.

One medical witness deplored the fact that the poor now ate white bread and drank tea, whereas in the past they had lived on 'oatmeal and milk', but on the other hand another assured the Committee that 'white bread properly made was as rich in nutritive properties as any form of brown bread'. In giving this opinion he was certainly expressing the current belief, founded on the results of the analysis of breads expressed in terms of protein, fat, carbohydrate and mineral ash, and on what was known of their digestibility. The differences between 'brown' and 'white' bread in respect of the main constituents are insignificant. They are also almost equally digestible. It was quite justifiable, therefore, at that time to doubt whether white bread was injurious to health when forming the chief part of the solid food eaten by the poor. Nearly twenty-five years were to elapse before the deficiences of the modern types of white bread in respect to vitamins and mineral salts were recognized, but it will perhaps be instructive to reveal at this point how great a difference it actually made to the nutrition of the poor. We can take as a convenient example the diet of a young child of 10 years of age — requiring about 2000 Cal. daily — and consisting in the one case of 1½ lb. of white bread and ½ oz. of margarine, of the type eaten by the poorer people early in the twentieth century, and in the other, of 1½ lb. of bread made from stone-ground flour and ½ oz. of butter. The amounts of protein, fat and carbohydrate being similar in the two diets, they would have been considered to be of equal nutritive value. The following table shows the important differences between the two diets in relation to a child's requirements.

	Stone-ground bread and butter	Unfortified white bread and margarine	Estimated needs per day
Iron mg.	13	7	11
Vitamin A i.u.	425	0	1500
Vitamin B₁ mg.	1.0	0.3	0.8
Nicotinic acid mg.	5.4	3.8	8
Vitamin D i.u.	8	0	unknown

Perhaps it is not inappropriate to give a short description of modern types of brown bread because it is sometimes assumed, erroneously, that they are equivalent to, or even identical with, wholemeal bread. In the old days 'brown' bread was baked from coarse wholemeal flours containing a large part of the bran and, sometimes, a proportion of rye or other cereal. It was a rough but nutritious food. The modern types of 'brown' bread date from the introduction of the roller-mill white flour about 1880. With very few exceptions they are baked from ordinary white flour with which has been mixed an appropriate proportion of bran. Sometimes a small amount of molasses is also added to make the colour a little darker. A few of the special brands of 'brown' bread contain a small proportion of germ and are, therefore, more comparable with wholemeal breads. The bran is useful in serving as 'roughage' but is probably even more valuable in the diet as a source of vitamin B_1. It is sometimes argued that white bread cannot be deficient in vitamin B_1 because yeast is used in its making and yeast is usually assumed to be rich in that substance. This is a fallacy. Even if the yeasts employed in making bread were very rich in B_1 — in actual fact bakers usually employed a type of yeast which is of peculiarly low vitamin content — the addition of a mere 30-60 oz. to a sack of 280 lb. of flour would not significantly raise the nutritive value of the loaves.

§ 2 THE FEEDING OF CHILDREN

The Committee which reported in 1904 gave considerable attention to the question of the feeding of children. It was well that they did so, for a dreadful state of affairs was revealed. It was established that breast-feeding was rapidly declining, to some extent because women were being employed on an increasing scale in factories but more because of chronic ill-health which made so many of them incapable of providing the necessary milk. How could a working woman rear an infant at her breast when she had been for years going to work early in the morning with nothing more than a cup of strong black tea? Probably her midday meal consisted of bread and jam and tea, and only at the evening meal at the end of a long tiring day was any cooked food eaten. 'Fish and Chips' from the little shop round the corner, a kipper or a few cheap sausages, with, perhaps, some highly seasoned pickles, then made some sort of semblance of a meal. No constitution could stand up to such a diet for long and it is not surprising to learn that factory inspectors, social workers and doctors were unanimous that chronic digestive troubles, bad teeth, anaemia and general debility were almost universal among working-class women.

The bad diet was one reason why so many of them could not produce milk to rear their infants. Animal experiments leave us in no doubt that interference with the flow of milk is one of the first signs of the effects of deficient diet. It is comparatively rare to find that malnutrition prevents pregnancy nor do dietary defects, with the possible exception of a lack of vitamin E, often produce an untimely termination of pregancy by causing a miscarriage. The history of the Siege of Paris and German records during the worst time of the food shortage during the First World War show that under-nourished women produce children, who, for the most part, are not much below normal weight, but they are seldom able to feed them. The reason is that when a woman is unable to nourish the child in her womb with material derived from her food there occurs a breakdown of certain of her own tissues and transport of this material to the developing embryo. Consequently, she loses weight, becomes anaemic and generally fails in health. The sacrifice of her own flesh and blood, for literally it is such, enables the young child to be born, not adequately nourished, it is true, but in such a condition that if given adequate diet it might ultimately be little the worse for the bad start. It will be obvious, however, that the mother would be left in a state of serious depletion after such an experience and that it might well be physiologically impossible for her to make further sacrifies in order to provide the materials from which her milk is made. Unless, therefore, her own nourishment were improved the flow of her milk might become meagre, and prematurely cease. Such was the case with many of the mothers in the poverty-stricken areas of our towns. As a substitute for the natural nourishment they gave their infants the cheapest food they could buy. In nine cases out of ten it was sweetened condensed skimmed milk. This was bad enough, for this product, excessively rich in sugar and almost wholly devoid of fat, was unsuitable for very young children and gave rise to much rickets and other consequences of defective nutrition, but some mothers were so poor that they were obliged to try to rear their babies on nothing better than flour and water.

A survey made in Sheffield in 1900 showed that over 60 per cent of the women in the working-class districts were feeding their babies on wholly unsuitable foods. With such an unpropitious start in life it is not surprising that the young children of the slums were found to be in a very bad way. Many of them did not get enough to eat. The 1904 report revealed that at least 33 per cent were under-nourished, not in the sense that they got bad food but that they actually went hungry. None of them got the right sort of food. Bread and jam was their almost unvarying meal.

Rickets, bad teeth and stunted growth were seen everywhere. One survey of school children in Leeds in 1902 showed that in the poorer districts no less than half had marked rickets while more than 60 per cent were suffering from carious teeth. An interesting point which this particular inquiry revealed was that the incidence of these defects was much smaller among the children of Jewish parents, the corresponding figures being 7 per cent and 25 per cent respectively. It is certain that this was due to better feeding, for it is a well-known fact that the Jews as a people take far more pains to give their children good food than do the English. For one thing, Jewish infants are nearly always breast fed. Secondly, the Jews have a sense of good living and even when poor will make almost any sacrifice to try to get wholesome food for their families. Naturally fond of rather rich dishes, the diet of the working-class Jews usually provides considerably more fat than that of the poor Gentile. Some fats, as we have seen, are particularly important when there is any danger of rickets. They are also lovers of fruit and will often spend money in this way when they can ill afford it. These facts undoubtedly explain the striking difference between the nutrition of the Jews and of the Gentiles in the same working-class districts.

The revelation that thousands of young children were living on starvation diets came as a considerable shock to the Committee, particularly when they were emphatically assured by leading educational authorities that a great part of the instruction in the Board Schools was being wasted because the wretched boys and girls came to school so hungry that they could not profit by the teaching. The Committee was forced to realize that a hungry child must be fed before it can give its mind to lessons, and they therefore turned their attention to the task of devising schemes whereby it would be possible to provide meals for necessitous children. This part of the inquiry led to an interesting revelation, namely, that the London School Board had considered but shelved a memorandum on the subject five years earlier. One recommendation which it contained was:

> That where it is ascertained that children are sent to school underfed it should be part of the duty of the authorities to see that they are provided, under proper conditions, with the necessary food.

The recommendations of the 1904 Committee led in 1906 to the Education Act (Provision of Meals). In one respect it was a great advance but in another it was unsound, in that by charging the cost to the rates it made it difficult to raise the money in the very poor districts where help was most needed. Nevertheless, it meant a great deal for the children whose only hope before the Act was passed was to be lucky enough to get a meal from one of the charitable organizations which were struggling to do something to ameliorate the terrible state of affairs. By 1911 more than 200,000 poor children were benefiting from free meals of one sort or another.

It must not be imagined that it was only the children of the poor who suffered from malnutrition in the early part of the twentieth century. The diets given to the boys and girls at many of the big public schools at that time were often defective, seldom, it is true, in amount, but very often in nutritive quality. The chief object of the school kitchen or the housemaster seemed to be to fill the boys up as easily as possible with large, stodgy and, of course, cheap meals. This meant that they got plenty of bread, porridge, hot dishes of meat and potatoes, and heavy suet puddings. Milk, fruit and salads seldom figured in the menus, not only because they were dear but because they were rather generally regarded as unnecessary luxuries and, in boy's schools, as 'namby-pamby' foods quite unsuitable for the development of brawn and muscle.

One of the more enlightened schools at that period was Christ's Hospital, which made up for its bad reputation in Charles Lamb's days by giving the boys an excellent diet. From Dr Pearce's records we learn that in 1901 the dinners provided new potatoes, fresh peas, garden greens, fresh lettuce, plenty of cheese, and quite often stewed fruit.[1] Unfortunately, there are no records of the height and weight of the Christ's Hospital boys at this period which would enable us to compare their physique with that of boys in other schools where the food was less good, or with that of the less fortunate, under-nourished children on the rolls of the elementary schools.

If the food given to many boys in the better-class schools was almost as bad as it had been in Dickens's time it was certainly equally true that many young girls suffered as severely as Charlotte Brontë had done. Here is the experience of a friend of Sir James Crichton-Browne.

There were fifteen of us boarders. We paid £150 a year, and we never had enough to eat. We rose at 7 a.m. and had breakfast at 8.30, consisting of weak tea, a thick bit of bread with a thin smear of butter. Butterine was substituted for butter until complaints were made, and then we had salt butter. Once a month a boiled egg was given at breakfast. Dinner, which came at one o'clock, consisted of two courses, soup and meat, or meat and pudding, vegetables being always served with the meat. But the meat was doled out in very small portions, and although second helpings were nominally allowed, they were regarded with disapprobation, and were scarcely worth asking for ... Tea at six o'clock consisted of weak tea and bread and butter as at breakfast, but occasionally jam of a livid complexion was substituted for butter. We were always hungry, and all our pocket money went on food. I was growing fast, and often felt faint and ill, but it would not do to complain, for a girl on the sick list was isolated and fed on gruel or arrowroot made with water.[2]

One wonders what proportion of the mothers of past generations had their health undermined in consequence of the ignorance and sometimes the greed of those who catered for them at school.

During the past thirty years or so the diets of children, both in private and elementary schools, have been improved in a very striking manner. To some of these changes we will refer when an account has been given of the discoveries which led to their being made.

---

[1] *Annals of Christ's Hospital*, 1901, E. H. Pearce.
[2] *Parcimony in Nutrition*, Sir J. Crichton-Browne, 1909.

§ 3 MATERNAL AND INFANT WELFARE

The year 1906 is memorable for an event no less important than the Bill which authorized expenditure on food for necessitous children. This was the first National Conference on Infant Mortality, held in London, at which John Burns, then at the head of the Local Government Board, acted as President.[1]

The death-rate among infants in the County of London had been over 200 per 1000 in the third quarter of the year — when the infantile death-rate is usually at its highest — for eight out of the ten previous years. In 1899 it had touched the unprecedented figure of 279 per 1000.

It is to the influence of this Conference and to Sir George Newman's book on infant mortality that we owe the beginnings of the Infant Welfare Movement. The Borough of St Pancras led the way in 1907 with a centre at which mothers could get advice about bringing up their children. Four years later when Mr Lloyd George forced his National Insurance Act through Parliament in face of strong opposition from the great body of the medical profession there were about a hundred such centres in operation. The movement won tardy but none the less welcome official backing in 1914 when the Local Government Board approved a system of grants to enable local authorities to assist such work, and in the following year an important step forward was taken by the decision in the Notification of Births Act (1915) to permit expenditure on the assistance of expectant mothers.

No one can estimate how many hundreds of thousands of lives have been saved as a result of that first Conference on Infant Mortality. With the exception of the years of the First World War, the infant death-rate has dropped steadily from the ghastly figures around 220 per 1000 to its present level of little more than 20 per 1000. Better feeding has been responsible for saving a large proportion of these lives. Mothers have been encouraged to feed their children at the breast whenever possible, and have received valuable advice on their own diet. They have been taught that unboiled or un-pasteurized milk is a potential source of disease and that sweetened condensed milks, especially the skimmed varieties, are not suitable foods for infants. It has been made possible for mothers to obtain supplies of dried milks of good quality. These are free from infective organisms and, when properly recon-stituted, form a highly nourishing food for babies. More recently, modern knowledge of the role of the vitamins has been put to practical use by in-structing the mothers in the proper use of fruit juices and cod liver oil.

The years before the outbreak of the First World War saw the turn of the tide, and the Infant Welfare Movement was not the only indication that

[1] *The Early History of the Infant Welfare Movement*, G. F. McCleary, 1933.

things were changing. Experimental research in medicine and nutrition was expanding rapidly in every direction. In 1913 there came into being, as a direct result of Lloyd George's National Health Insurance Act of 1911, a body known as the Medical Research Committee. It was an entirely new departure for it represented the Government's admission of its responsibility not only to encourage but actually to participate in investigating the nature and cause of disease.

One of the first subjects to which attention was given by this new body was a study of rickets. A comprehensive plan of investigation was drawn up but, unfortunately, the outbreak of hostilities in August 1914 made it necessary for them to turn their attention to more pressing matters and to shelve a large part of the inquiry on rickets.

§ 4 PRISON AND INSTITUTIONAL DIETS

The knowledge which was gained in the last decade or so of the nineteenth century enabled the experts to say with much greater certainty than before whether the diets provided in prisons and workhouses were adequate for the needs of the inmates. It is not surprising, therefore, that many of these diets came up for reconsideration in the light of the new ideas regarding the need for protein, fat, carbohydrate and calories.

The first to be severely criticized were the prison diets, which, at the end of the nineteenth century, were still based on Sir James Graham's scales of 1864. Here is an account by one who had suffered from them.

The scene was the House of Commons; John Burns was speaking on the Prison Bill. In restrained but none the less telling language he recounted his own experiences when imprisoned for six weeks for being concerned with the Labour demonstration in Trafalgar Square in 1887.

I have had No. 1 diet, bread and oatmeal . . . I went into prison with a strong constitution and I was there for six weeks. I never made any complaint. But what is 6 oz. of bread? It is as much as the Hon. gentlemen take with their chop and potatoes, and cabbage and spinach. I had the bread at 5.30 p.m. and nothing till 7.45 next morning. I am not ashamed to say that at 1 or 2 o'clock in the morning I have wetted my hands with my spittle and gone down on my hands and knees in the hope of picking up a stray crumb from the meal I had had ten hours before. By that diet you break down and enfeeble a man's constitution.

The Class I diet to which he referred was for short-term prisoners. It was an inadequate ration, even less nutritious than when it was approved in 1864.

It consisted mainly of bread, 18 oz. a day, but in addition the prisoners received 8 oz. of potatoes on one day, 6 oz. of pudding on another, and a bowl of soup on a third. It gave a man about 45 g. of protein, none of which came from animal sources, and rather less than 1500 Cal. Even quantitatively it meant semi-starvation. But it was worse than that. More certainly than John Burns suspected, it was a diet that would undermine a man's health. From about 1880 the bread was wholly white which meant that the prisoner was so restricted in vitamin B_1 that it is surprising that cases of oriental beri-beri did not occur. Perhaps they did and went unrecognized. No one suspected what the change from wholemeal to white bread would mean; below we show what was the inevitable consequence.

	18 oz. wholemeal bread	18 oz. unfortified white bread	Estimated daily needs of a moderately active adult man
Vitamin B_1 mg.	0.9	0.3	1.2
Nicotinic acid mg.	19	3	12
Iron mg.	12.5	5.5	12
Calories	1300	1360	3000

The level of intake of vitamin B_1 below which there is real danger of beri-beri, particularly if the diet is rich in starch or other carbohydrates, is about 0.2 mg. per 1000 Cal. Thus the Class I diet was almost a beri-beri diet. Equally serious was the complete absence of vitamin A, except for any small quantities of carotene present in the soup.

Other evidence, equally damning, showed that it was undoubtedly true that the prisoners in English gaols were badly undernourished. The outcry led to the appointment of another Departmental Committee which, accepting expert medical advice, recommended improvements which certainly brought the diets up to adequate levels so far as proteins and calories were concerned. This was all that the knowledge at that time could achieve. The importance of the qualitative composition of the diet was then almost entirely unsuspected.

How the problems were tackled can be illustrated by the manner in which Dr Dunlop estimated the needs of the convicts in the Scottish prisons. He found that on a diet supplying 3500 Cal. no less than 82 per cent of the men lost weight when engaged in breaking stones for the best part of eight hours a day. The men complained bitterly that they did not get enough to eat. Dunlop then got the authorities to provide them with extra food so that their calorific intake was raised to 3900. A change was soon apparent. The men began to put on a little weight and their complaints turned on the quality rather than the quantity of their meals. A balance was struck at the intermediate ration of 3700 Cal. Complaints were reduced to a minimum and the men were able to perform their work without fatigue or loss of weight. On this evidence, regarded as adequate at the time, the diet for this form of hard labour was fixed at 3700 Cal.

About this time the diets in workhouses were very much better than those in the prisons. The Local Government Board's inquiry in 1897 had led to a complete revision of the diet sheets and the new ones came into operation in 1901. A typical week's meals are given below.

	Breakfast	*Dinner*	*Supper*
Sunday	Bread, 8 oz. Margarine, ½ oz. Tea, 1 pt.	Boiled Bacon, 3 oz. Pease pudding, 12 oz.	Bread, 8 oz. Margarine, ½ oz. Cocoa, 1 pt.
Monday	Bread, 8 oz. Porridge, 1½ pt.	Potatoes with milk, 24 oz. Bread, 2 oz. Cheese, 2 oz.	Bread, 8 oz. Vegetable broth, 1 pt. Cheese, 2 oz.
Tuesday	Porridge, 1½ pt. Skim milk, 1 pt.	Vegetable broth, 1 pt. Bread, 4 oz. Cheese, 2 oz. Dumpling, 8 oz.	Bread, 4 oz. Porridge, 1½ pt.
Wednesday	Bread, 2 oz. Porridge, 1½ pt. Treacle, 1½ oz.	Boiled bacon, 3 oz. Bread, 4 oz. Potatoes, 12 oz.	Porridge, 1½ pt. Skim milk, 1 pt.
Thursday	Porridge, 1½ pt. Skim milk, 1 pt.	Coffee, 1 pt. Bread, 8 oz. Cheese, 3 oz.	Bread, 8 oz. Vegetable broth, 1 pt. Cheese, 2 oz.
Friday	Bread, 2 oz. Porridge, 1½ pt. Treacle, 1½ oz.	Boiled bacon, 3 oz. Bread, 4 oz. Potatoes, 12 oz.	Bread, 6 oz. Gruel, 1½ pt.
Saturday	Bread, 4 oz. Porridge, 1½ pt.	Vegetable broth, 1 pt. Bread, 4 oz. Cheese, 2 oz. Suet pudding, 8 oz.	Bread, 8 oz. Skim milk, 1 pt.

(In addition to the above, a lunch consisting of 4 oz. bread and 1½ oz. cheese is allowed daily.)

Such meals provided an adult with quite a good intake, according to the accepted views of the time, which, generally speaking, were based on Voit's figures.

	Protein	Calories
Men	137	3560
Women	115	3000
Voit's standard	118	3055
(for an adult man)		

The Local Government Board's new diets for children were also fairly good, far better indeed than many that the expensive private schools provided. From the age of 3 to 8 they got a pint of milk a day and often ½ a pint of skimmed milk in addition, while up to the age of 16 there was ½ a pint of milk on three days of the week and ¾ of a pint on three others. This gave a very good measure of protection against vitamin and mineral deficiencies. The only items which can be critized in the light of modern views were white bread and margarine. Probably for the first time in the history of official care of children the calorific intake was adequate; from 3 to 8 years of age it was about 1825 and from 8 to 16, 2740 a day. The protein supply was also good, being respectively 66 and 87 g. daily, a reasonable proportion being derived from milk.

§ 5 WHAT ARE PROTEINS?

The first matter to be cleared up was the important question of the nutritive value of the proteins. We have already shown that Liebig taught that the proteins which form part of both animal and vegetable foods are compounds which are readily converted after assimilation first into blood and then into the material of flesh and other tissues. It will also be recalled that gelatin had somewhat perplexed him, because although obviously very like other proteins, it seemed to have no value as a 'flesh-forming' food. To account for this he offered the unconvincing explanation that its function was to form the gelatinous material of bones and tendons rather than the substance of muscles and other tissues. It was an explanation which for lack of a better one was generally accepted until about 1912. Then the true facts were revealed.

The essential discovery was made as a direct result of the brilliant series of researches which the German chemist, Emil Fischer, and his collaborators made during the first ten years or so of the century.

These experiments revealed that Liebig had been misled by the results of his rather primitive analyses into thinking that all the chief plant and animal proteins had the same composition. It was true enough that many of them contained approximately the same proportions of carbon, nitrogen, etc., but this evidence was no longer sufficient. Fischer and his pupils probed much deeper. They discovered that there is a very wide variety of proteins in natural foods and that although most of them have different composition they are in one respect alike. Without exception they proved to be compounds formed by the combination together of a large number of smaller units which, as a class, the chemist calls amino-acids.

It is unnecessary to go into the question of the chemical nature of these units. Suffice it to say that proteins are built up of some twenty-two separate amino-acids arranged in many different designs. Since all or some of them may combine together, and in different amounts to form the proteins, it will be clear that the latter class of compounds exhibit both variety and complexity.

The amino-acids are often, and quite appropriately, termed the 'building stones' of the proteins. A very simple illustration will show how they are related to the natural proteins, for it would be quite impossible to give any sort of diagrammatic portrayal of a large and complex protein molecule. We can represent six of the amino-acids, all chemically distinct, by the letters a, b, c, d, e, f. By combining together they could form many arrangements such as:

a-b-c-d-e-f
a-c-d-b-e-f

In this simple fashion we can illustrate the manner in which the 'building-stones' are combined together in the proteins, but it must be borne in mind that instead of six units and only one of each, nature uses hundreds of molecules of some or all of the twenty-two or more units that exist. Clearly, therefore, the number of possible arrangements of these units is astronomical. Some of these arrangements represent the natural proteins and a differentiation between them is based not only on the number of the amino-acid units found to be present but on the proportion of each one.

It will be helpful, perhaps, if one forms a mental picture of a protein as a mosaic composed of at least twenty-two different coloured stones, each representing a different amino-acid. If there is a large number of each type of stone the complexity and variety of the patterns which could be constructed would be very great. We will find that this simile serves usefully to illustrate other facts about the proteins.

The next important point which Fischer's researches established was that during digestion of protein foods the bonds between the individual amino-acid units are broken and the 'building-stones' are set free. It is not an immediate process, but a gradual one, requiring first the action of the digestive enzymes in the gastric juice, then a supplementary action by the agents, also enzymes, present in the pancreatic and intestinal juices.

In this manner the big protein molecule is eroded and broken down during its passage through the stomach and small bowel, until it is completely, or very nearly completely, degraded into its constituent amino-acids. It is these units which pass through the wall of the intestine and reach the blood and tissues. The breakdown of the protein in digestion can be represented by a gradual loosening of the material uniting the separate pieces of the mosaic so that finally each one is detached.

Liebig, it will be remembered, had thought that protein was absorbed unchanged, but by about 1912 it was conclusively proved that he was mistaken and that it is only after being fully digested that the material of protein is absorbed in the form of its constituent units. The process of breakdown requires about four hours in the case of easily-digestible protein foods such as underdone meat, chicken, eggs or milk. About one hour is occupied by gastric digestion, the other three by progressive degradation in the upper part of the intestines.

It will be realized that it is much more convenient from the point of view of nourishing the tissues that the proteins should be broken down to their constituent units, because these then become available for the building up of the proteins of the body. It would be of little use if the proteins were absorbed unchanged because none has a composition quite identical with those of the body.

If one examines the 'building-stones' of which the proteins are composed it is found that there are important differences, not only in respect to the particular amino-acids which are found present, but also to the proportions of each one. Using again our simple illustration of letters we might represent three different proteins by the following arrangements:

a-b-d-a-c-f-k
a-k-k-b-h-e-g
b-g-g-k-m-s-f

Now, it will be at once apparent that on full digestion these proteins will give rise to an entirely different mixture of 'building-stones'. It is these differences which determine the nutritive value of proteins as foods.

§ 6 FOOD VALUE OF PROTEIN

To return to our useful illustration of the mosaic; if one wished to lay a pavement of a certain pattern in one spot, and had available a short distance away a mosaic of identical size and design, it would be a very simple matter to loosen all the fragments of the one and relay them where desired. That is exactly what happens when meat is used as food by a growing child. The proteins of mutton or beef are very nearly identical, as regards their amino-acid make-up, with those of the tissues of the child. It is just a question of breaking down the one, transporting the constituent units through the wall of the bowel and rebuilding them in almost identical form in the growing muscles and organs. A cannibal could, therefore, claim that he has sound scientific justification for his practice.

Supposing, however, that we wish to build a mosaic of a certain design but have available only the materials provided by breaking up another mosaic of quite different character. There might not be all the different colours we needed or there might be an insufficient number of some. What could be done? In the first place, it might be possible to make some of the missing pieces ourselves. If, however, this were impossible the mosaic would have to remain uncompleted until the requisite fragments were obtainable.

This is exactly what happens in the body. Our tissues have the power to make some of the protein building-stones, but not others. The second group of amino-acids are termed the essential amino-acids and there are eight of them. When they are not provided in sufficient amount in the food the formation of new tissues stops at once for lack of building material; that is, growth ceases. If some, but not enough, are provided, growth is retarded.

Now, let us return to the case of gelatin, which, as we have seen, was recognized a hundred years go to be of exceptionally poor nutritive value. Chemical analysis reveals that it completely lacks the essential amino-acid, tryptophan, and is poor in others. It is for that reason that it is useless as a tissue-building food. This explains why weight is lost when gelatin is the only protein in the diet.

§ 7 BIOLOGICAL VALUE OF PROTEINS

It is obviously important to have the proteins graded so that their 'tissue-building' value can be assessed. The results of much experimental work on animals and man combine to give the proteins of milk and egg the highest biological value, closely followed by the proteins of meat and fish. Next come cereal protein, then the proteins of pulses and those of nuts. Gelatin, being deficient in one essential amino-acid is useless by itself for body-building, but because it is relatively rich in the amino-acid lysine, which wheat proteins lack, it can supplement the proteins of wheat to form a mixture of higher biological value than that of bread proteins. Thus, beef tea and toast can benefit an invalid.[1] The main practical conclusion to be drawn from all recent work on the nutritive value of proteins is that it is sound dietetic practice to eat a mixture of proteins, of both animal and vegetable origin.

It will be appreciated that when the experts of 1910 expressed the view that a man required not less than 120 g. of protein a day the statement meant very little. Nevertheless, there was about this time a very violent controversy on the subject of man's need for protein. We have already mentioned it but it will help our present discussion if brief reference is again made to it.

It started with the publication of Russell Chittenden's book, *Physiological Economy in Nutrition*, in 1905. This American physiologist could not understand what purpose was served by the large amounts of proteins eaten every day by adults. Obviously a child needed protein because it was growing and had to obtain material for the construction of its tissues, but why, he asked, is it so readily accepted that a fully grown man requires more than a growing boy of 12 or so? It was known at that time, indeed it had been suspected by Liebig, that protein which is not utilized in the body for tissue-building is broken down and oxidized, just as are carbohydrates and fats, to provide energy for work or for maintaining the warmth of the body.

Chittenden resolved to make an experiment on man and did so by feeding a number of soldier and student volunteers for several months on special diets which provided rather less than half the amount of protein regarded as necessary for an adult. At the end of the trial the subjects were stated by Chittenden to be in excellent health and good physical condition. Indeed, he implied in his writings that they had benefited not a little by the reduction of their protein intake. One of the findings, to which he attached no little importance, was that they excreted less uric acid. Coming at a time when certain medical circles were finding in uric acid the scapegoat for a whole list of human ailments his observations made a considerable sensation. Indeed, they gave the 'uric-acid bogy' such a boost that Harley Street did well out of it for twenty years, while the patent medicine manufacturers are still finding it an unusually paying line. Actually there is no substantial evidence to show that uric acid is in any way harmful to the normal person. It is produced by the breakdown of certain types of protein, which are present both in plant and in animal foods, and has, so far as is

[1] 'Nutritive Value of Vegetable Proteins and its Enhancement by Admixture', Harriette Chick, *Brit. J. Nutr.* (1951), V, 261.

known, no relation whatever to high blood pressure, or to many other conditions for which it has been widely blamed. The most up-to-date authorities on gout even exonerate uric acid from a primary role in that disease. The sinister advertisements showing sharp-edged crystals of uric acid as the cause of severe pain in joints and limbs are just nonsense. The pain arises from inflammation of the surfaces of the bones which form the joint and cannot be related to crystals of uric acid which do not exist.

Chittenden's views were soon attacked. It must be remembered that nothing was known at that time about the biological value of proteins; all the proteins with the exception of gelatin were regarded as equal.

Sir James Crichton-Browne was one of the first to join the fray. In a scholarly and interesting little essay entitled *Parcimony in Nutrition* (1909) he repudiated most of Chittenden's claims. One argument appeared to him to be incontrovertible. The Class 1 diet of the prisons, of which John Burns had such vivid memories, supplied just about the amount of proteins, 45 g., that Chittenden thought sufficient for a full-grown man. Why, Crichton-Browne asked, was its effect on the prisoners so harmful?

Then came Major McCay's careful survey of the diets of the Indian races.[1] This, too, seemed to provide convincing evidence that wherever one found people living on a high intake of protein, particularly animal protein, there one found good physique, physical strength and manly courage.

Little or nothing came of the dispute until the fundamental facts regarding the nutritive value of the proteins had been discovered. At once light was thrown on the discrepancies, because it was realized that the nutritive value of the proteins are not identical. It was then learnt that Class 1 prison diet was defective not because it provided only 45 g. of protein, but because that protein was almost entirely derived from bread. Had the protein been in the form of meat or milk the diet would have been much more nutritious.

It is necessary to add that in spite of many advances in our knowledge of the part played by the various components of our diet the experts are still divided on the question of the essential needs of an adult for protein.

We know that a large proportion of the protein eaten by a fully grown person is digested, absorbed and then burnt as a source of energy just as are the carbohydrates or fats. This is simply because it is not required for tissue-building. Why, then, do we still advise such a person to eat 70 or 100 g. a day? Protein foods are, by comparison with carbohydrates, expensive, and if they are to a large extent used only as a source of heat it would be more economical to take the equivalent amount of sugar or bread. We do not yet know the answer to this question.

[1] *The Protein Element in Nutrition*, D. McCay, 1912.

There is one advantage, however, in recommending a fairly high intake of proteins of high biological value. Many of the foods which supply them are also good sources of vitamins and other valuable nutrients. Thus, for example, a pint of milk provides not only about 18 g. of animal protein, but 680 mg. of calcium, from 400-800 international units of vitamin A, nearly 0.3 mg. of vitamin B_1 and nearly 1 mg. of riboflavin.

§ 8 THE DISCOVERY OF THE VITAMINS

We have already recounted how in 1881 a young assistant named Lunin, working in Bunge's laboratory, came very near to discovering the vitamins when he attempted to rear young mice on a mixture of purified proteins, carbohydrates, fat and minerals, compounded so as to resemble the composition of milk, and which according to current theories, should have provided all that was required for nutrition. Unfortunately, he did not carry his investigation further and the highly significant comment which his teacher made was soon forgotten.

On the other side of the world the medical authorities of the Dutch East Indies had for a long time been perturbed by the prevalence of beri-beri and the high death-rate among the natives. The Dutch Government decided to send a Commission out to the Colony to investigate the disease. It was the year 1886 and it is natural, so short a time after Pasteur's great discoveries had astounded the world, that the leaders of the Commission, Professors Pekelharing and Winkler, should think in terms of germs and infectivity. After a year's investigation during which they were assisted by a young Army doctor, Christian Eijkman, who had been seconded for the purpose, they returned to the Netherlands having discovered a germ, a micrococcus, which they had reason to suspect might be the cause of the disease. As they were due to return and much work remained to be done, it was arranged that Eijkman should be seconded for a further period in order to carry out the necessary investigations. For two years he concentrated his attention on the possibility that the disease was caused by an infective agent; then, a chance observation gave him what ultimately proved to be the essential clue. Scientific workers often deplore the inadequacy of the funds available for their research institutes, but it proved a blessing in disguise for Eijkman. The hospital at which he was studying had so restricted a budget that the laboratory assistant was obliged to feed the chickens which were kept for experimental purposes on the food left over from the ward kitchens. Eijkman observed, to his surprise, that a number of the birds developed a curious inability to walk and showed other symptoms which suggested that they were suffering from beri-beri. The first and natural conclusion was that they had become infected by the responsible germ, but this was soon dispelled by the unexpected observation that when the character of the food was changed the birds promptly recovered. Eijkman and his newly appointed assistant, Grijns, immediately left their bacterial cultures and began to investigate the composition of the different diets. It was found that the disease appeared in hens after only a few weeks' feeding on a diet of white, polished rice and could be cured with extraordinary rapidity by administering either unpolished rice or the material which is removed when it is polished.

It should be explained here that the polishing of rice was introduced towards the end of the nineteenth century as a method of making it appear more attractive for table use. When the outer husk of the rice grain is removed it has a curious greyish-red colour due to a very thin pigmented layer. When cooked in this form it has rather an unappetizing appearance. The coloured layer can be removed, however, by rubbing the grains between specially prepared surfaces in a machine. This is termed polishing. It is very important to note that the process does more than merely remove the pigmented layer, it also tears away the tiny germ which is tucked into one end of the grain. A grain of ordinary domestic white rice shows a little notch at one end which formerly held the germ. Like the germ of wheat, that of rice contains valuable nutrient salts and a good proportion of the vitamins of the grain.

Eijkman and his colleague were soon satisfied that the disease which the chickens developed was due to faulty diet and thought first in terms of the accepted theories about food. Polished rice is poor in fat and contains a very small proportion of mineral salts. Accordingly experiments were made in which these deficiencies were made good by adding appropriate fats and minerals. The additions were of no avail. These chickens also developed the condition resembling beri-beri. Then Grijns examined the polishings and found that he could prepare extracts which were curative in a very striking degree. The importance of this discovery lay in the fact that the amount of extract which produced a cure was so small that it did not add appreciable quantities of the previously recognized food constituents to the diet. This fundamental discovery dates from 1901, and within a year or two it was conclusively proved that the human disease beri-beri is essentially the same disorder as that which Eijkman had observed among his hospital chickens.

Eijkman's researches interested his former teacher, Pekelharing, who realized that they were undermining all the accepted theories regarding the essential principles of diet. He himself began at the University of Utrecht a series of experiments, similar in character to those which Lunin had made twenty years or more before, but he planned his with the definite object of proving or disproving whether a properly balanced mixture of protein, fat, carbohydrate and mineral salts is sufficient to maintain life and good health. Unfortunately, the conclusions he reached from these experiments were published in a Dutch medical journal and escaped the notice of most people outside Holland. Nevertheless, they were definite and provided the most impressive support for Eijkman's contentions. It is worth while to give some of his actual words.

'It has often been said that our food is adequate if it contains certain quantities of albumen, carbohydrates, fats and salts ... Yet physiology has demonstrated long since, that if food is to have its true value something more than these must be present ... It is impossible to keep an animal alive by feeding it with albumen, fat, carbohydrates, the necessary salts and water, *even if the quantities of these are amply sufficient* ... Such a substance occurs in milk ... If white mice are fed on bread baked from casein, albumen, rice meal, a mixture of all the salts that should be present and if water is their only drink *they die from deficiency* ... At first all goes well ... The bread is eaten readily and the mice look healthy ... Soon they grow lean, their appetite diminishes and within four weeks all are dead ... But if milk is given instead of water they keep in health, *notwithstanding that the quantities of albumen, lactose and fat they take with the milk are insignificant by comparison with those in the bread they consume. ...*

'I only wish to emphasize that an unrecognized substance occurs in milk which is of paramount importance for nutrition even in minute quantities ... If it is lacking the organism loses the ability to utilize the well-known principal components of the food, appetite is lost *and with apparent abundance the animals die of starvation.*'[1]

The views that Pekelharing had expressed were new. The animals that failed to thrive on the artificial food did so in spite of the fact that there was plenty of protein, of carbohydrate, of calories and of salts available, but when a minute trace of something found in milk was added to their diet it made all the difference between life and death.

Soon confirmatory proof of the existence of a new and very important class of food component was forthcoming. A German biochemist, Dr Stepp, discovered in 1909 that the nutritive value of foods is greatly reduced if all the fatty components are extracted. To his surprise, however, he also found that replacement of the extracted material by pure fats did not make good the deficiency. It could only be made good by replacing the whole

[1] The full details of the early experiments of Professor Pekelharing were kindly supplied by the late Professor G. Grijns, formerly of the Agricultural High School, Wageningen, who also provided the translation of the passage from the account of Pekelharing's Lecture published in 1905 (*Nederlandsche Tijdschrift v. Geneeskunde*, 51).

of the extracted material. He had, although he did not fully realize it at the time, discovered the fat-soluble vitamins.

Finally, in 1912 Professor Hopkins, later Sir Frederick Gowland Hopkins, demonstrated by a convincing series of experiments that animals decline in health on a diet lacking the essential vitamins even when they are eating sufficient protein, fat, carbohydrate and mineral salts to supply all their requirements. He at first referred to the newly discovered substances as the 'accessory factors of the diet'; it was a non-committal and not altogether satisfactory term because it was one which might also cover condiments and flavouring substances, which can fairly be regarded as 'accessories'. Funk coined the name 'vitamine' and this, with its original final *e* discarded[1] in deference to certain accepted rules of chemical nomenclature, has now been universally adopted.

§9 EXPERIMENTAL SCURVY

The previous discussion of scurvy should have made it clear that even after nearly five hundred years' experience of the disease very little was known about it. It was generally believed that it could be cured by fresh fruit and herbs, but this had been common knowledge among sailors since the early sixteenth century. Many people still suspected that salt foods had a good deal to do with its causation, but opinions were sharply divided as to whether fresh meat was a cure. Some people put their faith in lime juice; others asserted that they had found it useless. Nothing could better illustrate the halting progress of human knowledge when all there is to build upon is the random and uncoordinated impressions of individuals. There is no reason for thinking that we should know any more about scurvy today than we did in 1800 if another chance observation arising from a feeding experiment had not provided a means of making precise studies of the disease. Vitamin research owes a lot to chance observation, although Pasteur spoke truly when he said 'chance favours only him who is prepared'.

In 1907 two Norwegian scientists, Drs Holst and Fröhlich, were invited by their Government to investigate a disease known as 'ship beri-beri' which was affecting the health of seamen in the Navy. They had reasons for suspecting that improper food was responsible and they decided to try to reproduce a similar disease in animals by feeding them on the type of diet the sailors were getting; they doubtless had in mind the success which had followed Eijkman's discovery of the relation between chicken and human beri-beri. The Norwegian scientists experimented on guinea-pigs. They

[1] A procedure suggested by J. C. Drummond, see *Biochemical Journal* (1920), XIV, 660.

were not successful in reproducing a condition similar to the disorder they had hoped to study, but they observed that the animals developed a condition curiously like human scurvy. Closer examination revealed that it was scurvy. Holst and Fröhlich quickly appreciated that they had discovered a valuable means of producing the disease.

The first result of experimental studies of their experiments was convincing proof that scurvy arises as a result of lack of something in the diet. Throughout the centuries of the history of scurvy this idea had only once been clearly stated, by Bachstrom in 1734, and his views had soon passed into obscurity. The next outcome of Holst and Fröhlich's work was that it was found possible to use guinea-pigs as a means of assessing the relative value of antiscorbutic foods. For example, it required only a few weeks of experimentation to establish what exactly were the relative values of lime juice and lemon juice. This particular test immediately cleared up one of the most disturbing of the many discrepancies in the tangled history of the disease and one which might never have been elucidated had progress depended on empirical and uncontrolled trials by seamen and explorers whose judgment, in any case, was usually influenced by strong prejudices.

The guinea-pig also played a noteworthy part in the actual isolation of the vitamin itself. It was first separated as a pure crystalline substance in 1932 by a young Hungarian scientist, Szent Györgi, who was in fact searching for something of a totally different character. When he first obtained the crystals he did not suspect that he had isolated the essential antiscorbutic principle. At about the same time, however, two American scientists, Drs King and Waugh, isolated the same compound from lemon juice. Neither of these substances could have been immediately tested for antiscorbutic potency if animal experimentation had not been resorted to. It would have been useless to wait for cases of human scurvy to appear. They are rare, and even had one or two been available it would have been unfair to postpone a certain cure by treatment with lemon or orange juice while a substance of entirely unknown value, and which for all that was then known might have been either inactive or even toxic, was tried; for it must be borne in mind that the isolation of the pure vitamin from lemon juice had involved many stages of chemical treatment, after each of which it was necessary to make tests in order to see in which fraction the active material was concentrated.

The animal experiments proved that a minute amount of the crystals prevents or cures scurvy in guinea-pigs. Then, and only then, was it reasonable to try its effect on scurvy in man. It produced prompt recovery. The next step was taken by the organic chemists whose skill and ingenuity soon enabled them to discover that the vitamin was chemically very closely related to a member of the class of the sugars, of which there are many besides the common ones, glucose, cane-sugar and milk-sugar. The chemists next attempted to convert this particular sugar into the vitamin by appropriate chemical treatment. It proved successful and the synthesis of the vitamin had been achieved.

A few years before these discoveries were made we had a tragic reminder of the effect of the ravages of acute scurvy. In early December 1915 General Townshend, retreating after the failure of his attack at Ctesiphon, decided to make a stand at Kut-el-Amara. Within a few days he was surrounded by the Turks. By Christmas Day it had been found necessary to reduce the rations of the garrison and before long further reductions were enforced. By the beginning of March the white troops were subsisting on 1 lb. 4 oz. of horseflesh, 10 oz. of bread and a little oatmeal. The Indian troops had 10 oz. of barley flour, 4 oz. of barley, a little *ghee* (native butter) and a handful of dates. These restricted diets caused two deficiency diseases to appear. The English troops began to fall victims to beri-beri because their bread was white and their diets as a whole deficient in vitamin B_1, whereas the Indian troops became scorbutic as a result of the lack of fresh vegetables in their diet. It is interesting that the white men were protected against acute scurvy by their small ration of horse-flesh. Fresh meat is by no means rich in ascorbic acid but providing it is not cooked too long it may serve to prevent the more obvious symptoms from appearing. On the other hand, the Indians escaped beri-beri because they ate whole barley, but developed severe scurvy when, on religious grounds, they refused the ration of meat.

Before General Townshend capitulated at the end of April he had nearly 1100 cases of severe scurvy and 150 of beri-beri out of his small force of about 9000 men. This serious loss of fighting strength might have been prevented had it been possible, as it would be today, to drop from an aeroplane a small packet containing a few ounces of pure vitamins B_1 and C. There is a cruel irony in the fact that an aeroplane did drop a small packet to bring relief to the starving garrison; it contained opium to deaden the pangs of hunger.

This was not the only occasion on which our forces in Mesopotamia suffered from scurvy. In fact it became a considerable menace before the authorities learnt how to cope with it. At first they showed a pathetic faith in lime juice such as was supplied to the Navy, but on the whole it proved unreliable. This led to the investigation into the value of other antiscorbutics which revealed that lemon juice is so much more powerful as an antiscorbutic than lime juice. After this discovery was made late in 1916 our forces in the East were provided with supplies of preserved lemon juice or with vegetables which were specially grown in garden plots near the front lines. There are probably many people who will remember the thin, pallid, insipid 'marmalade' which was all that could be procured in England during the latter part of the First World War. It was prepared from the residues of lemon pulp from which the juice had been expressed to make antiscorbutics for the fighting forces.

CHAPTER XXIV

THE APPLICATION OF THE NEWER KNOWLEDGE OF NUTRITION

by Dorothy Hollingsworth

§ 1 TRENDS IN FOOD SUPPLIES

UNTIL the nineteenth century no quantitative information existed on the total volume of British food supplies, so that it is impossible to calculate the nutritive value of the national diet over the centuries for comparison with estimates for the twentieth century. In the last quarter of the nineteenth century, however, official statistics of food production became available and it was then possible to obtain a more complete quantitative picture of the national diet. A Committee of the British Association in 1881 was appointed 'for the purpose of inquiring into and reporting on the present Appropriation of Wages, and other sources of income, and considering how far it is consonant with the economic progress of the people of the United Kingdom'. The report of this Committee[1] gave, for the first time, the distribution of the national income on different foods with some estimates of consumption. The following information is taken from the report. Yearly consumption of flour (of about 71 per cent extraction) was about 280 lb. per head, of which roughly half was imported and half home-grown. Consumption of potatoes, of which just over 10 per cent was imported, was 296 lb. per head. Of the quantity of vegetables and fruit home-produced there was no account, but the Committee estimated expenditure at half that on potatoes, or 0.25d. per head per day net or 0.32d. including distribution costs. Consumption of meat was about 90 lb. and fish about 18 lb. per head — for both these foods London was better supplied than the rest of the country. Butter and cheese together amounted to 20 lb. per head, rather more than half of which was home-produced. No estimate was given for milk and egg consumption, though the expenditure on both together was given as 0.66d. per head per day net or 0.78d. including distribution costs. Excluding sugar used for brewing, sugar consumption was about 64 lb. per head. Consumption of beer was 28 gallons per head per year (or over 4 pints a week at a cost of 7d.) and of spirits over a gallon per head per year. The Committee remarked

---

[1] *Report of the Fifty-first Meeting of the British Association for the Advancement of Science,* August-September (1881), LI, 272.

that the 'consumption of imported articles of food and drink has largely increased of late years' and added:

A large consumption of articles of food in great part imported is a sign of general prosperity, and is conclusive to greater effectiveness of labour. There is no reason to suppose that home production has diminished of late years, except indeed as the consequence of deficient harvests on special years. The increasing imports therefore denote so much additional food consumed by the people. Mr. Stephen Bourne (one of the members of the committee . . . said: To be thus dependent upon extraneous sources for so large a portion of the national food may probably, to some minds, be the occasion of much anxiety, as rendering our existence precarious, and as being derogatory to our national pride; but provided our circumstances be such as to preclude it resulting in financial embarrassment we shall find it to be in every respect advantageous, or at least to have so many benefits connected with it as to far outweigh any consideration of an opposite character.'

The next estimate of British food resources was that prepared by the Committee of the Royal Society in 1916 for the years 1909-13.[1] In a Presidential Address delivered to the Royal Statistical Society on June 17th, 1930, Sir Alfred (then Mr A. W.) Flux of the Board of Trade compared the pre-war estimates with corresponding data for 1924-28.[2] Estimates were made by the late Sir Albert (then Mr A. E.) Feavearyear for the years 1924-27 and 1932 and by the Market Supply Committee for 1934 and 1935. These last were revised in consultation with the Board of Trade and the Agricultural Departments to give the data used by the Advisory Committee on Nutrition of the Ministry of Health in its First Report.[3]

Both Flux and the Ministry of Health Committee pointed out that the data for 1909-13 are not strictly comparable with those for later years, because at that time the United Kingdom included the area and population of what is now Eire. Although allowance was made for the change in the numbers of the population of the United Kingdom at various dates, it was not possible to estimate the probable effect of the change in the consumption habits of the population caused by the transference of Eire, a predominantly rural area, from the United Kingdom. If the food supplies of Eire had been included in the 1934-35 estimates the main differences would have been slightly smaller consumption of meat and fish and rather larger consumption of milk, eggs, butter and vegetables and potatoes.

[1] Cd. 8421, 1917.
[2] 'Our Food Supply before and after the War', A. W. Flux, *J. Roy. Stat. Soc.* (1930), XCIII, 538.
[3] *Ministry of Health. Advisory Committee on Nutrition. First Report*, 1937.

TRENDS IN UNITED KINGDOM FOOD SUPPLIES FROM 1880 TO 1954
(lb. per head per year)

	1880 (i)	1909-13 (ii)	1924-28 (iii)	1934-38 (iv)	1941 (iv)	1944 (iv)	1947 (iv)	1950 (iv)	1952 (v)	1954 (vi)
Dairy products										
Total as milk solids	n.a.	33	35	38	41	49	49	54	52	52
Liquid milk	213	219	217	217	265	308	306	347	342	334
Cheese	8	7	9	9	8	10	9	10	8	9
Meat (carcase wt. incl. bacon and ham)	91	131	129	129	99	110	96	112	100	124
Poultry and game	n.a.	5(a)	6(a)	9	6	4	7	7	8	6
Fish	18	41	41	26	16	20	32	22	23	21
Eggs	11	16(a)	15(a)	28	25	27	25	31	28	30
Butter	12	16	16	25	10	8	11	17	11	14
Margarine	0	6	12	9	18	18	15	17	19	18
Other fats	n.a.	4(b)	6(b)	19	18	19	14	19	20	22
Sugar(c)	64	79	87	98	67	71	82	83	88	105
Potatoes	296	208	194	182	188	275	286	246	238	222
Other vegetables (incl. pulses) and tomatoes	n.a.	83(a)	106(a)	127	123	140	142	132	124	132
Fruits (incl. nuts)	n.a.	69(a)	118(a)	104	30	52	89	86	87	102
Wheat flour	280	211	198	194	237	234	225	206	202	187
Other cereals	n.a.	26	16	16	20	19	17	17	18	15

n.a. — not available.

(a) Including domestic production.
(b) Excluding home-produced lard which is included in meat.
(c) Excluding sugar for brewing.

Sources (i) British Association, *Report of Committee on Appropriation of Wages* (1881), LI, 272.
(ii) Royal Society Committee, *The Food Supply of the United Kingdom*, Cd. 8421, 1917.
(iii) A. W. Flux, 'Our Food Supply before and after the War', *Journal of Royal Statistical Society* (1930), XCIII, 528.
(iv) *Ministry of Food Bulletin*, No. 720, 1953.
(v) *Board of Trade Journal*, July 9th, 1955.
(vi) Ibid., August 11th, 1956.

The statistics of food supplies in the United Kingdom have improved since 1939, so that there now exists a series of estimates, which takes account of home production, imports and stock changes for each year from 1940 onwards. The estimates for the pre-1939 years have also been revised. The methods by which these data have been compiled were described in 1944 by a Committee of the Combined Food Board[1] and the complete series can be obtained from reports of the second Ministry of Food and the present Ministry of Agriculture, Fisheries and Food.[2] There also exist the

[1] *Report on Food Consumption Levels in the United States, Canada and the United Kingdom*, Combined Food Board.
[2] *Ministry of Food Bulletin*, No. 720, p. 6; Ibid., No. 755, p. 8; *Board of Trade Journal*, July 9th, 1955; Ibid., August 11th, 1956.

records provided by the National Food Survey which was started in 1940 to supply information on the adequacy of the diet of the urban-working class, and which was extended in 1950 to cover the whole population at a time of rising prices and inflation.

Mr E. M. H. Lloyd[1] has recently summarized the data on trends in national food supplies between 1880 and 1951, deriving his estimates from the sources already mentioned. The preceding table is based on Lloyd's summary, but has been expanded to include information on poultry and game, fish, fats other than butter and margarine, vegetables and fruits. Different post-1939 years have been chosen to illustrate, from the nutritional aspect, the effects of wartime and post-war conditions.

The estimates for 1934-38 onwards are comparable with each other (their nutritional value is given in Appendix B), but not so closely with those for earlier years. In spite of the imperfections of the earlier data, the trends that the series reveal are probably sufficiently trustworthy to provide a background to a discussion on the application of nutritional knowledge to the problem of feeding the population in the twentieth century.

§ 2 FIRST WORLD WAR[2]

When hostilities broke out in 1914 the position was an interesting one, because scientists in England held more advanced views on nutrition than those in Germany. The latter were still wholly absorbed in estimates of proteins, fats, carbohydrates, minerals and calories, and had failed to show any interest in the new discoveries which were beginning to reveal the existence of vitamins. It was a difference of outlook that persisted throughout the First World War and that was not without influence on the direction of the policy in regard to food problems adopted by the Governments of the two countries. The years of the First World War, like those of the Second, produced a wide variety of problems that were essentially nutritional, some of which had close relation to peace-time problems, but all of which called urgently for attention and study. The 1914-18 war provided the first occasion in history when the scientist was in a position to study such problems by precise methods and to offer advice on their solution. The application of nutritional science to the problem of feeding the British population has been accelerated by national danger. Recruitment for the South African War first revealed the poor physique of large sections of the population; the

---

[1] E. M. H. Lloyd (1952), *J. Proc. Agricultural Economics Society*, X, 174.
[2] Much of the material in this section was taken from Chapter XXIV, 'The War' of the first edition of *The Englishman's Food*.

1914-18 war provided an opening for the first attempt to use the findings of science in the feeding of the nation. It took the depression and unemployment of the 'thirties to cause the nation to consider by what means sufficient food of suitable nutritional composition could be provided at a cost within the means of all sections of the population. When the Second World War struck in 1939, sufficient scientific, medical and economic facts were available to make it possible to apply from the outset the accumulated knowledge of the previous forty years.

In August 1914 neither side had any suspicion that the successful solution of food problems would play a big part in determining victory. It has been stated that the *War Book* of the British Government, which contained the plans for ensuring the safety of the country in case of war and for conducting a campaign in France or Belgium, made no reference to food questions.[1] When Germany opened the campaign her plans were based on the confident assumption that the struggle would be fierce but brief. When disillusionment came her rulers were slowly forced to realize that the problem of feeding their people was just as serious as that of breaking the power of the enemy on land and sea. Disillusionment came to England too; but not until the unexpected scope and success of the submarine warfare made it clear that it was by no means impossible for our island to be starved into capitulation.

Germany was the first to suffer. The position was reviewed by a Committee of German scientists when the war had lasted a year.[2] They were still hopeful that the bare needs of the population could be provided by home production, but it was soon impossible for the Germans to hide from the world the gap in their armour. Signs of malnourishment were beginning to appear in the towns where food was short. Doctors were reporting that children were showing retarded development, pallor and debility, and that a rise in the incidence of rickets, tuberculosis and other diseases was already obvious. The comfortable middle-class citizen was finding that his weight was steadily falling and that he was much more susceptible to colds, influenza and other infections than in normal times. In the autumn of 1916 Germany's position was desperate and she was within a month or two of capitulation from exhaustion when Mackensen brought temporary relief by his brilliant and lightning quick conquest of Rumania.

Meanwhile, Britain was having to face the effects of submarine warfare after a temporary lull in the summer caused by indignant American protests. By October the toll of sunken ships had reached an alarming total. For the first time the public learned that nearly two million tons of shipping had been

---

[1] *British Food Control*, Sir William H. Beveridge, 1928. We have drawn liberally upon the wealth of information contained in this volume of the *Social and Economic History of the World War* prepared under the auspices of the Carnegie Endowment for International Peace.
[2] *Die deutsche Volksernährung und die Englische Aushungersplan*, P. Eltzbacher, 1915.

sent to the bottom. Until then no steps more far-reaching than the appointment of a Sugar Commission to regulate imports and supplies of sugar had been taken to protect the food supply of the people; this Commission had been appointed in the first week of the war when two-thirds of the usual supply was cut off by the isolation of central Europe. A Royal Commission on Wheat with similar powers was hurriedly appointed, but Mr Runciman, speaking in the House of Commons as President of the Board of Trade, expressed the view of the Cabinet that there was no need to appoint a Food Controller or establish a Ministry of Food. He was emphatic. 'We want to avoid any rationing of our people in food.'[1] That was in October 1916.

After so definite a pronouncement of the official view it came as a distinct shock to the nation when scarcely a month later Mr Runciman announced that the Government intended to appoint a Controller immediately and to assume almost unlimited powers of control over food supplies and prices. The change had been brought about by an alarming rise in food prices and by the growing suspicion of the public that they were being victimized by profiteers. Shortly afterwards Mr Asquith's government fell and the Controller was not appointed until the Second Coalition came into power under Mr Lloyd George's leadership in early December. The choice fell on Lord Devonport.

His acceptance of office coincided with the presentation of an important report to the Government. Before he left the Board of Trade Mr Runciman had appreciated the need to obtain an accurate estimate of the minimum food requirements of the whole population. His Department had statistics giving the imports of foods in times of peace, while the Board of Agriculture had estimates of the production of food at home, but these data did not indicate the smallest quantity of food necessary to keep going. He wisely approached a Committee of the Royal Society that had been appointed a little earlier with the object of providing a panel of scientists capable of advising on physiological matters relating to the war. They had already advised against restricting the importation of fruit. It was the official view that oranges, lemons and apples were dispensable luxuries and that with heavy demands on cargo accommodation in ships it was advisable to use all available space for transporting wheat and meat. It was a reasonable official attitude but the Royal Society Committee had good grounds for taking another point of view. Only a few months previously General Townshend and his gallant little force beleaguered in Kut-el-Amara had been forced to capitulate to the Turks, a tragic event, hastened by the ravages of scurvy and beri-beri.

The Army medical authorities were beginning to appreciate that deficiency diseases might be responsible for loss of man-power in some of the theatres

[1] *Hansard*, 86, H.C. Deb. 15 (October 17th 1916).

of war. Scurvy had spread and become very troublesome in Mesopotamia after the tragedy of Kut, no less than 11,000 men being invalided from this cause in 1916. At home scientists were following with great interest the researches in progress at the Lister Institute of Preventive Medicine in London by Miss (now Dame) Harriette Chick and her colleagues, who were attempting to find foods which would give protection against scurvy and beri-beri. The Royal Society Committee had this work in mind when they warned the Government that there would be risk, if the importation of fresh fruit were cut off, that the health of the people would be harmed as a result of a lack of 'essential subtle principles'.

The next valuable service rendered by the Royal Society Committee was the preparation of the estimate of the food resources and food requirements of the nation which Mr Runciman had desired. This thorough and comprehensive survey, which has already been mentioned as the second estimate of British food resources, showed that the pre-war (average 1909-13) home-production and imports of food had been sufficient to provide on the average 87 g. protein, 100 g. fat and 440 g. carbohydrate supplying 3091 Cal. per head daily. Allowing for the smaller consumption by women and children, the amounts 'per man' were estimated at 113 g. protein, 130 g. fat, 571 g. carbohydrate and 4009 Cal. In comparison the requirement of an average workman doing an average day's work was considered to be 100 g. protein, 100 g. fat, 500 g. carbohydrate and approximately 3400 Cal. The Committee concluded that the food supply had not only met requirements in the past, but had provided a margin for waste during transport and marketing and in the home.[1]

For the first time an estimate of our need for food was drawn up in metric tons of protein and milliards of calories. The survey was reassuring so far as the immediate future was concerned, for it was found that the food available was sufficient to provide the fighting forces with 140 g. protein and 4300 Cal. and the civilian population with 106 g. protein and 3859 Cal., both expressed per man per day. But the Committee found it necessary to sound a warning that, whereas there was still available a margin of about 5 per cent above 'the minimum necessary for proper nutrition' the prices of certain foods were tending to rise and that this movement was an indication of approaching scarcity that would need careful watching; otherwise inequalities of distribution would arise unless steps were taken to ensure the equitable distribution of the available food throughout the population. The warning was opportune and the conclusion of the Committee sounds such a modern note that it is worth-while to quote it:

[1] *The Food supply of the United Kingdom*, prepared originally as a confidential document, December 9th, 1916, and later published as Cd. 8421, 1917.

The Committee, as physiologists, desire to lay stress on the fact that in buying food the labouring population is buying energy — the power to do work. Increased cost of food . . . means increased cost of production. If the rising prices curtail for any class of the community its accustomed supply of food, its output of work will, of necessity, be reduced. It is important to remember that a slight reduction of food below the necessary amount causes a large diminution in the working efficiency of the individual.

The new Ministry of Food did not start well, partly on account of Lord Devonport's reluctance to accept scientific advice. He seemed unwilling to believe that scientists could know more about food than one who, like himself, had spent a lifetime as a provision merchant and he made many mistakes that aroused criticism both in official circles and in the press. No amount of hard work, for he killed himself overworking at his task, could make up for the blunders caused by his ignorance of the simplest facts about the functions of foods. In February he launched an appeal for voluntary rationing, suggesting that purchases of essential foods should be limited to 4 lb. of bread, 2½ lb. of meat and ¾ lb. of sugar per head per week. Such a plan ensured only 1200-1300 Cal., or less than half the requirement of a man doing light work. To obtain the rest it would be necessary to increase considerably the consumption of potatoes, butter, margarine or milk, the necessary supplies of which were simply not to be had, apart from any question of expense.

Having these facts in mind the Committee [of the Royal Society] views with concern the loyal attempts which schools and charitable institutions are making to comply with the published voluntary ration.

Confirming the truth of these remarks, the boys at Christ's Hospital showed a sharp fall in weight during the summer term as a result of restricting their bread supply.

At the time the distribution of sugar was giving rise to difficulties and to a growing volume of complaint. Lord Devonport planned economies by restricting its use for confectionery and sweet cakes. Sir William (now Lord) Beveridge has given a picture, as disturbing as it is amusing, of a meeting of the higher chiefs of the Ministry at which they 'sat in solemn inquisition round the library table, passing from hand to hand in judgment a selection of ₅ugared cakes bought as specimens that morning; the exhibits later furnished a sumptuous tea for the typists in the sugar department'.[1]

In April 1917 Lord Devonport launched another ill-advised venture, the

[1] *British Food Control*, Sir William H. Beveridge, 1928.

'meatless' day, which was at once attacked by the scientists who pointed out that it would lead to a reduction in the consumption of home-produced food at the expense of imported grain. At the same time they revealed the seriously misleading statements which had been made in a *Food Economy Handbook* issued by the Ministry for the guidance of the public. One statement absolutely false as the Royal Society memorandum of 1916 clearly showed, was that 'before the war the nation could live on the food it wasted'. Even more serious was the allegation, also wholly untrue, that 'if you are eating meat you are better without bread: starch and meat together double the stomach's work'.

The confidential memoranda sent to the Minister by the Royal Society Committee in April 1917 were fearlessly outspoken and did not hide the fact that they thought disaster lay ahead. A rising toll of torpedoed ships and increasing irregularities of supplies were making the food position much more serious. In spite of this menace and the warning of rising prices, only wheat, flour and sugar were under Government regulation and control. Fears of an even more serious shortage had, however, led to the consideration at the Ministry of plans for a rationing scheme, which gravely alarmed the Royal Society Committee. It appeared that officials were thinking of including bread and flour in the scheme. Immediately the Committee pointed out to the authorities that unlimited supplies of a cheap form of energy were necessary if the working efficiency of the civil population was to be maintained. They expressed the belief that the mass of the people sustained by patriotic impulses would tolerate almost any deprivation in a national emergency providing there was enough food to satisfy hunger. Therefore, urged the Committee, however much it may be found necessary to restrict the consumption of meat, eggs, milk, butter and other important foods, leave bread and flour outside the scheme for as long as possible.

The Committee drew attention to the desirability of killing off a certain carefully estimated proportion of cattle, sheep and pigs, the number of which had increased since 1914, on the ground that livestock are wasteful transformers of energy, because an animal expends a large proportion of the energy of its food as heat given off by its body, and in movement. As food supply this is entirely lost, the return in flesh being 8 to 16 per cent of the energy value of the animal's food, and in milk about 35 per cent.[1] This again was an opportune warning. The area required to raise meat can be better employed in a time of shortage by producing cereals or potatoes.

There was no sign that the sound advice tendered by the Committee was

---

[1] *The Efficiency of Farm Animals in the Conversion of Feedingstuffs to Food for Man*, I. Leitch and W. Godden, Commonwealth Bureau of Animal Nutrition, Technical Communication No. 14, July 1953.

welcomed at the Ministry, and the Committee, feeling that they would be failing in a national duty if they did not reiterate it, submitted a series of memoranda, each more strongly worded than the last. They prophesied disaster if the supply of the chief and cheapest forms of energy, bread and flour, were reduced by rationing before such a step was absolutely inescapable.

In May 1917, Lord Devonport, broken by his sincere if often misguided efforts to cope with a task beyond his powers, resigned because of ill-health and in the following month Lord Rhondda took over. Almost at once there were signs of a more vigorous and enlightened direction. But within a few months events provided proof of the reality of the very dangers which the Royal Society Committee had foreseen.

It was clear by the summer of 1917 that the distribution of some foodstuffs would have to be improved. The shortage and high price of sugar was causing discontent in some parts of the country and there were signs of shortage of meat and fats. Between June and October a violent and bitter controversy raged among officials as to whether sugar should be rationed on a household or an individual basis, and in October a puzzled public which had already filled in the 'household registration' forms was asked to start all over again and to fill in new forms entitling them to individual cards. The new scheme came into force as the New Year dawned and proved an immediate success. Everybody was at least assured of half a pound of sugar a week.

Other signs were ominous. Prices were rising and distribution was chaotic. As the year drew to its close the grim sight of food queues standing in the wet and foggy streets warned the Government that it would not be wise to delay any longer its powers to ration and control all the important foods. The mechanism for this had been prepared in November and on February 25th, 1918, a scheme for rationing meat (by value), butter and margarine (by weight) came into force in London and the Home Counties. It seems clear that the Government feared that the people would react unfavourably and mistrusted the assurances of their scientific advisers that a well-planned measure would be unlikely to disturb morale if everyone was treated alike and if plenty of a cheap source of energy, such as bread, was available to stave off hunger and to enable people to work without undue fatigue.

During the next few months public confidence was won by the smooth working of the system and by carefully chosen propaganda. By the summer of 1918 the Government had taken control of all the important foods, and in one year its turnover amounted to over £900,000,000. Perhaps the most striking feature of this time of rationing in England was the negligible extent to which evasion and illicit trading occurred, an experience repeated in the

Second World War. By comparison with other countries they were almost non-existent. Rich and poor, the great hotel and the small East End eating house, were treated alike and it was no easier to get a little extra sugar in Mayfair than it was in Bethnal Green. In fact, the well-to-do were rather worse off than the poorer people because the rations of meat represented a much greater reduction of their usual consumption. There was, of course, a good deal of grumbling, which was hardly surprising, as there was much to put up with.

By the end of November 1916 the first 'war bread' of about 76 per cent extraction had appeared. Owing to the subsequent steady rise in the percentage of extraction of flour, bread took on a dirty greyish colour. The Royal Society Committee had advised the Ministry in 1917 that an extraction of flour equivalent to 80 per cent of the whole wheat represented the most economical distribution between its use as flour for human food and as offal for feeding livestock. In February 1917 extraction of up to 81 per cent was authorized and admixture with 5 per cent of flour derived from barley, rye or oats made compulsory. The extraction rate rose from 78 per cent in October 1917 to about 92 per cent in March and April 1918, when there was an acute shortage. Later it fell, as supplies came in, to about 87 per cent where it remained until control ceased. At various times soya and potato flour and other materials as well as other cereal flours were mixed with wheaten flour, so that the war bread was not attractive. It was at its worst in the first half of 1918, but at least everyone got as much as he wanted.

Fat American bacon, at which many people grumbled, began to arrive in the early summer of 1918. Although disliked it helped to compensate for a reduction in the meat ration. From 4 oz. in the early part of the year the weekly ration of bacon rose to 1 lb. The population felt very keenly the inadequacy of the rations of butter and margarine which amounted to 4 oz. weekly for both fats from January to June 1918, and 5 oz. from then onwards. Butter was often lacking and the ration was made up with margarine, which was then by no means an attractive product. Manufacturers could not select oils suitable for its manufacture. They were obliged to use anything they were lucky enough to get. In addition, it was not then known that butter is a good source of vitamin A and also contains some vitamin D, whereas margarine, without fortification, lacks these vitamins. The general shortage of fats and sugar produced cravings in many people, particularly in children. It was noticed, for example, that children at school who in normal times tended to dislike fat developed a strong desire to eat every piece they could get hold of and the desire for sweets became almost an obsession not only with children but with many adults.

That we emerged from the conflict with the morale of our civil population comparatively unshaken can be fairly attributed to the fact that we never went hungry, another event which foreshadowed the Second World War. The scientists had been right in their predictions that the people would stand a great deal of hardship in the way of food restrictions providing they could get anough food to keep warm and do their daily work without fatigue, and providing they could rest assured that all classes were being treated alike.

It does not follow that because the British population did not suffer prolonged hunger, as did the civil populations of Germany and Austria, they were unaffected by the eighteen months or more of restricted diet. One would suppose that there must have been a sharp rise in the incidence of rickets in young children. Compared with peace-time, the diet had tended to become richer in carbohydrates, poorer in calcium and increasingly deficient in vitamin D. This could have had only one consequence, an increase in the number of rachitic children. There is no statistical evidence that it occurred, because there is no sound information about the prevalence of the disorder in towns in 1914. What is certain is that the survey reported by the Medical Research Council in October 1917 indicated that not less than 50 per cent of the children in industrial populations were affected[1] and Dr Corry Mann, who had an intimate knowledge of conditions in the poorer areas, gave it as his opinion that the incidence of rickets, which had been declining just before the war as a result of the activities of the newly established Maternity and Infant Welfare Centres, had risen appreciably by 1919.[2]

The survey[3] compiled by the then medical officer of Christ's Hospital, Dr G. E. Friend, from a large mass of data representing observations covering the twenty years from 1913 to 1933, provides a valuable insight into the effects of the diets of the First World War. Up to the spring of 1917 the diet of the boys was much the same as it had been before 1914. Taken as a whole it was a good diet, except that fruit and vegetables did not figure in it to the extent that would be recommended today: in 1913 they were not regarded as essential food for the growing boy. In the summer of 1917 when an attempt was made to limit the consumption of bread in response to the Government's appeal for voluntary restriction, the average calorie intake fell from the peace-time level of rather less than 2700 daily to about 2500. Immediately a loss of weight was shown by a considerable proportion of the boys. When the rationing of fats was introduced, butter was replaced by a small ration of margarine. Fortunately, as the boys were by this time allowed to make up the deficiency with bread the energy intake was not further

[1] 'A Study of Social and Economic Factors in the Causation of Rickets', Margaret Ferguson and L. Findlay, *Medical Research Committee, Special Report*, No. 20, 1918.

[2] 'Rickets: the Relative Importance of Environment and Diet as Factors of Causation', H. Corry Mann, *Medical Research Council, Special Report*, No. 68, 1922.

[3] *The Schoolboy, A Study of his Nutrition, Physical Development and Health*, G. E. Friend, 1935.

reduced; on the contrary, it tended to return to normal. The replacement of butter by margarine had one curious result, although at the time a relation between them was unsuspected: there was a surprising increase in the number of fractured bones. Another observation made later was that the unusual fragility of the boys' limbs seemed to persist after the beginning of 1919 when the school kitchens were again able to provide an ordinary diet. Having Mellanby's recently published work on the cause of rickets in mind, Dr Friend suspected that a vitamin deficiency might be responsible and it then struck him that although the boys were getting what was more-or-less a pre-war diet, the school authorities had not replaced the margarine by butter. The Governors agreed in 1922 to make the change and almost at once the incidence of broken bones returned to its usual level. It would be difficult to find a more striking illustration of the influence of a mild vitamin deficiency, which was detected only because the diet and physical condition of the community were under such close observation.

The examination of the Army recruits for the South African War had, as we have pointed out, caused alarm owing to its revelation of the extent to which physical disability was rife. The same disturbingly high proportion of men judged unfit for active service was found in the 1914-18 war, but the findings were much more significant and much more serious than those which shook Whitehall early in the century. Then, not a few had accepted the comforting view that a large proportion of those who volunteered for service represented a class of poverty-stricken down-and-outs among whom undernourishment was to be expected. They refused to believe that the working-class population as a whole was affected to that extent. No such view could be retained after the operation of the Military Service Acts of 1916. For the first time in our history every male in England, Scotland and Wales between the ages of 18 and 41 was medically examined. A vast and invaluable mass of statistical information about the state of the nation's health was obtained. There could no longer be any question of evading the seriousness of the position, for the proportion relegated to category C was high.

Fortunately, there was in existence a body competent and anxious to give attention to such matters, the Medical Research Committee, which had been established in 1913, and which, with the grant of a Royal Charter in 1920, became the Medical Research Council. They decided that one of the most pressing matters to be investigated was the cause of rickets. A comprehensive co-ordinated scheme of inquiry had been planned and, although the exigencies of the war held up much of the work, one part was completed. The late Sir Edward Mellanby was asked to reinvestigate the relation of calcium and phosphorus to the causation of rickets. To do this he decided to produce the disease experimentally in animals, so that he might be able to study the intake and output of bone-forming elements with greater precision than is possible in studies on infants or young children. He turned to the current theories of the origin of the disease, of which there were many, and thought it worth while to investigate the claim that a diet rich in carbohydrate and poor in fat tends to produce faulty bone formation. His experiments showed that young animals soon get rickets if their diet contains vegetable oils, such as linseed oil, but grow sound healthy bone when butter or cod liver oil is included. Following up this clue he discovered the part played by one of the fat-soluble vitamins and established that rickets is essentially a vitamin-deficiency condition. This was the foundation of modern views on the cause and treatment of the disease.

In 1918 the Medical Research Committee, acting in co-operation with the Lister Institute, appointed a joint Sub-Committee on Accessory Food Factors to co-ordinate and stimulate investigations in the newly developed field of nutritional study. One of the first practical results of the work of the Accessory Food Factors Committee was the decision in 1919 to send a team of scientists to Vienna to study the conditions of severe malnutrition which were a sad legacy of the war privations. Dr (now Dame) Harriette Chick was asked to take charge of the mission. On their arrival they found acute food shortage, that there had been actual starvation and deaths from hunger oedema, that scurvy was common among infants and that a marked increase in the incidence and severity of rickets had been noted. The Austrian doctors knew little or nothing of vitamins and had not heard of Mellanby's discoveries on the cause of rickets. Professor von Pirquet, a leading authority on the feeding of children, frankly admitted that he 'had little expectation that it [the scientific mission] would lead to results of much practical value'. He added:

At that time I was of opinion that a vitamin deficiency in ordinary diet was a very exceptional occurrence . . . With regard to the etiology of rickets, I held the view that it was an infectious disease, widely prevalent in this part of Europe.[1]

The painstaking researches of Dr Chick and her colleagues, working in the face of very great difficulties in the poverty-stricken atmosphere and gloomy depression of post-war Vienna, conclusively established the practical significance of the facts which had recently come to light in experimental vitamin research. To quote once again from Professor von Pirquet:

The crucial experiment was thus successfully made. The British workers succeeded with the accuracy of a laboratory experiment, in a city where rickets is extremely prevalent, in maintaining a large

[1] 'Preface to Studies of Rickets in Vienna (1919-22)', *Medical Research Council, Special Report,* No. 77, 1923.

number of artificially fed babies free from the disease, and further in the same wards, were invariably successful in healing children admitted with rickets already developed.

It was the dawn of a new era. It was no longer possible to dismiss the vitamins as interesting curiosities related to conditions and diseases unfamiliar to most English medical men. The time had come when the assessment of the nutritive value of the diets of European populations had to take into account the newly discovered factors.

§ 3 BETWEEN THE WARS[1]

Rationing and control of foods did not end with the Armistice in 1918. The close of the war found the Ministry of Food in control of nearly everything that man could eat or drink, and it held unparalleled reserves of food. The Cabinet decided in May 1919 that the Ministry should complete its life by the end of that year. This, however, did not prove to be possible and it became clear that some control whould have to be exercised beyond that date. Indeed, the situation made inevitable the re-registration of customers at appropriate retailers for butcher's meat, butter and sugar. Meat rationing, however, finished on December 15th, 1919, the rationing of butter on May 30th, 1920, and of sugar on November 29th, 1920. March 31st, 1921 saw the end of the control of flour milling and of the Ministry itself, though the liquidation of accounts lingered on until after 1927.

Beveridge's[2] conclusion was that the direct lessons from the work of the first Ministry of Food, being entirely concerned with the control of livestock and the rationing system, were small. Nevertheless, the First World War had a far-reaching influence, both direct and indirect, on our knowledge of the function of food and other food problems.. It was directly responsible for a great deal of technical investigation into methods of preparation, preservation, storage and transport. Emergencies had revealed how little was known about the changes that occur in foods under such treatment and it became obvious that the urgent problems which had to be solved as well as possible under the stress of war were only a fraction of those needing attention and for which a vast expansion of research was necessary. On the medical side there were demands for more extensive research into the physiological functions of foods. The medical services had been caught unawares by numerous food difficulties, not least of which was the appearance

[1] Some of the material in this section was taken from Chapter XXV 'A New Era' of the first edition of *The Englishman's Food*.
[2] *British Food Control*, Sir William H. Beveridge, 1928.

of deficiency diseases in more than one theatre of war. Some authorities were tentatively expressing the view that much of the physical unfitness revealed by the examination of the adult male population might have originated from faulty or inadequate nutrition.

All these influences tended to concentrate interest on the scientific aspects of food and nutrition. The outcome was a remarkable development of experimental research. In Great Britain an outstanding part in assisting and making investigations on nutritional questions was played by the Medical Research Council, which from its inception kept this line of inquiry in the forefront of its programme. The Department of Scientific and Industrial Research, through its Food Investigation Board, attended to the equally important problems of food technology, establishing research stations for the investigation of methods of preserving and storing perishable foods. It gave considerable assistance to many other types of research. Many commercial organizations interested in food also established research departments.

During the 'twenties it became clear that no reliable information existed about the actual food consumption of families or of individuals. Without such information it was impossible to test the validity of the belief that much of the physical disability revealed by the medical examinations of recruits was due to malnutrition.

This gap in knowledge led to the making of a number of surveys in selected areas of the country. They were usually based on house to house visits. One of the first was that instigated by the Scottish Committee for Child Life Investigation. Begun in 1919 and continued over nearly five years, it dealt with typical urban, rural and mining areas of Scotland.[1] This careful and detailed study was unfortunately made before the importance of dietary factors other than protein, fat and calories was fully recognized and for this reason many of the conclusions that were drawn from the observations were misleading. The inquiry did, however, establish that in the immediate post-war years there was no shortage of food in the areas surveyed. Nearly all the families seemed to be getting sufficient calories, although poverty forced the majority of them to purchase the cheapest forms of energy. The small size of the poorer town child was regarded as being a consequence of inferior 'inherited growth impulse' or 'racial influences' exaggerated by lack of fresh air and sunlight and by overcrowding. Other surveys confirmed that the vast majority of the working-class population was getting enough to eat. There was no longer the fear of actual hunger and semi-starvation that had haunted the man who lost his employment before the benefits of the National Insurance Act of 1911 came into operation,

[1] 'Poverty, Nutrition and Growth', D. N. Paton and L. Findlay, *Medical Research Council Special Report*, No. 101, 1926.

and that has been vividly described, for example, in the novel *Howards End* by Mr E. M. Forster.

> The boy . . . stood on the extreme verge of gentility. He was not in the abyss, but he could see it, and at times people whom he knew had dropped in, and counted no more. . . . His mind and body had been alike underfed because he was poor, and because he was modern they were always craving for better food.[1]

But a new danger had to be faced. The importance in nutrition of the 'protective foods' was beginning to be recognized and it was soon apparent that they were beyond the reach of a large proportion of the poorer people. When, in the depression which followed the post-war boom, the industrial barometer sank to a lower level than had been known to living memory and unemployment exceeded two million, whole zones of the industrial areas were reduced to poverty and desolation and their inhabitants to misery and despair. The records of dietary surveys made then all establish the same grim facts: The lowest wage-earners and the unemployed were just able to purchase sufficient calories to keep body and soul alive. A report to the Ministry of Health in 1929 described the terrible food conditions in the Welsh coal-fields, but the same distressing details were true of other areas in the country. The diets of the poor working people had become almost as bad as they were in the worst years of Queen Victoria's reign: white bread, margarine, jam, tea and fried fish. Meat was seldom eaten more than once a week, while fresh vegetables, other than potatoes, were rarely bought. Fresh milk was hardly ever seen.

It was important to obtain precise information about the critical range of income below which families could not afford the protective foods, milk, fruit and vegetables. Dr G. C. M'Gonigle, then the Medical Officer of Health for Stockton-on-Tees, was one of the first to appreciate this. In 1927 an 'unhealthy area' in his Borough was demolished and 710 inhabitants, all of them poor and many of them unemployed, were moved to a new and up-to-date housing estate built for the purpose. To everyone's surprise the next five years showed a rising death-rate among these people. For five years before they had been moved the mean rate in the unhealthy area had been 18.75 per 1000, compared with 13.96 for the whole of Stockton-on-Tees. In the new surroundings it averaged 26.71 during the next five years; the figure for one year was actually 32.48. Meanwhile the rate for the Borough as a whole had remained unchanged, and, even more significant, that for another bad area had fallen slightly from 22.16 for the first five years to

---

[1] *Howards End*, E. M. Forster. First published 1910.

20.45 in the second. M'Gonigle instituted detailed inquiries into incomes, expenditure, habits of life and any other factors which might have played a part and concluded that the people had been living for years in the danger zone of dietary insufficiency, not in respect to calories and protein but to good nourishing foods. The move to the new estate had involved them in an appreciable amount of additional expense, mainly in the form of larger rents, which had been sufficient to reduce their purchases of the more nutritious foods. They had fallen back, as the poor always must in such conditions, on the cheaper forms of energy such as white bread. The consequences were inevitable. Their health was impaired and their resistance to disease enfeebled. Perhaps the most striking feature of this unpremeditated experiment in practical human nutrition was the rapidity with which the influence of the change of diet was felt.[1]

In 1931, the Minister of Health, Mr Arthur Greenwood, considered that the position was serious enough to call for the appointment of an Advisory Committee on Nutrition to advise him 'on the practical application of modern advances in the knowledge of nutrition'. One of the first pronouncements of this panel of physiologists was on the importance of the protective foods.

Probably if the diet contains per person one pint of milk per day, if cheese is partaken freely, if one orange or one tomato or a helping of raw salad is taken daily, if 30 g. (a little over 1 oz.) of butter (or of vitaminized margarine) is given, and if some sort of fat fish, such as herring, appears on the winter menu once a week (or if in default of such fish half a teaspoonful of cod-liver oil is taken once a day) the mineral matter and the vitamin content of the diet is satisfactory.[2]

Viewed against the revelations of the inadequacy of the diets of the poor this passage struck an ironic note, but it was encouraging that an official statement stressed the importance of such foods.

The next task was to ascertain the lowest cost for which a diet adequate in all respects could be obtained, an exercise which was to occupy much attention until well into the Second World War. One of the first practical suggestions came from the Health Committee of the League of Nations, which in 1928, at the request of the French government, had placed the subject of nutrition on its programme. The diet suggested contained 2 lb. cabbage, 1 lb. carrots, 8 oz. apples, 8 oz. herrings, 6 oz. cheese and 5 pints milk a week, in addition to foods such as bread and meat. It provided about 2500 Cal. and 81 g. protein daily at a cost of 9¾d., and was regarded as

---

[1] *Poverty and Public Health*, G. C. M. M'Gonigle and J. Kirby, 1936.
[2] 'The Criticism and Improvement of Diets', *Ministry of Health Report*, 1932.

being 'moderately satisfactory' in other respects.[1] Much the same could be said of diets proposed by Dr G. P. Crowden, the cost of which in 1932 was roughly 1s. a head daily.[2]

In 1933 the British Medical Association appointed a Committee 'to determine the minimum weekly expenditure on foodstuffs which must be incurred by families of varying size if health and working capacity are to be maintained, and to construct specimen diets'. In a short time they produced a concise report giving advice on the composition of diets for limited incomes and estimates of the cost of providing adequate nourishment. Their estimates, based on prevailing market prices in 1933, ranged from 5s. to 6s. per man per week.[3]

Such estimates made abundantly clear the reason for the widespread malnourishment among the poorer classes. There were thousands of families in which nothing like these sums could be spared for food. In Hammersmith, for example, there were many families affected by unemployment where there was as little as 1s. 7d. per head to spend on a week's food, while even many of those in work were restricted to sums below 4s.[4]

In December 1935 an important paper was read by Mr E. M. H. Lloyd at a meeting of the Agricultural Economics Society in London. It was an analysis of the information relating to food consumption at different levels of income. Mr Lloyd's inquiry represented the first attempt to apportion the nation's expenditure on food, which was estimated at an average of 9s. per head per week, between the different income groups. The population was divided into six groups representing an average expenditure on food of 4s., 6s., 8s., 10s., 12s. and 14s. per week. These corresponded to a range of incomes from up to 10s. to over 45s. per head per week.[5] There was a very sharp increase in milk consumption with rising income from 1.1 pint per head per week in the poorest group to 5.4 pints in the richest. Expenditure on vegetables (other than potatoes) ranged from 1.5d. to 8.5d. per head per week and on fruit from 2.4d. to 20.0d. It appeared that half the population of Great Britain was getting insufficient dairy produce and fruit and vegetables.

In the same study Mr Lloyd reviewed the changes in food supplies over the preceding 100 years and reached the following conclusions:

Thus the broad picture is that in 1934, compared with a hundred years earlier, tea and sugar had fallen by more than half in price and had

---

[1] 'Diet in Relation to Small Incomes', *Quarterly Bulletin of the Health Organization, League of Nations*, Vol. II, No. 1, 1933.
[2] *Lancet* (1932), i.
[3] *Report of British Medical Association Committee on Nutrition*, 1933.
[4] *Report of the Medical Officer of Health for Hammersmith for the year 1931*.
[5] *Journal of Proc. Agricultural Economics Society* (1936), Vol. IV, No. 2.

increased five-fold in quantity per head; meat and fats had fallen in price and consumption per head had about doubled; the price of bread and flour was the same but consumption had nearly halved; and liquid milk, which is not imported, had more than doubled in price while consumption per head had remained unchanged at less than half the optimum level of a pint per head per day.

The data obtained by Mr Lloyd were made the basis of an analysis by Sir John (now Lord) Boyd Orr of the national food consumption in terms of calories, protein, mineral salts such as calcium and iron, and some of the vitamins.[1] This analysis showed that only one group, that in which the average weekly income per head was over 45s., had a surplus of all dietary constituents considered. All the others, representing 40 million of the population, were deficient to some extent, at least in respect to calcium. The intake of vitamin A was found to be lower than desirable in three groups, representing 22 million people, while the diet of the poorest group comprising 4½ million people was deficient in every constituent examined. 20 to 25 per cent of the children in the country were estimated to belong to this last group. (For comparison with these findings and also with the calculations of the nutritive value of the diet in earlier centuries selected data from the National Food Survey for years since 1942 are given in Appendix C.)

In previous centuries malnutrition could be traced to failure of harvests. In the 'thirties the inability of the farmer to sell his produce set in motion much of the mechanism that led to the economic depression. It was therefore in the interests of farmers throughout the world that Governments should find some way of expanding the markets for foodstuffs. Both in Britain and America a few experiments were being tried for the disposal of surplus milk and other foods in the form of relief to the unemployed and in the feeding of school children. The National Milk Publicity Council in Britain had been promoting sales of milk in schools since about 1927 by means of a scheme by which ⅓ pint of milk could be obtained for 1d. By 1933 the number of children taking advantage of the scheme was not far short of a million and in 1934 it was superseded by the scheme based on the Milk Act of that year, and operated by the newly established Milk Marketing Boards. This made milk available to children in elementary schools at a price, either to the school authority or the child's parents, of ½d. for ⅓ pint, the difference between this sum and the market price of liquid milk being borne by the Government; those from very poor homes could obtain it free. In about twelve months nearly half of those attending elementary schools were taking advantage of the scheme. By 1939 over half of those in grant-aided schools were taking school milk.

[1] *Food, Health and Income*, John Boyd Orr, 1936.

The first proposal to expand the market for food came from Australia, with its food-exporting interests. The notion of a 'marriage of health and agriculture' was first enunciated by Mr F. L. McDougall, later the Deputy Director of the Food and Agriculture Organization of the United Nations, and was put before the League of Nations in September 1935 by the Australian delegate Viscount (then Mr) Bruce. As a result the League of Nations established the Mixed Committee on the Relation of Nutrition to Health, Agriculture and Economic Policy which published during 1937 and 1938 a series of reports on nutritional problems, which have since formed the basis of national nutrition policies and of the nutrition policy of the Food and Agriculture Organization of the United Nations.

§ 4 SECOND WORLD WAR

The outbreak of war in 1939 found this country better fitted than ever before to apply the findings of nutritional science to the task of feeding the population. The Food Defence Plans Department of the Board of Trade had drawn up plans for rationing and distribution which were based on the experience of the First World War. The Ministry of Health had shown in 1937 in the First Report of its Advisory Committee on Nutrition in what respects the national diet should be improved. The Milk-in-Schools Scheme had been started. Since the passing of the Maternity and Child Welfare Act in 1918 any local authority had been permitted to supply cheap or free milk to poor mothers and children against a medical certificate. In 1935-36 the Milk Marketing Board, the milk trade and the Commissioner for Distressed Areas had co-operated in starting a cheap milk scheme for mothers and children in the Rhondda Valley, Whitehaven, Jarrow and Walker-on-Tyne and in August 1939 a permissive cheap milk scheme for mothers and infants had been introduced on an income basis: this was run by local authorities and ranked for an Exchequer Grant in Aid.

The second Ministry of Food was formally established by Order in Council on September 8th, 1939, and Mr W. S. Morrison, who, as Chancellor of the Duchy of Lancaster, had been the Minister responsible for the last few months of food defence planning became the first Minister of Food.

On October 16th, 1939, the late Professor J. C. Drummond (afterwards Sir Jack) was seconded from London University to the Ministry of Food as Chief Adviser on Food Contamination. He was appointed Scientific Adviser to the Ministry on February 1st, 1940, a position which he held with distinction until in 1946 he left government service for industry.

One of Drummond's first acts in the Ministry was to prepare a memorandum stressing the need for the co-ordination of all scientific investigations into food problems. Early in 1940 he submitted another 'on certain nutritional aspects of the food position'. In this notable document he reviewed the pre-war nutritional position of the United Kingdom and the probable effects on it of wartime conditions, particularly in relation to the poorer sections of the population. He stressed the need for providing bread of high nutritive value, for increasing the consumption of potatoes, oatmeal, cheese and green vegetables, for supplying not less than a pint of milk a day to expectant and nursing mothers and to all children up to the age of 15, and for fortifying margarine with vitamins A and D, recommendations which were the direct outcome of his knowledge of the science of nutrition, of the nutritional situation of the British population and of the history of the British diet. Many of his proposals were in due course put into effect and the account of wartime nutritional policy which follows is drawn in the main from his official papers and subsequent publications.[1] It is clear from the official documents on food prepared during the Second World War that Drummond's influence spread wide and that his stamp appeared in unexpected places. He had a flair for applied science, and he was uniquely placed by temperament and function to gather up the accumulated knowledge of nutrition and direct it outwards into schemes, administrative, practical or educational, to promote the adequate nourishment of the people and the economical use of foods. His special skill lay in his ability to judge when and how to apply his knowledge. He set out from the start not only to maintain but to improve the nutritional value of the diet,[2] an aim which could not have been realized, as it was, without the support of the second Minister of Food, Lord Woolton, who, according to Drummond, 'invariably balanced evidence and arguments on the psychological side against the recommendations of the scientists'.[3] Early in 1940 Drummond made strong recommendations against measures to reduce the country's total consumption of food, drawing on the experience in the First World War when (as he wrote) 'most unwisely and against expert advice, a campaign urging voluntary restriction in the consumption of foods, particularly bread, was launched by the Government' and when 'those who loyally responded suffered loss of weight and reduction of efficiency'. The first official indication of his influence on food policy appeared in May 1940 in the Ministry's import programme for the second year of war, to which was appended *A Survey of Wartime Nutrition*, setting out in detailed and quantitative form what were

---

[1] For example, 'Scientific Approach to Food Problems during the War', Sir Jack Drummond, *Nutrition: Dietetics: Catering* (1947), I, 47.

[2] See Obituary, 'Sir Jack Cecil Drummond, D.SC., F.R.I.C., F.R.S.', *Brit. J. Nutr.* (1954), VIII, 319.

[3] 'Scientific Approach to Food Problems during the War', Sir Jack Drummond, *Nutrition: Dietetics: Catering* (1947), I, 47.

in effect Drummond's own views on the type of nutritional strategy that the Ministry of Food should adopt. The scientific principles underlying this survey were not new — but neither were they universally familiar. It was, moreover, something of a novelty to apply modern concepts of nutrition to the job of planning the food supplies of a nation at war, and Drummond's unique contribution at this stage was his success in collaborating with statisticians and economists in producing a document that could form the practical basis of the national wartime food policy. In the survey he furnished estimates of the nutritional requirements of the population and showed that national food supplies before the war had been adequate in energy-rich foods but short in protective foods, particularly in those supplying calcium, vitamin A and vitamin B_1. He reviewed the dietary changes that occurred during the First World War — these showed a deterioration in the supply of minerals and of vitamins, particularly among the more vulnerable sections of the population — and indicated means by which the danger could be averted. Home production during 1940-41 was expected to provide about one-third of the nation's energy requirements, two-thirds of the calcium, one-third of the vitamin A, two-fifths of the vitamin B_1 and, as a result of the increased potato production, all the necessary vitamin C. The import programme was then considered and the resulting total food supplies assessed. As a result recommendations were made for increasing the supply of vitamin B_1, either by raising the extraction rate of flour or by fortifying white flour with synthetic vitamin B_1; for expanding the home production of milk and vegetables, including potatoes; for increasing the overseas supplies of cheese, dried and condensed milks, canned fatty fish and pulses; and for importing vitamin A and D concentrates to add to margarine. On the other hand it was recommended that imports of fruit (other than oranges), nuts and eggs in shell should be reduced as being wasteful of shipping. The impossibility of reducing energy-rich foods without impairing health was again emphasized.

The measures which were planned, and put into effect, to maintain and improve the nutritional position are summarized in the following table. These measures were superimposed on a general system of rationing which provided for all persons equal domestic rations of bacon, fats, sugar, preserves and sweets, equal domestic rations of cheese (except for certain classes of workers who were entitled to extra cheese for sandwiches), equal domestic rations of tea (except for children under 5 who got none) and domestic rations of equal value of carcase meat (with the modifications of a half-ration for children under 5 and, after the end of 1946, an extra allowance for underground coal miners). There were also systems of allocation of eggs and milk and the 'Points' rationing scheme by which non-perishable foods, mainly canned and dried, too scarce to ration, could be bought against special coupons. After the end of the war, when there was a severe world shortage of cereals, flour, bread and flour confectionery were also rationed. Bread rationing lasted from July 21st, 1946, to July 24th, 1948. Because of the severe winter and late spring, the 1947 potato crop was unusually small and the distribution of potatoes had to be controlled from November 9th to April 30th, 1948.

SUMMARY OF NUTRITIONAL MEASURES

Measure	Object	Class Benefited
(1) Steps to increase milk (milk solids) consumption. Increased milk production. Diversion of milk to liquid market. Increased imports of skimmed dried milk and cheese. National Milk Scheme (cheap milk for expectant mothers, infants and children up to 5 years). Milk-in-Schools Scheme (expansion). Milk Cocoa Drink Scheme (for adolescents). Milk Supply Scheme (to provide for differential rationing of milk).	To raise levels of intake of (a) Animal protein (b) Calcium (c) Riboflavin.	Primarily, the 'vulnerable' groups. Secondarily, the whole population.
(2) Addition of vitamins A and D to margarine.	(a) to make margarine nutritionally similar to butter. (b) To raise intakes of vitamins A and D. (c) To compensate to some extent for the shortage of eggs, which are one of the few natural foods rich in Vitamin D.	Whole population.

Measure	Object	Class Benefited
(3) Introduction of 85 per cent extraction flour and National bread.	(a) To remove all risk of vitamin B_1 deficiency. (b) To improve iron consumption. (c) To improve riboflavin and nicotinic acid consumption.	Whole population.
(4) Addition of calcium carbonate to flour.	(a) To raise calcium consumption. (b) To counteract any immobilizing influence on calcium of phytic acid in high extraction flour.	Whole population.
(5) Increased production and consumption of carrots and green vegetables.	(a) To maintain supply of vitamin C to compensate for reduction of fruit imports. (b) To improve vitamin A consumption.	Whole population.
(6) Vitamins Welfare Scheme; orange juice, cod liver oil, vitamin A and D tablets.	To ensure adequacy in respect to vitamins A, C and D during pregnancy and early life of children.	Pregnant women, infants and children up to 5 years.
(7) Communal meals, factory canteen meals, British restaurants, etc.	(a) To feed the workers 'on the job' and thus to provide a practical alternative to differential rationing. (b) To give a measure of flexibility to the rationing system. (c) To provide nourishing meals of good protein, vitamin and mineral content.	Whole population.

Measure	Object	Class Benefited
(8) Expansion of School Meals Service.	(a) To provide nutritious meals for children. (b) To give measure of protection against deficiencies of home diet.	School children.

Not specifically mentioned in the table, but of vital importance, was the task of increasing agricultural production to compensate for reduction in food imports. In spite of considerable agricultural efforts it was only possible to increase the energy value of home produced food from the pre-war level of about 900 Cal. per head per day (or 30 per cent of the total) to 1200 Cal. per head per day (or about 40 per cent of the total in 1943 and 1944). The volume of food imports, however, dropped from an annual average of over 22 million tons for the years 1934 to 1938 to 10½ to 11½ million for the years 1942 to 1944.[1] In a country at war and dependent on imports for about two-thirds of the energy value of its food supply, food technology became an essential tool of applied nutrition. All import programmes were reviewed so that priority could be given to foods with the highest energy value per cubic ton. Wheat was saved by raising the extraction rate of flour, animal feeding-stuffs were cut drastically, the average annual quantity of sugar imported over the three years 1942 to 1944 was reduced to about half the pre-war level, imports of vegetables to less than half the pre-war volume and of fresh fruits to less than one-tenth. In contrast imports of oilseeds and oils and fats (except butter) were increased, those of canned meat were more than quadrupled and of cheese about doubled and processed milk more than doubled. Space was saved by importing boneless meat and 'telescoped' carcases. The war saw the introduction of such unfamiliar foods as dried eggs and dried skim milk and the initiation of prodigious efforts to teach the population to compensate for the shortage of vitamin C from fresh fruits by eating raw vegetable salads or by cooking green vegetables conservatively.

Much thought and energy was devoted to technological problems, the most important of which probably concerned bread. All Drummond's early Ministry memoranda contain reference to the need for good quality bread of high vitamin B_1 content. As early as April 1940 he expressed the view that the right way to tackle the problem was to provide the public with bread

[1] 'How Britain was fed in War Time', *Food Control 1939-45*, H.M. Stationery Office, 1946.

baked from 82-85 per cent extraction flour. The decision taken in March 1942 to raise the extraction rate of all flour to 85 per cent was made to save shipping, but it could not have been the success it was without the scientific knowledge and technical skill which were developed mainly at the Cereals Research Station of the Research Association of British Flour-Millers under Dr T. Moran, who became Deputy Scientific Adviser of the Ministry. The subsequent history of the nation's flour policy is well known and is documented in a series of reports by Drummond and his colleagues, the Report of the Conference on the Post-War Loaf[1] and the Report of the Panel on the Composition and Nutritive Value of Flour.[2]

The development of dehydrated foods was another of Drummond's major interests. In a memorandum written in March 1941 on nutritionally desirable foods that might be imported from the United States, he noted that considerable quantities of spray-dried egg were available in California and possibly also Wisconsin and suggested that if sufficient dried skim milk could be secured it might be sold in small domestic packs. Dried eggs were imported under the Lend-Lease Act the following year and within nine months small packs of National Household Milk were on the market, and dried skim milk was also allocated for school and hospital meals. Dehydrated vegetables and minces were also produced, largely for use by the armed forces. Since the end of the Second World War important advances have been made in the production of compact (mainly dehydrated), long-storing foods at the Experimental Factory of the Ministry of Agriculture, Fisheries and Food which was established at Aberdeen in 1949.

Such changes in food supplies made it necessary to teach the public how to use unfamiliar foods like dried eggs and dried skim milk, and how to make the best use of cabbage and other green vegetables. This simple aim led to a widespread programme of cookery instruction and eventually of education in nutrition, by means of leaflets, posters, lectures and demonstrations. The central point of this national effort was probably the Food Advice Division of the Ministry of Food, which worked under Drummond's guidance, but its influence could not have been as wide or as lasting as it proved to be without the enthusiastic and trained support of countless teachers of domestic science, dietitians, school meals' organizers, hospital caterers and public health workers who demonstrated that simple nutrition could be taught and practised. This work of nutrition propaganda was much helped by the support of such bodies as the King Edward's Hospital Fund for London which published two memoranda on hospital diet in 1943 and 1945. The Fund and the Ministry of Health both appointed advisory dietitians before the end of the war, and in the thirteen years since the

---

[1] Cmd. 6701. November 1945.   [2] Cmd. 9757. May 1956.

publication of the Fund's Memorandum the whole concept of hospital catering in this country has changed for the better.

The war also brought advances in food legislation for the protection of the consumer. A new Food and Drugs Act of 1938 came into force after the outbreak of war. As the Ministry of Food was then in existence power under the Act was assumed by that Ministry in 1943 in the form of Defence (Sale of Food) Regulations and the wartime orders made by the Ministry grew into a comprehensive system of control over the advertising, labelling and composition of foods, with important new developments concerning, particularly, claims as to the nutritional value of a food, and with an advisory body in the shape of the Food Standards Committee.[1] Since then, Ministers have been given wider powers to protect the public against the sale of adulterated or injurious foods and drugs, misdescriptions in labels or advertisements, or the contamination of food in the course of preparation, distribution or sale by the Food and Drugs Act, 1955, which came into force on January 1st, 1956. The Food Hygiene Regulations, 1955, which closely affect all those engaged in the manufacture, packaging or sale of food came into force on the same day as the Act.[2]

§ 5 SINCE 1945

After the end of the Second World War the national diet suffered through the abrupt ending of Lend-Lease and the consequent need to switch purchases of food from dollar to non-dollar sources. The energy value of total food supplies fell slightly below 2900 Cal. per head per day, mainly on account of relatively low fat supplies. The population was vocal in its discontent, and the importance of palatability and acceptability of food supplies became abundantly clear. The data in Appendix B show that in many respects the 1947 diet was better than that of 1934-38, the most striking improvements being in calcium, vitamin B_1, nicotinic acid, protein (mainly in vegetable protein) and vitamin C. The first was caused partly by the 30 per cent increase in the supplies of dairy products (other than butter) and partly by the addition of 14 oz. calcium carbonate (*creta praeparata*) per 280 lb. sack of flour. Increases in vegetable protein and the vitamins of the B complex were mainly the result of increased consumption of flour of improved nutritional value (it was then of 85 per cent extraction). Increased vitamin C supplies were the result of greater potato and vegetable consumption which

[1] A symposium on 'Nutrition and the Pure Food Laws', was held by the Nutrition Society on March 3rd, 1951, and its Proceedings are published in *Brit. J. Nutr.* (1951), V, 363.

[2] *The Food and Drugs Act, 1955*, John A. O'Keefe and Robert Schless, Butterworth's Annotated Legislation Service, 1956.

more than compensated for the remnants of the wartime restrictions on imports of fresh fruits.

Since 1947 the fat content of the diet has increased by nearly 30 per cent. There has also been substantial improvement in vitamin A supplies which in 1954 were over 13 per cent greater than before the war. The small decreases in calcium, iron and vitamins of the B complex occurred mainly because of decreased flour consumption and changes in its nutritive value: in 1956 regulations were introduced requiring that all flour of less than 80 per cent extraction should be restored to the 80 per cent level with added iron, vitamin B$_1$ and nicotinic acid.

The rationing of the Second World War came quietly to an end in 1954. By 1949-50 the shortages of 1947 had been made good and it became possible to take controls off the food supply gradually and without losing the benefits which wartime policy had introduced. From 1953 onwards the national diet has been of greater value for all the nutrients commonly assessed than that available before the war.

As the trends in the supplies of the foods which are of greatest nutritional importance cannot easily be appreciated in the context of broad nutritional considerations, they will be treated separately.

§ 6 MILK AND MILK PRODUCTS

Lloyd has pointed out[1] that milk consumption per head was no lower in 1835 than it was a hundred years later. It seems, therefore, that for a century the consumption of liquid milk remained roughly constant, though milk products increased somewhat. Then, as part of the deliberate national nutrition policy, the consumption of milk and milk products was increased. The most marked rise in total occurred between 1941 and 1943, after which consumption remained steady until the gradual rise after 1948 to a peak in 1951, since when it has dropped slightly. In 1954, consumption of total milk solids was 38 per cent greater than in the pre-war years and of liquid milk alone 54 per cent greater.

The outbreak of war made complete control of the national milk supplies a necessity, and therefore the initiation of a system of milk priorities a possibility. The National Milk Scheme, which later became part of the Welfare Foods Service, was introduced in July 1940 and provided milk free or at a special price for all expectant mothers and young children irrespective of income. Another important measure implemented shortly afterwards by the joint action of the Ministry of Food and the Education

[1] *Journal of Proc. Agricultural Economics Society* (1936), Vol. IV, No. 2.

Departments was the expansion of the Milk-in-Schools Scheme. By the beginning of 1943 about three-quarters of the school population was taking milk at school, compared with just over half in 1939. School milk was taken by about this proportion of children until after it became free of charge in August 1946, since when 85-90 per cent of school children have taken it. The result of these measures together with full employment and the general rise in the standard of living is that the wide disparity between social classes in milk consumption revealed by the pre-war surveys no longer exists.

The results of the National Food Survey which has been in operation since 1940 indicate that in some ways size of family is a more important factor in determining adequacy of diet than income per family or social class. The Advisory Committee on Nutrition of the Ministry of Health made recommendations on the desirable milk consumption of persons of different ages. On the assumption that children aged 0-1 should drink 2 pints of milk a day and all other children and adolescents up to the age of 21 1 pint, expectant mothers 2 pints and other adults $\frac{1}{2}$ pint, the milk requirements of families of different size surveyed in the National Food Survey in 1950 have been calculated and compared with actual consumption.[1]

The comparison showed that in 1950 childless families, those with one child and those with adolescents were meeting their milk requirements, those with two or three children were almost doing so, but those with four or more children and those with both adolescents and children were failing to do so. No earlier data with which to compare these estimates exist, but later results have confirmed the findings of 1950. It is thus almost certain that the differences between the milk consumption of large and small families are not new. Indeed, milk consumption in large families is probably greater than it was before 1939, but the fact that they are taking less than the national average of milk in spite of the Welfare Foods Service and the Milk-in-Schools Scheme suggests that more education in milk drinking is required. This appears to be the more important in view of the recent finding of the Ministry of Health that children of small families tend to be of better physique than those of large ones.[2]

§ 7 MEAT, FISH AND EGGS

Trends in the consumption of meats, fish and eggs have followed different courses in the last seventy years. Consumption of meat and fish apparently increased most rapidly before the First World War. Writing in 1935 Lloyd

---

[1] D. F. Hollingsworth, *British Journal of Nutrition* (1951), V, 392.
[2] *The Health of the School Child, 1952 and 1953*, H.M.S.O., 1954.

stated that consumption of all meats, including poultry and game, had increased slightly by 1934-38 compared with 1909-13 and 1924-28, the increase being mainly in bacon and meat offal. He asked whether this was due to the growing popularity of liver and bacon, or to medical recommendation of liver as a cure for anaemia. He added that fish in the aggregate remained constant, but that herring had disappeared from the breakfast table to the extent of 50 per cent and that canned fish, mostly tinned salmon, had nearly doubled. Meat had in 1954 just about regained the pre-1939 level and fish consumption, which increased sharply in 1947 when meat was very short, was tending to decline. Egg consumption approximately doubled between 1909-13 and 1934-38, since when, apart from wartime shortages of shell eggs, it has not changed much.

§ 8 FATS

Changes in the consumption of fats have been very striking and in total have been markedly upward, except for temporary set-backs in both wars, with the result that the consumption of visible fats per head in 1954 was probably more than twice that in 1909-13 and may have been about four times that in 1880. The total contributions to the diet of fat from dairy produce, meats and fish have not varied much during the twentieth century: the great dietary changes are the result of the introduction of margarine towards the end of the nineteenth century – in 1909-13, as Flux stated, 'at least the substantial part of the fats used for making margarine was produced from animals fed and slaughtered in the United Kingdom' – and the introduction after the First World War of the method of manufacturing both margarine and cooking fats from hardened oils. As the consumption and composition of fats may be of considerable physiological importance an attempt has been made to calculate, on a comparable basis, for the years 1909-13 to 1954, the amount of fat in the British diet from animal and vegetable sources, and from sources of which no constitutent was hardened by hydrogenation and of which some were so hardened. The results of the calculations are shown in the table on the next page.

Three features are clear from the table: Total fats estimated per head have increased by about 40 per cent during the last forty years, but not steadily. Animal fats and fats from non-hardened sources have fluctuated with the general food supply above and below the 1909-13 level and in 1954 were not much above it. Fats from vegetable sources, and from sources some constituents of which have been hydrogenated, have increased almost continuously during the forty years.

FAT SUPPLIES IN THE UNITED KINGDOM
(g. per head per day)

	Total	Animal Sources	Vegetable Sources	Sources containing no hardened fats	Sources containing some hardened fats
1909-13	98	90	8	98	0*
1924-28	109	94	15	96	13
1934-38	130	107	23	116	14
1941	114	80	34	87	27
1944	124	90	34	102	22
1947	106	75	31	82	24
1950	131	93	38	101	30
1952	122	82	40	93	29
1954	136	97	39	106	30

* 6 per cent of total fats in 1909-13 are estimated to be margarine which was not hydrogenated.

§ 9 SUGAR

Lloyd, writing in 1935, considered that the five-fold increase in sugar consumption was the most significant change in the nation's diet during the preceding hundred years. After reduction during the Second World War to the 1880-1928 level it rose again after that war so that in 1954 it was greater than it had been in 1934-38. As Lloyd remarked in 1935 'from the nutritional standpoint this increase in the consumption of sugar is not so desirable as an increase in certain other foodstuffs, such as milk would have been'.

§ 10 VEGETABLES AND FRUITS

Statistics of the consumption of vegetables and fruits are notoriously unreliable. In 1904 they played such a small part in the diet of the urban working class that they were not represented in the Cost-of-Living Index, but in the last forty years, consumption per head of these foods, excluding potatoes, may have increased by something like 50 per cent, so that the old index, which was revised in 1947, failed to reflect their increasing importance in the diets of all sections of the community. It is impossible to calculate the meaning of the long-term change in precise nutritional terms, but, in general, it can be stated that it must have meant improvements in the supplies of β-carotene (the precursor of vitamin A) and vitamin C as well as the other vitamins and mineral salts which are widely distributed in fruits and vegetables.

Before 1939 there were marked class differences in the consumption of vegetables and fruit and even now the taste for these foods is a mark of middle-class status. Consumption per head of vegetables, estimated from expenditure, by the poorest group was less than half that of the richest while that of fruit was just under one-third.[1] In comparison recent National Food Survey Reports[2] show a very small class difference in vegetable consumption, but the consumption of fruits ranges from one-half to three-quarters in the lowest and intermediate social classes compared with the highest. The present differences have an influence on vitamin C intake. The highest social class and also the families with few or no children differ from the remainder in that they obtain absolutely more total vitamin C than other groups and relatively more from fruit and tomatoes. The other groups obtain a higher proportion of their vitamin C from potatoes. The point in relation to family size is even more strikingly made when the expenditure on these foods is considered: whereas the addition of each child to the household is accompanied by an increase in household expenditure on potatoes, no such increase occurs for green vegetables and none for fruits and tomatoes after the second child.[3]

§ 11 CEREALS AND POTATOES

The consumption of the two cheap foods, cereals and potatoes, fluctuates inversely with the supply of animal foods, fats, sugar, fruits and other vegetables. Potato consumption has not yet returned to the low 1909-13 level and, with the general improvement in standard of living, and therefore presumably in the number of cooked meals served, it may never do so.

The consumption of wheat flour is, however, already below the 1924-28 and 1934-38 levels, though flour still takes such an important place in the diet, providing nearly 30 per cent of its energy and protein value, that arrangements have been made to safeguard its nutritional value as regards iron, vitamin B_1 and nicotinic acid. All flour must contain either naturally or by restoration minimum amounts of 1.65 mg. iron, 0.24 mg. vitamin B_1 and 1.60 mg. nicotinic acid per 100 g. flour.

Lloyd[4] commented in 1935 that the greatest change between 1909-13 and the diet of the 'twenties and 'thirties was the fall in 'the nursery group of cereals — rice, tapioca, sago and arrowroot. The revolt against the milk

---

[1] *Food, Health and Income*, John Boyd Orr, 1936.
[2] *Domestic Food Consumption and Expenditure*, 1953, H.M.S.O., 1955; ibid., 1954, H.M.S.O., 1956.
[3] Ibid., 1952, H.M.S.O., 1954.
[4] *Journal of Agricultural Economics Society* (1936), Vol. IV, No. 2.

pudding of our childhood days appears to have more than halved the national consumption of rice, tapioca and sago . . . This eclipse of the milk pudding, which is no doubt connected with the growing popularity of fruit, may have contributed to the apparent fall in milk consumption'. Comparing data for 1954 and 1934-38 it is clear that this trend has continued: rice, starch and 'other farinaceous foods' are at little more than half the pre-war level, though breakfast cereals have more than doubled.

§ 12 DIETARY PATTERN

The extent, in terms of dietary pattern, of the changes in food supplies over seventy years, can perhaps best be illustrated by comparing the sources of calories in the national food supply as in the following table, which illustrates strikingly the increasing dependence on fats at the expense of cereals and potatoes.

ESTIMATED PERCENTAGE DISTRIBUTION OF UNITED KINGDOM CALORIE SUPPLIES
1880-1954*

	1880	1909-13	1924-28	1934-38	1941	1947	1952	1954
Grain and potatoes	55	42	38	34	44	42	38	33
Animal products	21	25	25	25	22	23	24	26
Fats and oils	5	11	14	18	16	14	17	18
Sugar	13	16	16	15	11	13	14	16
Other foods	6	6	7	8	7	8	7	7
	100	100	100	100	100	100	100	100

*Data from Dr N. C. Wright.

It is difficult to assess the effect of these trends in food supplies on the health of the community: it has so far proved impossible to disentangle the conflicting effects of the social changes and disturbances of family life which have occurred in the United Kingdom during and since the war from the improvements in medical treatment and the introduction of new drugs. But it is known that even during the war health, as revealed by vital statistics and the growth rates of children, improved and that these improvements have continued. It is reasonable to assume that increased supplies of body building and protective foods for all classes have played their part in these improvements, a view expressed in the Report of the Chief Medical Officer of the Ministry of Education for the years 1939-45[1] where 'the brilliantly successful

[1] *The Health of the School Child*, H.M.S.O., 1947.

food policy' was listed as one of the three main factors responsible for the improvement and maintenance of a satisfactory state of nutrition of the public elementary school child. On the negative side the long-term increase in the consumption of fats and their changed composition over the last forty years may have some bearing on the increased incidence of coronary disease which has been described[1] as having reached epidemic proportions; the increasing consumption of sugar, a 'dead' source of calories which does not carry with it the vitamin B_1 necessary for its metabolism, may have some bearing on the incidence of dental caries which has not been arrested; and the increasing processing of the foods in our diet may have as yet unproved undesirable physiological effects.

This survey of changes in food supply and policy over forty years cannot be completed without a further brief reference to the spread of knowledge on the relation of food to health. Much was accomplished during the Second World War when, owing to rationing and control, it was difficult to obtain an ill-balanced diet. In the doubts that at present assail us as to the subtle dangers to health of too much of the wrong kinds of foods the lessons of wartime nutrition should not be forgotten. For it remains true that the foundations of good health are laid in the early years of life and that if boys and girls are properly nourished until maturity is reached they will be the better fitted to withstand hardship and privation in later life. It remains for us to be certain as to the nature of 'proper nourishment', a necessity which points to the need for more research on the problems of human nutrition. This urgent need has been expressed in a recent letter to the *Lancet* by Professor A. C. Frazer.[2] 'We live in a world in which scientific knowledge is applied more and more to fields that affect our everyday life. If this is to be done safely, scientific applications must rest on a sound foundation of knowledge. It is this foundation that is inadequate in this, as in many other fields . . . The remedy is to give much greater support to food research as a whole, which must include the utilisation as well as the composition of food, and to ensure that the greater proportion of this support is used for long-term studies designed to increase the general knowledge in this field. There is no other way of ensuring that a progressive policy involving the application of scientific advances to food technology can be followed with safety and confidence.' Such a call merits a prompt response, for 'proper nourishment' or the 'perfect' balance of diet is one of the secrets of human well-being.

This is no new discovery; over two hundred years ago the French dietitian

---

[1] 'Coronary Thrombosis: a modern epidemic', J. N. Morris, *Health Education Journal* (1956) XIV, 36.
[2] 'Research on Food', A. C. Frazer, *Lancet* (1956), ii, 197.

Lemery put into words opinions which were strangely prophetic of our feelings about nutrition in the nineteen-fifties:

> In the mean Time, if Foods contribute so necessarily, to the Preservation of Life and Health; they also produce the greatest Part of those Distempers, to which we are subject, and many Times, by the ill Use of them, cause even Death itself. All which being set together, we may easily see, that the Groundwork of our Preservation, consists chiefly in a knowledge of suiting Foods to every Constitution, as it best agrees with it; and so the Knowledge we ought to be most desirous of, should be that of Foods.[1]

[1] *A Treatise of all Sorts of Foods*, L. Lemery, translated by D. Hay, 1745.

APPENDIX A

Some of the diets mentioned in the text are given below in terms of foods per day or per week.

Fifteenth-century peasant diet (*per day*)

(i)
1 pt. milk
1 pt. whey
2 oz. cheese
1 oz. bacon
2 lb. maslin bread
2 oz. pease

Fifteenth-century diet Meat-eating classes (*per day*)

(ii)
4 oz. cheese
1½ lb. meat
6 oz. herring
1 oz. fat
1 lb. bread
1 pt. wine
1 qt. ale

Seventeenth-century diet when 'White Meats' became scarce (*per day*)

(iii)
3½ oz. cheese
2 lb. bread
9 oz. pease

(iv)
Without cheese

Sailors' Diet 1615 ('*Britaine's Busses*') (*per day*)

(v)
8 oz. cheese
4 oz. bacon
4 oz. butter
1 lb. biscuit
3 oz. oatmeal
1 gall. beer

Diet of St Bartholomew's Hospital 1687 (*per day*)

(vi)
1½ oz. cheese
1 pt. milk pottage
4 oz. beef or mutton
1 pt. broth
1 oz. butter
10 oz. bread
3 pt. beer

Navy Ration 1745 (*per week*)

(vii)
12 oz. cheese
4 lb. salt beef
2 lb. salt pork
8 oz. butter
7 lb. biscuit
2½ lb. oatmeal
2 pt. pease
7 gall. beer

Navy Ration 1811 (*per day*)

(viii)
1¾ oz. cheese
4½ oz. beef
2¼ oz. pork
⅞ oz. butter
¼ oz. suet
⅞ oz. sugar
1 lb. bread
3 oz. flour
1 qt. beer

Gloucester Gaol 1815 Daily average (*per day*)

(ix)
1½ oz. cheese
3½ oz. beef
14 oz. potatoes
1½ lb. bread
2 oz. oatmeal
Pease pudding twice a week

Dr Kitchener's Estimate 1826 (*per week*)

(x)
6 lb. meat
½ lb. butter
½ lb. sugar
4 lb. bread
2 oz. tea
1 pt. porter

APPENDIX A

SIR JAMES GRAHAM'S PRISON DIET 1843

Less than 7 days' confinement		*21 days-6 weeks' confinement*
Class I		*Class III*
(per week)		*(per week)*
(xi)		(xii)
Meat	0	6 oz.
Potatoes	0	64 oz.
Soup	0	2 pt.
Bread	112 oz.	140 oz.
Gruel	14 pt.	14 pt.

PRISON DIET 1864

	Class I	*Class III*
	(per week)	*(per week)*
	(xiii)	(xiv)
Cheese	0	2 oz.
Potatoes	24 oz.	60 oz.
Indian meal pudding	18 oz.	0
Suet pudding	0	24 oz.
Soup	0	2½ pt.
Bread	128 oz.	144 oz.
Gruel	0	14 pt.

An attempt has been made to analyse these diets and to compare them with modern estimates of requirements. The calculations give no more than very rough estimates. It is a difficult task to determine accurately the actual intake of food constituents even when it is possible to analyse portions of the meals and to ascertain the amount consumed. Food varies so much in its composition, e.g. the proportion of fat in meat, that even with careful sampling errors may arise. With no more detailed items than '1 lb. of beef' or 'half a pint of gruel' to work on, it is only possible to make what are often called guestimates. The approximate nutritional value of diets is expressed per day.

DIET

		Require-ment (*)	(i)	(ii)	(iii)	(iv)	(v)	(vi)	(vii)	(viii)	(ix)	(x)	(xi)	(xii)	(xiii)	(xiv)
Energy Value	Cal.	3,000	3,200	4,750	2,850	2,450	5,800	2,350	5,500	2,900	2,600	2,050	1,600	2,100	1,400	2,450
Protein	g.	87	100	190	110	90	150	70	160	80	90	70	50	70	50	80
Fat	g.	n.a.	60	190	40	10	250	80	180	100	50	120	20	30	5	40
Calcium	mg.	0.8	1.6	1.3	1.1	0.3	2.6	0.9	1.9	0.7	0.6	0.1	0.5	0.6	0.2	0.7
Phosphorus	g.	n.a.	2.8	4.2	2.3	1.7	3.7	1.7	3.7	1.9	2.0	1.2	1.3	1.7	1.0	1.8
Iron	mg.	12	17	39	25	24	24	14	36	18	24	18	14	19	13	19
Vitamin A	i.u.	2,500	1,450	2,800	1,300	tr.	6,350	3,200	1,750	1,450	500	1,150	300	800	tr.	900
Vitamin B_1	mg.	1.2	1.9	1.5	2.3	2.3	1.9	1.1	2.6	1.6	2.2	0.8	1.4	1.8	1.3	1.9
Riboflavin	mg.	1.8	2.8	3.7	1.3	0.8	3.9	1.7	4.0	1.5	1.3	1.3	1.0	1.3	0.5	1.3
Nicotinic acid	mg.	12	22	68	33	33	84	40	100	46	33	28	17	24	19	24
Vitamin C(†)	mg.	20	?	?	14	0	?	25	?	?	30	0	0	20	7	20
Vitamin D	i.u.	n.a.	9	950	14	0	100	25	26	22	5	19	0	0	0	4

n.a. — not available.
(*) Moderately active man. British Medical Association. Committee of Nutrition, 1950.
(†) Very uncertain owing to the impossibility of assessing vegetable consumption and of estimating losses in cooking.

APPENDIX B

NUTRITIONAL VALUE OF SUPPLIES PER HEAD PER DAY MOVING
INTO CONSUMPTION IN THE UNITED KINGDOM

		1934-8 (iii)	1941 (i)	1944 (i)	1947 (i)	1950 (i)	1952 (ii)	1954 (iii)
Protein—Animal	g.	43	36	41	45	47	43	46
Vegetable	g.	37	47	46	46	42	41	36
Total	g.	80	82	87	91	89	84	82
Fats — all sources	g.	130	113	124	106	131	122	136
Carbohydrate	g.	378	368	386	390	378	378	393
Calcium	mg.	688	698	1,039	1,142	1,157	1,095	1,108
Iron	mg.	13.2	12.9	16.2	14.6	15.3	13.4	13.8
Vitamin A	i.u.	3,700	3,480(§)	3,680(§)	3,700(§)	3,970(§)	3,620	4,270
Vitamin B₁ (*)	mg.	1.3	1.5	2.0	1.8	1.7	1.7	1.7
Riboflavin	mg.	1.6	1.6	2.1	1.9	1.9	1.8	1.8
Nicotinic acid	mg.	13	13	16	16	15	14	15
Vitamin C (*)	mg.	93	81	106	110	101	96	96
Energy value Cal. (†)		3,000	2,820	3,010	2,880	3,050	2,950	3,130
Energy value Cal. (‡)		3,110	2,930	3,110	2,980	3,150	3,060	3,240

(*) Without allowances for cooking losses.

(†) Calculated according to the convention adopted in 'Nutritive Values of Wartime Foods', *Medical Research Council War Memorandum*, No. 14, 1945.

(‡) Calculated according to the convention adopted in *Food Composition Tables for international use*, Food and Agriculture Organization, 1949.

(§) Revised.

Source of data (i) *Ministry of Food Bulletin*, No. 720.

           (ii) *Board of Trade Journal*, July 9th, 1955.

           (iii) Ibid., August 11th, 1956.

APPENDIX C

SELECTED DATA FROM THE RESULTS OF THE NATIONAL FOOD SURVEY
ENERGY VALUE AND NUTRIENT CONTENT OF DOMESTIC FOOD CONSUMPTION
INTAKE AND PERCENTAGES OF REQUIREMENTS (*) MET

Intake per head per day

		1942	1944			1952		
		Urban Working Class (i)	Urban Working Class (ii)	Middle Class (ii)	Slum-Dwellers (ii)	National Sample (iii)	Class C (iii)	Old Age Pensioner Households (iii)
Energy value	Cal.	2,269	2,387	2,403	2,404	2,447	2,482	2,341
	%	n.a.	97	101	101	99	97	101
Protein	g.	74	73	74	75	77	78	73
	%	n.a.	99	106	103	104	103	115
Fat	g.	n.a.	94	98	92	94	93	90
	%	n.a.	n.a.	n.a.	n.a.	n.a.	n.a.	n.a.
Calcium	mg.	672	868	948	843	1,043	1,046	988
	%	n.a.	89	101	83	108	107	112
Iron	mg.	13.5	13.5	13.9	13.3	13.0	13.2	12.0
	%	n.a.	109	110	110	106	107	90
Vitamin A	i.u.	2,980	3,170	3,630	2,790	3,550	3,410	3,070
	%	n.a.	133	147	121	148	144	112
Vitamin B$_1$	mg. (†)	1.19	1.38	1.34	1.42	1.28	1.30	1.20
	%	n.a.	141	143	150	131	128	131
Riboflavin	mg.	1.54	1.76	1.87	1.67	1.64	1.62	1.56
	%	n.a.	118	129	115	109	104	111
Nicotinic acid	mg.	11.9	13.9	14.0	12.9	12.9	12.9	12.2
	%	n.a.	143	149	137	131	128	133
Vitamin C	mg. (†)	38	40	42	35	53	51	44
		n.a.	181	191	160	244	234	199
Vitamin D	i.u.	100	106	123	105	148	150	128
		n.a.	n.a.	n.a.	n.a.	n.a.	n.a.	n.a.

n.a. — not available.

(*) Based on the Recommendations of the Committee on Nutrition of the British Medical Association, 1950.

(†) With allowances for cooking losses.

Sources (i) *The Urban Working-Class Household Diet 1940 to 1949*, H.M.S.O., 1951.
    (ii) *Studies in Urban Household Diets 1944 to 1949*, H.M.S.O., 1956.
    (iii) *Domestic Food Consumption and Expenditure, 1952*, H.M.S.O., 1954.

INDEX

ABERGELE FAIR, 190
Abernethy, Dr John, 398
Aborigines, teeth of, 165
Abstinence from the Flesh of Animals, 397
Academia dei Lincei, 119
Académie française, 350; des Sciences, 119-20, 359
Accessory Food Factors Committee, 441-2
Accum, Frederick, 289-93
Acescent foods, 234-8
Achard, 205
Acids, amino, 75, 416-18 (*see* Proteins)
Addison, Joseph, 253
Admiralty, The, 261, 264, 268, 270, 317-22
Advisory Committee on Nutrition, 445
Agricultural Chemistry, 284-5
Agricultural Economics Society, 431, 446, 456, 460
Agriculture: Board of, 173, 175-6, 177, 285-7, 433; eighteenth-century, 171-84; experimental, 177; medieval, 17-19; nineteenth-century, 279-87; seventeenth-century, 92-4
Akikuyu, 163
Alcohol, effect of, 338-9
Ale, 32-3 (*see also* Beer and Wine): seventeenth-century, 112-14; sophistication of, 43; 'ale-conners', 43-5
Alkalescent foods, 234-7
Alum, in bread, 187-90, 292, 295
Alva, Duke of, 29
Amino acids, 75, 416-18
Anaemia, 130-1, 389-90
Anatto, 195
Andrews, John and Sidney, 298
Animal protein, in diet, 451
Annals of Agriculture, 177
Anne, Queen, 171; enclosures under, 174-6
Anson, G., 262
Antirachitic vitamins, 149-51
Antiscorbutics, 77, 137, 391, 425
Aperitifs, 337
Apothecaries, The, 118
Appert, Nicholas, 317
Aquasparta, Duke of, 119
Aquavitae, 115, 337
Arable farming, increase in, 29
Arbuthnot, Dr John, 236
Aristotle, 65
Armstrong, Sir Alexander, 394-5
Armstrong, George, 246, 248

Army, rations of, 103, 329, 344; recruiting for, 387, 404
Arnaldus de Villa Nuova, 68
Artisans, meals of, 54-7, 218, 434; *Appendix A,* 465-7
Ashley, Sir Anthony, 30
Asquith, Mr (*see* Oxford, Lord)
Asses' milk, 69, 71, 124-5, 194, 375
Asses' milk, artificial, 375
Assize of Bread, 41, 106, 118
Athletics, and diet, 354-5
Aubrey, T., 235, 262

BACHSTROM, JOHANNES, 260, 425
Bacon, consumption of, 458; and eggs, 51-2, 335; imported, 331
Bacteria, 326
Baker, Sir George, 201-2, 254
Bakers: Brown, 41; eighteenth-century, 186-190; medieval, 41-3; nineteenth-century, 290-5; White, 41
Bakewell, Robert, 177, 184
Ballexserd, M., 249
'Balls', for improving beer, 200
Banquets, 57-9, 215-18, 308
Banting, William, 400
'Banyan' days, 227
Barclay, Capt. Robert, 354
Barlow, Sir Thomas, 377
Barnet Fair, 190
Barton-Wright, E. C., 352
Bate, Dr G., 153
Bateman, Thomas, 271
Bayly, Walter, 128
'Bay-salt', 261
Beaufroy, Mark, 201
Beaumont, Dr William, 347-9
'Beauty Training for Ladies', 335
Beddoes, T., 266
Bedford, 4th Earl of, 97; 5th Earl of, 97, 107, 111, 145
Beer: adulteration of, 43-5, 199-200, 290-4; 'balls' for improving, 200; bottled, 333; copperas in, 200-1; coriander seeds in, 199; eighteenth-century, 198-200; introduction of, 32-3; nineteenth-century, 290-1; seventeenth-century, 112-14; sophistication of, 43-5; vitamin B in, 114
Beet-sugar, 205
Bennett, H. S., 19, 52
Bennett, John, 382, 385, 388

Beri-beri, 84-5, 413, 421-2, 424, 426, 433-4
Berkeley, Lord, 143
Beveridge, Sir William, 432, 435, 442
Beverwyck, Johan van, 155
Billingsgate Market, 191
Bills of Mortality, 152-3, 160, 271-2, 379
Births and Deaths Registration Act, 312
Bissett, Charles, 259
Black Death, the, 26
Black, Joseph, 232, 266
Black, W., 272
Blake's 'land carriage' scheme, 185-6
Blane, Sir Gilbert, 252, 265, 269-70
Board of Agriculture, 173, 175-6, 177, 285-7, 433
Board of Trade, 315, 393, 429-30, 433, 448, 468
Boate, Arnold, 154, 156
Boate, Gerard, 154
Boke of Husbandry, 19
Boleyn, Anne, 23
Bones: growth of and stature, 166-8, 443; structure of, 147-9
Bonhomme, Citoyen, 273
Book of Orders, 56
'Boon-work', 49
Boorde, Andrew, 21, 38, 44, 51-3, 72, 75, 137
Booth, R. G., 352
Bourne, Stephen, 429
Boyle, The Hon. Robert, 117, 119, 123, 126-7, 144, 232
Bradley, R., 180-1
Bramble, Matthew, 190-2, 201, 209-11
Brande, Prof. W. T., 285
Brandy, 116; 'British', 116, 202; faked, 202; French, 202
Brawn, 53
Bread: adulteration of, 187-90; aerated, 299; agene in, 298; alum in, 187; Assize of, 41, 106, 118; barley, 74, 174; black, 42; bleaching of, 298; brown, 48, 296; and butter, 213-14; composition of, 297-8; decline in consumption of, 299; eighteenth-century, 186-90; inadvisability of rationing, 435; manchet, 43; maslin, 43, 48; medieval views on, 74; mineral salts in, 42-3; National, 452-4; nineteenth-century, 295-9; post-war loaf, 454; price of, 62, 106, 171, 181; rye, 174, 296; seventeenth-century, 105-6; short-weight, 42; 'Standard', 187; vitamins in, 451-3; war, 438; white, 43, 187, 297-9, 388-90; white lead in, 188; yeast in, 299
Breakfast, English, 335
Breast-feeding, decline of, 373-4, 407
Breviary of Healthe, The, 137
Brewers, 44, 198-201
Brewers' Company, 59
Brewing, 43, 198-201
Brillat-Savarin, 334
'Britaine's Busses', 102-3, *Appendix A*, 465-7
British Association, 285, 346-7, 370, 428, 430, 446

British Medical Association, 446, 467
Broedingur, 274
Brontës, the, 340; Charlotte, 410
Browne, Sir Thomas, 159
Bruce, Viscount, 448
'Bubby-pots', 246
Buckingham Palace, sanitary condition of, 310-11
Budd, Dr Richard, 228
Buer, M. C., 271
Bullein, William, 30, 72, 82
Bunge, Prof. G., 362, 421
Burghley, Lord (*see* Cecil, William)
Burns, John, 412-13, 420
Burton, Robert, 100, 122, 125, 126, 130
Butchers, 34-5
Butchers' Company, 216
Butter, 40-1, 303-4; eighteenth-century, trade in, 195; views on, 239; 'Epping', 195, 304; 'May', 74, 132; medieval, views on, 73-4; nineteenth-century, 303-4; price of, 41, 54; seventeenth-century, 105; twentieth-century, 438-40; vitamin A content of, 76; vitamin D content of, 74; 'butter-men', 41, 304; buttermilk, 194; wartime shortage of, 438, 440
Byng, The Hon. John, 202

CABBAGES, 20, 21, 30; English cooking of, 220; as field crop; 'great Scotch', 182; improved variety of, 31; for soups, 59
Cadman, Thomas, 115-16
Cadogan, William, 248, 254
Caius College, 124
'Cakes' for cattle-feeding, 179, 287
Calcium, 450-1, 455
Calcium/phosphorus ratio, 147-53, 157
Calorie(s): energy value of, 453; human requirements of, 255, 360; sources of, 461
Cambridge Crew, diet of, 354
Campbell, Robert, 128, 214
Canals, development of, 186, 195
Canning, 317-22
Capsicum: in beer, 199; in mustard, 290
Carbohydrates, in diet, 440-1; oxidation of, 352
Caries, dental, 161-4, 385-7, 462
Carolina rice, 221, 227
Carpenter, John, 42
Cartier, Jacques, 135-6
Casein, in milk, 76
Castel of Helth, The, 53, 65-6, 68, 72, 137
Cattle plague, 24, 301, 304, 314, 331
Cavendish, The Hon. Henry, 232
Caxton, William, 68
Cecil, Hon. Mrs. Evelyn, 20, 30-1
Cecil, William (Lord Burghley), 22, 64
Cereals: consumption of, 460-1
Cereals Research Station, 454
Chadwick, Dr, 310-11
Chameau, 143

Champagne, 339
Charitable Institutions, diets in, 56, 222-8
Charles I, 95, 154
Chaucer, Geoffrey, 22-4, 41
Cheadle, Dr W. B., 377, 381-2
Cheese: eighteenth-century trade in, 194-5; medieval views on, 73; price of, 103, 173
Chemistry, agricultural, 284-5
Chevaline (*see* Horse-flesh)
Cheyne, Dr George, 256, 259, 397
Chick, Dame Harriette, 352, 419, 434, 441
Child labour in factories, 283
Children, feeding of, 70-1, 76-7, 225-8, 244-9, 331-2, 373-9, 407-10, 415
Chittenden, Russell, 419-20
Chlorosis, 130-1
Chocolate, drinking, 106, 116-17, 205
Cholera, 311
Christmas pudding, 337, 'pye', 112
Christ's Hospital, 56, 101, 104, 114, 227-8, 341-2, 410, 435, 439
Cicill, Princess, 60
Cider, 32, 54, 113; lead in, 201
City Madam, The, 108
Clare Market, 195
Claret, price of, 54
Claridge, John, 176
Clark's hydrometer, 203
Clerkenwell Prison, 229
Clinker, Humphrey, 229
Clover, for cattle-feeding, 182; 'great', 92
Clusius, Carolus, 31
Cobbett, William, 30, 279-81, 327
Cockburn, Dr William, 143
Cocculus indicus, 199, 290
Cod liver oil, 149-51, 452; and rickets, 149, 275-6, 382-4, 441; and tuberculosis, 384-5
Coffee, 106, 116-17, 205; coffee houses, 116
Cogan, Thomas, 62, 71, 74
Coke, Thomas (Earl of Leicester), 177, 181
Coldbathfields Penitentiary, 353, 370
College of Physicians, 153, 155, 245-6, 254, 261, 264-5, 364, 404
College of Surgeons, 364, 404
Collins, Emmanuel, 188
'Colloppes and egges', 188
Colyer, Sir Frank, 165
Combined Food Board, 430-1
Compendyous Regyment, 21, 38, 44, 75
Compleat Confectioner, The, 215
'Concentrates' for cattle-feeding, 286
Constipation, 131-2
Cook, Capt., 267-9, 315
Cook's Oracle, The, 334
Cooking, English, 53, 218-21, 334-5; French, 213-15; Italian, 213
Cooks and Pastelers, ordinance of, 35
Cookshops, 35-6, 55, 105, 218-21, 332-3
Convict ships, scurvy in, 264, 393
Cooper, Sir Astley, 345
Copper, in foods, 196, 291

Copperas, in beer, 200, 290, 294
Coram, Thomas, 244
Coriander seeds, 199
Corn: cheap supplies for the poor, 55, 87; price of, 91, 100, 171
Corn Laws, 279; Repeal of, 283
Cornaro, Luigi, 254
Coronary diseases, 462
County surveys, 173, 176, 194, 250
Court, S. D. M., 300
Covent Garden Market, 97
Cow's horn, as feeding bottle, 69; cow's milk, composition of, 248, 378; cow-sheds, in London, 193-4, 299-300
Cranmer, Archbishop, 59-60
Crawford, Adair, 241-2
Crichton-Browne, Sir James, 410
Criminal Law, revision of, 283
Crisp, Sir Frank, 20
Cromwell, Oliver, 113
Crops, 18-19, 30, 92-3, 178-83, 286
Crowden, Dr G. P., 446
Crowley, Robert, 27
Culinary Chemistry, 290
Cullen, William, 237-8, 241-2, 251, 253, 261, 272-3
Culpeper, Nicholas, 96, 155
Curiosities of Literature, 30
Currency, debasing of, 28, 100
Curtilage, 20

DAIRY PRODUCE, 29, 49, 193-5, 430, 446 (*see also* Butter, Cheese, Milk and 'White meats')
Dalton, John, 356
Darbey, Dr Robert, 275
Dauglish, Dr, 299
Davenant, C., 91, 101
Davy, Sir Humphrey, 285, 290
Deadly Adulteration and Slow Poisoning, 292
Dehydrated foods, 454
Defoe, Daniel, 178, 185, 218
Denmark, eye diseases in, 81
Department of Scientific and Industrial Research, 443
Description of England, 20, 49, 55, 60
Description of London, A, 36
Deserted Village, 176
Devonport, Lord, 433-5, 437
Dica's hydrometer, 203
Dica's lactometer, 194
Dickens, Charles, 282, 309, 333, 340, 364-5
Diet: and athletics, 354-5; Banting's, 400; comparison of, *Appendices A, B and C*, 465-9; in charitable institutions, 56, 222-8; evaluation of, 355-7; high-protein, 78-80; in hospitals, 56, 104, *Appendix A*, 465-7; in nineteenth/twentieth-centuries, 428-63; in orphanages, 225-8; in prisons, 228-31, 366-72, 412-14, *Appendix A*, 465-7; in schools, 56, 101, 104, 114, 225-8,

340-2; in seventeenth-century, 130-1; theories regarding essentials of, 76-7, 361-2; vegetarian, 396-9; in workhouses, 56, 222-5, 363-6, 414-15

Dietary deficiencies between the wars, 443-5; pattern (1880-1954), 461-3

Digestion, views on (seventeenth-century), 125-8; (eighteenth-century), 240-1

Discourse of the Husbandrie used in Brabant and Flanders, A, 92

Disease: Barlow's (*see* Scurvy, infantile): the English (*see* Rickets); of London (*see* Scurvy)

Diseases of London, 271

D'Israeli, Isaac, 30-1

Distillers' Company, 115

Dodds, Sir Charles, 298

Donkin, Bryan, 318

Dossie, Robert, 177, 179

Dotheboys Hall, 340

Drake, Sir Francis, 115

Drake, Richard, 115

Drummond, Sir J. C., 114, 150, 315, 319, 389, 424, 448-9, 453-4 (*see also Preface*)

Dundonald, Earl of, 284

Dutch East India Company, 117, 140

Dwarfism, 167

Dysentery, 332

EAST INDIA COMPANY, 95, 117, 139-40, 142

Ebers Papyrus, 80-1

Eden, Sir Frederick, 23, 56, 60, 204, 206-10, 223-4, 250

Education Act (Provision of Meals), 409

Edward I, 38; Edward IV, 27, 60

Eggs, consumption of, 428, 458; dried, 454 (*see also* Dairy produce)

Eijkmann, Christian, 421

Elizabeth, Queen, 51, 68, 115, 128, 137; teeth of, 165

Ellis, William, 178

Elyot, Sir Thomas, 53, 65, 72, 137

Enclosure Acts, 280

Enclosures, 26-9, 49, 174-6, 206, 280

Engels, Frederick, 281-4, 307, 329-30

Englands Happiness Increased, 93-4

English Physitian Enlarged, The, 96, 155

Epidemics, 26, 88, 311, 332

'Epping' butter, 194, 304

Erasmus, 72

Ergotism, 86-7, 252

Eskimoes, diet of, 79

Essay on Bread, An, 189

Essay on Tea, 259

Eugalenus, 141

Evelyn, John, 94, 99, 106, 119-21

'Everlasting Syllabub', 215

Excess of Diet, Statute against, 60

Eye diseases, 80-2, 128-9, 251-2, 387-8

FABRICIUS OF AQUAPENDENTE, 119, 121

Factory Act, 283; factory workers, meals of, 328-32

Factories, H.M. Inspector of, 405

Family Oracle of Health, The, 335-8, 346, 375, 379, 386

Farmers, meals of, 52-4, 97

'Fasting Woman of Tutbury' (*see* Moore, Ann)

Fats, 455, 458-9

'Feaster's Morning Draught', 338

Feavearyear, Sir Albert, 429

Feeding-bottles, 69, 246-7, 374

Fertilizers, agricultural, 284

Field of the Cloth of Gold, 59

Fielding, Henry, 197

Filby, Dr F. A., 188

Fischer, Emil, 415-16

Fish, 38-40, 63-4, 185-6, 191-2, 307-9; canned, 458; and chips, 407; liver oils, 150; price of, 40, 192

Fishmongers' Company, 39-40

Fitz Stephen, William, 22, 36

Fleta, the, 19

Flour, 43, 428, 450, 454; agenized, 298; composition of, 454; 'Graham', 397; milling technique, 388 (*see also Preface*); nutritional value of, 454; self-raising, 299; stone-ground, 43

Flux, Sir Alfred, 429-30, 458

Food, acescent, 234-8; adulteration, 117-18, 195-6, 289-93, 455; alkalescent, 234-7; amount required, 254-5; antiscorbutic, 74-5; body building, 461; chemical preservation of, 325-6; classification of, 344-9; cravings for, in childhood, 438, in pregnancy, 70; dehydrated, 454; eighteenth-century estimates, 256-8; energy value of, 357-9, 435, 455; estimates of national requirements, 434; imports, 429, 450-1, 453; of Jews, 408-9; nineteenth-century estimates, 333-4, 354-7, 361-2; nutritional value of (*see Appendix B,* p. 468); preservation of, 313-26, 443; prices, 29, 35, 54-5, 62, 100-3, 107-12, 171-3, 181, 183, 208, 216, 219, 222-3, 228, 250-1, 272, 279, 304, 308-9, 314, 322, 325, 336-7, 433, 445-7; production of, 17-33, 279-87, 450; protective, 444-5, 450, 461; *proximate principles of,* 361; quality of, 34-46, 105-6, 185-96, 288-301, 303-8; rationing, 437-8, 450-6; in seventeenth century, 130-1 (*see also Appendix A,* pp. 465-7); sold in streets, 39, 96-7, 191; supplies in the United Kingdom (1880-1954), 430; tinned, 314, 318-22; twentieth century, 429-63; wartime deficiencies, 439-50; Food and Drugs Act, 294, 455; *Food Economy Handbook,* 436; Food Investigation Board, 433; Welfare Foods Service, 456-7

Forbes, Duncan, 204

Fordyce, Sir William, 247, 272
Forestus of Delft, 134, 141, 155
Forster, E. M., 444
Forster, John, 93
Forster, William, 236, 239, 244, 247, 273
Foundling Hospital, 225, 244-9
'Four-bottle' men, 212-13
Frankland, Sir Edward, 311, 358
Franklin, Benjamin, 242
Frazer, Prof. A. C., 462
Friend, Dr G. E., 227, 341-2, 439-40
Frölich, Dr, 424
Fruit: 'cures', 399-400; dried, 22, 54; eigh-
    teenth-century, 182-3, 192-3; views on,
    235, 249; import of, 22-3; medieval, 20-3;
    views on, 68-9; nineteenth-century,
    views on, 336, 379; price of, 107-11, 183,
    192, 216, 336-7; seventeenth-century,
    110-11; views on, 125; suspicion of, 68-9,
    125, 237, 249, 336, 379; Tudor, 30;
    twentieth-century, 459-60; in wartime,
    433, 450, 460
Fuller, Thomas, 156
Funk, Casimir, 424
'Fysshe Dayes', 63-4

Gaddesden, John of, 67
Galen, 68, 75, 81, 119, 121, 123, 155
Galileo, 119
Game Laws, the, 210
Gamgee, Prof., 307, 316, 324
'Garbelling', 37, 118
'Gardener, Mayster Ion', 20
Gardens: market, 22, 96-7, 192-3; medieval,
    20-3; monastery, 20; seventeenth-cen-
    tury, 94-6; Tudor, 29-31
Gardiner, Lady, 124, 128
'Garnish', 229
Garrison, F. H., 68
Gaskell, Mrs, 340
Gay Lussac, 313
Gelatin, 350-1, 415-19
General Treatise of Husbandry, A, 180
George III, 172, 185, 199, 289; enclosures
    under, 174
George, Miss M. D., 271
Gerard, John, 22, 30, 31, 137-9
Germany: malnourishment in 1914-18 War,
    432; rationing in, 256
Ghee, 74
Giantism, 167
Gibraltar, Siege of, 252
Gilks, Dr J. L., 79
Gilbert, Joseph, 286
Gin: drunk by wet nurses, 244; in eighteenth
    century, 196-8, 204, 229, 244; faked, 197-
    8; given to babies, 244; imported from
    Holland, 166; introduction of, 116; in
    nineteenth century, 333, 374; in prisons,
    229; Gin Lane, 197; gin shops, 196
Gladstone, William, 333, 339

Glands: pituitary, 167; thyroid, 167
Glanville, Prof. S. K., 81
Glasse, Mrs, 215
Glasshouses, introduction of, 94-5
Glisson, Francis, 151-6, 166, 377
Gluttony, 252-4
Goldner, Stephen, 320
Goldsmith, Oliver, 176
Good Thoughts in Bad Times, 156
Gouernance of good healthe, 72
Gouernayle of Helthe, 68
Gout, 74, 213, 254
Graham, Sir James, 368-9, 317, 412
Graham, Sylvester, 397
Grains of Paradise, 200, 294
Gras, N. S. B., 23
Graunt, Capt. John, 160
Great Beam, the, 37
'Green-sickness' (see Chlorosis)
Greene, Robert, 35, 41
Greenwood, Arthur, 445
Grijns, Dr C., 422
Grocers' Company, The, 56, 118
Grocers, Mistery of, 37
Grosley, M., 187, 191, 214, 219
Grosseteste, Robert, Bishop of Lincoln, 19, 67
Growth rate, of children, 461
Guillemeau, Jacques, 69-70, 82
Guy's Hospital, 346
Györgi, Szent, 425

Hakluyt, Richard, 22, 31, 37, 39, 57, 63
Hales, John, 28-9, 50
Hales, Stephen, 166
Hanway, Jonas, 198, 208, 221-2, 231, 244, 246-
    7, 256, 259
Hardy, John, 201
Harington, Sir John, 68, 71-2
Harriott, Thomas, 31
Harris, Dr Walter, 123, 159, 247-8
Harrison, William, 20, 33, 41, 49, 60, 63, 88
Hartley, Miss Dorothy, 20-1, 25, 77
Hartlib, S., 92
Harvey, Gideon, 141
Harvey, William, 119, 121
Hassall, Dr, 293-5, 299-300, 303-4, 313, 356
'Hasty Pudding', 209
Hawkins, Sir John, 137
Hawkins, Sir Richard, 137-8, 140
Haygarth, J., 254
Health Committee of the League of Nations,
    445
Health of the School Child, The, 457, 461
Healths Improvement, 97-8, 128-9
Heberden, William, 312
Helmont, Jan Baptist van, 125-6, 233
Henderson, Dr Alexander, 343-4
Henry IV, 57 (of France), 70
Henry VI, 37, 44
Henry VIII, 23, 44; armour of, 167
Hentzner, Paul, 44, 165

Her Majesty's Stationery Office, 453 (*see also*
  Appendix C, p. 469)
Herbs, 20-1, 30
High Protein diets, 78-80
Hippocrates, 65, 81, 127
History of Pediatrics, 247
History of the School of Salernum, 67-8
Hogarth, William, 197, 213
Hohenheim, Phillipus von (*see* Paracelsus)
Hollingsworth, Miss D. F., 428, 457 (*see also*
  Preface)
Holst, Dr, 424
Holt, John, 194, 250
Home, Francis, 284
Hopkins, Sir Frederick Gowland, 362
Hops, introduction of, 43-5
Horder, Lord, 298
Horse-flesh, 308
Hospitals, diets in, 56, 104; *Appendix A*, 465-7
Houghton, John, 92
Howard, John, 229-30
Howard, Lord William, 96, 144-5
Howards End, 444
Human milk, composition of, 248, 378
Humoral doctrine, 65-6, 122
Hunger-oedema, 88, 330, 441
Hungers Preuention, 98
Hunter, John, 242
Hutton, Catherine, 209, 211
Hydrometer, 120, 203
Hypercalcaemia, 151
Hythe, sculls at, 164-5

'IATRO-CHEMISTS', 123
Ignis sacer, 86
Indian troops, rations of, 426
Industrialization, growth of, 279
Infant foods, 374-9, 411
Infant mortality, 69-70, 244-6, 373-4, 405, 411
Infant welfare, 411
Infants, feeding of, 69-70, 244-9, 373-9, 407-9,
  555
Inn meals, 219-21
'Invisible college' (*see* Royal Society)
'Iodine theory', 384
Ireland: diet in, 209, 329; eye diseases in, 388;
  famine in, 330; potatoes in, 93, 180-1,
  327, 330; rickets in, 154-6
Ireland's Natural History, 156
Iron, amounts in food, 130-1, 390
Iron deficiencies, 130-1, 388-90 (*see also*
  Chlorosis)

JACKSON, H., 189-90, 195, 198, 200-1
Jago, W., 298
James I, 95, 109
James I (of Scotland), 60
Jams, cheap, introduction of, 332
Jebb, Sir Richard, 180
Jekyll, Sir Joseph, 197
Jerusalem artichokes, 93

Jewell House of Art and Nature, The, 36, 45,
  338
Jews, food of, 408-9
Joan of Navarre, 57
John, King, 41
Johnson, G. W., 20-2
Jongh, L. J., de, 383, 385
Joule, 357
Journal of Natural Philosophy, 274, 289
Journal of the Society of Arts, 177, 295-6
Jus faldae, 19

KAY, DR, 275, 331. 382
King, Dr, 425
King, Gregory, 101
King Edward's Hospital Fund, 456
'King's Pike Ponds', 39
King's Ward Prison, 229
Kitchiner, Dr, 333-5
Klaproth, Prof., 205
Kut-el-Amara, 426, 433
Kwashiorkor, 158
Kymer, Gilbert, 54, 72

LABOURERS, MEALS OF, 101-3, 206-10, 327-9
Lactometer, Dica's, 194
'Lady Morgan's Toothbrush', 386
Lamb, Charles, 227, 410
Lambe, Dr, 397-8
Lancet, 292-5, 299, 300, 302, 304, 313, 341,
  348, 352, 355-6, 364, 374, 379, 381, 382,
  384, 388, 446, 462
'Land carriage' scheme, Blake's, 185-6
Laplace, 242
Latimer, Bishop, 27
Lavoisier, 242, 266, 343, 357
Lawes, John, 286
Laxton, open field system at, 17
Lead: in cider, 201, 292; in food, 291-2; in
  wine, 202, 292
Leadenhall Market, 190
League of Nations, 445-6, 448
Leathersellers' Company, The, 23
Leersum, Dr van, 80
Leeuwenhoek, Antony van, 119
Lemery, Louis, 234, 463
Lemons, 23, 109, 111, 192; use of, in scurvy,
  140, 145, 391-2, 425-6
Lend-Lease, 454-5
'Lenten meats', 23, 52
Leprosy, 84
Letheby, Dr, 293, 311, 328-9, 356, 358
Letter on Corpulence, A, 400
Letters on Chemistry, 358
Leyden, University of, 141, 143, 152-4, 242
Liber Albus, 43
Liebig, Baron Justus von, 285, 346-7, 349,
  350-3, 358, 375, 398, 415, 417, 419
'Liebig's Extractum Carnis', 352
Lime-juice, use of, in scurvy, 392-6, 424-6
Lind, James, 133-4, 136, 259, 265-6, 268

Linseed, for cattle, 286-7
Linseed oil, use of, in rickets, 441
Lister Institute of Preventive Medicine, 434, 441
Lister, Lord, 325
Literary Gazette, The, 291
'Livergrown', 160 (*see also* Rickets)
Livestock, 23-5, 184; maintenance of, in war-time, 436
Lloyd, E. M. H., 431, 446, 456-7, 459
Lloyd George, David, 411, 433
Locke, John, 100-1
London, bakers in, 41-2; bread in, 41-2; Bills of Mortality in, 152-3, 160, 271-2; civic authorities of, 34-5, 38-41, 43-6, 96, 118; coffee houses in, 116, 205; cookshops in, 35, 55, 105, 218-21, 333; cow-sheds in, 193, 299-300; dairy produce in, 40-1, 118, 193-5, 299-300, 303-4; 'Disease of' (*see* Scurvy); fish in, 38-40, 185-6, 191-2, 307-9; fruit in, 22, 96, 183, 192-3; gardens in, 22; markets in, 22, 34-5, 38-9, 96-7, 118, 183, 190-1, 250; meat in, 34-5, 117-18, 190; milk in, 40-1, 191, 193-4, 299-301; vegetables in, 22, 96-7, 182-3, 192-3, 250; water supply of, 358; whey houses in, 117; *London and Country Brewer, The*, 199-200; *London Spy, The*, 192; *London Tradesman, The*, 214
Lowndes, Thomas, 261
Lunin, N., 362, 421, 422
Lydgate, John, 42
Lying Detected, 188-9

MacBride, Dr D., 259, 262, 267, 269, 339
MacKay, Dr Helen, 131
Mackenson, 432
Maerland, Jacob van, 81
Magellan, Fernandus, 134
Magendie, François, 296, 345-7, 350, 375
Maize, 221
Malfi, Duchess of, 70
Malmsey, 32
Malnutrition: in 1900, 403-7; traced to harvest failure, 447
Malpighi, 119
Mangel wurzel, introduction of, 180
Mann, Dr Corry, 76, 439
Manning, Dr Joseph, 188
Manor servants, meals of, 52-3
Manuring, artificial, 284-6
Maoris, teeth of, 163
Margarine, 281, 296, 304-7, 440; vitaminized, 307, 449, 451; shortage of, in 1914-18 War, 438; Margarine Act, 306
Marggraf, 205
Market gardens (*see* Gardens, market)
Markets: fish, 38-9, 191, 307; meat, 34-5, 105, 117-18, 190-1, 307
Markhams farewell to Husbandry, 92
Markham, Gervase, 92, 98

Markham, Dr Peter, 188-9
Marling (soil), 19, 92
'Marmelade', 54, 62
Marrow, vegetable, introduction of, 340
Marzipan, 37
Masai, diet of, 79
Maslin, 19; bread, 43, 48; flour, 43
Maternal and Infant Welfare, 411-12; centres, 439
Maternity and Child Welfare Act, 448
'May' butter, 74, 132
Mayer, J., 255
Mayerne, Sir Theodore, 115
Maynwaring, E., 141
Mayow, John, 127, 232
'Mayster Ion Gardener', 20
McAdam, John, 288
McCance, Prof. R. A., 76
McCarrison, Sir Robert, 82
McCay, Major, 420
McDougall, F. L., 448
Mead (*see* Metheglin)
Mead, Dr Richard, 202, 261
Meals: of artisans, 54-7, 105, 218-21, 333-4, 337; of factory workers, 207, 329-30, 403-8; of farmers, 52-3; of labourers, 206-10; of manor servants, 52-3; of peasants, 47-52, 209; for school children, 453; times of, 55, 60, 106, 211-12, 335; of townsmen, 54-7, 105-6, 213-21, 329-33, 403-8; of wealthy classes, 53-4, 57-63, 210-18, 335-40; *Appendix A*, 465-7
Meat: canned, 317-22, 331; consumption of, 458; eighteenth-century, 190-1; and gout, 254; imported, 453; markets, 34-5, 105, 117-18, 190-1, 307; national supplies of, 430; medieval, 34-5; views on, 75; nine-teenth-century, 307-9; powdered, 97; preserved, 25, 97, 313-14, 316-17; price of, 35-6, 49, 100; refrigerated, 323-5; seventeenth-century, 97-8, 105; 'sub-stance' of, 122; tainted, 34-6; twentieth-century, 457-8
'Meatless' day, the, 436
Medical Research Council, 76-9, 131, 412, 439-43
Medical Times and Circular, 308
Medicina Statica, 126
Mège-Mouries, 296, 304-5
Mellanby, Sir Edward, 149, 298, 440-1
Mellanby, Lady, 160, 162
Memoirs of Agriculture and other Oeconomical Arts, 177
Mendel, Lafayette B., 82
Merchant Shipping Act, 393
Mertens, Dr, 266
Merton College, 62
Metcalfe, the Rev. William, 397
Metheglin, 32
Method of Treating Fevers, 127
Methuen Treaty, The, 113, 212

Metropolitan Water Board, 312
Meux, Mr, 199
M'Gonigle, Dr, 444-5
Military Service Acts, 440
Milk: adulteration, 299-307; asses, 69, 71, 124-5, 194, 375, (artificial) 375; concentrated, 376-7; condensed, 301-3, 332, 375, 377; cows', composition of, 248, 378; dried, 301-3, 411, 454; eighteenth-century, 193-5, views on, 237, 247; numan, composition of, 248, 378; medieval, 40-1; views on, 71-2; nineteenth-century, 299-301, 428; views on, 372-9; pasteurization, 301; price of, 56, 99, 194, 456; prohibition of preservatives in, 326; for school children, 76, 447-8, 451-7; scrofula from, 300; seventeenth-century, 117; views on, 123-5; twentieth-century, 429-63; in workhouses, 225; milk-women, 193-4; Milk Act, 447; Milk-in-Schools Scheme, 447-8, 451, 457; Milk Marketing Board, 447-8; National Household Milk, 454; National Milk Scheme, 456
Millbank Penitentiary, 330, 366
'Miller of Billericay' (see Wood, Thomas)
Miller, F. J. W., 300
Miller, W. D., 161
Mineral salts in fruit and vegetables, 459
Ministry of Agriculture, Fisheries and Food, 430-1, 435, 442, 448, 454-8, 468 (see also Preface)
Ministry of Education, 461
Ministry of Health, 310, 326, 429, 444-8
Misson, M., 105-6, 110-12, 114, 116
Mitchell, John, 292
Modest Apology in Defence of the Baxers, 188
Mollenbrook, Andreas, 145-6
Monasteries, 20-1, 32
Moore, Ann, 343
Moore, Sir Norman, 67
Moran, Dr T., 298, 454
More, Sir Thomas, 29
Moritz, Charles, 220-1
Morris, J. N., 462
Morrison, W. S., 448
Muffett, Thomas, 97, 100, 106, 121, 122, 124, 128, 129
Mulder, 349
Muscular work, and nitrogenous foods, 353
Museum Rusticum et Commercial, 177, 179
Mussels, 39

Names of Herbes, The, 137
Napoleon III, 305
Nares, Sir George, 394-5
National Food Survey, 430, 447, 457
National Health Insurance Act, 411-12, 443
National Milk Publicity Council (see Milk Marketing Board)
National Milk Scheme, 456
Nature of Bread, The, 188

Navigation Act (1651), 113
Navy, rations of, 262-5, 344; Appendix A, 465-7
Nevell, George, Archbishop of York, 59
New Zealand, dental caries in, 163
Newgate Market, 190
Nicholson, William, 274, 289
Night-blindness, 80-2, 388
Nightingale, Florence, 396
Nitrogenous foods, and muscular work, 353; value of, 349-52
Nonnes Preestes Tale, 23, 48
Norfolk, wheat grown in, 178
Northumberland, 5th Earl of, 23, 61
Notification of Births Act, 411
Nutrition, the newer knowledge of, 428-63; cereals, 460-1; dietary pattern, 461-3; fats, 458-9; food supplies, 428-31; potatoes, 460-1; sugar, 459; in the First World War, 431-42; in the Second World War, 448-55; between the wars, 442-8; since 1945, 455-6; Advisory Committee on Nutrition (Ministry of Health), 429
Nutrition, science of, 343-62
Nutrition Society, 455
Nutritional measures, summary of, 450
Nyctalopia (see Night-blindness)

O'CONNOR, FEARGUS, 280
Offal, 75, 78
Oilcake, as cattle-food, 179, 287
Olympic athletes, and diet, 355
Orange 'cure', 400
Oranges, 62, 192; use of, in scurvy, 139, 145; Vitamins Welfare Scheme, 452
Oriel College, 62
Orphanages, diets in, 225-8
Orr, Lord Boyd, 79, 447, 460
Osborne, T. B., 82
Osmazome, 351
Oxford Colleges, times of meals at, 214
Oxford Crew, diet of, 354
Oxford, Lord, 433
Oysters, 39, 106, 191-2, 309

PACKARD, F. R., 68
'Pale Ale', 333
Paracelsus, 123, 127, 129, 234
Parcimony in Nutrition, 320, 410
Parkinson, John, 32, 59, 95
Parkyns, Boothby, 180
Parr, Catharine, 22
Parry, Admiral Sir W. E., 390-1
Pasley, Admiral Sir Thomas, 261-2, 269
Pasteur, Louis, 44, 301, 311, 321, 325, 378, 424
Paston Letters, The, 23
Pasteurization, 301, 378
Patent Law, 115
'Patent Masticators', 387
Pavlov, Ivan, 349

Pavy, F. W., 325, 329, 353, 373
Paynell, Thomas, 68
Peaches, medieval, views on, 69
Pearce, Dr E. H., 227, 410
Peasants, diet of, 75-7; Appendix A, 465-7
Pease-pudding, 25
Pechey, John, 144, 340
Peel, Sir Robert, 283, 386
Pekelharing, Prof., 362, 421
Pellagra, 84-5
Pennant, Thomas, 199, 201
Pepperers, The, 37
Peptic Precepts, 335
Pepys, Samuel, 106-7, 117, 119-20, 124-5
Percival, Dr T., 275
Perry, 32
Philosophy of Manufacturers, 331
Physiological Economy in Nutrition, 419
Physiologie du Gout, La, 334
Pica, 70
Picrotoxin, 199
Pigeon-lofts, 25, 97-8
Pirquet, Prof. von, 441-2
Plague, the, 26, 88
Platt, Sir Hugh, 36, 39, 44-5, 51, 71, 93
Playfair, Dr Lyon, 346, 353-6
Plowman, Piers, 18, 21-2, 24, 34, 48, 52, 61
'Plumb-pudding', 225
Plutarch, 72
Poaching, 24-5, 98, 210
Poison Detected, 187-9
Polycronycon, 19, 47
Poor Law Amendment Act, 283, 363
Port, 212-13; faked, 203, 290
'Portable soup', 315
'Portynggales', 62
Potatoes: as antiscorbutics, 228, 366-7, 393;
    'Canadian' (see Jerusalem artichokes);
    disease of, 330; in eighteenth-century,
    180-1; introduction of, 31; in Ireland,
    327, 330; in seventeenth-century, 93;
    price of, 183; sweet, 31; twentieth-cen-
    tury, 460-1
Poultry, 23, 25, 28, 35, 46, 48, 50, 54, 55, 58,
    61, 62, 99, 106-10, 122, 185, 191, 207,
    430, 458
Practical Farmer, The, 179
Practical Treatise on Diet, 343
Priestley, Joseph, 232, 266, 339
Pringle, Sir John, 243, 267, 315
Prisons, diets in, 228-31, 366-72, 412-14;
    prison hulks, diets in, 231, 264, 393
Proteine, 350
Proteins, 415-21, 451; biological value, 75-82,
    349-51, 418-21; discovery of, 345; food
    value of, 417-18; malnutrition, 158; need
    for, 75-6; high-protein diets, 78-80
Proximate Principles of Food, 361-2
Puddings, 112
Punch, 116
Punch, 293-4, 312

Purchas His Pilgrimes, 79, 139, 142, 274

QUEENHYTHE MARKET, 37-40, 56
Quip for an Upstart Courtier, A, 45-6

Rachitide, De 153-4, 272
Racine de disette, 180
Radnor, Lord, 354
Raglan, Lord, 396
Railways, introduction of, 288
Raleigh, Sir Walter, 31
Rathgreb, Jacob, 39
Rationing in England, 437-8, 450-6; 'points'
    scheme, 450
Ravens' livers, use of, in rickets, 159
Reaumur, Vicomte de, 239
Refrigeration, 323-5
Regemorter, Dr A., 153
Regimen Sanitatis Salerni, 67
Research Association of British Flour Millers,
    454
Rhondda, Lord, 437
Rice: importation of, 101; Carolina, 221, 227;
    polished, 422
Rickets, 147-68, 271-6, 376-7, 379-84, 432,
    439-41; and cod liver oil, 275-6, 382-4;
    etiology of, 440-1; ravens' livers, use of,
    in, 159
Roads, turnpike, 185, 288
Robert, Duke of Normandy, 67
Robertson, W., 272
Rogers, Thorold, 22, 55, 100
'Rogues and vagabonds', 50
Roller-mills, 388-90; introduction of, 297-8
Rosa Angelica (Rosa Medicinae), 67
Ross, Sir John, 318, 390-1, 395
Rothamsted Experimental Station, 286
Rowlandson, Thomas, 213
Rowntree, Seebohn, 403-5
Royal Commission on Wheat, A, 433
Royal Society, 93, 119-20, 429-38
Royal Society of Arts (see Society of Arts)
Royal Statistical Society, 429-30
Rugg, H. Hodson, 299-300
Rugge's Diurnal, 117
Rum, 203
Rumford, Count, 257, 296, 330, 355
Runciman, Walter, 433-4
Rye, 93, 178; cheap supplies for the poor, 56,
    87; ergot in, 86-7
Rye bread, 43, 48, 174, 296 (see also Bread,
    maslin)

SACK, PRICE OF, 54
Saffron, 37
'St Anthony's Fire', 86
St Bartholomew's Hospital, 56, 104, 145
St James's Market, 190-1
St Martin, Alexis, 347-9
St Paul's Churchyard, 22, 96
St Thomas's Hospital, 388, 392

Sailors' diet, 102-3; *Appendix A*, 465-7
Salads, 22, 54, 59, 79
Salaman, Redcliffe, N., 31, 181
Salernum, School of, 67-9, 73
Salt: and scurvy, 261; trade in, 39; salts, eighteenth-century, views on, 234
Salters' Company, 39-40, 58
'Sampson Syllogism', 188
Sanctorius, 126
Sanfoin, for cattle-food, 182
Sanitation, 309-12
Sassure, Theodore de, 285
Scandinavia, scurvy in, 133
Sceptical Chymist, The, 123
Schenk, Dr, 382
Schnirdel, Hulderike, 79
Schools, diets in, 56, 101, 104, 114, 225-8, 340-2, 409-10, 447-8, 451-3
Science, modern birth of, 118
Science of nutrition, 343-62,
Scotland, diet in, 60, 209, 329
Scrofula (*see* Tuberculosis)
Scurvy, 133-46, 235, 252, 259-70, 330, 390-6, 433-4, 441; experimental, 424-7; infantile, 377-9; in Crimea, 395-6; scurvy-grass, 139, 144-6, 259
Sennertus, 141
Serious Reflections, 195
Sewage disposal, 310
Sharpey, Prof. William, 356
Sheep farming, 23, 28
Shelley, P. B., 397
Silver, fall in price of, 172
Simon, André, 32
Simon, Sir John, 311
Sinclair, Sir John, 175, 177, 280, 285, 296, 313, 354
Skinners' Company, 62
Skreel, Prof., 190
Slare, Fred., 129, 238
Slave-trade, 263-4
Sloane, Sir Hans, 251
Smith, Dr Edward, 59, 325, 328-9, 332, 353, 370-2
Smith, Mrs Henderson, 394
Smith, Dr Southwood, 310-11
Smith, William, 229-31, 237-8, 254
Smithfield Market, 220, 325
Smollett, Tobias, 190, 192, 194-5, 201, 209, 211, 218, 228-9, 261
Society of Arts, 177, 179-80, 183, 185-6, 295-6, 307, 314, 316, 318, 321, 324, 329, 352, 356, 372
Soda-water, 339
Soil analysis, introduction of, 285
Solanus of Ephesus, 155
'Soteltes', 57
Soup, 51; dried, 315-16; Hanway's, 221-2, 256; 'portable', 315; Rumford's, 257-8
Soup-kitchens, 257, 316
'Spagyrists', 123

Spallanzani, Larazzo, 239-40
Spence, James, 300
Speenhamland system, 283, 363
Spices, 36-8, 118
Spirit drinking, 115-16, 197-8
Spirit, taxation on, 197-8, 333, 339
Spitalfields Market, 183, 193
Stafford, William (*see* Hales, John)
'Staffordshire blanks and prizes', 25
'Standard' bread, 187, 227
Star Chamber, diet of, 109-10
Stark, William, 242-4, 256
Starvation, 87-8
Stature and bone growth, 166-8
Statute of Monopolies, 115
Steele, Richard, 214
Stefansson, 79
Stepp, Dr, 362, 423
Stevens, William, 240
Still, Dr G. F., 246-7
Stockfishmongers, the, 39
Stone, 82-4
'Substance' of meat, 122
Sugar, 37, 204, 459; acescence of, 238; price of, 38, 112, 205; and teeth, 161, 165, 385-7; in wartime, 433, 435; beet sugar, 205
Sulphites, in food preservation, 316, 326
Sundrie new Artificiall Remedies, 51
Surgions Mate, The, 142-3
Survey of Wartime Nutrition, A, 449
Swedes, as cattle-food, 180
Swinfield, Richard de, Bishop of Hereford, 54
Sydenham, Thomas, 127, 130, 144
Syhoroc, 189
Sympathetic magic, 127

TANGIER, ARMY AT (RATIONS), 103
Tatler, The, 214, 259
Tea, 116-17, 198, 203-5, 329; green, 203; price of, 117
Teeth: of aborigines, 165; carious, 161-4, 385, 462; early English, state of, 164-6; formation of, 160-1; of Maoris, 163; of Masai warriors, 163; in New Zealand, 163; in nineteenth century, 385-7; and sugar, 161-4; in Tristan da Cunha, 161
Tellier, Charles, 425
Tenant farmer, the, 26, 32, 171
Teonge, The Rev. Henry, 110
Thacker, R., 103
Thames, the: fishing in, 38; refuse, fat collected from, 305-6; sewage in, 311
Thompson, Flora, 281
'Three-field system of agriculture', 18
Thudichum, Dr, 307
Times, The, 281, 305-6
Tinned foods, 317-22
'Toad-skin', 81
Toast, 214
'Tooth preservers', 386
Tomato, introduction of, 340

Torrington Diaries, 219
Tournesole, 45
Townshend, Charles, Viscount, 177
Townshend, General, 426, 433
Townsmen, meals of, 54-7, 105-6, 213-21, 329-33, 403-8
Trawlers, development of, 309
Treacle, 332
Trinity College, Oxford, 111
Tristan da Cunha, dental caries in, 161
Trotter, T., 262-3, 266, 268
Trusler, Rev. Dr, 190-3, 218, 245
Tuberculosis, and cod liver oil, 384-5
Tuberculosis, bovine, 330, 332, 380
'Tuck-box', 111, 342; tuck-shop, 342
Tucker, Josiah, 193, 221
Tull, Jethro, 177-8
Turberville, Daubeney, 129
Turner, William, 137
Turnips: as cattle-food, 178-9; introduction of, 92
Turnpike Acts, 185
Tusser, Thomas, 18, 19, 25, 52-3
Twist, Oliver, 364-5
'Two-field' system of agriculture, 18
Typhoid, 332

UNIVERSITY COLLEGE HOSPITAL, 385
Ure, Dr Andrew, 283, 300, 331, 364
Uric acid, 419-20
U.S.S.R., scurvy in, 136
Utrecht, Treaty of, 171

VASCO DA GAMA, 134
Vegetables: as antiscorbutics, 77; cooking of, 77, 334; consumption of, *Appendix A*, 465-7; deficiencies of, 336, 341; dried, 314-15; eighteenth-century, 192-3, 219; views on, 235, 237, 253-4; medieval, 20-2, 54, 77; nineteenth-century, 334, 340-1; prices of, 96, 108, 111, 183, 193, 208, 250, 336-7; seventeenth-century, 92-4, 95-6, 102, 110-11; views on, 125; twentieth-century, 459-60; Tudor, 30-1
Vegetarian diet, 396-9
Vermoolen, Dr, 83
Verney, Edmund, 111
Verney, John, 108, 158
Verney, Lady, 158
Verney, Molly, 114
Verney, Mun, 158
Verney, Ralph, 114
Verney, Sir Ralph, 102, 124, 158
Victoria, Queen, 310, 403, 444
Vienna, malnutrition in, 441
Vinegar, adulteration of, 195-6
Vineyards, decay of, 32
Vintners' Company, 46
Vitamins, discovery of, 362, 421-4;
    vitamin A, 74, 77-9, 80-2, 413; in bread, 463; in butter, 342, 438; β-carotene, 74, 77,

413, 459; in dairy produce, 76-8; deficiency, 77-8, 80-4, 128-30, 345, 387-8, 438; and eye diseases, 80-2, 128, 251, 345, 387-8, ; and fish liver oils, 81, 149, 276, 384; in fruit, 459; in meat, 78; and stone, 82-4, 129-30; supplies, improvement in, 456; tablets, 452; in vegetables, 77-8, 271, 459;
    vitamin B 'complex', 84-6, 455; in beer, 114; and beri-beri, 84; in bread, 43, 114, 388; deficiency, 345, 426; discovery of, 421-4; and gastric disorders, 84-5, 389-90; in meat, 352; and pellagra, 84; *vitamin B₁*, 84-5, 388, 407, 413, 455, *Appendices A, B and C*, pp. 467-9; nicotinic acid, 85, 114, 352, 388; riboflavin, 85-6, 114, 352, 451;
    vitamin C: deficiency, 77, 79, 133, 144, 426, 438; discovery of, 425; in fruit, 433; in infants' foods, 376-9; and scurvy, 144, 378 (*see also Preface*); in soups, 77; and teeth, 163; and vegetables, 455;
    vitamin D: in dairy produce, 74, 76; deficiency, 80, 272, 438-9, 441; and dental caries, 162-3; excess in infant diets, 151; and fish liver oils, 149-51, 384; and rickets, 148-51, 157, 160-1, 271-6; tablets, 452; and teeth, 160-3; in vegetables, 271;
    vitamin E, 407
Vitamins, adequacy in pregnancy, 452; deficiency and rickets 441 (*see vitamin D*); and flour, 450; Vitamin Welfare Scheme, 452
Vitriol, 'elixir' of, 264, 266, 392
Vitriol, oil of, 140, 143-4, 266
Vodka, 339
Voit, Dr, 360-1, 415

WAGES, 55, 99, 281, 284, 328
Walpole, Horace, 165
Walter of Henley, 19
Walton, W. S., 300
War(s): Crimean, 315, 395-6; First World, 83, 256, 431-42; Franco-Prussian, 305; of the Roses, 26; Second World, 445, 448-55, 462; Seven Years, 262; South African, 404, 431, 440
War Book, 432
War Bread, 438
Ward, Edward, 192, 218-19, 229
Water supply, 309-12, 358
Waugh, Dr, 425
Way to be Rich and Respectable, The, 173
Welfare Foods Service, 456-7
Wealthy Classes, meals of, 53-4, 57-63, 106-10; 210-18, 335-40
Weller, Sam, 309
Wellington, Duke of, 292
Welsh coalfields, food conditions in, 444
Weston, Sir Richard, 92, 179
Wet-nurse(s): for adults, 124; choice of, 69; decline in popularity of, 373; hire of, 245; and gin-drinking, 244

Wheat, 17-19, 174; bounty on, 91; and ergotism, 252; price of, 91; rise of, 178; storage of, 288-9; Royal Commission on Wheat, A, 433

Whey: eighteenth-century, 194; medieval views on, 49, 71-2; seventeenth-century, 105, 117

Whey-houses, 117

Whiskey, 115

Whistler, Daniel, 151-6

'White meats', 29, 49-50, 193-5; importance of, 75; and rickets, 157

Whittington, Richard, 42

Wierus, 141

Wilkinson, J., 268

Williams, Dr C. J. Blasius, 384-5

Willis, T., 141

Winchester College, 228

Wine: adulterated, 45-6, 201-2; duty on, 113, 212; eighteenth-century, 201-3; English, 32, 45; faked, 46, 201-2; French, 32, 45, 53, 113, 339; German, 32, 53, 113, 339; Levantine, 32, 53, 113; lead in, 202; nineteenth-century, 337-9; Portuguese, 113, 202, 212; seventeenth-century, 112-14

Wine Act, 113

Winkler, Dr, 421

Wolsey, Cardinal, 29

Wood, Thomas, 254

Woodall, John, 142

Woodforde, Parson, 211-12, 276

Wool Trade, 26

Woolton, Lord, 449

Workhouses, diets in, 56, 222-4, 363-6, 414-15

Worlidge, John, 92

Wright, Dr N. C., 461

Wynkin de Worde, 19

XEROPHTHALMIA, 80-2, 128-9, 251, 345, 388

YEAST, 299

Young, Arthur, 172, 179, 181-3, 185-6, 192-3, 195, 204, 207, 209, 256-7, 280-1

Zakushki, 339

Zoological Society, 383